W9-BYP-510

UNDERSTANDING THE POLITICAL WORLD

A Comparative Introduction to Political Science

NINTH EDITION

JAMES N. DANZIGER

University of California, Irvine

PEARSON
Longman

New York   Boston   San Francisco
London   Toronto   Sydney   Tokyo   Singapore   Madrid
Mexico City   Munich   Paris   Cape Town   Hong Kong   Montreal

To Lesley, Nick, and Vanessa

Acquisitions Editor: Vikram Mukhija
Executive Marketing Manager: Ann Stypuloski
Production Manager: Stacey Kulig
Project Coordination, Text Design, and Electronic Page Makeup: Electronic
   Publishing Services Inc., NYC
Cover Designer/Manager: Wendy Ann Fredericks
Cover Photos (clockwise from top left): Tibetan monks protest in front of the Chinese
   Embassy in Kathmandu, Tibet. © Narendra Shrestha/epa/Corbis. A Serb student chants
   an anti-Kosovo slogan during a march in protest of Kosovo's declaration of independence
   in the ethnically divided region, © Attila Kisbenedek/AFP/Getty Images. Argentina's
   president Cristina Fernandez de Kirchner reviews troops upon her arrival at Miraflores
   presidential palace, in Caracas, Venezuela, © Juan Barreto/AFP/Getty Images. A woman
   casts her ballot in Peshawar, Pakistan, © Paula Bronstein/Getty Images)
Photo Researcher: Julie Tesser
Senior Manufacturing Buyer: Alfred C. Dorsey
Printer and Binder: R.R. Donnelley and Sons
Cover Printer: Phoenix Color Graphics

For permission to use copyrighted material, grateful acknowledgment is made to the
copyright holders on page 501, which are hereby made part of this copyright page.

Library of Congress Cataloging-in-Publication Data
Danziger, James N.
   Understanding the political world: a comparative introduction to political science/
James N. Danziger.—9th ed.
   p.cm.
ISBN-13: 978-0-205-64459-9
ISBN-10: 0-205-64459-7
1. Political science. 2. Comparative government. I. Title.
JA66.D36 2009
320—dc22   2008023524

Please visit us at www.pearsonhighered.com

ISBN 13: 978-0-205-64459-9

ISBN 10: 0-205-64459-7

1 2 3 4 5 6 7 8 9 10—DOC—11 10 09 08

CONTENTS

PART THREE   Political Systems

CHAPTER 5   States and Nations   108

CHAPTER 6   Political Institutions I: Structures   134

PREFACE

When you consider the current political world, you might be reminded of Charles Dickens' famous observation "it was the best of times, it was the worst of times . . ." Is it? In fact, the final debate in this book, at the end of Chapter 15, considers that very question. It is noteworthy that when Dickens wrote those words, his world, centering in Victorian England, was in a state of tremendous change, as industrialization and colonialism were dramatically reshaping political, social and economic systems. And Dickens was writing about the French Revolution, a period which was equally turbulent.

In retrospect, neither of those periods was as tumultuous as our contemporary world. On the one hand, the combination of technologies, globalization, and government policies have lengthened our lives, increased the quantity and quality of material goods we enjoy, and opened us to an extraordinary range of experiences. There is a higher proportion of democratic regimes that at any time in history. And the recent Global Peace Index concludes that ". . . the number of armed conflicts throughout the world—both international and civil wars—has decreased dramatically since the end of the Cold War in 1990" (Economist Intelligence Unit 2008).

On the other hand, the combination of technologies, globalization and government policies are also associated with substantial human suffering. One billion people attempt to survive every day with a caloric intake below subsistence level and without sufficient clean water. The degradation of the environment continues at high speed, led by global warming, resource depletion, and spreading desertification. Tension and hostility between religions and across cultures seem extraordinarily high. Citizens' trust in their governments and in public officials has dropped substantially. And we live with the constant carnage and complex effects of terrorism and other forms of political violence. We seem incapable of stemming the steady proliferation of weapons of individual and mass destruction, whether conventional, chemical, biological, or nuclear.

In these best/worst times, it is essential to understand the political world and to act sensibly in it, since it is arguably the most critical domain in which our futures are being shaped. And thus we should consider whether the information, insights, and concepts of political science are useful. Can they help us understand the political world? Can they guide our actions in ways that improve the quality of our lives, individually and collectively?

As its title indicates, addressing such questions is at the heart of this book. The book attempts to link the central analytic concepts of political science that have emerged over decades of research to the realities of the political world in the early twenty-first century. Using contemporary and some historical evidence, the book emphasizes empirical research that illuminates the processes and structures of politics. The level of analysis ranges from the individual's political beliefs and actions through the politics of groups and countries to the dynamics of the international system.

This book asks the reader to assess whether it is possible and useful to develop generalizations about political phenomena. It combines attention to systematic descriptive analysis—the *what* questions—with efforts to explain underlying patterns—the *why* and *how* questions. And readers are continually reminded that they must consider the important normative questions about what *should* be done that are embedded in most issues about politics. Many topics are also presented in a manner that encourages the reader to think like a political scientist—to structure questions and assess evidence in order to make inferences.

This book is written for every person who wants to enrich his or her basic understanding of the political world and to learn how political scientists attempt to describe and explain politics. The reader might be in an introductory course in political science or comparative politics, but the book would also be useful for those taking a "capstone" course that integrates their political science studies. A reader might also be anyone who wants to think about the fascinating and confusing world of politics in a more informed and systematic way.

FEATURES

The ninth edition retains the conceptual framework of previous editions, focusing on politics at every level from that of the individual person to the level of the global system. To enrich our understanding, it employs a comparative perspective, considering evidence and examples from many countries in all regions of the world. This approach is guided by Aristotle's wise observation that all thinking begins in comparison and by a recognition that the political world is now truly global.

Thus, the organization of the book follows this logic. It provides the reader with a brief characterization of how political scientists study politics in a comparative framework, and then uses such a framework to focus on how to understand politics at the level of the individual and group, the different ways in which political institutions are organized, the dynamics of important political processes, and the key patterns of politics in major clusters of countries.

- Chapter 1 and the Appendix introduce the logic of political science and the methods of comparative political analysis.
- Chapters 2–4 examine both normative political theory and also the empirical study of political behavior at the individual and group levels, describing and explaining the causes of political beliefs and actions.
- Chapters 5–8 emphasize the structural and institutional elements of political systems, offering analytic concepts for characterizing the different ways in which people organize themselves politically.
- Chapters 9–12 analyze crucial political processes, such as public policy making and the exercise of power, political and economic development, politics across national borders, and political violence. Finally,

- Chapters 13–15 explain in detail how important groups of countries try to achieve their broad goals of prosperity, stability, and security within the complex international environment. These chapters provide specific analyses of the developed countries, the developing countries, and two sets of transitional developed countries—the postcommunist developed countries and the newly industrializing countries.

In addition, this ninth edition retains the following key features:

- More than 60 boxed discussions and debates provide memorable applications of key concepts such as power, authority, liberalism, and globalization, and issues such as the emergence of China as a global economic power, the debate over whether terrorism is ever justifiable, and the effects of colonialism and neo-colonialism on a developing country (Congo), the question of whether international humanitarian intervention violates national sovereignty, the future of the European Union, the different paths of political activism taken by Gandhi and Osama bin Laden, and the issue of whether interest groups are good for democracy.
- Continual use of country-based examples ground every topic in relevant, specific realities
- Presentation of current data and examples facilitate analysis and comparisons on many topics
- The extensive use of political cartoons and photographs illuminates themes in a manner that complements the textual discussions
- A recurring focus on political economy emphasizes the significance of linkages between the political system and the economic system
- An engaging, readable style

NEW TO THIS EDITION

Given the extraordinary rate of change in the political world, many examples and most quantitative data have been updated. In addition, there are the following significant differences from the previous edition:

- There is a substantial expansion in the analysis of the patterns of global terrorism and the behaviors and motivations of terrorists, especially in Chapters 4, 11, and 12.
- The coverage of political institutions has been strengthened with more detail and additional examples, particularly in Chapters 6, 7, 11, and 13.
- New sections in Chapter 10 explore the dynamics of change in political systems, highlighting transitions in the direction of greater democratization and political institutionalization as well as those in the direction of political decay and failed states.
- A more extensive analysis of the United Nations (Chapter 11) highlights the challenges and impacts of this major international organization on global politics and society.

- The social development index employed to classify the world's countries in Chapters 13–15 is both updated and expanded to include a richer set of indicators.

- Chapter 15 on the transitional developed countries is substantially rewritten to reflect the significant changes occurring in both the newly industrializing countries and the postcommunist developed countries.

- The popular "Debate" boxes on topics such as globalization, judicial review, and terrorism have been improved, and there are new debates on such topics as whether economic development is a necessary precondition for effective democracy, whether information and communications technologies are revolutionizing politics, and whether presidential or parliamentary government is preferable.

- To improve clarity and understanding, there are new diagrams, such as those examining the distribution of world value systems (Chapter 2) and the modes of political action (Chapter 3), and many tables throughout the book have been transformed from numeric lists into figures that do a better job of visually communicating political information.

- "On the Web"—a list of particularly useful and relevant Internet sites at the end of each chapter—has been updated and expanded.

- The readability of the text is enhanced by the use of a two-color design and a more integrated use of boxed discussions, as well as more streamlined explanations of political concepts and additional country examples to illustrate them.

SUPPLEMENTS

Longman is pleased to offer several resources to qualified adopters of *Understanding the Political World* and their students that will make teaching and learning from this book even more effective and enjoyable. Several of the supplements for this book are available at the Instructor Resource Center (IRC), an online hub that allows instructors to quickly download book-specific supplements. Please visit the IRC welcome page at www.ablongman.com/irc to register for access.

For Instructors

MyPoliSciKit for *Understanding the Political World* This premium online supplement features multimedia and interactive resources to help students better understand and critically engage political concepts. In addition to book-specific assessment, MyPoliSciKit includes case studies with streaming video, simulations, mapping exercises, ABC newsfeeds, and more to help students make connections between concepts and current events. With the Instructor Grade Tracker, instructors can easily follow student work on the site and their progress on each activity. MyPoliSciKit is available at no additional charge when packaged with this book. To learn more, please visit www.mypoliscikit.com or contact your Pearson representative.

MyPoliSciKit Video Case Studies for International Relations and Comparative Politics   This DVD series contains video clips featured in the MyPoliSciKit case studies for this and other Longman political science titles. Featuring video from major news sources and providing reporting and insight on recent world affairs, this DVD helps instructors integrate current events into their courses by letting them use the clips as lecture launchers or discussion starters.

Instructor's Manual/Test Bank (0-205-64460-0)   Written by James N. Danziger, this resource includes up-to-date chapter summaries, multiple-choice questions, essay questions, and ideas for classroom discussions.

Computerized Test Bank (0205644643)   The flexible, easy-to-master computerized test bank includes all of the items in the print test bank. The software allows instructors to edit existing questions and to add their own items. Tests can be printed in several different formats and can include features such as graphs and tables.

PowerPoint Presentation (Available exclusively at the IRC)   Organized around a lecture outline, these electronic presentations contains maps, figures, and tables from each chapter.

Digital Transparency Masters (Available exclusively at the IRC)   These downloadable transparency masters include all of the maps, figures, and tables found in the text.

For Students

MyPoliSciKit for *Understanding the Political World*   This premium online supplement features multimedia and interactive resources to help students better understand and critically engage political concepts. In addition to book-specific assessment, MyPoliSciKit includes case studies with streaming video, simulations, mapping exercises, ABC newsfeeds, and more to help students make connections between concepts and current events. With the Instructor Grade Tracker, instructors can easily follow student work on the site and their progress on each activity. MyPoliSciKit is available at no additional charge when packaged with this book. To learn more, please visit www.mypoliscikit.com.

***Longman Atlas of World Issues* (0-321-22456-5)**   Introduced and selected by Robert J. Art of Brandeis University and excerpted from the acclaimed Penguin Atlas Series, the *Longman Atlas of World Issues* is designed to help students understand the geography and major issues facing the world today, such as terrorism, debt, and HIV/AIDS. These thematic, full-color maps examine forces shaping politics today at a global level. Explanatory information accompanies each map to help students better grasp the concepts being shown and how they affect our world today. Available at no additional charge when packaged with this book.

***New Signet World Atlas* (0-451-19732-1)**   From Penguin Putnam, this pocket-sized yet detailed reference features 96 pages of full-color maps plus statistics, key data, and much more. Available at a discount when packaged with this book.

***Newsweek* Discount Subscription (0-321-08895-6)** *Newsweek* gets students reading, writing, thinking about what's going on in the world around them. When a discount subscription card is packaged with this book, students will receive a 12-week subscription for only 59 cents an issue. To learn more about this and other discount subscriptions to newspapers and periodicals, please contact your Longman representative.

***Careers in Political Science* (0-321-11337-3)** Offering insider advice and practical tips on how to make the most of a political science degree, this booklet by Joel Clark of George Mason University shows students the tremendous potential such a degree offers and guides them through: deciding whether political science is right for them; the different career options available; job requirements and skill sets; how to apply, interview, and compete for jobs after graduation; and much more. Available at a discount when packaged with this book.

ACKNOWLEDGMENTS

Many sources of ideas and information constitute the basis of *my* understanding about politics. Broadly, you should know that I was born and have primarily been educated in the United States. I have also studied, lived, and/or spent significant periods in Western and Eastern Europe, South America, Asia, the Middle East, and Africa. I have circumnavigated the global twice on Semester at Sea. The people I met and the events I experienced in all these places have certainly influenced my perceptions about politics.

More direct contributions to this book have come from my colleagues in political science and from the many students and others in the political world with whom I have interacted. I have drawn deeply and often from the ideas of these groups.

By the publication of a ninth edition, the layers of contributions and ideas to the construction of this book are deep, rich, and indescribable. In every edition, there is a list of people who added positively to that edition, and I continue to be grateful to them all. Explicit guidance and advice regarding the writing of this particular edition have come from several valuable sources: the cadre at Longman Publishers, including Vikram Mukhija, Elizabeth Daniel, Ann Stypuloski, Liz Hoens, Alfred Dorsey, Rona Tucillo, and Wendy Fredericks; Scott Hitchcock from EPS; scholarly colleagues who have offered useful suggestions; and students who have provided feedback on the book, including those who provided specific material, undergraduates Danielle Menard, Xenia Tashlitsky, and especially Benjamin Bohr. The reviewers, who offered very thoughtful and constructive commentaries for this edition, are Gregory Culver, University of Southern Indiana; Ric Epps, San Diego State University; Minton Goldman, Northeastern University; B. Guy Peters, University of Pittsburgh; and Lori Riverstone, University of Tennessee-Knoxville.

I am very grateful for the help provided by all these (and many unnamed) sources. Regarding the roads not taken and the missteps in this book, the responsibility is mine.

James N. Danziger

TO THE READER

The aim of this book is revealed by its title: It is meant to help you understand the political world. It assumes that you are willing to think about politics. It does not assume that you have substantial knowledge about politics or political science, or even that you know the difference between politics and political science. I hope that when you complete the book and any course in which you are reading it, you will feel that you have increased your knowledge about the contemporary political world.

The study of politics is full of fascinating questions. First are the questions about *what is*, such as: Who exercises political power, and what values and purposes guide them? Why do people accept political authority? How do people organize themselves politically? What causes individuals and groups to take political action? A second set of questions concerns *what ought to be*: Who should exercise political power, and what values should they pursue? Why should people accept political authority? How should political structures be organized? Why should individuals and groups act politically? People disagree sharply about answers to both these descriptive (what is) and normative (what ought to be) questions. In addition, the study of politics provokes a third set of questions regarding *what we can actually know* about the political world. Here also there are major disagreements about the appropriate methods for describing and understanding politics.

Although this book cannot resolve the underlying disputes, it offers you the basis for making sense out of politics at all three levels. As author, I make some basic assumptions: that you can think systematically about politics and make general statements about how politics works; that you will learn more about politics by considering the politics of many different places; that every observer of politics (certainly including you and me) has biases, only some of which can be understood; that you need a variety of sources of ideas and information before you can make informed and sensible decisions about the value disagreements pervading politics; and that this book is one such source that can be helpful to you. My efforts will be successful to the extent that *you* ultimately judge my assumptions to be correct (especially the last one...).

It is inevitable that you will be frustrated with the treatment of politics at some (many?) points in this book. I would say: Reader, be merciful! The study of politics is very complex. Gather bits of understanding where you can find them.

ABOUT THE AUTHOR

James N. Danziger is a professor and former chair of the Department of Political Science at the University of California, Irvine, where he also has served as campus-wide Dean of Undergraduate Education, Chair of the Academic Senate, and Associate Director of the Center for Research on Information Technology and Organizations. He is recipient of many honors and awards, including a Marshall Scholarship (to Great Britain), a Foreign Area Fellowship, a Woodrow Wilson Fellowship, Phi Beta Kappa, and an IBM Faculty Award. He received the first UC Irvine Distinguished Faculty Lectureship Award for Teaching in 1987 and the UC Irvine Distinguished Service Award in 1997. His Ph.D. is from Stanford University, and he has held visiting appointments at the universities of Aarhus (Denmark), Pittsburgh, and Virginia. His research has received awards from the American Political Science Association and the American Society for Public Administration. He has published extensively, particularly on information technology and politics, and he is on the editorial board of the International Journal of Electronic Government Research. He has been an active participant in local politics and especially enjoys playing sports, travel, music, and cinema.

UNDERSTANDING
THE POLITICAL WORLD

CHAPTER 1

POLITICS AND KNOWLEDGE

Dan Frazier thought he had found a great way to make some money and deliver a political message. He designed a T-shirt, for sale on the Internet, with large letters saying "Bush Lied." In very tiny letters, the shirt lists the names of every American solider who has died in the Iraq War since March 20, 2003. But Frazier's home state of Arizona and four other states passed laws attempting to prevent him from selling his T-shirts. These states had responded to requests from parents of dead soldiers arguing that their sons and daughters would not have supported Frazier's political message and that he had refused to remove those names from his shirt. The new state laws require that soldiers or their next of kin must give permission for the commercial use of their names. Frazier is now being defended by many people who believe that such restrictions are a clear violation of his right to free speech on political issues, as protected by the First Amendment to the American Constitution. Do you think Frazier should be allowed to sell these T-shirts?

Stop for a moment. I encourage you to reflect on this question for 20 to 30 seconds, rather than rushing ahead in order to complete your reading. Questions like this appear throughout this book. Your responses to these brief "reflections" should help you to clarify your own thinking on the subject under discussion. As novelist E. M. Forster said, "How do I know what I think until I see what I say?" So, do you think Frazier should be allowed to sell the T-shirts?

ON POLITICS

This issue captures some of the crucial themes that relate to politics. **Politics** is defined in a variety of ways. (The **bold type** indicates a Key Concept; these terms are listed at the end of the chapter and are included in the Glossary beginning on page 484.) Here are some of the most widely used definitions of politics:

Politics is the exercise of power.

Politics is the public allocation of things that are valued.

Politics is the resolution of conflict.

Politics is the competition among individuals and groups pursuing their own interests.

Politics is the determination of who gets what, when, and how.

All of these definitions share the central idea that *politics is the process through which power and influence are used in the promotion of certain values and interests.* Conflicting values and interests are clearly at the heart of the T-shirt example. In a free society, an individual has the right to make a political statement on almost any issue. But there are instances where free speech is not absolute. In Frazier's case, other people are deeply distressed by his political speech, because they think it exploits the names of their dead loved ones. Whose rights should prevail? If people cannot work out their conflicting values through discussion and compromise, must the government intervene? How does the government exercise its power to resolve the conflict?

Even if the government passed a law, the issue might persist. Frazier has been supported by influential national groups that defend First Amendment rights (e.g., the American Civil Liberties Union) and that challenged the state laws in the court system. Then the U.S. Congress considered passing a law that applies throughout the United States, with restrictions similar to those in the five states' laws. More broadly, what should happen if a political statement on a T-shirt uses extremely vulgar language? What if the statement is full of hateful references to a specific group (such as Jews, gays, African Americans)? What if it incites people to engage in violence? And is a statement treated differently when it is on a T-shirt in contrast to when it is proclaimed in front of a large audience? How will such free speech issues be handled? These are *political* questions.

As individuals, groups, and governmental actors make decisions about what is good or bad for society, and as they try to implement their decisions, politics is at work. For our purposes, politics is associated with those aspects of life that have *public* significance. Other aspects of life, in contrast, are understood to be private and thus are beyond the domain of politics. However, we shall see that what is considered "private" in one country may be considered "public" in another. Even your choice about the job you take, the religion you practice, or the music you listen to can be either a private choice or one within the public domain. Can you see why a government might conclude that these choices have public significance? Within each country, there is a constant debate about the appropriate areas for governmental action and the domains of life that should remain private and unrestrained by political action. Sometimes the term *politics* is used even more broadly than in this book to refer to competition over values in domains that are not truly public, such as the "politics of the family" or "office politics."

In almost every contemporary society, the area that is subject to politics is very large. Politics, usually via government, determines how much education you must have and what its content will be. Politics establishes the words you cannot utter in a public place, how much of your hard-earned income you must give to government, and how various governments spend that money to provide different groups with a vast range of benefits (e.g., education, roads, fire protection, subsidized health care, safe food, national defense, aid to another country, and so on). Politics determines whether you are allowed to use a certain drug, the amount of pollutants that your car can emit, how secure you feel against violence by others within your neighborhood and within the global system, and whether you receive unequal treatment in the allocation of benefits because of your ethnicity, gender, ideology, or some other factor.

TYPES OF POLITICAL KNOWLEDGE

Clearly, politics can affect our lives in many ways. Yet people differ greatly in their understandings about the nature of politics, the uses of political power, and the distribution of political benefits and burdens. If you have discussed politics with your friends, you probably have noticed that they differ in how much they know about politics and in their opinions about what constitutes good and bad political actions. Your understandings about politics and your decisions about whether to undertake specific political actions are grounded in your knowledge of politics. But what are the sources of your political knowledge? How do you make sense out of the many conflicting issues and statements about the political world that confront you each day?

Here, for example, are three political statements:

A "single-payer" national health insurance system is the only solution for solving the inadequacy of the United States' health care system.

In a democracy, men are more likely to vote than women.

The United States is the most peaceful, least warlike nation in modern history.

When you hear or read such a statement, you might take one of these actions:

Ignore it.

Accept that it is correct.

Reject it.

Try to assess it.

If you decide to assess it, you would probably ask questions such as: Is it based on accurate information? Is it consistent with other things that I know about politics? Does it influence any political actions I might take?

When you begin to ask assessment questions, and especially when you try to answer them, you are performing political analysis. At its core, **political analysis** is *the attempt to describe (to answer the* what *questions) and then to explain politics (to answer the* why *and* how *questions).* This book attempts to enhance your ability to do political analysis, to answer the *what, why,* and *how* questions about politics.

Suppose a group of people is instructed to give each of the three political statements above a "truth score," ranging from 100 percent (absolutely true) to 0 percent (absolutely false). Do you think anyone would give all three statements a score of 100 percent? 0 percent? What truth score would you give each of these statements? Did you give every statement a score of either 100 percent or 0 percent? Do you expect that most other people will report scores close to your own? Why?

It is reasonable to assume that few people, if any, believe that all the things they hear about politics are absolutely accurate and true. One reason to be suspicious of statements about politics is that they usually reflect the values and interests of the source of the statement.

The first statement was by Physicians for a National Health Program (2008), a not-for-profit organization of physicians, medical students, and other health care professionals. The second statement was made by political scientists Lester Milbrath and M. L. Goel (1982: 116) in a book summarizing the research on political participation. And the third was made by Ronald Reagan, president of the United States from 1981 to 1989, during his nomination acceptance speech to the Republican Party in 1984.

Unless you view all these sources as equally reliable, your knowledge of who made the statements might alter your truth score in some cases. If it does, can you explain why?

There are many sources of statements about politics—family, friends, television, books, newspapers, teachers, politicians. Such sources can provide information about politics, but the information can be unclear, contradictory, or wrong. You are surrounded by competing claims regarding the political world. How are you to determine what you do know about politics?

Political science is one way of attempting to establish such knowledge. As you will discover in reading this book, **political science** is *a set of techniques, concepts, and approaches whose objective is to increase the clarity and accuracy of our understandings about the political world.* You will learn how some political scientists try to think systematically about political phenomena in order to describe "political reality" and explain how politics works. You will also be introduced to some of the findings about politics that have emerged from the work of political scientists and other social scientists.

It was noted earlier that people have very different views about politics. Your friends probably differ in how much they know about such things as the names of the leaders of various countries, do not agree on such questions as how easy it is for a president to get a law passed, and have significant differences of opinion on political issues such as whether there should be a system of "free" health care for all citizens. An individual's understanding of politics is composed of three general types of political knowledge: (1) descriptions of political facts, (2) explanations of how and why politics occurs as it does, and (3) prescriptions of what should happen in the political world.

Description

Many bits of political knowledge offer a ***description***, which focuses on *what* questions and is usually based on one or more "facts." (A term printed in ***bold and italic*** type is a Key Concept that is listed at the end of the current chapter but is not in the Glossary at the back of the book.) They can be answered with relatively straightforward political facts such as these:

> The date the Soviet Union ceased to exist: December 25, 1991, with the resignation of Mikhail Gorbachev
>
> The number of states in Nigeria: 36
>
> The country with the highest gross domestic product (GDP) per capita in the world in 2008: Luxembourg

But on many questions about the political world, there are no indisputable answers. On some questions, it is difficult to get precise information. Suppose you want to know the number of countries with operational nuclear weapons. Seven countries acknowledge having operational nuclear devices (China, France, India, Pakistan, Russia, the United Kingdom, and the United States). One additional country (North Korea) tested a nuclear weapon and might have more that are operational. Experts believe that one more country (Israel) has nuclear weapons, and at least one additional country (Iran) is suspected of having a secret nuclear weapons program. Several others (Algeria, Argentina, Belarus, Brazil, Iraq, Kazakhstan, Libya, South Africa, and

BOX 1.1

Where in the World?

The section on "Description" briefly refers to 21 countries (and 1 country that no longer exists) on 5 continents. Do you have a clear sense of where they are?

There will be detailed discussions of many countries in this book. Knowing the location of a country and its geographic relationship to certain other countries is sometimes extremely important for an understanding of its political choices and actions. When such discussions occur, you are strongly encouraged to locate the country on a map. For this purpose, there is a world map on the front inside cover of this book.

Several recent studies have shown that American students are more ignorant of world geography than are students in most other countries. If that characterization applies to you, help change the situation by referring frequently to the map.

Ukraine) had or were close to having nuclear weapons but are now assumed to have backed away from nuclear ambitions (Federation of American Scientists 2008). Even the experts cannot reach consensus on the straightforward issue of which countries belong to the "nuclear club." Box 1.1 asks you an important question about these countries. Is your answer yes?

On other questions about politics, description requires assessments that raise complicated issues about power, interests, and values, thus making it difficult to reach agreement about the facts. Here are two examples:

Do nonwhites and whites in the United States enjoy equal treatment before the law?

Can a country legally invade another country that has not used military force against it?

Explanation

Many questions about politics are even more difficult to answer because they require political knowledge in the form of **explanation**, which attempts to *specify why something happens* and to *provide the reason or process by which the phenomenon occurs.*

Why is one in eight families "poor" in the wealthy United States? What causes a country (e.g., Zimbabwe) to have inflation higher than 2000 percent in a single year? Why does revolutionary violence overthrow the government in one country (e.g., Nicaragua) but not in another (e.g., its comparable neighbor, El Salvador)? Responses to these kinds of questions require explanation, not mere descriptive facts. Such questions can be among the most fascinating in politics, but adequate explanation is often difficult because patterns of cause and effect can be extraordinarily complex.

Prescription

Statements about politics often include claims or assumptions that certain choices and actions are more desirable than others. These represent a third form of political knowledge, prescription. A *prescription* is *a value judgment that indicates what* should *occur and* should *be done.* Thus a prescription deals with answers to questions about what ought to be, not merely description and explanation of what is.

For example, there are many possible prescriptive responses to this question: What should the government's role be in the provision of health care? Answers vary from the viewpoint that government should take absolutely no action that interferes with the private provision of health care to the viewpoint that government should meet the full range of health care needs at no direct cost to the patient. You can probably think of many positions between these two extremes.

The position you select is an element of your **normative political knowledge—** *your value judgments.* Notice that normative political knowledge combines three types of understanding: (1) your descriptive knowledge of certain facts (e.g., the alternative forms of health care that are available in a particular society); (2) your explanatory knowledge about why certain outcomes occur (e.g., the causes of unequal health care); and most important, (3) your priorities among competing values (e.g., how much you prefer equality, lower taxes, personal responsibility).

SOURCES OF POLITICAL KNOWLEDGE

Each individual's political knowledge is a unique combination of descriptive facts, explanations, and prescriptions about politics. What is the basis of such knowledge? This section describes three important sources: (1) authority, (2) personal thought, and (3) science.

Authority

The method of *authority* involves *the appeal to any document, tradition, or person that is believed to possess the controlling explanation regarding a particular issue.* Knowledge about politics can be based on three kinds of authority sources: (1) a specific authority, (2) a general authority, or (3) "everyone."

Specific authority sources.   A particular individual (but few others) might place great confidence in the knowledge he derives about politics from a specific authority source, such as a parent, teacher, friend, or famous person. Young people and those minimally interested in politics are especially likely to rely on specific authorities for much of their political knowledge. Chapter 4 will argue that specific authority sources powerfully influence some important political beliefs of most individuals. Can you think of a significant piece of your own political knowledge that you derived primarily from a parent, an influential teacher, or a public figure you admire?

General authority sources.   A general authority source is one that has substantial influence on a large proportion of people in a society. Examples are constitutions,

BOX 1.2

General Authorities and Normative Knowledge: The Role of Women in Politics

▶ Tens of thousands march in Washington, D.C., in support of an amendment to the U.S. Constitution that would guarantee equal rights for women.

General authorities are particularly powerful in providing normative knowledge. It can be extremely difficult to decide how to judge political issues, and in such cases, it can be helpful to find a widely accepted authority for guidance. For example, consider the question: What is the role of women in a country's politics? While some people see this as a straightforward question of fact, others view it as a normative question about what the role of women *should* be. In some societies, there is disagreement about this question, and many look to an authority source to provide the answer.

In the United States, the crucial source of authority for such questions is a *legal document*—the Constitution. The U.S. Constitution does not mention women. For nearly 150 years, this omission was interpreted to mean that women should be excluded from any political role, even from voting. Finally, political pressure resulted in a formal change within the source of authority, with the passage of the Nineteenth Amendment in 1920, which added language to the Constitution granting women voting rights (and, implicitly, all political rights exercised by men).

BOX 1.2 *(Continued)*

In Iran, as in the United States, the key source of authority on women's political rights is also a document, but in Iran, it is a *religious document*, the Koran. During the political regime of Shah Reza Pahlavi (1941–1979), women were encouraged to participate more fully in politics than a strict interpretation of the Koran might suggest. However, when the Ayatollah Khomeini (in power 1979–1989) replaced the shah, he insisted on a strict interpretation, and the political roles of women were significantly limited. After Khomeini's death, more moderate leaders again extended the political rights and activities of Iranian women for about a decade. Since then, political power is dominated by those who have acted to reduce women's political roles.

In contemporary China, the authoritative pronouncements of a *person*, Mao Zedong (who ruled from 1949 to 1976), established the contemporary political rights of women. Prior to the revolution of 1949, the role of women in China was defined by the religious traditions of Confucianism (discussed in Box 15.3). Most women were essentially the property of men, and they had few political rights. As part of Chairman Mao's efforts to transform Confucian tradition, he granted women full equality under the law, and women were encouraged to participate actively in all aspects of political life.

revered leaders, widely respected media or books, and religious teachings. General authorities are especially evident as a basis for normative political knowledge. (See Box 1.2 on the role of women in politics.)

"Everyone" as authority.   Sometimes we are convinced that something is true because it is a belief strongly held by many other people. If virtually "everyone" (i.e., the reference group to which you look for information and knowledge) seems to agree on a "fact" about politics, there is little reason for you to disagree or challenge that fact. One reason to place confidence in a belief strongly held by many people is the assumption that it is unlikely so many people will be incorrect. Such knowledge has stood the test of time, since it could have been challenged and repudiated in the marketplace of ideas. For example, you will probably find that virtually everyone you know agrees that political terrorism is bad.

Problems with authority as a source of knowledge.   However, there are fundamental problems with using authority as a way of knowing. This should be most obvious with *specific authorities*. You might think that your parent or best teacher or favorite celebrity has the correct view on an important political issue, but few of the other 6.6 billion people in the world have any confidence in this source of your political knowledge.

And, although "everyone knows that *X* is true," there is no guarantee that *everyone* is correct. First, as "Honest Abe" Lincoln observed, you can fool all of the people some of the time. Indeed, a political belief that is widely held might be particularly immune to careful assessment. Experiments in psychology have revealed the extent to which a person's beliefs can be altered by the beliefs of others. For example, if a subject hears several respondents (collaborating with the experimenter) all give identical wrong answers to a question, the subject can thereby be persuaded to change his mind about what he knows, even when he is correct. Second, "everyone" often consists mainly of people whose cultural background we share. If you reexamined the above example about terrorism with a different "everyone," it is unlikely that virtually everyone living under an oppressive political regime believes that political terrorism is bad.

It is common for citizens in most political systems to believe that the citizens of rival political systems have been brainwashed. We know that some beliefs of our rivals are incorrect. Isn't it likely that they are equally convinced that some of our strongly held beliefs are wrong?

There are even problems with *general authorities*. Sometimes, as when they are listing the countries with nuclear weapons or explaining why poverty exists, even the most competent general authorities might not have access to crucial information or might disagree about how to interpret the available data. And sometimes, even when a group accepts a single authority, there can be ambiguities and problems of interpretation. Consider again the normative issue of the political role of women (discussed in Box 1.2):

> In the United States, all branches of government continually interpret and apply the rather limited framework outlined in the Constitution. The strong political agitation for an "equal rights" amendment indicates that many people feel that the Constitution, even with the Nineteenth Amendment, still fails to ensure women of political rights equivalent to those enjoyed by men.
>
> Notice that women's political and civil rights in Iran have been extended and then severely limited several times in recent decades. The appropriate role of women in Iran's politics remains a highly contested issue, despite the Koran. Indeed, there is considerable difference of opinion within the broader Muslim world regarding how to interpret the Koran's authoritative prescriptions regarding women's roles in political life. In some Muslim countries, such as Saudi Arabia and Sudan, women's roles are greatly restricted. Yet Bangladesh, the "Islamic Republic of Pakistan," Indonesia, and Turkey are Muslim-majority countries that selected female heads of government (prime ministers) in recent years.
>
> In China, Mao Zedong remains the authority source on equality for women in political and social life. But his view was never accepted by some rural people who continue to follow the traditional Confucian norms. And while the top Chinese leaders follow Mao's pronouncements on women, the leadership now rejects Mao's authoritative pronouncements on other important subjects, especially on economic matters.

In short, it is common, and perhaps inevitable, for authority sources to offer inconsistent or conflicting knowledge claims about the political world. It is extremely difficult to differentiate between alternative authorities or even to establish widespread agreement on precisely what political knowledge a particular authority source provides.

Personal Thought

Have you ever insisted that some fact is correct because it seemed so "obvious" to you? It is possible to feel confident that you know something on the basis of your own reason, feelings, or experiences. This second source of knowledge does not rely on outside authorities; rather, it assumes that the individual can use his own powers of thought to determine what he knows about the political world. Such knowledge can be based on rationality or intuition or be grounded in personal experience.

Rationality.   An individual can rely on his own rational thought as a means for deciding that something is correct. On occasion, you probably have decided that a certain fact is true because it is logical or obvious—it just "makes sense." The underlying assumption is that such a knowledge claim is verified because it will seem self-evident to all reasonable people and needs no further justification. For example, the Preamble to the American Declaration of Independence claims that there are "self-evident" truths—that all men are created equal and that they have inalienable rights to life, liberty, and the pursuit of happiness.

Intuition.   Another form of personal thought is intuition. Here, one's knowledge is based on feeling, on a sense of understanding or empathy, rather than on reason. You have probably been convinced that something is correct because it *feels* right. For example, the key slogan of Barry Goldwater, the Republican presidential candidate in 1964, was an explicit appeal to intuition: "In your heart, you know he's right!"

Personal experience.   You can also be convinced that something is true because of your own personal experiences. For example, you might be convinced that government bureaucracies are inefficient because a specific agency handled your inquiries so ineptly. Or you might believe that different ethnic groups can live together in harmony based on your own positive experience in a multiethnic setting. Personal involvement in a dramatic event, such as witnessing a handgun murder or being physically harassed by the police, can have a particularly powerful impact on one's political beliefs.

Problems with personal thought as a source of knowledge.   A major problem with all three forms of personal thought as a source of knowledge is that there is no method for resolving "thoughtful" differences of opinion among individuals. This is most obvious with personal experience: because people have quite different personal experiences, they are unlikely to reach the same conclusions about what is true. Similarly, there is no reason to assume that different people will share the same intuitive feelings regarding what is true. Goldwater's poor electoral showing (he received only 39 percent of the vote) suggests that many people concluded (intuitively?) that he was not right, or perhaps they decided (rationally?) that he was too far right—too conservative ideologically.

Even rational thought will not necessarily enable people to agree on political facts. We do not all employ the same logic. Consider again the key knowledge claim cited earlier: "We hold these truths to be self-evident—that all men are created equal." This seems a clear appeal to rationality, a political fact that is self-evident to all thinking people. But what exactly does this claim mean? Do all men have equal physical or mental traits at birth? Do they grow up with equal opportunities? Are they equal before the law, regardless of the quality of legal help they can purchase? Are all women created equal, too? Many legal and political struggles in the United States during the more than two centuries since this "self-evident" truth was proclaimed have concerned precisely what equal rights *are* assured to every person in the American political system, with particular regard to race, gender, and age.

Science

In contrast to the two other sources of knowledge, science uses explicit methods that attempt to enable different people to agree about what they know. The goal of any science is to describe and explain—to answer *what, why,* and *how* questions. There are four essential characteristics of the **scientific method**:

1. Science entails a *search for regularities* in the relationships among phenomena.

2. Science is *empirical* in the sense that it is concerned with phenomena that can be observed, or at least measured.

3. Science is *cumulative* because it tentatively accepts previously established knowledge on a subject as the foundation for development of further knowledge. One can challenge existing knowledge, but it is not necessary to reestablish the knowledge base every time.

4. The method of science is *testable*. Its practitioners, "scientists," specify the assumptions, data, analytic techniques, and inference patterns that support their knowledge claim. They look for some analysis or evidence that would invalidate ("falsify") the claim. Other scientists can evaluate all aspects of the claim and can repeat the analysis to ensure that everyone reaches the same conclusion.

POLITICAL SCIENCE

Most contemporary political scientists attempt to use the scientific method to establish shared knowledge about the political world. Box 1.3 demonstrates how to apply the scientific method to one of the knowledge claims listed near the beginning of the chapter: that in a democracy, men are more likely to vote than women. This example reveals how political scientists structure the search for regularities and the methods that they use. This book will offer many examples of generalizations and empirical findings about politics that are based on the scientific method.

Within the framework of the scientific method, there are different ways of undertaking political analysis. (Some of the most important are explained in detail in the Appendix.) Each mode of analysis is distinct in terms of its assumptions, methods, use of data, and inference structures. However, all modes share a fundamental commitment: to discover regularities among political phenomena using approaches that are empirical, cumulative, and testable.

In the example of political analysis in Box 1.3, as in any scientific study, one's conclusions, as well as one's concepts, data, and methods, are subject to scrutiny and challenge by others. An analyst's conclusion is presumed to be correct until there is compelling criticism or contrary evidence that undermines it. Because many knowledge claims about politics concern complex phenomena, it is often difficult to establish with precision what we do know, even when we use the scientific method. Nonetheless, the scientific

BOX 1.3

Gender and Voting: Applying the Scientific Method to Politics Using the Appendix

This analysis of gender and voting is typical of one form of political analysis employed by political scientists. As you read through it, ask yourself whether you understand how to interpret Table 1.1, whether you know the kinds of data that would strengthen the analysis, and whether you think this is a functional or relational analysis (see pages 477–478). If you understand these terms and feel confident in answering such questions, you have a strong analytic basis for discussions later in the book. If you feel that you could use a bit more background on such issues, read the Appendix before you continue. It explains some of the major analytic approaches that are used in applying the scientific method to the study of politics, the types of empirical data that are employed, and the means of reaching conclusions through the use of such data. Even those readers with some analytic background will find the Appendix helpful as a review and as a means of checking their understanding.

Is it true that men are more likely than women to vote in a democracy? Let us briefly consider how you might analyze this claim by means of the scientific method. Remember that applying the scientific method entails formulating a question with precision, gathering and analyzing empirical evidence that is relevant to the question, and then proposing a generalization or conclusion.

1. *Examine existing evidence* that is relevant to the issue you are analyzing. In this example, it would be sensible to look in various sources for studies of voting by political scientists or other social scientists (e.g., Carroll and Fox 2006; www.gendergap.com; Lovenduski 2005).

2. With this background, *state the issue* you are examining in a precise manner. This particular issue is already stated in the form of a *hypothesis* (i.e., a proposition about a political fact): In a democracy, men are more likely to vote than women.

3. *"Operationalize" key concepts.* This means that you specify exactly what each concept means and how it might be measured. Defining political concepts such as democracy can be extremely difficult (as you will see in Chapter 7). In this example, let us tentatively propose that a political democracy is "a state with periodic elections in which most adult citizens are allowed to vote in order to select among genuine alternative candidates for public office." The probability of voting is operationalized as "the percentage of those eligible to vote who actually do vote on a major political office."

4. *Gather appropriate data.* You need a strategy for collecting evidence that is *valid* (i.e., it measures what it is supposed to measure) and *reliable* (i.e., it is accurate). You also decide what specific cases you are going to analyze. In this example, choose one or more democracies and certain specific elections for which you are going to

BOX 1.3 *(Continued)*

gather data. You might gather the relevant data from books or reports, or you might need to go "into the field" to measure the phenomena yourself. For this example, suppose you select the United States as the democracy, the presidential election as the vote on a major public office, and 1976 and 2004 as the elections for which you actually gather data. Do you think these are reasonable choices with which to assess the question? The survey data are displayed in Table 1.1. (Regarding the data in Table 1.1: These data are individuals' own reports, after the election, on whether or not they voted. The data were gathered for a carefully selected national sample of voters in a survey designed by academic researchers. Can you think of any problems with the validity of such data? How might more valid data be gathered?)

> **TABLE 1.1**
> **Participation of Eligible Voters in the U.S. Presidential Election, by Gender**

	1976		2004	
	% Men	% Women	% Men	% Women
Voted	77	67	62	65
Did not vote	23	33	38	35

5. *Analyze the evidence.* According to the 1976 data in Table 1.1, men do vote at a substantially higher rate than women (77 percent versus 67 percent). In 2004, however, the voting rate for women (51 percent) is slightly higher than that for men (49 percent).

6. *Decide what, if any, inferences can be made* about the issue on the basis of your evidence. This is where your analytic skills must be especially rich. The Appendix illustrates a statistical technique that can help you judge whether the difference in the data for women and men is greater than might be expected by chance. In the absence of such statistics, what do you think?

Is the evidence sufficient? Can you have confidence in a generalization about gender and voting in the United States based on only two elections? Table 1.1 probably would lead you to observe that you cannot generalize with any confidence until you have more data. In fact, if you did get comparable data for other presidential elections, you would discover that women have voted at a higher rate than men in every U.S. presidential election since 1980, and at a lower rate in every election prior to 1980. What is your inference now?

Among the reasons that the study of politics is so fascinating are that things are rarely straightforward and that they can change (sometimes quite rapidly). For the political analyst, this means that generalizations must be made with care and with attention to longitudinal patterns (i.e., patterns over time). If you wanted to establish a broad generalization about gender and voting, you would need voting data from several democracies, not just the United States.

Even with data from more elections, you still must assess whether you have analyzed the evidence correctly. Have you overlooked some other important variable that might affect the relationship between gender and voting? To deal with this

BOX 1.3 *(Continued)*

possibility, identify the factors that might affect voting rates among men and women. Many other explanatory factors might seem relevant: age, ethnicity, education, party identification, attitudes on key policy issues, and so on. By analyzing the relationships among various factors, you can gain a clearer understanding about the importance of gender in explaining varying rates of voter turnout. As an example of the kinds of subtle relationships that exist among different explanatory factors, the Appendix reconsiders the 1976 data. The analysis reveals that the apparent relationship between gender and voting in the 1976 data is virtually eliminated when the voter's education level is considered.

7. Ideally, the final stage of your analysis is to *offer a tentative conclusion* regarding the issue. Defensible conclusions in analyses of politics often require extensive data, thorough analysis, and consideration of several alternative explanations. Sometimes the phenomena are so complicated or the evidence is so mixed that no generalization is possible. In our example, the data seem too contradictory to support any clear generalization about gender and voting. Rather, more data and more thoughtful analysis are required. If anything, this brief analysis seems to support the conclusion that, in recent U.S. elections at least, men are not more likely to vote than women.

method does help people to identify more clearly the points on which they agree or disagree and, ultimately, to develop generalizations about politics.

Political science is composed of certain subfields that are usually defined by their specific subject matter, rather than by their mode of analysis. While there are different ways to categorize the subfields, four are prominent:

1. **Comparative politics.** This subfield *focuses on similarities and differences in political processes and structures* (Laitin 2002). Comparison might be cross-national (e.g., comparing the legal systems of Iran and Taiwan or comparing the voting patterns in 40 countries), or it might compare actors within a single country (e.g., comparing the welfare policies of the 50 American states). (While U.S. politics is sometimes treated as a separate subfield, it is best classified as a part of the subject matter of comparative politics.) Comparative politics covers a huge domain within political analysis, and it has many sub-subfields (e.g., public administration, political parties, development, individual political behavior, and public policy).

2. **International relations.** The *focus is on the political relations between countries, the behavior of transnational actors, and the dynamics within the worldwide system of states and groups.* Subjects within international relations include war, interstate conflict resolution, international law, globalization, regional alliances, colonialism, and international organizations. The study of foreign policy is also within this subfield.

3. **Political theory.** More precisely called political philosophy, this subfield *focuses on the ideas and debates dealing with important political questions.* Some of this work attempts to characterize and interpret the writings of major political theorists (e.g., Plato, Thomas Hobbes, Karl Marx, John Rawls), whereas other works

are original explorations of the political questions themselves (e.g., What is the nature of a just society? Why is there conflict between groups?). Political theory is *the source of many of the normative knowledge claims made by political scientists.* Much of the work in political theory is based on the methods of rationality or authority or on an appeal to moral truths, rather than on the scientific method.

4. **Boundary-spanning subfields.** Political science is an eclectic field that often links with other fields of inquiry or, at least, that borrows and adapts ideas from other disciplines. Some work actually spans the boundary between political science and another discipline. While the subject matter of much of this work fits within one of the preceding three major subfields, we could list these hybrids as components of a fourth subfield, which would include political anthropology, political economy, political psychology, political sociology, and biopolitics.

POLITICAL "SCIENCE"?

Criticisms of Political Science as a "Science"

Not everyone agrees that it is appropriate and desirable to apply the scientific method to politics. Four different kinds of criticism have been aimed at political science.

It is not a "real" science.   The first criticism is that political science is not "scientific" in comparison with "real" natural and applied sciences (e.g., chemistry, physics, engineering). Stimulated by Thomas Kuhn's book *The Structure of Scientific Revolutions* (1996), this view posits that there is general agreement on the four key elements that provide organization and direction within a fully developed science: (1) central **concepts**, which *identify and name crucial phenomena* (specifically, such as "the Iraq War," or generally, such as "war"); (2) **theories**, which are *sets of systematically related generalizations that provide explanations and predictions about the linkages between certain concepts* (in the form "If A, then B under conditions C and D"); (3) *rules of interpretation,* which indicate the methods that will establish whether the explanations and predictions posited by the theory are right or wrong; and (4) a list of questions or *issues* that are worth solving within the area of inquiry.

These four key elements are well developed and widely shared within the research communities of every natural and applied science. In contrast, researchers in political science (and other social sciences) have not agreed on a coherent set of concepts, theories, and rules of interpretation. As you will discover throughout this book, many different methods are used in political science. There is disagreement regarding the important issues that ought to be solved, little consensus on what theories or generalizations have been proven, and even great difficulty in operationalizing key concepts, such as "power" and "democracy."

Its subject matter defies generalization.   The second criticism is that it is impossible to develop a science of politics because of the subject matter. In this view, the political world is far too complex and unpredictable for systematic generalizations.

Politics is based on the actions and interactions of many individuals, groups, and even countries. Politics occurs in the midst of many changing conditions that can influence those actions. The range of variation in what people might do and in the conditions that might exist is so vast that clear "If A, then B" statements about politics are impossible. Thus it is not surprising that political analysts cannot precisely explain the causes of war, or why women vote differently than men, or what effect a law banning private handguns will have on crime rates.

Its "scientists" cannot be objective.   The third criticism is that the analysis of politics cannot be objective in the way assumed by the scientific method. The issues chosen for study and the manner in which variables are defined, measured, and analyzed are all powerfully influenced by the analyst's social reality (e.g., by his own culture, ideas, life experiences). In this view, no person (whether Sunni Muslim or agnostic, rural Nigerian or cosmopolitan Parisian, international lawyer or migrant farm worker) can be totally objective and unbiased in the way he tries to analyze political phenomena (see Box 1.4).

Its practice diverts attention from normative questions.   Finally, the fourth criticism faults the scientific method itself for not helping to answer the crucial normative questions of politics. Since the time of Aristotle (384–322 B.C.E.), classical political theorists have insisted that the ultimate aim of political analysis is to discover "the highest good attainable by action." In this view, political analysis is a noble endeavor because it helps determine what government and individuals *should* do so that valued goals (e.g., democratic politics, a good life, a just society) can be achieved.

However, even many of those who use the scientific method to study politics do not assume that it can achieve such goals. Max Weber (1864–1920), the influential German social scientist, argued that the scientific method is useful for describing and categorizing political and social reality. But, Weber added, it cannot provide answers to fundamental normative questions about goals and appropriate means. Weber (1958a: 152–153) approvingly quoted Russian novelist Leo Tolstoi's assertion that science can provide no answer to the essential question, "What shall we do, and how shall we arrange our lives?" According to this fourth critique, then, political science becomes an arid enterprise if its reliance on the scientific method discourages attempts to address essential questions about political values and political good (Strauss 1959; Wolin 1960).

Political Science as a Means of Understanding the Political World

These four main criticisms of a science of politics are important; you should assess them throughout this book. In general, this book will make the case that, despite the complexity of politics, generalizations are possible—each political phenomenon is not *sui generis*, a unique thing. If political "science" means the attempt to apply the scientific method in order to understand the political world better, it is desirable to use such systematic and analytic thinking. And if we are to share *any* knowledge about the political world, we need methods to reach some interpersonal agreement about political facts. Although political science lacks precise concepts and theories,

BOX 1.4

How's Your Bias?

In its idealized form, the method of science might be value free. But in the analysis of politics, it is impossible for the analyst to describe and explain without being influenced by his own values. You should remember this fact as you consider the arguments and information in this book. It is likely that most readers (including the author) have lived primarily in Western democratic countries. As you will see in Chapter 4 and as you should recognize when you react to the claims throughout the book, your attitudes and judgments are biased by your experiences and your political socialization.

As I wrote this book, I attempted to be sensitive to my own political biases (I recognize some of them, but others are subconscious) and to be fair in describing, analyzing, and generalizing about different political systems. But throughout the book, value judgments are embedded in every choice about what content is included and how it is presented. The chapters are based on my study of social science research (mainly in the English language) and on my personal experiences, which have occurred in many parts of the world. I am aware that my writing includes many explicit or implicit evaluations and that it might reflect political reality or my biases (as an American, a man, etc.). It is important that you assess issues of bias whenever you encounter claims about politics, from any source.

It will take far more than this book to help you make your own judgments regarding political reality. As you read, try to become more conscious of *your* biases, which will undoubtedly influence your ultimate assessments of politics and even your openness to any claims made about the political world.

it does enable us to develop better concepts, improved methods, and sound generalizations, and thereby it makes the study of the political world an exciting intellectual challenge.

This book assumes that understanding politics is extremely important. As Austrian philosopher of science Karl Popper (1963: 227) suggests, "We must not expect too much from reason; argument rarely settles a [political] question, although it is the only means for learning—not to see clearly, but to see more clearly than before." In the face of fundamental value conflicts and the potential for massive political violence among individuals, groups, and countries, political knowledge might reduce our misunderstandings and misconceptions. Thus it can be the grounds for greater tolerance and wiser value judgments about normative political issues. Moreover, enhancing *what* we know about politics should make us more effective in knowing *how* to behave politically—as voters, political activists, and political decision makers. The study of the political world is of crucial importance to the creation of humane social life. Ultimately it is up to you, as you read this book, to decide what can be known about politics and whether you think political "science" is feasible.

WHERE IS THIS BOOK GOING?

Just as there are different approaches to political science, there are different ways to introduce you to the political world. This book is organized to lead you along one route to understanding. But there are other routes, including reading the book in a different order than beginning at Chapter 1 and finishing with Chapter 15 (for example, I think it would be helpful for you to read the Appendix now; it has also been suggested that Part Two could be read after Parts Three and Four).

"Man is the measure of all things," observed the ancient Greek philosopher Protagoras (c. 490–421 B.C.E.). In that spirit, this book begins its exploration of the political world at the most personal and individual level. It initially examines what individual men and women think about politics and how they act politically (Part Two). The book then focuses primarily on the politics of large collectivities of people that we call states and that are organized politically as governments. Thus, Parts Three, Four, and Five offer perspectives and explanations from political science regarding how states and governments are organized for political action, how political processes occur, and how countries are attempting to fulfill their political goals in the challenging conditions of the early twenty-first century.

Part Two, "Political Behavior," begins in Chapter 2 with a description of basic political theories and an assessment of the kinds of *political beliefs* that people hold. It continues in Chapter 3 with a consideration of the *political actions* that people and groups undertake. Chapter 4 moves from description to explanation: Can we explain *why* people seem to think and act in certain ways?

Part Three, "Political Systems," is about the politics of large numbers of people—about how the political world is organized and about the *structures of government*. Chapters 5 through 8 address such questions as: What is a state? How are the political system and the economic system linked? What features distinguish democracies or dictatorships? What are the responsibilities of such political structures as the bureaucracy or the legislature?

Part Four, "Political Processes," emphasizes the *key dynamics of politics*. Chapter 9 characterizes the public policy process and details three major explanations for how political power is distributed and how policy decisions are made. Chapter 10 explores the important processes of political change and development. The vital issues of politics across borders and the manner in which states and other transnational actors cooperate and compete are central to Chapter 11. The various forms and causes of political violence are analyzed in Chapter 12.

Part Five, "Politics Among States," focuses on the actions and challenges facing *countries in the contemporary political world*. Chapters 13 through 15 consider countries at different stages of development as they pursue the general goals of prosperity, security, and stability in the complicated global system. Finally, the Appendix explains major concepts in political science, including four important frameworks for engaging in political analysis.

Whatever the order in which you read sections of this book, I hope it will enhance *your* understanding of the political world.

KEY CONCEPTS

authority (as a knowledge source)
concept
description
explanation

normative political knowledge
political analysis
political science
politics

prescription
scientific method
theory

FOR FURTHER CONSIDERATION

1. What do you think is the most serious obstacle to a "science" of politics?

2. Which authority have you relied on most extensively as a source of your knowledge about politics? What is the biggest shortcoming of this source?

3. What is the most important question that political science should attempt to answer? What might prevent political scientists from answering this question adequately?

4. Many people insist that most of their political knowledge is based on their own rational thought processes. What might be wrong with this claim?

5. Do you think political scientists can play an important role in government, or are they just intellectuals who can only stand on the sidelines and analyze politics?

6. Which statement about the political world proposed within this chapter do you think would receive the greatest variations in "truth scores" among citizens in your society? Which statement would receive the greatest score variations between your society and another one that you identify? Why do you expect variation in the assessment of these statements?

FOR FURTHER READING

Almond, Gabriel. (1989). *A Discipline Divided: Schools and Sects in Political Science.* Newbury Park, CA: Sage. One of the major scholars of comparative politics assesses the diversity of approaches to political science and the possibility of a science of politics.

Carlisle, Rodney, Ed. (2005). *Encyclopedia of Politics: The Left and the Right.* Newbury Park, CA: Sage. This clever and comprehensive (1,100 pages) two-volume set (the "left" volume examines progressive/socialist thinking and the "right" examines conservative and classical liberal perspectives) contains more than 450 readable and interesting articles that concentrate on the "isms" and many, many other interesting themes, as elaborated by historical and contemporary thinkers from many parts of the world.

Goodin, Robert, and Hans-Dieter Klingemann, Eds. (1996). *A New Handbook of Political Science.* New York: Oxford University Press. Articles by well-known political scientists discuss the central concepts, institutional issues, and recent empirical research in many important subfields.

Katznelson, Ira, and Helen Miller, Eds. (2002). *Political Science: State of the Discipline.* Centennial ed. New York: W. W. Norton. In only(!) 993 pages, a strong set of political scientists offer essays (sponsored by the American Political Science Association) on the current insights and debates on central issues related to core concepts in the discipline, such as the state, democracy, political institutions, participation, and modes of political analysis.

Kuhn, Thomas. (1996). *The Structure of Scientific Revolutions.* 3rd ed. Chicago: University of Chicago Press. A short, understandable, and enormously influential discussion of how sciences develop and overturn paradigms, first published in 1962.

Manheim, Jarol B., Richard Rich, Lars Willnat, and Craig Brians. (2006). *Empirical Political Analysis: Research Methods in Political Science.* 6th ed. New York: Pearson Longman. A very effective and understandable presentation of the primary methods that political scientists utilize in the attempt to understand politics and develop defensible generalizations, focusing on a full range of qualitative and quantitative approaches.

Pollack, Philip H. (2005). *The Essentials of Political Analysis.* 2nd ed. Washington, DC: CQ Press. Using many interesting examples and communicative language, the book explains how to use empirical data and quantitative analysis (especially the use of the Statistical Package for Social Sciences—SPSS) in the study of political phenomena.

Popper, Karl R. (1968). *The Logic of Scientific Discovery.* London: Hutchinson. A major and widely respected statement of the philosophy and application of the scientific method.

ON THE WEB

http://www.apsanet.org/

This Web site for the American Political Science Association, the major organization for political scientists in the United States, provides links to a variety of activities and opportunities associated with political science professionals, including online papers from the national conference and articles from *PS: Political Science and Politics.*

http://www.psqonline.org/

Political Science Quarterly is America's oldest continuously published political science journal and brings you the world of politics.

http://www.etown.edu/vl/

The rich and extensive set of links on this Web site, "WWW Virtual Library: International Affairs Resources," includes numerous sites for each region as well as links to many key international topics that are as varied as international organizations, environmental issues, world religions, media resources, health, and human rights.

http://www.realclearpolitics.com

A daily compendium of many of the most interesting stories about politics available on the Internet, with an almost exclusive focus on U.S. politics.

http://www.lib.umich.edu/govdocs/polisci.html

The University of Michigan library has compiled an in-depth listing of political science resources on the Web, including a compilation of numerous interesting articles on politics and political science, both historical and current.

http://polsci.colorado.edu/RES/

Similar to the University of Michigan's site, this "WWW Resources for Political Scientists" from the University of Colorado provides a variety of useful links to key sites in the professional literature.

http://www.psr.keele.ac.uk/

Richard Kimber's Political Science Resources page includes an extensive listing of sites on such topics as political theory, political thought, constitutions, elections, political parties, international relations, and British politics.

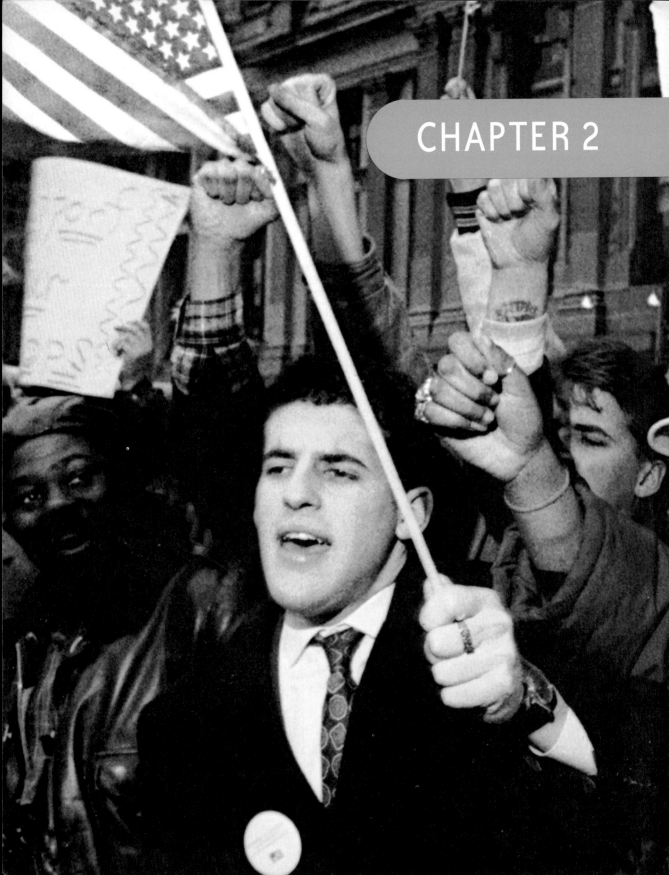

CHAPTER 2

POLITICAL THEORY AND POLITICAL BELIEFS

You stop at a Burger King to eat. While ordering your food, you see some acquaintances motioning you to join them. As you sit down, someone you don't know is saying, "The U.S. invasion of Iraq was totally immoral. The United States had no right to cause all that suffering, and it cost America billions of dollars that should be spent dealing with poverty at home!" She looks directly at you. What would you do in this situation?

CHAPTER OUTLINE

- Normative Political Theory
- Individual Political Beliefs
- Belief Systems
- Political Culture
- Looking Ahead

Many reactions are possible. You might feel indifference, anxiety, or even anger. You might be silent and act as if this has nothing to do with you. You might change the subject or say you have no opinion. You might indicate that you agree with her, or you might heatedly dispute her assertions.

Your responses to this incident offer interesting evidence about your reactions to the political world. Some of your responses might involve what you think (your political ideology and your political beliefs), and others might involve what you do (your political actions). This combination of beliefs and actions is the essence of the domain of political science called *political behavior,* or **micropolitics**. It is called micropolitics because the key object of study is the smallest political unit—the individual as a thinker and actor in the political world. Micropolitics can also include the study of the political beliefs and actions of groups, such as families, committees, and juries.

Part Two of this book explores themes in the study of micropolitics. Initially, this chapter focuses on **normative political knowledge,** *the fundamental ideas that can be the basis of an individual's beliefs and actions.* This first section also describes three key *political ideologies* that are prevalent in Western political thought. Second, the chapter examines the basic elements of an individual's *political beliefs,* which are grounded in a person's orientations toward the political world. Third, the chapter considers the configurations of beliefs held by individuals, a cluster called a *political belief system.* Finally, it attempts to characterize the dominant patterns of political behavior for an entire society—its *political culture.* Chapter 3 will then undertake an examination of individual political action and the activities of groups in the political world. Chapter 4 assesses alternative explanations for the sources of people's political beliefs and actions.

NORMATIVE POLITICAL THEORY

Should an individual resist a government policy on drug use with which she disagrees? Why? By what means? With what goals? Should government provide for the poor? Why? By what means? With what goals? As each of us attempts to answer such questions, we must grapple not only with the facts and realities of the situation, as we understand them, but also with our underlying beliefs about the role of government and the rights of the individual. Political questions are often very difficult to resolve because they are embedded in fundamental values and core beliefs that are subject to deep disagreement. Notice that the preceding questions are essentially *should* questions and are best classified within the domain of normative knowledge claims. Thus the subfield of political science that focuses on these kinds of questions is called normative political theory (a.k.a. political philosophy).

There are various approaches for thinking about the core questions of normative political theory. One way to frame some of these questions is to consider a basic issue: Why do we need a government? This can provoke further questions about why and how people associate with each other, about how government should function, and about how people and government should interact. Plato, Aristotle, Confucius, Thomas Hobbes, John Locke, Karl Marx, and John Stuart Mill are among the many important thinkers who have offered profound, provocative, and influential ideas about these basic normative questions regarding the relationships among individuals, the state, and society. Such political questions remain important and fascinating. This section describes some of these questions and a few of the many answers that are proposed. You might notice that many of the remarks by normative political theorists use descriptive statements (claims of how things actually are) that are not well supported empirically to justify their assertions of what should be.

Thomas Hobbes

As an example of normative political theory, consider this brief description of the ideas of Thomas Hobbes (1588–1679) regarding the appropriate relationships between people and government. In Hobbes's seventeenth-century England, serious succession problems after the death of Queen Elizabeth resulted in social chaos and civil war, as several different hereditary lines claimed the throne. One king reigned for seven years and then was executed, as Cromwell's Puritans took over government. The Puritans were replaced 11 years later by the "restoration" of the Stuart line of kings on the throne. Influenced by this turbulent context, Hobbes developed a normative theory that was based on his values and assumptions about political and social life.

▶ **Thomas Hobbes.**

In his major work, *Leviathan* (1651/1958), the Oxford-educated Hobbes argued that a powerful state should be established and should be obeyed. He grounded this argument in key assumptions about human nature and social life. First, Hobbes asserts that although people are generally rational, they are also influenced by their passions, fears, and aggressive instincts. Second, Hobbes claims that people are essentially selfish—they act to serve their own interests and to protect themselves from harm. And third, he asserts that before there is government, people live in a "state of nature" in which all individuals have equal rights and are free to do whatever they want.

Self-serving individuals living in the state of nature can enjoy obvious benefits from this situation of total freedom, but there are also potential problems. The desires and behaviors of different people might conflict. If one person claims a piece of land and someone else claims the right to hunker down on it, a conflict is likely. The conflict might be resolved amicably, but in the absence of a governing authority, there might be no agreement. Thus conflicts are inevitable and some (perhaps most) people will occasionally treat others unfairly or even use violence to further their desires. The likelihood of conflict and violence led Hobbes to conclude that life in the state of nature is "solitary, poor, nasty, brutish and short."

How, asks Hobbes, can the state of nature be overcome? His answer is that everyone will agree that it is in their individual self-interests to protect themselves from the nasty and violent behavior of others. To gain this protection, Hobbes claims, everyone will give up certain individual freedoms to a powerful authority that all must obey. This powerful authority has the right to establish rules and laws that protect everyone and also has the right to use whatever means are necessary, including force, to ensure compliance with the rules. This powerful authority is a government. And *the agreement to allow such a government to rule* is called the *social contract.* In the social contract, all the people cede power to the ruler in exchange for the promise that the ruler will protect their freedom, their rights, and their property. The ruler is empowered by the social contract but is not limited by it. As long as the ruler protects everyone from serious social disorder, the ruler must be obeyed.

In his political theory, Hobbes provides strong answers to important questions about how people should associate with each other, why government is necessary, and what powers government should have. Not all normative political theorists accept Hobbes's claims about the state of nature, the need for a powerful monarch, and the limitations on the people's right to resist. Thus other political theorists offer perspectives that are quite different from that of Hobbes. John Locke, for example, emphasizes the rights of the ruled to resist a monarch that does not meet their needs. Karl Marx exhorts the ruled to use whatever means are necessary to overthrow any oppressive ruling group and to establish a society in which all the people share political and economic power equally. Despite the enormous expansion in the complexity of society, the economy, and government, contemporary political theorists continue to address the relationships among individuals, society, and the state.

Political Ideology

Hobbes's political theory is one of the several dozen most famous and widely studied in the Western world. Some would also call it a political ideology. For our purposes, let us define a **political ideology** as *a comprehensive set of beliefs about the political world—about desirable political goals and the best ways to achieve those goals.* Thus it is a set of beliefs about the political world that characterizes what is and what should be, and it might also offer strategic ideas about how to make changes in the direction of that preferred situation. Among the many different political ideologies that can be identified in the contemporary world, three very broad ideologies are widely discussed in Western societies: classical liberalism, conservatism, and socialism. Prior to describing these three general ideologies, we describe three key issues that can help us distinguish analytically among such ideologies, based on their assumptions and value judgments about (1) individual human nature, (2) the proper relationship between the individual and society, and (3) the desirability of establishing certain kinds of equality among individuals.

Individual human nature. The "nature versus nurture" debate centers on disagreements about whether a person's fundamental beliefs and behaviors are determined primarily by innate needs and values with which she is born, or whether those beliefs and behaviors are mainly a product of her environment and experiences. The implications of nature and nurture for political beliefs and actions will be assessed in Chapter 4. In this section, our focus is on the key assumptions that political ideologies make about an individual's innate nature (e.g., the extent to which individuals are selfish or sharing, violent or nonviolent, emotional or rational) and about the adaptability of individuals (the extent to which they can be taught or induced to act and think in a way that is against their innate nature).

Individual and society. What is the proper relationship between the individual and society? One view is that the highest value in social arrangements is individual liberty and freedom of action. Alternatively, the collective good is seen as paramount, and individual freedom must be constrained to achieve those results that most benefit the overall society.

Equality.   To what extent should there be equality in terms of what individuals do and the benefits they acquire? One position is that there should be legal equality—that every person should be equal before the law, have equal political rights, and enjoy equality of opportunity. An alternative position is that there should be material equality—that every person deserves a comparable level of benefits and goods. This second position places a high value on equality of conditions, adding social and economic equality to legal equality. A third position posits that people and situations are intrinsically unequal and that it is neither possible nor desirable to attempt to legislate any kind of equality.

While there is broad agreement regarding the general perspective of each major ideology, be aware that every ideology is subject to varying interpretations across groups and especially across cultures. This variation is particularly evident for the term *liberalism*, which has both a traditional meaning (presented later in this section) and a very different meaning at the beginning of the twenty-first century. Similarly, the ideology of socialism in its Marxist-Leninist form is quite distinct from its democratic socialist form.

Conservatism

Conservatism *attempts to prevent or slow the transition away from a society based on <u>traditional values</u> and social hierarchy.* As the word suggests, the essence of conservative ideology is to conserve the many valued elements of the system that already exists. What the conservative wishes to preserve varies with the time and place, but certain underlying elements are highly valued. Particular importance is placed on stability, tradition, and loyalty to God and country. The relationship of the individual to society and an antipathy to egalitarianism (i.e., equality of conditions) are at the core of conservatism.

The individual.   Conservatism makes two key assumptions about human nature. First, individuals are not consistently rational. In many situations, people are emotional and are unable to reason clearly. Thus individual rationality is not usually a sound basis for decisions about appropriate social or political behavior. Second, individuals are inherently unequal in intelligence, skills, and status. Some individuals and groups are superior to others, and it is clearly preferable that those from the superior groups should be in positions of power in society and in government.

Individual and society.   Individuals have a basic need for order and stability in society. They belong to different groups that are unequal in power, status, and material possessions. Social harmony is maintained when these various groups work cooperatively together. Traditional values and ethics provide the guidelines for group cooperation and individual behavior. And it is the role of institutions such as the family and the church, as well as government, to communicate and enforce these values.

Individual liberty is valued, but only within a framework of mutual responsibility. No majority or government should have sufficient power to abridge the rights of others. But, even more important, no individual or group has absolute freedom to do whatever it wants; rather, each should behave in a manner consistent with society's traditional values. The superior groups should be allowed to enjoy the benefits and exercise the responsibilities associated with their position, but they also should protect the weak from severe hardships, a responsibility that the French term *noblesse oblige*—"the obligations of the nobility."

Existing values and social organization have evolved slowly and have survived the test of time. Tradition and religion, rather than reason, are viewed as the most reliable sources for guiding society, since they support stability and temper change. In the words of one British conservative, "The accumulated wisdom and experience of countless generations gone is more likely to be right than the passing fashion of the moment" (Hearnshaw 1933: 22).

Equality.   Since inequality is a natural aspect of society, it is foolish and even dangerous to seek egalitarianism. Forced equality is unwise because it disrupts the natural, cooperative hierarchy among groups, causes social conflict, and endangers the fundamental goal of order and stability. Attempts to force equality are also unacceptable because they directly undermine individual liberty, which is of greater importance than equality.

Edmund Burke (1729–1797), a British Member of Parliament, was an articulate spokesperson for conservatism. Other important advocates were British Prime Ministers Benjamin Disraeli and Winston Churchill and, to a lesser extent, American Founding Fathers James Madison and Alexander Hamilton. Many who are now called conservatives or neoconservatives are really more closely aligned with the philosophy of classical liberalism (discussed in the next section).

In those contemporary situations where government has become strong, and especially where government uses its power to equalize wealth and status, conservatism argues for a return to traditional values, for a contraction of government, and for the individual freedom to be unequal. Many of the contemporary political actors who come closest to the spirit of conservatism are in certain countries in Asia and the Middle East (e.g., Brunei, Kuwait, Nepal, and Saudi Arabia) where social hierarchy, order, and traditional values are celebrated. Most contemporary conservatives are pragmatic and recognize that a return to eighteenth-century society is impossible. They accept some of the government policies implemented in their societies to equalize status and income. But even here the rationale is to change in order to preserve, as the British Conservative Party has put it. The conservative perspective is sympathetic to government intervention if the goal is to maintain or return to traditional values, such as patriotism, family, morality, and piety. Thus a conservative government might actively expand its military power to influence other countries, support a state religion, or make abortion illegal.

▶ **Edmund Burke.**

Classical Liberalism

The ideology of **classical liberalism** *places the highest value on individual freedom and posits that the role of government should be quite limited.* In part, this ideology emerged (in the sixteenth through eighteenth centuries) as a response to rigid, hierarchical societies, such as those in feudal Europe. Intellectuals and those in commerce, among others, desired to be free from the constraints imposed by the dominant political, economic, and religious institutions in their society. They posited that each person should live responsibly but also should be allowed to live in the manner dictated by her beliefs and to enjoy fully the benefits of her efforts, with minimal limitations from these stifling institutions.

The individual.   John Locke (1632–1704), a primary theorist of classical liberalism, describes individuals in a "state of nature," prior to the existence of government (see his *Second Treatise of Government* 1690). Each person enjoys natural rights to life, liberty, and property. Moreover, each person is rational and has the ability to use her reason to determine the sensible rules (the "laws of nature") that shape how she should live. Essentially, every individual is capable of deciding rationally how to pursue her own needs and to avoid harming others. Notice two important contrasts with conservatism: (1) each person is rational and responsible and is the best judge of what is in her self-interest; and (2) there is no higher value in classical liberalism than the freedom of the individual to pursue her natural rights. (Notice also that this state of nature is far more benign than the one described by Hobbes.)

John Locke.

Individual and society.   A person's full capabilities can be realized only if she is not limited by a social order in which tradition and hierarchy are dominant. Such a social order would not only restrict individual freedom but also stifle progressive change and growth. And no one is forced to accept the authority of government. Individuals can consent to be governed—choosing to "contract" with a minimal government, the main roles of which are limited to clarifying the laws of nature and enforcing the occasional violations of those laws. (See Box 2.1 if you are wondering why all this doesn't sound "liberal.")

For similar reasons, classical liberals celebrate a laissez-faire economy. Each person should be free to pursue her economic goals by any legal activity and to amass as much property and wealth as possible. Individual actors are guided by enlightened self-interest, and the overall economy is structured by the "invisible hand" of the market. Both are unconstrained by government regulations. This vision of the "market political economy," associated with the writings of Adam Smith (1723–1790), will be explained in detail in Chapter 8.

Equality.   Equality before the law (equality of opportunity) is important, but government should not attempt to create material equality (equality of outcomes). People pursue their interests in different ways and with different levels of success. Even in situations of hardship, government action is undesirable because it can undermine individual initiative and independence. Thus government should have no significant role in addressing inequalities.

Among the many political thinkers associated with classical liberalism in addition to John Locke and Adam Smith are Jeremy Bentham (1748–1831) and John Stuart Mill (1806–1873). More contemporary advocates of classical liberalism (some of whom are labeled "neoconservatives") include economists F. A. Hayek and Milton Friedman and political commentator William F. Buckley. Part Five of this book will reveal that many contemporary political regimes are powerfully influenced by classical liberalism. Its emphases on limited government, individual liberty, and laissez-faire economics are among the central themes in many debates about policy and government action.

BOX 2.1

Whither Liberalism? Is That Liberal or Conservative?

If you are an American, you probably have noticed that the description of classical liberalism given in this chapter, emphasizing limited government, is quite different from the political beliefs currently called "liberal" in the United States. In the political language of today, a liberal in America is understood as someone who supports substantial government intervention and policies that increase equality of condition, not merely equality of opportunity.

This confusion of terminology is partly due to developments during Franklin Delano Roosevelt's tenure as U.S. president (1933–1945). Faced with a devastating economic depression, Roosevelt argued for a "New Deal" in which the central government had a clear duty and responsibility to assist actively in economic recovery and in social action. While not proposing the expansive government role in the economy and the egalitarianism proposed by socialism, he did insist that government must be very active in solving economic and social problems. Among other things, government must actively regulate business, create jobs, and distribute extensive welfare services to the citizens, including cash payments and increased public provision of education, housing, health care, and so on.

To avoid the politically negative label of "socialism," Roosevelt called himself and his policies "liberal," contrasting them with the "conservative" policies of others (mainly Republicans, such as the previous president, Herbert Hoover) who emphasized limited government, laissez-faire economics, and individual freedom. Notice that in the general language of political ideology, what Roosevelt was calling conservatism was really classical liberalism, and what he was proposing was a very modest version of democratic socialism.

Eventually, Roosevelt's terminology was widely adopted in the United States, and thus political discourse in the United States is characterized as a debate between liberals and conservatives, even though the ideologies of both groups combine, in different amounts, elements of classical liberalism and democratic socialism. In this book, the traditional ideology of liberalism will be called "classical liberalism" to distinguish it from the current understanding of liberalism as an ideology of big government and egalitarianism.

Socialism

For **socialism**, *the most important goal is to provide high-quality, relatively equal conditions of life for everyone, with an active state assisting in the achievement of this goal.* Many were still impoverished and exploited in the nineteenth-century world, despite the emergence of industrialization and democracy. Socialism evolved as a distinctive ideology among those who were concerned about the plight of people who had relatively little economic, social, or political power. They were dissatisfied that neither conservatism nor classical liberalism revealed much concern for improving the conditions of these groups. Socialism articulated a vision through which economic and political power could be directed to benefit all groups in society.

The individual.   In the socialist perspective, people are not innately selfish and aggressive. If anything, humans are social and caring by nature. To a large extent, individuals' attitudes and behaviors are determined by the environment in which they live and learn, not by invariant features of human nature. Consequently, it is crucial to create an environment that encourages individuals to place the highest value on cooperation and sharing and to believe that the most important goal for each person is to increase the collective good of all.

Individual and society.   While individual rights and freedom are valued, the most important value is the good of the society as a whole. Thus the individual's interests must be subordinated to, or at least coordinated with, the overall interests and needs of everyone in the society. All groups, from national organizations (e.g., trade unions) to local organizations (e.g., social clubs) to the family, must encourage these attitudes of cooperation and service to the common good.

The government has a crucial role, both through education and civic training and through policies that provide every citizen with good material living conditions. Thus government must take an expansive role, ensuring that every citizen has access to quality education, shelter, health care, jobs, and financial security against economic uncertainty.

Equality.   Both the organic, hierarchical world of conservatism and the individualistic, self-serving world of classical liberalism result in societies in which there are huge disparities of material conditions, status, and power. From the socialist perspective, these disparities cause misery, deep alienation, and pervasive conflict in the society.

Thus the ideology of socialism centers in a deep commitment to use the power and policies of the state to increase the material as well as the social and political equality of all its members. Such equality is believed to transform people into fulfilled, happy citizens who willingly contribute to the common good.

There are significantly different variations within the ideology of socialism. Among these, two major variations should be distinguished: Marxist-Leninist socialism and democratic socialism.

Marxist-Leninist socialism.   The **Marxist-Leninist** variant of socialist ideology begins with three assumptions regarding the changes necessary to produce equality and social justice. First, the old socioeconomic order will resist change by every means available, and thus change will require violent overthrow of the old order. Second, the transformation to socialism will be complex and difficult. To achieve the desired equality of conditions, a powerful government must be installed. Among the government's most important tasks is the restructuring of the economic system, with public ownership of all the major resources in the society and the production and distribution of goods and services for human need (see Chapter 8 on the command political economy for a fuller discussion of this point). And third, a small, dictatorial leadership group must be empowered to manage the government and to effect the complex changes in the economy and society. When relative equality is achieved, both the small leadership group and the powerful government supporting it can be eliminated. They will be replaced by decentralized, citizen-run politics and an efficient administration.

The core elements of this version of socialism are the theories of Karl Marx and its modified practical applications by V. I. Lenin in the Soviet Union and Mao Zedong in China. These variations of socialism are often called communism, Marxism, or revolutionary socialism, as well as Marxist-Leninist socialism. In the last 60 years, this version of socialism has been attempted in more than 60 countries, ranging from A (Albania, Angola, Algeria) to Z (Zimbabwe). Most of the major regimes that implemented Marxist-Leninist socialism have since abandoned it (see especially Chapter 15 on the postcommunist countries). However, groups in many countries are still inspired by the vision of Marxism and work, legally or illegally, to promote its values.

▶ **Karl Marx.**

Democratic socialism.   The other major variation within socialist ideology is **democratic socialism**. This variant also treats egalitarianism as its primary goal, but it assumes that the *changes can be effected by a government that comes to power and rules by democratic means,* not by violence and repression. This government's authority is derived from consent of the governed in elections. In democratic socialism, the state's policies emphasize the substantial reduction of inequalities in material conditions, power, and status, but they do not attempt to achieve complete equality of material conditions. The approach to change is gradual, placing continued importance on the protection of individual rights and freedoms, even as it transforms the socioeconomic order. The government might own some of the major economic resources in the society and it strongly regulates much of the economy, but it does not attempt to plan and control all aspects of the economic system (Przeworski 1985, 1993).

The ideology of democratic socialism is rooted in such utopian socialists as Thomas More (1478–1535), Robert Owen (1771–1856), and Claude-Henri St. Simon (1760–1825); in Fabian socialists such as George Bernard Shaw (1856–1950), Sydney Webb (1859–1947), and Beatrice Webb (1858–1943); and in revisionist Marxists such as Karl Kautsky (1854–1938). The ideology has been partially implemented in the contemporary "social market systems" present in such countries as Denmark, Germany, and Sweden (see Box 13.1 in Chapter 13). It is also advocated by some of the political elites in the postcommunist countries of Central and Eastern Europe (see Chapter 15).

One vision of democratic socialism was articulated by the British economist Sir William Beveridge in a major policy statement to the British government in 1941. Beveridge argued that in a society operating according to the tenets of classical liberalism, there are five tragic effects on some people. Thus the government should act as a "welfare state" (Castles 2004), implementing policies to overcome each of these five effects:

1. *Disease:* to be combated by public provision of subsidized or free health care services, including doctors, treatment, hospitals, and medicines.
2. *Want:* to be eliminated by public provision of sufficient money and other services to raise people above poverty.
3. *Squalor:* to be reduced by state provision of publicly owned and subsidized housing affordable to all.
4. *Ignorance:* to be eliminated by universal, free public education.
5. *Idleness:* to be overcome by government policies that insure meaningful work for every person.

Some Further Points About "Isms"

The preceding section identified three major political ideologies that characterize the political belief systems of many citizens in Western countries. There are many other significant political ideologies in the contemporary political world, at least some of which are "isms." Box 2.2 briefly characterizes the essence of some of the political "isms" that you might encounter. There are also broader systems of religious-social beliefs that have great political importance, including Christian fundamentalism, Islamic fundamentalism, Confucianism, and Hinduism. It is almost impossible to understand politics in the contemporary world without considering the influence of these religious "isms" on beliefs and actions. To advance your knowledge regarding particular belief systems, you might take a course in political theory, political ideology, or world religions, or pursue the "ism" of interest at the library or via the Internet.

The next section will suggest that few individuals adhere absolutely to any one of these political ideologies. Almost no one has a complete grasp of the details and subtleties of any ideology, and even fewer are prepared to accept without reservation every element of an ideology. Some "true believers" do adhere almost totally to a particular ideology, and these people are the genuine ideologues. A larger set of people are substantially influenced by one or more ideologies. They have developed their own system of political beliefs, which is a combination of basic principles from particular ideologies with ideas from other sources. And in most societies, many people have only rudimentary and inconsistent political beliefs that are shaped by perceptions of underlying principles of one or more political ideologies. Yet an "ism" can be a powerful force influencing people and shaping history.

In the twentieth century, for example, both communism and fascism had particularly strong impacts. The role of communism will be explored later, especially in Chapter 8 and Chapter 15. Box 2.2 provides a basic definition of fascism. **Fascism** is antisocialist—it emphasizes an organic social order and thus opposes the idea of class struggle among groups—and it is antidemocratic—it views competitive, multiparty politics as divisive and destabilizing. While several twentieth-century regimes included strong elements of fascism, it is most closely associated with Italy under

BOX 2.2

A Brief Primer on Political "Isms"

In politics and political theory, there are many "isms"—systems of beliefs that address how societies should function, how people should live and what they should value, and how political systems should operate. Entire books are devoted to each of the "isms" below, but here they are characterized in 40 words or less to give you an orienting idea (dangerously simplified?) about the core vision regarding any "ism" with which you are unfamiliar. The references in parentheses indicate the chapters in this book where some of these "isms" receive greater attention.

Anarchism—a moral-political ideal of a society that is untouched by relationships of power and domination among human beings; there is an absence of organized government.

Authoritarianism—a system in which the political rights and interests of individuals are subordinated, usually by coercion, to the interests of the state. (Chapter 7)

Capitalism—linking politics to the political economy, it is a system dominated by a (laissez-faire) market economy in which economic actors are generally free from state constraints. (Chapter 8)

Collectivism—a doctrine holding that the individual's actions should benefit some kind of collective organization such as the state, a tribe, or the like, rather than the individual herself.

Communism—based on the theories of Karl Marx, the essential goal of this system is the socialization of societal resources, with the state owning land, labor, and capital and using them to promote the equal welfare of all citizens. (Chapters 8 and 15)

Conservatism—a belief in the virtue of preserving traditional values and social institutions and of promoting loyalty to country, reliance on family, and adherence to religion.

Corporatism—a political economy in which there is extensive economic cooperation between an activist state and a few groups that represent such major economic actors as large industry, organized labor, and farmers. (Box 8.3)

Environmentalism—advocacy of the planned management of a natural resource or of the total environment of a particular ecosystem in order to prevent exploitation, pollution, destruction, or depletion of valuable natural resources.

Fascism—a system in which the unity and harmony of government and society are of central importance, and forces that might weaken that unity are repressed; a top leader is usually viewed as the embodiment of the natural will, and all individuals are expected to obey the leader's will.

Feminism—a diverse social movement promoting equal rights and opportunities for women and men in their personal lives, economic activities, and politics.

Liberalism—an emphasis on the primacy of the freedom and rights of the individual, relative to any constraints imposed by the state.

Libertarianism—an extreme version of liberalism, advocating the right of individuals to act freely and unconstrained by the state as long as they do not harm other people.

BOX 2.2 *(Continued)*

Marxism—a set of ideas based on the writings of Karl Marx, who argued that society is composed of competing classes based on economic power, that class struggle and change are inevitable, and that the desired goal is the equal distribution of welfare in the society. (Chapter 8)

Nationalism—a deep commitment to the advancement of the interests and welfare of the core group (based on location, ethnicity, or some other crucial factor) with which an individual identifies powerfully. (Chapter 5)

Pacifism—a belief that the highest political and social value is peace and the absence of violence.

Socialism—a system committed to utilizing the state, the economy, and public policy to provide a high-quality, relatively equal standard of living for all and, usually, to support democratic political processes. (Chapters 8 and 13)

Totalitarianism—a system in which the state possesses total control over all aspects of people's lives, including their economic, social, political, and personal spheres. (Chapter 7)

Benito Mussolini (1922–1943) and Germany under Adolf Hitler (1932–1945). In Germany, Hitler's particular version of fascism was driven by several key ideological elements. First, it held that the top leader is the embodiment of the national will and must be obeyed. Second, it inspired nationalistic fervor, with powerful loyalty to the homeland. The German leadership combined these ideas with a celebration of the superiority of the German race. This produced a virulent racism that became a justification for the brutal treatment of Jews, gypsies, homosexuals, and other "undesirable" groups,

▶ **Fascism in Germany under Adolf Hitler was among the most effective and destructive mass-mobilization ideologies in modern history.**

including the extermination of more than 6 million in the concentration camps of Europe. And all of these ideological elements, under Hitler's charismatic leadership, resulted in Germany's expansion beyond its borders, provoking a war (World War II) that spread across three continents and caused more than 51 million deaths. The death and suffering associated with communism and fascism in the twentieth century are compelling evidence that political ideologies can be more than bundles of ideas debated by intellectuals.

INDIVIDUAL POLITICAL BELIEFS

Can you describe your thought processes when you were asked, at the beginning of this chapter, how you would respond to the incident at Burger King (challenging your views about the U.S. government's policies on Iraq and on poverty)? Your reaction might have been based on deep and fundamental principles grounded in your political ideology. But if you are like most people, your reactions are probably best described in terms of a combination of three other factors: (1) your factual *knowledge* about the political world—for example, why the United States sent troops into Iraq, how much the military effort cost, and the level of poverty in the United States; (2) your *feelings*—for example, antagonism or indifference to such a strong criticism of the United States and its actions; and (3) your powers of *assessment*—for example, an attempt to judge whether the action in Iraq was, in fact, immoral and whether it is appropriate for the government to spend billions of dollars of taxpayers' money on either a war in Iraq or a war on domestic poverty.

Types of Orientations

These different aspects of your reactions typify the three types of orientations that constitute our individual *political beliefs*. As we explore the concept of political beliefs in this section, notice that this is a somewhat different perspective than the concepts of political theory and political ideology considered above. A specific political belief might be guided by a political theory, but it also might have no basis in fundamental assumptions about the individual, society, and the state. A specific political belief might be a component of a political ideology, but a political belief is not necessarily part of a coherent political ideology. These distinctions should become clearer as we characterize the three types of orientations, called cognitive, affective, and evaluative.

A person's **cognitive orientations** include *what she believes are political "facts."* Such facts might be correct and accurate, or they might be totally wrong. (Recall our discussion of "truth scores" in Chapter 1.) This knowledge might include such facts as the names of political leaders; the policies supported by particular politicians, political groups, or nations; events in political history; the features of constitutions; or the procedures and actions of a governmental agency.

Affective orientations include *any feelings or emotions evoked in a person by political phenomena.* For example, what (if any) feelings are stimulated in you when you come across the following?

You see someone burning your national flag.

You read about a deadly terrorist attack in an area where you have friends.

You are faced with the option of voting in an election and you don't like the candidates.

You are present at a political demonstration supporting a policy of which you strongly approve.

The nature and intensity of your feelings in these situations are instances of your affective orientations.

Finally, an *evaluative orientation* involves your *synthesis of facts and feelings into a judgment about some political phenomenon.* If you become aware that your government has proposed a policy that restricts the right of a woman to have an abortion, this might stimulate many different thoughts—your knowledge about the constitutional rights of an individual to freedom of action and of the state to limit those rights; your religious, moral, or scientific beliefs about the status of a fetus; your personal knowledge of the experiences of people who have been involved in decisions about abortions; your assessment of the arguments made by spokespersons for and against the proposed policy. In short, your judgment about a political issue can be grounded in many different kinds of cognitive and affective orientations that are combined into an evaluation. Ultimately, many of the attitudes that you would identify as your "fundamental political beliefs" are likely to be based on evaluative orientations and reflect any underlying political ideology that you embrace.

Identifying Specific Beliefs

There are several stages in building our conceptual understanding of political beliefs. If we want to understand *one* person's political orientations, we might begin by identifying one or a few specific beliefs she holds. Does she know the name of the country's chief executive? How does she react to news that her state's governor has just prevented the execution of a convicted murderer? What is her opinion on a proposal to reduce the number of nuclear weapons stockpiled by her country?

A similar analytic strategy can be used to determine what *many* people think about a specific issue. When *the attitudes of many people are gathered, aggregated, and summarized,* they constitute the most widely available data about people's political orientations: *public opinion polls.* Virtually every day, the media provide data on the percentage of people who hold a certain opinion regarding a political issue. For example, a public opinion poll might report data on the question, "Do most Germans support the entry of Turkey into the European Union?" On the basis of this poll, you might decide you know what Germans think about the issue. This information seems a stronger basis for a knowledge claim than a discussion with a few German friends or even a statement by a German political leader.

However, public opinion polls should be interpreted with care. In assessing the information, you should consider such questions as these: Did those who conducted the poll have a bias toward a particular result? Were the questions or the possible responses worded in a way that might distort people's opinions? Were those asked for an opinion a representative sample of the group to whom the opinion is attributed? Are different interpretations of the data possible? Even when the pollsters

are unbiased, there are numerous instances in which their estimates are inaccurate (e.g., there can be errors in their predictions of how the population will vote in an election).

BELIEF SYSTEMS

Beyond the identification of specific beliefs of individuals, other interesting analyses can focus on the array of their political beliefs. The term **political belief system** refers to *the configuration of an individual's political orientations.* A related concept used by political psychologists is a person's "opinion schema." This is a network of cognitive, affective, and evaluative orientations that serves as a basic framework, guiding a person as she organizes her existing political knowledge and processes new information in order to establish an opinion on a particular subject. Thus a person derives her belief on a specific issue from a more general orientation that is guided by some broad principle(s) (Dalton 2008: 28; Niemi and Weissberg 2001).

To examine a person's belief system, you can ask a series of questions:

1. What is the *content* of the beliefs—that is, the subject matter and the nature of the beliefs?

2. What is the *salience* of the beliefs—that is, the importance or significance the person attaches to the beliefs?

3. What is the level of *complexity* of the beliefs?

4. Is there a *consistency* among subsets of beliefs that suggests a series of general principles from which specific beliefs are derived?

5. How *stable* are the beliefs over time?

6. Do the beliefs *motivate* the person to undertake any political action(s)?

Some empirical research on the nature of belief systems has focused on the belief systems of the political elite or of the "mass public"—that is, of ordinary people in the society. The most intensive, analytic research has focused on belief systems in the United States, and this work has been particularly influenced by the analyses of Philip Converse (1964). In general, Converse argues that a belief system has two levels of information. One level includes relatively straightforward *facts or opinions,* such as the opinion that American public schools should not allow Christian prayers during class time. The second level is *constraint knowledge,* in which more abstract and overarching concepts (such as liberalism and conservatism) operate to shape and link ideas. In the school prayer example, a person might base her opinion on constraint knowledge about the constitutional separation of church and state or about free speech issues.

Belief Systems Among Mass Publics

On the basis of his empirical analyses of (American) individuals' belief systems, Converse (1964) concludes that there are important and predictable differences between the elite and the mass publics in the nature and structure of their belief systems. As you might expect, the belief systems of individuals in the mass public are simpler and narrower, and they are organized far less by constraint knowledge than are those of members of the elite. Within the mass public, Converse distinguishes five gradations in the level of conceptualization in people's belief systems. Only about 15 percent of members of the mass public have substantial constraint knowledge in their belief system across a range of issues. And almost half of the U.S. public is characterized by the two lowest levels—extremely simplistic political beliefs and "political ignorance."

While there has been continuing debate regarding the precise nature of political belief systems among mass publics, most researchers agree on certain generalizations about the citizens of Western democracies (i.e., the United States, Canada, and the Western European and Scandinavian countries). Like nearly every other generalization about politics, the following six generalizations are broadly accurate for "most people" but are subject to many qualifications and some exceptions:

1. Political issues have low salience compared with other concerns in people's lives. Although Aristotle called the citizen *homo politicus,* or "political man," most people do not locate political issues in the center of their interest and attention space.

2. People tend to focus attention on concrete issues and have minimal grasp of the abstract political concepts that serve as constraint knowledge.

3. Interest and knowledge are greater on immediate, short-term issues than on longer-term ones.

4. While people's fundamental beliefs are relatively stable, there can be considerable volatility in their short-term political opinions, which tend to shift when subjected to modest changes in political information. This volatility might be due to limited interest or to the sheer difficulty of trying to understand complicated political questions.

5. Significant inconsistencies can exist across political beliefs, in the sense that a person can hold contradictory positions. (For example, an American might express support for the First Amendment right to free speech but deny the right of an Islamic fundamentalist to speak at a public meeting or the right of the Ku Klux Klan to hold a public rally.)

6. The content of beliefs is often inaccurate. (In one survey, for example, half the Americans questioned did not know how many U.S. senators serve their state.)

The basic ideas of Converse (1964) and others have been challenged by those who acknowledge that the mass public might have a minimal grasp of political information and ideas but argue that people *are* able to fashion reasonable political opinions. In this view, members of the mass public use simple rules of thumb to make sense of issues. They focus most of their attention on some issue areas (e.g., foreign policy, race relations, and economic concerns) and have little knowledge of other issue areas, and they receive considerable guidance from information provided by the elite and the media (Dalton 2008: ch. 2; Lupia and McCubbins 1998; see also Chapter 4).

Another challenge to the view that most people have simplistic belief systems is the viewpoint that individuals develop structured ways of thinking about the world but that these ways are not similar for everyone. Thus it is argued that the analyst must first study and understand how particular people think, not merely ask questions about their specific beliefs, and then look for a pattern in their responses. When the analyst specifies a person's structure of thinking, her political attitudes might be generally consistent and coherent within this structure (Rosenberg 1988, 2002). This is an intriguing, alternative way to analyze the mass public's political beliefs that could change our unflattering picture of most people's belief systems, but there is not much empirical support for it. Moreover, even with these refinements, most research continues to reveal a mass public whose political belief systems seem neither rich nor sophisticated.

Belief Systems Among Elites

The **political elite** is a term for *those who have relatively high levels of interest, influence, and involvement in political life.* Some actually hold positions of political responsibility, and most communicate their knowledge and beliefs about politics to others. The belief systems of the elite are regarded as particularly important because the elites are presumed to have a major role in politics and because they can strongly influence the beliefs of the mass public.

Overall, Converse (1964) and others conclude that generalizations regarding the belief systems of the elites are the opposite of those for the mass public on each of the six points listed in the preceding section. For the most part, the belief systems of the elite are characterized by relatively high levels of salience, abstraction, accuracy, complexity, stability, and breadth. Constraint knowledge is well developed and influences most specific opinions. Despite the emphasis on consistency among beliefs, individuals in the elite can support core values that are in conflict. In contrast to those in the mass public, those with an elite belief system can reconcile differences within their constraint knowledge. This enables them to integrate conflicting information as they generate political opinions (Rosenau and Holsti 1986).

All individuals with sophisticated belief systems do not necessarily share the same core beliefs. For example, some people might have a coherent system of beliefs that support the protection of an individual's civil liberties, while other people's constraint knowledge and specific opinions consistently support the right of the government to limit individual liberties substantially in the protection of social order (Sniderman et al. 1991). Those characterized as utilizing an elite belief system are far more likely to be guided by a clear political ideology. Given that the more powerful political actors in most societies are guided by relatively well-developed political ideologies, the study of elite belief systems remains important and intriguing.

POLITICAL CULTURE

Some analysts attempt to identify broadly shared patterns of political orientations that characterize a large group of people. The objective is to develop generalizations about the political culture of the group. **Political culture** is normally defined as *the configuration of a particular people's political orientations*—that is, the generalized belief system of many. For this reason, political culture is not precisely a topic in micropolitics, but it is examined here because it is embedded in individual-level analyses.

Most commonly, it is the political culture of a country or of a major (ethnic or religious) community within a country that has been studied. The composition of the group that is studied depends on the interests of the researcher. It might be the people of a geographic community (e.g., Londoners, English, British, or Europeans) or of a community of shared identity (e.g., Sikhs in the Indian state of Punjab, Sikhs in the Indian subcontinent, or all Sikhs in the world) or of a community of shared meaning (e.g., French Canadians or all French-speaking peoples).

National Character Studies

A traditional approach that attempts to capture the essence of a people's political culture involves **national character studies** (Inkeles 1997). When someone is described as being "soooo French," you might think of her as being sophisticated, romantic, and volatile. At one level, we recognize immediately that such a characterization is a stereotype that does not fit the majority of individual subjects. Yet most of us, including people in the political world, use these kinds of labels (at least occasionally) as a shorthand method of describing groups or nations. Indeed, Franklin Delano Roosevelt (U.S. president from 1933 to 1945) observed that "the all-important factor in national greatness is national character."

Some political analysts have tried to specify the national character of certain countries and then to predict or explain their political behavior on the basis of such characteristics. Typically, these studies do not claim that everyone fits the national character profile, but they maintain that the profile is accurate for the politically relevant strata. For example, Ervand Abrahamian (1993) analyzes what he terms the "paranoid style of Iranian politics." He describes the consistent tendency of the political leaders and the mass public to fear foreign plots and conspiracies meant to subvert the culture and create societal chaos. He traces this political belief system to a "national culture" characterized by pessimism, subservience, egotism, dishonesty, and distrust of others. While he acknowledges that colonial dealings with the British and Americans provide Iranians with ample grounds to distrust foreigners, Abrahamian argues that the character of the population is excessively paranoid. He details how this has resulted in disastrous consequences, undermining the Iranians' capacity to develop cooperative internal politics based on coalition building, the ability to compromise, and tolerance for domestic opposition.

A controversial analysis based on broad notions of supranational character is Samuel Huntington's (1996) description of nine global "civilizations." These civilizations are the highest level of cultural identity among humans, with the nine groups differing in history, language, culture, and especially religion. The groups, which are also somewhat regionally based, are African, Buddhist, Confucian, Hindu, Islamic, Japanese, Latin American, Orthodox (Russian), and Western. Huntington predicts that clashes among these civilizations are now the fundamental source of international political conflict and will be the most likely cause of the next global war.

National character studies are criticized by many analysts as impressionistic and loaded with gross generalizations that greatly oversimplify political reality. Consequently, most scholars dismiss national character studies as caricatures with little capacity to account for the complex actual political behaviors within a country. However, the more thoughtful analyses of national character, based on dominant patterns of beliefs and behaviors, can provide fascinating insights into both the political culture and the political actions taken in a society, and such culture-based explanations are quite evident in recent research (see Box 15.3 in Chapter 15).

Survey Research

There is a more systematic and scientifically acceptable method for establishing the nature of a political culture—the use of *survey research*. This involves *taking a carefully selected sample of the population and then asking each person a series of questions that aims to tap individual political beliefs and actions*. The researcher then aggregates each person's responses, searching for patterns or configurations that profile the political culture of the sample and, by inference, that characterize the political culture of the population from which the sample is taken.

The first major study of this type is *The Civic Culture* by Gabriel Almond and Sidney Verba (1963). Lengthy interviews were conducted with a large sample of citizens in each of five countries. The data were then aggregated and analyzed in a diversity of ways to provide rich descriptions as the study contrasted the quite different political cultures of Italy ("alienated"), Mexico ("alienated but aspiring"), the United States ("participant"), the United Kingdom ("deferential"), and (West) Germany ("detached"). Another of the notable early studies found widespread similarities in the social and political concerns among citizens in many democratic countries. Personal desires for a happy family life, a decent standard of living, and good health were most important, and political concerns centered on fears about war and political instability (Cantril 1965).

The most comprehensive recent comparative surveys of political culture are the World Values Survey (WVS). Ronald Inglehart and collaborating scholars have conducted five "waves" of these surveys (in 1981, 1990, 1995, 2000, and 2006), and the survey now includes individuals from more than 80 countries containing more than 85 percent of the world's population. Samples of adults in these countries are asked many questions about their opinions regarding politics, societal needs, personal values, and so on. A few examples of these questions are:

- If you had to choose, which one of the things on this card would you say is most important? And which would be the next most important?
    a. Maintaining order in the nation.
    b. Giving people more say in important government decisions.
    c. Fighting rising prices.
    d. Protecting freedom of speech.

- Locate your opinion on a 10-point scale between these two statements:
    1 = The government should take more responsibility to ensure that everyone is provided for.
    10 = People should take more responsibility to provide for themselves.

- To what extent do you agree or disagree with this statement (5-point scale):
    Politicians who do not believe in God are unfit for public office.

- Generally speaking, would you say that most people can be trusted or that you need to be very careful in dealing with people?
    a. Most people can be trusted.
    b. Need to be very careful.

The recent research from the WVS has attempted a comprehensive characterization of cross-cultural variation in "people's prevailing value orientations." The analyses posit that, while the variations are complex and extensive, it is possible to define two critical dimensions in value orientations. The first dimension ranges from strong values of survival and material security to strong self-expression values. *Survival values*, also termed **materialist values**, exhibit high concern for economic and physical security, as supported by strong national defense, order maintenance, and economic growth. In contrast, *self-expression values*, also termed **postmaterialist values**, emphasize a subjective well-being and quality of life, as supported by a more esthetically satisfying environment, freedom of expression, and more personal power in social and political life. Inglehart (2005; see also Dalton 2008) suggests that data from Western democracies reveal a substantial increase in the proportion of citizens classified as postmaterialists since the early 1980s, especially because younger cohorts include a larger share of individuals who embrace self-expression values.

The second dimension is strong *traditional values* versus strong *secular-rational values*. The traditional set of values focuses particularly on the importance of religion and its teachings. Thus there is a rejection of such behaviors as abortion, divorce, suicide, and homosexuality. There is also strong support for deference to authority, national pride, and patriotism. In contrast, secular-rational values are opposite on all these matters, exhibiting substantial tolerance for nontraditional behaviors and less emphasis on the need to respect authority and teach obedience. Empirical data reflect a general trend toward secular-rational values in most industrial societies, but traditional values have remained strong in many societies where religions still have a powerful influence (Norris and Inglehart 2004).

Figure 2.1 provides a simplified characterization of some of the key elements that compose each of these two dimensions. This research claims that the more an individual's orientations are clustered in the secular-rational and the self-expressive direction on these key values, such as political freedom, free expression, tolerance, and trust, the greater the individual's orientation toward reliance on human choice and action. In contrast, greater support for values such as religiosity, respect for authority, national pride, and traditional family values leads to an orientation that supports constraints on human action. In addition to mapping these value clusters for each individual, the researchers have aggregated the scores of individuals in order to establish the overall pattern for each country. Scholars have computed country-level scores on the two general dimensions in each of the 80 countries, plotted them, and then identified eight clusters of countries that distinguish eight broad political cultures: Protestant Europe, Catholic Europe, English-speaking, South Asia, Africa, Latin America, Confucian, and ex-Communist (Welzel 2007).

The extensive empirical research on political culture, as it has become more precise in its methods and more cautious about cultural biases, has revealed the considerable variability in political culture within a country, across individuals, between groups, and over time. Chapter 4 will examine some of the factors that might account for differences in the political beliefs of individuals within a society. But it is also evident from the survey research that many societies do have a distinctive political culture—a general configuration of political beliefs that is similar to that in some countries and different from that in many other countries.

LOOKING AHEAD

Chapter 2 has begun our exploration of micropolitics. It has introduced you to normative political theory—the exploration of how individuals, government, and society ought to operate. The subfield of political theory is arguably the oldest in the study of politics, and its perennial questions about the good society and the appropriate role of government remain as intriguing and as contested as they were at the time of Plato. This chapter has also described the key topics in the empirical study of political beliefs—what individuals know and think about politics. Analysis can

Individual-Level Values

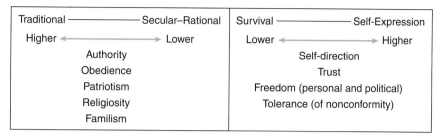

Collective-Level Values

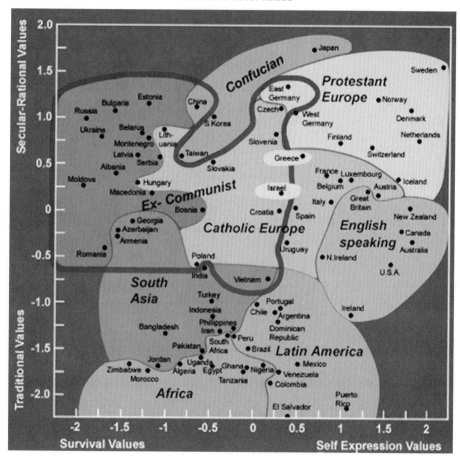

▶ **FIGURE 2.1**
Dimensions of
Human Values
at the Individual
and Collective
Levels.
Source: Inglehart and
Welzel 2005.

focus on a single person or on a group, and it can assess a single belief or an array
of beliefs across many issues. While examining specific beliefs can be quite interesting, political analysis contributes most when it attempts to generalize about the
belief system of a person or a group. A belief or belief system can be analyzed in

terms of its cognitive, affective, and evaluative components. The balance among these emphases and the composition of the group sharing a belief system, as well as the content of the beliefs, vary considerably when one is examining political ideologies, political cultures, mass belief systems, or elite belief systems.

The next step in micropolitical analysis is to move beyond description and develop explanations of political behavior (see Chapter 4). However, we must first look at the second general form of political behavior, political actions. Thus the focus of Chapter 3 is the array of political actions in which an individual or group can engage.

KEY CONCEPTS

affective orientation
classical liberalism
cognitive orientation
conservatism
democratic socialism
evaluative orientation
fascism
Marxist-Leninist socialism

materialist values
micropolitics
national character studies
normative political
    knowledge
political belief system
political culture
political elite

political ideology
postmaterialist values
public opinion polls
social contract
socialism
survey research

FOR FURTHER CONSIDERATION

1. What are your general beliefs about human nature? Are these beliefs consistent with your most important beliefs about how people ought to behave and do behave politically??

2. What do you think is the most sensible assumption and the most questionable assumption of conservatism? Of classical liberalism? Of socialism??

3. Can you characterize your own political belief system? For example, what are your three to five most salient political beliefs? Do they deal with the same general content area??

4. If you were to analyze the political belief system of another person on the basis of five questions, what questions would you ask?

FOR FURTHER READING

Almond, Gabriel, and Sidney Verba. (1963). *The Civic Culture.* Princeton, NJ: Princeton University Press. This is a landmark empirical, comparative study of the political cultures of different countries.

Ebenstein, William, and Alan Ebenstein. (1991). *Great Political Thinkers: Plato to the Present.* 5th ed. Fort Worth, TX: Harcourt Brace. This collection includes extensive excerpts from many major political theorists, supplemented by very helpful editors' introductions.

Fromm, Erich, Ed. (1965). *Socialist Humanism.* New York: Doubleday. Prominent social scientists and political philosophers expound the virtues of socialism.

Griffin, Roger, Ed. (1998). *International Fascism: Theories, Causes, and the New Consensus.* New York: Oxford University Press. A diverse and thorough selection of writings on fascism, by both fascists and antifascists, exploring the strong appeal of this ideology to many individuals and groups during the mid-twentieth century and also at the beginning of the twenty-first century.

Huntington, Samuel P. (1996). *Clash of Civilizations and the Remaking of the World Order.* New York: Simon and Schuster. As described in this chapter, the author offers a sweeping and controversial analysis of major cultural groupings at the global level, where identity, especially religious and cultural, is the dominant force shaping the beliefs and actions of individuals. He further argues that these nine cultural systems ("civilizations") that he characterizes as Western, Islamic, Japanese, Latin American, African, Sinic (Chinese), Hindu, Buddhist, and Orthodox (Russian) have reshaped the patterns of world politics in the post–cold war era and are a major source of conflicts.

Inglehart, Ronald and Christian Welzel (2005). *Modernization, Cultural Change and Democracy: The Human Development Sequence.* New York: Cambridge University Press. Building on his important earlier work (Inglehart 1989, 1997), the author and his coauthor further develop detailed analyses based on the World Values Survey that characterize the nature of and shifts in political culture across more than 75 countries.

Love, Nancy S., Ed. (2006). *Dogmas and Dreams: A Reader in Modern Political Ideologies.* 3rd ed. New York: Seven Bridges Press. A solid reader that includes important writings by many key theorists of the three major "isms" as well as anarchism, fascism, and feminism.

Mayer, Lawrence, and Erol Kaymak. (1998). *The Crisis of Conservatism and the Rise of the New Right in Western Democracies: Populist Revolt in the Late Twentieth Century.* Armonk, NY: M. E. Sharpe. An interesting exploration of the activities of ideologically driven and rather alienated populist groups that have their roots in traditional conservatism but have diverged substantially from it in both their attitudes and their political styles.

McLellan, David, Ed. (2007). *Marxism After Marx.* 4th ed. New York: Palgrave. An excellent set of readings exploring the many versions of Marxism that have continued to have great significance to the field of political theory.

Murray, Charles. (1997). *What It Means to Be a Libertarian.* New York: Broadway Books. A brief, readable application of libertarian ideology to many contemporary issues (e.g., abortion, education, drugs, economic regulation, free speech), written by one of America's most controversial social critics.

Nisbet, Robert. (2001). *Conservatism: Dream and Reality.* Piscataway, NJ: Transaction. A short, illuminating discussion that traces the development of conservative thought and its significance in contemporary politics.

Putnam, Robert D. (1993). *Making Democracy Work: Civic Traditions in Modern Italy.* Princeton, NJ: Princeton University Press. Using communities in northern and southern Italy as his cases, the author develops a significant, and widely cited, argument about the role of political culture in sustaining democracy, and especially about the crucial importance of "social capital"—the citizens' willingness to engage and interact with each other.

Pye, Lucian W. (1985). *Asian Power and Politics: The Cultural Dimensions of Authority.* Cambridge, MA: Belknap. The author presents an intriguing account of the varying political cultures in East Asia. See also Pye's *The Mandarins and the Cadre: China's Political Cultures* (Ann Arbor: University of Michigan Press, 1988).

Sniderman, Paul M., Richard Brody, and Philip E. Tetlock. (1991). *Reasoning and Choice: Explorations in Political Psychology.* New York: Cambridge University Press. A careful assessment of the extent to which Americans in the mass public actually do reason about political choices, focusing on such issues as racial attitudes, poverty, civil liberties, and AIDS.

Spencer, William. (1995). *Islamic Fundamentalism in the Modern World.* Brookfield, CT: Millbrook. A sensitive and informative discussion of the diverse ideologies and approaches associated with those generally termed Islamic fundamentalists.

Tucker, Robert, Ed. (1978). *The Marx–Engels Reader.* New York: Norton. An extensive selection of the important writings, with commentaries, from the major theorists of revolutionary socialism, Karl Marx and Friedrich Engels.

ON THE WEB

http://www.nationalgeographic.com

National Geographic has offered rich information and photographs from locations around the world for nearly a century. Some of this material is informative about culture and society in many places, including insights about political culture.

http://jkalb.freeshell.org/web/trad.php

This site offers an interesting and very diverse array of links to materials associated with "traditionalist conservatism worldwide." Links range across political perspectives from various countries from conservatism in many of the world's religions to extreme-right fringe groups.

http://www.intellectualtakeout.com

The Center for the American Experiment, whose goal is to promote conservative thought and perspectives on political issues, has set up this site specifically for college students.

http://free-market.net

This is the portal of the libertarian belief system and provides many sources that are guided by this ideology.

http://internationalsocialist.org

The site of the International Socialist Organization, an association promulgating the Marxist-Leninist perspective, and publisher of the *Socialist Worker* newspaper and the *International Socialist Review* journal.

http://socialist.org

The site of the international democratic socialist movement, it contains information about the people, ideas, and events important to the movement.

http://www.independent.org/archive/pol_ideology.html

The Political Ideology Link Archive, produced by the Independent Institute, provides access to a comprehensive list of various online opinion articles and book reviews tied to political ideology.

http://www.fordham.edu/halsall/mod/modsbook18.html

The Internet Modern History Sourcebook includes a number of links related to important works on both liberalism and feminism.

http://www.liberal-international.org/

This Web site serves as the electronic home of Liberal International, a worldwide federation of liberal political parties.

http://www.feminist.com/

Feminist.com is an online community designed to promote feminism and women's rights. The site contains a number of articles and speeches related to feminist thought.

POLITICAL ACTIONS

Help us get drunk drivers off the road so you and I can drive without fear. Please don't leave it up to the "other guy." We need you. . . . My husband was nearly killed because of a drunk driver. The driver of a pickup truck crossed the center line and struck us head-on. My husband suffered a broken arm and severe head injuries. As a result of a concussion he contracted spinal meningitis and almost died. I had broken bones myself.

After the crash, I was angry and hurt. But rather than sitting back and feeling sorry for myself, I turned my energies toward working against this problem of drinking and driving. I joined the Mothers Against Drunk Driving crusade because MADD fights to make our roads safe . . . for you, me and our loved ones.

Since our founding in 1980, we've made a great deal of progress—Congress passed a national Minimum Drinking Age Act . . . judges nationwide now impose stiffer drunk driving sentences . . . and government is taking drunk driving more seriously. Yes, we've made progress. But there's so much more to be done . . . . Please help us continue our fight.

—Micky Sadoff, MADD solicitation letter

Chapter 2 considered the nature of people's political beliefs. Ultimately, the more important issues regarding the individual in politics might be questions about what people *do* politically, not merely what they think. For instance, in the incident at Burger King described at the beginning of Chapter 2, the most relevant questions from the perspective of the political world would be: What did you *do*? and What did you *say* to the woman?

In this chapter, we examine the prominent modes of actual political behavior that people engage in. Moreover, many individuals, such as Micky Sadoff, decide that they can be more effective politically if they act with others rather than alone. Thus, instead of engaging in a lonely act of protest, a person could join a huge demonstration; instead of writing a letter requesting a change in public policy, a person could join an organization that speaks for thousands of people.

Broadly, **political participation** is the term that is applied to *all of the political actions by individuals and groups*. The explicit objective of most political participation is *to influence the actions or selection of political rulers* (Nelson 1993: 720). What is the range of behaviors that a person might undertake in the political world? At one extreme are people who are obsessed with politics, see political implications in most of life's actions, are constantly involved in political discussion and action, and want to make political decisions for others. At the other extreme are people who have absolutely no interest in politics, pay no attention to political phenomena, and engage in no politically relevant actions. (In some instances, such as not voting in an election to indicate dissatisfaction, not doing something can also be a type of political participation.) The first half of this chapter focuses on individual political action in the context of the range of actions between the two extremes just described.

An individual acting alone can engage in virtually the same political actions as a member of a group. The actions of groups can be analyzed on some additional dimensions because of their size and structure. Thus the second half of this chapter considers the activities and types of the two major forms of political groups: interest groups and political parties.

INDIVIDUAL POLITICAL ACTIONS

Modes of Political Activity

There are various ways to classify the modes of individual political action. Some of the most extensive empirical and cross-national analyses of political participation, by Sidney Verba and his colleagues (Verba and Nie 1972, 1975; Verba, Nie, and Kim 1978), focus on four broad categories of political participation: (1) voting; (2) campaign activities (e.g., attending rallies, working on a campaign, contributing funds); (3) personalized contacts (e.g., communicating with a politician via letter, e-mail, or meeting); and (4) communal activities (e.g., participating in a group or club that tries to promote civic and community life). However, more recent empirical studies have become more inclusive, including less conventional forms of political actions, such as participation in demonstrations, protests, or riots.

Figure 3.1 classifies the modes of individual political action in terms of two dimensions. The first dimension considers the extent to which the action is generally viewed as more or less conventional. While there are differences in what various people would

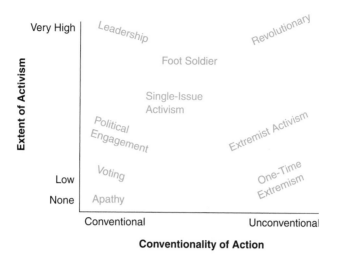

consider more or less conventional, there is definite variation from left to right. The second (vertical) dimension reflects the extent to which the individual is politically active, ranging from someone who is completely inactive to a level of political activism at which the individual truly lives and breathes politics. Figure 3.1 suggests labels for those who are associated with certain types of political actions. At the four (corner) extremes are those who are totally apathetic about politics, those who have made a full-time vocation of politics as elected officials, those revolutionaries who are passionately committed to transforming the existing political system, and those who are provoked into a rare but highly unconventional action. While we will explore some of these types of political actors and actions throughout this book, we can characterize a few of the main types here. It should be noted that a particular individual might operate in different action domains at various times, although most can be labeled by their dominant activity (Dalton 2008: chs. 3, 4; Rueschemeyer, Rueschemeyer, and Wittrock 1998; Verba, Schlozman, and Brady 1995: ch. 3). For example, an elected official will almost certainly vote, even a revolutionary might still vote, and a conventional voter might at some point be mobilized to participate in a more unconventional action, such as a violent demonstration.

Political Activists

Although the more routine modes of political action (listed in the middle and bottom of the left side of Figure 3.1) constitute the vast majority of actual political behavior, most of us are particularly interested in the extraordinary actions of the ***political activists*** *who seem to "live politics."* They might hold government office, spend many hours furthering a political idea or leader, or even risk their freedom and life in the pursuit of a dramatic change in the political order. At least three different types of political activists can be identified: foot soldiers, extremist-activists, and political leaders.

Foot soldiers.   ***Foot soldiers*** are those *activists who do the basic work of politics.* They link the government and the top political leadership to the masses by performing such tasks as raising money for candidates or political issues, working in the local offices of political leaders, communicating the views of top leaders to

"I didn't protest this war, but I'll try to protest the next one."

citizens, and regularly voicing their opinions to political leaders. In most countries, foot soldiers are members of political parties or groups with a political mission, although such membership is not necessarily synonymous with political activism.

Extremist-activists. *Extremist-activists* are *outsiders who are willing to engage in extensive political action in pursuit of their vision of an ideal political world,* which would require a dramatic shift in the nature of the existing system. "Extremism" is a subjective and relative concept; a person is politically extreme only in comparison with some standard position, typically the broad center of the existing political order. Like foot soldiers, extremist-activists might engage in some conventional political activities inside the system. However, what distinguishes them is the willingness to engage in intensive modes of unconventional political action. Some individuals can be classified as extremist-activists if their political goals or tactics locate them on the margins of the existing political system and political culture. Members of environmental activist groups such as Earth First! in the United States and the violent, anti-foreigner activists in many countries in Western and Eastern Europe are examples.

Political analysts have focused considerable attention on individual extremist-activists who are the most unconventional and fully engaged, the revolutionaries. A *revolutionary* is a person who desires to overthrow the existing political order and to replace it with a very different one, using political violence if necessary (see Chapter

12). Some revolutionaries, such as Mao Zedong (China), Fidel Castro (Cuba), Ayatollah Khomeini (Iran), and Nelson Mandela (South Africa), eventually attained leadership roles in their political system after years or even decades of struggle. (Two examples are featured in Box 4.4.) Others, including Che Guevara (Cuba, then Bolivia) and Steve Biko (South Africa), died in the struggle and became martyrs to those committed to revolutionary change.

Many extremist-activists are a radical version of foot soldiers, serving as the members of such organizations as the Revolutionary Armed Forces of Columbia (FARC), Osama bin Laden's worldwide al-Qaeda ("the Base") network, and the Tamil Tigers, the separatist group in Sri Lanka. But an increasing proportion of the extremist-activists operate as members of small, relatively independent groups, and occasionally there is a "lone wolf" extremist who acts virtually alone. There is strong contemporary interest in extremist-activists who are willing to use *any* tactics and *any* level of violence to achieve their goals. These individuals are often labeled as "terrorists" because of their extreme tactics, and particularly their willingness to direct violence against those who are not actively engaged in political struggle (for more details, see Chapter 12). Most extremist-activists operate in relative obscurity, eventually burning out and dropping out, being captured by the state, or dying as a result of political violence.

Political leaders.   Many of us are fascinated with such ultimate political activists as Fidel Castro, Winston Churchill, Adolf Hitler, Nelson Mandela, and Mao Zedong. These top political leaders are distinctive because they succeed in capturing supreme political power within a government and using it with extraordinary energy and effect (whether good or bad). Their titles vary by country and level of government and include chairman, chancellor, dictator, governor, king, mayor, president, prime minister, and supreme leader, among others. A top political leader might put his substantial political power and position to admirable purposes, might implement reprehensible policies, or might accomplish virtually nothing. These political leaders have been the subject of more descriptions, analyses, and evaluations than any other type of actors in the political world. They will frequently be the subjects in this book.

Political Participation Studies

After categories of political action are established, a basic research question is: How many people participate in each category, both within and across various national political contexts? In studying participation, Milbrath and Goel (1982) argued that less than 5 percent of the United States' population can be called "gladiators"—those people who engage at high levels in the more demanding forms of political action, such as protests and extensive partisan political work. More recent empirical research reports that about one in five adults in the United States engages in no political activity and another one-fifth do little more than vote. This research also suggests that only about 5 percent of the population engage in a significant level of political activism (Verba, Schlozman, and Brady 1995: 50–54, 72–74).

Some empirical data compare levels of participation across countries. The most reliable comparative data measure voting in national elections. Table 3.1 provides these data for selected countries. The most striking observation about these figures is the huge variation in voting levels, ranging from a reported 98 percent in Vietnam to only

▶ **Political leaders who capitalize on celebrity and media attention can be formidable.**

23 percent in Egypt. Notice the very high voter turnout in countries such as Vietnam, Cuba, and North Korea (which reports voting participation at 99 percent). In such countries, voting is primarily a symbolic act that is supposed to express support for the existing political leadership, not an action in which citizens select their leaders.

While almost every country in Table 3.1 now offers the voters a choice among candidates, there is considerable variation in the extent to which the choice is genuine and the votes really do determine the top leadership. In some countries (e.g., Singapore, Azerbaijan), one group is virtually assured of victory; in others (e.g., Algeria, Myanmar), the top leadership or the military has repudiated the election if it does not approve of the electoral results. Even a country with one all-powerful political party can offer choices. China, for example, defines itself as a multiparty state although it is totally dominated by the Communist Party. Yet the 2,979-member National Peoples' Congress does have a significant number of elected members from eight minor parties that provide broader representation of various groups within Chinese society. It is even possible for candidates to run for the Congress as independents. However, since there are several stages of voting leading up to the final election, nearly every candidate who is not approved by the Communist Party is eliminated.

These variations in voting alert us to a general problem in cross-national analyses of micropolitical data—the same action or belief might have quite different meaning and significance in different settings.

It is even more difficult to do empirical, cross-national comparisons between other modes of individual political participation. Even more than with voting, the same act can vary in meaning in different political and cultural environments. For example, the significance and potential personal risk of a public political protest are far greater for a person in North Korea than in South Korea, and greater in both those countries than for someone in Sweden.

> **TABLE 3.1**

Voting Participation in Selected Countries: Percentage of Eligible Adults Voting in Most Recent Major National Election

% Turnout	Countries
95–100	Vietnam, Cuba
90–94	Belarus
85–89	Chile, Indonesia
80–84	Denmark, Italy, Turkey, Brazil, France, Iraq, Taiwan
75–79	Germany, Australia, South Africa, Spain, Palestine (territory), Mongolia
70–74	Argentina
65–69	Uganda, Finland, Hungary, Japan, Ukraine, Canada, Costa Rica
60–64	Israel, Portugal, United Kingdom, Iran, South Korea
55–59	Mexico, India, Syria, Russia, Singapore
50–54	Poland
45–49	Zimbabwe
40–44	Pakistan
35–39	United States, Algeria
30–34	Colombia
25–29	
20–24	Egypt
15–19	
10–14	
5–9	
0–4	

Source: Wikipedia, http://en.wikipedia.org/wiki, 2007.

The most consistent finding in recent comparative research on participation in democracies is clear: most people do not regularly engage in high levels of political activity (Dalton 2008; Rueschemeyer, Rueschemeyer, and Wittrock 1998; *World Values Survey* 2006). Apart from voting, which *is* a political act done by many/most citizens, high levels of persistent political activity tend to be uncommon in most political systems. For example, Dalton (2008: tables 3.3–3.5) reports that fewer than one in ten citizens engages in active, partisan activities in the four Western democracies.

A second broad finding is that some citizens are willing to engage occasionally in more activist modes of political participation. While very few citizens participate in violent protests against people or property, Table 3.2 indicates that a significant number of people perform certain less-conventional political acts, including some actions that require considerable effort or risk. In about half of the countries listed in the table,

"I'M HAVING SECOND THOUGHTS ABOUT THE ELECTION... I'M NOT SURE I VOTED AGAINST THE RIGHT PERSON."

15 percent or more of the citizens have engaged in at least one "challenging act" (e.g., a lawful demonstration, boycott, or building occupation). The photograph that opens this chapter depicts citizens engaged in a demonstration against government policy, while other citizens protest against their protest. Skinheads and Ku Klux Klan members march in opposition to the celebration of Martin Luther King Jr.'s birthday in Tennessee, flanked by African-Americans who mock them with fascist salutes.

These cross-national differences underscore the third broad observation based on these empirical participation studies. There is substantial variation from country to country in the proportion of citizens who undertake various forms of conventional and unconventional political action. In the data in Table 3.2, rates of activity (from highest to lowest) between countries often vary by a ratio of 3:1 or higher (except for voting). For example, three out of four Canadians have signed a petition, whereas fewer than one in 20 Nigerians has done so. And about one in three Italians and Swedes has participated in a lawful demonstration, compared with about one in 20 Uruguayans. In some countries, there can be an explosion of protest behavior and political violence against the regime during periods of unsatisfactory political or economic conditions. Such political behavior includes strikes, violent demonstrations, insurrections, and revolutionary action.

In democratic countries, about which we have the most systematic empirical data, the evidence generally supports the conclusion that most people employ the conventional modes of voting and contacting public (elected or appointed) officials as the key means of achieving political objectives. But data such as those in Table 3.2, which report a notable level of unconventional activities involving protest or political

▶ **TABLE 3.2**
Levels of Less-Conventional Political Actions in Selected Countries (Mode of Political Action)

Country	Sign Petition	Boycott	Demonstrate Lawfully	Occupy Building
Australia	78%	21%	18%	2%
Belarus	9	3	19	0.3
Brazil	47	6	25	3
Bulgaria	6	2	9	1
Canada	76	22	20	3
Chile	16	2	14	2
Denmark	50	10	27	2
France	51	11	31	7
Ghana	7	3	7	3
Great Britain	75	14	13	2
Hungary	25	3	9	0.2
India	17	11	8	1
Italy	44	10	34	4
Mexico	28	9	10	4
Nigeria	4	5	9	5
Japan	51	7	9	0.1
Poland	19	5	9	2
Russia	9	2	20	0.5
South Africa	13	11	10	2
South Korea	40	16	14	2
Sweden	71	33	30	0.8
Turkey	19	9	9	0.7
United States	71	18	15	2
Uruguay	34	4	4	7

Note: About 1,500 respondents in each country indicated whether they had engaged in each political action.
Source: World Values Survey, 1995–1997, 2001.

violence, reveal that individuals' choices of political action might not conform to the democratic model. It is also clear that many people continue to rely on nongovernmental channels to achieve objectives that could be pursued by contacting public officials.

Although systematic, comparative data on less democratic and nondemocratic countries are limited, it seems that the reliance on nongovernmental channels and the incidence of unconventional political behavior are greater (and vary more substantially) there than in democratic systems. In some less democratic countries, state repression deters the great majority of citizens from participation. And there are also countries characterized by "de-participation," as the political leadership has weakened or even eliminated the mechanisms that enable citizens to engage in political actions (Nelson 1987: 116–120).

GROUP POLITICAL ACTIONS

Recall the letter from Micky Sadoff of MADD at the beginning of this chapter. Rather than suffer privately, Sadoff decided to take political action. She became a leader, and ultimately the president, of MADD. This group has developed into an effective nationwide organization in the United States. MADD recruits members and solicits contributions and then uses its resources to lobby politicians to pass more aggressive policies for punishing drunk drivers.

Sadoff's story is dramatic, but it illustrates the most common reason people join political groups. A person might want to influence the actions of his government but might believe that his individual actions will not make any difference. People tend to feel that they are relatively powerless in politics when acting alone—but there might be strength in numbers. If a person joins with many others in a political group, it is possible that the group can exercise influence in the political world because of the group's numbers, organization, and capabilities.

Although a few political activists can have a major impact on politics, most individuals, most of the time, have a minimal effect on political decisions and actions. Even in democracies, casting a vote is their primary political act. But if huge numbers of votes are cast (more than 100 million votes are cast in a U.S. presidential contest), one person's vote is politically insignificant.

To have a greater impact, an individual's best strategy is to combine his political actions with those of others through a political group. Groups are extremely important in politics because they are often the major mechanism through which individuals are linked to the political system—hence their label as "linkage institutions." Some political groups, such as a major political party, can have wide-ranging goals and a huge membership. Other groups, such as MADD, are more narrowly focused in their objectives and have limited membership. And extremist groups, such as al-Qaeda, might have few members but can still pursue extensive, radical agendas. The rest of this chapter describes the nature and activities of various kinds of political groups and political parties.

As an analytic concept, a **group** can be defined as *an aggregation of individuals who interact in order to pursue a common interest* (see also Chapter 9). It is the pursuit of a common interest that is most crucial to this definition, since the individuals do not necessarily interact directly with one another. The factor that distinguishes a political **interest group** from other groups is that *the common interest the group pursues is a political objective*—an interest in a particular policy or action that might be taken.

A distinction is usually made between political interest groups and political parties, although both types fit under our general definition of political group. A political group enters the special category of **political party** when the group seeks not merely to influence political decisions, but also to place its members in the actual roles of government, such as chief executives and legislators. Although this distinction can become rather fuzzy among the most politically active groups, we shall treat political parties as a category different from other types of political interest groups.

POLITICAL INTEREST GROUPS

Activities of Political Interest Groups

All political interest groups share the common objective of attempting to influence the allocation of public values. But such groups can employ a variety of strategies to achieve this purpose (Baumgartner and Leech 1998).

Political action.   The most direct methods to achieve political objectives involve some form of political action. Such action might be taken by all group members or by some members who formally or informally represent the entire group. Depending on the political system, this might entail voting and campaign activities to influence the selection and action of political authorities. Or the group might attempt to communicate its interest to political actors by such techniques as letters, personal contacts, petitions, rallies, or political violence.

Provision of material resources.   Political interest groups also can provide goods or services to political actors. Such a strategy assumes that providing goods and services will influence decision makers to be more favorably disposed toward the interests of a group. Each political system develops its own rules about the methods and amounts of money or goods that can be given legitimately to political actors. The line between legal and illegal provision of money and goods varies dramatically across political cultures. In some political systems, all it takes to shock people is the revelation that an interest group has given a political actor a small gift, but in many political systems, it requires a multimillion-dollar kickback to a politician to upset citizens and provoke action.

The United States is one of the countries where interest groups contribute extraordinary amounts of money to political actors. In the 2004 elections, for example, interest groups contributed more than $1.5 billion to congressional candidates (Center for Responsive Politics 2006). Most of these contributions are legal, although some are not (e.g., in 1997 the Democratic Party returned more than $1 million to questionable donors, and President Clinton was widely criticized for "renting the Lincoln bedroom" for overnight visits in the White House by big contributors).

The ethics of a system in which political interest groups can make huge contributions is increasingly questioned. It is obvious that money is given in the expectation of influencing public policies. Although cause-and-effect relationships are hard to establish, there are striking linkages between groups' campaign contributions and beneficial legislation. In the 1996 election in the United States, for example, tobacco companies contributed $11.3 million; soon after, legislation was passed directing a 15-cent-per-pack cigarette tax to a fund offsetting lawsuits, a benefit estimated at $50 billion. Oil, energy, and natural resource firms contributed $18.3 million and then gained $18 billion in benefits from exemptions from the passage of an alternative minimum tax

▶ Greenpeace activists demonstrate against genetically-modified papaya outside the Thai Ministry of Agriculture.

law (O'Connor and Sabato 2004: figure 16.3). No one knows the amount of illegal resources that are distributed, although in most countries, scandals regarding bribes and kickbacks seem to be reported with increasing frequency. In 2007, for example, former Philippine President Joseph Estrada was found guilty of taking more than $85 million in bribes during his presidency. And China reported 17,000 bribery cases involving more than $575 million between August 2005 and December 2006 (Chinese Consulate-General 2007). This is not a new phenomenon. In a wry comment on American politics, humorist Will Rogers once observed that "our Congress is the best that money can buy."

Exchange of information.   Another activity performed by some interest groups is providing data and information to those within the government. The interest group may have specialized information that policy makers would find difficult or impossible to obtain from other sources. These private groups are stakeholders with a vested interest in the public policies that emerge, and so most actively provide data that support their own interests. For example, in the early 1980s, the U.S. Congress began considering a law requiring mandatory air bags as a safety restraint in automobiles. In determining whether to pass such a law, legislators were particularly influenced by information provided by automobile manufacturers (whose data indicated that air bags were costly, would reduce fuel economy, and would not substantially reduce overall injury levels in automobile collisions). This critical information, from a highly interested party to the decision, was an important reason behind the refusal of Congress to require air bags (Reppy 1984). Later in the decade, a barrage of counterinformation from another powerful interest group, the insurance industry, persuaded Congress and the public that air bags could save lives and lower insurance premiums. This resulted in laws requiring air bags.

In many countries, as the scale of government and the reach of public policy have expanded, many organizations in society need detailed, inside information about what the government is doing or intends to do that might affect their organization. Thus Salisbury (1990; Salisbury et al. 1991) has concluded that American interest groups in Washington, D.C., now spend more time gathering information *from* the government that is relevant to their organizations' interests (e.g., changes in rules or laws) than they do providing information *to* the government that might influence its policies.

Cooperation.   Major interest groups can also exert influence through their compliance or noncompliance with the government policy process. In many countries, government actors understand that policy is implemented more successfully when it is acceptable to the affected interest groups. There are many countries (especially industrial democracies such as France, Japan, South Korea, and Sweden) in which government cultivates a special relationship with the interest group representatives of major economic organizations, such as business, labor, and farmers. When such interest groups can help the government implement policy, they enjoy a privileged position. Governance based on close cooperation with major sectoral interest groups is called **corporatism** (see Box 8.3). For example, the British ministry responsible for agriculture and food works closely with the interest group representing the food manufacturers so that the manufacturers, rather than the government bureaucracy, take most of the responsibility for inspecting and monitoring food hygiene (Wilson 1991). Obviously, an organization benefits greatly when its interest group persuades the government to allow the organization to regulate itself.

Constraints on a Group's Behavior

Each interest group must decide what mix of activities is most likely to serve its political agenda. This mix depends on many things, including the nature of the group's political resources, the objectives it pursues, and the political environment in which it operates.

Political resources.   A group's **political resources** are *those elements, controlled by the group, that can influence the decisions and actions of political actors.* The political resources that are most effective differ according to the situation and the political system. The preceding section emphasized the potential impact of financial resources and information, but certain other political resources can also be influential: control of factors of production, social status, legality, special knowledge or skills, ability to mobilize large numbers of people who pressure the government, capacity for social disruption, and access to decision makers. Various groups usually have dramatically different levels of all these political resources. An interest group's behavior depends on the kinds of resources it has available and its decision to use a particular mix of resources.

Objectives.   The *objectives* that interest groups pursue in the political world are as diverse as the different policy issues upon which the government might act. One group might want one specific thing, such as a subsidy for growing wheat, while another group might have very broad objectives, such as a set of policies to eliminate poverty. The groups' strategies and the probability that they will be successful are related to the groups' political objectives. In general, an interest group is advantaged to the extent that its objective (1) is quite similar to existing policy and (2) is a value allocation that the political system has the capacity to make. For example, the Greenpeace groups in France and Germany are more likely to influence government policies on safer disposal of nuclear wastes than on stopping the development of new nuclear power stations, and these groups have little chance of achieving their goal of worldwide nuclear disarmament.

Political environment.   At the most basic level, the demands that groups can make and the actions they can take depend on the boundaries of acceptable political action within the particular *political environment*. Every example of interest group action given thus far in this chapter has focused on a group operating in a democratic political system. An essential feature of democratic systems is that interest groups have extensive rights to make political demands and engage in political actions. Yet there is some disagreement about the extent to which interest groups contribute to healthy democratic processes (see The Debate in 3).

In democracies such as Great Britain, Italy, and Japan, professional representatives of interest groups (lobbyists) are as much a part of the accepted set of governmental actors as are elected legislators and their staffs. In Japan, it is common for senior government officials to "descend from heaven" (*amakudari*) to a high-paying lobbyist's job for a major corporate interest. In the United States, 35,000 full-time professional lobbyists are registered in Washington, D.C., and one analyst contends that the total number of people engaged primarily in lobbying activities is more than 80,000 (that is, more than 140 professional lobbyists per member of Congress) (Birnbaum 1993). In contrast, repressive political systems tolerate only a very narrow range of interest group activities that are in opposition to the leadership. Such groups, and especially their leaders, usually face extensive harassment and punishment from the

THE DEBATE IN 3

How Interested Are Interest Groups in Democracy?

For as long as democratic governments have existed, there has been ambivalence about political interest groups. On the one hand, democratic theory is grounded in the idea that individuals can and should form political interest groups to influence the selection of officials and to promote public policies that serve their goals. On the other hand, the press, the public, and even some governmental officials are often heard blaming a country's problems on "special interests," which are effective in influencing government to enact policies that serve the interests of specific groups but are not in "the public interest." Do interest groups hinder the democratic process or facilitate it?

Interest Groups Facilitate Democracy

- Interest groups are a fundamentally important set of actors in a democratic system because they enable citizens to organize into groups of sufficient size to communicate their concerns and demands in a clearer, more amplified voice to policy makers, especially to the national government.
- Interest groups are especially valuable in representing and supporting those groups whose views are not effectively represented by any of the political parties.
- In a single country, thousands of interest groups can operate at the same time, representing the interests of different groups of people. Because there are so many groups whose voices are heard, no one interest group will go unchecked and become too powerful and influential relative to the others.
- Financial contributions from interest groups enable candidates to purchase the expensive media that allow them to communicate their ideas to many citizens and thus enhance the citizens' capacity to participate knowledgeably in the democratic process.
- Interest groups play a very beneficial role in the public policy process. They provide public officials with an enormous amount of relevant, specialized information that public agencies might not be able to gather efficiently and that supports good policy making.
- Interest groups serve as an expert watchdog over legislation or policies that public officials might try to implement but that are based on error or are self-serving. By articulating such concerns, interest groups add a valuable level of accountability and monitoring to the process of democratic governance.

Interest Groups Hinder the Democratic Process

- Most interest groups work to garner support for a single or narrow set of goals, often at the expense of the interests of the broader society.
- Many interest groups have large professional staffs that work 24/7 to promote their goals. Ordinary citizens rarely have this level of expertise and time commitment for political action, and thus the interests of these ordinary citizens are not as well promoted in the policy process as those of special interests.
- Interest groups have specialized information and data that they provide to government officials. Although such information can be quite influential in the policy process, it can also be heavily biased in favor of the interest group's position on issues.
- Special interest groups are the major source of funds to many political actors. Campaign contributions and other "goodies" can be the source of considerable corruption as they purchase access to and influence with public officials. Meanwhile, most other citizens, who lack such financial resources, are seriously disadvantaged in gaining access and influence.
- Interest groups form an unnecessary layer that insulates citizens from their government and discourages them from engaging in direct democracy.

More questions . . .

1. Can you think of any effective interest groups whose actions are a positive force in making your government work in a more democratic manner? Can you think of any effective interest groups that actually undermine democracy? Are your choices closely linked to *your own* interests and values?
2. Does a system of strong and active interest groups increase or decrease the effectiveness of political parties?
3. Can you imagine an effective political system that has no organized interest groups?

authorities. Nonetheless, groups periodically emerge to articulate demands for political, social, and economic changes. Occasionally, the state responds positively to these demands. Some interest groups are eventually granted a major role in the political process. This happened in South Africa to the African National Congress, which began in 1912 as an interest group to promote the human rights of black Africans, was later a government opposition movement, and then an outlawed violent protest group (in 1961); finally it became the country's major political party whose leaders (Nelson Mandela and Thabo Mbeki) were elected presidents of the country. Other groups have successfully engaged in a combination of political violence and mass mobilization to overthrow the existing regime, as did the Sandinistas in Nicaragua in 1979.

In general, however, one of the key features of a repressive political system is its capacity to stifle or crush opposition interest groups. Such groups therefore operate on the margins of the political system, ranging from small revolutionary cells such as FARC in Columbia to organized groups such as the Buddhist monks in Myanmar to mass movements such as the democracy demonstrations in China in 1989.

Types of Interest Groups

Gabriel Almond proposed a relatively simple and widely accepted taxonomy of four types of political groups (Almond et al. 2008): (1) associational, (2) institutional, (3) nonassociational, and (4) anomic.

Associational interest groups.   The first type, the **associational interest group**, is *organized specifically to further the political objectives of its members.* One example is the British Medical Association (see Box 3.1). Another example is Common Cause, an American interest group whose citizen-members pay a membership fee to support the lobbying activities of a central staff. The leadership of Common Cause identifies political issues of significance to the group's members and then attempts to mobilize political action (such as letter-writing campaigns and press releases) in support of a particular position on the issue. The group also provides decision makers with information and data and contributes funds to some political candidates.

Institutional interest groups.   This type of group has been formed to achieve goals other than affecting the political system, but it also pursues political objectives. Most occupational and organizational groups recognize that the decisions of the political system sometimes have major impacts on their own interests. Thus they have a formal or informal subunit whose primary purpose is to represent the group's interests to the political system. For example, the University of California is a large institution of higher education, but its interests are strongly affected by local, state, and national policies on educational funding, research funding, regulation of research, discrimination in admissions and hiring, tax law, patent law, collective bargaining, and many other policies. Consequently, the university has full-time professional and student lobbyists on each campus, in Sacramento (the state capital), and in Washington, D.C.

Nonassociational interest groups.   These groups are fluid aggregates of individuals who are not explicitly associated with a permanent organizational entity but who share some common interest regarding certain issues and become politically active on an issue. A loosely structured organization might temporarily emerge to plan

BOX 3.1

The British Medical Association: An Effective Associational Interest Group

The British Medical Association (BMA), a professional organization for doctors in Great Britain, exists primarily to provide technical and professional information to 139,000 member doctors and to protect the standards and practices of the medical profession on matters of education, training, qualifications to practice, and malpractice.

The BMA is a good example of an effective associational interest group because, in protecting the professional and financial interests of its members, its professional staff and members take many actions to influence the policies of the British government regarding the health care system. Some areas of obvious interest to the member doctors are the training of doctors, pay issues, client choice of doctors and hospitals, and the quality and quantity of medical facilities.

The BMA also is concerned about public policies regarding such issues as advertising by professionals, judicial rulings on liability, personal and business taxation policies, certification of health care paraprofessionals (e.g., chiropractors), support for medical research, and so on.

Given the wealth of its members, the BMA can contribute substantial amounts of money to influence policy makers directly or to finance public information campaigns. Its members command respect from political actors because of the doctors' high status and social standing. The BMA is also a source of vast information and expertise about health care issues for those public officials who must formulate and implement health care policy. But the BMA's greatest leverage on political actors is its capacity to cooperate or withhold cooperation, since it can powerfully influence the extent to which most doctors support the nationalized health care system in Britain. Thus the British Department of Health works extremely closely with the BMA, as the interest group representing most doctors, in all public policy decisions relevant to health care.

and coordinate political activities, but the group will be temporary and relatively informal, and once the issue has lost its immediate salience, the group will disappear. If an interest group emerges in your community to stop a building development, or to recall a public official, or to promote a particular law, it can be categorized as a nonassociational interest group.

Anomic interest groups.   These groups are short-lived, spontaneous aggregations of people who share a political concern. These people participate in a group political action that emerges with little or no planning and then quickly stops after the action is completed. For Almond, a riot is the clearest example of an anomic interest group—the participants tend to share common political interests or grievances that they express through a generally disorganized outpouring of emotion, energy, and violence. A political demonstration is a somewhat more organized version of this type of interest group activity.

POLITICAL PARTIES

An interest group is transformed into a **political party** when *the group attempts to capture political power directly by placing its members in governmental office.* The political party is the broadest linkage institution in most political systems because most parties are overarching organizations that incorporate many different interests and groups. While countries can have thousands of political interest groups, most have only a handful of political parties.

Activities of Political Parties

Political parties in most countries engage in six broad activities, or functions: (1) serve as brokers of ideas, (2) serve as agents of political socialization, (3) link individuals to the system, (4) mobilize and recruit activists, (5) coordinate governmental activities, and (6) serve as organized sources of opposition to the governing group.

Serving as brokers of ideas.   The first, most central activity of political parties is to serve as major brokers of political ideas. Many individuals and political groups have interests and demands regarding the policies of government. A crucial function of political parties is to aggregate and simplify these many demands into a few packages of clear alternatives. To the extent that political parties are effective in this activity, they dramatically reduce the complexity and scale of the political process for the decision maker, who must perceive and respond to the individual and group demands, and for the voter, who must select political leaders whose overall policy preferences are closest to his own.

While all political parties are brokers of ideas, parties can be differentiated into two broad categories—ideological and pragmatic—on the basis of their intensity of commitment to those ideas. *Ideological parties* hold major programmatic goals (e.g., egalitarianism, ethnic solidarity, Islamic fundamentalism) and are deeply committed to the implementation of these goals to achieve comprehensive changes in the sociopolitical order. Ideological parties are usually extreme within the context of their particular political culture. The Islamic Salvation Front in Algeria, the North Korean Communist Party, Sínn Fein in Northern Ireland, the American Libertarian Party, and the German Green Party (see Box 3.2) are examples of ideological parties.

In contrast, *pragmatic parties* hold more flexible goals and are oriented to moderate or incremental policy change. To achieve electoral success, pragmatic parties might shift their position or expand the range of viewpoints they encompass. Parties of the center are characteristically pragmatic parties. Examples include the Christian Democrats in Germany, the Congress-I Party in India, the Institutional Revolutionary Party (PRI) in Mexico, and the Democratic Party in the United States.

Facilitating political socialization.   A related activity of political parties is their socialization of people into the political culture (see Chapter 4). In many political systems, most people develop a clear "party identification." This means that a person trusts one political party to represent his political interests. The person's political beliefs and actions are influenced by information that a political party provides or by the person's perceptions of what the party supports. Even if a person does not have strong party identification, political parties can be an important source of his

BOX 3.2

Let's Party! The Rise of the Green Party in Germany

Few political interest groups transform into successful, modern political parties. The Green Party in Germany seems to have achieved this transformation. It began as a diverse set of loosely affiliated interest groups in the 1960s and declared itself a political party in 1980. Its electoral fortunes in the national legislature have gone up and down (starting with 3.7 percent of the seats in 1983, dropping as low as zero seats in 1990, and currently holding 8.3 percent of the seats).

Where did the Green Party come from? Like all political groups, it began with people who wanted to influence politics. In the late 1960s, some West Germans were displeased with their government's support of U.S. actions in Vietnam and Southeast Asia. Some also believed that their government, and the entire "establishment" in their society, had been corrupted in its quest for ever expanding power and wealth. Some had other policy concerns, including the huge inequalities in wealth and welfare within their society and among countries, the discrimination against certain groups such as women and ethnic minorities, the frightful buildup of nuclear weapons by the superpowers, and the degradation of the environment.

People with these political beliefs, energized mainly by young countercultural Germans, demonstrated, marched, and formed local protest groups. Dissatisfied with the policies of the national parties, these groups began to elect some of their members to local office, especially in larger cities. The most dynamic people in these local groups developed a national network, and in 1980 they formed a national political party, Die Grünen (the Greens).

The common concern that attracted many individuals to the Green Party was its commitment to preserving the environment. In Europe, the Greens became the first important party representing the "postmaterialist, self-expressive values" discussed in Chapter 2.

The Green Party remains an ideological party, and its party platform includes strong antiestablishment elements. The party ideology emphasizes the transformation of Germany: from capitalism to a system in which workers own and control industry; from a militaristic, NATO-based country to one that becomes neutral, eliminates nuclear weapons, and stops preparing for war; and from a leading postindustrial society to one that uses only those technologies that do not damage the environment.

The Green Party had a substantial impact on German politics in the 1980s but struggled for electoral support in the early 1990s and then became a somewhat uneasy junior partner in a governing coalition with the large Social Democratic Party (1998–2005). It opted to remain outside the conservative-led 2005 "grand coalition" of parties under Angela Merkel. The future of the Green Party at the national level remains uncertain. Will it be outflanked by the more radical Left party or absorbed by the large Social Democratic Party in the left center? Can it avoid self-destruction caused by the strong ideological differences among its moderate and more radical factions? Some analysts suggest that this party is too wild to last much longer.

political knowledge since they provide easily understood reference points regarding politically relevant information.

Linking individual and system.   In its role as a linkage institution, a political party connects individuals and the political system. Most individuals rely on political groups to represent their interests within the political system. More than other groups, political parties function in a general manner to formulate, aggregate, and communicate a coherent package of demands and supports. And, if the party gains political power, it can attempt to implement those demands on behalf of the individuals whose interests it serves. Thus political parties greatly facilitate the individual's sense of integration into the political process.

Mobilizing and recruiting political activists.   The political party offers a well-organized and obvious structure within which a person can direct his political interests. It is a source of political information, of contact with other politically relevant individuals and groups, and of effective access to the political system. In many political systems, involvement with a political party is the primary mechanism through which individuals are drawn into roles as political foot soldiers and, ultimately, as political leaders. Often it is political parties that select the candidates for political positions or have the power to place people directly in positions within the political system. Whether one is considering a highly democratic polity such as Great Britain or an extremely nondemocratic one such as China, most or all individuals in key executive and legislative positions have achieved these positions through recruitment and selection by a political party.

Coordinating governmental operations.   The fifth major activity of political parties is to coordinate the actions of the government. The political party can encourage or require its members to work together to achieve shared policy goals. It can establish an internal hierarchy, with party leaders (e.g., in the U.S. Senate, majority and minority

▶ **Mobilizing citizens to political action is one important function of political parties, as in this rally for the United National Congress Party in Trinidad.**

leaders, whips, committee chairs) controlling the actions of party members in the conduct of government. The parties can also provide mechanisms for facilitating cooperation and regulating conflict among different parties. Leaders of several parties might form a coalition to secure majority support for certain policies. Such coalitions are especially important in legislatures in which no single party commands a majority. Political parties can also establish forms of power sharing in the conduct of government business. For example, the parties can agree to formulate executive or legislative committees in a manner that reflects the political strength of the various parties.

Serving as sources of opposition.   Finally, where the political system has more than one party, the parties not participating in the governing group can serve as an explicit and organized source of opposition. The function is most fully institutionalized in Great Britain, where the major out-of-power party in Parliament is explicitly designated as "Her Majesty's Loyal Opposition." The party should oppose, but never obstruct, the actions of the governing party, since the opposition party remains loyal to crown and country. In Britain, the opposition party is guaranteed control of a specified amount of time during legislative sessions. The opposition leaders receive salaries to serve as a "shadow government," with a member of the opposition serving as the alternative and potential future replacement for each top official in the government. Hence there is a "shadow prime minister," a "shadow minister of defense," and so on, who articulate what they would do if they held ministerial positions as the governing party.

DOING POLITICS

Politics comes alive when people engage in political action. The participation in a protest march, the attempt to persuade a friend to share your political perspective, even the act of voting can be a moment of heightened experience. Acting alone or with others, the individual who takes political action can seek to serve his own most crass self-interest or the altruistic goal of global prosperity.

This analysis has indicated the diverse modes of political action as well as the rather modest levels of such actions reported by most people. Some people are shocked that so many citizens do not even bother to vote in a country such as the United States. Others are surprised that anyone really thinks that one person's involvement in politics, whatever the level of commitment, will make any difference in the grander scheme of things. Political participation is a crucial topic for analysis because people's actions are at the heart of the political process.

In this chapter, you have been introduced to the methods and findings of micropolitical analysis. Could you undertake such an analysis yourself? Yes! Before you conclude this chapter, Box 3.3 shows you how you might do it by studying your own peers.

To this point in the book, our treatment of micropolitics has focused mainly on description and taxonomy—on what people believe about politics and on what political actions people undertake. For a richer analysis, however, we must at least attempt to answer the *why* questions: Why do people engage in a particular political action? Can we explain the apparent differences in people's political beliefs? Explaining political beliefs and actions is the central topic in Chapter 4.

BOX 3.3

Measuring Students' Political Behavior: An Example of Micropolitical Analysis

Let us consider how you might study the political participation of American college students. Do you consider yourself an active participant in the political world? How many different types of political actions have you engaged in during the last three years? How might you assess whether most college students are politically active? Using the methods of survey research, you might begin to analyze your own or others' political activity level. Here are the key steps:

1. *Conceptualizing variables.* Our objective is to describe and explain college students' political participation. The first task of such an analysis is conceptualization.

BOX 3.3 *(Continued)*

This entails developing a set of concepts that clarify and elaborate on the basic idea(s) you wish to analyze. Which specific behaviors do you want to study: Reading a political blog? Voting? Contacting officials? Signing petitions? Participating in political demonstrations? There are many possibilities.

2. *Operationalizing variables.* Once you have decided which modes of participation you will study, you need to define them more carefully so that you can delimit those instances where the activities have actually occurred. This process is called *operationalizing* variables. You detail how key concepts are identified and measured in actual research settings. This can be more complicated than it seems. For example, to operationalize the concept of voting, do you want to distinguish between voting in national elections and all other elections? Do you want to determine the proportion of elections in which the person voted? Do you want to focus only on recent activity? Notice that many such questions merit consideration when you operationalize a major political variable, and these must be resolved before you gather data.

3. *Collecting data.* Now you collect data. This step entails identifying the population (the set of subjects) you wish to study and developing a strategy to gather empirical data that measure your operationalized variables. Assume that the population for your study is the students at your college (notice that this is an extremely limited sample for generalizations about "all college students").

Typically, it is not feasible to gather data for everyone in the group about whom the analyst wishes to generalize, and so a procedure is developed to sample a subset of the group. This can be done by gathering data for anyone who is willing to respond, by selecting people at random, or by devising a more sophisticated sampling strategy that ensures adequate representation of respondents with certain key characteristics (e.g., age, gender, ethnicity, socioeconomic class, region). Professional public opinion pollsters and social scientists usually use these more sophisticated sampling strategies.

In your study, you might not have time to gather data for all the students at your college (and certainly not all college students in America), so you might randomly select one out of every 50 students in the student directory to serve as your sample. It would be simpler to study the students in your political science class, but consider why a study of your political science class is likely to be more biased than a study of the sample from the student directory.

The next problem is deciding how to collect data about each student's actual political behavior. Since you cannot observe the behavior of all students, you probably have to settle for asking them to report their own political activity through some form of personal interview or questionnaire. To elicit accurate responses, you need an approach that enables the respondent to understand what you are asking and to answer honestly. Your method must also ensure accurate recording of the responses.

4. *Analyzing data: creating variables.* Once you have gathered the data, you must organize the data in forms that enable you to analyze them. You might just compare the percent of each answer to each question. But analysts usually want to engage in richer data analysis. So, for example, you might try to create a taxonomy of different types of participants (e.g., apathetics, voting specialists, foot soldiers, etc.). Or you could

BOX 3.3 (*Continued*)

compute a "political action score" for every respondent, as a sum of how many different activities each respondent reports. You could make this score more subtle, by considering the frequency with which the respondent engages in the various activities or by giving greater importance in the overall score to more demanding or unconventional activities. You can see that there are many creative and interesting ways in which to combine the data. Most contemporary political analyses attempt to develop these more complex variables because such measures allow for richer findings and generalizations.

Notice that virtually all the decisions in the analysis, and especially those about measurement and variable creation, are made by *you*—the individual political analyst. There are no fixed rules regarding these decisions, although they are not arbitrary. The analyst must attempt to make decisions that are reasonable in terms of the analytic issues being considered and that are defensible, since others might question these decisions in the spirit of the scientific method.

5. *Analyzing data: description and explanation.* With your data and variables, you can now *describe* the political behavior of college students in your study. Here are some of the questions you might examine:

What are the most frequent political behaviors that the students undertake?
How frequently do the students discuss politics face to face? Online?
What percentage are politically apathetic?
What percentage have participated in political demonstrations?

As you will find in Chapter 4, political analysts are rarely satisfied with answers to these kinds of descriptive questions. Whenever possible, they also attempt to generate more *explanatory* statements that search for general patterns among the behaviors or indicate the conditions that seem to cause certain types of political behavior. To do this in your study, you would need to gather additional data about your respondents, such as their personal characteristics, background experiences, and political beliefs. Then you might be able to offer tentative answers to such questions as these:

Do students who discuss politics more frequently also have higher grade point averages?
Are older students more politically active than younger students?
Is political protest more common among social science majors than among science majors?
Is party identity correlated with parents' income level?
Is ethnicity associated with interest in politics?

As you can see, there are many fascinating questions that you can examine as you become a more insightful political analyst. For example, are college students different politically from young people who do not attend college? It would also be interesting to examine these questions across different cultures. For example, what are the similarities and differences in the political behavior of students in different regions or different countries? As political scientists gather more extensive databases and use more refined analytic techniques, they can begin to develop stronger generalizations about the nature and causes of political beliefs and actions.

KEY CONCEPTS

associational interest group

corporatism

extremist-activists

foot soldiers

group

ideological party

interest group

political activists

political environment

political participation

political party

political resources

pragmatic party

FOR FURTHER CONSIDERATION

1. Why might the absence of a political action be viewed as an act of political participation?

2. Apart from voting, what political action do you think is most important?

3. Imagine that you could engage in a conversation with the political activist, contemporary or historical, who most fascinates you. Whom would you choose? Why? What would you ask him or her?

4. Should there be any limits on people's actions to influence political decision makers? What principles can you offer to justify any such limitations?

5. What is the most unconventional political action in which you have engaged? If the same circumstances arose now, would you behave any differently? Why?

FOR FURTHER READING

Ackerman, Peter, and Jack DuVall. (2001). *A Force More Powerful: A Century of Non-Violent Conflict.* New York: Palgrave. A series of engaging case studies set in many countries (e.g., Chile, Denmark, Poland, Serbia) reveals how political activism grounded in strategies of nonviolence (e.g., strikes, protests, boycotts) has achieved major political change in the face of repressive regimes and dictatorial leaders.

Beah, Ishmael. (2007). *A Long Way Gone.* New York: Farrar, Straus and Giroux. A dramatic and remarkable autobiography of a Sierra Leone boy who is captured and trained as a child soldier. He describes his violent world and how he escapes it and establishes a new life for himself.

Bohlen, J. (2000). *Making Waves: The Origins and Future of Greenpeace.* Montreal: Black Rose. The fascinating history of an international group committed to fighting governments and huge corporations in order to protect the environment, with a special focus on its activist leaders.

Cigler, Allan J., and Burdett Loomis, Eds. (2006). *Interest Group Politics.* 7th ed. Washington, DC: CQ Press. Thoughtful essays on how interest groups operate in the American political context in an era characterized by a huge infusion of money into the policy process, single-interest politics, social movements, and the Internet.

Florini, Ann, Ed. (2000). *The Third Force: The Rise of Transnational Civil Society.* Washington, DC: Carnegie Endowment for International Peace. Interesting studies of the impacts of global citizen activists—groups whose members and activities cross national boundaries as they strive to alter state policies on such important issues as nuclear non-proliferation, human rights, sustainable development, and corruption.

Genovese, Michael A., Ed. (1993). *Women as National Leaders.* Newbury Park, CA: Sage. Detailed and interesting case studies of late–20th-century female political leaders, such as Corazon Aquino, Benazir Bhutto, Violeta Chamorro, Indira Gandhi, and Margaret Thatcher, assessing their leadership styles and whether they seem to govern differently than men.

Greenwood, Justin. (2003). *Interest Representation in the European Union.* Basingstoke, England: Palgrave Macmillan. An exploration of the roles, behaviors, and impacts of various types of interest groups (e.g., business, "the public," professional groups, labor) in the context of the EU as a supranational policy-making body that also must link with state governments and a multitude of interest groups.

Hoffman, Abbie. (1989). *The Best of Abbie Hoffman.* New York: Four Walls, Eight Windows. A selection of the funny, irreverent writings on radicalism and revolution by one of the key leaders (now deceased) of the student radical movement of the late 1960s and a member of the "Chicago 7," tried for conspiracy after the riots at the 1968 Democratic Party convention in Chicago.

Loader, Brian D., Paul G. Nixon, Dieter Rucht, and Wim van de Donk, Eds. (2004). *Cyberprotest: New Media, Citizens, and Social Movements.* London: Routledge. A useful set of essays exploring how the new ICTs (information and communication technologies) are being utilized in Europe by activists (citizen groups and social movements) in an attempt to mobilize other citizens and also pressure governments to respond to their demands.

Lowi, Theodore. (1979). *The End of Liberalism: The Second Republic in the United States.* 2nd ed. New York: Norton. An incisive critique of the shortcomings of politics dominated by interest groups.

Ma Bo. (1995). *Blood Red Sunset: A Memoir of the Chinese Cultural Revolution.* New York: Viking. A harsh, gripping autobiography of a young person drawn into the fervor of Mao Zedong's Cultural Revolution. A Red Guard working on a hopeless program to create farmland in Mongolia, Ma Bo is transformed from a true believer into an embittered man fighting to clear himself from charges that he is a reactionary.

Meisner, Maurice, and Gareth Schott. (2006). *Mao Zedong: A Political and Intellectual Portrait.* London: Polity Press. An illuminating biography of one of the most remarkable leaders of the 20th century, emphasizing both his personal qualities and his enormous impacts on the evolution of politics and economics in China.

Meyer, David S., Valerie Jenness, and Helen Ingram, Eds. (2005). *Routing the Opposition: Social Movements, Public Policy, and Democracy.* Minneapolis: University of Minnesota Press. A diverse set of essays examining the impacts on public policies of "social movements"—organized group social protest activities that are typically focused on a single issue area. Based on analyses of social movements in such policy areas as prison reform, immigrants' rights, and the organic agriculture movement, the studies explore how the very different approaches and agendas of policy makers and those participating in social movements interact.

Rueschemeyer, Dietrich, Marilyn Rueschemeyer, and Bjorn Wittrock. (1998). *Participation and Democracy East and West: Comparisons and Interpretations.* Armonk, NY: M. E. Sharpe. The current patterns of participation and activism are compared and analyzed, grounded in studies of the Czech Republic, Germany, Hungary, Norway, Poland, Sweden, and the United States.

Volgy, Thomas J. (1999). *Politics in the Trenches: Citizens, Politicians, and the Fate of Democracy.* Tucson: University of Arizona Press. A political science professor offers a brief, highly readable and revealing description of the challenges and actual experiences of political leaders in American local politics, based on his many years as a local government elected official and his interviews with more than 300 elected officials.

ON THE WEB

http://www.politics1.com/parties.htm

This site offers a directory and description of U.S. political parties.

http://www.ifex.org

The International Freedom of Expression Exchange represents more than 50 groups committed to human rights and civil liberties and describes current situations of concern.

http://www.idea.int/index.cfm

The International Institute for Democracy and Electoral Assistance (IDEA) provides information about current democratic practices and various relevant databases for more than 100 countries, including comparative data on voter turnout for both presidential and parliamentary elections covering the period since 1945.

http://www.greenpeace.org

Greenpeace's Web site describes some of the key initiatives taken by this global, action-oriented interest group.

http://www.protest.net

Protest.net provides a comprehensive calendar of upcoming protests and political rallies taking place around the world. The site lists upcoming protests by both geographic region and political issue.

http://www.internationalanswer.org

This Web site serves as the electronic home of International ANSWER, an antiwar coalition. This electronic portal provides a wealth of information in regard to antiwar movements taking place throughout the international community.

http://www.wsu.edu/~amerstu/smc/smcframe.html

This site, developed by Washington State University, provides a number of links and articles related to both American and global social movements.

http://www.amnesty.org/

Amnesty International has been dedicated to human rights causes for well over 40 years. The site provides information on a variety of topics ranging from refugees to arms control.

http://civicyouth.org

CIRCLE (Center for Information and Research on Civic Learning and Engagement) promotes research on the civic and political engagement of Americans between the ages of 15 and 25. The organization's Web site offers a variety of interesting data and studies on this topic, including research papers on youth participation and strategies for mobilizing young adults into political participation.

CHAPTER 4

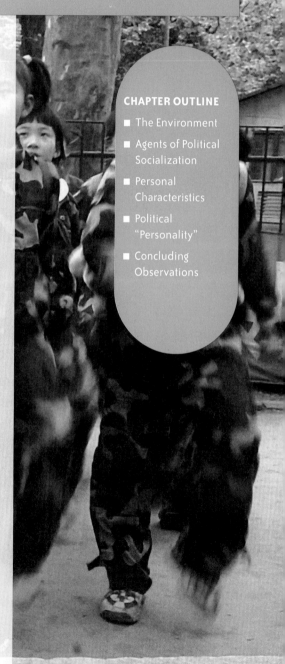

INFLUENCES ON BELIEFS AND ACTIONS

A friend who is skeptical about political science confronts you with a challenge. She brings three adults into the room and announces that one is an elected public official, one has never voted in a single election, and one has participated in many violent political protests. You must decide who has done what. You can ask each person two questions that make neither a direct nor an indirect reference to the three kinds of political behavior. How would you try to solve this problem? What questions would you ask?

In Chapters 2 and 3, we *described* people's political beliefs and political actions. Some of the most interesting questions in political analysis are the *why* questions: Why do individuals hold particular political beliefs and engage in certain political actions? Figure 4.1 indicates four broad types of explanatory factors that might account for individual political behavior: (1) the environment, (2) agents of political socialization, (3) personal characteristics, and (4) personality and human nature. This chapter considers these four types of influences on the political beliefs and actions of individuals, from the apathetics to the activists. Thus it provides ideas about the kinds of clues and questions that might help you respond to your friend's challenge.

THE ENVIRONMENT

In the national election in Vietnam in 2007, it was reported that 98 percent of the adults voted, whereas in the United States, only about 37 percent of the citizens voted in the 2006 national election. What best accounts for this difference? In Vietnam, voting is an obligatory act, a required gesture of support for the current political leadership, rather than a genuine selection among candidates—indeed, there is no choice. Most Vietnamese vote because a comrade who does not vote risks unwanted scrutiny by Communist Party authorities. In the United States, voting has always been a voluntary act, and there are no sanctions for not voting. Thus the citizen decides whether her sense of civic responsibility or her desire to affect the outcome on ballot choices merits the effort of going to vote. The Debate in 4 asks whether it is actually rational to vote.

The example of voting in Vietnam and the United States is suggestive of how a person's *environment—the broad context in which an individual lives*—can powerfully influence her political behavior. In its most comprehensive form, the environment includes literally everything outside the individual. It obviously includes political elements (e.g., governmental procedures, public policies, specific political events and actors), but it also includes elements of the social and cultural system (e.g., religious foundations, attitudes toward such characteristics as ethnicity, gender, and class), elements of the economic

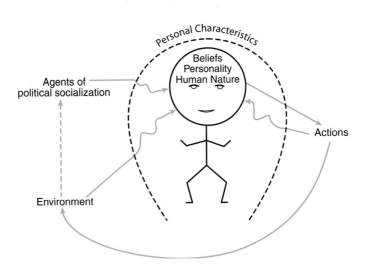

▶ FIGURE 4.1

A framework for explaining individual political behavior

THE DEBATE IN 4

Should a "Rational" Person Vote?

You know that you ought to vote in a democracy so that you can help determine policies and political leaders. However, from the perspective of rational choice theory, you are "irrational" if you vote in a major election. **Rational choice theory**, also known as *public choice theory* (see the Appendix), assumes that *actors (individuals or organizations) are rational and calculating*. Actors can establish the costs and benefits to themselves of the outcome associated with an action that they might take, and they can select the most rational strategy to maximize the benefits relative to the costs. If you have studied microeconomics, you might recognize that this description is rather like the "economic man," another version of this rational actor. Some analysts apply rational choice theory to questions addressed in political science. It is this theory that inspires the question of whether a truly rational person should vote in a major election.

A Rational Person Should Not Vote

- It is important to consider the personal *costs* associated with voting. Minimally, you expend time and energy to register to vote, to find the polling place, to wait in line and cast your ballot, and to get to the next place you want to go.
- There are even more serious *costs* related to your efforts to try to understand the issues that you think are most important, to determine which candidates endorse policies that are closest to your preferences, and to calculate how much you will actually benefit from each policy the candidate might promote. (These analyses can be particularly difficult on the complicated ballot propositions on which you are expected to vote.)
- Even if you cannot think of things you would rather do with all that time and energy, the *benefits* side of the calculation is more daunting. If your candidate is elected, how confident are you that she will be directly responsible for enacting policies that serve your needs and desires?
- And most significantly on the *benefits* side, as a rational actor, you must ask: What is the chance that my vote will make a difference? In U.S. national elections, about 100 million votes are cast for the presidency. The probability that there will be a tie so that one vote (yours or anybody else's) will determine the outcome of the election is infinitesimally small—certainly less than one in a trillion. So what is the point of voting?

A Rational Person Should Vote

- Your vote matters as part of the set of votes from a larger group that shares your interests. If everyone in your group acted "rationally" and did not vote, the loss of the total set of votes might be large enough to affect the outcome of the election.
- The rationality of voting increases in an election in which few votes are cast or in which you think the outcome will be close. This is particularly true in local elections, where the margin between candidates can be quite small. Recent national elections in the United States have also been characterized by some very close races. In Nevada in 1998, for example, Harry Reid, the victor for the U.S. Senate seat, received only 459 votes more than John Ensign out of more than 415,000 votes cast. In 1994, a Connecticut seat in the House of Representatives was determined by fewer than 10 votes out of more than 158,000. And the Florida vote in 2000 (Bush versus Gore) revealed that the difference of only a few

hundred votes *can* actually determine who is elected president.

- The argument against voting is based on a flawed basic premise, because the fact is that most people are not rational calculators. They make most decisions in their lives (e.g., whether to marry, whether to enroll in a class, whether to drive very fast) without any clear idea of the precise costs and benefits to them.

- Voting can provide an individual with many benefits besides crass self-interest. Voting can serve as an expression of citizenship, social solidarity, and political communication. You might vote because you love your country and want to support its democratic traditions, because you recognize the dangers to society if people do not exercise the privilege of voting, because you want to be a small part of a large voice saying yes or no to political leaders, or because you want to show support for the group(s) with which you identify.

More questions . . .

1. Do you think the political world (and society more generally) would be a better place if everyone did act solely in terms of the costs and benefits to herself personally?

2. Younger voters in most countries, and certainly in the United States, have the lowest turnout rate of any age cohort (Wattenberg 2008). Do you think this can be explained by rational choice theory?

3. Rational choice theorists need to explain why about 100 million Americans behave irrationally in national elections. This is what such theorists call the "paradox of participation" (Riker and Ordeshook 1973). Of course, they sometimes point to the 100 million people who do not vote and suggest that at least half of the population *is* rational. Why *do* people vote?

order (e.g., level of economic prosperity and development), and the physical features of the environment (e.g., topography, natural resources). For some analytic questions, it might also be important to distinguish between the environment as measured "objectively" by the analyst and the environment as perceived "subjectively" by the individual who is attempting to understand and act in the political world.

For any particular political belief or action, there are various possible effects from an environmental stimulus. An element of the environment might activate, repress, transform, or amplify a person's political behavior. Most elements of the environment are likely to have little or no effect at any given moment, so the task of the political analyst is to identify those few environmental elements that do have especially significant effects on political belief or action and to explain how these effects occur.

Since the environmental context is, at least in theory, of enormous scope, it is helpful to consider different ways in which the environment might affect behavior: political, social, cultural, economic, and physical. Here are two examples regarding the *political environment:*

1. **Effects on information about politics.** In Myanmar (Burma), the government strictly limits the available information about politics, so many citizens have only a minimal knowledge of the current politics of even their own country. In the United States, the politically interested citizen has access each day to hundreds of hours of television and radio programming and has available even more reading materials and Internet sites with information about worldwide political events.

2. **Effects on individuals' political party involvement.** From the late 1940s to the late 1980s, Romania had only one legal political party, the Communist Party. Party membership, open to only about 10 percent of the population, was essential for any citizen who wanted to hold political office or gain major advantages in the society, such as quality housing (see Chapter 15). Currently, Romania has dozens of active political parties, and 24 hold seats in the parliament. Party membership and opportunities to run for public office are now open to all citizens. However, party membership no longer affords the advantages that existed during the communist period, and thus the proportion of Romanian adults who are active party members of *all* political parties is actually lower now under multiparty democracy than it was during communism.

Moreover, the broader *social, cultural, economic, and physical environments* can have more indirect but no less powerful influences on a person's political behavior than the political environment. If the dominant religion in the cultural environment has traditionally relegated women to a secondary role, as in Saudi Arabia's adherence to the sharia laws of Islam, it is likely that few women will be involved in politics. If the social environment has an undercurrent of racism, as in France, this will affect many aspects of the political behavior of both the majority and minority racial groups.

The impact of the environment on political behavior is sometimes hard to predict. If poverty is widespread in an economic system, will this influence the probability of political rebellion? On the one hand, such poverty might produce a frustrated population who will be responsive to a revolutionary movement promising future prosperity, and it might inspire a particular person to become very active in such a movement. On the other hand, the people might be too concerned about basic survival to have the time or energy to engage in political action.

It should be evident from these examples that many aspects of the environment might influence political beliefs and actions. The analyst must be sensitive to possible environmental effects when attempting to provide an adequate explanation for a particular political behavior.

AGENTS OF POLITICAL SOCIALIZATION

Each person has a complex blend of political beliefs—of cognitive, affective, and evaluative orientations regarding political phenomena. (These three kinds of orientations were defined in Chapter 2.) Even individuals who live in the same environment can hold very different political beliefs. Political socialization research attempts to explain the sources of individuals' political beliefs.

Political socialization can be defined as *the processes through which individuals acquire their orientations toward the political world.* An understanding of how this process works is of obvious importance not only to political analysts but also to those, especially political leaders, who wish to influence people's political beliefs and actions. Plato (c. 428–347 B.C.E.) observed that society's most important function is civic training, instructing citizens regarding the nature of their social and political world and their proper roles in that world. The appropriate content and style of such political socialization are subject to debate, since one person's vision of proper civic training might be viewed by another person as indoctrination and brainwashing.

Among political scientists, the emphasis in political socialization research has been on analyzing the *agents of political socialization—the major sources of political training and indoctrination.* The key concerns have been to identify these agents and to explain the processes through which they affect individuals' political orientations. There has been considerably less attention, and very limited empirical success, in linking the activities of specific agents of socialization to individuals' actual political actions. In this section, we discuss some of the most important agents of political socialization: the family, schools, peer groups, the media and culture, and events.

The Family

The family is the first, and often the most powerful and lasting, agent of political socialization. The political orientations of most individuals are deeply influenced by the behaviors and beliefs they experience in the family environment. Before individuals are capable of making judgments for themselves, they have absorbed perceptions about the political world from conversations overheard within the family. For example, most seven-year-old children in the United States already identify with one political party and have affective orientations toward both major parties (Jennings, Markus, and Niemi 1991).

Even the pattern of interactions between parents and children can have political implications. If the family is very hierarchical, with the father or mother ruling with an iron hand, preventing discussion, and using strong sanctions for disobedience, the child might assume that this is the appropriate pattern of authority relationships in the society. If the family tends to discuss issues before it makes rules or decisions, the child might feel more strongly that she has the right to participate actively in decisions, even in the political world.

Some leaders have viewed the family as a major obstacle to their political agendas. For example, Mao Zedong deeply opposed the traditional loyalties taught by Confucianism, which stresses obedience to the kinship group, to elders, and to males (see Box 15.3). When Mao was in power in China (1949–1976), he wanted every Chinese person to accept the equality of all individuals, regardless of age or gender. He also insisted that individuals should work cooperatively for the good of everyone in the society (the key slogan was "serve the people"). Mao identified the family as the major obstacle to these goals, called the family the "citadel of oppression" in society, and experimented with attempts to eliminate the nuclear family. When these attempts failed, Communist Party members put enormous pressure on families to "revolutionize" themselves by shedding their Confucian thinking and traditional behaviors. Even today, China's government engages in extensive early socialization, as in the training of Shanghai children shown on pages 80-81.

Schools

From the perspective of political authorities, schools can be the state's most valuable agent for political socialization. Schools offer the opportunity for sustained and highly controlled contact with youth at the extremely impressionable age when many political beliefs can still be molded. Apart from the family, the classroom is the most important microcosm of society that most young people experience. The teacher is the authority figure, who rewards thinking and behavior that conform to what is deemed desirable by the society and who sanctions or withholds rewards from those who fail to conform. In most societies, students are taught to accept the authority of the teacher, to suppress their own desires, to value the symbolic rewards offered by the education system, and to interact with their peers in the manner approved by the school system. Moreover, in every school system, there are rituals that support the political system. These might include songs, chants, or activities that express allegiance to political leaders or symbols.

Also important in shaping the student's understanding of the political world is the school curriculum. Educational authorities can control what subjects are taught, what textbooks contain, what content is tested, and even what teachers say and do. An extreme form of this central control over education was achieved during the French Fourth Republic (1946–1958). It was said that the minister of education in Paris could look at her watch and specify exactly what chapter in what textbook the children of a certain age were studying at that moment all over France.

Every textbook and every lesson in school are selective and thus contain biases in what is emphasized, what is ignored, and how meaning and value are established. Sometimes the level of indoctrination seems extreme, especially to those unsympathetic to the message. Here are four examples. As you read them, try to guess what subject is being taught and the country from which each example is taken.

1. Add *not* to the following sentence: "The Iranians are brave."

2. Our forefathers believed, and we still believe today, that God himself made the diversity of peoples on earth. . . . Interracial residence and intermarriage are not only a disgrace but also forbidden by law. It is, however, not only the skin of the Betas that differs from the Alphas. The Beta stands on a much higher plane of civilization and is more developed. Betas must so live, learn, and work that we shall not sink to the cultural level of the Alphas. Only thus can the government of our country remain in the hands of the Betas.

3. Imperialism knows no other type of relations between States except domination and subjugation, the oppression of the weak by the strong. It bases international relations on abuse and threat, on violence and arbitrariness. Between January 3 and June 10, 1961, Gamma military airplanes violated Delta airspace 3 times in the month of January, 15 in February, 17 in March, 9 in April, 8 in May, and 10 in June. What was the average monthly number of violations of Delta airspace by Gamma military airplanes?

4. Which of the following descriptions of America is incorrect?
   a. The world's leading arms-exporting country.
   b. The world's most heavily nuclear-armed country.
   c. The world's leader in chemical weapons research.
   d. The world's most peace-loving country that never once was at war with other countries.

Were you able to identify likely settings for these educational examples? The first one is from a 2002 sixth-grade Arabic language textbook in Iraq (Robinson 2003). The second one is an excerpt from a South African textbook on race relations during the era of apartheid (1948–1988, substitute "whites" for "Betas" and "nonwhites" for "Alphas") (Thompson 1966: 100). The third is mathematics as it is framed for Cuban children (substitute "Cuban" for "Delta" and "North American" for "Gamma") (Fagen 1964: 68). And the fourth is from a 2003 history test for South Korean eighth-graders (Demick 2003).

These extreme examples reflect the manner in which political authorities can influence the content of educational materials in order to buttress the view of the political world most aligned with their own interests. While subject matter in the schools of most countries is less openly political than these examples, school systems of *every* country present materials that are supportive of that country's politics and dominant cultural norms.

Have you noticed anything odd about the use of the pronouns *he* and *she* in this book? To counter the male dominance in the language of many American textbooks, I alternate masculine and feminine pronouns in odd and even chapters. If you were conscious of the "strange" use of gender references in Chapter 2 and this chapter, your reaction may be indicative of the subtle way in which your cultural norms are reinforced by language and education.

Peer Groups

Persistence is the rule for political attitudes and behaviors that are learned early from parents and schooling. However, according to the *life cycle* interpretation of political socialization, learning never stops entirely. As the importance of parents diminishes and after formal schooling ends, peer groups become an increasingly significant influence on many people's political socialization. *Peer group* is a general term that includes friends, neighbors, and colleagues from the workplace or clubs and organizations.

The section on " 'Everyone' as Authority" in Chapter 1 suggests the attraction of bringing one's views into closer conformity with those of relevant peer groups. In general, a person is more likely to be accepted by her peers if her beliefs and actions are consistent with those in the peer group. Also, it is possible that there is a subtle tendency for a person to be influenced by what "people like me" think and the individual's social context (Agnew 2003; Jennings, Markus, and Niemi 1991).

In many cases, peers and others influence a person's political views via a *"two-step" communication flow* (Bennett 2008; Zaller 1992). People with greater interest and knowledge of politics absorb new information from various sources (*step one*). Then they relay what they have learned to others (*step two*), especially those in the mass public whose political beliefs are less salient and developed (recall Chapter 2). In general, direct communications from peers allow for a rich exchange of political information, since such political messages have the immediacy, credibility, and power of face-to-face interaction.

As noted earlier, China used the peer group as a major mechanism for political socialization, especially during the period under Mao Zedong. Small groups on collective farms, in factories, and in other workplaces not only were required to discuss their political beliefs and actions but also were supposed to monitor the political behavior of everyone in the group. If a person's views or actions strayed from the "mass line," the group applied various types of pressure to help the person recognize and rectify her errors and return to the proper political position. If this pressure failed, more aggressive forms of peer pressure, including public ridicule (and ultimately imprisonment), were employed to force the person to conform. In China, peer pressure reached an extreme form during the Cultural Revolution in the late 1960s. Groups of true believers organized themselves as the "Red Guard" and engaged in widespread peer pressure, repression, and violence against any Chinese who did not conform to Chairman Mao's ideology (Meisner and Schott 2006).

Peer influence is also a powerful factor in the radicalization of many of the "home-grown" terrorists who are becoming a significant threat in many countries. There is considerable evidence that individuals, especially young adult males, who feel alien-ated and alone as part of a cultural and religious minority find encouragement and direction in a small group of peers who gather informally. As they share their ideas and frustrations, they begin to radicalize each other and to discuss how they could strike out at those in their country who antagonize them. In some cases, these ideas move from imagination to actual plans to act, usually by committing violent acts. Some analysts refer to this peer political socialization resulting in terrorist thinking and action as the BOG ("bunch of guys") theory (Sageman 2008). These small peer groups, which usually have no direct connection with larger, known terrorist orga-nizations such as al-Qaeda, are emerging in many countries, from Europe and North America to Asia, North Africa, and the Middle East. Two recent examples of terror-ists who emerged from such groups are the two Anglo-Indians who rammed an auto-mobile filled with explosives into the Glasgow Airport terminal in summer 2007 and the 23-year-old American Muslim who planned to detonate hand grenades in a Chicago mall in 2006 (Meyer 2007).

The Media and Culture

Very few of us directly experience the great majority of political phenomena about which we claim knowledge. For most adults, *the media,* especially television, radio, and the press, are the major sources of political information. Dan Nimmo and James Combs (1990: xiii) argue: "Few people learn about politics through direct experience. For most persons, political realities are mediated through mass and group communi-cation, a process that results as much in the creation, transmission, and adoption of political fantasies as it results in independently validated views of what happens." They claim that each of us creates a personal vision (a "fantasy") of political reality, based mainly on what is communicated to us by such information sources as other people, the mass media, and popular culture. Regardless of how fantastic our politi-cal visions are, it is important to understand that the media can be a crucial agent of political socialization for either stability or change.

These information sources really do *mediate* between the individual and most political reality. While most media content is not explicitly political, much of it does contain subtle information that influences how one thinks about politics and society. Exposure to television and radio is extensive in most countries. Thus the individual is bombarded with messages about values, lifestyles, and so on. While sweeping gen-eralizations about the impacts of the media on people's political beliefs and actions are not possible, two broad observations can be offered.

First, the research generally concludes that few people absorb media information in a way that significantly changes most of their political attitudes or actions. Rather, people interpret and retain media information selectively to reinforce their existing atti-tudes. And many people, especially those with less sophisticated political belief systems

And now we get to watch them govern

and minimal political knowledge (see Chapter 2), do not even pay much attention to the media that provide political information. The media-based information for such people often comes from a politically knowledgeable peer who, as described previously, seeks information from the media and then transmits such information to others.

Second, however, there is considerable evidence that the media are increasingly important in shaping many people's understandings of specific political phenomena. The mass media are especially significant in *drawing people's attention to some political phenomena rather than to others*—an impact called **agenda setting**. Also, a person can be influenced by absorbing the overall tone and key themes in the media coverage of an issue (Iyengar 1994).

For most people, the media have their greatest impact during situations of political drama (e.g., war, major political crises, elections). Newspapers are still credited with the greatest effect on knowledge about politicians and issues among the most educated people (Davis 1998; Graber 2001). However, for the reasons suggested in Box 4.1, television is regarded as the most important source of political information for the largest number of people in Western democracies (Dalton 2008: table 2.1). Moreover, it is at least possible that for many young people, the Internet, even more than television, has become the key source of political information (Center for Media Education 2001). The easy access to powerful search engines and vast online resources from around the globe and the capacity to participate in discussion environments such as blogs offer individuals extensive opportunities to use the new media to reinforce or alter their political orientations and to inform their political actions. Indeed, the full set of contemporary information and communications

BOX 4.1

What You See Is What You Get

It is often asserted that television has become *the* most powerful form of communication now shaping peoples' political orientations. The vast expansion of channels and content now accessible wherever satellite or cable technologies are available has made this viewpoint even more compelling. While the empirical evidence regarding this assertion is not conclusive, there are some significant reasons television might be such an important force in political life.

1. *High exposure.* Citizens in both industrial countries and developing countries watch increasing amounts of television each year. In the United States, for example, most adults spend as many hours with the mass media (predominantly television) as they do at work, and their children spend more hours watching television than attending school. Many other societies in both the developed and the developing world are also reaching these levels. There is growing evidence that such a high level of exposure to television has an impact on a person's social and political values, even if little of the programming is explicitly political (Savage and Nimmo 1990).

2. *The power of the visual.* The biochemistry of the human brain affects the impact of television. Generally, the brain responds strongly to visual cues and less to written text. Moreover, visual input produces direct emotional arousal, which is the most potent neurochemical condition for learning and attitudinal change. Because the images on television are generally simple and can evoke strong emotional response, they generate information that is easy to process and has a relatively high impact on learning and attitudes (Masters 1992).

3. *Agenda setting.* People's immediate views on politics are greatly influenced by what they believe to be important. Television, and especially television news, focuses on certain political issues, people, and events and not on others. Most people tend to identify as significant those political topics that are "in the news" and think topics that receive little or no media coverage are not very important. Thus television increasingly sets the political agenda by establishing what issues are worthy of attention and public concern (Iyengar 1994).

4. *Priming and framing effects.* Television "primes" viewers about a political topic by providing information about how they should understand the topic, the kinds of information that are relevant, and the criteria that they should employ to evaluate it. Television "frames" the topic by providing viewers with a broader structure and context within which to consider it. Television generally simplifies complex issues by using specific and dramatic examples to explain a topic. For example, television news typically examines an issue—say, poverty—by creating a visually engaging story involving specific poor people, not by emphasizing the basic

BOX 4.1 *(Continued)*

societal dynamics that generate poverty. Thus television's treatment leads viewers to attribute responsibility for a political issue to the personal shortcomings of individual actors. It discourages viewers from recognizing underlying social, political, and economic forces that have created the problem and are appropriate targets for solutions (Iyengar 1994).

Many people rely on television to provide them with information about the political world. As television directs our attention to the simple, the visual, the individual, and the evocative on only selected political topics, our ability to understand and evaluate politics in complex and subtle ways atrophies. Many researchers argue that these factors account for some of the most undesirable features of contemporary politics: the prevalence of simplistic political discourse based on sound bites, the decline of political parties, single-issue politics, negative political campaigns, and spin doctors who further distort the media's presentation of politics (Graber 2001, 2005; Kellner 1990; Neuman 1999).

It is interesting that people who are currently reaching adulthood in developed countries increasingly view the Internet (e.g., Web sites and blogs) as their key source of information. Some argue that this enables individuals to focus almost exclusively on sources that reinforce their existing political viewpoints and that this "selective exposure" is dangerous for healthy democracy (Sunstein 2002). Is it possible that Web-based narrowcasting might be an even less desirable source of political information than the simplistic broadcasting of television?

technologies (ICTs) have so much potential impact that some argue they are fundamentally transforming all aspects of political life (see The Debate in 9; Bimber 2003; Chadwick 2006).

As noted in Box 4.1, much of what you know about the political world from the media is contingent on what topics the media choose to expose you to and what content the media select to report. Like textbooks, the media are not neutral; someone has selected the subjects and content.

In many countries, the major media are owned and controlled by the government or by members of the wealthy, dominant class in that society. The print and broadcast media are free of substantial government censorship in less than two-fifths (38 percent) of all countries, and these countries include only 18 percent of the world's population (Freedom House 2008). Through their ability to control the media,, most governments have had a significant resource for political socialization, exposing people to "news" and information that reinforced the government's view of the political world. And there is empirical evidence of a recent global decline in press freedom (Freedom House 2008).

Of course, you are not completely passive in the process. In most countries, people can choose among alternative media sources and can attempt to evaluate the truth of what they read, hear, and see in the media. And the recent explosion of telecommunications technologies (such as satellite television transmissions and the Internet) has made it increasingly difficult for a government to control all the sources of information reaching its citizens. Consequently, most governments are becoming less effective in shaping people's political beliefs through the media, even as the media are an ever more important source of people's political "reality."

Culture offers an interesting alternative to the media and to other agents of political socialization. Culture, like the media, can be extensively controlled by the dominant political order in a society and can be used to reinforce the state's view of the political world. Cuba, like many of the communist states in the past, has generally insisted that culture must meet the standards of "socialist realism," which means that no art, theater, or cinema is to be produced that is abstract or, most important, that fails to celebrate the virtues of socialism, Cuban style.

Culture need not reinforce the dominant order, however. It can inform and criticize subtly, by means of metaphor and symbol, in ways less likely to be interpreted as a direct challenge to the established authorities. This is especially true in societies where there is considerable censorship of the media and state control of most sources of public information. During the 1980s, for example, an extensive body of fiction, cinema, poetry, theater, art, and music emerged with political content critical of the state's views in still-communist countries such as East Germany and Poland (Larkey 1990). Culture can also be openly subversive, directly attacking mainstream values or advocating opposing values. For example, Jamaican reggae music offers a revolutionary vision of an alternative social and political world for its people. While most contemporary Anglo-American music has little explicit political content, this kind of expression can be found in some rap music and in songs by such performers as Charlie Daniels, U2, and Bruce Springsteen (Coles 2003).

Events

The general effects of the environment on political beliefs and action have already been discussed. While the context of everyday life has slow, evolutionary effects on a person's political behavior, a particular event can act as a sudden and powerful agent of political socialization. For example, Sarah Brady shifted from a "politician's wife" to a tireless activist on behalf of gun control legislation after her husband, James Brady, President Reagan's press secretary, was shot and paralyzed in a 1981 assassination attempt on the president. Another example of mobilization after a dramatic event is the transformation of Micky Sadoff into a MADD activist (recall the example at the beginning of Chapter 3).

While an extraordinary event can transform a person's political behavior, it is also possible that the general flow of events during an entire period can influence political orientations, especially of individuals who "come of political age" during the period. For example, the combined impacts of such events as American military involvement in Vietnam and Southeast Asia, the hippie culture, and the Nixon presidency seem to have had strong effects on the political understanding of many Americans who were reaching adulthood during the late 1960s. And young people currently growing up in the West Bank and Gaza are deeply affected in their political beliefs and actions by the intense rhetoric and chaotic ultraviolence emanating from the Israeli government and military, the Palestinian Authority, and such groups as Hamas.

PERSONAL CHARACTERISTICS

As one part of your strategy for responding to the challenge offered at the beginning of the chapter (to link the three people to specific political behaviors), you might consider their physical appearance or **personal characteristics**. The research suggests that you can make some broad inferences about a person's political behavior on the basis of certain "objective" personal features. Sometimes called *demographic characteristics,* these include both visible characteristics, such as age, gender, and ethnicity, and less visible ones, such as education, income, social class, and occupation. What underlying dynamic might link personal characteristics with political behavior?

Personal characteristics can be thought of as *filters* that influence how the environment and the agents of political socialization affect an individual's political behavior. For example, the relevance of the environmental factor of Islamic fundamentalism will have very different effects on the political beliefs and behaviors of Saudi men and women. Similarly, the current impact of parents as agents of political socialization is likely to be far greater for their offspring of age 4 than of 44.

Much of the empirical research on political behavior attempts to establish and clarify the relationships between personal characteristics and specific political beliefs or actions. No single personal characteristic is a certain predictor of political behavior, but empirical research (based on relational analysis) in many countries indicates that some personal characteristics are associated with certain political beliefs and actions. And when key personal characteristics seem to reinforce each other, you might have greater confidence in a correct prediction about political behavior. Of particular interest to researchers (and to politicians) have been studies indicating who is more likely to vote and identifying factors that seem to explain the particular voting choice.

For example, can you think of any personal characteristics that might inform your prediction of whether a particular person voted for George W. Bush or John Kerry in the 2004 U.S. presidential election? Table 4.1 (like the example of correlational analysis in the Appendix) provides actual data for exploring those linkages. Do any personal characteristics seem to be associated with a tendency to vote for a particular candidate? In addition to comparing a category across candidates, another reasonable technique for answering this question is to determine whether there are instances where the candidate's percentage for a category (e.g., high school graduates) is noticeably different from the candidate's percentage of the total vote.

While most of the differences are not dramatic, some demographic characteristics do seem to correlate with support for a particular candidate. Notice, for example, that the probability of voting for Bush was substantially higher among those who had any of the following characteristics: Protestant religion, Caucasian ethnicity, and being married. People's probability of voting for Kerry was especially high among African Americans, Chicano Latinos, and Asian Americans; those who were unmarried; those under 30 years old; and Jews.

Although there are some clear associations among variables, we cannot conclude that any personal characteristic actually *caused* a person to vote for a particular candidate (see the distinction between correlational and causal analysis in the Appendix). And when several personal characteristics are associated with voting choice, we also cannot determine which of them are the most powerful predictors of candidate choice

> ▶ **TABLE 4.1**
> ## Voting Choices in the 2004 U.S. Presidential Election, by Personal Characteristics

Total	Percent of All	Bush (51%)	Kerry (48%)
Gender			
Male	49	53	46
Female	51	49	50
Gender and marriage			
Married men	31	59	40
Single men	16	40	58
Married women	30	57	42
Single women	19	35	64
Ethnicity			
African American	10	14	86
Asian American	3	34	64
Caucasian	79	57	42
Chicano/Latino	5	45	54
Age			
18–29	20	43	55
30–44	32	52	47
45–64	36	54	45
65 and older	12	55	45
Education			
High school diploma or less	48	54	45
Some college	26	45	51
College degree or more	52	49	50
Religion			
Protestant	51	61	38
Roman Catholic	25	55	44
Jewish	4	26	74
Annual family income			
Under $20,000	10	46	51
$20,000–$39,999	20	47	52
$40,000–$59,999	20	51	48
$60,000–$74,999	15	53	46
$75,000 and over	35	54	45

Note: Due to rounding, not all categories total 100%.
Source: Los Angeles Times exit poll (http://www.latimes.com/timespoll).

without statistical analysis (such as regression analysis, a statistical technique that identifies how much variance in the dependent variable—vote choice, in this case—can be attributed to each subject's level on various independent variables). Nonetheless, Table 4.1 does provide reasonable support for our assumption that personal characteristics are sometimes associated with political behavior.

While generalizations are always difficult, there is some consistency in the empirical research on the personal characteristics of those who do *vote* (in political systems where there are genuine voting choices). In general, a higher probability of voting is correlated with such characteristics as membership in organizations that have explicit interests in politics (e.g., political parties, unions), higher education, higher income, higher social class, greater age, and male gender. Incidence of voting is also associated with the person's political beliefs, especially a strong identification with a party, a greater sense of personal capacity to influence the political world ("political efficacy"), and better understanding of the available political choices.

Research findings on *other modes of political behavior* are less extensive and less consistent. As in the taxonomies of participation, the cross-national studies by Verba and his colleagues (Verba and Nie 1972; Verba, Nie, and Kim 1978) remain among the most influential in identifying the individual characteristics that correlate with each mode of political action. Participation in campaign activities is especially linked with higher education, higher income, and male gender. Socioeconomic characteristics are also most strongly correlated with the likelihood that a person engages in communal activities, and identification with a particular social group (religious, ethnic, or linguistic) can be extremely important if there are political cleavages associated with these group differences. Contacting government officials personally is least clearly related to personal characteristics, and some research suggests that the decision to engage in personal contacts depends more on whether the person has an effective private means to gain her objective or whether she must rely on contacting public officials to achieve this objective. Contacting officials might be the type of political action that has increased most during the last several decades (Verba, Schlozman, and Brady 1995), and it is increasingly facilitated by e-mail and other digital communications innovations.

In studying *extremist-activists,* many analyses attempt to specify the personal characteristics that typify a particular type of activist relative to the general population. For example, many of the Muslims who have engaged in terrorist acts are young adult males who are well-educated and come from middle-class families (Berrebi 2007; Sageman 2004). The rural extremist-activists who are engaged in a struggle for control over land in Asia and Latin America tend to be male, poor, and of limited education. Urban activists who promote leftist ideologies (e.g., Marxism, environmentalism) are generally characterized as being well educated, middle class, mainly young, and only slightly more likely to be male than female. Right-wing urban activists are more varied. Those promoting an ethnic or racist position (e.g., neo-Nazism) tend to be young, male, working or lower class, and somewhat lower in education. But those promoting causes such as the antiabortion movement are more middle aged, female, middle class, and relatively well educated (Dalton 2008: ch. 4; Meyer and Tarrow 1997).

Overall, what do you expect to be the personal characteristics of *top political leaders* in a given society? Perhaps the broadest generalization is that leaders' personal characteristics tend to be quite consistent with those of the socially dominant groups within their society. Why do you think this occurs? Among the most common shared characteristics, across many societies, are high education, upper-middle-class or upper-class background, adherence to the society's dominant religion, and male gender.

Given our general fascination with extraordinary political actors such as presidents, charismatic leaders, and revolutionaries, it is interesting to assess whether particular environments, socialization experiences, or personal characteristics seem to account for the political behavior of these individuals. Box 4.2 briefly describes the

BOX 4.2

You Go Your Way, I'll Go Mine

The two young men have some common roots. Both are born into societies ordered by traditional social systems of hierarchy and male domination and by strong, fundamentalist religion. Both are sons of prosperous professional fathers who are devout and emphasize the importance of orthodox religion in the home. Each young man displays high intelligence and receives an excellent education.

As young adults, each trains successfully for a professional career and enters that career. Each is shocked by his exposure to religious or racial discrimination and by the severe deprivation that characterizes the lives of the great majority of people in his society. Each becomes a deeply devout follower of his religion. These beliefs, along with family background, training, and experiences, cause each to develop a powerful commitment to the independence of his people from foreign powers, who each believes are the source of oppression and injustice. Each decides to devote his life to political activism and to engage in extreme political acts, as necessary, to achieve his vision of social justice. But the two men follow very different paths.

The first man travels to another country to join the revolutionary struggle against a major colonial power. He is trained and supported in guerrilla warfare tactics (see Chapter 11) by the U.S. Central Intelligence Agency and becomes an effective leader. After successfully defeating the foreign power, he returns home to Saudi Arabia to work in the family business. However, he is deeply offended by the presence and influence of foreigners in his religion's holiest lands. His open commitment to the expulsion of foreigners and the establishment of a pure religious state results in conflict with the authoritarian regime in his homeland. He is harassed by the regime, his citizenship is revoked, and he is forced to leave the country. He moves to another country in the region, but powerful foreign governments force his expulsion from this country as well. He returns to the country where he had fought on behalf of the revolution and is given protection.

By this time, he is convinced that his righteous cause can be advanced only by extreme acts of violence. He uses his considerable personal wealth ($300 million) and his ideological vision to establish a loosely connected international network of small

BOX 4.2 *(Continued)*

groups of extremist-activists. Eventually he has loyal, highly trained operatives living in more than 60 countries. He calls upon all his followers to use whatever means are necessary to serve their cause: freeing their lands from foreign occupiers and influences. Members of his network are linked to many acts of international terrorism. These include the bombing of the World Trade Center in New York City in 1993; a massacre of tourists in Luxor, Egypt, in 1995; and the bombings of the U.S. embassies in Kenya and Tanzania in 1998. Many plots are unsuccessful, including an attempt to fly a hijacked airplane into the Eiffel Tower and assassination attempts on President Hosni Mubarak of Egypt, Jordanian Crown Prince (now King) Abdullah, and Pakistani Prime Minister Benazir Bhutto. The man is identified as the mastermind behind the most brutal terrorist attack ever undertaken in the United States, with hijacked passenger airplanes crashing into the two towers of the World Trade Center and another into the Pentagon on September 11, 2001. These attacks result in more than 3,000 deaths as well as worldwide fear and disruption of both travel and financial markets. The CIA labels his al-Qaeda organization "the most dangerous terrorist organization in the world," a $25 million reward is offered for his capture, and he becomes the prime target in the "war on international terrorism" initiated by U.S. President George W. Bush.

In response to criticism that he targets "innocents" and supports terrorism, he comments:

> Each action will solicit a similar reaction. We must use such punishment to keep your evil away from Muslims, Muslim children and women. American history does not distinguish between civilians and military, and not even women and children. Americans are the ones who used the bombs against Nagasaki. Can these bombs distinguish between infants and military? America does not have a religion that will prevent it from destroying all people.
>
> Your situation with Muslims in Palestine is shameful, if there is any shame left in America. In the Sabra and Shatilla [Lebanon refugee camps] massacre, a cooperation between Zionist and Christian forces, houses were demolished over the heads of children. Also, by testimony of relief workers in Iraq, the American-led sanctions resulted in the death of over 1 million Iraqi children. All of this was done in the name of American interests. We believe that the biggest thieves in the world and the terrorists are the Americans. The only way for us to fend off these assaults is to use similar means. We do not differentiate between those dressed in military uniforms and civilians; they are all targets in this fatwa [death decree]. (*Source:* http://abcnews.go.com/sections/world/dailynews/terror_980609 .html)

The second man witnesses the whites' racism against Indians while serving as a lawyer in South Africa. To resist such injustice, he develops a strategy of political activism. This strategy, inspired by an American, Henry David Thoreau, as well as by his own religious principles, emphasizes civil disobedience. His fundamental principle is *ahimsa*—nonviolence in thought as well as in action. He advises his followers:

BOX 4.2 *(Continued)*

"Not to submit; to suffer." He is repeatedly jailed for his nonviolent resistance to laws that he believes are unjust. He assumes that the opposition will discredit itself by its repressive responses to nonviolent protest.

Returning to his native India, he begins to organize protests demanding independence from the British imperialists. His protest techniques continue to be based on nonviolence and *satyagraha*—soul force. In contrast to brute force, soul force provokes constructive change through positive action and reconciliation, not through harming and angering the enemy. He observes, "My experience has shown me that we win justice quickest by rendering justice to the other party." He becomes an extraordinarily powerful and inspirational leader through his theatrical acts of civil disobedience and his personal sacrifices, including extended fasts, lengthy marches, and sexual abstinence. His nonviolent activism captures world attention, and his Indian followers expand to the tens of thousands. His supporters call him *Mahatma*—great soul. His tireless political activism, in deed and in word, contributes substantially to the developments that lead, three decades later, to the granting of independence to India by the British. His life of struggle is not a complete success, however. He fails to prevent the division of India into separate countries dominated by Hindus and Muslims, a struggle bloodied by 1,000,000 deaths. He fails to persuade Hindus to repudiate the divisive and unjust social caste system. And he is assassinated by a Hindu extremist within months of India's independence. (This discussion is based on Broomfield 1982.)

Osama bin Laden (1957–) and Mohandas K. Gandhi (1869–1948), despite their early similarities, diverged onto nearly opposite paths of political activism in the pursuit of their personal visions of social justice and human liberation.

▶ **Osama bin Laden.**

▶ **Mohandas Gandhi.**

environment, socialization, and personal characteristics of two remarkable political activists. Do these factors seem relatively comparable for the two men? Do these factors seem to produce similar political behavior?

POLITICAL "PERSONALITY"

The three types of explanatory factors discussed to this point either are outside the person (the environment and agents of political socialization) or are surface characteristics (e.g., age, ethnicity). However, some political analysts insist that an adequate explanation of political behavior requires explication of the *political personality*—*the deeper psychological dynamics inside the individual that affect her response to political stimuli.*

Personality

Personality can be broadly defined as the propensities within an individual to act in a certain way, given a particular context. If someone is usually cheerful or aggressive or thoughtful under a variety of circumstances, this style of behaving could be called a *personality trait* of that individual. The cluster of basic personality traits that dominates an individual's attitudes and behavior is what most people mean when they talk about someone's personality "type." It seems plausible that personality could influence the political beliefs and actions of any individual. Most of the empirical research examining political personality has focused on the beliefs and actions of political activists. Political personality analyses are found in biographies, in opinion pieces in the media, in our conversations about top political leaders, and even in leaders' own speeches and writings.

Normative approaches. People have always had strong opinions about the kind of personality that a political leader *ought* to have. What personality characteristics do you think are desirable in a political leader? Perhaps no one is better known for advice about the kind of personality a political leader needs than Niccolò Machiavelli (1469–1527), author of *The Prince* (1517/1977). Machiavelli believed that society tends toward disorder, in part because events are substantially dependent on *fortuna*—a combination of chance, fate, luck, and unpredictable circumstances. The political leader must act decisively to overcome *fortuna*. She must think strategically, suppress moral judgments, and act with fierce resolve.

"Everyone sees what you seem to be," Machiavelli (1517/1977: ch. 18) observed; "few know what you really are." Thus the leader must combine the qualities of the lion (aggression, bravery) and the fox (cleverness) and must make the citizens completely dependent on her every decision and action. In the pursuit of the good society, the leader must be single-minded and, if necessary, ruthless in order to achieve her desired ends. Machiavelli insisted that the effective political leader will face many situations where the ends justify the political means, even if ethical behavior must be sacrificed: "To preserve the state, he often has to do things against his word, against charity, against humanity, against religion.... [H]e should not depart from the good if he can hold to it, but he should be ready to enter on evil if he has to" (Machiavelli 1517/1977: ch. 18). Most politicians work hard to project certain personality traits that they think will appeal to their followers (e.g., honesty, responsiveness, compassion, thoughtfulness); few contemporary politicians want to be characterized as "Machiavellian."

Empirical approaches.   While some studies offer normative perspectives on political personality, most contemporary studies are empirical and aim to explain the behavior of top political leaders and activists. These studies attempt to identify their key personality traits (such as idealism, aggressiveness, frustration, and so on) and then link those traits to specific political beliefs and actions.

Political personality approaches can delve quite deeply, explaining the psychological needs, drives, or experiences embedded in the person's psyche that are the underlying forces resulting in her political behavior. In this perspective, activist political behavior is seen as a response to a person's psychological life history. For example, Harold Lasswell (1960), one of the intellectual founders of behavioral political science, argues that the activist political personality is motivated primarily by the drive to overcome a low sense of self-esteem. However, the systematic empirical evidence suggests that most top political leaders actually rank higher on measures of self-esteem and psychological well-being than does the average adult (Sniderman 1975).

One personality-based analysis has posited that the behavior of political leaders can be explained by their responsiveness to some combination of seven "incentives" that they connect powerfully with political action: (1) the urge to solve public problems; (2) the need to be accepted by others; (3) the search for fame and glory; (4) the desire to follow their conscience in serving society; (5) the pleasure derived from competition and manipulation of others; (6) the satisfaction from commitment to a grand mission; and (7) the desire for praise and adulation (Woshinsky 1995: ch. 11).

Some of the most detailed analytic work develops an extensive *psychobiography* of the individual political activist. Such analyses attempt to provide information about political activists' personalities and to explain how such information helps us make

better sense of how and especially why they act as they do. Erik Erikson (1958, 1969), among the most influential scholars in this tradition, adopts a Freudian framework to reveal the crucial importance of child rearing and early socialization through adolescence in determining the activist's later political behavior. (See Erikson's psychobiographies of Martin Luther [1958] and Mohandas Gandhi [1969] and Lucian Pye's [1962] application of Erikson's approach to analyze an entire class of political leaders in postcolonial Burma/Myanmar.)

Empirical, personality-based approaches have also been used to account for the behavior of other types of political activists, such as student radicals. As someone who has experience with other students, what do you hypothesize about the student radicals? Are student extremists different from other students in their intelligence or idealism or independence? Are student radicals of the left different from student radicals of the right? While a few empirical studies identify some student radicals with substantial personality disorders, the research generally concludes that student radicals tend to be more intelligent, creative, idealistic, and independent than the nonradicals. It also has been shown that these generally favorable qualities apply to those student radicals whose ideology is extremely progressive or extremely conservative (Fendrich 1993; Kerpelman 1972).

Recently, there has been particular interest in analyzing the psychology of those who engage in terrorist acts. While the backgrounds and even the personalities of terrorists vary, it has been suggested that many do share some traits. They can be troubled by high levels of loneliness, alienation, and isolation. As noted above regarding the impact of peers, they can seek to overcome this through the sense of belonging provided by a small strong network of friends ("BOGs"). These individuals can also be very frustrated because they feel that the political and social conditions they value have been denied them by others whose actions are illegitimate and against whom they are willing to retaliate with violence. Some recent terrorists also have very strong religious convictions and are prepared to engage in any necessary actions to protect and promote their religion (Juergensmeyer 2003; Sageman 2004; Victoroff 2005).

Human Nature

Some of those who offer a psychological explanation for political behavior do not focus on individual personality or even on a particular culture; rather, they emphasize a more generalized conception grounded in *human nature—innate motivations and invariant drives shared by all people.* At some time, most of us have engaged in a discussion about the possibility of a utopian society. Typically, someone takes the position that a benign utopia is not possible because humans are imperfect—men and women are intrinsically selfish or violent. The person who makes such an argument is linking the political behavior of individuals and groups with notions about innate (and possibly universal) human nature.

Certain political psychologists address this issue, asking whether there are innate human motivations that affect political behavior. The links between human nature and political behavior raise fascinating issues. Are there fundamental elements of human nature that cannot be significantly altered by socialization and institutions? Some theorists claim that nearly all human behavior is based on essential biological/genetic foundations (see, e.g., the sociobiology approach of Edward Wilson 1978; Masters 2001). From an opposing perspective, it is assumed that people's social values and behavior, if not their basic nature, can be shaped via proper socialization and enlightened institutions. Such shaping of people into a cooperative society is the theme of *Walden Two,* a novel by behavioral psychologist B. F. Skinner (1948). However, the power and danger of such pervasive socialization are a central theme in Aldous Huxley's (1932) classic novel *Brave New World.*

In general, one claim underpinning the human nature approach seems reasonable: we are not merely the product of our environment. But the crucial issue relevant to understanding politics is the extent to which individual personality and human nature *cause* political behavior. Are some innate characteristics of human nature so invariant that they are subject to only minor modifications from particular patterns of political socialization and from specific political environments? Empirical social science has yet to provide decisive answers to these questions about nature versus nurture in relation to politics.

CONCLUDING OBSERVATIONS

Our exploration of micropolitical analysis has continued with a consideration of primary explanations for individuals' political beliefs and political actions. The research and theories that attempt to answer the *why* questions about political behavior emphasize four types of explanatory factors: the environmental context, the agents of political socialization, personal characteristics, and political personality. The basic assumption is that some combination of these factors influences the kinds of political stimuli to which people are exposed, the manner in which they interpret these stimuli, and their responses to the stimuli.

The *environment* presents the individual with stimuli and opportunities as well as with obstacles to certain political beliefs and actions. While a person can ignore or misperceive these broad environmental constraints, they do constitute a framework that guides, and to some extent determines, political behavior. In most micropolitical research, the analyst can (and should) identify the major features of the environment that might affect the probability that an individual will manifest certain political beliefs or actions.

In a similar manner, an individual's *personal characteristics,* such as age, gender, social class, and education, can have a powerful cumulative influence. First, they can serve as a set of filters that influence the kinds of political phenomena to which the person is exposed. Second, they can influence the expectations that others have regarding how the person ought to think and act politically. The empirical evidence is sometimes quite clear (as are the data on voting in the 2004 U.S. presidential election) that certain personal characteristics (in a given environmental context) correlate significantly with particular political beliefs and actions. Thus personal characteristics, such as the environment, can be understood as a set of forces that influence the nature and intensity of individual political behavior but do not determine that behavior.

The inadequacy of either the environment or personal characteristics as a complete explanation for most individual political behavior is reflected in the fact that people with comparable personal characteristics or people who operate in a similar environment do not necessarily manifest identical political beliefs or actions. For example, of two intelligent 19-year-old Chicanas at the same university, one might be an activist deeply involved in Democratic Party politics and the other might be politically disinterested and inactive. Similarly, consider the divergent paths of political activism pursued by Mohandas Gandhi and Osama bin Laden, despite notable similarities in their characteristics and environments. While the environment and personal characteristics might not provide a total explanation, a strong case can be made that these factors do tend to set the boundaries within which much political behavior occurs.

The attempt to build an empirically validated causal theory of the effects of *political socialization* on political behavior is intriguing. A major analytic shortcoming in most of the political socialization research has been the difficulty in demonstrating empirically that there is a clear causal linkage from a specific agent of socialization to a particular belief, and then to a politically relevant action. In most instances, researchers lack the methodologies and the data-gathering instruments to measure how the messages of various agents of political socialization are absorbed, interpreted, and responded to by people. Rather, the researchers must attempt to infer what socialization agents have been important by asking individuals to recall the major sources of their own political beliefs.

Despite these empirical difficulties, the study of political socialization has been useful in increasing our understanding of the major forces that influence how people learn about and evaluate political phenomena. In their attempt to use the agents of political socialization, political regimes display their own belief that these socialization processes can either create and preserve popular support for the existing political order or create a new political consciousness. Research suggests that where the agents of political socialization are ineffective or provide contradictory messages, a person's political behavior will tend toward apathy or, in a few cases, toward producing the totally committed political activist. While the precise linkages among agents of political socialization, political beliefs, and political behavior have yet to be empirically verified, this area of inquiry remains an important one for political scientists.

The explanation of micropolitical behavior by *political personality* is perhaps the most intriguing of the four sets of factors. The political behavior of ordinary men and women is seldom analyzed using explicit, personality-based approaches. Most of the personality-based work has examined activists, such as radicals, terrorists, and top leaders.

Personality-based approaches are the explanatory framework for political behavior that has been least fully explored by means of social scientific inquiry. These approaches use some of the same evidence as the other approaches. For example, this approach might explain political personality in terms of the relationship of the individual to a social group, as would an explanation based on the peer group as an agent of political socialization. Thus personality is difficult to isolate from other forces—the environment, personal characteristics, and political socialization and learning—that intervene between human nature and political behavior and that shape personality. To a large extent, the psychological perspective differs from the other approaches less in the evidence it examines than in the more subjective, psychoanalytic framework within which the evidence is interpreted.

We began this chapter by asking whether it is possible to explain political beliefs and actions. In general, analyses can rarely prove that any of the four types of explanatory factors we examined is almost always *the* basic causal factor for a particular micropolitical behavior. Nonetheless, the evidence summarized in this chapter suggests that relevant knowledge about each of these four sets of explanatory factors can provide significant insights regarding political behavior.

KEY CONCEPTS

agenda setting

agents of political
    socialization

environment

human nature

personal characteristics

political personality

political socialization

rational choice theory

FOR FURTHER CONSIDERATION

1. Which agent of political socialization has been strongest in influencing *your* key political beliefs? Which of your key beliefs have been least influenced by this agent? What accounts for the agent's minimal influence on these beliefs?

2. Under what conditions are personal characteristics likely to have particularly powerful effects on an individual's political beliefs or actions?

3. To what extent are people either a blank page on which political beliefs can be written ("nurture") or genetically determined actors ("nature")? Do you think this overall assessment is valid for you?

4. In a contemporary society, what conditions cause schools or the media to be the more powerful source of people's political orientations?

5. What is your assessment of Machiavelli's advice to the leader that ethics, the leader's word, and even "the good" must sometimes be sacrificed to achieve desirable ends?

FOR FURTHER READING

Calderisi, Robert. (2007). *The Trouble with Africa: Why Foreign Aid Isn't Working.* London: Palgrave. A controversial explanation, which focuses particularly on a "national character" analysis, for the difficulties that most African countries have faced in achieving economic development.

Erikson, Erik. (1969). *Gandhi's Truth.* New York: Norton. Applying his rich psychobiographical approach, Erikson explains the crucial points of development shaping the personality and political style of Mohandas Gandhi.

Esposito, John, and John Voll. (1996). *Islam and Democracy: Religion, Identity and Conflict Resolution in the Muslim World.* New York: Oxford University Press. By means of a sensitive analysis of both Arab and non-Arab Islamic countries, the authors conclude that the core elements of Islam, as a system of beliefs, can be compatible with certain forms of participatory government.

Gobodo-Madikizela, Pumla. (2003). *A Human Being Died That Night: A South African Story of Forgiveness.* Boston: Houghton Mifflin. A psychologist who was a member of the Truth and Reconciliation Commission in South Africa explains the importance of this public acknowledgement process in creating a new peace and reducing the likelihood of future ethnic and racial atrocities.

Hayhoe, Ruth. (1992). *Education and Modernization: The Chinese Experience.* New York: Pergamon. An insightful analysis of the impacts of education on the political socialization process and on culture and modernization in China, from Confucianism to Marxism.

Huxley, Aldous. (1932). *Brave New World.* London: Chatto and Windus. A chilling vision of a society in which the state effectively uses socialization and material conditions to control the thoughts and actions of citizens.

Khadra, Yasmina. (2007). *Sirens of Baghdad.* Trans. John Cullen. London: Heinemann. A compelling novel that describes the conversion of a gentle, idealistic Iraqi college student into a disillusioned survivor in war-torn contemporary Iraq and then into a violent, nonreligious radical activist.

Lawrence, Bruce, Ed. (2005). *Messages to the World: The Statements of Osama Bin Laden.* London: Verso. The known commentaries by the leader of al-Qaeda provide insights into his worldview and strategies.

Mandela, Nelson. (1995). *Long Walk to Freedom.* Boston: Little, Brown. In his autobiography, Nelson Mandela provides a compelling narrative of his extraordinary life of political activism against racial injustice and apartheid, culminating in his election as president of South Africa.

Masters, Roger. (1989). *The Nature of Politics.* New Haven, CT: Yale University Press. A fascinating exploration of the biological bases of people's political beliefs and actions.

Nixon, Richard M. (1962). *Six Crises.* New York: Doubleday. Richard Nixon, one of the most controversial American presidents, provides a revealing self-assessment of his reactions to six critical events in his early political career.

Sears, David O., Leonie Huddy, and Robert Jervis, Eds. (2003). *Oxford Handbook of Political Psychology.* New York: Oxford University Press. This award-winning book employs the insights of psychology to examine such issues in the political world as the impact of personality, political socialization, information processing in opinion formation, emotion and politics, gender and political behavior, and styles of conflict resolution.

Skinner, B. F. (1948). *Walden Two.* New York: Macmillan. A renowned behavioral psychologist presents his conception of a setting in which socialization is used to create a benign and cooperative community. An intriguing counterpoint to Huxley's *Brave New World.*

Stern, Jessica. (2003). *Terror in the Name of God: Why Religious Militants Kill.* New York: HarperCollins. Based on detailed interviews with many terrorists, this interesting and accessible analysis of the psychology of terrorists and the nature of terrorist organizations focuses mainly on Muslims but also discusses Christian and Jewish terrorists.

Thomassen, Jacques. (2006). *The European Voter.* New York: Oxford University Press. A thorough comparative analysis and explanation of the changing voting behavior of citizens in many European countries.

Wattenberg, Martin. (2008). *Is Voting for Young People?* New York: Pearson Longman. This short book uses empirical data from the United States in comparison to other democracies to assess the political inactivity of young Americans, relative to their European peers and older Americans, and to argue for more political activism.

Wolfenstein, E. Victor. (1967). *The Revolutionary Personality: Lenin, Trotsky, Gandhi.* Princeton, NJ: Princeton University Press. A classic study of three great revolutionary leaders from a psychoanalytic perspective.

Zimbardo, Philip. (2007). *The Lucifer Effect: Understanding How Good People Turn Evil.* New York: Random House. A distinguished psychologist explores why behaviors such as organized genocide and the abuses at the Abu Ghraib prison in Iraq occur. His central argument is that it is not one bad person enticing others into highly unacceptable acts, but rather that groups collectively turn to such behavior in response to their social environment and the organizational system in which they function.

ON THE WEB

http://www.americanrhetoric.com/informationindex.htm

The News and Information Index from American Rhetoric is an extremely rich set of links to newspapers from around the world, other online news sources, magazines, search engines, polling databases, and legal databases.

http://www.umich.edu/~nes/nesguide/nesguide.htm

Data and analyses from the American National Election Study, the major survey of American political opinions and behavior (1948–2004). The material on the Web site addresses such topics as the role of personal characteristics, ideology, and partisanship on political beliefs and actions.

http://www.cddc.vt.edu/feminism/

The Feminist Theory Web site, developed at the Center for Digital Discourse and Culture at Virginia Tech University, provides a large number of links to information on beliefs, as well as groups and movements, that are inspired by a feminist perspective on political and social issues in many countries.

http://www.cnn.com/WORLD

The site for CNN, the 24-hour, U.S.-based international news organization.

http://www.itn.co.uk

World news and British news from Independent Television News, based in London, are provided.

http://www.webdopresseweb.ch/

"Webdo" is a Swiss-based link that enables you to access current articles in a diverse set of newspapers from many countries and in a variety of languages.

http://www.nytimes.com

This is the site for key articles and information from one of the premier newspapers in the United States.

http://www.worldnews.com

WorldNews provides an electronic news portal with international sites in multiple languages categorized by geographic region and subject.

http://news.bbc.co.uk

The Internet home of the British Broadcasting Company, this site offers world political, business, scientific, and entertainment news from a British perspective.

http://news.google.com

Using the same technology as in the Google Internet search engine, this site provides access to thousands of different news sources.

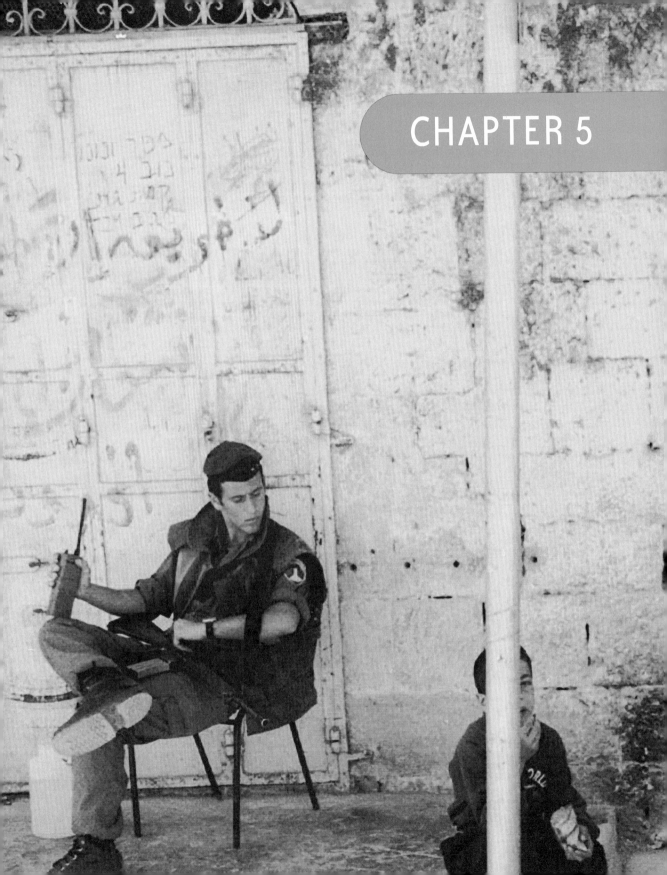

CHAPTER 5

STATES AND NATIONS

" O, Canada! Our home and native land! True patriot love in all thy sons command . . ." Voices fill Toronto's Maple Leaf Gardens as the Maple Leaf hockey game is preceded by the singing of the national anthem. But then as the vocalist intones, "O Canada! Terre de nos aieux, ton front est ceint de fleurons glorieux!" there are boos and catcalls. The national anthem continues to glorify the same native land of brave forefathers and heroic exploits. What has happened?

The lyrics are now a symbol of the conflict and disagreement within Canada. Canada is a single territorial space with one government that is attempting to rule a population in which "all thy sons" (and daughters) are deeply split into two groups that share neither culture nor identity. The English-speaking Canadians and the French-speaking Canadians are unable to establish harmonious coexistence within the same state. Many argue that the only solution is separation of Canada into two distinct countries.

The disjunction between state boundaries and peoples with shared identities, a central theme of this chapter, is a fundamental problem in many countries. It is arguably the greatest cause of violence and death in the contemporary political world. While Chapters 2–4 primarily considered the political beliefs and actions of individuals, this chapter expands the scale of our subject substantially, focusing on large collectivities of people. Initially, this chapter examines and distinguishes two crucial concepts: *state* and *nation.* This is followed by a discussion of the *political system,* a third major concept used to analyze these collectivities.

THE STATE

Anthropological evidence suggests that early social organization among humans was probably based on small living groups of family or kin. As suggested by humanistic psychologist Abraham Maslow (1954), human groupings formed so that people were better able to meet their physiological, safety, love, and belonging needs. As groupings became larger, tribes or bands were formed on the basis of more extensive kinship ties. It might be argued that the first "state" emerged when a multiplicity of such tribes combined under some leadership structure and some pattern of organization. In this conception, there have been states since ancient times, in the sense that a state exists when there are distinctive leadership roles, rules for social interaction, and a set of organizational arrangements to identify and serve collective needs (see Box 5.1).

A Legal Definition

The social scientific concept of the state, however, is a relatively modern one, based on the legal notion that the **state** is *a territorially bound sovereign entity.* The idea of sovereignty emerged in the sixteenth and seventeenth centuries. In current interpretations, **sovereignty** is *the premise that each state has complete authority and is the ultimate source of law within its own boundaries.* Sovereignty is the key element in the legal concept of the state. It is a basic assumption of international politics and is reflected in a fundamental principle of the United Nations, the sovereign equality of all member states. This means that, before the law, Cambodia is equal to China, Jamaica is equal to Japan. While sovereignty has legal standing and moral force in international law, the reality of international politics is that a state's sovereign rights depend ultimately on whether the state has sufficient power to enforce its position. Thus it is not likely that, when major national interests are at stake, China will yield to Cambodia merely on the basis of Cambodia's sovereign rights.

BOX 5.1

The States of the "State"

"State" is among the most extensively used concepts in political science, and it has various meanings. A source of confusion for American students is that they are accustomed to thinking of a state as one of the 50 units of subnational government in the United States, such as Illinois or Alabama. This is one appropriate meaning of the concept. However, in the general language of political science, *state* usually refers to the set of organizational units and people that performs the political functions for a national territorial entity, such as France, Indonesia, or Nigeria. In this chapter, and in this book, the term *state* will usually denote this full array of governmental units and people within the society.

You should also be aware that the language of political science often treats the state as though it were a single actor. For example, consider the statement (below) in the discussion of sovereignty that "a state has the right to resist . . . any aggression." In reality, the state is composed of many people who behave as individuals but whose combined behaviors are characterized as if they were performed by a single actor. In this book, there are other collectivities (e.g., the group, the political party, the army, and the bureaucracy) that are complex aggregates of individuals but discussed as though they operate as a single actor.

Associated with the idea of sovereignty is the doctrine of **territorial integrity**, which holds that *a state has the right to resist and reject any aggression, invasion, or intervention within its territorial boundaries.* As with the more general notion of sovereignty, a state's protection of its territorial integrity depends on the state's capacity and political power.

It might seem there are many relatively clear examples of a state's territorial integrity being violated, such as the Iraqi army's invasion of Kuwait in 1990, but there is often considerable disagreement over claimed violations of territorial integrity. First, territorial integrity is a fuzzy concept when there is a *dispute over boundaries.* For example, both Canada and the United States claim that certain fishing waters are within their territorial boundaries, and each state attempts to exclude the other's commercial fishing fleets from its territorial waters. In this case, the dispute has been settled by adjudication. But border disputes can also become a cause of violence between states, as when Iran and Iraq both claimed certain land along their mutual border, precipitating a war in 1980 (see Box 14.3).

Second, attempts to exercise sovereignty can be disputed when there is *disagreement about who the legitimate rulers are.* In Angola, for example, three contending groups each claimed to be the legitimate ruling group of the resource-rich country at independence in 1975. Each group controlled parts of the country and each had outside "assistance" (money, arms, troops) from such actors as Cuba, South Africa, the Soviet Union, the United States, and the United Nations. This struggle over sovereignty resulted in a devastating civil war that ravaged the country for more than 25 years (1975–2002). The toll included complete collapse of the economy, 4.5 million refugees, tens of thousands who lost limbs to millions of land mines, and the death of more than 1.5 million Angolans (Central Intelligence Agency 2008). Similar conflicts over sovereignty have arisen recently in Congo, Sudan, Somalia, and the Spanish Sahara.

Third, the international community has become less sensitive to the protection of sovereignty when there is strong evidence that the government is committing *serious human rights violations* against its own citizens. This has led to intense controversies about whether sovereignty has been violated. One recent example is the Sudan, a country of 35 million people with the largest land area in Africa. Even before a bloody 21-year civil war (northern Arab Muslims versus southern black non-Muslims) ended (in 2005), a new conflict emerged (in 2003) in the western region, Darfur. More than a dozen rebel groups fought for Darfur's autonomy on behalf of the ethnic groups in the region, who are mainly black non-Arabs. Darfur's rebels were resisting the Sudanese central government's support for the migration onto their lands of Arab settlers fleeing severe drought in the north. The government, dominated by northern Arabs, also provided support for informal bands of Arab militias (the Janjaweed) who fought against the rebels but who also drove Darfur's civilian population off its land through a brutal campaign of ethnic cleansing, based on murder, mutilation, torture, and rape.

When the United Nations proposed sending in a peacekeeping force on humanitarian grounds, the Sudanese government strongly objected, arguing that the basic situation was an illegal civil war. In this view, the problems in Darfur were an internal matter over which the government had complete sovereign rights, and the insertion of a large-scale outside force would constitute a foreign invasion. The Sudanese government's objections were a major reason that the UN did not intervene directly in Darfur during four years in which more than 200,000 were killed and 2 million became refugees. The UN finally did move forward with a humanitarian intervention by a large peacekeeping force in late 2007, overcoming the Sudanese government's objections regarding sovereignty.

A rationale for these "humanitarian interventions" within sovereign states was offered by former UN Secretary-General Kofi Annan when he accepted the 2001 Nobel Peace Prize awarded to the United Nations: "The sovereignty of states must no longer be used as a shield for gross violations of human rights. When states undermine the rule of law and violate the rights of individual citizens, they become a menace not only to their people, but also to their neighbors, and indeed the world" (Holley 2001). However, others are concerned that the increased use of such justifications undermines weaker states, since sovereignty can be one of their best protections under international law from military intervention by outside powers (Sassen 1996). Even current UN Secretary-General Ban Ki-moon has been much more cautious about violating state sovereignty. The Debate in 5 explores this tension between sovereignty and intervention.

THE DEBATE IN 5

Does Humanitarian Intervention Violate State Sovereignty?

A controversial issue in recent years is whether it is acceptable for states and international actors to use force (or the threat of force) against a state that is suspected of or is abusing the fundamental human rights of its own citizens. This is sometimes justified as "humanitarian intervention" by those taking the actions (Falk 2003; Holzgrefe and Keohane 2003). However, the state that is the target of such an intervention can object that this is a clear violation of its sovereignty and hence of international law. Disputes over the clash between these principles have recently become serious issues regarding such countries as China, Congo, and Sudan. Is humanitarian intervention an acceptable action if it violates a state's sovereignty?

Protecting Human Rights Takes Precedence Over State Sovereignty

- The international society of states now defines sovereignty in terms of a bundle of both rights and obligations. Respect for human rights to "life, liberty, and security of person" is among those obligations, by virtue of the Universal Human Rights Declaration (adopted by the United Nations in 1948) and other treaties. Thus a state that inflicts gross and widespread atrocities on its own population has forfeited some of its rights and cannot insist that humanitarian intervention violates its sovereignty.
- In 2005, the United Nations General Assembly explicitly asserted its "responsibility to protect" people by humanitarian intervention when a government does not safeguard its own peoples' lives, particularly in cases of ethnic cleansing or other forms of large-scale state violence against its population, such as

▶ **Is there a level of human suffering in Sudan that justifies outside intervention despite the state's objections?**

widespread torture or extensive use of imprisonment without due process.
- Democratic states have a particular responsibility to take whatever actions are necessary to prevent other states from abusing individuals' human rights, because this demonstrates their commitment to democratic principles

and their willingness to act beyond national self-interest.

- If no outside group intervenes to stop a state from serious violations of human rights, the state might engage in even more extensive and unacceptable acts of violence against its own citizens.

- Moreover, if no outside group intervenes to stop a state from serious violations of human rights, other states might be emboldened to violate the human rights of their own citizens.

State Sovereignty Takes Precedence Over Outsiders' Concerns About Human Rights

- State sovereignty is a central premise of international law. This core principle provides a state with almost complete authority to implement policy decisions within its own borders. A state's right to this "exclusive internal jurisdiction" is violated if another state or group intervenes within its borders without its consent. In accordance with international law, the state can respond by any means necessary to defend its territory.

- Despite the idealized notion of universal human rights, different cultures have significantly different interpretations of individual rights and the conditions under which such rights have been violated. It is not clear that these predominantly Western conceptions of human rights should take precedence over the country's own standards.

- It can be very difficult for outside actors to determine the precise level of the purported violations of human rights within another country. Even more importantly, there are no universally accepted standards regarding the level at which human rights violations become so gross (that is, so extensive, severe and persistent) that outside intervention is justified.

- Nearly all states accept the principle that no single country or group of countries has the right to intervene, yet such interventions do still occur without international sanction (e.g., NATO in Kosovo). While some argue that the Security Council of the United Nations does have the legitimate right to authorize intervention, this view is not universally accepted and is usually contested by the state in question.

- Humanitarian intervention, when associated with severe economic sanctions and military invasion, can cause more harm to the population than the human rights violations that prompted them. This problem is compounded when intervening states do not follow international norms that require an intervention to be proportional to the human rights violation.

More questions . . .

1. How severe and extensive must a violation of human rights be in order to justify the intervention of other countries into the internal affairs of a sovereign state? Who can legitimately judge the level of violation?

2. Should international actors respond any differently if there appear to be human rights violations but they are being committed by groups within a country, not just the government?

3. Is it acceptable to cause widespread suffering and destruction within a country in order to end the perceived human rights abuses?

A Structural-Functional Definition

As an alternative to defining the state in terms of its legal standing, it can also be defined by the key organizational *structures* that operate as "the government" and the key *functions* that the state performs. In this structural-functional perspective, the

state might be defined as *the organized institutional machinery for making and carrying out political decisions and for enforcing the laws and rules of the government.*

For Max Weber (1864–1920), the great political sociologist, the one function that distinguishes the state from all other organizations is its monopoly on the legitimate use of force and coercion in the society. That is, only the state has the right to use violence to enforce the society's laws and decisions.

The "state-centered" definitions of the state offer a more expansive conception: the state's essential functions are to maintain order and to compete with other actual or potential states (Levi 2002; Skocpol 1979: 30). The state is an autonomous actor, composed of public officials making decisions. The state has goals, broadly under-stood as the "national interest," that it attempts to achieve against resistance from both domestic and international actors (Morgenthau 1993; Kahler 2002). The particular way in which a state's structures are configured has crucial effects—on the content of public officials' policy preferences, on the determination of whose preferences will be adopted as those of the state, and on the state's effectiveness in implementing those policy preferences in the society.

A widely used approach emphasizing the structures and functions of the state is based on the work of Gabriel Almond and his colleagues (e.g., Almond et al. 2008). Their conceptual framework is based on two central questions:

1. What functions must be performed if the state is to persist?
2. What structures perform these necessary functions within a given state?

Chapter 10 will present a recent elaboration of this basic structural-functional approach called "capabilities analysis." In the classic version of this approach, Almond identifies eight *requisite functions*—that is, functions that must be performed in every state (Almond et al. 2008: ch. 2):

1. *Political socialization* is the processes through which individuals acquire their cognitive, affective, and evaluative orientations toward the political world.
2. *Political recruitment* is the processes through which people are drawn into roles as political activists.
3. *Political communication* is the mechanisms by which political information flows through society.
4. *Interest articulation* is the low-level communication, by individuals and groups, of what they need or want from the state.
5. *Interest aggregation* is the transformation of all these political needs and wants into a smaller number of coherent alternatives.
6. *Policy making* is the process by which the state establishes laws, policy decisions, and value allocations.
7. *Policy implementation* is the actual application of such laws and policy decisions.
8. *Policy adjudication* is the interpretation and resolution of disagreements regarding what the policies mean and how they should be implemented.

Given these functions, analyses using Almond's approach have primarily attempted to identify the particular structures within a state that are most significant in the performance of each function and to describe how the structures contribute to performing each function. While it might seem obvious at first glance that a certain structure always performs a particular function, more reflection (and later chapters) will suggest that the situation is more complex. For example, it is not simply the case that Congress performs the policy-making function in the United States. Many policy decisions are made by the president, by cabinet departments, by the bureaucracy, by the courts as they both interpret and reshape laws, by structures at the local levels of government, and by citizens through electoral initiatives.

In most contemporary societies, virtually every political function is performed by a variety of structures. Many of these structures are part of the state, but others are nonstate actors, such as interest groups, religious organizations, media, social groups, private businesses, and international organizations. Thus the central questions in structural-functional research address the characteristic processes of each structure and the subtle interrelationships among structures as they contribute to a given function. These questions are especially germane in comparative research, where the analyst attempts to specify how the structure-function patterns vary among states.

The Domain of State Action

One other way of characterizing the state is to define its appropriate domain of action. When we examine "appropriate" rather than "actual" state action, the central question is normative rather than descriptive or analytic. A normative question asks how something *should* be rather than how it is (recall Chapter 1). Many of the most fascinating and fundamental issues in the political world have normative components. Political scientists attempt to distinguish the normative elements of their discussion from the descriptive-analytic elements, but as Chapter 1 observed, there are always subtle normative judgments organizing the manner in which every political question is examined.

A fundamental, unresolved debate in everyday political discussion, as well as in political theory, concerns how extensive the state's role in society should be. Everyone agrees that the boundaries of state activity should be limited to *res publica,* a Latin phrase meaning "things of the people." But what "things" should be included? And how expansive should the state's involvement with these things be?

In contemporary political thought, certain broad views regarding the appropriate boundaries of *res publica* are associated with the three political ideologies (the major "isms") outlined in Chapter 2. In the *conservative view of the state,* one important domain of state action is military power, which functions to protect and promote the country's interests abroad and to defend against intervention by other states. Internally, the expectation is that the state will use its monopoly of force to maintain social order and to protect private property rights. State policy will also be used to preserve traditional values, especially regarding family life, religion, and culture.

As suggested in Chapter 2, a view of *res publica* based on classical liberalism is more limited. Similar to the conservative view, the state must defend the country's sovereignty against external aggression or influence. However, the *liberal view of the state* has great confidence in the dynamics of the free market to motivate and coordinate human behavior. Thus the state should be mainly a night watchman, a low-profile policeman who ensures the basic safety and freedom of every individual.

Thomas Paine's (1737–1809) slogan captures this perspective on *res publica:* "That government is best which governs least." In its extreme form, the domain of appropriate state action is reduced to almost nothing, a perspective termed *libertarianism.*

There are several different interpretations of the domain of state action across the major variants of socialism described in Chapter 2. The *democratic socialist view of the state* is that the state must constrain the powerful and self-interested groups whose behavior will harm the collective good of the society. Also, the state must intervene to provide assistance to the many groups in the society that are deeply disadvantaged by the workings of the system and must enact policies that ensure greater equality of condition. The *Marxist view of the state* is that most states are expansive and repressive, serving mainly to preserve the interests of the dominant class in the society. In the words of V. I. Lenin (1870–1924), the Soviet revolutionary leader and theorist, such a state is "a body of armed men, weapons, and prisons." After a successful revolution, however, a more benign and positive Marxist state can be installed. Its domain of action is to implement any policies necessary to serve the fundamental goal of equality of political, economic, and social resources in the society. Some Marxist socialists assume the state will ultimately be eliminated (in Marx's words, the state will "wither away"), but even in this view, organizational structures would remain to administer policy. *Anarchism* is an extreme form of this view of the state, since the state actually does disappear. This does not mean a situation of chaos and disorder; rather, it is a stateless society where individuals and groups organize spontaneously to create a society in which all people participate and all benefit from the goods and services that are produced.

While these three views of *res publica* are dominant in Western political thought, there are other conceptions that do not emphasize a unique, political "state." For example, in some societies dominated by an all-encompassing religion, there is no political state that is independent of the religious order. In fundamentalist Islamic regimes, sharia law, the law of Islam, establishes a religious state that defines all aspects of social life, including the content of *res publica.* And throughout history, many societies have had no distinct political order. For instance, no specifically political structures existed in most precolonial African societies. Rather, the rules governing the society were based on tradition, as interpreted by community leaders (such as tribal elders or religious authorities).

THE NATION

The concept of the nation has a psychological and emotional basis rather than a legal or functional basis (as the concept of the state does). A **nation** is defined as *a set of people with a deeply shared fundamental identification.* Different factors might be the basis of such identification: shared descent (belief in a common kinship or history), shared culture, shared geographic space, shared religion, shared language, or shared economic order. The nation is a community of understanding, of communication, and of trust (Connor 1994).

Most people feel some identity with a variety of different reference groups or communities, such as a religion, local community, ethnic group, social club, and sports team. In the usage here, what distinguishes a nation from other reference groups is that the nation is a major group, beyond the family group, with whom a person identifies very powerfully. It is an essential division between "us" and "them." The strength of a person's primary national identity depends on the relative importance he places on various identities and the extent to which the most important identities reinforce this basic conception of "us" versus "them." Thus **nationalism** is *a powerful commitment to the advancement of the interests and welfare of an individual's own nation,* with minimal concern about the conditions of those outside the nation.

The best situation for effective governance is a **nation-state,** which is *an area that has both the territorial boundaries of a single state and a citizenry who all share the same primary national identity.* Only a few modern states have the combination of common culture, history, ethnicity, religion, and language that results in a strong sense of shared nationality among nearly all the citizens governed by the state. Japan is an example of a relatively homogeneous nation-state.

Occasionally, one nation is split into two states, such as North and South Korea. In such cases, the citizens often dream of reunification, even when their governments and ideologies differ fundamentally. This occurred in Germany, which was split into communist East Germany and capitalist West Germany after World War II. In 1990, citizens of the single German nation were reunited in a single country after nearly half a century of antagonistic separation into two very different states.

The reality of the contemporary world, however, is that most countries are *multinational states,* which *include significant groups whose fundamental identities are associated with different nations.* When these nationality identities are very strong and are based on *religion, race, and/or ethnicity* (also sometimes called **ethnonationalism**), they can produce intense animosity and violence between groups within (and between) states (Connor 1994; Conversi 2004; Snyder 2000).

These problems have been evident in many of the states that gained independence after 1945 with territorial boundaries that were based on the arbitrary administrative decisions of colonial powers, not nationality differences. Many of these states have experienced traumatic nationality conflicts, and few of these conflicts have been permanently resolved. There are reports every day of struggles such as those of the Tibetans in China; the Tamils in Sri Lanka; and the Kurds in Turkey, Iran, and Iraq. The Israeli soldier and the Palestinian on pages 108-109 each believes that this land in Hebron belongs to *his* nation. The example of the Indian subcontinent in Box 5.2 illustrates the kinds of differences that exist between states and nations and how they can generate instability and political violence.

Even in some of the more established states, nation-based cleavages frequently explode (sometimes literally). When the Soviet Union, the world's most multinational state, collapsed in 1991, it was replaced by 15 states that were generally organized on nationality grounds. However, the large nationality minorities in many of them (e.g., Chechens in Russia) have waged extensive nation-based struggles. The bloody nationality violence in Eastern Europe was based on devastating ethnic battles among the Bosnians, Croatians, Kosovars, Macedonians, Serbs, and others in the former Yugoslavia (see Box 15.2). Even this carnage is overshadowed by the horrendous ethnic conflict in Rwanda and Burundi between the Hutus and the Tutsis. More than 100,000 (mostly Tutsis) were slaughtered in Rwanda in only 100 days in 1994, and more than 300,000 Hutus and Tutsis were killed in ethnic conflict in Burundi between 1994 and 2006.

BOX 5.2

State and Nations:
The Indian Subcontinent

The problem of discontinuities between nations and states is often most severe in states that have gained independence within the last 60 years. The Indian subcontinent exemplifies these problems. The vast Indian subcontinent was a feudal society divided into many small kingdoms ruled by kings (*maharajahs*). Starting in the sixteenth century, the riches of India were pursued, and often exploited, by many traders, including the British, Dutch, French, and Arabs. The states from which these traders came began to struggle for dominance over the Indian trade, and the British finally gained hegemony in the eighteenth century after defeating the French. From that time until 1947, the Indian subcontinent was the major jewel in the British imperial crown, treated as a single territory under colonial rule.

After a lengthy and often violent campaign of political and social action by Indian nationalists, the British granted the subcontinent independence in 1947. However, despite the desires of the British and the efforts of some Indian leaders such as Mohandas Gandhi (recall Box 4.2), the subcontinent was deeply split on the basis of religion between Hindus and Muslims. Since it seemed impossible to fashion a single state out of these two nations, two states were formed in 1947: India, which was predominantly (82 percent) Hindu; and Pakistan, predominantly (90 percent) Muslim.

The situation was further complicated by the concentration of Muslims in two geographically distinct areas in the northeast and northwest regions of the subcontinent. As a consequence, Pakistan was composed of two parts, separated by more than 1,500 miles of rival India's territory. Many Hindus in Pakistan and Muslims in India were forced to leave their homelands and migrate to the new state sharing their religion. The hostility and bloodshed associated with the partition resulted in a million deaths. There have been periodic violent boundary conflicts ever since. The ownership of nuclear weapons by India and Pakistan since 1998 accentuates the need to resolve the conflicts between the two states.

While the major religious difference on the Indian subcontinent was generally resolved by this partition, many other nationality problems remained. For example, since 1947 India and Pakistan have disagreed about which country should control the region of Jammu and Kashmir. At independence, India was given control of the region, although the majority of the population was and remains Muslim. Disputes over control of the region have resulted in more than a half-century of military conflicts and intermittent guerrilla war, despite persistent United Nations involvement.

Within Pakistan, an even more substantial nationality dispute emerged after independence between two major ethnic groups, the Punjabis and the Bengalis. When the Bengalis, who are dominant in East Pakistan, won a national election, Punjabi-dominated West Pakistan attempted to reassert political power through its control of

BOX 5.2 *(Continued)*

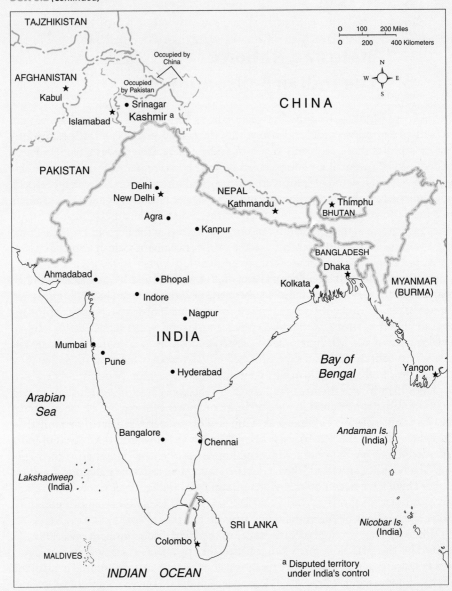

the military. When the Bengalis attempted to form their own independent nation-state (with some support from India), a terrible civil war resulted. After hundreds of thousands of deaths from war and starvation, the Bengalis of East Pakistan won the civil war and created a new sovereign state, Bangladesh, in 1971.

BOX 5.2 *(Continued)*

And while India is dominated by Hindus, major nation-based cleavages continue to plague the country, creating tremendous barriers to forging a single identity as a nation-state. There are 21 official languages in addition to the two "national" languages, Hindi and English, each understood by only about one-third of the population. In all, there are about 1,650 different dialects in India, most of which are mutually unintelligible.

Moreover, India has at least five major religious groupings: Hindu, Muslim, Sikh, Christian, and Buddhist. Hindu nationalism has increasingly been expressed through a political movement, resulting in the growing power at the regional and national levels of Hindu parties, particularly the Bharatiya Janata Party (BJP). The BJP, which dominated the government from 1998 to 2004, is the most serious threat to a secular Indian government since independence. With the increase in Hindu nationalism, violence against Christians and Muslims has risen significantly.

Most of the non-Hindu groups are regionally concentrated, enhancing their identity as religion-based nations. One major source of political unrest in India since 1980 has been the Sikhs, who are concentrated in the northwest part of India called the Punjab. The Sikhs have a very strong identity as a religious community and an ethnic group. Their sense of nationality is heightened by their belief that they are discriminated against politically by the Hindus. The Sikhs have occasionally been militant in demanding greater political autonomy, and since the early 1980s, some have insisted on full independence to create the nation-state of Khalistan. After the Indian army stormed the Golden Temple, the Sikhs' holiest shrine, to drive out Sikh militants who had taken refuge there, Indian Prime Minister Indira Gandhi was assassinated in 1984 by two Sikhs among her private guard.

Rajiv Gandhi succeeded his mother as prime minister, only to be the victim of another nation-based dispute. The Indian army had intervened on the neighboring island-country of Sri Lanka in an attempt to limit the extremely violent ethnically based civil war between the native Sinhalese and the Tamils, who had migrated to Sri Lanka from Southern India. Tamils in Sri Lanka have been angered by the lack of support from India and by the treatment they received from the Indian army. In 1991, Rajiv Gandhi was assassinated by a Tamil woman who had strapped a bomb to her body. In sum, the many deep cleavages in India, based on religion, ethnicity, culture, and region, have exposed the state to persistent instability, conflict, and nation-based carnage.

Meanwhile, the agitation of the Quebequois in Canada, the Basques in Spain, and the Irish Catholics in Northern Ireland are testimony to the possibility that even centuries-old states might split apart. Some scholars predict that the current reorganization of states based on nationality identities will produce more than 50 new states and that nation-based conflicts might remain the major cause of violence and instability (Barber 1995; Hechter 2000; but also see Sadowski 1998).

A broad class of nation-based groups is sometimes given special consideration. *Indigenous peoples* is a term for more than 370 million people in about 70 countries.

Each of these 5,000 distinct nations is understood to be a "first people" who originally inhabited a geographic area as "natives," but who were then subjugated by an invading nation. In nearly every case, these nations have virtually no political or social power and their culture is marginalized or suppressed by the dominant culture. Since the early 1970s and most recently with the Declaration of Rights of Indigenous Peoples (2007), the United Nations has been concerned about protecting such groups against discrimination and against efforts to destroy their nationality identity and culture. Some of these nations have become more politically assertive, demanding autonomy, although most countries resist providing their indigenous peoples with special political rights.

THE POLITICAL SYSTEM

While concepts such as state and nation are extremely useful, political scientists have sought an additional, more general and analytic concept to describe the structures and dynamics of organized politics at all levels. Many political scientists use some version of the concept of the political system developed in the work of David Easton (1953, 1965). Easton was searching for an analytic concept that would facilitate the development of a general theory of politics. He found the basis for such a concept in the notion of general systems theory used in biology.

Systems in General

The essential concept is a *system,* which is a group of components that exist in a characteristic relationship to each other and that interact in regular patterns. Because the components are interdependent, change in one component will have some effect on other components. Such change can cause minor or even major alterations in how the total system functions. In a mechanical analogy, an automobile engine can be viewed as a system, a set of components interacting in a regular way. If one spark plug is dirty, the performance of the automobile-as-system will be substantially altered; if the spark plug is removed, the system might not work at all.

The same interdependency of components is evident in human systems, such as families, sports teams, factories, and bureaucracies. The components of human systems—people in roles—are more likely to vary in the range of their actions than are the components of most mechanical systems, making their performance far more variable and less predictable. Human systems function relatively smoothly as long as most of the components (the people) interact within a tolerable range of expected action. For high performance, some human systems, such as a symphony orchestra or a drill team, require far more rigid adherence to predictable roles than others, such as a jazz combo or a basketball team. Because of people's capacity to adapt and improvise, human systems can sometimes adapt effectively to unexpected circumstances. But human variability can also result in system performance that is disorganized, with negative or even disastrous effects.

The Political System Defined

For Easton (1953, 1965), the **political system** is a system of behavior, and it is defined by its distinctive activities, the *authoritative allocation of values for a society.* This definition is central to the idea of a political system as it is used in this book and in many political analyses. Thus it is appropriate to examine each aspect of the definition in greater detail.

Values.   *Values* are those things that have significance and importance to people. We can discuss **political values** in terms of *the idealized abstractions that inspire or justify much political action:* liberty, equality, freedom, justice. Political values can also be defined more concretely: They can be *material goods,* such as a decent house or road system; they can be *services,* such as quality health care or protection from crime; they can be *conditions,* such as clean air or security from national enemies. Values can also be *symbolic goods,* such as status. In addition to positive values, there are negative values, such as coercion or imprisonment, polluted water, epidemic disease, and so on. (Notice that this social scientific concept of values is broader than the notion of values as moral judgments that people use to guide their actions.)

By definition, values tend to be scarce resources—either there is an insufficient amount of a given value to satisfy everyone, or the enjoyment of one value by some requires a loss of value to others. To use an example from the preceding paragraph, there is no political system in which all citizens have housing they would consider adequate. There are people who would view their housing as too small, or too expensive, or in the wrong location, or lacking in sufficient luxuries. Even if a state could provide everyone with identical housing, some would be dissatisfied because they want better housing or because they object to the use of their taxes to subsidize the housing of others. A state's vast arsenal of nuclear weapons may make one person feel secure while making another person extremely insecure. One person might favor more state expenditures on missile systems, while another would prefer to spend more resources on housing, and a third might prefer lower taxes rather than either weapons or housing. Every possible value distribution entails trade-offs between different values as well as some inequality in the benefits and burdens linked to each person. Thus there are always disagreements, competition, and even violent conflict over whose values will be served and whose will not. What are *your* top two values for your society? For yourself?

Allocation.   Pierre Mendes-France, a distinguished French premier (1954–1955), observed that "to govern is to make choices." *Allocation* refers to such choice making—to the process by which decisions and actions are taken to grant values to some and deny values to others. Value allocations occur at every moment when decisions are made to alter or even to sustain the existing distribution of values. Making these decisions and actions in the face of competition and conflict over values is a central aspect of politics.

Authoritative.   Value allocations are *authoritative* when the decisions are accepted as binding by those people affected by the decisions. One of the most fascinating questions in political analysis is: Why do people accept the authority of the political system to allocate values in a manner that is not to their direct advantage? That is, why do people accept the imposition of taxes, policies, and laws that they judge to be undesirable for themselves? The discussion in Box 5.3 suggests some of the reasons people accept the authority of the state.

BOX 5.3

Why Do People Accept Authority?

There are many answers to the question of why people accept the **authority** of the state. In the classic definition, authority is voluntaristic. **Authority** is based on a subjective belief in the *legitimacy* of the state: *a person willingly accepts the decisions of the state as binding because it is "the right thing to do."* The individual's judgment that the state's authority is legitimate might be grounded in one or more of the following phenomena (see Weber 1958a: 295–301):

- *Law.* The individual believes that the laws of the state are rationally established, purposeful, and enacted with formal correctness by appropriate public actors, and thus compliance with those laws is proper behavior.
- *Tradition.* The individual is influenced by a long-standing habit among most people in the society to accept patterns of authoritative action.
- *Charisma.* The individual is persuaded by a dynamic leader whose personal qualities are so extraordinary that the leader wins the individual's trust and unquestioning support. (Among the examples of twentieth-century charismatic political leaders are Winston Churchill, Adolf Hitler, Nelson Mandela, and Mao Zedong.)
- *Social contract.* Most broadly, classical political theorists such as Thomas Hobbes (1588–1679; recall Chapter 2) and John Locke (1632–1704) suggest that acceptance of the state's authority is due to a "social contract" in which each individual sacrifices certain personal values to a state whose actions ensure that social order will replace the violent state of nature.
- *Socialization.* The effective efforts of the agents of political socialization might convince (indoctrinate?) the individual that the state has authority to make decisions and that obedience is proper, without relying specifically on any of these other sources of authority.

In many contemporary states, explanations of the acceptance of the state's authority by most citizens are often based on a more explicit assessment of material incentives or sanctions:

- *Individual utility.* The individual is satisfied with the array of values that the state provides specifically to him, or with the broad values provided to all citizens, such as economic growth and social stability, to which he attaches great importance.
- *Fear of sanction.* The individual might fear the negative values, such as deprivation of valued benefits, coercion, imprisonment, or even death, that the state can inflict on him if he openly challenges the state's authority. With sanctions, the line between authority and power exercise might have been crossed.

BOX 5.3 *(Continued)*

The debate over the legitimacy of the state's authority is a perpetual one. A fascinating literary expression of the authority debate is the classic play *Antigone*, by the Greek dramatist Sophocles (496–406 B.C.E.). Antigone violates a rule set by Creon, who is not only her uncle (and potential father-in-law) but also the king. In defense of social order, Creon argues, "He whom the State appoints must be obeyed to the smallest matter, be it right or wrong....There is no more deadly peril than disobedience" (Sophocles 1967: 144). In a similar way, contemporary political analyst Samuel Huntington (1968: 7–8) observes: "The primary problem is not liberty but the creation of legitimate public order. Men may, of course have order without liberty, but they cannot have liberty without order."

Ultimately, Antigone decides to do what seems morally correct to her, and she breaks the law. Thus Antigone represents the other side of the debate, which is characterized by eloquent defenders of the individual's right and even the obligation to resist his state's authority when he believes the state is wrong. In "Civil Disobedience," American philosopher Henry David Thoreau (1817–1862) writes: "If [the law of the state] is of such a nature that it requires you to be the agent of injustice to another, then, I say, break the law. Let your life be a counter friction to stop the machine. What I have to do is to see, at any rate, that I do not lend myself to the wrong which I condemn" (Thoreau 1849/1981: 92).

In some cases, the objective of resistance to authority is social change. Mohandas Gandhi's essential strategy in resisting British rule in India was repeated episodes of (generally) nonviolent resistance to a system of laws and authority that Gandhi judged to be immoral. Civil disobedience also was used by Martin Luther King Jr. and others in the civil rights movement in the United States during the 1960s to protest laws that failed to prevent discrimination on the basis of race. In other cases, the resistance to established authority is more aggressive, and the objective is establishment of a new political order. Karl Marx and Friedrich Engels, in the famous *Communist Manifesto* (1848/1978: 500), conclude: "In short, the Communists everywhere support every revolutionary movement against the existing social and political order of things. . . . They openly declare that their ends can be attained only by the forcible overthrow of all existing social conditions. Let the ruling classes tremble at a Communist revolution. The proletarians have nothing to lose but their chains. They have a world to win. Working men of all countries, unite!"

Despite such stirring calls to question authority, most people usually do obey the commands of others who seem to be in positions of authority. In a famous series of disturbing social psychology experiments, subjects were told by a researcher to administer increasingly powerful electric shocks to another person (who was collaborating with the researcher to fool the subject). Despite the (fake) shrieks of pain from the person they were shocking, most subjects continued to increase and administer the electric shocks when told to do so (Milgram 1974). At some point, almost everyone justifies the unjustifiable by relying on the "I was only following orders" defense that is particularly associated with Nazi war criminal Adolf Eichmann (1906–1962).

BOX 5.3 *(Continued)*

*"It would appear that the sequinned youngster is preparing to challenge
the authority of the silver-backed alpha male."*

For a society.   The final element in Easton's definition of the political system is meant
to solve the difficult analytic problem of defining the boundaries of the political world.
Easton limits the domain of the political system to those areas where values are being
allocated "for a society"—that is, to those values where the state must act to protect
and serve the public's interests. Recall the notion of *res publica*—"things of the people." The political system, in establishing the range of value allocations included in
res publica, also sets the boundaries of its own domain of action.

Every political system defines its boundaries of legitimate action differently. This
crucial point is reflected in the contrasting views of the role of the state discussed earlier in this chapter. We shall see throughout this book, and especially in Part Five, that
some political systems allocate values in virtually every aspect of their citizens' lives,
while other political systems intervene minimally. One political system might provide
a total health care delivery system to all citizens, with no direct charges for doctors,
hospitals, or treatment, whereas another system might subsidize only hospitalization
for the very poor. One political system might require schools to provide daily religious instruction, while another system might forbid schools from engaging in even
the general discussion of religious philosophies.

It should be noted that Easton's definition seems to cover only national political systems. The idea of a political system for an entire society serves the purposes of this book well, since the book focuses primarily on countries. But analytically, a political system could exist at any level, even one that does not have ultimate authority. This concept could certainly apply to subnational political systems (including such American examples as states, counties, and municipalities). It could also apply to a supranational system that encompasses more than one state (e.g., the European Union). Perhaps a more generalized definition of the political system might be "the authoritative allocation of values *for a collectivity.*"

Conceptualization of the Political System

Easton's (1965) conceptualization of the political system, characterized in Figure 5.1, is based on the idea of an *input-output system* within a broader environment. This means that, within an environment, the system receives certain phenomena as inputs, does some processing of those inputs ("conversion" in the figure), and then generates outputs back into the environment. The elements in Figure 5.1 are described more fully in the following sections.

Environment.   The *environment of the political system* is the name given to *all those activities that are not included within the state's activity domain of res publica.* Thus it encompasses all those physical and social domains where the authoritative allocation of values for the society is *not* the dominant activity. Do not think of the environment as a separate physical area; the political system often operates in the same physical environment as other subsystems, such as the economic environment (e.g., the inflation rate or water resources) and the social environment (e.g., religious beliefs or ethnic relations). The activities in the "intrasocietal" environment are occurring in the same spatial area as are the activities performed by the political system. The environment is vast because it includes not only all the activities within the society but also an "extrasocietal" environment that includes virtually every activity in the world that is external to the territory of the state.

While any aspect of this enormous environment might affect the political system, only a few aspects are considered in any particular analysis. That is, the environment

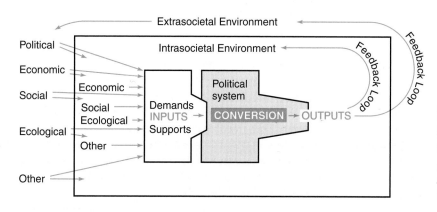

▶ **FIGURE 5.1**

Conceptualization of the political system

Source: Based on Easton 1965: 31.

provides opportunities and obstacles, resources and constraints that are relevant to the functioning of the political system. For example, there might be a shortage of fossil fuels within the state (i.e., in the intrasocietal ecological system). This *input* might provoke the political system to take some action (policy decision) to ensure more fuel for its citizens and its economy. Among the various policies the political system might adopt are these:

- Stimulate additional fuel production within the society through subsidies for exploration.
- Reduce fuel consumption through a very high fuel-use tax.
- Encourage innovative alternatives by supporting research and development of synfuels.
- Obtain fuel resources from outside the state by using military force to capture some other state's fuel resources.

Can you think of other feasible policy responses to this problem in the political system's environment?

Demands and supports.   Among the inputs from the environment, the most direct are demands and supports. ***Demands*** are *wants or desires for particular value allocations.* Demands might come from individuals, groups, or systems either within or outside the society. When a citizen prefers lower taxes, or more expenditure on health care, or greater regulation of corporations, or a freeze on nuclear weapons construction, these preferences become demands to the political system when they are communicated directly by the citizen or by other actors such as spokespersons, interest groups, or political parties. (This process corresponds, in the functional language described earlier in the chapter, to interest articulation and political communication.)

Supports are *actions by individuals or groups that indicate either favorable or unfavorable orientations toward the political system.* These actions can be directed toward individual *actors* in the political system (e.g., France's Nicolas Sarkozy, Venezuela's Hugo Chavez), toward elements of the *regime* (e.g., the prime minister, the supreme court, the municipal council), or toward a broad *political community* (e.g., the Sikhs, Francophones [all peoples speaking French], the Third World, dar al Islam [the World of Islam]). Support can be positive, as when a person pays taxes, serves in the state's military, salutes the flag, or votes. Support can also be negative, through actions that criticize or oppose the political system, such as a person refusing to pay taxes, avoiding military service, burning the flag, or defacing the ballot.

Conversion.   At the heart of the political system framework is *conversion*—the process by which political actors assess demands and supports within the context of the relevant environmental forces and then determine what values will be allocated to whom. In Easton's own discussions, the conversion process is treated a bit like a black box, in the sense that little detail is provided about how decisions are made.

Many analysts, however, have been especially interested in studying how the political system actually does make policy decisions and allocate resources. Chapter 9 will describe in detail an analytic model of the public policy process that defines a series of key stages, from problem definition to implementation and evaluation. Chapter 9 also compares three widely proposed general explanations of the decision process: the *class approach,* the *elite approach,* and the *group approach.* In each approach, a different mix of groups in society (the dominant class, the small ruling elite, or a diversity of private groups) has the greatest influence on the conversion process; the explanation of the role of the political system also differs in each approach.

Outputs.   Once political decisions have been made and implemented, they become *outputs* of the political system. Some outputs are visible and obvious, as when the political system authorizes the development of a new missile system, spends the money to build the missiles, and points them toward its enemies. But it is sometimes quite difficult to identify the decisions (outputs), since they might involve subtle actions, secret policies, or even "nondecisions" that perpetuate the existing value distribution or bury issues. For example, if some people demand government subsidies for small farmers and the government does nothing, there has been an allocation decision even though no visible policy action can be identified. A policy might also be implemented in a multiplicity of ways for different people, making it difficult to specify exactly what the policy output is. For example, the state might have a law that a person cannot kill another person, yet then the state does not mete out identical punishment to all those who kill.

Most analysts distinguish outputs from **outcomes**, which are *the impacts of the decisions taken and implemented by the political system.* Ultimately, it is the impacts of the political system's policy choices that really affect people's lives. The essential questions are: What difference did that policy choice (that value allocation) make? How does the implemented policy affect people's health, welfare, security, knowledge, and self-worth? How does it influence their life, liberty, and pursuit of happiness? Even more than in the analysis of outputs, it can be extremely difficult to identify with precision the overall outcomes of a policy and its effects on particular individuals and groups.

Feedback.   The final component in the systems approach is the "feedback loop." It is assumed that outputs will result in outcomes that alter aspects of the environment and thus will affect the next round of demands and supports reaching the political system. *Feedback* is the term applied to the dynamics through which information about the changing nature of the political system and its environment is monitored by the system. Political actors are supposed to monitor this information because changes in the environment, inputs, and the political system might require the political actors to revise the value allocations they have previously made. In Figure 5.1, feedback is drawn as a loop to emphasize the continuous interdependency among components in the system.

System Persistence

For Easton (1965), the underlying question is: How does a political system persist in a world of change? The political system is embedded within a complex and changing environment. Political decision makers must maintain a delicate balance of forces: the environments must be prevented from constraining or overwhelming the political system and must be exploited for the resources and opportunities they present; political actors must be sensitive and accurate in their perceptions of the effects of all other components in the system; demands must be managed so that they are not irreconcilable and do not overload the resources available; positive support must be nurtured and negative support discouraged or suppressed through some mix of value alloca-tions that maintains the loyalty or acquiescence of the citizens. In short, the conver-sion process must operate with political skill and political will.

If the political system's performance is poor, there can be many negative conditions: a reduction in the quality of citizens' lives; loss of support for those in positions of power and even for the institutions of the political regime; increasing problems from the inter-nal and external environment; a rise in disorder. At some point, if there is insufficient political skill, political will, or resources to respond effectively to these conditions, the persistence of the political system could be at risk. Many national political systems have, in Easton's terms, failed to persist in the last two decades, including Iraq in 2003, the Soviet Union, East Germany and Czechoslovakia in 1989, Sierra Leone in 1996–1998, and South Africa in 1994. Chapter 10 will explore more fully the issues of major politi-cal system change, severe political decay, failed states, and system transformation.

The Utility of the Political Systems Approach

Political scientists disagree about the utility of the political systems approach. Some think it is a flawed conceptual framework for political analysis. Crucial concepts are defined in several different ways, and clear operational measures have never been devel-oped for these concepts. Moreover, the theory linking the concepts is not specified with much greater precision than is indicated in Figure 5.1. And the approach has provided few predictions or hypotheses that are subject to rigorous empirical measurement and testing. Therefore critics dismiss the political systems approach as a nontheoretical and nonempirical abstraction that does little to advance a science of politics.

Few political scientists expect that the political systems approach will live up to the early hope that it might become the basis of a "real science" of politics (recall pages 14–21 in Chapter 1). Still, the approach has been influential as a *metaphor*—a concep-tual framework that describes how the political system operates and that suggests key variables and their linkages. It encourages the analyst to think of politics in terms of political actors, structures, and processes that constitute a system that is dynamic and adaptive as it constantly interacts with its environment(s). The political system is open, in the sense that the environment and inputs generate forces that affect the system and to which it must respond. And the political system is itself an active force, since its decisions and actions are aimed at modifying and shaping its environment and inputs by means of a constant flow of outputs. Many political scientists use this con-ceptualization of the political system, either consciously or subconsciously, when they attempt to explain the dynamic processes of politics.

THREE MAJOR CONCEPTS: A REPRISE

This chapter has focused on three major concepts that characterize large political entities. First, *state* is a concept that emphasizes the legal standing of these govern-mental entities, the necessary functions that they perform, and the organizational structures through which they take action. The discussion of three alternative views of the appropriate domain of state activities reveals the considerable range of differences in defining *res publica*, "things of the people."

Second, *nation* is a concept indicating a mental state characterized by a sense of shared identity among a set of people, distinguishing "us" from "them" in the sociopolitical world. Multinational states face particularly strong challenges from the instability that can result from different nation-based identities. The Indian subcontinent is an example of the widespread problem of disjunction between state and nation.

Third, the notion of the *political system* attempts to provide political scientists with the basic analytic concept for building a general theory of political entities. It specifies the crucial components in a dynamic and adaptive system whose essential function is the authoritative allocation of values for its society. The concept of political system is one abstraction that facilitates discussion and analysis of the major political units in the world. In Chapters 6 and 7, our discussion of these political units will become more concrete as we examine the actual political institutions and structures in contemporary political systems.

KEY CONCEPTS

authority	inputs	political system
conservative view of the state	liberal view of the state	political values
	multinational state	*res publica*
demands	nation	sovereignty
environment of the political system	nationalism	state
	nation-state	supports
ethnonationalism	outcomes	territorial integrity
indigenous peoples	outputs	

FOR FURTHER CONSIDERATION

1. Do you think there are circumstances in which a country's sovereignty should be violated? What is the most serious problem with your position on this question?

2. Do you identify with more than one "nation"? Is there any conflict between these identities? Under what types of circumstances might a person's multiple nationality identities produce serious internal conflicts?

3. To what extent is it possible to align states and nations in the contemporary world? Would doing this be desirable?

4. Develop a dialogue between person A, who believes that the authority of the state must be obeyed under virtually all conditions, and person B, who believes that the authority of the state can be disputed in any situation in which B substantially disagrees with the state's decision.

5. Describe several situations in which the decision-making capacity of the most powerful actors in the political system is almost completely constrained by factors in the extrasocietal or the intrasocietal environment.

FOR FURTHER READING

Barber, Benjamin R. (1995). *Jihad versus McWorld*. New York: Random House. An incisive analysis of current world trends, in which there is a simultaneous globalization of culture and economics on the one hand and the breakdown of peoples into distinct and hostile nationality groups on the other.

Barnett, Michael N. (1998). *Dialogues in Arab Politics: Negotiations in Regional Order.*. New York: Columbia University Press. Focusing especially on the views of key leaders of Middle Eastern Arab states and their attempts to create effective interstate relations, this study also offers insights about the struggle to define nation and state, given the complex identities based on Arabism, Islam, tribes, and countries.

Connor, Walker. (1994). *Ethnonationalism: The Quest for Understanding*. Princeton, NJ: Princeton University Press. A detailed analysis of the nature of and the imperatives driving the strong identity with nation as opposed to state, enriched by many illuminating examples.

Hutchinson, John, and Anthony Smith, Eds. (1995). *Nationalism*. New York: Oxford University Press. Hutchinson, John, and Anthony Smith, Eds. (1995). *Ethnicity*. New York: Oxford University Press. These two "Oxford Readers" offer an exceptional selection of short excerpts relevant to understanding each concept. Each book includes perspectives from a wide variety of social scientists, historians, social theorists, and others.

Kaufman, Stuart J. (2001). *Modern Hatreds: The Symbolic Politics of Ethnic War*. Ithaca, NY: Cornell University Press. The manipulation of ethnonationalist sentiments to serve the political goals of leaders is described in a set of intriguing case studies.

Kesey, Ken. (1962). *One Flew over the Cuckoo's Nest*. New York: New American Library. A funny, gripping novel (made into a film) that, at its core, considers the virtues and costs of defying institutional authority.

Krasner, Stephen D., Ed. (2001). *Problematic Sovereignty: Contested Rules and Political Possibilities*. New York: Columbia University Press. An exploration of how changes in the global system are shaping and being shaped by the role of sovereignty, which is now a far more "contested" (i.e., debated) concept.

Marx, Anthony W. (2003). *Faith in Nation: Exclusionary Origins of Nationalism*. New York: Oxford University Press. This study emphasizes the way in which nation-based identity is created mainly by excluding groups, especially based on religious differences, as an intentional strategy to establish nationalism and consolidate governmental power.

Paul, T. V., John Ikenberry, and John Hall, Eds. (2003). *The Nation-State in Question*. Princeton, NJ: Princeton University Press. These essays explore the continuing power and central importance of the state, despite the enormous forces undermining the state from both nation-based identities and globalization.

Philpott, Daniel. (2001). *Revolutions in Sovereignty: How Ideas Shaped Modern International Relations*. Princeton, NJ: Princeton University Press. In tracing the evolution of the concept of sovereignty, during both the early period of state formation and the postcolonial period, the author reveals how political forces have altered the meaning and nature of sovereignty in the relations among actors in the international system.

Rashid, Ahmed. (2002). *Jihad: The Rise of Militant Islam in Central Asia*. New Haven, CT: Yale University Press. Author of the widely discussed *Taliban* (2000, Yale University Press), Rashid offers a rich account of the rapid emergence of religious nationalism in the "stans" of Central Asia (e.g., Tajikistan, Kazakhstan). This dynamic has been driven particularly by poverty, corruption, and a reaction to the suppression of Islam under Soviet rule as well as the events in such neighbors as Afghanistan and Pakistan.

Snyder, Jack. (2000). *From Voting to Violence: Democratization and Nationalist Conflict.* New York: W. W. Norton. In exploring four different types of nationalism (civic, ethnic, revolutionary, and counterrevolutionary), the author examines the relationship between nationalism and other dynamic forces, especially democratization, political leadership, and political violence.

Sorensen, Georg. (2001). *Changes in Statehood: The Transformation of International Relations.* New York: Palgrave. A useful taxonomy of states (modern, postmodern, and postcolonial) is the basis for an exploration of how states attempt to achieve their security goals as they respond to pressures from external and internal forces.

Taras, Raymond, and Rajat Ganguly. (2008). *Understanding Ethnic Conflict.* 3rd ed. New York: Longman. In addition to a helpful conceptualization of the nature of ethnic conflict, there are revealing case studies of the problems of nation and state in such settings as Canada, Eritrea and Ethiopia, Sri Lanka, and the former Yugoslavia.

Thoreau, Henry David. (1849/1981). *Walden and Other Writings.* Ed. J. W. Krutch. New York: Bantam. These essays, especially "On Disobedience," constitute one of the most influential arguments in English for resisting authority.

ON THE WEB

http://www.atlapedia.com

Atlapedia provides diverse statistical information and various maps for each country as well as recent political history.

http://cwis.org

The Web page of the Center for World Indigenous Studies, an independent, nonprofit organization emphasizing the distribution of knowledge about the issues and status of indigenous peoples (nations not coterminous with states) and promoting greater autonomy of power to such peoples.

http://www.ipl.org.ar

The Internet Public Library provides links to numerous reference books, newspapers, and magazines about various countries.

http://www.cia.gov/cia/publications/factbook/index.html

The Web site of the U.S. Central Intelligence Agency includes the CIA World Factbook, a detailed and relatively up-to-date compilation of information about the political, economic, geographic, and demographic characteristics of every country.

http://www.un.org/esa/socdev/unpfii/

The official site of the United Nations Permanent Forum on Indigenous Issues.

http://www.state.gov/www/ind.html

Operated by the U.S. Department of State, this site has country reports and information on international organizations, human rights, and numerous other topics related to foreign policy and international relations.

http://www.countryreports.org

Country Reports provides comprehensive reports for most countries and also includes access to international news and reference maps.

http://www.un.org/Pubs/CyberSchoolBus/infonation/e_infonation.htm

Infonation, developed by the United Nations, provides the latest statistics for all UN member states.

http://www.economist.com/countries/

This site, produced by the publishers of the *Economist,* a respected British newsmagazine, contains detailed country profiles and links to international news resources.

CHAPTER 6

POLITICAL INSTITUTIONS I: STRUCTURES

I n framing a government which is to be administered by men over men, the great difficulty is this: you must first enable the government to control the governed; and in the next place oblige it to control itself.

—*James Madison*

Along with the other American Founding Fathers, James Madison grappled with many questions regarding how to design a set of political structures and institutional arrangements that would result in an effective government. What responsibilities should be reserved for the political executive? How large should the legislature be? How should its leaders be selected? How powerful should the administration be? What should the relationship be between the courts and the other branches of the government? Should subnational governments be under the control of the national government? Like the Founding Fathers, leaders in every country establish and later modify these structures and arrangements in the attempt to create a government that can achieve valued goals.

These issues are the central topics of Chapters 6, 7, and 8. Chapter 7 will examine forms of institutional arrangements regarding such matters as executive–legislative relationships, the party system, and citizen democracy. Chapter 8 will analyze the alternative frameworks through which the political system and the economic system are linked. Chapter 6 provides an analysis of the four major structures that are basic components of most contemporary political systems: *legislatures, executives, administrative systems,* and *judiciaries.*

Chapter 5 made the analytic distinction between certain *functions* of governance, such as policy making and policy adjudication, and the institutional *structures* that might be involved in performing those functions. This distinction between functions and structures can be confusing because there is a tendency to identify a certain function with a certain structure. For example, one might assume that the national legislature is the structure that dominates the policy-making function. However, the distinction between function and structure is useful because, minimally, structures other than the legislature might be significantly involved in policy making. For instance, in the United States, major policy-making activities are performed not only in the Congress but also by the chief executive (the president), the upper levels of the administration (the cabinet departments), and the judiciary (particularly the Supreme Court). In China, the national legislature has almost no real power over the policy-making function, which is carried out by the Communist Party and the political executive.

This chapter emphasizes the primary functions that are typically performed by each of the four major institutional structures. As you read, remember that each major structure can perform a variety of functions in a particular political system and can be composed of many different substructures. For these reasons, the discussions emphasize broad patterns and generalizations, although there are always exceptions and variations across the many national political systems.

THE LEGISLATURE

Most states (about 96 percent) have a **legislature** as one of their basic structures of governance (Derbyshire 2000). Among the names of legislatures (which can have one or two "houses") are the Senate and the House of Representatives (United States), the Senate and the Chamber of Deputies (Chile, Mexico, and Venezuela, among others), the Legislative Assembly (Costa Rica), the National People's Congress (China), the Majlis (Iran), the National Assembly (Egypt and Tanzania, among others), the

Lok Sabha and the Rajya Sabha (India), the Knesset (Israel), the House of Representatives and the House of Councillors (Japan), and the House of Commons and the House of Lords (United Kingdom).

Roles of the Legislature

Legislatures have always been *structures in which policy issues are discussed, assessed, and enacted.* Indeed, the roots of the name of the first modern legislature, the British Parliament, suggest this crucial function—the French word *parler* means "to talk." Most early legislatures were created to provide advice to the political executive, typically a monarch, and to represent politically relevant groups. Many legislatures have also been responsible for a second major function—enacting public policies. The roots of the word *legislature* are the Latin words *legis,* meaning "law," and *latio,* "bringing or proposing." Some of the earliest legislatures, such as the Roman Senate (c. 500 B.C.E.–100 C.E.), had great power to discuss and enact laws.

Most legislatures are supposed to have three broad roles: (1) enacting legislation, (2) representing the citizenry, and (3) overseeing the executive. In this discussion of these roles, be aware that it is difficult to generalize about the actual functions of the legislatures in all contemporary political systems for several reasons. First, these functions are often different from those specified in the state's normative rules, such as those in constitutions. Second, the functions of legislatures vary considerably from state to state. Third, they vary through time within a state. Fourth, even in one time period, the role of the legislature within a state can vary by issue and by the personalities of those involved.

Enactment of legislation.   It might seem obvious that legislatures draft, modify, and then ratify public policy in the form of legislation. In some political systems, many laws are initiated and written by the legislature. However, most contemporary legislatures do not play the dominant role in the policy-making function; rather, it has passed to the executive.

The essence of the legislature's power in the policy-making process is, in most political systems, a constitutional provision that a majority vote of the members of the legislature is required to authorize the passage of any law ("legislative enactment"). One of the most important responsibilities of the legislative majority is the power to enact laws that raise revenue and authorize its expenditure on public policies ("the power of the purse"). In some systems, legislatures have special committees that thoroughly assess and can amend all proposed legislation under the committees' jurisdiction.

Representation of the citizenry.   A second major role of the legislature is to represent, within the governing process, the opinions and interests of the citizenry. Most legislators are elected by some set of the eligible voters, and it is assumed that a key responsibility of a legislator is both to reflect and to serve the interests of those voters.

However, the concept of *representation* is not straightforward because there are at least four different views of the "interests" that a legislator might attempt to represent: (1) the group that is most dominant in the legislator's constituency, possibly a social class, religious group, or ethnic group; (2) the political party to which the legislator owes loyalty; (3) the country as a whole, whose broad interests might transcend those of any group or party; or (4) the legislator's own conscience, which provides moral and intellectual judgment about appropriate political behavior (a position made famous in a brilliant justification by British parliamentarian Edmund Burke in his 1774 "Address to the Electors of Bristol" [1790/1955: 219–222]).

Is it possible for a legislator to represent all four voices simultaneously? Most contemporary legislators do not feel it is necessary to do so, for these reasons:

- Some legislators hold office in undemocratic systems where their actions are dictated by the political leadership, and thus they act as little more than "rubber stamps." This position characterizes the behavior of a legislator in Cuba or Libya, for example.
- Some legislators are deeply committed to adhering to their political party's line, or they must obey the party to survive politically. This is usually the situation for members of the British House of Commons, for instance.
- Some legislators have such deep loyalty to a particular ideology or to certain societal norms that they rarely feel obligated to consider how they might represent other groups or policy positions. Certain members of committed religious parties, such as BJP in India or Shas in Israel, have this perspective, as do some members of extremely ideological parties.

In many political systems, legislators occasionally trade votes and compromise their positions on some policy issues to ensure greater support for the issues about which they care most deeply. But in only a few political systems are many legislators sufficiently unconstrained that they often try to balance all four competing views of representation. Some members of the U.S. Congress can be characterized in this way. They attempt to balance legitimate but competing interests and group pressures that reflect different views on policy against pressures from their party, their assessment of the national interest, and the guidance provided by their own conscience.

Oversight of the executive.   The third major role of legislators concerns their interactions with the executive. In general, the legislature is responsible for overseeing the political executive's actions. The legislators in some systems have substantial capacity to influence what the executive does. The legislature might have the constitutional right to select the executive, to authorize major policy decisions by the executive, and to approve the chief executive's selection of key appointments. In some systems, such as in India, the president is actually chosen by the legislature (although it is the prime minister, not the president, who is the most powerful executive officer).

Many legislatures have the right to approve the executive's selection of major appointments. The Israeli legislature must approve the cabinet as a whole. The U.S. Senate has the right to "advise and consent" on such presidential appointments as cabinet members or Supreme Court justices. The Senate's 1987 rejection of Judge Robert Bork, President Reagan's nominee for the Supreme Court, is an example of a legislature asserting its power over appointments. In parliamentary systems, the cabinet and prime minister hold office only if they have the confidence of the majority of the members of the legislature, and the cabinet's policies are enacted only if they are approved by the legislative majority (see Chapter 7).

A second area of legislative oversight involves the right of the legislature to scrutinize executive performance. In many political systems, there are regular procedures by which the legislature can question and even investigate whether the executive has acted properly in implementing public policies. At a minimum, the legislature serves as a discussion and debating chamber. Subjecting the political executive's plans and actions to public debate serves as a modest check on executive power. Many legislatures have a regular opportunity, during their legislative sessions, to question the specific plans and actions of particular members of the executive. In Britain, Italy, and South Africa, for example, ministers in the executive cabinet must appear before the legislature and respond to legislators' questions or criticisms about any actions taken by their department.

Most legislatures also have formal investigatory powers on a continuing or a case-by-case basis. The 2003 parliamentary investigation of Prime Minister Tony Blair (regarding the basis of his claims that Iraq had weapons of mass destruction and whether this justified Britain's military intervention) is an example of such oversight. In addition, some legislatures have followed Sweden's innovative idea, setting up an *ombudsman—an independent agency that investigates complaints* regarding the actions of the executive branch and its administrative units. If legislative questioning, committees, or the ombudsmen discover inappropriate behavior by the executive, they put significant political pressure on the executive to correct it. Of course, if the executive resists such pressure, the ultimate resolution of the dispute entails either legal adjudication or, in most cases, a power struggle between the executive and the legislature.

The most fundamental power of oversight held by some legislatures is their capacity to overturn the government. In a parliamentary system, the legislature can require or pressure the executive to resign from office by a vote of censure or of no confidence, or by defeating a major bill put forth by the executive (see Chapter 7). In Italy, for example, the legislature forced the executive to resign about once a year (on average, 1951–1994). Even in presidential systems, the legislature has the power to overturn the executive by means of the extraordinary process of impeachment, though this is rare. In 1992, Brazilian President Fernando Collor de Mello resigned after being impeached by the National Congress on corruption charges. In the United States, no president has been removed from office because of impeachment and conviction. However, in 1868 President Andrew Johnson was acquitted on the House of Representatives' impeachment charge by only one vote in the Senate, Richard Nixon avoided an impeachment trial in 1974 only by resigning, and Bill Clinton was acquitted by the Senate on two articles of impeachment brought by the House in 1998.

Legislative Structures

Number of houses.   There is one very visible difference in the structural arrangements of various legislatures—the number of houses (often called *chambers*). There are **unicameral (one-chamber) legislatures** in 63 percent of the countries that have legislatures (Derbyshire 2000). The presumed advantages of a unicameral system are that political responsibility is clearly located in one body and that risks of duplication or stalemate between parallel legislative bodies are eliminated. More than two-thirds of the countries with a strong central government (see Chapter 7 on these "unitary states") have unicameral legislatures, including Algeria, Bulgaria, China, Costa Rica, Denmark, Finland, Greece, Hungary, Israel, Kenya, New Zealand, South Korea, Sweden, Taiwan (see its legislature in action on pages 134–135) and Tanzania.

Since 1990, there has been a considerable increase in the proportion of countries that have *bicameral legislatures*—those with two separate chambers. Bicameral systems are especially prevalent in countries that are federations (states in which a central government and regional governments share power). Bicameral federations include Australia, Brazil, Canada, Germany, India, Mexico, and the United States. There are bicameral systems in 31 percent of the unitary states, including France, Great Britain, Italy, and Japan (Derbyshire 2000).

Given the apparent advantages of a unicameral system, what is the justification for two chambers? There are two main arguments. First, two legislative houses ensure more careful deliberation on issues and laws. Second, the two houses can be based on two different and desirable principles of representation. In about two-fifths of the bicameral legislatures (e.g., Germany and the United States), one house represents the regional governments and the other house more directly represents the numerical and geographic distribution of citizens. Some upper houses also represent functional groups in the society, as in the Republic of Ireland, where members are appointed as representatives of such groups as agriculture, labor, industry, culture, and public services.

Over time, some bicameral systems have evolved toward unicameral systems, especially in cases where the need for extensive checks and balances within the legislative branch has not seemed compelling, where representation in the "people's" chamber has seemed adequate, and where the problems of overlap and stalemate between the two chambers have increased. Some political systems, such as those of Sweden and Costa Rica, have constitutionally abolished one chamber. In others, such as Norway and Britain, the powers of one chamber have been so reduced that it can only delay, but cannot veto, the decisions of the more powerful chamber. In fact, the United States is now the only bicameral political system in which the regional upper chamber (the Senate) is more powerful than the popularly based lower chamber (the House of Representatives) (Derbyshire 2000). Does Nebraska have a good reason for being a U.S. state with a unicameral legislature while all of the other state legislatures are bicameral?

Size of legislatures.   The number of members in legislatures varies enormously, with some houses having fewer than ten members and others having thousands of members (e.g., the National People's Congress in China has 2,979 members). The single house or the lower house typically represents "the people," with legislators elected proportionately to the population. In general, there is a positive correlation between a country's population and its number of legislators (a ratio defined mathematically as a "cube root law" by Taagepera and Shugart 1989: 174–179). However, among the more populous countries, there is no obvious principle for determining the optimal numbers of legislators. In the U.S. House of Representatives, 435 members are elected, a ratio of 1 member per 692,000 people. Of the 165 countries with a legislature, only India has a higher ratio of population to members than does the United States. The United Kingdom, with less than one-third the U.S. population, has 659 elected members in its House of Commons, a ratio of 1 member per 92,000 citizens. More than half of all countries have a ratio of fewer than 65,000 people per representative (Derbyshire 2000).

Can you think of an appropriate criterion for deciding the number of members in a country's legislature? For example, are there reasons the upper house in the United States (the Senate) has two rather than three—or four or more—representatives from each state?

The Decline of Legislatures

Many observers claim that for more than 100 years, there has been a general decline in the power of legislatures relative to executives and bureaucracies. Is this true, and if so, why? Actually, it is very difficult to provide a definitive answer to these questions about relative power using the techniques of cross-national empirical analysis. In large part, this is because the precise measurement of power continues to be a puzzle for which political science has no clear solution (see Box 6.1).

Given the difficulty of assessing political power with precision, is it possible to provide *any* answer to the question of measuring the decline of legislative power? Developing an empirical test that could do so is challenging. It requires measuring and comparing the power not only of the legislature but also of the executive and the bureaucracy at several points in time and across several (many?) countries. Since no studies have provided a rigorous analysis of this issue, we might begin with a more modest question: Is there evidence that contemporary legislatures display significant political weaknesses?

A few types of circumstantial evidence do suggest legislative weakness. To begin with, the legislature is essentially a rubber stamp for the actions of a powerful political executive in about one-sixth of contemporary political systems. Among other political systems, several factors point to the relative weakness of legislatures.

First, most legislatures do not provide a coherent structure within which power can be concentrated and exercised effectively. Many legislatures have relatively slow and cumbersome procedures for the lawmaking function, especially where there are regular legislative committees that amend legislation. This complexity in the legislative process is even more evident in bicameral systems, since there is often disagreement between the two chambers.

Second, most legislatures react to policy initiatives from the executive more than they create policy. The legislatures almost never have the level of support services that is available to the executive. Their budgets, facilities, staff sizes, and even the legislators' own salaries are significantly lower than those of top members of the executive and administrative structures. Similarly, the technical expertise and knowledge resources available to legislatures are far less than those of the executive and administrative structures, a major liability when legislators attempt to deal with the complex subjects facing governments in modern societies.

Some analysts have argued that a third, more social-psychological weakness of legislatures exists: most citizens desire clear, dynamic, and singular political leadership, but legislatures are typically composed of many people who most citizens feel are either indistinguishable or offer too many different identities. In the United States, for example, it is usually possible to answer this question: What does the president think about issue *Y*? But how does one answer the corresponding question: What

BOX 6.1

The Problem of Defining Power

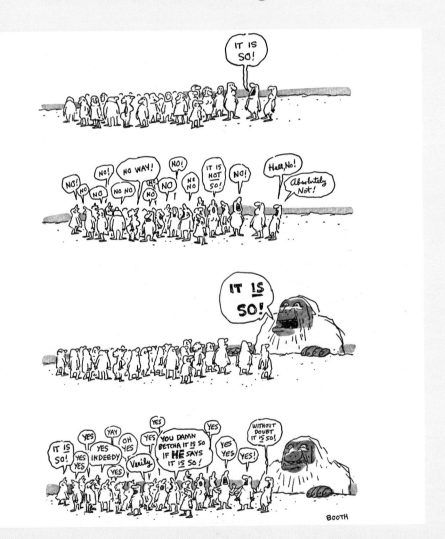

Few discussions about politics can occur without direct or indirect reference to power. There is general agreement that **power** *is exercised when A (one actor) induces B (another actor) to behave in a manner in which B would not otherwise behave.* This emphasizes a causal relationship between what A wants and what B does. The two actors can be two individuals or groups or even countries.

BOX 6.1 *(Continued)*

The key question, of course, is: How does A exercise this power over B? Many political scientists and other social scientists have grappled with this question. (For different views, see Bachrach and Baratz 1962; Boulding 1989; Dahl and Stinebrickner 2003; Lukes 2005; and Wrong 1995.) Kenneth Boulding (1993) suggests that there are three major varieties of power:

1. *Force* (coercive power). Here, A indicates to B that unless B does what A wants, A will cause something to occur that B does not want. The concept of "power politics" is usually understood as a situation involving force—typically based on coercion or at least the credible threat of coercion by A. A might inflict direct bodily harm on B using an instrument of force (e.g., guns, bombs, torture), or A might impose undesirable conditions on B (e.g., imprisonment, discriminatory treatment). Of course, B might not yield to A's threat of force, responding, for example, with a counterthreat. Also, B might resist A's actual use of force with counterforce, resulting in a fight.

2. *Exchange* (economic power). A can have economic resources that alter B's behavior. This exercise of economic power could be coercive, in the sense that A might prevent B from enjoying certain economic benefits. For example, A might refuse to sell or give to B an important resource that B needs (e.g., oil, economic aid) unless B meets A's demands. Alternatively, A and B might engage in a more cooperative arrangement, where A promises a resource to B (e.g., a trade agreement, a bribe) if B does what A desires.

3. *Mutuality* (integrative power). Power can also be exercised if B perceives a shared commonality with A. In this case, B conforms to A's demand because B feels a bond of affection or loyalty to A. For example, B might decide that A has legitimacy—that B should obey A because A is worthy of exercising authority (recall Box 5.3). Thus B feels a moral or social obligation to yield to A. Integrative power is the least coercive and most subtle form of power exercise; it is probably most widespread in the world of political relationships. It is a power relationship because it causes B to do something that A wants but that B would not otherwise do.

Notice that these three forms of power cover an enormous range of processes. Many situations involve a complex mix of these dynamic processes, and it is hard to specify which particular type of power has actually caused the observed behavior. These kinds of conceptual and empirical problems have led most political scientists to admit, often with embarrassment, that operationalizing and measuring one of the central concepts in political science remain elusive. However, because most people share a broad common understanding of the idea of power, it is reasonable to continue to refer to it. And it is worthwhile to attempt to analyze empirical questions regarding the relative power of legislatures, executives, and other political actors.

does the legislature think about issue *Y*? There are not only two chambers and two parties but also a great diversity of different opinions among the individuals and factions within the legislature. In a sense, even though legislatures usually have spokespersons and leaders, no one can truly speak for the legislature. One might even conclude that the legislature in a democratic society tends to fulfill one of its roles *too* well: its members too accurately represent the diversity of political beliefs among the society's population, and thus they speak with many voices.

Although the power of legislatures has not kept pace with that of other institutions, especially the executive and the administration, not all legislatures are impotent or dying institutions. Certain national legislatures remain extremely powerful political structures, such as those in Italy, Japan, Sweden, and the United States. In most other relatively democratic political systems, legislatures have significant impacts on the authoritative allocation of values through their roles in enacting legislation, in representation, and in oversight. And in virtually all societies that have a legislature, its members can exercise political power in many subtle ways. At the least, legislative members have dramatically more political power than most other citizens.

EXECUTIVES

The historical evidence indicates that as long as there have been political systems, there have been individuals or small groups who assume top leadership roles. Such leaders have the responsibility to formulate and especially to implement public policy, and they can be broadly called the *executive structure*. The word *executive* comes from the Latin *ex sequi*, meaning "to follow out" or "to carry out." Thus the particular role of the executive is *to carry out the political system's policies, laws, or directives*.

One might be tempted to generalize that a few individuals emerge as the leadership cadre in *every* political order. But there are some historical counterexamples, especially from Africa and Asia, of societies that are *acephalous*—that is, "without a head." In such systems, many people in the community share power somewhat equally as a collective leadership. Nonetheless, in most systems, a few people do assume the positions of executive power.

At the apex of the executive structure, there is usually an actor who can be called the chief executive. In a national political system, this might be a single person with a title such as president, prime minister, chief, premier, supreme leader, or queen. Or the top executive leader can be a role filled by two or more people. In this case, there might be a president and a prime minister (as in the French example described in Box 7.3) or a group exercising shared executive leadership (e.g., a junta).

A broader definition of the executive includes not only the chief executive but also the entire administrative system. Such a definition derives from the notion that the policy implementation function (the "execution" of policy) is shared by the chief executive and the administration. The top executive group cannot survive without the continuing support of an extensive system of people who interpret, administer, and enforce its policy directives. However, we examine the chief executive and the administration in separate sections of this chapter so that we can differentiate analytically among the major structures in most political systems.

Roles of Executives

Leadership roles. In the contemporary political world, political leadership is almost always identified with chief executives. The leadership role entails taking the initiative in formulating, articulating, and implementing goals of the political system. The effective chief executive becomes the spokesperson for the aspirations of the people, attempts to galvanize the people's support for these goals, and develops strategies that facilitate their accomplishment.

To a large extent, the chief executive takes the initiative in policy formation. Executive policy leadership is especially crucial during times of crisis because the executive structure has the potential for a level of coherence and unanimity of action that is often lacking in the legislature. Moreover, in most political systems, the chief executive has the capacity to veto, either directly or indirectly, the legislation that the legislature initiates. Increasingly, even the drafting of legislation is a function dominated by the executive, since many major bills require the expertise and policy direction of the chief executive and its staff.

Symbolic and ceremonial roles. The actors in the executive role usually function as the unifying symbol of the entire society, becoming the ultimate mother/father figures for the people. This is especially true when the chief executive has a strong image, like such leaders as Libya's Muammar Qaddafi and King Mswati III in Swaziland (see Box 9.1). The executive's presence becomes central to many of the society's rituals and ceremonies, whether it is the Japanese emperor's wedding, the Kenyan president's official send-off of the national team to the Olympic Games, or the British queen's Christmas Day televised message to her subjects.

Supervision of the administration. In virtually all contemporary political systems, the executive has primary responsibility for implementing the policies and laws of the political order. At the apex of this administrative hierarchy, which might include millions of public employees in the state's departments, bureaus, and agencies, is the top group of the executive structure. Most systems have an executive cabinet, with each member directly and personally responsible for some major area of administration. Given the scale and complexity of the activities in each area, these top executive actors can neither know nor control all of the actions that occur within their domain. Nonetheless, they are supposed to set the broad guidelines for policy implementation, and in many political systems, they are accountable for any major failures that occur. In parliamentary systems, for example, the minister of a department will usually resign if there is a serious shortcoming or blunder in her area of responsibility.

Supervision of the military and foreign affairs. Given the state's monopoly of the legitimate use of force, the top political executive usually has direct control over the military (including internal security forces). In such cases, the top executive is the commander in chief of the entire military system of the state, including personnel and other resources (aircraft, nuclear weapons, military intelligence, and so on). The chief executive must set policy and supervise the organization and utilization of the state's military capabilities, a task that can have the most serious consequences for the security and well-being of the society.

Associated with control of the military is the executive's responsibility for foreign affairs—the state's relations with other states. As Chapter 12 will describe more fully, the relations between states involve complex patterns of cooperation and conflict, as each state attempts to accomplish its own goals in the international environment. The chief executive (or the chief executive's delegates) represents the state in its dealings with other countries. Particular significance is often attached to situations where the chief executives of different states meet directly, as in a state visit or a "summit conference." In fact, such meetings among heads of state typically are symbolic gestures of cooperation or occasions for ratifying agreements that have been reached by the chief executives' representatives. But the concentration of the states' political power in the chief executives is so great that such meetings can provide opportunities for major breakthroughs in the relations between the states.

Structural Arrangements

Fused versus dual executive.   Many political systems have a **dual executive**. One actor, the ***head of state***, *performs the more ceremonial aspects of top leadership*, while another actor, the ***head of government***, *is responsible for the more political aspects*. The main advantage of the dual executive is that citizens can be angry or hostile toward the head of government while still remaining loyal to the nation and to the political system through their affection and support for the more ceremonial head of state.

Constitutional monarchies are obvious examples of political systems with a dual executive. In these systems there is a ruling king or queen (e.g., Queen Elizabeth II in Britain, Queen Margrethe II in Denmark, or Emperor Akihito in Japan) and also a prime minister or other head of government. The monarch has little or no power to make authoritative value allocations but serves mainly symbolic or ceremonial functions, as an embodiment of the nation and the people. Monarchs with limited powers also operate in some less democratic countries, such as King Norodom Sihamoni in Cambodia. Some countries have attempted to create a dual executive without a monarch, establishing a second executive office as head of state (such as the presidency in Germany, India, and Ireland) that is typically insulated from the daily struggles of politics and thus can be a symbol of national unity. In countries where the culture is deeply grounded in a religious belief system, the head of the religion can function like a head of state, as in Iran, where the president and legislature lead the political system, but the religious leader, Ayatollah Ali Khamenei (the "Leader of the Islamic Republic and of the Nation"), also has formidable power over aspects of political life.

Most political systems have a ***fused executive***. Here *a single actor fulfills both the ceremonial roles associated with the head of state and the political functions associated with the head of the government*. In such cases, it can be difficult or impossible to distinguish (dis)loyalty to a partisan political leader from (dis)loyalty to the nation. Clever chief executives use this fusion of roles to their advantage, "wrapping themselves in the flag." Such executives criticize or even punish their opponents by claiming that they are traitors to the political society (even though the opponents are usually criticizing only the political actions of the leader). For example, Zimbabwe's President Robert Mugabe used this tactic very effectively to intimidate and eliminate his rivals.

▶ **The British Parliament opens yearly with Queen Elizabeth II, the head of state, delivering a speech written by the prime minister, the head of government. The speech outlines the legislation that the prime minister's government will introduce. The queen comes to the House of Lords, whose members surround the Law Lords (the highest judiciary group, wearing white wigs). By tradition, the prime minister and the members of the now-powerful House of Commons symbolically "demand" entry into the chamber and stand in the back of the House (they are not visible in the photo).**

Some political systems have two actors who perform parts of the chief executive role but are not really dual executives in the sense described in the preceding paragraphs. For example, there are countries (e.g., France and Russia) where both a prime minister and a president perform essentially political functions, although one usually has a stronger claim to the head-of-state role (see Box 7.3). Some political systems have a political executive but also have a monarch who, in addition to serving as head of state, is a powerful political actor. Bhutan, Kuwait, Morocco, and Swaziland are examples where the monarch is the head of state and also has greater political power than the prime minister.

The executive.   While the term *chief executive* refers to the one person or small group at the apex of the executive structure, **executive** is a broader term, including *all the people and organizational machinery that are below the chief executive in the executive structure.* Thus the executive encompasses upper- and middle-level decision makers in all the departments, agencies, and other administrative units that are in the chief executive's chain of command. As was noted earlier, a definition of the executive far broader than the one in this book might also include the entire administrative system.

In theory, and usually in practice, this is a hierarchical system of political control, in the sense that the actors in the executive structure are supposed to follow the directives of the chief executive. But the chief executive's power over the rest of the executive is rarely absolute. There are many reasons the chief executive's directives might not be carried out:

- Units within the executive might be too disorganized to act effectively.
- The executive might lack the resources to carry out policies in the manner desired by the chief executive.
- Some units might be more involved in competing against other units than in coordinating their actions to meet the chief executive's policies.
- Units might misunderstand, resist, or defy the chief executive.

Can you think of other reasons?

The Age of the Executive?

Although chief executives have nearly always been evident, and usually ascendant, in political systems, some analysts call the twentieth century the "age of the executive." This label reflects the apparent concentration of power in executives and the relative decline of legislatures' powers. What might account for this concentration of power? To some extent, this is a chicken-and-egg issue: The reduced capacity of many legislatures to take coherent and decisive state action is linked to the emergence of coherent and decisive executives.

In comparison with legislatures, the executive structure tends to be more streamlined and less prone to stalemate and inaction. Also, the executive, centered in a single person or small group, can offer a unified focus for a mass public that either desires simplicity and clarity in an age of great complexity or wants a form of heroic leadership.

The chief executive typically speaks with one voice and, when effective, can assure the people that political power will be exercised with certainty and efficiency to respond to the pressures and demands in the society and in the international environment. Even if a chief executive cannot deliver, she can at least promise decisive leadership in a manner that no other political structure can.

Can you think of any conditions under which a state might be dominated by a structure *other* than the political executive?

THE ADMINISTRATION

While the chief executive is the top manager of the policy implementation function, the administration consists of the thousands or even millions of public employees who do the ongoing business of interpreting and implementing the policies enacted by the state. These employees are divided into organizational units called by such names as departments, ministries, agencies, and bureaus. The state's military and police forces are often a particularly crucial component of the administration.

The administration is the machinery of government without which the political system could barely function. The units perform such important activities as maintaining order, collecting revenues, keeping records, providing public goods and services (e.g., roads, education, solid-waste disposal, health care, monetary aid for the needy), and regulating or controlling the factors of production (e.g., production of steel, provision of transportation, growth and distribution of food).

Bureaucracy as One Form of Administration

In most discussions, administration and bureaucracy are synonymous concepts, but in the attempt to clarify our language of political analysis, it is helpful to distinguish them. In this view, **administration** is the general term used to describe *the machinery and the processes through which rules and policies are applied and implemented.* **Bureaucracy** is a particular structure and set of processes through which the administration can operate. Its definitive description is by Max Weber, the great German sociologist we first encountered in Chapter 1. Structurally, bureaucracy is characterized by *hierarchical organization and specialization by means of an elaborate division of labor.* Weber also defined the concept of bureaucracy by a key process: its members (1) apply specific rules of action to each case; therefore, the resulting treatment of each case is (2) rational, (3) nondiscretionary, (4) predictable, and (5) impersonal (Weber 1958a: 196–244).

Some readers may have regularly been treated by public administrators in ways that are consistent with these features because some countries have deeply incorporated this bureaucratic style. But there are also many contemporary political systems, and even more examples historically, where public administrators often treat people unpredictably and personally. Situations such as that in the imaginary country of Delta (see Box 6.2) are widespread. Personal contacts and bribes (in various societies called *chai, baksheesh, mordida,* or *dash*) are often essential for success in dealing with the administration. Indeed, in some societies, people view a style of administration like

BOX 6.2

"Dealing" with the Administration in Gamma and Delta

An imaginary example might help illustrate the contrast between a classic bureaucracy and an administrative system that does not meet Max Weber's criteria. Two citizens, A and B, each intend to undertake an identical activity: to open and operate a small shop selling tea and pastries in the market district.

In the country of Gamma, both Citizen A and Citizen B apply to the Ministry of Business, where an employee requires each to complete a standard form and to pay a fixed application fee. An inspector from the Ministry of Health examines the premises to ensure that all health and sanitation regulations are met. When rat droppings are found in both premises, both A and B are obliged to hire an extermination service. Each receives the health certificate only after pest eradication and a second inspection. Both A and B open their shops.

In the country of Delta, Citizens A and B make the same application. However, A is a member of the dominant ethnic group and B is not. When A applies to the Ministry of Business, she is given a form to complete by the clerk, also a member of her ethnic group, and the form is approved. When B applies, she is told that the maximum number of permits for the district has already been issued. After lengthy discussion, B telephones her cousin, who is an important politician in the local government. B's cousin contacts the undersecretary in Delta's Ministry of Business on behalf of B, and the application form is now provided and permission is granted. When the inspector from the Ministry of Health examines A's shop, she finds rat droppings. The inspector says she will not issue the certificate, and so A offers the inspector a substantial amount of money if she will ignore the problem. The inspector takes the money and then issues the certificate. When the same inspector goes to B's shop, she again claims to find evidence of rats. When the inspector can show B no evidence, B demands her certificate. The inspector shrugs, provides the name of the only extermination service she "guarantees," refuses to issue the certificate to open the shop, and leaves.

The contrast between the two imaginary cases is clear. The administrators in Gamma behave in accordance with the bureaucratic ideal. Both A and B receive fair and identical treatment, and all rules of procedure are scrupulously followed. In Delta, however, the treatment of A and B is very different. A manages to succeed because she is a member of the favored ethnic group and she is willing to bribe an inspector. Citizen B overcomes the hurdle of her unfavored ethnicity because she has an influential contact, but she fails to open her shop because she is not willing to offer the inspector a bribe or hire the extermination service that would give the inspector a kickback.

that in Delta as normal and even appropriate because they assume individual treatment and personal favors are preferable to rigid application of the rules.

Is there a reasonable argument against a Weberian-style bureaucracy? In complex societies, calling an organization "bureaucratic" is not usually intended to be a compliment. Some criticisms of bureaucracy are really directed at all large administrative structures that exercise increasing control over people's lives and that seem too large and powerful. But at its heart, the "bureaucracy" label has come to connote a system that is too inflexible and impersonal. The application of rules is so rigid that extenuating circumstances tend to be overlooked, and every individual is treated as merely a number. Bureaucrats themselves are seen to be relatively free of political accountability because they are protected by professional norms and hiring and firing rules that give them quasi-permanent tenure and insulate them from political pressure.

Despite criticisms of its occasional excesses in practice, most people in contemporary political systems conclude that the Weberian bureaucracy is the best administrative form because they prefer an administrative system that is overly rigid and impersonal to one that is based on corruption and personal favoritism. Many countries claim to be operating according to the ideals of Weberian bureaucracy, but there are enormous differences in the extent to which such ideals are consistently applied, especially in environments where they are contrary to traditional practice.

Administrative Functions and Power

The scale of activity of a state's administrative structure depends on that political system's definition of *res publica* (recall page 116). In political systems that penetrate a larger sphere of the society and economy, there is a corresponding need for more extensive administrative structures, since the administration is the basic apparatus through which the state interprets, implements, and monitors its policies. The administrative structures in contemporary political systems perform, more or less extensively, five broad functions:

1. *Provision of public goods and services.* The essential work of the administrative structure is the implementation of policy. Administrators must constantly interpret and apply public policies that provide public goods and services to individuals and groups.

2. *Regulation and enforcement of public policies.* Administrators are also responsible for interpreting and applying many public policies that set guidelines for the behavior of individuals or groups. These can vary greatly, from monitoring collusion among corporations to enforcing traffic laws to protecting the civil rights of ethnic minorities.

3. *Provision of knowledge.* Many administrators develop great expertise within their specialized areas. This knowledge can be of enormous utility for virtually every decision and action undertaken in that area by the political system.

4. *Information management.* Administrators are responsible for the collection, storage, and analysis of huge amounts of information about the people and processes in the society. This information provides a crucial database—for recording activities and conditions in the society, for measuring the nature and impact of public

policies, and for informing many ongoing decisions and actions related to the allocation of public values.

5. *Extraction of resources*. In roles such as collector of revenues from citizens and businesses or operator of state-owned companies producing goods and services, the administrative structure is in charge of many tasks that generate resources for the political system.

This brief list of functions suggests the enormous breadth and depth of the administrative structure and its activities. Some observers argue that in the complex, extensive, and knowledge-based political systems of the early twenty-first century, the power of the bureaucracy is supreme. Although the administrators are, in theory, "servants" of their political masters and clients, it might be that, in reality, these roles are reversed. Bureaucrats have such unmatched knowledge and experience in their specialized domains that generalist politicians rarely have sufficient expertise to question the bureaucrats' information, recommendations, or actions (Weber 1958a). Also, their power to grant or withhold benefits provides them with considerable leverage over clients. Career administrators have quasi-permanent tenure, while politicians and clients come and go. The modern bureaucracy has such wide-ranging power and competence that it is typically credited with maintaining political systems when executives and legislatures are ineffective, as in the Third and Fourth Republics in France and in many modernizing states in Africa and Asia. Max Weber himself might have had the last word when he observed that "in the modern state, the actual ruler is necessarily and unavoidably the bureaucracy" (1958a: 211).

THE JUDICIARY

In a Hobbesian state of nature (see Chapter 2), disputes among people would normally be resolved by force or the threat of force. In such a setting, "might makes right." Thus a primary reason for the social contract is to authorize the state to intervene in the potential and actual disputes among individuals and groups by creating and enforcing rules regarding proper forms of interaction. Every society holds that those who violate its rules and laws (i.e., its policies) must be sanctioned. The specific rules in a given society are born out of its unique culture, history, and politics; however, a commonality within all legal systems is that there are usually ambiguities regarding the rules:

What does the rule mean?

Has a rule been violated?

Who are the "guilty" actors?

How serious is the offense?

What sanctions are appropriate?

These kinds of ambiguities are resolved through the adjudication function in every political system. Many political systems have established judicial structures whose primary role is, or at least appears to be, adjudication.

Aspects of Adjudication

The **adjudication** function attempts to *interpret and apply the relevant rules or laws to a given situation.* When the issue involves *civil law*—the rules regarding relations between private actors (individuals or groups)—the main objective of adjudication is to *settle the dispute.* Examples of such rules include divorce, contracts, and personal liability litigation.

When an individual or group behaves in a manner interpreted as an offense against the social order, adjudication can be an important mechanism of *social control.* This is the area of *criminal law*, and examples of offenses are murder, substance abuse, theft, bribery, extortion, and environmental pollution. The state represents the public interest and protects the social contract, ensuring that the relations among actors are within the boundaries of "acceptable social behavior." Just as the definition and scope of *res publica* differ greatly across political systems, the definition of acceptable social behavior varies dramatically. In some political systems, social control entails little more than regulation of the conditions under which people can do physical and economic violence to one another. In contrast, other political systems view mere public criticism of the political order or its leaders as a violation of acceptable social behavior punishable by imprisonment or death.

In some instances, adjudication can center on *arbitration regarding the behavior of the political system itself.* This is especially evident in cases involving *constitutional, administrative, or statutory law*—the rules concerning the rights and actions of the political system. The main issues for adjudication involve questions about the legitimate domain of action by a governmental actor in its relations with other governmental units or private actors. Such a dispute might concern a highly technical disagreement over the implementation of a specific policy (e.g., is a person with vision correctable to 20/400 qualified to receive state-subsidized services for the "visually impaired"?), or it might raise fundamental constitutional questions about the distribution of political power (e.g., can the chief executive order the military into a violent confrontation with another country if the majority of the legislature opposes the action?).

Judicial Structures

Most, but not all, political systems have specialized structures of the **judiciary**—*the system of courts and personnel that determines whether the rules of the society have been transgressed and, if so, whether sanctions ought to be imposed on the transgressor.* (Some broad definitions of judicial structures even include agencies of law enforcement, such as police and security forces, as well as agencies that apply sanctions against rule breakers, such as jails and prisons, although in this book, these are considered administrative structures.)

In the United States, the adjudication function is closely linked with explicit judicial structures. The United States has one of the world's most complex judicial structures, with its Supreme Court and extensive system of federal, state, and local courts, including judges, prosecuting attorneys, defense attorneys for the indigent, court clerks, and so on.

While there are significant cross-national variations, most political systems have a hierarchical system of judicial structures, with appeal processes possible from lower- to

*"Do you ever have one of those days when every-
thing seems unconstitutional?"*

higher-level courts. Most judicial systems also have subsystems that are responsible for
different aspects of adjudication. For example, the French judicial structure separates the
criminal and civil law system from a second system that handles administrative law. In
Ukraine, one major system handles criminal and civil law, and a second major system is
composed of special prosecutors who monitor actions in all types of cases and who can
challenge, retry, or even withdraw cases from the regular courts. In Great Britain, one
major judicial system is responsible for criminal law and a second handles civil law.

Among the contemporary countries that do not have judicial structures as part
of the government are the Islamic countries that adhere to sharia law. Sharia is the
divine law, detailed in the Koran and further elaborated in the *hadith*, the teachings
of Muhammad. It is sharia, not the laws of humans, that is the dominant judicial framework in such countries as Iran, Saudi Arabia, and Sudan. The Koran prescribes all
aspects of social, spiritual, and moral life. As part of that prescription, the sections on
law provide the details of what in Western jurisprudence includes criminal law, civil
law, and administrative law. Sharia is strictly applied by religious courts, and even the
punishments for violations of the law are specified in the Koran.

The constitutions of many states include provisions meant to create an "independent" judiciary. The notion that a judicial system can be independent does not mean
that the judiciary is *apolitical*. The legal system and the set of judicial structures in *every*
political system are political. Most importantly, adjudication, by its very nature, entails
crucial decisions about the allocation of values and meanings for a society. Also, the
judicial officials in most systems are either appointed by those with political power or
are elected in a political process by the voters.

The judiciary in some political systems does have the capacity to display independence. By exercising the power of **judicial review**, *judicial structures can reinterpret or even revoke the policy decisions of the other political structures.* About one in ten states has a strong system of judicial review, including Canada, Colombia, Germany, India, Israel, Italy, Mexico, Norway, Switzerland, and the United States. Recent research has revealed that judicial structures in many advanced democracies have exercised increasing power to redefine and overturn the actions of the other branches (Koopmans 2003: ch. 4; Stone Sweet 2000, 2004). The Debate in 6 questions whether such judicial review is actually consistent with democratic premises.

However, even when judicial structures do strive to maintain some political independence, they still might respond to external pressure. First, the judiciaries in nearly

THE DEBATE IN 6

Is Judicial Review Democratic?

In essence, judicial review means that an independent judiciary has the right to assess the constitutional legitimacy of any legislation enacted by the legislature or any policy action implemented by the executive. The judiciary can uphold the authority of the government regarding the policy, or it can rule that the government's action violates fundamental laws, especially the constitution. Judicial review was one of the founding principles of the U.S. Constitution, as a key method of ensuring there was a strong countervailing power that prevented the legislature and executive from overstepping their authority. Currently, more than half the world's democratic countries have some form of broad and significant judicial review. However, some critics argue that essential features of judicial review are actually inconsistent with the basic values and principles of a democratic society. Is judicial review democratic?

Judicial Review Is Undemocratic
- The hallmark of democracy is that those who have great power over the laws of the society should have a direct mandate from the people by means of election. Yet in most countries, the judges who exercise the extraordinary power of judicial review are not elected by the people. Thus Alexander Bickel, a distinguished professor at Yale Law School, argues that judicial review is undemocratic because "it thwarts the will of representatives of the actual people of the here and now; it exercises control, not on behalf of the prevailing majority, but against it."
- The judges making these decisions cannot be held accountable, since they cannot be removed from office except in extraordinary circumstances (i.e., impeachment) and they typically serve for life. Thus the people have almost no capacity to replace the judges who make fundamentally important decisions about the restraints on the rulers or the rights of the ruled, a hallmark element of democracy (see Chapter 7). Indeed, it is arguable whether the people have any significant influence on what cases the judges consider or any direct input into the decisions that the judges make.
- Crucial interpretations and decisions can hinge on a bare majority vote by a tiny number of

The Debate in 6 *(Continued)*

people. The highest constitutional court in most countries makes decisions by simple majority, with fewer than 15 judges. In the United States, for example, a fundamentally important judicial ruling can be made by only five members of the Supreme Court, even when four of their colleagues on the Court totally disagree with them.

- The grounds for a decision in cases of judicial review can be highly subjective. There can be deep disagreements among the judges about how the basic legal documents of the society should be interpreted and applied to specific cases.

- In short, crucial rulings about actions by the government are made when a handful of unelected and unaccountable individuals use their own subjective reasoning to offer a contested interpretation of documents and statutes that can be generations old. And "the people," the elected chief executive, and the elected national legislature have no recourse but to accept this judgment (Waldron 2006). What could be more undemocratic in a democratic society?

Judicial Review Supports Democratic Processes

- Virtually all countries are representative democracies, not direct democracies. Supreme power rests with the citizens, who then exercise that power to elect officials to serve them. Those officials, in turn, appoint many others to play important roles in governance. Even in countries where top judicial officials are appointed, their authority is derived directly from the elected officials, whose power is based on popular consent. Thus empowering appointed judges is fully consistent with democratic principles.

- Once appointed, high court judges are independent of those in other powerful roles in the political system. Unlike most other political actors in a democracy, judges engaged in judicial review do not need to curry favor in order to raise money for reelection and they have no need to compromise their positions in order to make deals with others in the political system. Thus they are able to make reasoned interpretations of the fundamental laws of the land, as well as rule on specific actions by the current legislative and executive branches, based solely on their constitutional merits.

- A just democracy must be guided not only by majority rule but also by a commitment to protect the rights of the individual and minorities against a "tyranny of the majority." An independent judicial leadership, including judicial review, is a key element in such protection. In making decisions on constitutional rights of the weak as well as the strong, these judges are not pressured or constrained by the current whims of the electoral majority, since they do not need to stand for reelection.

- In Federalist 78, Alexander Hamilton explains that judicial power does not "by any means suppose a superiority of the judicial to the legislative power. It only supposes that the power of the people is superior to both; and that where the will of the legislature, declared in its statutes, stands in opposition to that of the people, declared in the Constitution, the judges ought to be governed by the latter rather than the former. They ought to regulate their decisions by the fundamental laws."

- In most democracies, the judges who are engaged in judicial review are highly qualified legal experts. They generally have years of experience in the legal system and their judicial decisions are bound by the statutes as well as precedents. While they might occasionally disagree on the interpretation of a constitutional issue, most of their decisions are by clear and unambiguous majorities and reflect shared analyses.

Is Judicial Review Democratic or Not

all contemporary states are ultimately dependent on other political structures, especially the executive and the administration, to enforce their decisions. Secondly, when judicial officials displease the dominant power group, they can often be ignored, replaced, or even eliminated. The conflict between President Franklin D. Roosevelt and the U.S. Supreme Court in the 1930s (see Box 6.3) is a notable example of a process that occurs continually in a subtler manner—the impact of external political power on judicial processes and decisions. A far less subtle example is Argentina during the 1970s, when more than 150 high-level judges "disappeared," and it is speculated that the Argentine government ordered their executions.

Third, since the people in top judicial positions have usually been socialized by those in the culture's dominant socioeconomic groups, they are likely to share the values of those groups when they make judgments. Thus one key consideration regarding an *independent* judiciary is assessing the extent to which the judicial structures make decisions and take actions that are *not* substantially influenced by their common political orientations with and dependence on other powerful social, economic, and political structures in the society. While the rituals of the judicial structures offer the appearance of protecting impartial "justice," the reality is that the judicial structures in many, perhaps most, countries serve the political and economic elite and a truly independent judiciary is a rarity.

CONCLUDING OBSERVATIONS

Traditional political science assumed that a detailed description of political structures is the best means to explain how politics works. But empirical research revealed considerable diversity in the roles of particular political structures. Key political functions might occur in a wide variety of structures inside and outside of the formal governmental arrangements. In response, there was a period during which political structures were viewed as so malleable that they were treated as secondary elements, merely forming one of the contexts where various political, economic, and social groups manuever as they interact to allocate values for the society. More recently, many scholars have reemphasized the importance of institutional arrangements. For these "new institutionalists," the particular configuration of political structures can powerfully shape political actions and outcomes (March 2006). For the "neostatists," the structures of the state—its institutional arrangements, the actors who have major roles in its institutions, and its policy activities—are autonomous and have fundamental impacts on political, economic, and social life (Evans 1997; Evans, Rueschmeyer, and Skocpol 1985; Levi 2002).

BOX 6.3

Packing the Supreme Court: FDR Versus the Judicial Branch

There is a constant interplay of power between the judiciary and other structures. A classic example occurred in the United States during President Franklin D. Roosevelt's New Deal (1933–1940). Roosevelt drafted and pushed through Congress a series of sweeping laws meant to use national government policies to pull the country out of the Great Depression. However, the Supreme Court consistently ruled these laws unconstitutional, since the New Deal legislation gave powers and functions to the central government that far exceeded its constitutionally defined roles, as the Court interpreted them. After considerable grumbling and frustration, Roosevelt devised a different strategy for influencing the Court. Since there was nothing in the Constitution that limited the Court to nine justices, Roosevelt announced that he would significantly increase the number of members on the Supreme Court, appointing new justices sympathetic to the New Deal policies.

Congress blocked President Roosevelt's initiative to expand the Supreme Court. But his appointment of two replacement justices and his threat to "pack" the Court were followed shortly by a change of heart on the Court regarding the constitutionality of New Deal legislation. By 1937, the Court majority no longer blocked the central government's expanded activities. While it cannot be proven empirically that Roosevelt's threat to increase the size of the Court changed the judicial reasoning of the justices, it was punned at the time that "a switch in time saved nine."

Thus precise, behaviorally oriented and process-based analyses of politics now treat political structures more richly. A full understanding of the political world requires a clear grasp of the essential features of executive, legislative, administrative, and judicial structures. Institutional structures are the skeleton and organs of the body politic. Just as one could explain certain biological functions and processes of the body without explicit reference to the skeleton and organs, so one could explain certain functions and processes of the political system without reference to structures. But such an abstract description of a biological organism would be incomplete without indicating the way in which the structures constrain and shape the functions. Similarly, attempts to describe or explain politics, especially in actual settings, are much richer and more complete if they include a characterization of how political institutions constrain and shape the political process. The next chapter will extend further the explanation of how the structures interact to produce different forms of the body politic.

KEY CONCEPTS

adjudication   fused executive   ombudsman
administration   head of government   power
bicameral legislature   head of state   representation
bureaucracy   judicial review   unicameral legislature
dual executive   judiciary
executive   legislature

FOR FURTHER CONSIDERATION

1. Whom should a legislator represent on policy decisions? Develop an argument justifying your order of importance in representing the following: those groups who voted for the legislator, the constituency, the legislative coalition, the political party, the party leader, the nationality group, the country, the legislator's own best judgment.

2. Evaluate whether, on balance, it would be desirable to have an administrative system that is relatively flexible and is sensitive to unique, individual circumstances in the handling of each case.

3. The discussion of the judiciary asserts that every set of judicial structures is political. Is the notion of an independent judiciary a sham?

4. What are the benefits and shortcomings of a political system that has a weak chief executive? A fused chief executive?

FOR FURTHER READING

Abraham, Henry J. (1998). *The Judicial Process: An Introductory Analysis of the Courts of the United States, England, and France.* 7th ed. New York: Oxford University Press. A clear introduction to the theory and practice of judicial decision making in the three countries, as well as reflections on the judicial process in other countries.

Campbell, Colin. (1998). *The U.S. Presidency in Crisis: A Comparative Perspective.* New York: Oxford University Press. Informative studies of recent U.S. presidents are related to analyses of top leaders in Australia, Canada, and the United Kingdom. The author argues that these chief executives have become ineffective, particularly because increasingly they are political outsiders who operate independently of the party and no longer work productively with their administrative structures and their staff.

Derbyshire, Denis, with Ian Derbyshire. (2000). *Encyclopedia of World Political Systems.* New York: M. E. Sharpe. A useful inventory of the forms of contemporary political institutions, as well as detailed descriptions of each national political system.

Hess, Stephen. (1996). *Presidents and the Presidency.* Washington, DC: Brookings Institution. A series of thoughtful essays on executive leadership and power spanning two decades by a leading scholar of the modern American presidency.

Koopmans, Tim. (2003). *Courts and Political Institutions: A Comparative View.* Cambridge: Cambridge University Press. Koopmans, a former law professor and judge in the

European Union, offers a persuasive analysis of the increasing power of the courts to engage in judicial decision making and to exercise influence and control over the actions of other political structures. The cases of Britain, France, Germany, and the United States are at the center of the study, but other constitutional court systems are also examined.

Morgenstern, Scott, and Benito Nacif, Eds. (2002). *Legislative Politics in Latin America.* Cambridge: Cambridge University Press. This lengthy book includes illuminating comparative studies of the different styles of legislatures and the alternative strategic behaviors of legislators in numerous Latin American countries.

Morris, Norval. (1992). *The Brothel Boy and Other Parables of the Law.* A distinguished legal theorist presents a set of fictional short stories, set in Myanmar (Burma), as a mechanism to explore some of the most controversial issues of the law and justice.

Osborne, David, and Ted Gaebler. (1993) *Reinventing Government.* New York: Penguin. An influential critique of large bureaucratic government and a framework (using examples from the United States) of how to make government more responsive and entrepreneurial.

Peters, B. Guy. (2001). *The Politics of Bureaucracy: A Comparative Perspective.* 5th ed. New York: Routledge. A rich, analytic comparison of the behavior and power of bureaucracies in many countries.

Pitkin, Hannah F. (1972). *The Concept of Representation.* Berkeley: University of California Press. A thorough descriptive and normative exploration of political representation.

Sparrow, Malcolm K. (2000). *The Regulatory Craft: Controlling Risks, Solving Problems, and Managing Compliance.* Washington, DC: Brookings Institution. Writing as much for those who work in the public service as for scholars, Sparrow offers a positive and persuasive argument in support of administrative regulation, detailing the role of regulators as important innovators and protectors of the public interest within the policy process.

Stone Sweet, Alec. (2004). *The Judicial Construction of Europe.* Oxford: Oxford University Press. The author characterizes the considerable expansion of power of the European Union court system in shaping the political behavior of individual actors, the nature of the political system, and the functioning of the EU itself.

Von Mettenheim, Kurt, and Bert Rockman, Eds. (1997). *Presidential Institutions and Democratic Politics: Comparing Regional and National Contexts.* London: Johns Hopkins University Press. Essays in a comparative perspective as well as focused on a single country that examine the behaviors and institutional frameworks of top executives.

Wilson, James Q. (1990). *Bureaucracy: What Government Agencies Do and Why They Do It.* New York: Basic Books. An interesting analysis of the performance of the American national administration, identifying both the value and the flaws of the system.

ON THE WEB

http://www.gksoft.com/govt/en
Governments on the Web provides a comprehensive database of governmental institutions on the Internet. The site contains 17,000 entries from 220 different countries.

http://thomas.loc.gov/home/legbranch/cis.html

http://www.loc.gov/rr/news/fedgov.html

http://www.uscourts.gov

These three Library of Congress sites provide information about the legislative, executive, and judicial branches of the U.S. government.

http://www.fedworld.gov

This site provides a huge central information network of the U.S. federal government, with searchable access to agencies and departments, documents, databases, and so on—a comprehensive site for searching for, locating, ordering, and acquiring government and business information.

http://www.thisnation.com

This electronic textbook provides an in-depth look at American politics and includes links to other American government-related Internet resources.

http://www.usa.gov

The U.S. government's Official Web Portal provides a wealth of government-related material, including access to the Internet sites of every major U.S. government agency.

http://lcweb.loc.gov/rr/news/extgovd.html

This site allows you to browse through Library of Congress electronic government resources.

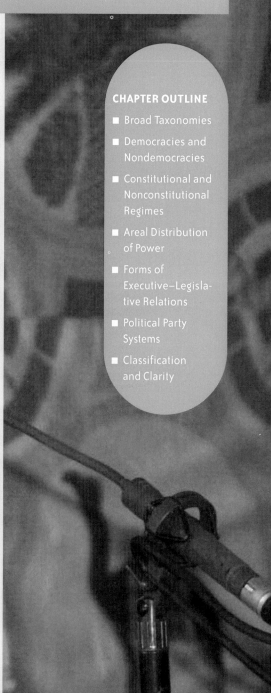

CHAPTER 7

POLITICAL INSTITUTIONS II: INSTITUTIONAL ARRANGEMENTS

Democracy is:

a. an agreeable, lawless . . . commonwealth, dealing with all alike on a footing of equality, whether they be really equal or not.

   —Plato, c. 427–347 B.C.E., Greek philosopher

b. the theory that the common people know what they want, and deserve to get it good and hard.

   —H. L. Mencken, 1880–1956, U.S. journalist

c. a system where no man is good enough to govern another man without that other's consent.

   —Abraham Lincoln, 1809–1865, U.S. president

d. the substitution of election by the incompetent many for appointment by the corrupt few.

   —George Bernard Shaw, 1856–1950, Anglo-Irish playwright

e. all of the above

f. none of the above

We know that all political systems are not democracies. But what constitutes a democracy? We know that all political systems are not identical. But are they all different? A basic task in political analysis is to determine whether there are some criteria by which political systems can be classified. This chapter considers various ways in which the structural elements of a political system can be arranged.

BROAD TAXONOMIES

Consider these 21 countries:

United States	Iraq	El Salvador
Libya	Kenya	South Africa
Kuwait	Poland	Saudi Arabia
Japan	Italy	Laos
Cuba	Thailand	United Kingdom
Zimbabwe	Venezuela	Philippines
Singapore	Russia	China

Can you make any distinctions among these political systems? Try. Do your distinctions enable you to establish two or more categories and then place each of the 21 countries into one but no other categories? Would other people agree with your classification?

When you attempt to classify countries by some criteria, you are engaged in **taxonomic analysis** (as discussed in the Appendix). Developing a taxonomy is often the first stage in political analysis because it groups cases to reduce complexity, to facilitate comparative analysis, and then to aid the development of generalizations. You might group countries on the basis of their political cultures or aspects of their political structures, such as the division of power among different levels of government or the type of party system. You might distinguish democracies from nondemocracies. Or you might use a nonpolitical criterion to categorize countries, such as their levels of economic development, their regional locations, or their size.

This chapter explores several ways in which political systems might be classified on the basis of their key *institutional arrangements*—that is, the ways in which certain key political structures are organized. The discussion should be useful both in the sense that it provides *analytic information* about the taxonomies used in the study of political systems and, in the broader sense, that it provides *descriptive information* about the basic differences among actual political systems. No single taxonomy is used in all political analyses because each taxonomy emphasizes different aspects of the political world. The choice of a taxonomy depends on the interests of the political analyst. This discussion begins by considering the classification of political systems using the venerable concept of *democracy*.

DEMOCRACIES AND NONDEMOCRACIES

One of the most common ways to classify political systems is to distinguish democracies from nondemocracies. From our education, as well as our other socialization and experiences, most of us have an intuitive sense about which countries are democracies and which are not. However, the concept can become slippery when we try to apply it. North Korea calls itself the *Democratic* People's Republic. Is it? Sri Lanka calls itself the *Democratic* Socialist Republic. Is it? El Salvador, France, Kenya, and Libya also consider themselves democracies. Are they? "Democracy" has become such a highly valued label that most states, except a few systems ruled by a hereditary monarch, claim that they are democratic. Is virtually every contemporary political system to be called a democracy? If not, what general label do you give to countries that are not democratic? "Dictatorships"? "Communist systems"? "Totalitarian regimes"? "Authoritarian systems"?

While we work toward acceptable definitions and labels, let us use "dictatorship" as the opposite of democracy. To begin to clarify your thinking, use your current understanding of democracy and dictatorship to classify the seven political systems in the first column of the list of countries at the beginning of the chapter. If you have been raised in the United States or Western Europe, you probably view Japan, the United States, and possibly Kuwait and Singapore as democracies, and Cuba, Libya, and Zimbabwe as dictatorships.

The qualification in the preceding sentence regarding the site of your upbringing is a crucial one—it alerts us to a fundamental problem with any such discussion. Chapter 4 attempted to persuade you that how one understands and uses political labels is dependent on one's own political socialization and political environment. Thus you should not assume that people from other cultures will necessarily agree with your labels.

It might be argued that this problem regarding interpersonal differences in assessments underscores the virtue of the scientific method. The scientific method requires the analyst to specify what a particular concept means with great precision and in an empirically measurable manner. This method might be the only way in which people with fundamentally different ideological views could agree on which of the states are democracies and which are dictatorships. The discussion in this chapter will proceed in the spirit of the scientific method, although the author acknowledges his own lifetime socialization, which is grounded in the political conceptions of the American and Western world.

How might individuals with dramatically different political worldviews attempt to agree on the accuracy of the classifications suggested earlier? For example, consider these issues:

- Libya calls itself a *jamahiriya*—Arabic for a "state of the masses"—in which the people rule through local councils and leader Muammar Qaddafi (shown on pages 162-163) holds no official title. Assume that local councils do make some decisions and that we are able to establish empirically that the majority of the Libyan population supports the Qaddafi government (this is arguably the case, although we do not know it empirically because there are no genuine elections or reliable public opinion surveys in Libya). Under such assumptions, is Libya a dictatorship?

- The same issue might be raised regarding Cuba under Raul Castro. By what criteria is Cuba undemocratic when a far greater proportion of people vote in Cuban elections and the government provides far more extensive social benefits to all its citizens than is the case in the democracy of either the U.S. or Japan?

- By what criteria is Zimbabwe not a democracy when President Robert Mugabe defeated other candidates in three straight elections (in 1990, 1996, and 2002) and his party won less than half of the seats in a 2008 legislative election?

■ By what criteria is Singapore a democracy when virtually all members of the national legislature have, since independence (in 1959), been members of a single political party, despite party competition in each election?

In asking and responding to such questions, you begin to establish the standards that must be applied when you attempt to distinguish between democracy and dictatorship. These kinds of questions also underscore the importance of defining with precision the concepts that we use in political analysis.

Defining Democracy

What are the necessary and sufficient conditions for democracy? In its classic sense, true *direct democracy* (also known as **participatory democracy**) is government of and by the people—there is *active, direct participation by all citizens in the authoritative allocation of values.* Realistically, there is no such political system; indeed, Jean-Jacques Rousseau (1712–1778) claimed that only a society of gods could be a true democracy. If our definition is less stringent, democracy might entail the relatively equal capacity of all citizens to influence the allocation of values. It would be difficult to make a persuasive case that this condition holds in *any* political system, including Japan or the United States. In *every* political system, some are more equal than others. In every political system, some make public policy decisions and others observe.

An alternative concept is **representative democracy**, a system in which the *citizens elect people to represent them in the political process and to allocate values on their behalf* for the society. Another general term used to describe a representative democracy is a *republic.* In fact, the majority of the countries in the world, in their formal title, call themselves republics (examples, from the A's: Republic of Albania, Democratic and Popular Republic of Algeria, People's Republic of Angola, Argentine Republic, Republic of Armenia, Republic of Austria, Republic of Azerbaijan; you might think some of these A "republics" are not particularly democratic).

Kuwait seems to meet this criterion for representative democracy because its citizens elect representatives. Yet few would classify it as a democracy, since about half of its resident adult population (those who cannot trace their Kuwaiti ancestry to 1920) are not allowed to vote in legislative elections and the chief executive, the Emir, is appointed from the ruling Al-Sabah family.

Thus the definition needs to be refined to specify that the elections for representatives must be held under conditions of *universal (adult) suffrage.* Cuba meets this condition, but few would consider it a democracy because, among other reasons, there are very limited choices for governmental office—there is only one candidate per district and nearly every candidate is a member of the single (Communist) party.

Is the definition of democracy adequate if it further stipulates that the elections provide voters with alternative choices among representatives? Since Cuba actually does allow alternative candidates (from the single party) to be nominated, it seems the definition should also specify that the choices must be genuine. Even with this clarification, there are cases, such as Singapore, where numerous parties offer candidates, but more than 95 percent of legislators are elected from one party. Thus even the notion of genuine choices among alternative candidates can be ambiguous. This set of conditions does seem to define an *electoral democracy: a political system in which virtually all citizens periodically vote in order to select political leaders from among alternative contenders.*

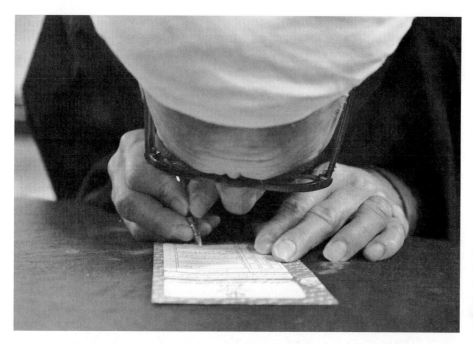

▌**An Iranian cleric considers his vote in the election of the national legislature.**

However, even more conditions might seem appropriate in defining democracy. It also seems important to establish the periodic right of the people to have the genuine capacity to retain or reject those serving as their political leaders. This additional condition, called the ***limited mandate***, means that the electorate grants the authority to govern (the mandate) for only a short, fixed (limited) period of time and then the electorate has the opportunity to select representatives again.

Even more broadly, should a complete definition of democracy have more than electoral components? Perhaps a democracy not only must ensure voting rights among alternatives and a limited mandate but also must allow the citizens and the media to exercise such freedoms as speech, assembly, and political opposition. We can classify a political system as a **liberal democracy** when *citizens enjoy not only electoral democracy but also these more extensive political rights and civil liberties regarding participation, personal freedoms, and opposition.* Some scholars include additional elements, such as an independent and neutral judiciary and civilian control of the military (Diamond 2000).

Perhaps we can now establish one possible set of sufficient, as well as necessary, conditions for a **democracy**: *governance by leaders whose authority is based on a limited mandate from a universal electorate that selects among genuine alternatives and has some rights to political participation and opposition.*

This is a modest notion of democracy, since it guarantees the people little more than political rights and the occasional opportunity to select among the competing elites who govern them. It is clearly less than a full participatory democracy, where there would be active, direct rule by all the people, who would be empowered to make policy decisions themselves by referenda or some other means (see Barber 2004; Dahl 1971, 2006; Schumpeter 1950). Yet even with the modest definition above, only two (Japan and the United States) among the first seven political systems in the list on page

164 are clearly classified as democracies. Singapore is more problematic, since the extent to which there is genuine contestation is unclear. Not only does one party win nearly all the legislative seats, but also the last several presidents of Singapore have been elected by "default" because a governing panel declared that only one candidate was qualified to run. While all seven systems encourage some forms of political participation and allow some political opposition, the authority of the political leadership in Cuba, Kuwait, Libya, and (probably) Zimbabwe is not based on its electoral selection, by universal suffrage, among genuine alternatives, or for a fixed period of time.

Most definitions of democracy focus on process. However, some argue that a genuine democracy not only must guarantee appropriate processes of empowering and replacing leaders but also should deliver desirable policy outputs (value allocations) from those authorities. Such a process-and-output conception of democracy might include such benefits for all citizens as quality education, employment, health care, housing, other forms of social welfare, and such conditions of life as a sense of personal safety and a healthy environment. While it might seem reasonable that a democracy should "deliver the goods," there is usually substantial disagreement about the nature of this package of goods, and thus the contents of policy decisions are part of the political process but do not define democracy (see Chapter 9).

There is also the idea that public officials in a democracy should be accountable. For example, Austin Ranney defines democracy as a form of government in which power to make decisions or select public officials is granted to all adult citizens, based on majority rule, and in which "having ascertained the people's preferences, public officials must then put them into effect whether they approve or not" (Ranney 2001: 114). Notice that the first part of Ranney's definition refers to the processes of selecting political authorities, while the second part requires responsiveness to citizen preferences. But how do we establish whether decision outputs do reflect the "people's preferences"? Are they determined by yesterday's opinion polls? By the insights of the public officials? By an assumption that the voters in the previous election were approving the complete array of policies discussed during the campaign by the victorious leaders? None of these measures seems promising.

This consideration of how the citizens' policy preferences are expressed raises associated questions about the **electoral system**—*the framework by which the citizens' votes select those candidates who receive a limited mandate to govern.* How are the electorate's votes converted to the selection of a particular set of representatives? Do you have a clear answer to how this should be done? In fact, in most countries, it is not a simple matter of counting votes (LeDuc, Niemi, and Norris 2002; Norris 2004). Box 7.1 suggests that choosing the best method for converting votes to seats is not as straightforward as it might seem. Could a political system that meets all the other conditions for democracy be faulted because its conversion of votes to seats puts some voters at a substantial disadvantage?

This extensive discussion might help you identify the criteria that *you* think are necessary for an adequate definition of democracy. (It is certainly possible that your definition will differ from any of those suggested here. You should, however, be able to justify your criteria.) Can you now articulate a conceptual definition of democracy and use it to classify the political systems in the list on page 164? Do you think your friends will accept your definition and classifications? Would a Cuban or Libyan student accept it? You might be surprised how difficult it is to develop a generally accepted definition of this most widely used political concept.

BOX 7.1

How Much Is Your Vote Worth? Converting Votes into Political Representation (via the Electoral System)

The Debate in 4 considered how much casting a vote is worth to an individual—especially a rational person who evaluates all the personal costs and benefits connected with that action. At another level, every political system that allows its citizens to vote for elected officials must determine how those votes will be converted into a distribution of political representatives (LeDuc, Niemi, and Norris 2002). How much is one vote worth to the political system?

When All Citizens Vote for a Single Office

When there is an election for a single office, such as a national president or a regional chief executive, the most obvious approach is that the winner is the individual who garners the largest number of votes. But some political systems complicate this straightforward approach by allowing preliminary elections in which some candidates are eliminated (e.g., primary elections in the United States) or in which candidates can volunteer to drop out after a first electoral round (e.g., the French elections for the legislature). Even more countries require that the winner receive a majority of the votes; if no candidate receives a majority in the first round, there is a runoff election between the two top vote getters.

The United States is one of the few presidential democracies that does *not* allow its citizens to elect their chief executive directly. Even if most Americans were previously unaware of the actual dynamics of electing their president, they were confronted with some notable facts in the close and contested Bush–Gore 2000 election: *Fact:* Your vote for president can count for absolutely nothing, because if your candidate does not gain the largest share of votes in your state, all the state's electoral college votes are cast for another candidate. *Fact:* One presidential candidate can garner the largest share of votes nationally and not be elected, because the winner is the candidate who wins a group of states that hold a majority of the electoral college votes. *Fact:* In 1824, 1876, and 2000, the presidential candidate with the largest popular vote was not elected. Does this seem right? *Fact:* If there is no majority in the electoral college, every state gets a single vote in the election of a president. Does it seem right that California, Wyoming, New York, and Rhode Island would all have equal impact on the selection of the president?

When All Citizens Vote for a Legislature

The conversion of votes into representatives in a legislature can require some interesting decisions. First, how many representatives will be elected from each district? It is possible to elect one representative per district, as in the U.S. House of Representatives (although not the Senate). But many political systems have more than one representative

BOX 7.1 *(Continued)*

per district, depending on the population in the district, with as few as one and as many as 39 representatives per district (Taagepera and Shugart 1989: table 12.1). At the extreme, some countries (e.g., the Netherlands, Israel) treat the entire country as one giant electoral district. Can you think of a sound argument for having all the legislators elected by everyone?

Second, how is the number of votes converted into the number of legislative seats? Table 7.1 presents a possible distribution of votes among candidates from four parties that are distributed ideologically from right (Party A) to left (Party D). In a *plurality* system (column [*b*]), used in most countries with single-member districts, each voter casts a vote for a specific candidate, and the candidate with the largest number of votes wins. The virtue of this approach is that the representative is the candidate who is the top choice of the largest number of voters in the constituency. In column (*b*) of Table 7.1, can you see a serious problem with this plurality victory for the candidate of Party A?

In a system of *proportional representation (PR)*, which is primarily used with multimember districts, candidates from each party are elected in proportion to their party's share of the total district vote. For example, if a district had 20 legislative seats, the outcome would be as shown in column (*c*) of Table 7.1. Can you see how this distribution of seats was determined? The calculations within PR systems can become very complicated if "leftover" votes are transferred to other districts or are pooled nationally for certain additional legislative seats.

An increasing number of countries have attempted to combine favorable aspects of both the PR and plurality approaches in a *mixed-member (MM)* system. Such

▶ **TABLE 7.1**

Converting Votes to Elected Officials: Number of Representatives Elected per District in Each Electoral System

	(a) Percentage of Votes	(b) Plurality	(c) PR	(d) Preferential	(e) Approval
Party A	31%	1	6	0 (38%)	0 (46%)
Party B	15%	0	3	0 (0%)	1 (75%)
Party C	29%	0	6	1 (61%)	0 (69%)
Party D	25%	0	5	0 (0%)	0 (54%)

Note: Regarding this hypothetical example: In the proportional representation (PR) system, 20 seats are distributed among competing parties in the district, whereas there is only one seat per district in the other three electoral systems. In preferential voting, it is assumed (in this example) that the votes for Party B split evenly between A and C on the second count, and then all of D's votes go to C on the third count. In approval voting, it is assumed that each voter judges any candidate adjacent to his first choice to be acceptable. The percentages in parentheses (for the preferential and approval voting systems) reflect the ultimate percentage of voters who support a particular party's candidate, given these assumptions.

BOX 7.1 *(Continued)*

systems were implemented in more than 40 countries during the 1990s, including Italy, Japan, and Russia (Shugart and Wattenberg 2001). There are many variations. In some systems (e.g., Mexico), there is direct plurality voting for part of the legislature, and additional seats are distributed by proportional representation. In other mixed-member systems, the particular representative who is elected is the person preferred by the largest number of voters in the district, but the party's total number of representatives in the entire legislature is proportional to its national electoral success.

Most political systems use one of the many variations of either plurality or PR voting, but other calculations are possible. A few political systems (e.g., Australia) employ *preferential voting*. Voters rank candidates in order of preference, and then the votes for the candidate with the lowest total are redistributed to those voters' second choices. Votes of each remaining bottom candidate continue to be redistributed until a majority candidate appears (see column [*d*] of the table).

Some scholars have argued that a better system than any of these is *approval voting* (see column [*e*]), in which voters can vote for as many of the candidates as they find acceptable. The winner is the candidate who is acceptable to the largest proportion of the electorate (Brams and Fishburn 1983).

Table 7.1 reveals that each of these alternative approaches can produce a different outcome! Which approach makes most sense to you? As you reflect on the virtues of these broad alternatives, you might notice that every system is flawed in some manner. No system perfectly mirrors the voters' preferences in the composition of a representative legislature. Compared with plurality systems, PR systems and mixed-member systems tend to enable more parties to gain seats in the legislature, which is good for representing the diversity of citizens' preferences. However, such multiparty legislatures can be less likely to produce a coherent governing majority, a desirable quality of most plurality systems. Alternatively, it might be argued that although the candidate of Party B is the first choice of the fewest citizens, he enjoys the broadest support among all voters and is the best "consensus candidate"—a virtue of approval voting.

So, how much is your vote worth? How much should it be worth? How should votes be converted into a fair distribution of representatives? These are intriguing political puzzles.

Defining Nondemocracies

How about *nondemocracies*? What concepts can be used to characterize those systems that are not democratic?

Dictatorship.   One conventional concept used to define nondemocracies is *dictatorship*. A stringent definition of a "dictator" might be a ruler with absolute power and authority (independent of any consideration of the process through which power was acquired). Can any one person or even a small group exercise "absolute" power? Would a system not be a dictatorship if the ruler were unable to exercise absolute power? Alternatively, **dictatorship** might be better defined in terms of *the absence of a limited mandate*—a critical factor in our definition of democracy. That is, if the citizens have no regular and realistic opportunity to replace the political leadership, then the political system is a dictatorship. Clearly, an unpopular ruler or ruling group that has forced the population to accept its authority is dictatorial. However, even a political leadership that has popular support from the majority but does not provide opportunities for the population to renew the mandate in competition with alternative leaders could be defined as dictatorial. This definition seems to characterize the situation in Libya under Qadaffi, and in Cuba under Fidel and Raul Castro. (Interesting problem: What about a hereditary ruler who is widely supported by the citizenry, as in Kuwait?)

Authoritarian regime.   The most common concepts that political scientists have applied to nondemocratic systems are totalitarian or *authoritarian regimes*. Many authoritarian regimes, like dictatorships, lack a limited mandate. But what distinguishes **authoritarianism** is another dimension: *the political actions and decisions of the ruler are not constrained, while the political rights and freedoms of the citizens are significantly limited.* In other words, under authoritarianism, the population has few, if any, political rights. An authoritarian regime places severe restrictions on the activities of individuals and groups who desire to influence the allocation of values by the political system. The great majority of the population is not allowed to participate in any political activities except those expressly encouraged by the regime. In most instances, this means that occasional public expressions of support for the system, such as mass rallies, are the only forms of political behavior that are acceptable (Linz 1993; Wiarda 2004).

Citizens are not permitted to question the political institutions, procedures, or public policies of an authoritarian regime. However, the nonpolitical aspects of people's lives, such as occupation, religion, and social life, are not generally under the direct control of the political system. In some countries, these other areas of life are still significantly controlled, but the control is by traditional societal values or by overriding religious values, not by the political system. Singapore, as well as Libya and Zimbabwe, could be characterized as authoritarian regimes.

Totalitarian regime.   In a *totalitarian regime*, the definition of *res publica* becomes total. Thus, under **totalitarianism**, *the political system's allocation of values and its control penetrate into virtually every aspect of its people's lives.* The totalitarian political system demands complete obedience to its extensive rules regarding culture, economics, religion, and morality. It prescribes and proscribes the behavior and even the thoughts of its population in almost every domain of existence. Every political system intervenes occasionally in such domains, but the defining characteristic of the totalitarian regime is its constant and pervasive efforts to control totally the lives of its population.

All organizations are subordinated to the totalitarian state. Every activity of the individual citizen is subject to scrutiny by the state in the name of the public interest. The state might define the acceptability of films and plays, determine what jobs individuals will have, prohibit the activities of organized churches, prevent families from moving without approval, and so on.

Totalitarian regimes, even more than authoritarian regimes, depend on the use of extensive coercion for their survival. The state employs its military, internal security forces, and other instruments of violence to suppress any citizen or group that challenges its authority. To sustain its pervasive control, the totalitarian regime also makes extensive use of the agents of political socialization, especially the media, the educational system, and cultural forms. Often the totalitarian state is dominated by a single leader, venerated in a cult of personality, and by a single political party. There are no limits on the mandate of the leadership of a totalitarian regime. George Orwell's novel *1984* (1949/1967) is a literary vision of the totalitarian state, and other recent examples include Afghanistan under the Taliban, Cambodia under Pol Pot (see Box 10.4), North Korea, and Sudan.

Some nondemocracies can be located on a continuum between totalitarianism and authoritarianism. These are authoritarian regimes whose political systems extend their control into important nonpolitical domains but do not exercise the totality of control associated with absolute totalitarianism. Belarus, Congo under Mobuto Sese Seko (1965–1997) (see Box 11.3), Indonesia under Suharto (1966–1998), Iran, Myanmar, and Saudi Arabia are examples along this continuum of countries that are not totalitarian regimes but do assert extensive control over culture, religious practice, and social life.

A Democracy–Nondemocracy Continuum

Consideration of several of the cases among the first seven countries in our list, especially Singapore, Kuwait, and Zimbabwe, suggests that there are gradations of democracy among political systems. None of these cases is an example of totalitarianism because significant areas of life are free from extensive political control. None of these countries is even fully authoritarian because citizens have some limited rights to criticize and oppose the leaders (although see Box 13.2 on behavioral controls in Singapore). In all three countries, the citizenry occasionally votes, which can result in turnover within the national legislature. A selection process with no real election determines Singapore's top executive, whereas Zimbabwe's leader retained power for many years in flawed elections, and Kuwait's top leaders are hereditary.

Few, if any, actual political systems are perfect examples of democracy or its opposites. Do you think it is appropriate to think of democracy and dictatorship as two ends of a single continuum? Are democracy and authoritarianism two ends of a continuum? Or democracy and totalitarianism? Not all political analysts are consistent in how they employ these concepts. In this book, at least, dictatorship, authoritarianism, and totalitarianism will all be treated as modes of politics that contrast with democratic regimes. *Dictatorship* will especially emphasize the absence of a limited mandate for the political leaders. *Authoritarianism* will connote a more encompassing array of nondemocratic practices and significant controls over citizens' political behavior. And *totalitarianism* will be used to describe systems whose oppressive control goes far beyond the strictly political sphere into personal and social life as well.

Notice that the dictatorship dimension differs in an important respect from the authoritarian and totalitarian dimensions. Many authoritarian or totalitarian regimes are dictatorships. However, there are instances where people elect their leaders but the political system substantially limits the people's personal and political freedoms. Thus, as in Singapore and Iran, there can be an authoritarian regime with relatively nondictatorial leadership. Indeed, since the early 1990s, many countries that were previously nondemocratic, especially in Latin America, the former Soviet bloc, and Africa, have engaged in serious attempts to establish democratic political systems, although they might fall short of liberal democracies (Schedler 2006).

What proportion of national political systems is democratic? The precise number of countries in this "wave of democracy" (a key theme in Chapter 10 and in Part Five of this book) ebbs and flows yearly as some countries establish democratic systems while others retreat or revert to nondemocratic systems. Freedom House (2008) is an organization that uses the various conceptualizations of democracies and non-democracies to analyze this question.

First, Freedom House identifies those countries that meet the minimal conditions for an electoral democracy. Second, those countries that do not meet these conditions can be classified as nondemocracies. Third, Freedom House analyzes the extent to which each country, whether an electoral democracy or not, grants its citizens the *political rights* (e.g., to form political parties promoting genuine alternatives, to allow contestation in elections) and *civil liberties* (e.g., religious and ethnic freedom, press freedom) that define a liberal democracy.

Freedom House has developed a widely cited scale, with a country scoring from 1 to 7 points on political rights and from 1 to 7 points on civil liberties. A country's combined average score on the two measures can range from 1.0 points, the most extensive liberal democracy, to 7.0 points in the world's most repressive regimes. Based on actual conditions, a country is classified as "free" (1.0–2.5 points), "partly free" (3.0–5.0), or "not free" (5.5–7.0) (Freedom House 2008).

If a country is *an electoral democracy but its citizens' political rights and civil liberties are significantly limited*, the country can also be classified by yet another term, ***illiberal democracy*** (Zakaria 2003). Venezuela under president Hugo Chavez is an example. There are multiparty elections with universal suffrage. In the 2005 election for the legislature, opposition parties were active. However, those parties ultimately boycotted the election due to intimidation by the government and fear of vote-rigging. Only 25 percent of the electorate voted and all the seats were won by pro-government candidates. Government has also increased its extensive control of media and cracked down on the activities of opposition groups. Thus, Venezuela is classified as an electoral democracy, but its current scores on political rights (4) and civil liberties (4) are so low that it is only "partly free" and meets the criteria to be classified as an illiberal democracy.

There is considerable disagreement about whether it is desirable for groups like Freedom House to label a country a democracy if it significantly limits its citizens' political rights and civil liberties. What's in a name? On the positive side, it is suggested that if a country is called an electoral democracy, its leaders will feel considerable pressure to hold periodic elections and to allow some democratic practices involving citizens' rights and liberties. Moreover, the practice of periodic elections emphasizes the need for a renewable leadership mandate provided by the electorate. On the negative side, it can be argued that if the political elite can claim that the international community calls their country a "democracy," this helps legitimize a regime that governs by rigged elections and violates its citizens' political rights and civil liberties. There is no compelling empirical evidence that calling a country an "electoral democracy" is a positive causal factor in the transition to a genuine democracy.

Table 7.2 indicates the classifications of selected countries by Freedom House, circa 2007, and Map 7.1 graphically displays the regional differences in the distribution of countries on these measures. According to that analysis, 123 (64 percent) of the 193 countries are electoral democracies. However, 27 percent of the electoral democracies (17 percent of all countries) are illiberal democracies, and thus only

> **TABLE 7.2**
> ## Classification of Selected Countries by Level of Freedom and Regime Type, Circa 2007

	Freedom Score	Liberal Democracy	Electoral Democracy	Nondemocracy
Free	1.0	Costa Rica 1,1*		
		Sweden 1,1		
		Poland 1,1		
		United States 1,1		
	1.5	Japan, 1,2		
		South Africa 1,2		
		South Korea 1,2		
	2.0		Argentina 2,2	
			Brazil 2,2	
			Mexico 2,2	
	2.5	India 2,3	Indonesia 2,3	
			Serbia 3,2	
Partly Free	3.0	Thailand 3,3	Turkey 3,3	
	3.5		Sierra Leone 4,3	
	4.0		Nigeria 4,4	
			Venezuela 4,4	
	4.5			Singapore 4,5
	5.0			
Not Free	5.5			Cambodia 6,5
				Egypt 6,5
				Russia 6,5
	6.0			Congo 6,6
				Swaziland, 7,5
				Vietnam 7,5
	6.5			China 7,6
				Saudi Arabia 7,6
	7.0			Myanmar 7,7
				Syria 7,7

*Scores: The first score is political rights, the second score is civil liberties, with 1 = the highest score and 7 = the lowest score. A country's "Freedom Score" is the average of these two component scores.
Source: Freedom House 2008.

▶ MAP 7.1   **Map of Freedom.**

Source: Freedom House, http://www.freedomhouse.org.

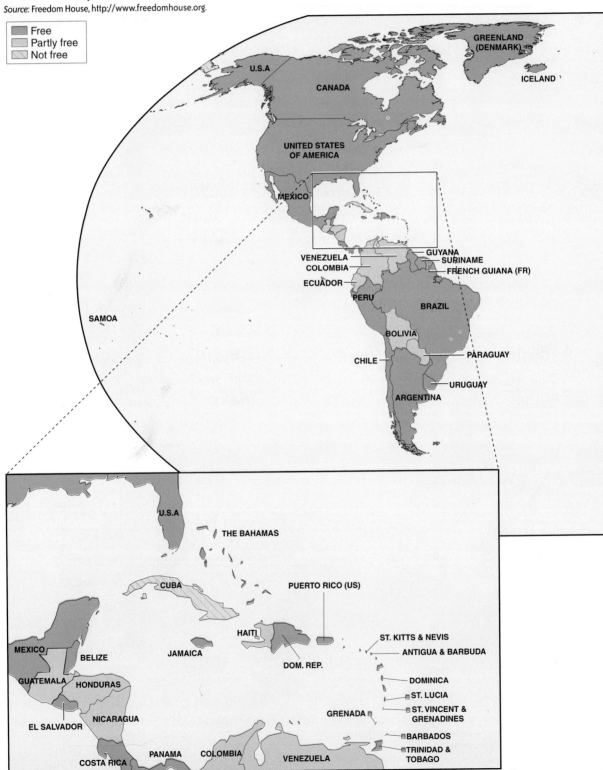

Free
Partly free
Not free

Free
Partly free
Not free

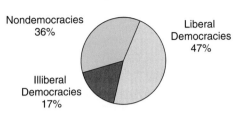

Percentage of World's Population

Not Free 37%

Free 46%

Partly Free 17%

Percentage of Countries

Nondemocracies 36%

Liberal Democracies 47%

Illiberal Democracies 17%

▶ **FIGURE 7.1**

Distribution of countries and people in terms of democratic regimes and practices

Sources: Freedom House 2008; Puddington 2008.

47 percent of the countries in the world are liberal democracies (electoral democracies with full freedoms) (Puddington 2008). Figure 7.1 indicates the current proportion of countries that are liberal democracies, nondemocracies and illiberal democracies as well as the proportions of the world's population that are free, partly free, or not free.

To report these same data from the "underside," 36 percent of the countries are not at all democratic. And fully 54 percent of the world's population live in countries that do not provide the extensive political rights and civil liberties associated with democracy. Generally authoritarian regimes rule 17 percent of the world's population, who are "partly free," while 37 percent of the world's population are "not free" and live in repressive conditions approaching totalitarianism (Freedom House 2008).

Now that we have explored some of the complexities of defining political systems on a democracy–nondemocracy continuum, do you have a clearer notion of how you might define and operationalize democracy?

CONSTITUTIONAL AND NONCONSTITUTIONAL REGIMES

A related classification of political systems also emphasizes aspects of the relationship between the rulers and the ruled. In this schema, the key question is whether the political system abides by the provisions in the state's constitution or fundamental laws. A **constitutional regime** *operates in terms of the rule of law and ensures effective restraints on the power holders*, as defined within the constitution. In contrast, a **nonconstitutional regime** is characterized by *unchecked political power, and the structural arrangements of the constitution are not upheld*. In theory, at least, a state might scrupulously follow a deeply repressive and undemocratic constitution imposed by the political leadership and thus qualify as a constitutional regime. However, those who make this distinction typically assume that the guarantees within the constitution provide for a generally democratic and humane political order.

Constitutions

At the heart of most political systems is a **constitution**, *a set of statements describing the fundamental rules of the political system.* The constitution declares the existence of the state, and it expresses three crucial sets of rules. First, the constitution allocates governmental activities, defining what actions are within the domain of *res publica* and what political structures will perform these various actions. Second, it establishes the formal power relationships among the political structures, indicating the conditions under which each is independent or dependent on the actions of the others. Third, the constitution limits the power of the rulers and guarantees the rights of the ruled by defining the maximum extent of the state's authority over its citizens and by enumerating citizens' freedoms and benefits from the state.

The actual drafting of every constitution is either directly or indirectly controlled by those with political power in the society. Many groups in a society might offer interpretations of what the constitution means and how it ought to be applied to particular circumstances—governmental officials, courts, political parties, interest groups. Ultimately, the force of the constitution depends on the will of those with political power to enforce its provisions.

Most constitutions are a single written document, like the U.S. Constitution. However, some political systems do not have such a document; their fundamental rules are embedded in major statutes, precedents, and legal decisions, as in Great Britain's "unwritten constitution" or in Israel's "basic laws." While early constitutions tended to be relatively short and general, some recent constitutions are quite detailed. The Nigerian Constitution has 245 articles, and the Indian Constitution has 395 articles. The language of constitutions is also becoming increasingly similar because drafters liberally borrow ideas and even specific language from other countries. For example, more than three dozen countries have borrowed Abraham Lincoln's felicitous phrasing regarding government "of the people, by the people, and for the people."

Although the idea of a constitution has a certain timeless quality, the constitutions of political systems are always changeable. Most countries periodically alter their constitutions. For example, India has added nearly 100 amendments to its constitution in 60 years. And at some point, many countries have abandoned their existing constitutions and ratified new ones in an attempt to rejuvenate their political systems. (Box 7.2 discusses the interesting history of the 1947 Japanese constitution.) New constitutions have recently been adopted in Afghanistan (2004), China (2004), Colombia (2005), Congo (2006), Finland (2000), Iraq (2005), Kyrgyzstan (2006), Serbia (2006), Swaziland (2006), Thailand (2007), and Zimbabwe (2005). The process does not always succeed. In 2005, Kenyan citizens rejected a new constitution proposed by President Mwai Kibaki. And the parliament of the European Union adopted a new constitution in 2004, but key member states (e.g., France and the Netherlands) have subsequently voted against ratification.

Few constitutions provide a precise description of how the political system actually works. Yet constitutions are significant. In the turbulent debate over the creation of Spain's new constitution in 1978, the distinguished historian Julian Marais insisted, "If the constitution does not inspire respect, admiration and enthusiasm, democracy is not assured." Even if the state makes major diversions from its constitution's provisions, the constitution remains a moral yardstick against which to measure actual

BOX 7.2

Constitution by Fiat: Japan

One of the most extraordinary constitution-drafting episodes occurred in Japan. The Japanese operated under the Imperial Meiji Constitution from 1889 until they were defeated by the Allies at the end of World War II. After the war, Japan was under the control of the American occupation forces, led by General Douglas MacArthur. Concerned about possible communist influence in Japan, both MacArthur and officials in Washington, D.C., insisted that the Japanese write a new democratic constitution. A newspaper leak revealed that a Japanese commission charged with writing the new constitution was unwilling to propose major changes in the Meiji Constitution. Thus, in February 1946, MacArthur took decisive action. He convened a group of 17 American military officers stationed in Tokyo

▶ Entitled "The Real Japanese Diet," this racially antagonistic 1946 American cartoon suggests that the Japanese will be reformed by a "Diet" (the actual name of the Japanese legislature) imposed by the United States.

Source: Library of Congress

and told them that he wanted a constitution for Japan in one week. The group included four lawyers but no one with constitutional expertise, no political scientists, and no one who was deeply knowledgeable about Japanese culture.

Using their knowledge of the American political system and their imperfect understanding of the British parliamentary system, the group completed the constitution in just eight days! The English version was translated into two forms of Japanese: formal bureaucratic language and common Japanese. Some of the Americans' perspectives were so alien to Japanese culture and political traditions that some concepts in the new constitution, such as "civil rights," were not even words in the Japanese language and required new ideographs. The constitution copied much of the preamble to the U.S. Constitution and referred to George Washington, President Roosevelt, and even Douglas MacArthur. The Japanese political leadership was shocked by and deeply opposed to the new constitution, but it was faced with a variety of even more undesirable threats (especially the possibility that the emperor would be tried as a war criminal). Consequently, the leadership capitulated and accepted the "MacArthur constitution." The Japanese cabinet presented the constitution to the Japanese public as its own. It was passed almost unanimously in the legislature, and it became binding in May 1947.

This constitution, written by inexpert foreigners, has been in force in Japan since 1946. It was not amended for nearly 50 years and it seems to have worked, in the sense that the Japanese have maintained a stable and working political system in the subsequent 60+ years. Can you explain this constitutional "success"? Perhaps the military officers developed a sound constitutional framework for the governance of contemporary Japan. Perhaps the constitution is primarily a symbolic document and its details are unimportant for the actual functioning of the political order. Or perhaps this was an early example of Japan's postwar skill: taking an American product, reflecting on how to improve upon it, and modifying it into a superior product.

performance, and it is a persistent reminder of the high ideals and goals that have been set for the political system.

Constitutional Regimes

The defining feature of a *constitutional regime* is that the state attempts to fulfill the provisions of its constitution. A political system becomes more fully a constitutional regime to the extent that it abides by the three sets of rules described above. Compliance with the constitutional limits on the rulers' power and the provision of the rights guaranteed to the ruled are particularly important. In the short run, at least, those who have political power in the society greatly influence whose interpretation of the constitution will prevail and how the constitution's provisions will be implemented. In constitutional regimes, the interpretations are generally reasonable and judicious, and the implementation is fair (Sunstein 2001).

Among constitutional regimes, it is not always the case that compliance with the rules is complete. Even the limits on the state and the rights of the citizens are not absolute and are not absolutely implemented. Disagreements over interpretation of the constitution occur, practice and precedent can result in a gap between the rules and standard practice, and political actors sometimes willfully bend the rules to serve their agendas. Some states implement a "temporary" suspension of major constitutional provisions in response to circumstances that seriously threaten the stability of the society. A regime becomes less constitutional when the disparity becomes larger between the provisions in the constitution and the actual politics of the society.

Nonconstitutional Regimes

Almost every political system occasionally violates or ignores some principle in its constitution. But the political system can be called a *nonconstitutional regime* when there is persistent nonenforcement of constitutional provisions, especially regarding crucial limits on rulers or rights of the ruled. In this sense, most authoritarian and totalitarian regimes are nonconstitutional.

Various sets of conditions can result in nonconstitutional regimes. First, some political systems (e.g., Bhutan, Saudi Arabia) simply do not have a constitution and are governed by hereditary rulers, religious principles, or traditions that guarantee no rights to the ruled and place few limits on the rulers. Second, leaders in some political systems simply ignore with impunity the basic rules in the constitution (e.g., Myanmar, Vietnam). Third, in some countries (e.g., Sierra Leone, Somalia), the rule of law collapses because the social order disintegrates through natural catastrophe or severe political violence. And fourth, there are instances where either the entire constitution or major constitutional rights are suspended "temporarily" but then are not restored for a lengthy period. In Israel, for example, this temporary suspension of constitutional rights (there is no written constitution) has persisted since independence in 1948.

AREAL DISTRIBUTION OF POWER

With the exception of small political systems serving only a few thousand citizens, most political systems have found it desirable or necessary to create governmental structures at several levels. The *areal distribution of power* describes the allocation of power and functions across these levels of government. National political systems, in particular, can be classified into three major forms: (1) unitary states, (2) federations, and (3) confederations.

Unitary State

In a **unitary state**, *a central government holds all legitimate power*. While the central government has indivisible sovereignty, it can delegate power or functional responsibilities to territorial units, which have such names as departments, regions, or prefectures. These peripheral governments serve only at the convenience of the central government, which can revoke their power or functions at any time. More than 70 percent of the current countries are unitary states. Examples include China, France, Japan, the United Kingdom, and most Latin American and Asian political systems.

Why are most contemporary states unitary? Its major advantage is the clear, hierarchical authority. While there might be a conflict between the central and the peripheral governments, the center's superior constitutional power is clear, and center–periphery stalemates are uncommon. In addition, because all citizens are loyal to the governmental authority embodied in the national government, citizens tend to identify with the country as a whole, rather than with regional authorities.

Federation

A **federation** has *a constitutional division of power and functions between a central government and the set of regional governments*, which have such names as states, provinces, or cantons. In contrast to a unitary state, there is an explicit sharing of power among levels of government in a federation, and no level has legal power to dominate any other level in all policy domains. The essence of a federation is coordination, not hierarchy.

There are five major rationales for a federation:

1. *Large size.* Many states become federations to distribute governmental power where there is a huge area to be governed. Fewer than 25 states are federations today, but this group includes nearly half the land area of the world. Most of the largest states are federations, including Brazil, Canada, India, Mexico, Nigeria, Russia, and the United States. During the constitutional debate in the United States, Thomas Jefferson observed, "Our country is too large to have all its affairs directed by a single government."

2. *The prior existence of strong states.* A federation can be an acceptable compromise when strong peripheral governments create a central government. In the formation of the United States, for example, the already strong state governments were unwilling to give up the bulk of their power to a central government, as in a unitary state. Rather, they agreed to delegate certain functions to the new central government while retaining all other "residual" powers for themselves.

3. *The attempt to create unity or accommodate diversity.* Chapter 5 described the serious problems of conflict between states and nations, especially in the newer states. Federations appear to bond diverse nations into a unified state while still recognizing the different nations' diversity and desire for power in the regional governments. The peripheral governments represent major ethnic, linguistic, religious, or other nation-based characteristics of regions. India is a federation with 28 states, most of which are related to linguistic-ethnic dominance in the area and a few of which are related to religious dominance.

4. *The desire to concentrate power and resources.* In some instances, a federation is created to combine several states into a stronger political system. In the effort to create Arab unity and to expand the political and economic power of the state, Egypt has several times attempted to forge federations with its neighbors Syria, Yemen, Iraq, and Jordan. Federations of strong states are often short-lived because the prior states are unwilling to sacrifice sufficient power and resources to a potent central government.

5. *The desire to disperse political power.* In contrast to the preceding rationale, a federation can be established to prevent the overconcentration of power in the central government. After the trauma of Hitler, West Germans formed a federation to prevent the emergence of another overly powerful central government. The bulk of legislative power was granted to the central government, but most power to administer and adjudicate the laws is held by the Länder (regional) governments.

Confederation

A **confederation** is *an association in which states delegate some power to a supranational central government but retain primary power.* It is a loose grouping of states in which each state's membership, participation, and compliance to the central government are conditional, depending on the state's perception of its own national interest. Confederations are usually created when states decide that the performance of certain functions is enhanced by structured cooperation with other states. To facilitate such cooperation, the states establish permanent supranational machinery. The United Arab Emirates is a confederation of ministates, and the United Nations is a confederal structure containing more than 190 member states. Confederations can emphasize economic cooperation, such as the European Union (EU), or military cooperation, such as the North Atlantic Treaty Organization (NATO).

Although confederations can serve many useful functions for member states, their activities and even their very survival are always contingent on the members' continuing support. A member state will often refuse to comply with confederation policies that conflict directly with the state's definition of its own national interest. Disagreements among the members can necessitate negotiation and compromise, as in the periodic adjustments within the EU regarding such issues as farm subsidies to member states and a common monetary policy. A confederation can wither if the supragovernment is ineffective, as in the case of the Articles of Confederation in colonial America, or if members refuse to support its directives, as in the League of Nations after World War I.

Table 7.3 indicates some of the major advantages and shortcomings of each approach to the areal distribution of power. While each has relative advantages under certain conditions, none is without considerable drawbacks, and none can ensure the effective functioning or even the survival of a political system. The general trend toward the centralization of political power within states has meant that the distinctions between unitary states and federations are less clear than in the past and that confederations have become particularly fragile.

▶ **TABLE 7.3**
Relative Strengths and Weaknesses of Areal Distributions of Power

Form of Areal Distribution	Strengths	Weaknesses
Unitary state	Clear authority	Hyperconcentration of power
	Decisive control	Weak representation of diversity and minorities
	No stalemates between center and periphery	
Federation	Representation of diversity	Duplication and overlap of power
	Checks on center's power	Conflicts over ultimate power
	Creates unity	Sluggishness; compromises
Confederation	Facilitates cooperation	Conditional compliance
	Power retained by subunits	Instability
		Limited power

FORMS OF EXECUTIVE–LEGISLATIVE RELATIONS

Another conventional method of classifying and especially of describing political systems is by defining the pattern of power and interaction between the legislative and executive structures. The taxonomy in this section emphasizes the two most common patterns through which the executive and the legislative structures interact to perform the functions of policy making and policy implementation: the presidential form and the parliamentary form of government. Three other types of executive-legislative arrangements are also examined: the hybrid, council, and assembly systems.

Presidential Government

The crucial feature of **presidential government** is the *separation of executive and legislative structures.* Figure 7.2 portrays the electoral chain of command that is supposed to order the relationships between citizens and major political structures. In separate electoral decisions, the citizens select the chief executive (usually called the president) and the members of the national legislature. This electoral process provides both the president and the legislature with independent mandates to represent the citizens in the governing process. The term length of each is predetermined, and thus the tenure in office of each is not dependent on the other (except in the rare case of impeachment of the chief executive).

The separation of executive and legislative powers is explicit and intentional, in order to ensure a system of checks and balances in the policy-making and policy-implementation processes. Primary responsibility for policy making (debating, modifying, and enacting policies as law) resides in the legislature. Although the chief executive can veto legislation, the legislature can override that veto. Primary responsibility for the implementation of policy is with the president, who has control of the government's administrative departments. The president also appoints a cabinet, whose members are responsible for overseeing policy in the government's administrative departments and are controlled directly by the president.

In practice, it is common to find considerable interdependence and blurring of functions between the executive and legislative structures, and especially for the president to have substantial involvement in the policy-making function. The United States is the model example of presidential government, and it is also found in many

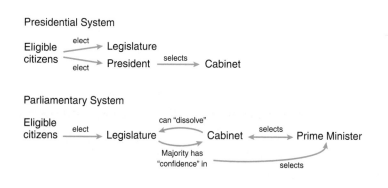

▶ **FIGURE 7.2**
Presidential and parliamentary systems of government

Latin American and some African and Asian states, including Brazil, Ivory Coast, Kenya, Mexico, Sri Lanka, Venezuela, and the Philippines.

Parliamentary Government

In contrast to the presidential system, the crucial element of **parliamentary government** is the *fusion of executive and legislative functions and structures.* As is indicated in Figure 7.2, the people elect the legislature (the parliament), whose majority empowers a cabinet, which then empowers one of its members to be the chief executive, typically called a prime minister or premier. The maximum length of the legislature's mandate is often five years, but its term can be shorter under the circumstances described next. The complex relationships among cabinet, legislature, and prime minister merit further detail.

Cabinet and legislature.   The cabinet is a collective leadership group of 6 to 30 people who are, in most systems, also members of the legislature. The cabinet is responsible to the legislature. This means that the cabinet serves only as long as it can retain the "confidence" of the majority of the members in the legislature. While serving, the cabinet has primary responsibility for both the policy-making and policy-implementation functions. Although policies must be voted into laws by the legislative majority, it is the cabinet that devises, drafts, and implements most policies.

In an intriguing manner, the cabinet and the legislature are at each other's mercy. At any time, the legislative majority can pressure the cabinet to resign, either by a negative vote on a major piece of legislation proposed by the cabinet or by a general motion of "no confidence" in the cabinet. Also at any time, the cabinet can "dissolve" the legislature, requiring immediate new elections. In the subsequent election, voters select a new legislature, whose majority then identifies a cabinet it will support, and the process begins anew. Thus the cabinet and the legislature are rather like two gunfighters standing gun-to-gun in a spaghetti Western: each has the power to eliminate the other, but each might also be destroyed in the exchange. Since new elections put everyone's position in jeopardy, it is more common for the cabinet to resign or reconstitute itself than for the cabinet to dissolve the legislature.

Legislature and prime minister.   In the parliamentary system, the prime minister (or premier or chancellor or whatever the chief executive is called) is not directly elected by the citizens to be the top leader. The prime minister is the member of the legislature who is supported as chief executive by the majority of the legislature. This executive can be removed at any time by a no-confidence vote of the legislature and might also be obliged to resign if the legislature defeats a major legislative initiative of the prime minister. The prime minister directs the overall thrust of decision and action in the legislative process.

Cabinet and prime minister.   The balance of power between the cabinet and the prime minister can be subtle, although both depend on majority support of the legislature. Traditionally, a cabinet that had legislative support could select one of its members to serve as prime minister. The prime minister was *primus inter pares* in the cabinet—"first among equals." The prime minister exercised broad policy leadership within a collective decision-making body. If a cabinet majority no longer supported a prime minister, the prime minister either resigned or attempted to reconstitute a cabinet that supported him and was supported by the legislative majority.

In many contemporary parliamentary systems, however, there has been a substantial shift of power from the cabinet to the prime minister. In these systems, the electorate selects legislative candidates from a party committed to support a particular prime minister. If a legislative majority can be created, its leader becomes prime minister. The prime minister then appoints the members of the cabinet and clearly dominates the cabinet in the governmental process. In Figure 7.2, the two-headed arrow between cabinet and prime minister indicates these alternative patterns of power.

Thus the parliamentary system is characterized by the fusion of executive and legislative functions because the cabinet and prime minister formulate policies, guide their passage through the legislature, and administer policy through the administrative departments. However, the actual policy process in a parliamentary system depends on whether there is a coherent majority group in the legislature.

There are both "stable" and "unstable" parliamentary systems. In a stable parliamentary system, there is a clear majority in the legislature (such a majority may be composed of either one party or a coalition). This majority provides the cabinet and prime minister with sufficient legislative support to enact their policy program, without the problems of stalemate and confusion of accountability that can result from the separation of powers in the presidential system. Australia, Canada, Denmark, Great Britain, and Japan are examples of parliamentary government systems that are usually stable.

In contrast, an unstable parliamentary system often emerges when there is no coherent legislative majority. Instead, policy making requires agreement within a coalition composed of multiple parties that tend to disagree on some important policy issues. If the legislature votes no confidence in the cabinet or defeats it on a major bill, the cabinet usually resigns. Then the media report that a parliamentary government has "fallen" or that there are efforts to form a "new government" (a new cabinet, actually). The new cabinet might have almost all the same people as members, or it might have a different set of people, drawing its majority support from different groups within the legislature. In general, prime ministers in unstable parliamentary systems are weaker than those in stable parliamentary systems.

Unstable parliamentary systems have been prevalent in contemporary legislatures that have strong ideological differences and multiple political parties. Italy has had an average of one cabinet (new government) per year since 1945. During the French Fourth Republic, the parliamentary system was so volatile that the average cabinet served for only 11 months; one cabinet lasted less than six hours!

Hybrid Systems

An increasing number of political systems attempt to blend desirable aspects of both the presidential and parliamentary systems. These **hybrid systems** *have a prime minister and an elected legislature that can both enact and implement policies, but they also have a president* (elected for a fixed term and having some independent executive powers) who, as a single individual, can act with decisiveness (Elgie 1999; Shugart and Carey 1992).

Some hybrid systems function more like parliamentary systems: The president has limited power, and the prime minister and cabinet exercise most of the control. In India, for example, the president is elected by the legislature for a five-year term and has notable responsibilities, including the appointment of state governors and the right to take over governance of the states during emergencies. However, the prime minister is the dominant political power in the system, with the president performing mainly ceremonial roles, such as appearances on national holidays. Germany, Austria, and Ireland are other examples of this style of the hybrid.

In other hybrid systems, there is a more balanced sharing of power between the president and the parliament. In Finland, for example, the presidential executive controls the administration and has oversight powers. Although the president does attend meetings on major legislation and both the president and the prime minister must sign a law before it is enacted, the cabinet and legislature undertake most of the legislation. In these more balanced hybrids, the relative powers of the president and the prime minister/cabinet vary, depending on the constitutional rules, the personalities of the officeholders, and the political situation in the society (see Box 7.3 on the French hybrid system).

BOX 7.3

A Hybrid System in Action: France

Many recent constitutions establish a hybrid model in which both a president and a prime minister have significant political power. A central issue is whether two independent executives can share power effectively. An early example of this complicated system is the French Fifth Republic, based on the "de Gaulle Constitution" of 1962. France created this hybrid to overcome the highly unstable parliamentary government system of the Fourth Republic. The premier (prime minister) and cabinet are responsible for the day-to-day functioning of the government, as in a parliamentary system, but the president (an office Charles de Gaulle fashioned for himself as a condition for his return to government) has extensive power and the freedom to exercise it. The president is elected popularly for a fixed term, and he selects a premier, who selects a cabinet. The cabinet controls the budget and legislative agenda as in a normal parliamentary system; however, the president can dissolve the legislature while retaining the cabinet. And Article 16 in the constitution provides that the sweeping powers of the presidency may be exercised whenever the president *alone* deems the political situation to be dangerous for the country.

De Gaulle served as the first president of the Fifth Republic from 1958 to 1969. He was an extraordinarily powerful man, and he demanded extraordinary power. He established a precedent that the president can act far more extensively than the constitution allows. He dominated every premier who served during his presidency. The presidents after de Gaulle (from Pompidou to Sarkozy) have continued to follow the de Gaulle precedent, exercising considerable power.

BOX 7.3 *(Continued)*

Many people felt that the French "dyarchy" (dual rule) would lead to a constitutional crisis as soon as a premier and cabinet challenged the president's extensive power. The first strong test of the French hybrid finally occurred between 1986 and 1988, when Socialist President François Mitterrand was faced with a legislative majority dominated by conservatives. But Mitterrand accepted the situation, appointing the conservatives' leader, Jacques Chirac, as premier. Despite strong ideological differences between the president and the premier-cabinet-legislative majority, there was a reasonable sharing of power and authority, which the French call *cohabitation.* President Mitterrand continued to be very active in foreign policy but allowed the premier to control the domestic policy agenda. From 1993 to 1995, a conservative legislative majority produced a second period of cohabitation. A weakened Mitterrand acknowledged that "it is not the task of the president of the Republic to govern" (Safran 2003: 169–172).

In 2000, the French altered a 127-year pattern, voting to shorten the presidential term from seven years to five years, ostensibly to increase the political accountability of the president. Since 2002, there has been no cohabitation because both the president and the prime minister are from the coalition of conservative parties. After these varied periods of cohabitation, the powers of the president in the French hybrid system seem to be sufficiently limited and institutionalized to survive the conflict inherent in a dyarchy. Through constitutional safeguards and precedents, the hybrid system in every country must establish an effective power balance between its two executives.

Hybrid systems have been implemented in virtually all the countries that emerged from the Soviet Union and in the postcommunist countries of Central and Eastern Europe. In nearly all these countries, the position of president has the greater power, including the right to dismiss the prime minister. However, the prime minister is responsible to the elected legislature and has direct control of the government. In most of these countries, the president does periodically exercise his right to dismiss the prime minister, an act that can relieve temporarily the citizens' dissatisfaction with the failures of the political system. But many of these hybrids have faced major governability problems (see Chapter 14), which suggests that the more ambiguous power relationships of the hybrid structure are not necessarily desirable.

Council Systems

In **council systems,** *a small group shares collective leadership and is responsible for both executive and legislative functions.* Although one member of the group might be deemed the leader for symbolic reasons, all members of the council are equal in constitutional terms, and they make decisions and actions based on the will of the council majority or, ideally, on council consensus. In American local government, the weak-mayor–council system and the boards of commissioners/supervisors (prevalent in many counties, school districts, and special districts) are council systems. Also, many tribal societies in Africa were traditionally ruled by a council of elders who collectively made decisions that were binding on the members of the tribe.

In many situations in which a small collective group forcefully removes the top leader, the group initially shares power. When the group that has taken power is from the military, this council-type group is called a *junta*. There were numerous juntas in Latin America and Africa in the latter half of the twentieth century (e.g., in Algeria from 1992 to 1999; in Argentina from 1976 to 1983), although Myanmar is one of the few current juntas. In most cases, council rule evolves into more dictatorial rule as a single political leader increasingly dominates the others.

Assembly Systems

In **assembly systems**, *collective leadership is exercised by a large group, usually constituted as a legislature.* There might be an executive officer, but the legislature is clearly dominant. Switzerland has an assembly system in which the legislature dominates the collective seven-member executive council that it elects. Most confederations, such as the United Nations and the European Parliament (the elected legislative wing of the EU), are assembly systems in which legislatures delegate administrative power to an appointed executive. The New England town meeting in American local government is an extreme version of the assembly system because all citizens directly participate in key decisions and oversee the administration of policy.

In theory, most communist states are assembly systems because the constitution grants most power for policy making to the legislative body. In reality, however, the legislatures in such states have traditionally rubber stamped the policies and administration of a single leader or a small collective leadership group, as in China and North Korea. In fact, few, if any, national political systems operate as true assembly systems, since power for policy making and policy implementation rarely remains dispersed among a large group of relatively equal rulers.

Which Form Is Optimal?

Which form of executive–legislative relations is best? If there were agreement on this question, we might reasonably expect most states to have adopted the same form of government. In fact, however, each form has its strengths and weaknesses, as reflected in the Debate in 7.

POLITICAL PARTY SYSTEMS

Another taxonomy for political systems is based on political parties. **Party systems** are generally classified according to *the number of political parties* and *the interactions among the parties in the governing process.* In the comparative study of political parties, there are usually four types of party systems: (1) two-party systems, (2) multiparty systems, (3) dominant-party systems, and (4) one-party systems. The distinguishing features of each type are described in this section, and representative examples are identified in Figure 7.3.

THE DEBATE IN 7

Which Form of Government Is Preferable: Parliamentary, Presidential, or Hybrid?

A central issue regarding governmental institutions is the normative question: Which arrangement of executive–legislative relations is preferable? Countries vary in the manner in which they organize executive–legislative relations. Initially, most modern countries established either the parliamentary form or the presidential form. Yet many of the countries that have dramatically transformed their governmental structures in the last several decades have opted for a hybrid. The current diversity suggests that no one form is clearly preferred in all cases. Since this three-way debate remains unresolved, it is useful to consider the key arguments regarding the strengths and weaknesses associated with each of the three major forms of executive–legislative relations.

The Parliamentary Form Is the Most Effective Institutional Arrangement

- The fusion of executive and legislative powers eliminates potential executive–legislative conflicts that can result in deadlock in presidential or hybrid systems. This singular authority structure ensures that as long as the governing majority (party or coalition) maintains its cohesiveness, this group is responsible for every stage of the policy process, and there are few roadblocks to the passage and implementation of any policy.
- This concentration of political control also ensures that there is a clear system of accountability. The successes or failures of policy can be associated directly with those who are part of the governing coalition. If citizens are dissatisfied, they know which parties to vote against in the next election,

and the citizens know whom to reelect if they are satisfied.
- If the chief executive loses the support of the governing majority, he can be replaced at any time and in a relatively rapid political process that does not require a national election or the trauma of an impeachment trial.

The Parliamentary Form Has Serious Problems

- A coherently organized majority exercises great, unchecked power because it can streamroll policy through virtually all opposition, since it controls both the legislative process and also the agencies that administer policy in every area. Even in its most benign form, the system is not well structured to encourage compromise, to protect against a tyrannical majority, or to ensure that minority concerns are represented during public policy making.
- The chief executive is not always directly elected by the public because he can be selected and also changed by a vote of the legislature at virtually any time, without any direct input from the citizens. It is quite possible for the citizens to be stuck with a chief executive that they did not vote for and that the majority does not support.
- Parliamentary systems are often plagued by uncertainty and instability, which stems from the chief executive's capacity to dissolve the legislature at any time and the legislature's ability to vote no confidence in the executive at any time. In addition, this perpetual vulnerability of the executive and the legislature can result in extensive strategic game-playing,

despite the apparent fusion of executive and legislative actors.

The Presidential Form Is the Most Effective Institutional Arrangement

- In presidential systems, citizens have the power to elect their top executive leader directly. The voters explicitly choose a president, who serves for a fixed term in office without legislative intervention (except in the extraordinary circumstances of impeachment).
- This directly elected president can act as a singular leader and an embodiment of the political will of the national majority, and not someone who happens to have emerged from a backroom deal in the legislature or in response to short-term disfavor in public opinion.
- Presidential systems are more stable because presidential and legislative elections occur in regular, fixed intervals so everyone knows exactly when the next election will occur and new mandates for power will be given.
- The separation of executive and legislative power provides a healthy system of checks and balances, preventing abuse of power and ensuring more careful consideration of policy before it is adopted and implemented.

The Presidential Form Has Serious Problems

- Presidential systems often obscure which policy-making structure is responsible for the impact of a particular policy. Executive and legislative power can be exercised by different groups who can, rightly or wrongly, accuse each other of policy failures. Thus accountability is often unclear, even if the executive and legislative majorities are from the same political parties, and especially when there is a split in power between the two branches.
- Perhaps even worse, the separation of power enables the legislature and the executive to block each other's actions if they do not fully share a political agenda. The legislature can refuse to pass executive-supported legislation, while the executive can veto policies adopted by the legislative majority and can use its control over all administrative agencies to distort or even block the intent of legislative policy. Such circumstances can produce interbranch conflicts, policy stalemates, and governmental paralysis.
- The fixed terms of both the executive and the legislature provide predictability at the cost of flexibility and responsiveness. An ineffective legislature cannot be forced to face the electorate until the end of its term. And, short of a traumatic impeachment, a highly unpopular chief executive cannot be replaced before the end of his lengthy, fixed term and can hold onto power with minimal support from either the legislature or the citizenry.

The Hybrid Form Is the Most Effective Institutional Arrangement

- The hybrid combines the best of both the parliamentary and presidential system. It takes advantage of the parliamentary form's fusion of executive and legislative power among a prime minister, cabinet, and legislature to ensure greater policy coherence, from conception to adoption to implementation.
- The hybrid also provides an independently elected presidential-type executive who can represent the national will and can act decisively when the cabinet and legislature fail to respond to a critical situation.

The Hybrid Form Has Serious Problems

- As is often a problem for presidential systems, a significant risk with hybrids is the potential for major power struggles, especially between the cabinet and prime minister on one side, and the president on the other side. The situation is made worse by the fact that the constitution is usually ambiguous about the conditions when one or the other is dominant in the policy process.
- The hovering presence of the president does not usually reduce the inherent problems of

the parliamentary form, such as excessive concentration of power in the majority and the uncertainty and instability due to the constant threat of dissolution.

And in case you were wondering . . .

A *council system* has the virtue of distributing power among a manageable number of people, but there is a strong tendency for collective leadership to result in persistent internal power struggles as one or a few members attempt to assert their dominance. And while *assembly*

systems are the best approximation of a genuine representative democracy, they lack the clear and decisive executive leadership that people in most contemporary states seem to want and complex modern political systems seem to need.

More questions . . .

1. Which system makes most sense to you?
2. Can you think of any conditions (e.g., the party system, aspects of the political culture, etc.) that might make different forms preferable?

Two-Party Systems

A *two-party system* is characterized by two major political parties that alternate in governmental power. Each party has a realistic possibility of forming a governing majority, although the electoral success of each party varies over time. In some countries the two major parties have distinct ideologies (as in Great Britain and Hungary), but in others (e.g., Honduras), the two major parties can have substantial ideological overlap. The United States is a classic two-party system, since one of only two parties almost always has a majority of seats. As Figure 7.3 indicates, the Democrats won 54 percent of the seats in the House of Representatives in the 2006 election, virtually the same percentage held by the Republicans in 2004. Hungary moved quickly in the postcommunist era from having a large number of parties to a system in which only two major parties dominate. Minor third parties typically arise in two-party systems, but these parties have limited power unless a major party needs their support. Currently, there are few pure two-party systems because minor parties frequently prevent either of the two major parties from achieving a majority. In Honduras, for example, the Liberal and National parties alternate in power although neither controls 50 percent of the seats in the legislature (Figure 7.3). Great Britain is now sometimes called a "two-party plus" system because it is dominated by two major parties (Labour and Conservative) but there is a significant third party (the Liberal Democrats, with about 10 percent of the seats) as well as several regional parties (such as the Scottish Nationalists).

Multiparty Systems

As you might expect, a *multiparty system* has more than two parties whose participation can be essential in the formation and activities of government. In parliamentary systems, this means that the creation of a legislative majority (a government) might require a coalition of two or more parties (see Chapter 8). Most contemporary political systems have some form of multiparty system.

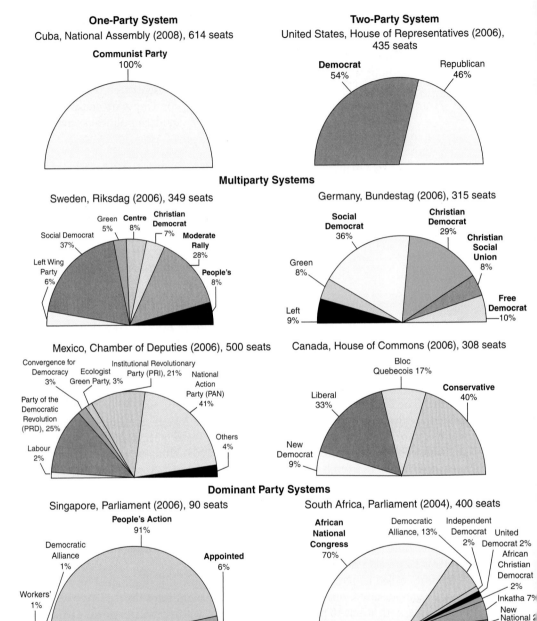

FIGURE 7.3 Examples of party systems (governing parties in **bold**)

Working multiparty systems. In a "working" multiparty system, several clusters of parties tend to be willing, after each election, to cooperate in order to form a governing majority. For example, several center- and right-oriented parties might form one group, with social democratic and socialist left parties constituting another.

This is the case in Sweden, where the government majority is usually dominated by the Swedish Social Democratic Party with support from the Green Party and Left Party. However, in 2006, the four- party center-right coalition was successful in winning a majority of the seats. These parties cooperate as an effective working group (Figure 7.3; see also Box 13.1). Denmark also has a stable system of seven major parties with coalitions of the left and the right. Currently, the Liberal (Venstre) Party leads a three-party conservative coalition.

It is also possible to have a working multiparty system in which parties across the ideological spectrum are willing to cooperate in a long-standing governing coalition. A notable example of this situation is Switzerland, where four major parties, ranging from right wing to center left, have shared governing power in every election since 1959, and the general viewpoint is that it is undesirable for any one of the parties to govern independently. A more unique form of this broad array of parties is Germany's current "grand coalition" (Figure 7.3). In the German election of 2006, neither multiparty coalition gained a majority of seats. Rather than creating a minority government, the leading parties of the two blocs agreed to create a "grand coalition" in which the governing cabinet includes nearly all of the major rival parties (the two leftist parties refused to participate) under the leadership of Angela Merkel, leader of the Christian Democrats. Such grand coalitions are unusual, existing mainly in times of national crisis, and thus is it unclear how long the German coalition will survive.

In some countries, multiparty systems have stabilized as groups of parties have organized themselves into two relatively stable blocs that compete for power. Citizens are reasonably confident that, even when they vote for a party that cannot win a majority of seats, their party is committed to cooperating with particular parties to form an effective and stable governing group. Italy, which had experienced decades of highly unstable multiparty government, introduced a new electoral system in 1996 in an attempt to create more party coherence. After some initial turbulence (ironically, a total of 251 parties put forth candidates in the 1996 election), the system seemed to have stabilized with two major alliances, each led by the major party in the bloc: the People of Freedom group (victors in the 2008 election) and the Democratic Party group. Chile is another example, where six parties each have a substantial proportion of seats, but these parties have formed two blocs that currently operate almost like a two-party system.

Unstable multiparty systems.   Multiparty systems are often unstable. In these cases, no party is close to a majority and differences in party ideology prevent temporary coalitions from forming long-term blocs. In such cases, it can be difficult to form a governing majority after an election and even more difficult to maintain it. After a long period of dominance by one party (see below), Mexico now has three parties (PAN, PRD, and PRI) that have had substantial electoral success and are clear rivals; they are unlikely to cooperate with each other in a coalition (Figure 7.3). Thus in recent elections, no party commands a legislative majority in Mexico, and it can be very difficult to pass legislation. Israel presents a more extreme example of the challenges in some multiparty systems (Figure 7.3). The largest party in the 2006 election was actually a new centrist party, Kadima, which holds only 23 percent of the seats in the legislature. It is attempting to govern in a complex coalition including parties of the left, the center, and conservative, ultra-religious parties.

In such party systems, there is usually a point where the government's policy on an issue induces a coalition partner to withdraw its support, causing a crisis for the government. In parliamentary systems, such a crisis often leads to the resignation of the government or the dissolution of the legislature. In presidential or assembly systems, this situation tends to produce paralysis in the legislature. Clearly, the difficulty of forming a governing majority among multiple parties increases as different parties are more firmly committed to their unique ideological orientations.

New democracies seem especially prone to a proliferation of political parties. In 2005, more than 300 parties competed for votes in Iraq. And in the initial years (after 1989) of democratic politics in the postcommunist states of Central and Eastern Europe, as many as 200 parties competed for political power. While there has usually been a significant reduction in the number of effective parties in the postcommunist states (as in the example of Hungary), many are still dealing with somewhat unstable multiparty systems. When many parties win representation, it has been extraordinarily difficult to form the stable coalitions necessary for coherent policy making.

Even more established political systems grapple with the challenges of achieving stability in situations with multiple competing parties. Canada has multiple parties but has had some recent periods in which the system approximates a "two-party plus" model. However, in the 2006 elections, neither of the two largest parties, the Liberals and Conservatives, was able to secure a majority or stable support from one of the two other major parties, the socialist New Democrats or the regional Bloc Quebecois (Figure 7.3). Thus the Conservatives initiated a period of minority

▶ Energetic campaigning and the powerful party organization of PRI enable virtual unknown Enrique Pena Nieto to win the gubernatorial election in Mexico's largest state.

government, a system that can be quite unstable in a multiparty system, depending on the political issues that dominate the agenda.

Dominant-Party Systems

In a *dominant-party system*, the same party repeatedly captures enough votes and seats to form the government, although other parties are free to compete. In Figure 7.3, Singapore is a clear-cut case of a dominant party. The People's Action Party wins nearly all the seats in the legislature in every election (since the first full general elections in 1959), although as many as 20 other parties put up candidates. In South Africa, the African National Congress (ANC) emerged as the key movement engaged in peaceful and violent resistance to apartheid. Under the leadership of Nelson Mandela and now Thabo Mbeki, the ANC has evolved into a dominant party, increasing its proportion of legislative seats in each election in the post-apartheid period (since 1994), with 11 other parties currently holding seats (Figure 7.3).

Eventually, a dominant party usually loses support and becomes a competitor in a multiparty system. This happened to Japan's Liberal Democratic Party (LDP), which was a dominant party in Japan for more than 40 years after the ratification of the 1947 constitution (recall Box 7.2). But scandals involving LDP leaders and changing attitudes among the Japanese electorate are among the reasons that the LDP lost its legislative majority in 1993 and has been less dominant since then, although it did garner a strong majority in the 2005 election. Other parties that lost their overwhelming electoral dominance after decades in power are the Congress Party in India and Mexico's Institutional Revolutionary Party (PRI).

One-Party Systems

In a *one-party system*, a single party is directly supported and favored by the governing group, and any other parties are elected, if at all, with explicit permission from the government. Some authoritarian regimes do not tolerate the existence of any political parties other than the single party that represents the state and its vision of political order, as in Myanmar, North Korea, and Sudan. Any party that expresses opposition to the ruling party is viewed not as the "loyal opposition" but as disloyal or even seditious (in other words, it is seen as stirring up resistance or rebellion against the government). There are currently few one-party systems in a technical sense, given the high ideological premium associated with the appearance of democratic processes. Thus some form of party competition is introduced although the ruling party maintains near-total control. In Cuba (Figure 7.3) and China, for example, the Communist Party allows other parties to elect a few representatives. In Syria, all parties are government controlled, and the ruling group is guaranteed the great majority of legislative seats.

No-Party Systems

The taxonomy should have a category for those political systems that have no political parties. Historically, many political systems had no organized parties. But only a few contemporary political systems do not allow political parties. Such countries as Kuwait, Oman, and Swaziland have banned political parties, either because the rulers do not want any organized bases of opposition to their authority or on the grounds that parties divide people's loyalty to the society. The latter argument is a primary justification given for the nonpartisanship (lack of political party affiliations or organization) of candidates for public office in many American local governments.

CLASSIFICATION AND CLARITY

Most theorizing about political systems begins with some classification scheme. Classifying political systems into a taxonomy can be straightforward, especially when the categories are based on clear institutional characteristics (e.g., federations, confederations, and unitary states). But many of the most interesting classifications (e.g., democracies and dictatorships) are challenging because political systems tend to be complex mixtures of characteristics that do not fit tidily into any category. In addition, any classification is time specific because evolutionary and revolutionary processes can change the nature of a political system.

There are at least three important reasons for classifying political systems. First, such classification can provide us with useful descriptive information about political systems. Most people have a vague sense that other political systems are different from their own, and by describing how various political systems are organized between central and peripheral units or between executives and legislatures, we expand our grasp of alternative forms of governmental structures.

Second, the classification of political systems helps us to undertake political analysis—to identify patterns of similarities and differences among the political systems of the world. Rather than positing that every political system is unique, the development of a taxonomy assumes that some generalizations can emerge from analyzing groups of these systems. Sets of political systems that share important characteristics can be compared with each other, or compared with sets that do not share those characteristics. Such taxonomies provide us with a basis for thinking more clearly about the kinds of generalizations that we can articulate. Comparative analysis can then increase our confidence regarding what we know about the political world.

Third, the taxonomies in this chapter might encourage us to specify with greater precision what we mean by value-laden terms such as *democracy* and *dictatorship*. In this manner, the analytic study of political institutions improves our understanding of how these terms are most appropriately used as thoughtful descriptors rather than as mere rhetorical labels.

Ultimately, developing greater precision in our use of key political concepts and increasing our knowledge about the political world can do more than clarify our thinking. They can also enhance our ability to evaluate the nature and desirability of the political structures in our own nation and in other countries, and to decide whether there is a "best" form of government.

Would you argue that one form of areal division of power and one form of executive–legislative relations and the same constitution are best for *all* states? Or might the best institutional arrangements be contingent on the major goals and key characteristics of the particular political society? As a closing puzzle, if your country were to convene a constitutional convention now, would you argue in favor of retaining all of the governmental forms that currently exist in your political system? Why, or why not?

KEY CONCEPTS

assembly system
authoritarian regime
authoritarianism
confederation
constitution
constitutional regime
council system
democracy
dictatorship
direct democracy

electoral democracy
electoral system
federation
hybrid system
illiberal democracy
liberal democracy
limited mandate
nonconstitutional
   regime
nondemocracy

parliamentary (cabinet)
   government
participatory democracy
party system
presidential government
representative democracy
taxonomic analysis
totalitarian regime
totalitarianism
unitary state

FOR FURTHER CONSIDERATION

1. What is your definition of a democratic political system? What are the minimal conditions necessary for a country to be classified as a democracy? If you opt for the definition used in this chapter, explain which elements of the definition are the most essential and the least essential for democracy.

2. In the late eighteenth century, the United States opted for a federal, presidential, two-party system with plurality elections. Given the situation at the beginning of the twenty-first century, what are the major shortcomings of each of these decisions? Speculate what politics in the United States might be like if the country became a unitary state with a parliamentary government or a multiparty system based on proportional representation.

3. Some analysts argue that democracy is not possible unless there are at least two political parties. Provide a critical evaluation of this viewpoint. In theory, might we expect any relationship between the number of parties and the extent to which the political system is democratic?

FOR FURTHER READING

Arendt, Hannah. (1973). *The Origins of Totalitarianism.* New York: Harcourt. The classic study of the forces underlying totalitarian regimes.

Barber, Benjamin. (2004). *Strong Democracy: Participatory Politics for a New Age.* Berkeley: University of California Press. A "twentieth anniversary edition" of an important book offering a persuasive argument that democracy can and should be based on active and extensive participation by the citizenry.

Bratton, Michael, and Nicolas van de Walle. (1997). *Democratic Experiments in Africa: Regime Transitions in Comparative Perspective.* New York: Cambridge University Press. Numerous examples are provided of the attempts to establish and sustain liberal democracy in the countries of sub-Saharan Africa, which, due to their history, informal institutions, and elite behavior, have been less successful in this transition than any other region.

Dahl, Robert, Ian Shapiro, and Jose Antonio Cheibub, Eds. (2003). *The Democracy Source-book*. Boston: MIT Press. This very strong collection of readings covers critical topics from the definition of democracy to issues of representation, constitutional regimes, and the impacts of democracy on individual countries and the global system. The (generally short) excerpts include both major historical thinkers (Locke, Rousseau, Madison) and important contemporary scholars (Dworkin, Pzeworski, Sen).

Elgie, Robert, Ed. (1999). *Semi-Presidentialism in Europe.* New York: Oxford University Press. An exploration of how similar forms of executive–legislative structures (hybrids with a directly elected president and a prime minister responsible to the legislature) can result in different patterns of politics and power.

Hesse, Joachim Jens, and Vincent Wright, Eds. (1996). *Federalizing Europe? The Costs, Benefits, and Preconditions of Federal Political Systems.* New York: Oxford University Press. From the perspective of developments within the European Union and its member states, the problems and prospects of federal forms of governance are debated.

Lijphart, Arend, Ed. (1992). *Parliamentary Versus Presidential Government.* New York: Oxford University Press. A wide-ranging set of readings examining the advantages and disadvantages of the two major forms of executive–legislative relations as well as hybrids.

Linz, Juan J., and Alfred Stephen. (1996). *Problems of Democratic Transition and Consolidation: Southern Europe, South America, and Post-Communist Europe.* Baltimore, MD: Johns Hopkins University Press. Based on illuminating examples from two continents, the authors explore the difficulties associated with the shift from authoritarian or communist regimes to democratic ones.

Norris, Pippa. (2004). *Electoral Engineering: Voting Rules and Political Behavior.* Cambridge: Cambridge University Press. A creative scholar considers the impacts of the various electoral systems being utilized by states with survey data and other empirical evidence from 32 countries in order to assess whether, given political culture, such "engineering" of institutional arrangements can influence political behavior, from voting to the building of social capital to democratic accountability.

Obinger, Herbert, Stephan Leibfried, and Francis Castles, Eds. (2005). *Federalism and the Welfare State: New World and European Experiences.* Cambridge: Cambridge University Press. Scholars explore the evolution of federal states (Australia, Austria, Canada, Germany, Switzerland, and the United States) in order to assess the interplay between this form of power distribution and the patterns of social welfare policies that emerge.

Wheare, K. C. (1980). *Modern Constitutions.* 2nd rev. ed. London: Oxford University Press. Although first written in 1951, this description of the content and impacts of constitutions is arguably still the best.

ON THE WEB

http://confinder.richmond.edu/index.php

Constitution Finder at the University of Richmond provides links to the constitutions and other key documents for most countries.

http://www.servat.unibe.ch/law/icl/index.html

The International Constitutional Law (ICL) Project provides English translations of constitutions as well as other textual material related to constitutions from more than 90 countries. It also cross-references those documents for quick comparison of constitutional provisions.

http://freedomhouse.org

The site of Freedom House, which includes current ratings for every country, along with topical discussions regarding those countries' levels of political rights and civil rights as well as press freedom and religious freedom.

http://mirror.undp.org/magnet/Docs/parliaments/Default.htm

This site explores a variety of issues regarding the functioning of legislatures and their relations with other branches of government, covers governing systems and executive–legislative relations within presidential, parliamentary, and hybrid systems along with information about political parties.

http://www.politicalresources.net/

This is a very useful and accessible site with information on many countries, including current data on party systems and the Web sites of most parties from each country.

https://www.cia.gov/library/publications/world-leaders-1/index.html

The Central Intelligence Agency manages this "World Leaders" database that lists the chiefs of state and cabinet members of all foreign governments.

http://wc.wustl.edu/parliaments.html

The Weidenbaum Center at Washington University in St. Louis provides a listing of the Web sites of most national parliaments.

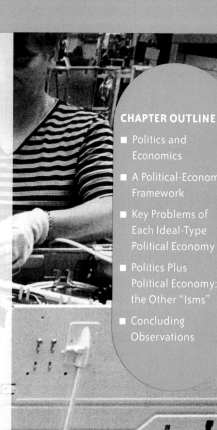

CHAPTER 8

POLITICAL ECONOMY

> In all the political systems of the world, much of politics is economics and most of economics is also politics. . . . For many good reasons, politics and economics have to be held together in the analysis of basic social mechanisms and systems.

> —*Charles E. Lindblom,*
> *Politics and Markets (1977: 8)*

This book is about the *political* world. But if Lindblom is correct, understanding contemporary politics requires an understanding of its linkages with economics. This *combination of politics and economics* is called **political economy**. This chapter explains this concept. First, it describes the connections between the economic system and the political system. Then it characterizes three different types of political economies: (1) the *market economy*, (2) the *command economy*, and (3) the *mixed economy*. Finally, it examines how these political economies are related to major "isms" in the political world, especially capitalism, socialism, and communism.

POLITICS AND ECONOMICS

Many of the decisions made by the political system can have significant impacts on the economy. Can you think of how the following government policies might affect the economy?

- No state involvement in the construction or repair of highways and roads
- State ownership of all factories producing cars
- Very high state taxes on the profits of businesses
- Full state financing of the provision of all medical services
- Absolutely no state restrictions on the right of foreigners to enter and work in the country
- State regulation of the prices of all basic foods

Similarly, the actions of major economic actors and the performance of the economic system can have a major impact on the political system. The political order depends on the economic system to generate income, goods, and services for the survival and prosperity of its citizens. For example, what policy responses might you predict from the U.S. government to the following economic factors?

- A lengthy nationwide strike by air traffic controllers
- The proposed sale of the country's major automaker to a Japanese corporation
- The discovery that there are fewer than five years' worth of underground oil reserves within the country's boundaries
- A virulent disease that requires the destruction of 80 percent of the country's poultry

The more one reflects on modern societies, the clearer it becomes that the political system and the economic system are inextricably entwined.

Understanding political economy requires a grasp of some basic economic concepts. This chapter describes a framework for the economic system that is similar in spirit to Easton's framework for a political system (see Chapter 5). The framework deals only with some core ideas that have been simplified considerably. However, this discussion does involve some complicated abstractions, so hang in there! (If you want the full treatment, take an introductory economics course or read an introductory economics book such as Heyne, Boettke, and Prychitko [2006]. For a political science perspective, see Wilensky [2002: ch. 2]).

A POLITICAL-ECONOMIC FRAMEWORK

The abstract model presented in Figure 8.1 is our starting point for understanding the idea of a political economy. The figure offers an extremely simple characterization of the way in which extraordinarily complex systems of production and exchange operate (see Blinder and Baumol 2008: ch. 8; Miller 2007: ch. 8).

Factors, Firms, and Households/Consumers

In the beginning (according to this model), there are three kinds of important productive resources—the three major *factors of production* (A) (see Figure 8.1). *Land* means the ground plus any raw materials (commodities such as coal ore and bananas) on or in the ground. *Labor* is human productive input (our common understanding of "work"). *Capital* is the nonhuman productive input from other resources (especially financial resources, machinery, and technology). Each factor of production is controlled by an owner who, in the language of economics, is referred to as a *household* (B).

Some actor called a *firm* (C) (in this book, the terms *firm* and *producer* are used interchangeably) attempts to acquire a combination of these productive resources (factors of production) in order to produce a *good* (D1). A good can be a product (e.g., a pencil, a nuclear missile) or a service (e.g., massage, transportation on an airplane).

A firm might be a single person who produces a good from her own resources. For example, a masseuse (massage giver) provides a massage through her own labor skills. Or a firm might be a large organization that uses many productive resources (of land and commodities, workers and capital). For example, a firm that produces something as simple as pencils needs such productive resources as wood, graphite, rubber, machines, and workers. The firm transforms these factors of production into the final good—here, pencils. Often some goods are acquired in order to make more complicated goods; these goods used in the firm's production process are called *intermediate goods* (D2). The pencil firm, for example, has probably acquired such intermediate goods as graphite (which it acquires from another firm that has mined and refined this chemical element) and wood (which has come from a firm that owns, cuts, and mills trees).

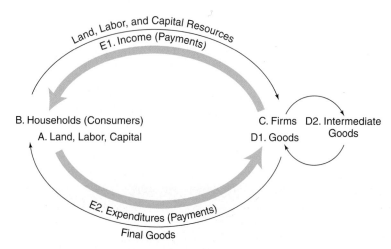

> **FIGURE 8.1**
> An economic system framework: the income-expenditures model

A household has a second role, as a *consumer*, when it wants to acquire a final good. A consumer offers something of value to the firm in exchange for the good that the consumer wants. What emerges between the household/consumer and the firm is a system of *payments* (E1 and E2 in the figure). A firm must pay something to those households that control the relevant productive resource(s) necessary for the firm to produce goods. And a household, in its role as a consumer, must pay something to the firm in order to get the final goods that it wants. Notice that any individual or group can act as either a consumer or a firm, depending on whether the individual or group is transforming productive resources into goods or is acquiring a final good.

The size of a payment (the price) is established when there is an agreement between one actor, who is willing to exchange (give up) something to get the good, and another actor, who is willing to give up the good for what the first actor offers. In the language of economics, each actor increases her **utility** (her overall happiness) in such an exchange because each has higher utility after the exchange than before it. So, for example, the actor who has grown a dozen tomatoes might have a higher utility when she exchanges them with someone who will give her whatever else she values highly enough to give up the tomatoes.

In every system, there are some good-for-good exchanges, called *barter trading* (e.g., the dozen tomatoes are traded for a massage). But most economies are dominated by exchanges where some form of currency (money) is the medium for the exchange. In good-for-money exchanges, the consumer gives the producer some amount of money in exchange for the final good (e.g., a tomato might be exchanged for $1, or a massage might be offered for $50).

If firms want to sell more massages than customers want to buy, the price of a massage is likely to come down. This is how **supply and demand** operate: if demand is low relative to supply, the price comes down; if demand is high relative to supply, the price goes up. In theory, with enough producers and consumers making exchanges, the price of a good reaches a perfect balance point between supply and demand, known as the *equilibrium point* (see Figure 8.2).

The payment by a consumer to a firm (E2) is usually a different amount than the payments by the firm for the productive resources used to produce that good (E1)

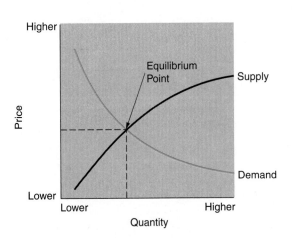

FIGURE 8.2

The relationship between the supply of a good and the demand for the good

▶ **The richest merchant in a Bedouin market in Egypt displays the goods she will sell, proudly wearing the chains of gold coins that attest to her entreprenuerial skills as a "firm" in a market economy.**

(Figure 8.1). A firm is successful if it can sell the good for more than it paid to produce the good. This return to the firm in excess of its payments is called *profit*. If the firm must sell the good for less than the cost of producing it, the firm suffers a *loss*. Obviously, firms normally try to increase their profit and to avoid loss.

Getting and Spending

In this way, the system of exchanges goes around and around. The households expend their resources on goods, and the firms provide the households with income as they pay for productive resources. Ideally, everyone is exchanging things of value for other things that they value even more. As the system becomes more complex, many actors are involved in the production and distribution of goods. In addition, some actors can operate as brokers, organizing and facilitating exchanges. For example, the grower of tomatoes sells them to a broker, who then markets the tomatoes to other consumers.

As the cycle continues, more and more goods are produced, bought, sold, and consumed by all the actors in the economic system. The complexity of the actual exchanges in most economic systems is beyond comprehension. As an example, see how long a list you can quickly develop of the number of different people who contributed some fraction of the value (the one dollar) that you pay for a tomato at the supermarket. (Think about the actors involved in the production and distribution of that tomato to you.) With sufficient time, you could probably identify hundreds of people who share in the resource that you have sacrificed (i.e., the payment you have provided in exchange for the tomato).

To the extent that others are willing to offer substantial payments in exchange for the factors of production or the goods that you control, you have more resource power. You have many choices regarding the use of your own resources. For example, if you have 12 tomatoes, you could (1) eat them all; (2) eat 6 and sell/trade 6 for as much money or goods as you can get; (3) eat 2 and sell/trade the rest to obtain a loaf of bread and a book of verse; (4) eat 2, sell/trade 2 for a loaf of bread, and use the remaining 8 and the bread to make 16 tomato sandwiches that you sell/trade (for as much as you can get); (5) give all the tomatoes to hungry people; or . . . the possibilities go on and on. And if you chose approach 2, 3, or 4, you would now have further choices to make with your new bundle of resources.

Presumably, you attempt to pursue a strategy that maximizes your utility (i.e., that results in your most preferred mixture of goods and resources) and hence enhances your life. Individuals (and groups) can have very different sets of preferences. One person might want to hoard money or food or precious metals; another might want to spend everything on consumption for personal pleasure. One person might actively seek the resources to own a mansion and a Mercedes-Benz, while another person might be happiest with minimal work and no possessions other than the bare necessities she carries in a backpack.

Of course, it is a tough world, and all people are not equally capable of maximizing their value preferences. A person's success in getting her preferred mix of goods and resources can be affected by such things as the kinds and amounts of resources she already controls, her skills in producing desired goods, the constraints in her environment, the actions of others, and even luck. Over time, there are likely to be huge differences in the mix of goods and resources controlled by different individuals and groups.

The State Joins In

We now have our first approximation of an abstract model of the economic system. The cyclical exchange of payments for factors of production and payments for goods becomes a perpetual motion machine. One very important addition to this simplified model is the political system. The state (F) is added in Figure 8.3, and the interaction

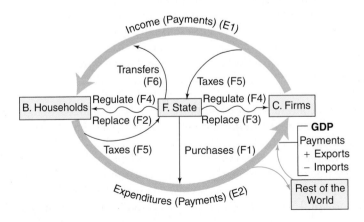

▶ **FIGURE 8.3**
A political economy framework

▶ **Every country tries to promote its exports. Here, the Canadian minister of international trade makes a pitch to persuade China's policy makers to open the huge Chinese consumer market to Canadian goods.**

between the economy and the state results in the dynamic processes we call the *political economy*. The state can powerfully affect the economic system in the six general ways labeled F1 through F6 in Figure 8.3. The state can:

- be a consumer, purchasing any good from a firm. (F1)
- replace (that is, be) a household, in the sense that it controls some or all factors of production. (F2) *Command economy   Cuba*
- replace (that is, be) a firm, producing any good. (F3)
- regulate the manner in which either households or firms operate by enacting policies that encourage or prevent certain behaviors by those other economic actors. (F4)
- tax (extract resources from) the payments to any actor. (F5)
- transfer payments to any actor. (F6)   *Eg- grants, aid to other country*

The state's patterns of action on these six dimensions distinguish the different types of political economies discussed below.

The World Joins In

The second important addition to our simplified model of political economy is nothing less than "the rest of the world." While Figure 8.3 could represent an economy at any level, it is most commonly understood as the national economy of a state. It is quite possible that there are exchanges of goods and factors of production that cross the boundaries of the state. In our model, *all those goods and factors of production that are sold to actors outside the state's boundaries* can be considered ***exports***. Thus, if the tomatoes or automobiles produced in the United States are sold to households in Mexico, these exports generate revenue for American firms (hence the exports arrow points inward in Figure 8.3). Exports are generally viewed as a positive for the economy, assuming the goods are sold for a profit, since they inject additional money into the system. Conversely, *the goods that a country's households purchase from another country* are **imports**. Thus, if the United States imports tomatoes or automobiles produced in Mexico, these imports result in money leaving the American economy (although the American households do get the goods).

Each state has major policy choices as it decides whether to influence the ease or difficulty of economic transactions that cross its borders. The state might be genuinely committed to "free trade" and thus make no effort to influence import and export activity. However, many countries do intervene in economic transactions that cross their borders in an attempt to serve their own needs and interests. Thus the state can discourage imports by taxing them on entry (tariffs) or by limiting how much of an import is allowed (quotas). In some cases, the state might even encourage certain imports. Similarly, the state can implement policies that facilitate or obstruct exports by its own firms. Can you think of reasons a state might restrict certain exports or encourage certain imports?

There have always been economic exchanges between states. In the last few decades, however, the scale and complexity of interstate exchanges have become extraordinary. There is now a vast "global economy" in which there is arguably more economic value in the economic exchanges that cross borders than in those that occur within countries. Chapter 11 will detail the forces of globalization, but the key point here is that states find it increasingly difficult to control their economy. First, many firms now operate "multinationally"; that is, they operate in multiple countries and can move their production from country to country, often very rapidly. Second, even more firms utilize factors of production and intermediate goods from multiple countries. Third, most large firms now sell their goods in multiple countries. Thus many consumers, especially in the more developed countries, purchase goods whose productive factors are not primarily from their home country. For example, consider whether the clothes you are wearing or your electronics gear are goods in which the majority of components were produced by firms inside your country. Probably not.

The global economy has many consequences for the national political economy. States have much less capacity to regulate the behavior of firms, to control the balance of imports and exports, and even to tax many economic transactions. Thus, for most countries, the actions of firms and households outside the state's borders are as significant for their political economy as those of economic actors inside their borders. The key impacts of such external actors will be particularly emphasized in Chapters 13–16.

The Grand Total

The total level of production in an economy is usually measured by one of two monetary figures that summarize "gross product"—the total value of all the final goods produced by a state's economic actors during a certain time period, adjusted for exports minus imports. *Gross domestic product (GDP)* is the total value of all final goods produced by all people within a state's boundaries, whether or not they are citizens (see Figure 8.3). The *gross national income (GNI)*—also called the *gross national product (GNP)*—includes the production of all citizens of the state, whether they are inside the state's boundaries or not. For comparisons, all amounts are typically measured in U.S. dollars. Although GNP is still the measure sometimes referred to in the United States, most international economic actors now opt for GDP as a more accurate indicator of a country's economic vitality, given the large numbers of noncitizens who produce goods within many countries. Box 8.1 indicates that the measurement and comparison of the total production of economies are subject to further refinements.

BOX 8.1

How Do You Measure Economic Prosperity?

Many important analyses require a measure of the economic prosperity of a country. The most widely used indicators are gross domestic product and gross national income. Since both measures are greatly influenced by the size of the country, attempts to compare the relative prosperity of the people in different countries have typically divided the productive total by the number of citizens (as "per capita"). However, as measures of a country's prosperity, both GDP per capita and GNI per capita have at least three important flaws:

1. They do not measure how the prosperity is distributed among the country's economic actors, and thus many citizens have an individual level of prosperity that is sharply different from their country's average production per capita.

2. Only the goods that actually enter the society's monetary sector are measured, while many other valued goods are ignored. These unmeasured goods include both household work and also goods in the "underground economy," particularly trade in illegal goods, barter trade, and the black market. In some countries, GDP and GNI are particularly misleading because such unmeasured goods are a significant proportion of total economic activity.

3. GDP/capita and GNI/capita are often used to compare the prosperity of one country versus another. However, there are huge between-country disparities in the exchange value of money. In two different countries, the same amount of money (converting local currencies into an international exchange currency, usually dollars) can buy much more or much less of the same specific goods (e.g., a pound of rice in Japan might cost 20 times as much as a similar amount in India).

Due to these cross-national disparities in the value of money, there is increasing use of a third prosperity measure that attempts to establish equivalent value, an index based on *purchasing power parity (PPP)*—that is, *correcting monetary indicators to reflect the amount of local currency required in that country to buy certain standard goods*.

If we use PPP indexing, India's GDP per capita of only $640 per year equates to $3,139 per capita in "purchasing power" (UNDP 2006: table 14). The purchasing

BOX 8.1 *(Continued)*

power of Japan's $36,182 is actually $29,251. In purchasing power dollars, the economic gap between the wealthier countries and the poorer countries usually decreases. Indeed, for many of the poorer countries, the purchasing power dollars are three to five times greater than GDP per capita dollars. However, it is important to note that when a country attempts to participate in the global economy, and especially when it attempts to import goods, the purchasing power of its currency is directly tied to international exchange rates, not to the price of bread at home (or PPP dollars), and its relative wealth or poverty remains.

Table 8.1 compares how GDP per capita and GDP per capita adjusted for PPP differ in 24 countries. The relative wealth of most countries across the two measures changes less than 20 ranks out of 210 economies. However, there are a few instances, such as China, where the gaps between gross product per capita and the correction for PPP are large. What might explain a disparity between the two measures, like that in China? More broadly, is there another indicator besides a gross product per capita measure that would be better at measuring the general prosperity in a society? Why?

▶ **TABLE 8.1**
Alternative Measures of Economic Prosperity

Country	GDP/Capita in PPP[a]	GDP/Capita[b]
United States	39,676	39,883
Canada	31,263	30,586
Sweden	29,541	38,525
Japan	29,251	36,182
Germany	28,303	33,212
Singapore	28,077	25,191
South Korea	20,499	14,136
Czech Republic	19,408	10,475
Poland	12,974	6,346
Russia	9,902	4,042
Mexico	9,803	6,518
Costa Rica	9,481	4,349
WORLD Average	8,833	6,588
Brazil	8,195	3,284
Turkey	7,753	4,221
Iran	7,525	2,439
China	5,896	1,490
Egypt	4,211	1,085
Syria	3,610	1,293

BOX 8.1 (Continued)

▶ TABLE 8.1   (Continued)

Country	GDP/Capita in PPP[a]	GDP/Capita[b]
India	3,139	640
Ghana	2,240	409
Angola	2,180	1,258
Nigeria	1,154	560
Kenya	1,140	481
Congo	978	1,118

[a]PPP=purchasing power parity, in U.S. dollars.
[b]In U.S. dollars.
Source: United Nations Human Development Report (2006: table 14).

TWO IDEAL-TYPE POLITICAL ECONOMIES

Based on the framework in Figure 8.3, we can distinguish two ideal-type political economies: *market economy* and *command economy*. An *ideal type* is a description of what a certain phenomenon might be like in its pure form, but it does not necessarily correspond exactly to any real-world example.

In distinguishing the market economy from the command economy, it's useful to consider five fundamental questions:

1. Who controls the factors of production?
2. Who determines what goods are produced?
3. Who establishes the value attached to different resources and goods?
4. Who decides how resources and goods will be distributed?
5. What is the role of the state?

The next two sections consider these questions for each ideal-type political economy. Table 8.2 summarizes the responses to each of these key questions. The table also provides answers for a "mixed" economy, which is less an ideal type than a real-world compromise between the two. (For other approaches that explain political economy, see, e.g., Heyne, Boettke, and Prychitko [2006] and Lindblom [1977, 2003].)

The Market Economy: Total Private Control

1. **Who controls the factors of production?** In the ideal-type **market economy**, there is *total private control*. The state has almost no significant role in the political economy. Thus every actor has direct, personal control over the use of all the factors of production that she owns. The laborer, the landowner, or the owner of capital decides who, if anyone, she will exchange her resources with and the amount of resources she will

> **TABLE 8.2**
Comparing Command, Market, and Mixed Political Economies

	Command	Market	Mixed
Who controls the factors of production?	The state owns all significant factors (land, labor, and capital).	Every private actor (household) controls her own factors.	The state and private actors each control some factors.
Who determines what goods are produced?	The state devises a detailed economic plan that specifies what level of each good will be produced. The system is supply oriented.	All actors (firms) make their own separate decisions about production in an attempt to maximize their own utilities. The system is demand oriented.	Some firms are under direct state control, but most make decisions in the market. The state regulates some actions of many firms and households. The system is mainly demand oriented.
Who establishes the value attached to different productive factors and goods?	The state sets the value (price) in all exchanges.	The market (via the "invisible hand") sets the value based on the equilibrium of supply and demand.	The market sets the value. The state regulates some prices to serve national priorities.
Who decides how factors and goods will be distributed?	The state's plan indicates who will receive which goods and in what amounts.	Distribution is based on a summation of the actions of all consumers and producers in the market.	The market is the main decision maker. The state intervenes in some cases to ensure that certain actors have access to particular goods.
What is the role of the state?	The state is dominant, controlling virtually all aspects of the political economy.	The state plays a minimal role in the political economy. The state enforces the "social contract," protecting all from violence or law breakers.	The state attempts to strike a balance between: • competition and state control • private profit and a sharing of societal resources

accept in that exchange. In a related process, each firm acts to maximize its profits through acquiring productive resources and then producing goods that can be sold to consumers (Lindblom 2003).

2. **Who determines what goods are produced?** All the firms' decisions about what goods to produce are based on their own assessments of how they can achieve maximum profit. If one thinks of an economy in terms of the supply and demand for goods, the market economy is demand oriented. The most important consideration for a firm that is deciding what to produce is this: What good can I offer that others will demand and for which others will offer the highest payments, in comparison with my costs of production? Thus the firm attempts to assess the demand for various goods in the market and then to acquire and transform certain factors of production in order to provide

whatever good it thinks will maximize its own profit. Overall, production is guided by what the famous Scottish economist Adam Smith (1723–1790) called the "invisible hand" of the market. This invisible hand is a summation of the self-serving actions of every household and every firm regarding their uses of the factors of production.

3. **Who establishes the value attached to different factors and goods?** Similarly, the invisible hand of the market establishes value. Each factor of production and each good that is produced through transformation of these factors are valued at their *opportunity cost*—the value (e.g., money, good, factor of production) that is sacrificed by someone in exchange for that factor or good. Hence nothing has value except to the extent that some other actor will exchange resources to obtain it. Usually many actors offer similar factors and comparable goods. This results in competition among households and among firms, as each one tries to gain the maximum payment from others in exchange for its own productive factors or goods.

Ultimately, the value of every productive factor or good is determined in this competitive market, based on both its supply and the existing demand for it (recall Figure 8.2). Competition is particularly intense where supply and demand are quite unequal. For example, if five workers (supply) will drill holes in metal and one firm needs only two workers with this productive factor (demand), the firm can bid down the resources it must pay for the work (this is usually a wage rate, but it can also include other resources, such as work conditions, benefits such as housing or health care, or shares of the firm's profits) by inducing the five workers to undercut each other's wage claim. Conversely, if only two workers are available with this skill and the firm needs five, the workers can bid up the resources that they will be offered.

A basic economic assumption in a market economy is the continual adjustment of supply and demand toward an equilibrium point. For example, some workers might move to a different place or offer a different labor skill if the wages for drilling holes get too low or there are too few jobs. And a firm might find a substitute for the labor it needs if hole-drilling labor is too expensive or too scarce to enable the firm to make a profit (e.g., technology, outsourcing). Can you think of other supply–demand adjustments that the workers or the firm might make?

4. **Who decides how productive factors and goods will be distributed?** Again, it is the invisible hand of the market, rather than anyone in particular, that determines who gets which factors and goods. As each person pursues her own private utility, economic actors accumulate dramatically different bundles of factors and goods, depending on their preferences, the resources they control, and their skill and luck in exchanging and transforming resources in the market.

5. **What is the role of the state?** The state is passive in the productive system, allowing private actors to operate in a relatively unconstrained manner. The state's primary obligations, under the social contract, are to prevent private actors from doing violence to each other, to protect private property rights, and to defend the state's sovereignty. In meeting these responsibilities, the state might purchase some goods and some productive factors, might levy minimal taxes, and might affect firms' import and export activities. Otherwise, state intervention in the economy is minimal.

The Command Economy: Total State Control

1. **Who controls the factors of production?** In the ideal-type **command economy,** *the state assumes total control of virtually all the significant factors of production.* The

state replaces or eliminates the role of private owners of labor, land, and capital. The state owns the land, the natural resources, the factories, the machines, and so on. The state even owns labor, in the sense that the state decides the conditions and purposes for which all individuals must offer their labor.

2. **Who determines what goods are produced?** In a sense, the state is a firm that produces virtually all major goods in the system. The state devises a detailed *economic plan* that specifies what level of each good will be produced from what combination of productive factors. Thus the state's plan makes production decisions that are supply oriented (in contrast to the demand orientation of the market economy). The state/firm attempts to use productive factors optimally to maximize the supply of goods that it has determined are most appropriate to produce.

3. **Who establishes the value attached to different factors and goods?** Since the state controls all the factors of production and is the firm producing all the goods, it also can set the values (i.e., establish the payments) for all exchanges within its boundaries. Competition is eliminated, since the state, rather than the market, establishes the payments for every factor of production and every good in the society. Thus the state tells a group of farmers to produce a million tomatoes and then sets the exchange value of those tomatoes. Similarly, the state decides which individuals will have jobs drilling holes, and it establishes the wages and benefits they receive for their work. The state is not completely free to set payments—for example, the scarcity of a productive resource can influence its cost—but given availability, value is set primarily by the state's decisions.

4. **Who decides how productive factors and goods will be distributed?** The state is equally active in the decisions about the distribution of goods to the population. The state's plan indicates who will receive which goods in what amounts. The plan could specify, for example, that automobile- producing factory X will receive 46 tons of steel each month, and that a town will receive three tomatoes per family per week. The plan can also indicate precisely where these goods will come from (i.e., steel from factory Y and tomatoes from farm Z). The crucial decisions about the distribution of goods are made by those with power to control the state.

5. **What is the role of the state?** Clearly, the answers to the preceding four questions indicate that the state has a dominant, even an overwhelming role in this ideal-type political economy. The state controls virtually all the important factors of production, plans the manner in which they will be utilized in the production of goods, establishes the official value of all resources and goods, and decides how the resources of the society will be distributed among individuals. In the command economy, profit is accumulated by the state, not by individuals. The state then determines how this profit will be used to serve its objectives and to provide goods to certain actors.

KEY PROBLEMS OF EACH IDEAL-TYPE POLITICAL ECONOMY

Table 8.3 lists several of the most important virtues of each of the two types of political economy. These benefits stem from the logic of each approach. In theory, the market economy is efficient and dynamic because profit-driven, self-serving behavior in a highly competitive environment encourages high levels of productivity and innovation. In theory, the command economy is effective and humane because society's resources are managed and distributed so that everyone benefits from the most desirable set of goods and services. These virtues are true, at least in theory. However, there are significant potential short-comings in the functioning of either the market economy or the command economy. These problems are also summarized in Table 8.3 and characterized below.

Market Economy

Resource inequality and hardship.   Substantial resource inequalities tend to emerge in a market economy. Competition is everywhere, and it tends to become ruthless. As every actor strives to maximize resources and control over the factors of production, some are extremely successful and others are total failures. Most important, the market system is indifferent to the hardships of those who do not succeed. Neither the successful actors nor the state intervenes to protect those who have minimal success. Over time, the rich tend to get richer (especially if they cooperate with each other) while the less successful tend increasingly to lack the resources for a secure and comfortable life.

Production for profit, not need.   A demand-oriented system of production does not necessarily produce goods that meet human needs. Rather, production decisions

▶ TABLE 8.3
Benefits and Problems of Market and Command Economies

	Benefits	Problems
Market Economy		
Competition	Energetic and efficient production	Ruthless interactions; huge inequalities in wealth and resources
Demand orientation	Goods' cost and quality responsive to consumers' desires	Creation of demand for and proliferation of goods that have limited social value
No central plan	Local decision and "invisible hand" stimulate innovation, facilitate freedom	Economic cycles of boom and bust, inflation and recession
Command Economy		
No competition	Work for common good; relative equality of wealth and income	Little initiative; shoddy products; low productivity; limited innovation
Supply orientation	Production and distribution for social and individual needs	Oversupply and shortages; lack of coordination
Central plan	Rational use of societal resources	Overcentralized control; lack of responsiveness to changing circumstances

are dominated by actors who produce those goods that they believe will result in maximum profit. Such goods might be extravagant, and there might be inadequate quantities of desirable goods for those who are relatively poor. For example, there might be an abundant supply of plastic surgeons to serve the rich, while large numbers of poor people lack adequate basic health care because private producers see too little profit in treating them and the state is not involved in the production and regulation of health care. Also, considerable resources might be wasted to create demand for more profitable products. For example, people can be persuaded that they need something that is inessential or that they should consume products that are more attractive or trendy, even if they are of lower quality (e.g., fashionable brands; high-fat, low-nutrition foods; and so on).

Severe economic cycles.   A third problem is that a market economy can experience major economic cycles. There is no guarantee that the very large number of private decisions about production and consumption (the "invisible hand") will mesh in a manner that ensures steady growth and prosperity for the economic system as a whole. The economy is prone to large swings toward either hyperactivity (causing inflation and scarcity) or serious economic slowdown (causing recession or depression), and the state does not intervene to counteract these swings. Fluctuations between boom and bust, even if infrequent, can be deeply disruptive to the productive system and especially to those actors whose limited resources make them vulnerable to bad times.

Command Economy

Limited incentives for efficiency.   The absence of competition in the command political economy can result in problems as serious as those from excessive competition. First, if the state controls wages and prices, there are no major economic incentives for firms to be efficient, for managers to be innovative, or for individual workers to work hard. Second, if there is no competitive market of alternative goods, there is minimal incentive to produce goods of high quality. People are obliged to accept goods that are unexciting or poorly made.

Unresponsive production.   The state's emphasis on a supply orientation means that production decisions are not directly responsive to consumer demand. The central planners' ideas of what people should want are not necessarily what consumers actually do want and will purchase. Thus the plan typically results in substantial oversupply of some goods and severe shortages of others.

Overcentralization and inflexibility.   Command economies are so centralized that they lose touch with the differences and complexities of individual firms and consumers. The central planners usually do not receive and react effectively to information regarding miscalculations and mistakes in either the development or the implementation of the state's overall plan. Such rigidity and unresponsiveness make the efficient use of productive resources unlikely. In short, the political economy that combines minimal competition, a weak demand mechanism, and inflexibility is prone to low productivity, inferior goods, and inefficient use of resources.

The Mixed Economy

Given the potential shortcomings of the ideal-type market and command political economies, is there an alternative? The **mixed economy** can be understood as *an attempt to combine the strengths of these two ideal-type economies while also minimizing their shortcomings.* As a hybrid, the mixed economy is not a "pure" ideal type. It compromises on each of the five major issues considered earlier (see Table 8.2).

1. **Who controls the factors of production?** Control of the means of production is shared between the state and private actors. The state owns or directly controls some of the major factors of production, such as those relating to key commodities (e.g., coal, oil, steel), key infrastructure systems (e.g., transportation, telecommunications), and key financial resources (e.g., banks). However, private actors (households) control a substantial share of the factors of production.

2. **Who determines what goods are produced?** Production decisions are primarily demand oriented, driven by the market mechanism. Half or more of all

▶ **Deal! The leaders of the fourth and second largest economies (in PPP), Prime Minister Manmohan Singh of India and Premier Wen Jiabao of China, sign a major trade agreement.**

production is done by private firms. Most public-sector firms (those owned and managed by the state) must interact and even compete with many private firms when acquiring productive resources and when selling goods to consumers. However, private firms and households are constrained by the state, which regulates the behavior of private actors and can implement an economic plan that specifies broad guidelines for all actors in the economic system.

3. **Who establishes the value attached to different productive factors and goods?** The value of most goods is established, as in a market economy, through the processes of supply and demand. But the state does intervene to ensure that national priorities are protected. For example, the state might establish the value of certain factors of production, including wages; it might set guidelines to control the market prices of key goods; it might regulate the manner in which households and firms collaborate and compete; and it might employ taxing and expenditures (purchases [F1] in Figure 8.3) to influence the productive system.

4. **Who decides how factors and goods will be distributed?** Decisions on the distribution of productive factors and goods are the most complicated element of the mixed economy. Private actors are allowed to make decisions and take actions that maximize their profits and their share of the resources. The state then intervenes through a variety of taxation mechanisms (F5 in Figure 8.3), extracting some of the payments received by every private actor. In turn, the state uses these taxes to purchase goods (F1) or as transfer payments (F6), both of which the state redistributes to certain actors in the social order. The state undertakes only a partial redistribution of resources (unlike the case in the command economy), leaving private actors with considerable resources and freedom to make their own decisions about production and consumption.

5. **What is the role of the state?** The mixed economy is a middle way between the market and the command political economies. The state's rules, actions, and direct involvement in the productive system are attempts to moderate and limit the market of private households and firms. The system blends a demand orientation and a supply orientation. The goals are to facilitate some competition while also mitigating the effects of ruthless competition, and to allow private actors to benefit from their skillful use of resources while also ensuring a certain level of necessary goods for the less successful actors. The great challenges for the state in a mixed economy concern striking a proper balance between competition and control, between a free market and a planned economy, and between private property and a sharing of society's resources. Real-world economies are so immensely complex and dynamic that the search for such a balance is continual and in some cases impossible.

POLITICS PLUS POLITICAL ECONOMY: THE OTHER "ISMS"

The Three "Isms"

One set of great "isms" in political analysis includes the ideologies of conservatism, classical liberalism, and socialism (see Chapter 2). Another set of "isms" explicitly links politics to political economy: capitalism, communism, and socialism. In twentieth-century politics, these were extremely emotive labels, endowed with powerful ideological content.

In their most straightforward form, capitalism, communism, and socialism correspond loosely to market economy, command economy, and mixed economy, respectively.

Capitalism is *a system in which private economic actors are quite free from state constraints, and the state engages in only limited efforts to shift resources among private actors.* It is founded on the philosophy of laissez-faire economics celebrated by Adam Smith, and it imposes the severe limitations on government activity that are associated with classical liberalism. While the freedom of economic actors from government intervention is critical, there is no assumption that capitalism requires any particular form of political processes to function efficiently (Thurow 1997).

Communism has as its centerpiece *the socialization of resources—the notion that the state must control society's land, labor, and capital.* The state must guide the utilization of all these major means of production with a central plan, so that the production and distribution of goods serve the best interests of the entire population. Although it is primarily an economic system linked to the command economy, communism also emphasizes an ideological commitment to economic and social equality among all its citizens. It typically posits that government and politics, like the economic system, must be guided powerfully by a unified leadership. Communism is generally associated with the theories of Karl Marx and with the economic systems that were developed in such countries as China (1949 to about 1990), Cuba (since 1959), North Korea (since the early 1950s), and the former Soviet Union (1917–1991).

Socialism is in the middle of the three "isms," and thus it is not precisely differentiated from the other two. It seeks *a complex balance between state involvement and private control,* in common with the mixed political economy. Some major productive resources are owned or controlled by the state, and the state actively intervenes in the economy, but most production decisions are private, and value is established primarily by supply and demand. While the policies in a socialist state attempt to reduce inequalities significantly, they do not aim for total economic equality. Sweden and Denmark are examples of what are known as democratic socialist systems (or "social market" systems, see Box 13.1) because they blend socialist economics with democratic politics. Some nondemocratic countries, such as China and Libya, also define themselves as socialist regimes because they claim that "the people" control society's major productive resources, but the political economy incorporates significant elements of the private market system. *Socialism* is a confusing term, in part because certain "communist" countries, such as Cuba and North Korea, are sometimes called socialist regimes, based on the manner in which Karl Marx and Marxists use the concepts of socialism and communism (recall Chapter 2, and see Box 8.2).

Communism is distinguishable from socialism in an analytic sense because the communist state (on behalf of "the people") attempts to control virtually all important factors of production in the society and has a fundamental commitment to total economic and social equality among all citizens. (Notice that such egalitarianism is not a necessary condition of the ideal-type command economy.) A socialist system, in comparison with capitalism, tends to use public policy to redistribute societal resources toward those citizens who are less advantaged economically, and the socialist state is substantially more involved in economic planning, regulation, and even ownership of some productive means than a state under capitalism (Przeworski 1985).

BOX 8.2

Communism Versus Socialism in Marxist Theory

It is worth noting that Marx and Marxist theorists use the terms *socialism* and *communism* in a different manner from either the political economy approach of this book or contemporary Western media and politicians. In Marxist theory, communism is a higher stage of political economy that follows socialism. In a *socialist system*, the state strives to achieve social control of resources (the means of production) by eliminating private property. As private property is eliminated, there will be a reduction in the presence of the different strata (classes) of citizens that are separated by substantial variations in the amount of private property that each controls. (A detailed description of the class approach to explaining politics will be provided in Chapter 9.)

In Marxist theory, *communism* emerges only when multiple classes (and the inevitable conflict between those classes) cease to exist. Thus most Marxists acknowledge that no "socialist" state (e.g., Cuba) has yet completely eliminated classes and the class struggle; in this sense, communism remains a goal. In the classless society, everyone will work for the good of all, not to gain private value. Under socialism, everyone provides resources (work) according to ability and receives resources according to that work, while under communism, everyone provides according to ability and receives according to need.

This book employs the common Western usage: communism exists if a state has nearly total control over the major factors of production. Given the recent shift away from communism (see Chapter 15), only a few contemporary states (e.g., North Korea) meet this criterion.

The Real World

It is possible to offer some generalizations about the political economies of contemporary countries. First, no country has a political economy that corresponds exactly to either the market economy or the command economy. Since these are ideal types, this fact is not surprising. While it is possible to locate countries generally along a continuum from a "pure" market economy to a "pure" command economy, all actual political economies are mixed. However, this does not mean that all political economies are basically the same—the mix of elements varies a great deal from country to country.

Second, regardless of how different states describe themselves, the concepts of communism, socialism, and capitalism might be best understood as broader, somewhat ideological labels that signify considerably more than the way in which each country's political economy is organized. For some countries, these labels also connote *sociopolitical* orders. Communism is viewed as a system that denies individual freedoms in noneconomic spheres and in which government does not depend on the consent of the governed. Capitalism signifies a system of self-interested individualism that denies the need for collective action to nurture society as a whole, to promote social values and culture, or to protect the ecology (Heilbroner 1994).

Third, every state engages in some regulation of some economic actors and some redistribution of resources. Politics and values play a powerful role in establishing exactly what kinds of interventions the state will undertake and what values and interests the state will serve. Thus understanding the mixed nature of actual political economies entails more than simply comparing the proportion of the GDP controlled by private actors versus the state.

In theory, at least, two countries might have the same overall levels of market freedom and state intervention in the economy (as well as the same level of taxation and the same share of GDP in the public sector) and yet be guided by very different philosophies. In one country, the state's role could be to limit the power of large firms, to ensure labor's participation in national economic policy making, and to facilitate domestic consumption. In another country, the state might be no less interventionist, but its involvement might be based on policies that support the growth of large firms, that suppress labor unions, and that channel citizens' resources into savings.

The latter profile is consistent with the political economies of some of the most successful industrializing countries of Asia, such as Singapore and South Korea, whereas countries such as Spain and Uruguay generally fit the first profile. These issues will be examined in more detail later in the book (in the study of economic development in Chapter 10, and in the comparative analyses of strategies for achieving prosperity in Chapters 13–15). The four examples that follow here suggest some of the features of actual political economies relative to ideal types.

Generally market and capitalist: Switzerland.   The sixth wealthiest major country in the world (measured as GDP per capita in purchasing power parity [PPP], CIA 2008), Switzerland, has a relatively weak central government. This decentralization of political power is linked to a political economy that strongly emphasizes private control and limited government involvement. Switzerland is ranked fourth among 143 countries on a measure of freedom of the economy from state regulation (Gwartney and Lawson 2007). Nearly all factors of production are privately owned, and most decisions and actions regarding the use of those resources are in private hands. Apart from defense expenditures and education, relatively few resources are allocated to the provision of public goods, given the wealth of the society. Central government spending is less than 15 percent of GDP, and total expenditure by all levels of government is 36 percent of GDP, among the lowest of all developed countries. Although still low, welfare spending rose substantially in the 1990s, generating a national debate about limiting public expenditure on social programs.

Generally mixed and capitalist: South Korea.   In South Korea, the state has little commitment to use the political economy for direct improvement of its citizens' quality of life. Apart from education, the state does not provide many welfare goods and services to its citizens. Government expenditures (by all levels) are only about 28 percent of GDP, the lowest among all relatively developed countries. It is not a purely capitalist system, however, because the state is extremely interventionist in promoting economic development. The state bureaucracy works very closely with firms to implement a comprehensive, collaborative strategy for economic growth, helping it to rise to 25th in the world on GDP per capita. This strategy has particularly favored the development of a few major Korean companies. Government loans, tax credits, and other subsidies are channeled to these companies, which are expected to operate and diversify in directions suggested by the government. In turn, the government has assured the companies of high profits and of a labor force that is well educated, disciplined, and unable to organize effectively for higher wages. The state has also used many hidden subsidies and import restrictions to provide competitive advantages in the international market to its export-oriented firms. Thus South Korea ranks only 32nd on the measure of economic freedom. (This "developmental-state" approach will be discussed further in Chapter 10.)

Generally mixed and socialist: Denmark.   Denmark is ranked ninth among major countries in terms of GDP per capita. The great majority of productive resources in Denmark are privately owned, and the state allows entrepreneurs considerable freedom of action, with a ranking of 15th on the economic freedom measure. However, the state is very active in guiding the Danish political economy. First, it enforces strong policies that regulate private economic actors, especially "corporatist" policies that control working conditions and environmental quality (see Box 8.3 on *corporatism*). Second, the state provides an extensive array of welfare services to the population, including income supplement programs, a comprehensive free health care system, state-subsidized housing for the elderly and for low-income groups, free child care and education from infancy through university, and an extensive public transportation system. More than 55 percent of GDP is spent by all levels of government, second highest among developed countries. And third, to finance these programs, the government collects various forms of taxes equal to more than 50 percent of the GDP.

Generally command and communist: Cuba.   In response to the global movement toward more market-oriented systems, Cuba has reduced its level of centralized state control over the economy. However, the state still owns and controls Cuba's major means of production, and there is a detailed central economic plan. Cuba is ranked 149th among the 154 countries on economic freedom (Heritage Foundation 2005). Agriculture and manufacturing operations remain collectivized, and the state controls many prices. The state promises work for all (although there is unemployment), and it sets workers' wages. Consistent with the ideals of communism, the state retains a fundamental commitment to control and allocate societal resources to serve human needs. There has been a strong emphasis on state spending on education and health care and on policies to equalize the distribution of land and income in order to increase equality among races, between genders, and between urban and rural citizens. Despite its rather low GDP per capita (95th in the world), government policies result in Cuba ranking in the top 50 countries in the world on the United Nations' index of quality of life for a country's citizens (see page 372).

BOX 8.3

From the "Ism" File: Corporatism

Many scholars refer to the political economy of some states by another "ism": corporatism. **Corporatism** is characterized by *extensive economic cooperation between an activist state and large organizations representing major economic actors*. The corporatist state identifies a few groups that control major productive resources. These "peak associations" (organizations that represent these big groups) usually include large industries, organized labor, farmers, and major financial institutions. The organizational leaders of the peak associations are given great influence in working with the state to answer key political economy questions regarding production decisions and the distribution of resources.

The idea is that there will be consultation, cooperation, and coordination among the state, big capital, big owners, and big labor, rather than conflict and competition. The peak associations have some autonomy from the state, but they are supposed to work together for common national interests. In short, corporatism blends features of capitalism (e.g., private ownership, private profit) and socialism (e.g., extensive state economic planning, coordination of major factors of production with the state's conception of the national interest).

Italy under Benito Mussolini created the first modern corporatist state—one with a strong fascist bent—between 1922 and 1943. Twenty-two corporations were established, including ones for chemical trades, textiles, lumber and wood, credit and insurance, and inland communications. Each corporation had owner, employee, and managerial representatives who met with state officials to develop economic policy (Macridis and Burg 1997: 220–226). Brazil, France, Japan, Peru, Portugal, and Spain are among the contemporary states with strong corporatist tendencies (see Royo 2002; Schmitter 1993; Wiarda 1997, 2004).

CONCLUDING OBSERVATIONS

This chapter has introduced you to an approach that classifies and characterizes political systems in terms of their political economies. These concepts are abstract and require the fusion of political science and economics. They are important concepts because the linkages between the political system and the economic system are fundamental and pervasive in the contemporary political world. Indeed, the two systems have become so interrelated in most states that it is difficult to separate them, except in an analytic sense. There is substantial variation in the extent to which the political system intervenes in the system of production and distribution of resources. At one extreme, the state can leave every activity to private actors; at the other extreme, virtually all economic activity is planned and controlled by the state.

In considering a system such as communism or capitalism, you might find it difficult to avoid strong normative judgments due both to your political socialization and to your tendency to identify an "ism" with particular states for which you have definite positive or negative feelings. For example, your evaluative orientations of communism might be negative because you associate it with the governments of North Korea or the former Soviet Union, states that you might have been socialized to distrust. It is certainly reasonable that you will make both analytical *and* normative judgments about the virtues and shortcomings of every form of political economy and every "ism."

Indeed, assessing the appropriateness of a country's political economy might be the most crucial issue in understanding its effectiveness in the contemporary political world. In recent years, the support for communism and the command political economy has substantially declined among the leaders and citizens in many countries. However, as you will see in Part Five, that decline has not necessarily led countries to adopt a full implementation of a market economy. It has not even meant that most political leaderships and most citizens have abandoned their support for all of the principles associated with a more command-oriented political economy or with communism.

Despite your own political socialization, you might reflect on a fundamental question: Is *every* state, regardless of its current economic and political development, best served by exactly the same political economy? If you allow for variations in the most appropriate form of political economy for countries in the current global system, you leave open many challenging and important questions about political choices, questions that will be considered from a variety of perspectives in the remainder of this book. This exploration will begin in Part Four, with chapters that examine crucial issues associated with political decision making; political, social, and economic change; and political violence.

KEY CONCEPTS

capitalism	gross domestic	mixed economy
command	product (GDP)	political economy
economy	gross national	profit
communism	income (GNI)	purchasing power
corporatism	gross national	parity (PPP)
exports	product (GNP)	socialism
factors of production	household (consumer)	supply
firm (producer)	imports	and demand
good	market economy	utility

FOR FURTHER CONSIDERATION

1. The economic productivity of command political economies has always been inferior to that of market political economies in comparable countries. What, then, might have been the attraction of this approach to many groups and to many countries between the 1950s and 1970s?

2. What would be the greatest benefit to individuals if the state played virtually no role in its political economy? What would be the most serious problem with such a system?

3. Are there measures other than the growth in GDP per capita that might indicate the success of a political economy? Why are leaders in most states so worried if there is no growth in GDP per capita?

4. Do you agree with those who contend that capitalism is so individualistic that it fails to protect the collective good?

FOR FURTHER READING

Courtois, Stephane, Nicholas Werth, Jean-Louis Panne, Adrzej Paczkowski, Karel Bartooek, and Jean-Louis Margolin. (1999). *The Black Book of Communism: Crimes, Terror, Repression*. Trans. Jonathan Murphy and Mark Cramer. Cambridge, MA: Harvard University Press.   A detailed and profoundly critical analysis of the history of communism in the twentieth century. Its core argument is that a series of regimes and ruthless dictators, ranging from Lenin and Stalin in the Soviet Union to Mao Zedong in China to Pol Pot in Cambodia to Kim Il Sung in North Korea, have led communist regimes that engaged in brutal "class genocide" in their societies, resulting in as many as one hundred million deaths. There are powerful chapter-length analyses of communist regimes on every continent.

Friedman, Milton. (1981). *Capitalism and Freedom*. Chicago: University of Chicago Press. The major contemporary explication of the classical liberal preference for a strong market economy with only limited state intervention.

Garson, Barbara. (2003). *Money Makes the World Go Around*. New York: Penguin. The controversial social critic offers a wonderfully readable exploration of the global economy by tracking the money in two small investments and revealing how that money has various effects on people around the world.

Heilbroner, Robert. (1994). *Twenty-First Century Capitalism*. New York: W. W. Norton. An economist and social critic outlines the challenges facing capitalism and the continuing need for the state to guide the market economy and serve the social good.

Kristol, Irving. (1978). *Two Cheers for Capitalism*. New York: Basic Books. A leading American neoconservative argues that capitalism is superior to alternative forms of political economy.

Levitt, Steven D., and Stephen J. Dubner. (2008). *Freakonomics: A Rogue Economist Explores the Hidden Side of Everything*. New York: Harper Collins. And now for something completely different: this book offers a playful and interesting wander through microeconomics, revealing how economic thinking can attack social issues and (often) offer unexpected conclusions.

Lindblom, Charles E. (1977). *Politics and Markets: The World's Political-Economic Systems*. New York: Basic Books. A rich comparative analysis of the relative merits of the political economies of modern socialism and capitalism.

Royo, Sebastian. (2002). *"A New Century of Corporatism?": Corporatism in Southern Europe—Spain and Portugal in a Comparative Perspective*. Westport, CT: Praeger. Detailed case studies of the last three decades in Spain and Portugal are the basis of an exploration of how technological and postindustrial changes have created the conditions for a resurgence of corporatism (see Box 8.3) in European settings.

Thurow, Lester. (1997). *The Future of Capitalism*. New York: Penguin. A leading economist critically assesses the strengths and weaknesses of capitalism as a political economy and as a system that must deliver prosperity to most of its citizens.

Westoby, Adam. (1989). *The Evolution of Communism*. New York: Free Press. A thorough and illuminating history of the development of communist thought and practice.

Yergin, Daniel, and Joseph Stanislaw (1999). *The Commanding Heights: The Battle Between Government and the Marketplace That Is Remaking the Modern World*. New York: Simon and Schuster. A sweeping, readable account of how major countries in Europe, Latin America, Asia, and North America embraced extensive state intervention in their political economies in the period after World War II and then shifted away from the mixed economy toward a stronger form of market economics in the last several decades.

ON THE WEB

http://imf.org/

The key documents and agreements among all states and for particular members of the International Monetary Fund (IMF), an organization that includes more than 180 countries that cooperate to sustain a smoothly functioning system of interstate trade and to provide loans and other financial assistance to countries.

http://freetheworld.com

A site containing reports and data from the Economic Freedom Network, a congeries of researchers "committed to bringing economic freedom and growth to all the countries of the world."

http://www.marxists.org

The Marxists Internet Archive offers links to numerous sources that make the case against capitalism as an economic system.

http://worldbank.org

The official site of the World Bank, an international consortium of banks and other major financial institutions, includes extensive economic data regarding the structure and performance of the economies of more than 180 countries.

http://www.wto.org/

The World Trade Organization (WTO) (see Box 11.2), which coordinates trade policy for about 150 countries, offers this Web site to provide key documents and agreements as well as sections that articulate and justify the WTO philosophy of open trade relations among countries.

http://globalexchange.org

Dedicated to a progressive agenda, this Web site includes links to articles and a section on the global economy that emphasizes fair trade, fair loan practices, and greater equality across countries and people.

http://www.freetrade.org/

From the Cato Institute, this site offers evidence for the benefits of free trade and the costs of protectionism, including various online studies and articles.

http://www.weforum.org/

The site of the World Economic Forum, an organization designed to allow world leaders to address global issues, contains a substantial amount of information on a variety of international economic issues (e.g., sustainable development, globalization).

http://efta.int/

The official site of the European Free Trade Association (EFTA) provides access to EFTA bulletins, conference information, and official documents.

http://www.capitalism.org

This libertarian-inspired site describes the core principles of a system of unconstrained, free market capitalism, including a useful glossary, links to articles, a newsletter, banners, and the unique "Capitalism Tour."

http://www.economist.com/

The electronic home of the *Economist*, a leading British news magazine, provides access to selected articles examining issues of political economy and world finance.

CHAPTER 9

PUBLIC POLICY, POWER, AND DECISION

F actoids:

Every year, the U.S. Congress considers 12,000 bills.

Every day, employees of the British National Health Service administer health care to 2.3 million patients.

Every day, public school teachers in China provide lessons to more than 300 million students.

Each year, Norway sends $477 per capita in aid to developing countries, while the United States sends $67 per capita in aid.

Syria spends 6.6 percent of its GDP on its military each year, while Libya spends only 2.0 percent.

The mayor of Los Angeles, California, required that his Bureau of Street Services fill 83,000 potholes during his first 14 weeks in office.

Politics has been defined (in Chapters 1 and 5) as a process through which power and influence are used to promote certain values that are allocated in decisions by those with governing authority. A national government can make a momentous decision, like the decision to declare war on a rival country or to join the European Union. A local government employee can act to fill a pothole or issue a building permit to a homeowner or organize a dance at a teen center. The government representatives of many countries can hammer out a joint treaty to limit greenhouse gases. A security unit can arrest a suspected terrorist. A government can pass a law making sex among certain consenting adults illegal. Each of these actions is an example of a "public policy." This chapter initially explores the concept of public policy. It then describes three basic theories that provide alternative explanations of how public policy is determined, and how the distribution of power shapes the process.

PUBLIC POLICY

A **public policy** is *any decision or action by a governmental authority that results in the allocation of a value*. These public policy decisions range enormously: in scale, in significance, in the number of people affected, in substantive area, in the power and role of the policy maker. Since the authoritative allocation of values is one essential definition of politics, the study of public policy is a key area of political science. Earlier chapters have emphasized that there are significant differences regarding what activities and what levels of those activities are within the domain of the diverse political systems in the contemporary world. The full range of differences is quite vast across all national, subnational, and supranational political systems, and thus the study of public policy spans a wide terrain.

Table 9.1 offers some representative examples of the variation in current public policy decisions made by seven national political systems. Notice that on nearly every policy decision reflecting the amount of the society's financial resources that the government has allocated to a particular public good, the highest allocations are at least three times more than the lowest. Brazil allocates nearly twice as much of its total economic base to government spending than does either India or China. But Brazil allocates only half as much on military spending than either India or China, nearly three times as much on public health care than India, and nearly twice as much on education than China. Russia requires males to complete compulsory military service and Sweden obliges males and females to fulfill mandatory national service (and the photo on pages 230-231 shows 19 year olds from both countries engaged in joint training). Two countries have abolished the death penalty, two retain the death penalty but have rarely used it in recent times, and three others average more than ten executions each year. This limited set of indicators offers reasonable evidence for the claim that each political system makes different public policy choices, thus producing its own unique blend of decisions.

How do we make sense of this array of public policies? There are several basic approaches to the study of public policy. One approach is based on the development of a taxonomy, which is then used to classify and compare various **types** of public policies. A second approach analyzes the various stages of the policy **process** and attempts to explain the dynamics at each stage. A third approach studies the **impacts** of a particular public policy, since what matters, ultimately, is a determination of what difference

▶ **TABLE 9.1**
Selected Public Policies in Seven National Political Systems

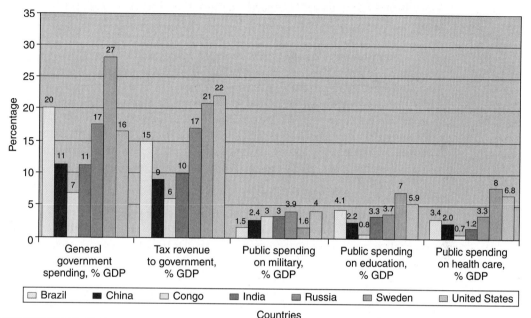

	Brazil	China	Congo	India	Russia	Sweden	United States
Policy on abortion	Only to save life or after rape	Yes, on multiple grounds	Only to save life	Yes, on multiple grounds	Yes, on multiple grounds	Yes, on multiple grounds	Yes, on multiple grounds; varies by state
Policy on death penalty	No, since 1889	Yes, for 60 crimes, ~200/year	Yes, but few known recent cases	Yes, but only two since 1995	Yes for 30 crimes, ~10/year	No, since 1921	Yes, in 32 of 50 states, ~16/year
Mandatory military service	Yes	Yes	No	No	Yes	Yes	No

*Estimate.

Sources: CIA (2007); UNDP (2007); WDI (2007); http://www.un.org/esa/population/publications/abortion/doc/unitedstates.doc; http://www.icj-cij.org/icjwww/ibasicdocuments/ibasictext/ibasicdeclarations.htm.

a particular public policy makes in the lives of individuals and groups. Finally, a fourth general approach is more **prescriptive**, evaluating public policy from the perspective of what policy ought to be implemented, given existing goals, conditions, and resources.

Taxonomies of Public Policies

Several criteria are used to classify different types of public policies. For example, policies can be distinguished by the broad *objective of the policy*: (1) *distributive* policies allocate values to provide particular goods and services (e.g., the building and maintenance of a system of streets and highways); (2) *redistributive* policies explicitly transfer values from one group to another group (e.g., a policy that provides subsidized housing to those with limited financial resources); (3) *regulatory* policies limit actions (e.g., a policy that prohibits a woman from having an abortion); (4) *extractive* policies take resources from some actors (e.g., a tax imposed by the government that takes a certain proportion of the personal income of a household); and (5) *symbolic* policies confer honor or disrepute on certain actors (e.g., a medal awarded to a soldier for bravery). Policies can also be classified by the *functional area* that is served, such as education, health, transportation, trade, public safety, the environment, or defense.

Analysis of the Stages of the Policy Process

This second approach analyzes a series of **stages of the policy process**—*the sequence of actions from the inception of an idea for policy to the point where the policy ceases to exist.* It is possible to analyze how a particular policy evolves at each stage: what actors participate in the stage, how they interact, how the policy is defined, and so on. Many public policy analyses focus on one specific stage and explore the dynamics of that stage of policy making in detail. Six stages are usually distinguished, as characterized in Figure 9.1.

1. Issue identification. Some actor decides that a condition in the environment requires a public policy response. For example, the national legislature decides

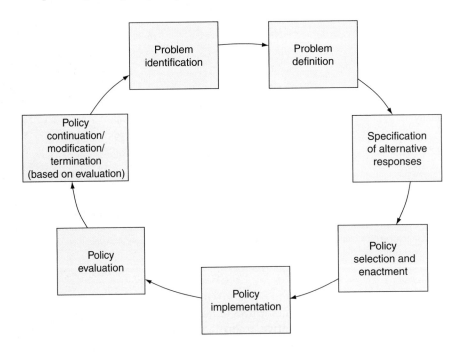

▶ **FIGURE 9.1**
The stages of
the public
policy process

that personal income taxes are too high; groups complain to the county board of supervisors that the traffic congestion has become a serious problem; the defense department gets secret intelligence that a rival state is developing a new nuclear weapons system; the state board of education receives annual testing data indicating that reading scores of elementary schoolchildren are very low. In all such instances, some policy makers or significant stakeholders must specify what the issue is and also define the results that they desire from a policy intervention. If important policy makers push the policy issue forward at this point, it becomes part of the agenda for action. Alternatively, it is possible at this stage that policy makers decide to drop the issue. To provide a concrete example of the policy process, Table 9.2 indicates how the issue of poor reading scores might evolve.

▶ **TABLE 9.2**

An Example of Each Stage of the Policy Process: Reading Skills of Urban Children

Stage	Action
Problem identification	Data indicate reading scores of urban children are too low. Set goal: Raise mean reading scores of 6th-grade children in urban areas by 10 percent in three years.
Problem definition	Target students: A proportion (too high) of students in grades 2–5 read two or more years below grade level. Target schools: Low reading scores are especially associated with families where English is not the first language and families in which parents have low education levels. Target schools where more than 20 percent of students come from such families.
Specification of alternatives	Intensive reading instruction in grades 3–5 for target schools. Or: Provide teachers in target schools with special training in reading pedagogy. Or: Provide reading specialist teachers for target students. Or: Provide computer-aided learning software to target schools. Or: Require an extra 30 minutes of reading instruction per day in target schools. Or: Reduce class size in grades 3–5 in target schools. Or: . . . .
Policy selection	▪ Local school board decides to provide three new reading specialists to work with target students. ▪ State board of education allocates funds to target schools for reading instruction software.
Implementation	▪ School superintendent meets with principals and they decide how to distribute the time of the reading specialists across the classrooms with target students. ▪ School technology committees train teachers to use reading software, principals require teachers to develop a plan for its use , and teachers implement it in the classroom.
Evaluation	Changes in reading scores will be analyzed in each of next three years. Teachers will report on the impacts of the new initiatives on the classroom. Continuation of the two policies will then be reevaluated.

2. **Problem definition**. Next, there is an attempt to explain why the problem exists and to determine what seem to be the causes of the problem. This is primarily an analysis stage, clarifying what the problem is, gathering relevant information that provides measures of the problem, and developing an understanding of the possible causes. Expert staff as well as interested stakeholders with knowledge of the policy domain can have a major role at this stage.

3. **Specification of alternatives**. There are efforts to develop various policy proposals that might respond to the problem, given the causes, a preferred result, and the likely obstacles. In addition, the resources necessary to implement each policy alternative are identified. There can be many such alternatives, depending on the policy problem. The costs (e.g., financial, political, organizational) of each alternative policy must be estimated, as well as the level of expected benefits.

4. **Policy selection**. At this stage, various political activities occur that result in the selection and enactment of a particular policy response from among the feasible alternatives. Alternatively, it is possible at this stage that policy makers will decide to do nothing, either by an explicit negative decision or by letting the policy issue disappear from the public agenda. Considerable negotiations, lobbying, compromises, and adjustments to the proposed policy are not uncommon during the political process culminating in a decision.

5. **Implementation**. In this stage, the policy is interpreted and actually applied in specific contexts. Those in relevant administrative positions typically take the lead role at this stage, determining how to convert the new policy into actual programs and activities, organize the necessary resources, and then actually deliver those programs.

6. **Evaluation**. The impacts of the policy are measured, and an assessment is made of whether these impacts are desirable. After some period of time (or never), new information is gathered to ascertain whether the policy has had any of the anticipated impacts, whether conditions (related to the policy domain or the political situation) have changed, and whether any unintended effects of the policy must be considered.

At any stage, but especially after implementation or evaluation, the policy might be continued, modified, or terminated. It is also possible that the circumstances at such a point will trigger another cycle of the policy process outlined above, possibly beginning with a new stage of issue identification. Also at any stage, many actors besides those authorized to make policy decisions (e.g., those stakeholders directly affected by the policy, taxpayers, administrators, those preferring that policy attention be focused on other issues) can attempt to influence the policy process.

Policy Impact Analysis

The last stage of the policy process described above, evaluation, is an especially significant mode of policy analysis. Ultimately, a crucial question is: What difference did the policy make? This can be considered in different ways. What have been the direct effects of the policy? Have there also been notable indirect effects? Who benefits and who is burdened by this policy? What are the nature and extent of those benefits and burdens? What have been the actual costs compared with the anticipated costs? On balance, is the overall situation improved because of the policy? These questions might be addressed by policy makers and their staffs, by interest groups, by affected publics, and by policy analysis scholars. Such actors attempt to measure the effects of the relevant policy and to compare those effects with the actors' political goals, given current conditions.

From policies that have broad-scale impact, such as the national government's decision about whether to go to war, to such a narrow policy action as a local government employee's decision on whether a homeowner has violated the building code by changing the color of his home, every public policy affects someone's interests. Thus there are always actors trying to influence and shape public policy decisions and to influence policy makers to make some decisions and not others. The views of those advocating a policy might be determined by careful policy analysis and policy impact studies, or they might be derived from ideological principles, or they might be influenced by an agent of political socialization or an authority source such as a political party or political leader (recall Chapters 2–4). The next section explores the public policy process from a very different perspective. It characterizes the process in terms of three broad explanations of how political power is distributed and wielded by different groups who control the policy-making process.

EXPLAINING PUBLIC POLICY DECISION MAKING

How and why does the political system decide to deal in one way or another with an issue like poor reading scores or nuclear proliferation or traffic congestion? A huge number of such specific questions are associated with one of the most obvious yet fascinating general questions in political science: *How does politics actually work?* How does a political system handle the incredibly difficult and complicated value allocations that are the stuff of politics? If someone from another country asked you how major public policy decisions are made in your country, what would you say? What key points would you emphasize?

Earlier chapters introduced many of the major actors and significant structures in the political world and indicated how these actors and structures operate. The first part of this chapter described the analytic concepts that model how the public policy process works. This section details three extremely "political" explanations of the public policy process: (1) the elite approach, (2) the class approach, and (3) the group approach.

Each approach provides a different explanation of how politics works, how influence is exercised, and what forces seem to shape the political decisions that result in public policy. No actual country or political system is likely to operate exactly like any of these three approaches. Rather, each approach is a rich illustration of a pattern of power and decision making that is prevalent in some systems. The three approaches also share two important analytic features:

1. All three are constitutive approaches (as a type of functional analysis; see the Appendix) in the sense that each attempts to define *the* fundamental unit of analysis that explains politics.

2. All three explain politics in terms of the interactions among aggregations of individuals who use the political system to pursue their own particular interests.

Our discussion begins with the elite approach.

THE ELITE APPROACH

Key Concepts

Two key concepts are central to the **elite approach**. First, *politics* is defined as *the struggle for power*. Second, the political world is characterized by ***political stratification***; that is, *the population is segmented into separate groups that are in layers (or "strata") with higher or lower amounts of power*. In the elite approach, there are only two major strata. The stratum that *does more of what there is to do* (in the public policy process) and that *gets more of what there is to get* (in the allocation of values) is called the **political elite**. The stratum that *does less and gets less* is called the ***mass***.

Elite theory can be visually represented by a power pyramid, as shown in Figure 9.2. Such a depiction emphasizes that the elite is composed of a relatively small number of individuals who are in a dominant position on top of the large mass. Notice that there is a third stratum between the elite and the mass. This is the ***political understructure***, composed of *political officials and state administrators who carry out the elite's policy directives*.

Major Theorists

The elite approach has been particularly grounded in the writings of European political theorists of the late nineteenth century, especially the Italians Roberto Michels,

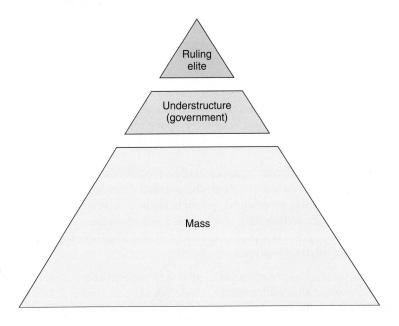

▶ **FIGURE 9.2**
Characterization of an elite system

Wilfredo Pareto, and Gaetano Mosca. In *The Ruling Class* (1896/1939), Mosca analyzes the political histories of a variety of political systems and concludes that they all have two strata: the political class (the elite) and the nonpolitical class (the mass). The political class controls all political functions, holds virtually all political power, and dominates the allocation of values. The basis of elite power has varied across time and location, but Mosca identifies broad historical stages during which the primary basis of elite domination has been military power, then religious control, then economic power, and most recently, technical knowledge. According to Mosca, the major role of the political system is as an instrument of the political class, serving the elite's interests in the allocation of values.

A well-known American application of the elite approach is *The Power Elite* (1956) by C. Wright Mills. Mills concludes that the power elite in American society is composed of those who control society's most powerful institutions: (1) the "warlords" in the military establishment, (2) the "corporation chieftains" in the economic sector, and (3) the "political directorate" at the top positions in the political system. Mills observes that the members of the elite share crucial values about how society in general, and the political system in particular, ought to operate. The members of the elite tend to come from similar social and educational backgrounds, to circulate among major positions in each of the three key institutional structures, and to have long-standing personal relationships with each other. Like other elite theorists, Mills does not claim the elite operates as a conspiracy that continually plots to retain control. But some of its active members do meet periodically to discuss common interests, and most of its members will act in concert during times of crisis (see also Domhoff 2005).

Most elite theorists focus on the elite itself—the identity and socialization of elite members, and how the elite maintains its domination through a variety of techniques, such as the manipulation of symbols, the strategic distribution of resources, control of the state, and the use of force. There is a normative element in the discussions of many elite theorists, indicating their disapproval of a system in which there is such a high concentration of political power serving only a small minority within society. But others respond that elite theory merely reveals the inevitable tendency for a few people to take control and to dominate the political order, while those in the mass willingly subordinate themselves to the few who are capable of giving coherence to political society.

The Public Policy Process

The process through which values are allocated is explained primarily in terms of the elite's actions. Some members of the elite decide that a particular public policy decision is in the elite's interest. They then discuss whether this policy should be enacted and how it should be implemented. When there is general consensus among those members of the elite who are concerned about the decision, representatives of the elite instruct the relevant members of the understructure to perform the policy-making and policy-implementation activities that serve the elite's interests.

In the elite explanation of the policy process, the active elites are subject to little direct influence from the mass or even from the understructure of governmental officials. The mass is politically apathetic and impotent, and policy is imposed on this large proportion of the population. The members of the understructure follow the elite's directives because they believe that their survival in positions of authority depends on the power and support of the elite.

The Prevalence of Elite-Based Political Systems

How many countries have elitist political systems? As noted in Chapter 7, at least two-fifths of contemporary countries (containing more than half the world's population) are nondemocratic systems. It seems reasonable to infer that most of these systems are dominated by an elite in the manner described by the elite approach.

However, the issue might be more complicated. Is it true that all the key conditions of elitism are met in every nondemocratic country? This empirical question could be examined in specific political systems (e.g., Congo, El Salvador, Saudi Arabia) by assessing these kinds of analytic questions:

- Does the political leadership act with unanimity on all major issues?
- Is there active and effective political participation by nonelite groups?
- Are some major political decisions responsive to nonelite demands, even when the decisions are contrary to the elite's interests?
- Is there dramatic inequality in the distribution of resources between the elite and the mass?

While definitive answers to these questions are difficult, our knowledge of political systems suggests that many contemporary states are generally characterized by elite rule. (Consider the brief description of Swaziland in Box 9.1.) The power to make crucial political decisions and the benefits from those decisions do seem predominantly concentrated in the hands of a small elite.

The issue can also be considered in a different way. Is it possible that a country classified as a democracy is actually run by an elite? That is, even if a political system meets such basic criteria of democracy as a limited mandate and freedom to criticize and oppose the leadership (recall Chapter 7), does this necessarily mean that the system is not elitist?

This question underlies a fierce debate among analysts regarding whether the elite approach best describes politics, even in many "democratic" political systems. Some, such as C. Wright Mills (1956; see also Parenti 2007), provide arguments and evidence that there is elite rule even in most democracies. In this view, a small proportion of the population dominates most significant political decisions and enjoys a hugely disproportionate share of the benefits from the value allocations made by the government.

Such empirical assessments of the elite approach, whether of a single city or an entire country, are highly controversial and ideologically charged, since they represent a direct attack on whether the place is a democracy. Moreover, conclusive proof of the elite approach in most political systems would be a massive undertaking, requiring the documentation of systematic elite dominance on a large number of key decisions across a variety of issue areas.

BOX 9.1

Elite Politics in Swaziland

One of the many contemporary examples of elite politics is Swaziland, a small African country between Mozambique and South Africa. While Swaziland was a British colonial protectorate (1902–1968), a local king (Sobuza II) became a hero of his people by leading the movement for independence (from 1921). After independence in 1968, Sobuza became the ruling monarch of the new country. A British-style parliament with competing parties was installed. Parties competed in three parliamentary elections, although the king's party dominated in each election.

In 1973, the king banned all opposition groups and declared that European government forms were "un-Swazi." Since then, political parties have been banned, and the nonpartisan parliament essentially affirms the king's decisions. The king personally appoints two-thirds of the members of the Senate and one-fourth of the members in the House. Indeed, according to Swaziland's official publications, even the method for selecting the next king is "a secret," except it is stipulated that he must be a young,

▶ **A day after being called back from high school in England and being crowned as the ruler of Swaziland, King Mswati III attends a party in the palace. The 18-year-old king moved quickly to establish rule under his personal control.**

unmarried prince. When Sobuza II died in 1982, the ensuing private power struggle among members of the royal family and the king's council resulted in the selection of King Mswati III.

In fact, everyone in Swaziland has always understood that real political power is concentrated in the king and his elite group of advisers, known as the National Council. Young King Mswati III quickly removed many of his rivals from positions of authority and elevated his own set of trusted advisers to positions of decision-making power. Under King Mswati III, as under King Sobuza, both policy making and the major sectors of the economy (the mines and most farmlands) are directly controlled by a king's council. Thus one key criterion of elite politics is

BOX 9.1 *(Continued)*

clearly met: virtually all major political decisions are made by a small group, and the mass of people in Swaziland have little direct impact on the policies or politics of the state.

Moreover, most of the benefits of policy are enjoyed by this elite, a second key criterion of an elite system. A clear indicator of this is the substantial inequality in the distribution of resources between the few rich and the many poor. Although Swaziland is in the middle of the country list on GDP/capita (PPP), the richest 10 percent of the Swazi population have one of the world's highest shares of total income (50.2 percent) and the country has a very high level of income inequality (see Table 13.4). In contrast, fully 69 percent of the Swazi population are below the poverty line, and the average life expectancy is only 32.5 years, the lowest among 222 countries (CIA 2007).

THE CLASS APPROACH

The **class approach** shares certain fundamental concepts with the elite approach, but it offers a very different explanation of the continuing dynamic processes of politics. The most important shared concept is *stratification*, the basic fact of *structured inequality* in the distribution of values in society.

The strata identified in the class approach are called classes, the second key concept. *Class* denotes *a large group of individuals who are similar in their possession of or control over some fundamental value*. The most fundamental value that distinguishes classes differs for different class theorists. Karl Marx (1818–1883), the best-known class theorist, differentiates classes primarily on the basis of a group's relationship to the major factors of production in the economic system (Marx 1867/1981: ch. 52). At the simplest level, Marx divides society into two classes: (1) the *capitalist class*, which includes those who own significant amounts of the major factors of production (especially financial resources, raw materials, and capital—the physical facilities to manufacture goods); and (2) the *proletariat class*, which includes those who own little more than their own labor.

Analysts suggest various modifications that refine Marx's distinctions between classes for most contemporary societies. First, most class theorists identify more than two major class strata, with each class characterized by its particular levels of social, political, and economic power. Second, some argue that it is *control* (rather than ownership) of the means of production that is most important. Third, others observe that in certain social systems, the key elements that distinguish different class strata are status, kinship, ethnicity, religion, or tradition-based authority (rather than ownership of the means of production). And fourth, still others posit that possession of information resources and knowledge has become the crucial resource distinguishing classes in postindustrial, high-tech societies (Castells 2000). In general, these analysts assert that there is strong empirical evidence for the continuing prevalence of class politics, even in developed countries (see, e.g., Dahrendorf 1959; Esping-Andersen 1990; Poulantzas 1973; Wright 1998).

Figure 9.3 provides two models characterizing class systems. Part A shows a characterization similar to the elite approach in its hierarchical and pyramidal form, and it also emphasizes a clear separation between multiple classes. Alternatively, part B highlights the overlap among classes. Here the boundaries between classes are permeable rather than distinct, there is more interdependence among classes, and some members of "lower" classes have as much or even more political power than those in the class above them (see Lenski 1966: 284).

The third crucial concept of the class approach is ***class conflict***. It is assumed that classes lower in the class system can increase their share of key values only at the expense of the classes above them. Given the fundamental inequalities in the distribution of values, struggle between classes is inevitable. The higher classes employ various strategies, and ultimately coercion, to prevent a significant loss of values (and of relative advantage) to the classes below them. Lower classes find that only violence enables their class to increase its relative share of values. Thus class conflict is systematic and ubiquitous, although its most visible and violent manifestations (such as strikes, riots, and rebellion) might be suppressed for periods of time if the higher classes are effective in their distribution of benefits and use of coercion.

The Public Policy Process

Most class analysts do not explain in detail how policy decisions are actually made. They assume that the common interests shared by members of a class will result in general consensus within that class regarding what public policy decisions should be enacted. Like elite theorists, class analysts view the political system as a set of structures that are subordinate to the dominant class. Thus members of this class either hold key positions of governing authority or directly control those who do. The interests of this class are well understood by those who can enact public policy. Consequently, the policies and actions of the state serve the interests of the dominant class, which attempts to maintain its domination and preserve the existing distribution of values.

Rather than focusing on the policy process, the class approach centers on the examination of the tactics of class domination and the dynamics of the class struggle. Not every value allocation by the state is coercive or of direct benefit to only the dominant class. The state might implement policies to shorten the length of the working day or to increase health care benefits to the middle classes. Such policies either ameliorate the worst conditions that might provoke violence or provide certain classes with advantages over classes below them. In such strategic uses of public policy, benefits are provided to some classes in an effort to buy their support or their acquiescence, or at least to dampen their propensity for conflict.

Despite such strategies, the systematic inequalities in fundamental values generate continuing conflict between classes in the society. Periodically, this conflict explodes into class violence. Ultimately, in an episode of class war, a lower class

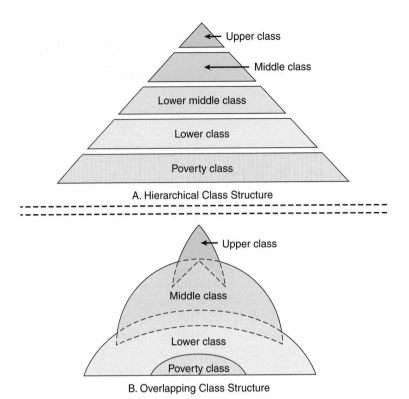

FIGURE 9.3
Two different
characteriza-
tions of class
structures
Source: Based on
Bill and Hardgrave
1981: 181.

succeeds in overthrowing the highest class. At this point, a new class gains dominance in the system, including control over the political system and superiority in
the distribution of values. In the view of Marx and many other class theorists, major
class conflict can end only when the elimination of dominant classes reduces the system to a single class, and hence society becomes classless. The state's policies then
serve all groups, and in the absence of class inequalities, there is no cause for further
conflict among groups.

THE GROUP APPROACH

The **group approach** offers a very different account of the political process. This
approach is grounded in the concept of the *group*, which is defined as *any aggregate
of individuals who interact to pursue a common interest.* A political group, as an analytic
concept, exists whenever individuals have a shared interest regarding some allocation
of values by the political system.

The explanation of *politics* as a complex web of group interactions has many
historical roots, but this approach is particularly identified with American social

scientists, especially *The Process of Government* by American political scientist Arthur Bentley (1908/1967) and the works of David Truman (1951) and Robert Dahl (1961, 1971, 1991), who is the modern political scientist most strongly associated with the development and defense of the group approach.

The group approach begins with the assumption that an individual's *group memberships are multiple and nonoverlapping*. That is, any particular individual can belong to many different groups. Individuals are not stratified into large, permanent groups as described by the elite and class approaches, because the aggregation of people who share a common identity on one political interest is not the same as the people who are part of groups formed for other political interests. Table 9.3 shows six hypothetical people whose group memberships overlap in different ways, depending on the issue. The second important assumption is that *many different political resources might influence those who make public policy decisions*. As discussed in Chapter 3, the kinds of resources that might be used to influence political decisions include money, numbers of supporters/voters, monopoly of expertise, political skill, access to information, legal rights, and status. It is also assumed that every individual (and hence every political group) has some political resources with which he can attempt to influence policy decisions.

In the group approach, *politics* can be understood as *the interaction among groups that are pursuing their political interests*. The role of the government is to manage the interactions within this giant system of interacting groups. Thus *public policy* is defined as *the balance point of the competition among groups on an issue at the time when government makes a policy decision*.

▶ **TABLE 9.3**
Group Memberships of Six Hypothetical Individuals in the United States

Groups	Person 1	Person 2	Person 3	Person 4	Person 5	Person 6
			Individuals			
Democratic Party	✓				✓	
Republican Party		✓	✓			
AFL-CIO union	✓					
Family Research Council			✓			✓
Mothers Against Drunk Driving		✓			✓	✓
NARAL	✓					
Pro-Choice America		✓	✓			
National Rifle Association	✓		✓			
Parent-Teacher Association	✓	✓				

Note: Each checkmark indicates a group with which the individual is affiliated. This distribution supports the concept of nonoverlapping (nonreinforcing) group memberships. An individual shares membership with different people across various groups and policy domains.

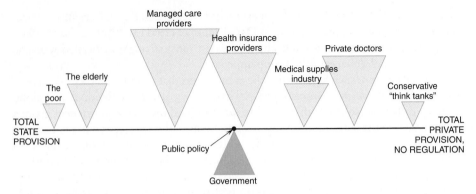

FIGURE 9.4

A group approach model of the policy process: a hypothetical policy decision

Symbols:
— = Continuum of possible public policies regarding health care policy

▽ = Interest group mobilized on this issue, with volume of triangle representing the group's political resources applied to the issue

▲ = Government, which determines the equilibrium point and ratifies that point as public policy

● = Public policy position, which is the equilibrium point in the competition among groups, given each group's political resources

The Policy-Making Process

Figure 9.4 provides a visual model of how a policy decision is made according to the group approach, using health care policy in a country such as the United States as the example. There is a continuum of possible policies, ranging from free state provision of all health care to all citizens at one extreme to total private provision based on fee-for-service at the other extreme. The analytic framework of the group approach can be summarized in five major steps:

1. Identify the key groups that have an active interest in decisions in this policy area.

2. On a continuum of possible policy outcomes, locate the preferred policy decision of each group.

3. Estimate the level of political resources each group employs to influence the decision regarding this policy (represented as a "weight" on the continuum, based on the total impact of the political resources that the group actually utilizes).

4. The "government" establishes the equilibrium point that balances the "weights" of the political resources mobilized by all groups.

5. This equilibrium point is described in terms of a public policy decision that corresponds to this position on the policy continuum. The decision corresponding to this point will be the political system's "authoritative allocation of values" (recall Chapter 5).

In this model, the particular functions of the government are to: (1) establish rules of the game for the group struggle; (2) determine the interests of competing groups and the levels of political resources mobilized by those groups; (3) find a public policy that approximately balances the positions of all active groups in terms of their interests and resources; (4) enact these balance points as public policy decisions; and (5) implement the resulting value allocations. Government, as an analytic construct in the group approach, is best understood as a neutral arbiter in the competition among groups.

In a more realistic interpretation, however, government is not merely an automatic weighing machine that totals the value of each group's influence resources. The government might have an ideological position and thus place greater emphasis on some objectives than others. For example, the government might enforce rules that help or hinder some groups in using their political resources, it might value some political resources more substantially than others, it might allow certain groups greater access to important information, or it might be more or less willing to find the financial resources necessary to implement a certain policy. In addition, certain elected and career governmental actors have their own personal and institutional interests (e.g., for political support, for growth of their unit's power, for personal wealth). When such interests are relevant, these actors can become active as groups that participate in the decision process (with obvious advantages because they are inside "the system").

Like all models, Figure 9.4 substantially simplifies reality. But it should help you to understand the logic of the group approach. A policy decision can change at any time if a different distribution of group interests is mobilized and the issue is taken up by policy makers. The group approach explicitly rejects the notion that a small elite or a single class dominates the resource allocation process. Rather, many different groups become active in the political process, but only on the narrow range of

▶ **Individuals and groups** *can* **influence the policy-making process in some political systems, as in this New England town meeting.**

issues relevant to their interests. Mobilized groups use their political resources to affect the decision. While a group might not always win, its participation can affect the policy decisions made in the area. Box 9.2 provides a case study from Robert Dahl's important book *Who Governs?* (1961), which reveals how a group can form and use its resources to influence public policy.

Critics of the group approach argue that the government/state, far from being neutral, is guided by a strong ideology and is especially responsive to powerful interests in the society. Thus some groups *are* likely to win almost every time they play the game of politics because they have a huge advantage in their political resources, such as wealth, access to decision makers, and political skill. Even though "the little people" might occasionally win a particular episode, the powerful groups in the system are persistent winners and big winners, and the system perpetuates very substantial inequalities in the distribution of benefits (Bachrach and Baratz 1962; Parenti 2007). Indeed, even in the metal houses case discussed in Box 9.2, the biggest losers are probably the poor families in New Haven for whom this housing would have been a substantial improvement over their existing conditions.

Before comparing the elite, class, and group approaches, it is intriguing to consider briefly the impacts on politics of the new information and communications technologies (ICTs). Some analysts argue that these ICTs are powerful political resources, which are having such substantial effects that they are actually "revolutionizing" how politics occurs in advanced countries. The Debate in 9 explores this issue.

THE THREE APPROACHES COMPARED

Which Approach Is Correct?

The three approaches offer powerful answers to the basic political questions of who gets what, why, when, and how. Which of these three approaches is correct? Is one the most accurate explanation of politics for all political systems? For most political systems at a given historical moment? Do different approaches account for the politics of particular systems? For particular kinds of issues?

Advocates of each position offer both theoretical and empirical evidence to show that the politics of actual systems correspond to the description provided in their approach. As an indirect method of providing support for their approach, advocates also cite considerable evidence indicating the inaccuracies and contradictions of the other approaches. As you might suspect, the debate has been most acrimonious between, on the one hand, supporters of the group approach and, on the other, supporters of the elite and class approaches, which both assume persistent stratification and deep inequality. Some scholars contend that virtually all political systems, even "democratic" ones, are elitist, in the sense that the policy process is guided by and generally supports the interests of a dominant elite (Domhoff 2005). In the United States, the debate has been most intense among those who study power at the local level, prompted by the dispute five decades ago between such "elitists" as sociologist Floyd Hunter (1953) and such "pluralists" (supporters of the group approach) as political scientist Robert Dahl (1961).

BOX 9.2

Group Politics in New Haven, Connecticut

The two Lebov brothers, wealthy local businessmen in New Haven, Connecticut, acquired 65 prefabricated metal houses from military surplus. They received permission from the city's building department to erect these houses on a site that was zoned for industry in a working-class neighborhood called The Hill. Their proposal also had the support of the mayor and the city's lawyer.

But the (mainly) Italian American residents of the neighborhood were outraged. They viewed the metal houses as an "instant slum" that would threaten the property values of their modest but well-kept houses and would bring African American residents to The Hill. Miss Mary Grava emerged as the improbable leader of the residents' opposition to the project. An elderly woman, she had never been involved in politics before this. She was tireless in contacting people who might influence the city's decision. She mobilized the residents to telephone members of the city council and others in city government and played Republican politicians against Democratic politicians in order to gain support from both groups for the neighborhood's opposition to the metal houses.

Under severe pressure from the neighborhood, the council drafted legislation to stop construction of the metal houses. But the Lebov brothers began building anyway, with added support from the local newspaper, which saw the houses as affordable housing for needy, low-income families. The city's lawyer ruled that the council had no legal power to stop construction. The council nonetheless voted to stop the project. The mayor vetoed the council's legislation. In response, The Hill residents organized a neighborhood association led by Mary Grava's brother, who happened also to be the mayor's godfather. This local association widened its base, gaining support from the middle-class League of Women Voters (which wanted to expand its membership among ethnic working-class groups), from the current mayor's chief Republican rival on the council, and from the Democratic candidate for mayor. The council overrode the mayor's veto. After an arson fire destroyed one of the metal houses, the fire inspector withdrew his support for the project. Ultimately, the metal houses were never placed in the neighborhood.

In Robert Dahl's view (1961), this is a compelling example of how people can organize into a political group when they care deeply about an issue and can combine their limited political resources to influence policy on the issue. In this case, "just plain folks" formed a group that fought city hall and beat the rich developers, the mayor, and the city's lawyer. (This section is based on Robert Dahl's seminal advocacy of the group politics approach, *Who Governs?* [1961: 192–199].)

vs. Class

the elite politics approach

THE DEBATE IN 9

Will the Communications Revolution Revolutionize the Policy Process?

The astounding recent expansion of information and communications technologies (ICTs), such as computers, cell phones, and satellite communications, has generated considerable talk of a revolution in how politics works (Chadwick 2006; Neuman 1999). The claim is grounded in Francis Bacon's famous observation that "information is power." The argument is that ICTs have substantially altered the distribution of who has information and how it is used in the policy-making process. Are these new technologies really revolutionizing politics?

"You asked us to build a computer which could replace the government."

A New Electronic Politics Is Rapidly Emerging

- Data and technical expertise have always been one important component in the policy process. The new ICTs have vastly expanded the data that are available and the rich ways in which the data can be analyzed and presented. Thus policy making has become much more technical and information driven, and those with the most compelling data are likely to prevail in key stages of the process, such as problem identification, problem definition, and evaluation.

- Electronic networks, such as e-mail, Web sites, and blogs, alter politics by facilitating the political mobilization of individuals and groups who did not participate or had no influence in the old power politics (Jensen, Danziger, and Venkatesh 2007). These ICTs have also generated "virtual political groups" formed from networks of individuals who are geographically dispersed and might never meet face to face. This virtual politics provides new means for engaging in various modes of political action, such as blogging to raise awareness of an issue, contributing funds online, sending e-mails to politicians, and so on.

- New electronic media have dramatically altered the availability of political information and the diversity of viewpoints. Media such as YouTube and blogs enable those with minimal resources to communicate potentially significant political information to a large audience, even if the mainstream media have ignored it. Also, the explosion of media outlets has created an unprecedented level of 24/7 coverage that stimulates constant one-upmanship and looser standards of accuracy among media competing for an audience and to be the first to break a story. Politics has never been subject to such relentless and sometimes shrill scrutiny.

- "E-government" provides powerful new modes of policy implementation. ICTs enable government to deliver services to citizens with ease and efficiency, as citizens complete many of their interactions with government bureaucracies online, from paying bills to completing applications to learning about the availability of services (Eifert and Puschel 2004).

- "E-democracy" opens new avenues for increased citizen participation in politics. Online voting can increase turnout and reduce electoral fraud. And more advanced uses of interactive media can allow citizens to participate directly in the policy process from anywhere, debating, expressing opinions, and even voting on policy choices (Becker and Slaton 2000).

Even with the New ICTs, It Is Basically Politics as Usual

- It is true that the policy process has become more analytic and data driven. However, those public and private elites who previously dominated the policy process are even more advantaged by these changes. They have the most extensive access to critical data, control the most powerful analytic tools and expertise, and can manipulate those data to serve their agendas.

- Those with substantial political power and resources have quickly learned that they can also penetrate the virtual world, from online networks to blogs in order to communicate their message, rally supporters, raise funds, and so on. Thus e-politics do not serve primarily as a forum for the relatively powerless and the unheard.

- The major media covering politics have changed, but not necessarily in ways that democratize politics. The concentration and globalization of major communications sources have resulted in vast media networks controlled by a few multinational corporations. One analyst predicts that soon "five to ten corporate giants will control most of the world's important newspapers, magazines,

The Debate in 9 *(Continued)*

books, radio and television outlets, cinema, recording industries, and video" (Frederick 1993: 124; see also Box 13.3 on media mogul Rupert Murdoch).

■ E-government is a welcome advance, but more efficiency and convenience in completing ordinary tasks like paying for parking tickets or applying for a dog license does not constitute a dramatic shift in the policy process or the distribution of political power.

■ Despite all these ICTs, citizens exhibit no greater knowledge about or interest in the political world, and political participation has not increased significantly as a result of these technologies (Bimber 2003). Moreover, few policy makers have much enthusiasm for most e-democracy initiatives. Most political actors discount e-mail, relative to others forms of communication from stakeholders, and reject electronic plebiscites, since they do not want to be bound by whoever is pushing those vote buttons in cyberspace.

■ Most empirical research has concluded that ICTs are essentially power reinforcing. Those elites and groups who already exercised greatest power over policy-making prior to the expansion of these technologies have been able to capture a disproportionate share of the power and benefits associated with the use of ICTs (Bimber 2003).

More questions . . .

1. Do you think government will be less able to control its citizens in a world where individuals have access to so many information sources?

2. If we employ the classic concept of revolution as a fundamental transformation, what impacts would ICTs need to make to *revolutionize* politics? Could they transform the manner in which political power is distributed and exercised or the nature and impact of political decisions?

Political scientists and other social scientists have yet to establish a critical test that reveals which of the approaches best describes or explains politics. After hundreds of studies in various political systems at the local, regional, and national levels, the disagreements among the advocates of the three approaches remain as deep as ever. To decide which approach provides the greatest insight into the politics of a particular political system, you might consider numerous conceptual and empirical questions, a few of which follow:

■ For the *elite approach*, look for evidence of actual collaboration among the elite in the formulation of public policy, the frequency with which the elite seems to lose on policy decisions of significance to its members, or whether there is a mass of citizens who are uninformed, inactive, and impotent regarding policy choices.

■ For the *class approach*, analyze whether the state almost always operates to serve the interests of a dominant class group, whether most people's interests and behaviors can be defined in class terms, or whether most significant social changes are directly attributable to violence.

■ And for the *group approach*, analyze whether there are persistent winners and persistent losers on policy decisions, whether the state applies rules and policies fairly and equally to all groups, or whether competition among groups can be fair if there are huge inequalities in the levels of political resources available to different individuals and groups.

Essential Similarities and Differences

The elite and class approaches share certain crucial premises. For both approaches, the fundamental feature of society is stratification—the unequal distribution of values across distinct groups. Also in both approaches, the government is one of the key mechanisms controlled by the dominant group, and the government's policy decisions are intended to maintain that group's domination.

But the elite and class approaches differ in their conceptions of the nature of the groups and their interactions. For the elite approach, there are two broad groups: the elite and the mass. Elite theorists mainly focus on the elite—its membership, the basis of elite domination, and the strategies employed by the elite to maintain its control. The mass is assumed to be inactive politically and is rarely analyzed in detail.

In contrast, most class theorists identify more than two distinct class groups and emphasize the dynamic interactions among the classes. There is substantial political energy inherent in the lower classes, who are the active agents of major political change. The class approach attempts to explain why class conflict is inevitable, how it manifests itself, and how it produces transformations in the sociopolitical system. In short, the elite approach tends to provide a top-down perspective in a two-group system, whereas the class approach often takes a bottom-up perspective that emphasizes the dynamic processes of conflict and change among multiple groups.

The group approach differs fundamentally from both the elite and class approaches, beginning with its rejection of the notion of social stratification. It conceptualizes a sociopolitical world composed of many groups, with each individual belonging to a variety of groups. Different groups emerge on each particular political issue, and each group has an array of resources that it can organize to influence decisions on that issue.

As groups compete to shape a public policy decision, the government is a relatively neutral referee that ensures the competition is fair; it is not the instrument of any particular group or class. There is a dispersion of power, of resources, and of benefits from policy decisions, not a pattern of "structured inequality." Everyone wins some and loses some, but the losers can always win on the next issue.

Vigorous and often hostile debate has persisted among the advocates of these three conceptions of how politics works. This debate is deep and serious, for it reflects fundamental disagreements about the very nature of society and politics. The elite and class approaches are based on a *coercive view of society*. Conflict and change are ubiquitous features of the relations among groups. Social coherence is maintained by means of power and constraint, of domination by the most powerful class and its agent, the state. In contrast, the group approach reflects an *integrative view of society*. Society is essentially stable and harmonious, in the sense that there is a moving equilibrium maintained by a "fair" competitive game, refereed by the state and played by many groups who accept the rules and the outcomes. Social coherence is grounded in cooperation and consensus (see Dahrendorf 1959).

The more analytic model presented in the first part of this chapter offers a different way of understanding the public policy process. Some of those who use that model tend to focus on providing an in-depth, empirical account either of the dynamics during a particular stage of the process (e.g., implementation) or of a specific policy domain (e.g., health care policy). There is an attempt to define how political institutions shape the process and to explore the behavior and interactions among various stakeholders. Policy analysis can also be employed to determine the most desirable response to a given problem, providing a prescriptive policy recommendation. The class, group, and elite approaches and the various approaches to public policy analysis provide you with a rich set of alternatives for responding to Harold Lasswell's (1960) classic question about politics: Who gets what, when, why, and how?

KEY CONCEPTS

class	group approach	political understructure
class approach	mass	politics
class conflict	political elite	public policy
elite approach	political resources	stages of the policy
group	political stratification	process

FOR FURTHER CONSIDERATION

1. What do you think is the single most important flaw in the assumptions or knowledge claims of the elite approach? The class approach? The group approach?

2. How might a class approach theorist challenge the basic assumptions of the group approach and the actual case of group politics presented in Box 9.2? How might a group theorist account for a case like the one described in Box 9.1?

3. In a sense, all political systems are elitist, since a few govern and many are governed. Does this observation seem accurate? Is it a persuasive basis for confirming the validity of the elite approach?

4. Are you and your peers characterized by nonoverlapping group memberships in the manner claimed by the group approach?

5. List six groups that have a political agenda and with which you have a membership or a strong identity. Ask a variety of friends to provide you with a similar list. How much overlap is there in your group affiliations? Does this seem to support the group approach tenet of nonoverlapping memberships? (To undertake a fuller test, you would need to survey many individuals from a variety of backgrounds.)

FOR FURTHER READING

Allison, Graham, and Philip Zelikow. (1999). *The Essence of Decision: Explaining the Cuban Missile Crisis.* 2nd ed. New York: Longman. This revised edition of Allison's seminal case study of the Cuban missile crisis in 1961 offers a superb presentation of three important models of the policy decision process that differ from those described in this chapter. These models emphasize: (1) "rational choice" by decision makers who engage in a dispassionate cost-benefit analysis of the expected utilities of different actions (recall the Debate in 4 and the Appendix); (2) "organizational processes" by which institutional routines shape policy due to actors' adherence to simple problem-solving strategies and standard operating procedures; and (3) "bureaucratic politics" whereby stakeholders' behaviors and choices are based on their personal values and the imperatives of their particular roles.

Anderson, James E. (2006). *Public Policymaking: An Introduction.* 6th ed. Boston: Houghton Mifflin. A solid text introducing the field of public policy analysis, with chapters focusing on the stages of the policy analysis framework presented in the first part of this chapter.

Balulis, Joseph, and Vickie Sullivan, Eds. (1996). *Shakespeare's Political Pageant: Essays in Politics and Literature.* Lanham, MD: Rowman and Littlefield. These articles offer a rich exploration of how the interplay of politics, power, and human nature is illuminated in the extraordinary plays of William Shakespeare.

Burki, Shahid J. (1991). *Pakistan Under the Military: Eleven Years of Zia ul-Haq.* Boulder, CO: Westview. A detailed description of elite rule in Pakistan under an authoritarian regime.

Chadwick, Andrew. (2006). *Internet Politics: States, Citizens, and New Communications Technologies.* New York: Oxford University Press. An excellent overview of most of the key topics regarding the interplay between politics and the Internet, considering the use of the Internet by government institutions, interest groups, social movements, and individual citizens and exploring such policy challenges as privacy and content control.

Curtis, Gerald L. (1999). *The Logic of Japanese Politics: Leaders, Institutions, and the Limits of Change.* New York: Columbia University Press. A fascinating account of how contemporary Japanese politics works, emphasizing competition among individuals and groups rather than consensus building, which is the more widely accepted explanatory framework for Japan.

Dahl, Robert. (1961). *Who Governs? Democracy in an American City.* New Haven, CT: Yale University Press. This remains the classic theoretical and empirical statement of the group approach to explaining politics.

Domhoff, G. William. (2005). *Who Rules in America? Power and Politics.* 5th ed. Boston: McGraw-Hill. The author updates Mills's *The Power Elite,* using more data and an elaborated theoretical base and reaching similar conclusions confirming that an elite governs the United States.

Evans, Geoffrey, Ed. (1999). *The End of Class Politics?: Class Voting in Comparative Context.* Oxford: Oxford University Press. In a series of revealing country-based studies, the contributors to this volume present a data-based case, grounded particularly in analyses of elections, that class politics continues to be a powerful force in certain developed countries and postcommunist developed countries.

Glazer, Amihai, and Lawrence S. Rothenberg. (2005). *Why Government Succeeds and Why It Fails.* Cambridge, MA: Harvard University Press. This readable analysis emphasizes the economic conditions that influence public policy in such domains as the regulation of personal behavior, welfare policy, and economic growth.

Ibsen, Henrik. (1882/1964). *Enemy of the People.* In *Six Plays by Ibsen.* Trans. Eva Le Gallienne. New York: Random House. A classic Norwegian play revealing the political processes by which self-interest and greed overwhelm the efforts of a good citizen to prevent his town from making a policy decision that will result in grave environmental damage and a risk to public health.

Kingdon, John. (1995). *Agendas, Alternatives, and Public Policies.* 2nd ed. New York: Addison-Wesley. The work that most fully explains the idea of agenda setting: how an issue emerges from many and becomes an important item drawing attention and action in the policy process.

Mills, C. Wright. (1956). *The Power Elite.* New York: Oxford University Press. A widely cited study that identifies the elite system underlying American national politics.

Moran, Michael, Martin Rein, and Robert Goodin, Eds. (2006). *The Oxford Handbook of Public Policy.* New York: Oxford University Press. A comprehensive (780 pages) treatment of public policy analysis, including all the major analytic approaches and all stages of the policy process.

Rubin, Barry. (1987). *Third World Coup Makers, Dictators, Strongmen, and Populist Tyrants.* New York: McGraw-Hill. Portraits of political leaders and the elitist regimes they dominated.

Skocpol, Theda. (1996). *Boomerang: Clinton's Health Security Effort and the Turn Against Government in U.S. Politics.* New York: W. W. Norton. A revealing case study of the policy process in the United States, describing how one policy proposal rose on the political agenda, pushed by a president, and then was crushed by an array of forces, including a shifting set of priorities, the strong mobilization of stakeholders and interest groups in opposition, and the impact of the media.

Tuohy, Carolyn Hughes. (1999). *Accidental Logics: The Dynamics of Change in the Health Care Arena in the United States, Britain, and Canada.* New York: Oxford University Press. An interesting description of group politics in the policy process in one important area—health care.

Wildavsky, Aaron. (1979). *Speaking Truth to Power.* Boston: Little, Brown. One of the most perceptive scholars of the public policy process, the late Aaron Wildavsky, offers many insights in this exploration of policy making and policy analysis.

Yang, Benjamin. (1997). *Deng: A Political Biography.* Armonk, NY: M. E. Sharpe. A compelling characterization of Deng Xiaoping, the shrewd leader who followed Mao Zedong to power in China. This book also provides an intriguing and illuminating account of an elite political system in action.

ON THE WEB

http://www.trinity.edu/mkearl/strat.html

This site provides a comprehensive look at the study of social inequality and contains a wealth of information on related topics such as gender stratification and homelessness.

http://www.washingtonpost.com/wp-dyn/politics/fedpage/columns/specialinterests/

The *Washington Post* Special Interests page contains a weekly column on lobbying and the influence of interest groups on government.

http://www.marxist.com/marxisttheory.asp

"In Defense of Marxism" is a comprehensive site that argues for the relevance of class theory and Marxism in the contemporary world, with essays and research on many political topics.

http://www.ncpa.org

The conservative National Center for Policy Analysis provides material and links to many current policy issues on its Web site.

http://www.urban.org

The Urban Institute describes itself as a nonpartisan economic and social policy research organization that focuses on policy analyses in such domains as education, health, crime, the economy, and international affairs.

http://www.movingideas.org

The Moving Ideas Electronic Policy Network offers many links to ideologically progressive material, think tanks, and blogs that address current policy issues.

http://www.angelfire.com/or/sociologyshop/CWM.html

This site offers a variety of links that explore the works and theories of elite theorist C. Wright Mills.

CHANGE AND POLITICAL DEVELOPMENT

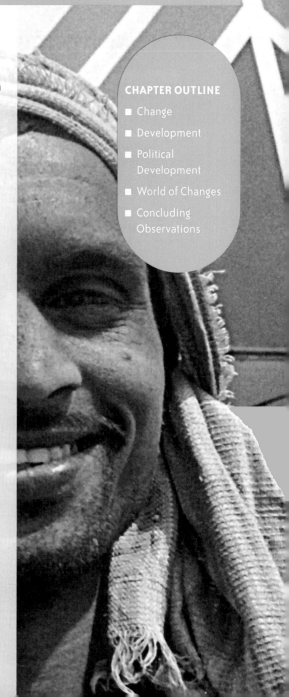

Oman is a medium-sized country of 3.2 million people east of Saudi Arabia at a strategic point on the Persian Gulf. Although Oman has a long history of trading with other countries, its rulers attempted to maintain an extremely traditional society, even in the late twentieth century. The sultan who ruled between 1932 and 1970, Said ibn Taimur, faced an especially strong challenge after 1964, when vast oil deposits were discovered in Oman. Fearful that this huge wealth would corrupt his people, the sultan took extraordinary steps to prevent modernization. He declared a moratorium on the building of roads, schools, houses, even hospitals. All ten Omani doctors were forced to practice abroad because the sultan distrusted modern medicine. Many modern objects were prohibited, including sunglasses, flashlights, and European shoes. One could be imprisoned for traveling after dark with any light other than a kerosene lantern. The gates of the capital were locked after sunset, and no one was allowed to enter or leave. The sultan even confined his son, Prince Qabus, to a house far from the capital because he feared the ideas that his son had brought back from his education in England.

But there was a group of Omani citizens who had some experience of Western culture through education, travel, or working with foreigners. These people increasingly chafed under the sultan's "backward" rule. Encouraged by the influential British elite in Oman, this group took action in 1970, overthrowing the sultan and replacing him with Prince Qabus. The new sultan and his advisers moved swiftly to bring improvements in the areas that his father had blocked. There was a massive school building program (from 16 to 490 schools), and Sultan Qabus University opened in 1986. Hospitals and many health clinics are operating, and an extensive road system has been built. Females are now being educated, and Omani citizens purchase many Western consumer goods. Despite fears of corruption from oil wealth, Oman has one of the lowest levels of corruption reported for any of the countries in the Arab world (Transparency International 2008). With a GDP per capita (PPP) of $19,100, Oman is now among the countries that score "high" on the Human Development Index (see Chapter 13). Many Omanis now have a lifestyle that attempts to balance the behaviors and morals of traditional Islamic culture and the material possessions of a wealthy, modernized society. (This discussion is based on Spencer 2008.)

CHANGE

The recent history of Oman illustrates the virtual impossibility of preventing *change* in any contemporary society. This chapter examines the concept of change and focuses on the nature and processes of development in a society and within its political system.

A few cultures have generally avoided the processes of change and modernization. For example, many of the Masai of the Serengeti Plain in East Africa live in a manner that has changed little from the ways of their ancestors of 50 generations ago. They continue to raise their cattle, ignoring the Kenya-Tanzania border and resisting the attempts of the Kenyan government to alter their long-standing cultural patterns of family and tribal life. But even the Masai have been affected by the modernization surrounding them. It has brought health care and disease, money from tourists and reduced land for grazing herds, education and cultural confusion.

There seems nowhere to hide from the forces of change. The Greek philosopher Heraclitus articulated this view in the fifth century B.C.E. His famous dictum "You can never step in the same river twice, for fresh waters are ever flowing in upon you" is an extreme version of the viewpoint that everything is in constant flux, that change is inevitable. It is presumed that just as individuals undergo a developmental sequence of birth, growth, maturity, decay, and death, social organisms (groups, organizations, societies) also have some form of evolutionary development.

On the opposite side of the debate about the inevitability of change is the wry French observation: *Plus ça change, plus c'est la mê me chose.* This translates loosely as "The more things change, the more they remain the same." Do you believe this? Is this a wise commentary about the human condition? An erroneous cliché?

There are ongoing disagreements about the desirability of change as well as its inevitability. One normative position, most aligned with modern rationalism, is that change is generally a positive force in human society. Change is the mechanism of growth, development, and progress, all of which are assumed to increase knowledge, extend control over the environment, and thus improve the human condition. This view is reflected in the ideas of Isaac Newton (1642–1727), Immanuel Kant (1724–1804), and Charles Darwin (1809–1882). In the contemporary world, it is especially prevalent among those who believe in the benefits of science and technology.

A contrasting position is that change and development have significant negative effects, perhaps so many that change is undesirable. Plato (c. 428–347 B.C.E.), Jean-Jacques Rousseau (1712–1778), and Sigmund Freud (1856–1939) are among those who argue that knowledge, civilization, and excessive control over the environment result in a loss of innocence, goodness, and happiness, and create the capacity for great harm and destruction. Material progress has been achieved at the cost of moral and spiritual decline. In this view, our capacity to increase our supply of food and material goods cannot be separated from our development of repressive and destructive forms of human interaction and technologies (e.g., weapons, chemicals) that degrade the environment and eliminate certain species of life, including, possibly, human beings. Most people now recognize the paradox that change and development simultaneously increase *and* reduce the quality of life. And most accept the serious problems and dangers associated with progress in order to enjoy the material benefits.

DEVELOPMENT

Characteristics of "More Developed" Human Systems

Contemporary changes of social, economic, and political systems are usually discussed in terms of development or modernization. While both of these concepts can be slippery, social scientific research usually avoids the concept of **modernization** because it is particularly fuzzy. What is "modern" depends very much on the particular historical moment and even on the values and culture of the analyst. For example, in the world of rapid social and technological change, what seemed modern in the United States 30 years ago (a world virtually without personal computers, DVDs, satellite television, AIDS, the Internet, and so on) does not seem so modern today.

The concept of **development** is also fluid, but more measurable. A social system is considered more developed when it displays certain key characteristics at relatively high levels. Development can also mean the processes through which these characteristics become more pronounced. More developed human systems exhibit several packages of characteristics that tap social, cultural, economic, political, and personal dimensions. These systems have three key dimensions (Bill and Hardgrave 1981: 63):

1. The *organizational* dimension: behaviors and actions by groups, institutions, and societies that are based on specialization, interdependency, and differentiation of roles and functions.

2. The *technological* dimension: the use of increasingly complex and sophisticated artifacts to produce useful goods and services and to control the environment.

3. The *attitudinal* dimension: cognitive, affective, and evaluative orientations that are dominated by scientific knowledge, rationality, secular values, and individualism.

The *technological* dimension is the core driver of **economic development**, which is of great importance to every state. Thus states attempt to identify and implement strategies that facilitate economic development, which they usually define by some measure of national economic product, such as GDP per capita or the rate of growth in GDP (described in Box 8.1). The expansion of available goods and services in the society offers the promise of a life that is more secure and more comfortable for at least some citizens.

Advances on the *organizational* and *attitudinal* dimensions are reflected by such social indicators as greater urbanization, expanded communications, more extensive social networks, improved efficiency, higher education levels, higher literacy rates, and greater social mobility. Most people assume that there are also societal benefits associated with increases on these dimensions, but there is less consensus about whether these aspects of development are always desirable.

The example of Oman reflects the concerns of some individuals in every developing society: that many of the changes associated with organizational and attitudinal development can have negative effects on deeply revered social and cultural values. In some countries, these negative changes are referred to as *Westernization* and are evident in attitudinal changes that shift toward *greater secularism, individualism, and materialism.* Groups that are strongly committed to sustaining tradition and religious values, such as those of Islam or Hinduism, can be very concerned by these types of changes within their countries.

Indeed, even economic development is questioned by those alarmed about the negative effects of unrestricted economic growth on the environment. Concerns for the environment center on both the *depletion of the earth's resources* (e.g., the destruction of the forests, shortages of water, overfishing and the overcultivation of the land to increase food production) and the *degradation of the environment* (e.g., global warming and solid waste associated with industrial processes and consumerism).

There are no agreed-upon measures for distinguishing sharply between systems that are developed/modern and those that are not. However, there is a broad distinction between the "developed countries" and the "developing countries," often based on a single measure of *economic* development—GDP per capita (recall Box 8.1). In Chapter 13 (e.g., Figure 13.1), this book will offer a broader set of criteria for categorizing levels of development, combining economic development with the three dimensions of social development discussed above. In this chapter, the more developed countries are those that are relatively high on productive output, urbanization, literacy, complexity, specialization, and secularization.

The Process of Development

Stage typologies.   Many scholars have attempted to define the process(es) through which development and modernization occur. One approach is to define a series of stages or phases that each society passes through. Best known are the simple typologies, many of which have only two stages, such as *traditional* and *modern, mechanical* and *organic, folk* and *urban, less developed* and *more developed.* These labels are so broad that they do not provide much conceptual clarity.

Karl Marx proposed a more complex typology in which most societies pass through six stages of development. A society's particular stage of development depends on the distribution of control over its major productive resources. Marx posited that there is an initial stage of *primitive communism*, in which all individuals jointly share control over any available productive resources. The development process then continues through a series of stages in which there are increasingly subtle forms of domination by some classes over others: *slavery*, then *feudalism*, and then *capitalism*. Eventually, capitalist systems are transformed into *socialist* and finally to *communist* systems, an ultimate stage in which all blend into a single class that shares control of resources (recall Chapters 2 and 8, including Box 8.2).

Response to key challenges.   Most explanations of the process of development do not assume, as Marx does, that there is a single, inevitable sequence of stages. Rather, analysts identify a series of key challenges in the developmental process. Different processes are possible, depending on the sequence in which the challenges occur, how the society responds to the challenges, and crucial features of the society and its environment. These challenges include the tension between traditional values and modern ones; the transition from a rural, agrarian society to an urban, industrial society; the transfer of social and political power from traditional elites to

Source: By permission
of Mike Luckovich
and Creators
Syndicate, Inc.

modernizing ones; and the fit among geographical territory, national identities, and state boundaries. For example, Barrington Moore (1966) uses detailed analyses of eight countries to define four different models of development based on how relationships evolved among key social groups, especially the landed aristocracy and peasants in the rural areas, and also the urban entrepreneurs and government bureaucrats. One of Moore's most powerful conclusions is that all forms of development are essentially revolutions from above, implemented by a ruthless minority and causing great hardship to the large majority of the population, which does not want these changes. Other theorists who also explain modernization in terms of the pattern of responses to key challenges facing the society include Cyril Black (1966) and Dankwart Rustow (1967).

Individual-level change.   Most analyses of development, whether emphasizing stages, sequences, or international political economy, focus on the macro-level structural dynamics—that is, on the organizational and technological dimensions of systems. But attention to the attitudinal dimension shifts the analysis to micro-level dynamics. This perspective emphasizes the social-psychological characteristics of the individual that might account for variations in rates and patterns of development (Inkeles and Smith 1999; Inkeles et al. 1985; Inkeles 1997; McClelland 1961). Such analyses are similar to the political behavior studies described in Chapters 2–4 (e.g., the shift from "materialists" to "postmaterialists" described in Chapter 2), although the focus here is on a broader array of beliefs (not just political beliefs).

In the attempt to establish the attitudinal traits associated with modernity, the work of Alex Inkeles and his colleagues (Inkeles and Smith 1999; Inkeles et al. 1985) is noteworthy. This group gathered extensive survey data from men in six developing countries (Argentina, Bangladesh, Chile, India, the "Oriental" Jews of Israel, and Nigeria). Statistical analyses have produced a set of seven qualities that the researchers believe constitute a "syndrome of modernity"—that is, the general attitudinal traits of a modern person in a developing society:

1. Openness to new experiences regarding both people and behaviors.
2. A shift in allegiance from those individuals in traditional authority structures (e.g., parents, religious leaders) to those representing modern institutions (e.g., government leaders).
3. Confidence in modern technologies (e.g., science, medicine) and a less fatalistic attitude about life.
4. Desire for social mobility for oneself and one's children.
5. Belief in the value of planning and punctuality.
6. Interest in local politics and community affairs.
7. Interest in news, especially national and international affairs.

▶ **This Samburu herdsman in a remote area of Kenya seems to balance tradition and modernity with ease.**

Inkeles and his colleagues conclude that there is remarkable similarity in these clusters of beliefs among the modern men in all six societies they studied. On this basis, they claim that the same traits are present in modern individuals in virtually all cultures (Inkeles et al. 1985: 102). Some believe that this uniformity of ideas is one part of a broader set of forces that are homogenizing everyone into a global economy, a global culture, and a global information network (Barber 1995; Friedman 2007). In the large literature on the traditional and modern personality, many issues are unresolved. For example, most studies have not established the existence of a single syndrome of modernity that exists across all cultures. Also, it is unclear whether most people are equally exposed to and equally changed by global culture.

In most developing societies, some people and groups enthusiastically embrace the new beliefs and new behaviors, while others cling tenaciously to the old ones. Box 10.1 summarizes a powerful literary account of the trauma some individuals experienced when tradition and modernity collide. Indeed, in some cases of religious fundamental-

BOX 10.1

How Ideas Undermine Culture: Things Fall Apart in Nigeria

You might understand individual-level change intuitively if you think about what happens to people when their existing values are challenged by education, other religions, or different cultures. The erosion of traditional values and behaviors can be rapid or slow. But as the Oman case suggests, it is difficult to prevent change in the face of major unsettling forces. The Koran recognizes the importance of personal values in shaping society, noting, "Lo! Allah changeth not the condition of a people until they first change what is in their hearts."

A rich illustration of these change processes is Chinua Achebe's 1959 novel *Things Fall Apart*, which describes the traumatic changes experienced by the Ibo people of Nigeria at the turn of the twentieth century. The novel's key theme is the conflict between the binding power of the Ibo's traditional views of life and religion and the disruptive ideas introduced into the culture by Christian missionaries and British colonial administrators. The story centers on the members of one Ibo village who are increasingly divided between those who continue to be guided by traditional patterns of behavior and religion and those who no longer accept those traditions.

The major character, Okonkwo, is a great farmer and a strong leader. He follows the traditional patterns rigidly, even participating in the murder, decreed by tribal law, of a boy he has treated like a son for years. This murder so alienates Okonkwo's own son that the son becomes one of the first in the village to be persuaded by the missionaries to convert to Christianity. Okonkwo continues to follow the traditions of

BOX 10.1 *(Continued)*

his tribe, and this results in a series of major setbacks, including being banished for seven years and losing his land and his possessions. Eventually, Okonkwo's anger and frustration at the collapse of Ibo village life lead him to murder a colonial administrator's messenger. Rather than be executed by the white men, he finally does violate a basic Ibo law by committing suicide.

Before Okonkwo dies, his friend Obierika articulates how these external ideas have caused the collapse of the village (and of Ibo) society. In a key passage, he says:

> Our own men and our sons have joined the ranks of the stranger. They have joined his religion and they help to uphold his government.
>
> If we should try to drive out the white men in Umuofia we should find it easy. There are only two of them. But what of our own people who are following their way and have been given power? They would go to Umuru and bring the soldiers . . . . [The white man] says our customs are bad; and our own brothers who have taken up his religion also say that our customs are bad. How do you think we can fight when our own brothers have turned against us? The white man is very clever. He came quietly and peaceably with his religion. We were amused at his foolishness and allowed him to stay. Now he has won our brothers and our clan can no longer act like one. He has put a knife on the things that held us together and we have fallen apart. (Achebe 1959: 161–162)

ism, it seems that leaders who display the activist and outward-oriented psychological traits associated with the syndrome of modernity are actually working to return the society to its traditional pattern of attitudes and actions (Banuazizi 1987).

Civil society.   The attitudinal changes in individuals are especially important when they create new patterns of interaction at the group or societal level. Thus one key consideration in assessing development is the extent to which a *civil society* has emerged. Attitudes particularly associated with the existence of civil society include tolerance of differences in opinions and behaviors, social trust, willingness to negotiate and to avoid violence in resolving differences, and a sense of shared identity with others. Some analysts conclude that, while a society could certainly be "developed" without being a civil society, these values of civility are crucial for sustaining effective community and democracy (Diamond 1999; Linz and Stepan 1996; Putnam 1993).

Culture and change.   Some studies of development have emphasized the importance of the culture in the processes of change. Since Max Weber's classic study (1958a) of the link between the culture of Protestant religions and the rise of capitalist political economies, there have been continuing efforts to clarify the relationship between broad cultural systems and economic development. Some, like Weber, have argued that Protestantism has motivated people to make substantial, even irrational, sacrifices of material consumption and the pleasures of life, inciting them to work extraordinarily hard and accumulate wealth rather than spend it.

A society infused with such values is associated with the transformation to a modern society and economy (Davis 1987: 223–234).

Weber (1951, 1958b) also applied an analysis of culture and religion to India and China to explain the absence of development there. But since the 1980s, there has been a dramatic surge of economic development among the Asian newly industrializing countries (to be discussed later in this chapter). Since these Asian countries have had substantially higher levels of development than most other countries employing similar development strategies, more recent explanations have emphasized how Asian culture has *facilitated* development (Davis 1987; Huntington 1987: 21–28, 1991; Pye 1985; and see Chapter 15, especially Box 15.4).

The Dynamics of Economic Development

The actual economic development of a country is the product of a complex set of actions by both major players (e.g., the government, large corporations, international banks) and small players (e.g., individuals as consumers and workers, small businesses) that is staggering in scale and incomprehensible in nature.

In the abstract, the discussion of political economy in Chapter 8 (look again at Figure 8.3) provides the key to understanding what is happening. Economic development occurs as more and more households and firms are engaged in ever higher levels of production and consumption. More goods (and, ideally, more diverse and complex goods) are produced, more income and expenditures are exchanged, and thus the GDP gets larger relative to the number of people sharing in the carnival of production and consumption. And a political economy is normally healthier and more vibrant if it is not only growing but also bringing in more income via exports to other countries than it sends out to pay for imports. Chapter 8 explored some of the general challenges facing every political economy in the quest for economic development. For every state, the underlying puzzle is: What should the political system do to facilitate economic development? In the latter part of the twentieth century, three competing visions guided the answer to this question in many political economies: statism, neoliberalism, and the developmental state approach.

Statism.   Between the 1950s and the 1980s, many developing countries (e.g., Brazil, Mexico, India, Tanzania) implemented versions of **statism**. This approach *emphasizes the importance of strong actions by the state to support and manage the system of production and distribution of goods*. The state extensively regulates the market and the actions of firms and households, and it protects firms from external competition. Many important areas of production are publicly owned and are operated as state enterprises (e.g., transportation, power, banking). The state also controls the prices of certain basic goods (e.g., foods, fuel), and it distributes many free or subsidized goods and services (e.g., shelter, health care), especially to less advantaged groups. The political economies of many communist countries (e.g., Bulgaria, China, Cuba) were extreme forms of the statist approach.

Neoliberalism.   Alternatively, many countries applied variations of **neoliberalism**. Grounded in the market political economy model (see Chapter 8), the guiding principle of the neoliberal approach is to *maximize the economic freedom of individuals, households, and firms*. Thus there is an attempt to limit severely the state's interventions in the economy, which are seen to undermine and distort the efficiency of the free market. Public expenditure is minimal, there is little government regulation of the economy, and direct foreign investment and free trade across state boundaries are encouraged. The state is mainly concerned with maintaining fiscal and monetary discipline (not spending much, keeping currencies stable) and facilitating the dynamics of the local, national, and global marketplaces. Since the mid-1970s, many countries have adopted versions of the neoliberal approach, especially due to two factors: the disappointing levels of economic growth achieved with the statist approach, and strong pressure from the international banking community and the global economy to embrace neoliberalism (Rodrik 2003; Linz and Stepan 1996).

The developmental state approach.   Some countries adopted a hybrid development strategy, combining elements of both the statist and the neoliberal approaches. Based on the Japanese model in the post–World War II period, this **developmental state approach** is grounded in three broad strategies:

1. *State-supported, export-oriented capitalism.* Aggressive capitalism is favored, and there are minimal governmental constraints on firms, as in neoliberalism. However, the state is very interventionist, providing strong support for firms by insulating the political economy from "politics," shaping the labor force via education, and enacting taxing and spending policies that promote the export of goods, encourage savings and investment, and discourage high levels of domestic consumption.

2. *Targeting market niches.* Firms and the state work cooperatively to produce particular goods that can be successfully sold in the international marketplace. Initially, modest-quality goods are sold at or below cost in order to capture a share of the market and gain consumer support. Gradually, prices and quality are increased. The balance of production shifts slowly from simpler, more labor-intensive goods such as textiles, shoes, and toys to more complex goods requiring sophisticated production technologies, such as electronics and automobiles. The state's policies (e.g., tariffs) protect producers against imported goods, although investment of foreign capital is usually encouraged.

3. *Agrarian support.* Government policy strongly supports efficient domestic food production. This element can include redistribution of land to small private farmers, subsidies on domestic food production, and tariffs on imported foods (Simone 2001; Woo-Cumings 1999).

As Chapter 14 will discuss in more detail, very few developing countries utilizing the statist approach achieved high levels of economic growth. Some developing countries employing neoliberalism have enjoyed periods of solid growth, but only a few have experienced sustained growth and prosperity. In general, most developing countries that have managed to achieve solid and sustained economic growth during the last four decades have pursued some variant of the developmental state approach. Many of these success stories have been in Asia, particularly China (see Box 10.2), Singapore, South Korea, Taiwan, and to a lesser extent Malaysia and Indonesia, and they are generally called the *newly industrializing countries*—**NICs** (see Chapter 15 for more details). Other developing countries that have attempted variations of the developmental state

BOX 10.2

Big NIC? China

As the world's most populous country (1.3 billion), China has always drawn attention. However, China's growing economic power has become one of the most widely discussed issues in the current global system. While still generally classified as a developing country (see Figure 13.1), China increasingly has the characteristics of a NIC— a newly industrializing country. Between 1980 and 1995, China's economic output and average income per capita quadrupled, and it still has a remarkably high rate of economic growth. It has rapidly created a substantial manufacturing sector, and it exports more goods than any other country. China is now the second largest economy in the world (in PPP) and is predicted by some to become the largest by 2015 (passing the United States).

Once the world's greatest civilization, China was a leader in science and the arts for many centuries. But for most of the nineteenth and twentieth centuries, China seemed an unlikely economic powerhouse, weakened by internal conflicts, devastating famines, pervasive corruption, and foreign intervention. Then, in 1949, the Communist forces under Mao Zedong gained power in China after a lengthy civil war. Since that point, China has undergone a remarkable transformation. What accounts for the turnaround?

Despite the open opposition to China by most other countries, especially the United States, "Chairman Mao" established a strong political system between 1949 and his death in 1976 and used it to change the social and economic systems as well. There were strict, totalitarian controls over the political life of the people under the guardianship of the oppressive Communist Party. There was an attempt to implement an extensive command political economy, with state ownership of virtually all productive means. Although there was considerable chaos (and more than 30 million state-caused deaths) in China under Mao, the period also laid the foundations for economic development. Among the many important changes were: the establishment of an effective central government; land reform; weakening of the rigid Confucian hierarchy of gender, age, and class; great improvements in health and education; and the transformation from an agrarian to an industrial nation.

Deng Xiaoping, Mao's successor (and China's most powerful leader from 1978 to the 1990s), followed a variant of the NIC strategy, given the constraints of China's size, stage of development, and Communist rhetoric. The political system has remained oppressive and authoritarian, firmly under the control of the party. Citizens enjoy few political or civil rights. However, Deng abandoned the statist approach and quietly embraced many aspects of the developmental state approach. He opened the economic system to market forces, a hybrid Deng called the "socialist market economy." Chided that he had adopted capitalism, the pragmatic Deng mused: "It doesn't matter if a cat is black or white, so long as it catches mice." Profit became not only an acceptable motivation but also a highly desirable one (another of Deng's famous comments is "to

BOX 10.2 *(Continued)*

get rich is glorious"). Under Deng, the share of industrial output under state owner-ship dropped from 78 percent to 26 percent, and virtually the entire agricultural system shifted from state communes to control by households. China moved aggressively into the global economy, including a rapid shift to manufacturing and to more sophisticated goods. China's total GDP and foreign trade each rose more than twelvefold, and both rural and urban income per capita increased more than tenfold.

Since Deng stepped down (1990), the political leadership has continued to manage the Chinese economy actively, and it has sustained an extremely high growth rate, due particularly to strong labor productivity gains and great success in exporting goods. Overall, the GDP has increased at an annual rate of 8 percent since 1978. A greater proportion of Chinese enjoy a high standard of material living than at any point in the history of the country. Yet many millions of Chinese still live in relative poverty, especially in rural areas, and increasing urban–rural inequalities in the distribution of wealth are creating substantial tension. China now accounts for one-fourth of all global economic growth. The Communist Party continues to resist increasing pressure for some loosening of its tight control over political life. The direction of the "big NIC's" development is arguably the most significant factor in the evolution of the world's economy in the near future. (This discussion is based on Meisner 1999 and World Bank 2008.)

strategy have had mixed success, with some achieving relatively high levels of multi-year economic growth (e.g., Argentina, Chile), others failing to sustain such growth (e.g., Brazil, Mexico), and still others having very little success (Stein 2006).

In the late 1990s, things seemed to go awry even in the more successful Asian NICs. Beginning in July 1997 with Thailand's currency problems, the booming economies of Asia suddenly and unexpectedly fell into a severe decline that was evident in negative GDP growth, high unemployment levels, and a huge decrease in the value of such assets as property and stocks (more details will be provided in Chapter 15). Although some countries with rapid economic growth seemed to avoid severe problems (e.g., China, Singapore), the economic "crisis" in Asia was soon followed by similar problems in other rapidly developing countries in Latin America (Mahon 1999).

The breadth and depth of these negative economic conditions resulted in more careful consideration of the flaws as well as the potential benefits of the developmental state model. A variety of problems were recognized, such as the state's overprotection of favored firms and inadequate regulation of the banking and monetary systems, the unrestrained speculation in land and the stock market, and increased inequality of wealth. Most of these economies have regained their economic momentum, but the economic turbulence produced renewed uncertainty in many developing countries about whether the developmental state approach is the best way to maximize broad economic growth and economic stability (Stein 2006).

Dependency within the international political economy.   With the exception of a few of the NICs, most developing countries have enjoyed only modest success in sustaining high economic growth during the postcolonial period (since about 1960). Why is this? Some analysts conclude that the difficulties facing the developing countries are due to their vulnerability to, and perhaps their dependency on, the countries that are highly developed. This view is most explicit in an explanation known as the dependency approach or as world systems theory.

The **dependency approach**, which has both ideological and descriptive elements, argues that *the "late developers" face difficult challenges because of their subordination to and dependence on the more developed countries and the transnational institutions they control in the current world.*

According to the *ideological* element, the key problem for current developers is a long history of exploitation by the more developed "capitalist/imperialist" states. These states have manipulated and controlled the political economies of the developing countries for decades or even centuries by means of their economic, military, and political domination of the global system. Indeed, one of the main reasons the capitalist states have sustained their prosperity since the mid-twentieth century is that they are still able to exploit the political economies of developing countries, especially through their broad control of capital, markets and prices, and technology. Thus they continue to reap huge profits at the expense of the less developed countries. In this view, the activities of the developed countries have not merely retarded the progress of the late developers, they have actually "deformed" (distorted and ruined) the efforts of the developing countries.

The *descriptive* element of the dependency approach provides a similar analysis but without heaping blame exclusively on the capitalist states. It posits an economic hierarchy in which economic actors take advantage of those below them in the global economic system. At the top of the heap is a **core**, composed of the powerful states, firms (especially multinational firms such as Siemens, Matsushita, and General Motors), and financial institutions controlled by the most developed countries (e.g., Germany, Japan, the United States). At the bottom of the heap on the *periphery* are the villages of the developing countries. In general, the states of the periphery remain suppliers of raw materials and providers of cheap labor for economies of the core states (Isbister 2006; Wallerstein 1974, 1980, 1991, 2004; Wiarda 2004).

The dependency approach asserts that many actors engage in exploitation. The resources of villages are exploited by local and regional economic actors, who are in turn exploited by national economic actors, who are exploited by the powerful core actors in the global economy. For example, analyses of Brazil have identified an exploitive alliance composed of three key sets of actors: (1) the multinational corporations, (2) the Brazilian capitalist class, and (3) the Brazilian state apparatus. Only the groups in the alliance, and especially the multinationals, gain most of the benefits from Brazil's rich resources, whereas the great majority of the Brazilian population remains poor and backward (Packenham 1998; Rocha 2002). Brazilian cartoonist Ziraldo offers his view of the rules of this game (p. 272).

Look again at the photograph at the beginning of this chapter. Why are these men smiling? Probably because they got free Pepsis. But the bigger story is that a major U.S.-based multinational corporation has just won a fierce political battle against Indian politicians and local cola manufacturers. Pepsi was granted franchising licenses in the huge Indian market, despite arguments from locals that a major multinational soft drink company would squash local producers and extract massive profits from the country.

ZIRALDO
Rio de Janeiro
BRAZIL

Source: Ziraldo,
CartoonArts
International/CWS.

Continuing dependency?   It is clear that the process of development is substantially affected by the current global economy. However, the four following arguments are offered by analysts who dispute the validity of the dependency approach. First, some argue that in the current global system, the developed capitalist countries behave no differently than other states (Weatherby 2008). Second, some note that the rapid economic development of the NICs contradicts key contentions of the dependency approach. In this view, the success of some Asian developing countries, relative to those in Africa and Latin America, suggests that cultural factors are more crucial to development than is the level of dependence on foreign capital or foreign companies (Fallows 1995; Huntington 1987, 1991). Third, serious internal problems in many developing countries, especially extensive corruption and conflicts between nationality groups, are major limitations on development (Calderisi 2007; Isbister 2006). And fourth, the low- and middle-income countries of the developing world, measured either as a group or by region, actually achieved higher average annual rates of economic (GDP) growth since the early 1990s than the developed countries (World Bank 2008: table 3).

In response to such arguments, dependency theorists observe that economic actors from the core have become more active in exploiting cheap labor in the periphery as well as its natural resources. This can generate a higher growth rate for a few years but that rate is unlikely to be sustained. Moreover, growth is extremely uneven—many developing countries experienced only minimal growth, and even in the developing countries with high growth rates, most of the actual benefits are enjoyed by elites, not by the great majority of the population. More than 40 percent of the people in the developing world live on less than $2 per day, and one in five averages only $1 per day (UNDP 2006). Worldwide, inequality is rising—the disparity in income between the top 20 percent and the bottom 20 percent of the population has nearly doubled in the last three decades, to a ratio of 50:1 (UNDP 2006).

POLITICAL DEVELOPMENT

To this point, this chapter has broadly considered development in all spheres of human activity, and particularly in the economic sphere. Let us now turn to the specifically *political* aspects of development. **Political development** refers to *the emergence of more extensive capabilities in the political system*, especially in the sense that political structures and processes become more specialized and more effective in managing internal operations and responding to the environment.

Characteristics of Political Development

Political development is typically measured by the extent to which a political system exhibits relatively high levels on the following four dimensions:

1. *Concentration of power in the state.* Most power and authority are increasingly centralized in a single state-level governmental system, and traditional sources of political authority weaken. The citizens agree that the state has the right to allocate public values and recognize their own responsibility to accept those allocations as authoritative. The formal-legal aspects of government (e.g., constitutions, laws) are well established.

2. *Specialized political structures.* Most key political functions are fulfilled by complex, organized political institutions such as legislatures, executives, political parties, and political interest groups. The actions of these institutions are generally guided by such bureaucratic principles as rationality and efficiency.

3. *Political institutionalization.* The citizens value and support the political structures and processes, which become more stable, and the citizens accept their political roles as participants in those processes of politics, as voters, foot soldiers, and so on (recall Chapter 3).

4. *Extensive capabilities of the political system.* The political system becomes better able to generate support, to respond to demands from its population, and to control the environment. Overall, its organization is more stable and coherent, its structures are more efficient, and its actions more effectively serve its goals and objectives.

A "capabilities analysis" of the political system (dimension 4) arguably provides the best set of indicators for assessing the level of political development. The late Gabriel Almond and his colleagues (2008) posit that a political system achieves a higher level of political development when it improves its effectiveness on any of five key capabilities:

1. *Extractive*: using human and material resources from the environment.
2. *Regulative*: controlling individual and group actions.
3. *Distributive*: allocating values through institutionalized structures and procedures.
4. *Responsive*: making decisions and policies that react to demands for value allocations.
5. *Symbolic*: manipulating images and meanings, and distributing nonmaterial rewards and values.

The Process of Political Development

Figure 10.1 presents one model of the process through which political development occurs. From this perspective, political development is essentially a *dependent variable*. (The **dependent variable** is *the phenomenon that changes in response to the impacts on it of other significant forces. Forces that can cause change* are called the **independent variables**. See the Appendix.) Thus the elements of modernization (the *independent variables*) provide the material and human resources that lead to the emergence of a developed political system. Greater economic capability produces goods that the political system can distribute. An urban population with increasingly modern beliefs is more willing to accept the authority of government and to participate meaningfully in politics. In essence, the political system develops more complex and specialized structures as a response to changes that are occurring in the society and the economy.

Conceptualizing political development as primarily a response to economic and social change is based on historical analyses of political systems that developed in the eighteenth and nineteenth centuries. However, the power and impact of the political system itself, as a causal force for change, are more evident when one analyzes the societies that have undergone substantial development during the last 50 years (Wiarda 2004).

This leads to a second perspective in which the political system is the crucial force (the independent variable) that causes development of the social and economic systems. Thus Figure 10.2 emphasizes the central importance of the political system as an agent of change in relation to other societal characteristics. As Kwame Nkrumah

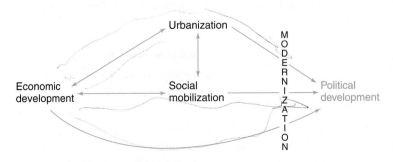

▶ **FIGURE 10.1**
Model of
development I

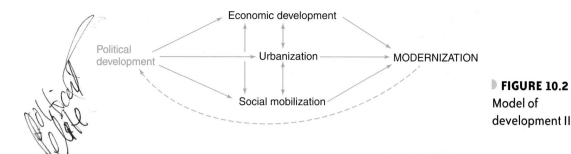

▶ **FIGURE 10.2**
Model of
development II

(1909–1972), the first president of Ghana, observed: "Seek ye first the political kingdom, and all else shall be added unto you." This widely quoted, nearly religious invocation asserts that if the political system is developed first, it can then serve as the instrument through which social and economic development is achieved. Public policy decisions by the political leadership can guide or even determine the direction of changes in individual and group behavior, the political economy, and the society.

According to Figure 10.2, change emanates from the domain over which the political elite has the most direct control—the political system. Thus an assertive political leadership can establish specialized political structures, expand the capabilities of the political system, and mobilize certain groups into the political process. The political leadership can then deploy these more developed political structures to enact public policies that empower governmental bureaucracies to perform new functions, assert state control over key human and natural resources, and allocate those resources in ways that result in social and economic development in such domains as the political economy, the educational system, the culture, national identity, the media, and religious practices.

Obviously, change and development in the political, social, economic, and other domains are interdependent; that is, they affect each other. But Figure 10.2 emphasizes the central role of political choice and politics as drivers for development. In this conception, development is shaped by the ideology, will, and actions of political actors rather than being driven by economic growth. A compelling example of a leader's explicit use of the political system as a powerful instrument to change many aspects of the society is Kemal Atatürk's efforts to modernize Turkey, described in Box 10.3.

Political Development as Democratization

In contrast to the capabilities analysis described above, some scholars (e.g., Cutright 1963) define political development as the establishment of the rule of law, legitimate elections, and representative institutions. Others object that this conception of a "developed" political system is extremely biased. Can you see why? What concept do such characteristics seem to measure?

You might answer that the preceding paragraph describes a *democratic* political system (recall Chapter 7). If you agree that the essence of political development is the capabilities of the political system to handle basic functions, it is possible to have a political system that is developed but nondemocratic (e.g., Cuba, China, Swaziland, Syria). However, it is certainly valid to conclude that one highly desirable outcome of political development is a system that is democratic.

BOX 10.3

Political Development and Modernization in Turkey

The modernization effort in Turkey is an example of "seeking the political kingdom first." Historically, the area of the Turkish nation was part of the large Ottoman Empire ruled by a sultan. After World War I, an army commander named Mustafa Kemal led a fierce military struggle for national independence. Victory resulted in the creation of the sovereign state of Turkey in 1922. Mustafa Kemal, who seized political power in the new republic, was committed to rapid modernization. At the time, Turkey had very traditional political, economic, and social systems, with Islamic law dominating the actions of the 98 percent Muslim population. The new leader decided that the key to modernization was to reduce the hold of Islam on the people.

▶ Thirty thousand Turkish students march to the mausoleum of Atatürk (photo on poster) to protest the antisecular education policies of the Islamist government. The banner reads: "The government will be overthrown, not the universities of the republic."

In a stroke of symbolic politics, Kemal began his modernization drive at the personal level. He changed his name to Mustafa Kemal Atatürk, the addition meaning "father of the Turks." (Kemal was also a fortunate name, since it means "perfect one.") Atatürk initially focused on political development, establishing a new state based on the principles of independence and democracy. A constitution was approved in 1924, executive power was granted to a president, the sultan was exiled, a legislature was elected, and a single political party was established. Atatürk thus created a political system with modern structures of governance and modern forms of political participation. This political system then became the instrument for Atatürk's broader efforts to reform Turkey.

From 1925 until his death in 1938, Atatürk employed his great

BOX 10.3 *(Continued)*

political power to implement three major sets of public policies that were meant to modernize Turkey and to separate it from the traditional Muslim world. First, he enacted laws that prohibited the wearing of religious garments in everyday life, abolished religious schools, and closed religious tombs as places of worship. Second, he encouraged the emergence and empowerment of a nationalist elite by such steps as creating a new Turkish language and banning the public use of other languages, replacing the Ottoman script with the Latin alphabet, and establishing Turkish literacy programs, especially in urban areas. Third, he established a new civil code (copied from Switzerland) to govern the legal relations between individuals and collectivities, relegating sharia law and the Koran to peripheral status in guiding public life. For example, he reduced the subordinate role of women, encouraging them to work, providing them with rights of divorce and inheritance, allowing them to vote and hold public office, and banning polygamy.

The effects of Atatürk's changes are evident in Turkey. While 70 percent of the population lived in villages in 1964, Turkey is now 66 percent urban. The economy, 75 percent agrarian in 1978, is nearly 90 percent industrial and service based. Turkey's 73 million people remain 99.8 percent Muslim, but the country now has the most educated and modern women in the Muslim world. From 1993 to 1996, Tansu Çiller was Turkey's first female prime minister. While gender inequality remains, about one-fourth of Turkish professionals are women, and the proportion of female doctors in Turkey is higher than in the United States.

Politically, the attempt to create an effective multiparty democracy in Turkey remains unfinished. There have been periods of serious social instability and governmental corruption, and three periods of military rule since 1960, although the military returned governmental reins to civilians in each case, once order was restored. For the first time since Atatürk, an Islamist party (the Welfare Party) came to power in 1996. When the government began to promote numerous policy changes based on Islamic principles and practices, the military responded with warnings and then forced the party from office in a "soft coup" that revealed the continuing power of the military in what is perhaps best characterized as an illiberal democracy (see Chapter 7). A reformulated Islamist party (AKP—Justice and Development) again took governmental power with majorities in the elections of 2002 and 2007. Despite continual attempts by AKP's prime minister to reassure the military of his support for Atatürk's secular society, he also guided the selection of an Islamist as president in 2007. This combination of political power and religious ideology has renewed the uneasiness of the military and secular elements of society, and the political situation is unstable.

Thus Atatürk's strong policies have not totally transformed Turkey. However, his legacy is an illuminating example of how a committed political leader can reform the political system and then use political power to achieve considerable social and economic development within a society, consistent with Figure 10.2.

test

Samuel Huntington (1991) suggests that there have been three long waves of democratization among modern states. The first occurred between the 1820s and 1926, when about 30 states established liberal democracies. Some of these then "reversed" (democracy was abandoned), until a second wave produced 36 democratic governments between 1945 and 1962. After another period of reversal, the third wave began in 1974. There are currently 123 electoral democracies. This is the highest proportion ever, having increased from 40 percent of the states in 1987 to 64 percent in 2007 (Freedom House 2008 and recall Chapter 7). Since 1990, the push toward democratization has been strong in many of the postcommunist states that emerged from the former Soviet Union and in Central and Eastern Europe and in some former military regimes in Latin America, Asia, and Africa (e.g., Chile, Ghana, Panama, South Korea, Taiwan, Uruguay).

What might account for the recent expansion of democracies? Consider the following six explanations.

First, the level of *economic development* has long been presented as a crucial factor. As suggested by Figure 10.1, economic development can cause changes in the social system that facilitate democratization. Greater wealth might reassure both citizens and leaders that the increased participation and demands associated with democratization can now be handled with less risk of instability because sufficient resources are available to meet those demands (Huntington 1991). The Debate in 10 explores whether economic development is a necessary prerequisite for democracy.

THE DEBATE IN 10

Is Economic Development a Necessary Prerequisite for Democracy?

Few research questions in political science attract more current interest than the attempt to identify the conditions that are most conducive to establishing democracy. Nearly 50 years ago, the distinguished social scientist Seymour Martin Lipset (1959) argued that economic development is the crucial prerequisite for democracy. Supported by the fact that all the most developed countries at the time were democracies, Lipset's thesis became the conventional wisdom. However, as a much more diverse set of countries has attempted to introduce democracy during the "third wave" of democratization, there has been considerable debate about whether economic development really is a *necessary* precondition for establishing and maintaining a democratic regime.

Economic Development Is a Necessary Prerequisite for Democracy

- The empirical facts support this linkage. Numerous comparative analyses indicate that there is a very strong correlation between a higher level of economic development and stronger democracy (Pei 1999). Most economically developed countries are democracies, while very few poor countries are democracies (Przeworski 2004).
- As indicated in Figure 10.1, economic development typically results in greater urbanization,

higher levels of education, and the development of a political culture with more trust and tolerance of diversity, all factors that are conducive to the emergence and maintenance of democracy (Spagnoli 2003).

- Economic development directly fosters the emergence of an educated and entrepreneurial middle class, whose members demand greater political voice and form the social-structural basis for effective democracy (Bueno de Mesquita and Downs 2005).
- Economic development results in more widespread prosperity, creating a larger proportion of the population who have the time necessary for active democratic participation. Conversely, in a society that lacks economic development, a substantial proportion of the population are so concerned with survival and economic advancement that they have little time or motivation to participate extensively in democratic life (Spagnoli 2003).
- The effects of economic development in raising education levels also promote greater political knowledge and awareness among the population, encouraging more extensive political participation.
- No democratic country with a GDP/capita of greater than $6,000 has ever abandoned democracy (Przeworski 2004). Thus, the prosperity that results from economic development is a crucial element in sustaining democracy.
- Economic development leads to greater access to a broader range of political information and more openness to global society. Such inputs reduce a nondemocratic government's ability to limit its citizens' exposure to disruptive political ideas that promote the concept of democracy and undermine authoritarian control.

Economic Development Is Not a Necessary Precondition for Democracy

- The empirical facts support this conclusion. A reasonable generalization from the hundreds of comparative empirical studies is that the conditions associated with the emergence of democracy are complex, multiple, and varied. That is, no single condition, including a high level of economic development, must always be present for the successful transition to democracy (Rueschemeyer et al. 1992; Spagnoli 2003).

- Economic development is not essential for establishing many of the critical preconditions for democracy in developing countries: effective political institutions, a working political party system, and a civil society in which groups share trust and tolerance (White 1998).

- Many authoritarian regimes have become very effective at resisting the demands for democracy supposedly associated with economic growth, as cases such as China and Singapore clearly demonstrate. Indeed, high-income countries that are nondemocracies are actually *less* likely to transition to democracy than middle-income countries that are nondemocracies (Bueno de Mesquita and Downs 2005; Przeworski et al. 2000).

- Many relatively poor countries have successfully implemented democracy. In fact, in the early twenty-first century, a substantially higher proportion of countries are democracies than are at high levels of economic development (Freedom House 2008).

- The spread of information and communications technologies and the Internet has reduced the significance of economic development in facilitating key preconditions of democracy, such as mechanisms for interest aggregation, shared cultural identity, and especially a community of communication (Klein 2001).

- Some of the most durable democracies in the developing world maintained their high levels of political rights and civil liberties during long periods of limited economic development and negligible economic growth. Examples include Botswana, Costa Rica, and India.

Second, *external actors* have been an important force in the shift toward democracy. The World Bank and the United States, among others, have been increasingly insistent that countries introduce democratic reforms as a condition for economic assistance. Also, the Catholic Church reduced its doctrinal emphasis on obedience to governmental authority, which led to a decline in citizen acquiescence to authoritarian regimes in such Catholic countries as Argentina and Brazil. And by the late 1980s, the Soviet Union under Mikhail Gorbachev was no longer willing to intervene in support of unpopular totalitarian leadership in East European states such as Hungary and Poland (Huntington 1991; Maxfield 1997).

Third, the *breakdown of authoritarian and totalitarian regimes* has provided a window of opportunity for democratization. In such cases, nondemocratic political systems have lost their capabilities to suppress the pressure for change. This seems to have been a particularly important factor in the states of the former Soviet Union and Central and Eastern Europe as well as in such countries as Argentina, Benin, and Chile (Linz and Stepan 1996).

Fourth, the expansion of democracy might be enhanced by *changing norms* that favor democracy. The perception has grown that many other countries are making the transition to democracy and that this is a right that citizens in all countries should enjoy. Thus citizens become more insistent that their leaders implement democratic reforms (Diamond 2003).

Fifth, nonviolent *"people power" movements* have become a crucial force for change in almost three-fourths of the countries that have democratized. There is a clear relationship between the strength of such movements and the level of democratic freedom that is achieved and maintained (Karatnycky and Ackerman 2006).

Sixth, another key factor is often the presence of *political leadership* committed to democracy. In many countries, new leaders gain broad popular support from civic movements and attain power based on their promise to pursue democratization as a central goal of the political system (as with Vicente Fox in Mexico, South Africa's Nelson Mandela, and Ukraine's Viktor Yushchenko). Indeed, so much ideological value is currently attached to democratization that nearly every political leader must at least declare her allegiance to expanding and protecting democratic processes in order to maintain her domestic and international support, although some leaders abandon this promise as they attempt to govern (Sorensen 2007).

WORLD OF CHANGES

Easton's model in Chapter 5 emphasized that the political system must attempt to respond to constant changes in its internal and external environments. Thus Easton (1965) asked: How can a political system persist in a world of changes? His answer is that the public policy process must result in decisions and actions that increase the support for the political institutions and the authorities and that manage the complex demands and challenges from the environment.

Thus political systems, like the global environment in which they function, are constantly engaged in both system maintenance and political change. Most political change is modest, resulting from the effects of (1) new policy decisions, (2) alterations in the way existing policy is implemented, or (3) variations in the inputs from the internal or external environments. In some political systems, we could probably identify thousands of small changes in a single week. Although political change usually results from the gradual accumulation of minor adjustments, it is more noticeable when there is a substantial shift. For example, there could be a major change from a dominant party to a multiparty system; from authoritarianism to electoral democracy; from a period of war to a period without military hostilities; from a statist political economy to a neoliberal one; from male-only to gender-neutral political rights; from an elected leader to a military dictatorship.

Even more *fundamental change in the nature of the political system or the political economy* can be called a **system transformation.** The emergence of a secular regime in Turkey under Atatürk, the destruction of the Saddam Hussein regime in Iraq, the dramatic alterations in the political system in Cambodia under Pol Pot (described in Box 10.4), and the abandonment of state socialism in Russia (see Box 15.1) are examples of system transformation. One striking feature of the political world in the last

BOX 10.4

Multiple Transformations of a Political System: Cambodia

The case of Cambodia illuminates a political system that has undergone five major transformations in a relatively short time span.

▶ **This memorial to the victims of the Pol Pot regime is close to the capital city of Phnom Penh. The sign indicates that 129 mass graves were found and 86 of them were opened, yielding the remains of more than 8,985 Cambodians executed in "reeducation camps."**

BOX 10.4 (Continued)

Cambodia I. The Cambodia of 1962 was a small, beautiful state in Indochina that had been granted its independence by France in 1953. It has been said that the most important activities in the lives of Cambodians were to dance, make love, and watch the grass grow. They were ruled under a rather authoritarian political system by Prince Norodom Sihanouk, a hereditary leader who attempted to balance the forces of the left and the right within Cambodia and to keep Cambodia on a neutral course.

However, in the late 1960s, Sihanouk was unable to prevent Cambodia from being drawn into the increasingly widespread and intense war in neighboring Vietnam, especially because of the underlying power struggle in the area between the Soviet Union, the United States, and China. Some Vietcong (the guerrillas attempting to overthrow the South Vietnamese state) took sanctuary in Cambodia, but Sihanouk insisted that Cambodian sovereignty prevented the United States and South Vietnamese armies from invading Cambodia to attack these Vietcong. Sihanouk also attempted to direct international attention to the "secret bombing" raids in Cambodia conducted by the American military but denied by the American political leadership.

Cambodia II. Because of Sihanouk's resistance to their military objectives, the Americans supported (and perhaps directed) a March 1970 coup in which Cambodian army leaders overthrew Sihanouk and replaced him with General Lon Nol, a rightist dictator who was generally viewed as a puppet of the United States. Under the Lon Nol government, there were dramatic changes in Cambodia's political structure and foreign policy and considerable changes in its domestic policy. This political system was maintained by the United States from 1970 to 1975. In turn, the Cambodian government and military assisted the U.S. military in fighting the communist insurgents. The guerrilla war by Cambodian communists—the Khmer Rouge—against the Lon Nol government escalated, and extensive fighting continued in Cambodia by the military forces of the United States, South Vietnam, the Vietcong, Cambodia, and the Khmer Rouge.

Cambodia III. With the collapse of the U.S. military effort in Southeast Asia, Lon Nol's government was among the casualties. Thus the Khmer Rouge came to power in April 1975 and created yet another political system, renaming the country Kampuchea. Under the communist regime of Pol Pot, Kampuchea experienced one of the most dramatic transformations in a political system during the twentieth century. The new government immediately relocated everyone from urban areas to the countryside, organized the entire population into collective farms that were really forced labor camps, and implemented a massive reeducation (indoctrination) program. In a brutal reign of terror, about one-third of Cambodia's population of 7 million was either killed or died during a total restructuring of the society.

Cambodia IV. The Vietnamese exploited this time of disruption, invading and conquering the Cambodians, their centuries-old enemies. In January 1979, the Vietnamese army installed a puppet government under Prime Minister Hun Sen (a dissident Khmer Rouge). Thus Pol Pot's barbaric regime was replaced with a new political system that operated as a satellite of Vietnam's communist government.

Cambodia V. After years of guerrilla warfare by groups loyal to the Khmer Rouge and Sihanouk, a treaty in Paris led to United Nations–supervised elections for a national

BOX 10.4 *(Continued)*

legislature in 1993. The election and subsequent constitution created a fifth political system, an odd combination bringing together many of the old adversaries. Sihanouk became king, a constitutional monarch with mainly symbolic power. His anticommunist son, Prince Ranariddh, as "first" prime minister, shared political power with communist Hun Sen, the "second" prime minister. The Khmer Rouge, who refused to participate in the election, continued a punishing guerrilla war and controlled large parts of the countryside.

This unstable system collapsed in 1997. After a brief civil war, Hun Sen's forces were victorious in a coup that deposed Prince Ranariddh, who was exiled. Key supporters of the prince's political party either fled the country or were executed. Meanwhile, rival forces within the Khmer Rouge captured Pol Pot, who was imprisoned and soon died. After two subsequent elections (1998 and 2003), uneasy coalition governments have been formed, with Hun Sen continuing as prime minister and the prince's party as the second largest in the legislature. Another son of Sihanouk (Sihamoni) is now king. The government controls the military and the national administration, although some rural areas still seem beyond the control of the central government. It remains uncertain whether any group can govern Cambodia effectively.

In summary, the political system of Cambodia has undergone five dramatic changes in less than 50 years. A phrase in the Cambodian national anthem aptly describes the country's recent history: "The bright red blood . . . spilled over the towns and over the plain." The life expectancy of Cambodia V is uncertain.

two decades has been the substantial number of such transformations. Chapter 15 will focus on political systems in which political and economic transformations have been particularly extensive in the past several decades: in the Soviet Union, Central and Eastern Europe, and the newly industrializing countries. In addition, later chapters will explore major transformations that seem to be occurring at the international level, generally associated with *globalization*. System transformation is rare. Incremental change is the norm.

Notice that both political development and democratization are narrower concepts than political change. Key actors in most political systems value changes that result in political development, understood as those changes that positively affect **political institutionalization**—*the depth of capabilities, stability, and citizen support for the political system.* We have noted above that, according to one dominant ideology, an additional goal of political development is **democratization**—those *changes that deepen and consolidate democratic processes* (Diamond 2003; Wilensky 2002). This view attaches considerable value to the transition from authoritarianism to electoral democracy to liberal democracy.

A second change goal valued by virtually all leaders in all countries is to achieve greater economic growth and development. As described in Chapter 8, the increasing capacity and complexity of the economic system and the production of a larger array of goods and services for consumption are the essence of economic development.

A related goal that is now frequently linked to this development model is neoliberalism, defined earlier in the chapter as the transition to full engagement in the global economy and a market political economy, and away from economic protectionism and from any remnants of a command political economy.

However, there is not global consensus about the desirability of either democratization or the neoliberal economic vision as necessary components of the development process. First, there are nondemocracies, such as China, Myanmar, Oman, and Ukraine, whose leaders aim to increase the capabilities of the economic system and the political system without substantially expanding the processes and institutions of democracy. Secondly, the elites in some countries, such as Venezuela and Ecuador, celebrate political development and democratization and strive for economic development but reject the strategy of neoliberalism. And third, in some countries, such as Iran, Sudan, and Saudi Arabia, the leaders' objective is to shape political and economic development to serve higher religious and social values.

Regardless of the directions of development envisioned by the political elites, it is usually very difficult for the elites to control the *directions* of change with precision. Samuel Huntington (1968, 1987) offers incisive commentary regarding the illusion of development. He describes many political systems that appear to have achieved a reasonable level of political development, which he defines in terms of political institutionalization, but then experience a substantial deterioration of political structures, processes, and roles. He calls this situation **political decay**—*a significant decline in the capabilities of the political system and its level of political institutionalization, and especially in its capacity to maintain order*. Political decay is evident in high levels of civil disorder—strikes, violent crime, riots, nation-based conflict, and rebellion.

Political decay can have multiple causes, but it is more likely when there are excessive demands on the political system, low levels of citizen support, pressure from the external environment, and ineffective governmental actions. Political decay can also be increased by destabilizing aspects of the development process, such as greater modernization, economic growth, urbanization, and communications. Modernization can undermine the traditional values and beliefs that sustained social order; economic growth produces new resources over which there is competition; urbanization concentrates heterogeneous groups into large, densely packed masses; expanded communications make these masses aware of the many resources and values that they do not currently enjoy.

Many political systems are confronted with challenging combinations of these causes of political decay. A political system might respond effectively to these challenges, by increasing the allocation of economic or political benefits to the population. If it is unable to generate and distribute these benefits, rising social, political, and economic frustrations can further reduce the support for the political system and accelerate the slide into political decay. In response to political decay, several scenarios can evolve:

- The political system cracks down on disorder, limiting the rights of protest groups, opposition parties, the free press, and so on, and deploying its security forces (e.g., the police, the military) to suppress any antiregime activities.
- A charismatic leader emerges. The leader gains the support and obedience of the people but only by personalizing power and thus weakening the overall processes through which power and political structures are institutionalized.

- The military—the one organization in most societies that *is* institutionalized— forcibly takes over political power under the justification of restoring order.

- In cases where no individuals or institutions have the capacity to reestablish social peace, disorder and violence become widespread and can result in civil war or revolution.

In each of the first three scenarios, one typical result is a shift toward greater authoritarianism. And in countries where there had been a deepening of democratic practices, these scenarios of political decay can lead to "democratic breakdown" and illiberal democracy. These trends are evident in most regions in recent years (Corothers 2002; Freedom House 2008; Schedler 2006; Wiarda 2004).

If the situation approaches the conditions of the fourth scenario, even the fundamental goal of state survival is under threat. When a political system loses its capacity to maintain basic order, it can be characterized as a *failed state.* Recent examples include Iraq, Sierra Leone, and the Sudan. Such widespread disorder can be almost akin to Hobbes's notion of the "state of nature." Life for most citizens truly is nasty, violent, and short, and many people engage in behaviors that are brutish. A failed state also creates dangers for other states in its region, due to disruptions caused by displaced populations and economic hardships. Box 10.4 describes the dramatic changes in the political system of Cambodia as it cycled through a chaotic period in which the political system was destroyed and recreated several times with devastating effects on its population.

CONCLUDING OBSERVATIONS

Ultimately, all political systems aim to increase their capabilities and thus achieve greater political and economic development. In general, most people assume that development in other countries should result in political systems and political economies that resemble those in their own country. It is debatable, however, whether all states should or even can follow the same developmental path. Some, perhaps most, newly developing countries might have characteristics that are not compatible with the patterns of development or the political structures and processes that "worked" in other countries, especially those that emerged in earlier eras.

The leaders in most countries try to assess whether the prior experiences and strategies of some other state provide a model for their own change and development. Even if leaders do select a model that seems compatible with their own goals and unique characteristics, achieving political development and political institutionalization and sustaining economic growth are extremely difficult for many countries in the contemporary world. The remainder of this book will continue to illustrate the extent to which the choices and actions of states are influenced and sometimes controlled by other actors in the global system and by limits on their own resources. This is a particular problem for states with low capabilities and minimal stability—that is, states that lack political institutionalization.

Huntington is certainly correct that the challenges to political development are great. There have been periods of major political instability even in some European and Latin American countries—and these countries had the advantage of a long period in which the structures of a modern state could evolve into more complex and effective forms and in which the citizens could come to accept and value their political system. In contrast to those countries, most states began creating their own modern political systems in the last 60 years. While these systems have the appearance of modernity—specialized political structures, widespread political participation, and so on—many lack the stability and value that come with a long evolutionary development.

The political elites in these states face many fundamental dilemmas regarding how to allocate public values effectively while maintaining political order, expanding political participation, and strengthening the political economy. How much political participation and opposition should be allowed? How large should the domain of *res publica* be? To what extent should the state control the political economy? What policies should regulate interactions with the global economy? What levels of which values should the state allocate to particular groups? In essence, can the political system shape political, economic, and social change? All states continually deal with these challenging issues, which will be recurrent themes in the remainder of this book.

KEY CONCEPTS

change
civil society
core
democratization
dependency approach
dependent variable
development
developmental-state
    approach

economic
    development
failed state
independent
    variable
modernization
neoliberalism
newly industrializing
    countries (NICs)

political decay
political
    development
political
    institutionalization
statism
system
    transformation
Westernization

FOR FURTHER CONSIDERATION

1. Most people in Western societies have been socialized to believe that change is associated with progress and is generally a good thing. However, the ideology of conservatism (as outlined in Chapter 2) does not make this assumption. What are the conservative's views about change? More broadly, can you specify types of change that would not necessarily be positive for a given political system?

2. The success or failure of the developmental-state strategy in certain developing countries is sometimes attributed to elements of culture. How important do you think a society's culture might be? Why? What factors other than culture might affect a country's capacity for rapid development?

3. Many countries have recently established democratic political processes. Is political decay inevitable in most of these countries? Why or why not? What strategies, general and specific, seem most promising in the attempt to avoid serious political decay?

4. Write a dialogue between two analysts: one contends that the dependency approach offers the best explanation for the failure of many countries to achieve development, while the second analyst argues that other factors best explain why some countries have limited development.

FOR FURTHER READING

Achebe, Chinua. (1969). *Arrow of God*. New York: Doubleday.   In themes similar to those in Achebe's highly acclaimed *Things Fall Apart* (1959) (see Box 10.1), this novel describes how West African villagers' beliefs in their local gods are undermined by a Christian missionary, leading to the disintegration of their cultural traditions.

Bales, Kevin. (1999). *Disposable People: New Slavery in the Global Economy*. Berkeley: University of California Press.   A powerful description of the emergence of new forms of human slavery, particularly among females and child laborers, in exploited work forces in such countries on the periphery of the global economy as Brazil, India, Pakistan, and Thailand.

Becker, Elizabeth. (1986). *When the War Was Over: The Voices of Cambodia's Revolution and Its People*. New York: Simon and Schuster.   A gut-wrenching description of Cambodia under the Pol Pot regime (Box 10.4).

Collier, Paul. (2007). *The Bottom Billion: Why the Poorest Countries Are Failing and What Can Be Done About It*. New York: Oxford University Press.   The author elaborates on four key reasons accounting for the development failures of the world's poorest peoples: civil wars, abundant resources that others covet, poor geography, and bad governance.

Diamond, Larry, Marc Plattner, Yun-han Chu, and Mung-mao Tien, Eds. (1997). *Consolidating the Third Wave Democracies*. Baltimore, MD: Johns Hopkins University Press.   In two volumes (*Themes and Perspectives; Regional Challenges*), diverse top scholars thoughtfully and comprehensively assess the issues and empirical realities associated with efforts to "consolidate" (institutionalize) liberal democracy in countries in every region of the world.

Harrison, Neil E. (2000). *Constructing Sustainable Development*. Albany: State University of New York Press. This brief, useful exploration of the various meanings attached to the concept of "sustainable development" concludes that the core values associated with the concept are inconsistent but argues nonetheless that there are policy actions that could advance sustainable development.

Huntington, Samuel P. (1991). *The Third Wave: Democratization in the Late Twentieth Century*. Norman: University of Oklahoma Press. A wide-ranging assessment of contemporary transitions to democracy by one of the major scholars of comparative development. The general argument about political institutionalization and political decay discussed in this chapter is fully elaborated in his earlier sweeping study *Political Order in Changing Societies* (New Haven, CT: Yale University Press, 1968).

Johnson, Chalmers. (1996). *Japan: Who Governs? The Rise of the Developmental State*. New York: W. W. Norton. An elaboration of his important earlier analyses of the Japanese development strategy (Johnson 1983a), this book provides a broader framework characterizing the government–industry cooperation that produced the "Japanese miracle" and has become the basis of the development approach taken by other Asian NICs.

Judd, Ellen, and Marilyn Porter, Eds. (1999). *Feminists Doing Development: A Practical Critique*. Useful articles and case studies examine development theory from a feminist perspective and provide strong examples emphasizing the crucial roles of women in development.

Lipset, Seymour Martin. (1988). *Revolution and Counterrevolution: Change and Persistence in Social Structures*. Rev. ed. Rutgers, NJ: Transaction Books. Provocative essays on the processes of change and development, with a particular emphasis on the effects of culture.

Rotberg, Robert I., Ed. (2003). *When States Fail: Causes and Consequences*. Princeton, NJ: Princeton University Press. The first part of the book is a series of essays examining the conditions under which states deteriorate to the point of possible death; the second part offers analyses of what can be done to prevent failed states and how to rebuild such states.

Sorensen, Georg. (2007). *Democracy and Democratization: Processes and Prospects in a Changing World*. 3rd ed. Boulder, CO: Westview. A wide-ranging discussion of the spread of democratic processes in many countries, defining the patterns and conditions under which democracy is viable and the likely evolution of various democratic systems.

Wiarda, Howard J. (2004). *Political Development in Emerging Countries*. Belmont, CA: Wadsworth. A sensible description of the major theories of development in the developing countries (see Chapter 14). It indicates how such frameworks as dependency theory, neoliberalism, globalization, and the developmental-state approach apply to the situation in such countries.

ON THE WEB

http://hdr.undp.org/en/reports

This is the site for the United Nations' Development Programme office, the source of the yearly Human Development Report.

http://worldbank.org

At the official site of the World Bank, an international consortium of banks and other major financial institutions, extensive economic data are available, including selections from the annual World Development Report as well as information on issues of development and trade.

http://www.iisd.ca/

The Web site of the International Institute for Sustainable Development offers information and essays on this topic, ranging from policy statements and economic data to book-length studies.

http://w3.acdi-cida.gc.ca/cidaweb/acdicida.nsf/En/Home

This site from the Canadian International Development Agency provides links to many sources of information about development issues, such as aid, economic growth, environmental impacts, and human rights issues.

http://www.un.org/esa/sustdev/

The home page of the United Nations Division for Sustainable Development, this site provides access to a wide variety of relevant UN resolutions and publications.

http://www.ulb.ac.be/ceese/meta/sustvl.html

The World Wide Web Virtual Library contains an extensive listing of Internet resources related to sustainable development and political change.

http://www.intl-crisis-group.org/

This is the International Crisis Group's "Crisis Web," which details the current crises within countries with serious levels of political decay and offers policy suggestions for conflict management and a return to political order.

CHAPTER 11

POLITICS ACROSS BORDERS

I magine an island state, Buena, blessed with temperate climate and rich natural resources that provide sufficient food and other necessities for the population. A few hundred miles to the south is a similar island, Malo, but Malo is cold and windy and has few resources to support its population. Each island is located about 50 miles off a large landmass composed of several states.

If you knew nothing more about either state, could you make any educated guesses about the political and economic relations these states have with each other and with the states on the large landmass?

CHAPTER OUTLINE

■ The Goals of States

■ Mechanisms of Cooperation Between States

■ Competition Among States

In considering the relations between the states of Buena and Malo, it would be reasonable to begin by assessing the resource situation of each state. Combining this with the location of each state, the following issues could emerge: Is either island state more in need of trading relations with outsiders? Does either state have strong reasons to protect itself from intervention by outsiders? How could such protection be accomplished? If either state establishes a military, what kind of forces would make the most sense? What kind of political alliance would each state be most likely to forge (with states on the landmass or with each other)?

One traditional method of thinking analytically about the actions of states is based on precisely these kinds of assessments. This method of **geopolitics** assumes that the geography of a state—that is, its physical characteristics (e.g., location, topography) and its natural and human resources (e.g., population size, fossil fuel resources, arable land, water)—might significantly affect the politics of the state (Parker 2000).

While only a few argue that "geography is destiny," it does seem reasonable to assume that a state's geography can be the source of both opportunities and constraints on its actions. Consider, for example, the effects on a state of conditions such as insufficient domestic food production, abundant fossil fuel resources, a small population relative to land area, the absence of any natural barriers separating the state from surrounding states, being snowbound eight months each year, enormous variation in yearly rainfall, or strategic location in a major international shipping lane.

It should be obvious that important features within a state's boundaries other than its geography, such as its political culture, the style of its major political leaders, and the nature of its political structures, might also powerfully affect the state's behavior toward other political systems.

The poet John Donne wrote, "No man is an island, entire of itself, every man is a piece of a continent." In the contemporary political world, it is clear that not even an island is insulated from the global society and economy. Indeed, our imaginary Buena and Malo (or actual islands such as Cuba, the Falklands, Great Britain, Japan, or Sri Lanka) will find that their politics are heavily dependent on what other state and nonstate actors are doing. In the model of the political system in Chapter 5, this point is made explicitly in the concept of the extrasocietal environment. The behavior of every political system is affected not only by its own characteristics but also by the actions of external actors in its environment. These external actors might include other states, "transborder" actors (actors whose political activities cross state borders, such as international organizations, multinational corporations, and nongovernmental organizations), and other external systems (such as economic, cultural, demographic, and social systems in other states or in the international system as a whole).

As globalization has dramatically increased the penetration of states by outside forces, many states expend much, and in some cases most, of their political energy on their relations with other states and with transborder actors. The *individual state's decisions and actions relative to such external actors* are called *foreign policy*. The *interactions among two or more states and external actors* are called **international relations**.

This chapter examines the politics across state borders. First, it details major goals pursued by all states. Second, it discusses the means by which states and transborder actors attempt to facilitate cooperation and resolve conflict. Third, it examines key forms of interstate competition, such as balance of power and colonial domination. The causes and use of force and violence across state borders will be considered in Chapter 12.

THE GOALS OF STATES

Realist and Idealist Perspectives on the State's "Motives"

To understand how states behave in relation to other actors in the global system, it is helpful to identify what motivates them. From this perspective, states can be analyzed, almost like individuals, as having motives and values that they attempt to pursue in the international environment. However, the context within which the states exist is different from the context for individuals because most analysts assume that the politics between states occurs in an international system that is *anarchic*. This does not mean that the system is chaotic, but that there is no overarching authority that can impose order and "good behavior" on all the states in their relations with each other and with other actors. Scholars attempt to explain how and why states interact in the ways that they do in the absence of such an authority. Two perspectives have especially influenced international relations theory: political realism and political idealism.

Political realism assumes that *people are naturally disposed to behave selfishly*. This same selfishness extends to the behavior of the states that people form. In the international system, there is no supreme authority that protects the states from predatory behavior by other states. Thus every state experiences "the security dilemma"— that no higher power will necessarily protect it—and the fundamental goal of each state is to ensure its own security and survival. A state's security increases to the extent it maximizes its own power (e.g., economic power, knowledge power, and especially military power) relative to the power of every other state. States are in constant competition for power, especially because power is a "zero-sum" commodity—an increase in power for one actor results in an equivalent decrease for others. There is no expectation that another state can be trusted, will avoid violence, or will act ethically. A state makes treaties or breaks them, makes war or cooperates with other countries for only one reason: to maximize its security goals.

In contrast, the crucial assumption of **political idealism** (also called *political liberalism*) is that *human nature is basically good*. People, and the states they construct, can be altruistic and cooperative. States have many goals, and aggressive, power-maximizing behavior is not inevitable. If a state's actions reduce the welfare of people in any country or increase interstate conflict and war, it is usually because of poorly designed institutions (e.g., governments, economic systems, legal systems), not because people are evil or selfish. For the political idealist, it is possible to establish an international system in which well-designed institutions can facilitate cooperative behavior among states and create a situation that is a "positive sum"—everyone is better off.

It is obvious that realism and idealism (and their recent elaborations, neorealism and neoliberalism, respectively) lead to very different explanations of a state's behavior toward other states (Kegley 2008; Keohane and Nye 2001; Mearsheimer 2001). They also provide contrasting prescriptions about how a state ought to respond to the actions of another state. Are you strongly oriented toward the realist or toward the idealist perspective? As you read, consider how the assumptions of realism or idealism alter one's interpretations of the topics in this chapter.

Major Goals

What major goals might a state pursue? The political system of each state assigns different levels of relative importance to a wide variety of goals. However, most can be subsumed under three overarching goals: *security*, *stability*, and *prosperity*. Each of these goals includes component goals that the political system might act to serve. The significance of each component goal and the capacity of the political system to achieve each goal depend on many factors, such as the state's relative tendency toward a realist or idealist orientation, geopolitical situation, history, culture, leaders, political structures, and interactions with other states. Notice that some of these factors depend primarily on dynamics internal to the state, and others are substantially affected by the actions of other global actors. Figure 11.1 illustrates this framework of basic goals. In the lists that follow, the major components of each overarching goal are presented in the general order of their priority for most states.

Security

1. *Survival* is the fundamental element of security. It entails the very existence of the state, such that other states do not conquer it and that internal forces do not destroy it.

2. *Autonomy* refers to the capacity of the state to act within its own boundaries without intervention into or control of its affairs by external actors.

3. *Influence* involves the state's ability to alter the actions of external actors in desired ways by means of persuasion or inducements.

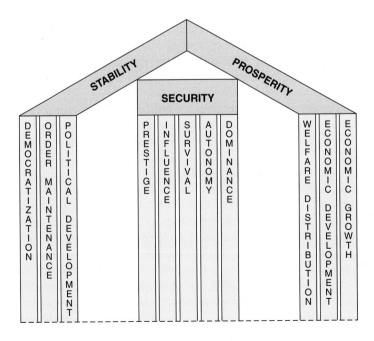

▶ **FIGURE 11.1**

Basic goals
of states

4. *Prestige* is the desirable situation wherein external actors admire and respect the state.

5. *Dominance* is the use of power or violence to enable the state to impose direct control over external actors.

Stability

1. *Order maintenance* is the capacity of the state to ensure social peace for its citizens through the prevention of individual and group violation of societal norms, especially those involving violence.

2. *Political development* refers to the concentration of political authority in a state that has strong capabilities to make and enforce effective policies and to gain support from its citizens (recall Samuel Huntington's conception of institutionalization in Chapter 10).

3. *Democratization* is the process of institutionalizing a democratic system of governance, which is achieved by allowing free elections and guaranteeing civil and political rights.

Prosperity

1. *Economic growth* refers to the increasing scale, complexity, and specialization of the productive system and of the goods produced.

2. *Economic development* is the capacity of the political economy to obtain, manage, and transform resources into valued goods.

3. *Welfare distribution* refers to the private or public allocation of adequate and increasing levels of valued goods to enhance the quality of life of the citizenry.

Notice that Figure 11.1 gives particular priority to security goals. While survival is a fundamental goal of every country, this priority on all security goals reflects the realist view. In some states, certain prosperity goals or stability goals are probably more important than some of the security goals, such as dominance. No state can fully achieve its desired level on all of these eleven major goals. Thus a state must make difficult trade-offs when pursuing multiple goals. For example, when a state makes a costly increase in the amount of welfare goods and services allocated to its citizens, it uses resources that it might otherwise have reinvested in the state's economic system to facilitate economic growth. This trade-off is often referred to as the fundamental policy choice of "growth versus welfare." In another example, resources that the state allocates to the military for major security goals are not available for either welfare or the production of consumer goods. This policy trade-off is characterized by the phrase "guns versus butter." Of the eleven major goals listed in Figure 11.1, which ones do you think are most complementary? Most incompatible?

The politics across state borders are usually characterized by cooperation or competition. The rest of this chapter explores these two dominant patterns in international relations. In most instances, a state realizes more benefits and fewer costs if it pursues its goals without using force against other states. However, the competition between states can escalate into conflict. The final section in Chapter 12 will examine those crucial situations where conflict resolution fails and the result is transborder violence and war.

MECHANISMS OF COOPERATION BETWEEN STATES

Diplomacy and Interstate Agreements

Do you agree with the proposition that, under most circumstances, a state is likely to accomplish more of its goals at lower costs if it can develop mutually advantageous cooperative arrangements with other states? From the neoliberal (contemporary idealist) perspective, a state has an inherent preference to establish arrangements through which such cooperation can be nurtured. Realists are likely to be more cynical about such cooperation, viewing such arrangements as strategic ones to be made or broken as they serve the state's national interest.

States formalize and coordinate their interactions through many mechanisms, the most widespread being *diplomacy*. Diplomatic practices enable a state's skilled representatives to engage in regular discussion and negotiation with the representatives of other states. Thus most states maintain an array of actors (e.g., ambassadors, cultural attachés) and institutions (e.g., embassies, trade delegations) whose objectives are to further interests shared with other states and to resolve potential problems by means of "normal diplomatic channels" and informal communications.

The essence of traditional diplomacy is sensitive and strategic face-to-face discussions between diplomats on behalf of their countries. However, modern communications technologies (e.g., videoconferencing) have provided new ways for leaders as well as diplomats to interact, allowing them to deal with each other directly, even if not in person. An interesting example of these new hybrids is "teleplomacy"— the use of broadcast television as a means for high-level communications between states. For example, during the "war on terrorism" begun in late 2001, U.S. President George W. Bush and al-Qaeda leader Osama bin Laden would not speak directly, but they did communicate with each other via television speeches, and they also used these broadcasts to persuade others to support their actions. In the world of 24/7 news media, political officials are aware that every public utterance is being recorded and might be accessible around the world to other political actors via some medium, ranging from Le Monde to CNN to YouTube.

More explicit cooperation among states is usually established by bilateral (between two states) or multilateral (among three or more states) agreements. Distinctions are sometimes made between three forms of these agreements: alliances, treaties, and regimes. *Alliances* are *informal or formal agreements between states that they will cooperate or assist each other* militarily, economically, or politically. During World War II (1939–1945), for example, both the Allied Powers (Britain and France) and the Axis Powers (Germany, Italy, and Japan) established alliances about cooperation and coordination if a war began. **Treaties** are also *interstate agreements that deal with the same areas but tend to be more formal and legalistic, and there is a stronger expectation of compliance*. These agreements can range from a straightforward arrangement for a cultural exchange between two friendly countries to a complex nuclear arms reduction pact between many hostile states. Most alliances and treaties involve a limited set of countries. For example, the North American Free Trade Agreement (NAFTA) is a treaty between three neighboring states to cooperate on a complex set of trade arrangements. And the European Union, described in Box 11.1, is an example

BOX 11.1

The More We Are Together: The European Union

According to some observers, the Soviet Union is dead and the United States is in long-term decline, but there is a new giant emerging in the world. It was born in the 1950s, when West European countries battered by World War II developed three cooperative communities regarding interstate trade, atomic energy, and coal and steel production. The underlying objectives were mutual self-help in economic redevelopment and military defense. It has evolved from a loose alliance into a powerful confederation that is the largest and wealthiest single consumer market in the world.

The six original countries (Belgium, France, Germany, Italy, Luxembourg, and the Netherlands) added six more during the 1970s and 1980s (Denmark, Greece, Ireland, Portugal, Spain, and the United Kingdom) and three more during the 1990s (Austria, Finland, and Sweden). Ten more were added in 2004 (Cyprus, the Czech Republic, Estonia, Hungary, Latvia, Lithuania, Malta, Poland, Slovakia, and Slovenia), and two in 2007 (Bulgaria and Romania). This European Union (EU) now has more than 497 million people and a combined GDP of more than $16.8 trillion per year, greater in both population and economic product than its nearest rival, the United States. With only 6 percent of the world's population, the EU is the source of more than 40 percent of international trade.

In the vision of its strongest proponents, the EU is becoming a true *supranational organization*—an international organization with autonomous policy-making and policy-implementation powers over national states that have ceded considerable sovereignty and have agreed to abide by its collective decisions, even when those decisions are not in the states' own national interests. The scope of EU decisions covers a vast array of policies that would normally be controlled by national political systems. In economic terms, this means that the EU is a single economic market in which people, money, and goods flow freely without regard to national borders. In military terms, a common foreign policy and joint armed forces would be under a single command. And in political terms, the goal is a "United States of Europe," with an elected European Parliament that passes legislation binding on all citizens, a council of ministers operating as a collective executive under a president, a court of justice serving as the interpreter and enforcer of laws that supersede the laws of individual countries, and a large administrative branch of "Eurocrats" applying the laws.

All the key elements of the EU are now in place, including the elected European Parliament of more than 730 delegates and all the other institutions previously described. As examples of the shared policies, there is now a common European passport and a common currency, the euro. Every country has been obliged to convert to the metric system. And labor and capital move freely between countries. However, some member countries are not prepared to concede a substantial share of their

BOX 11.1 *(Continued)*

sovereignty to the EU, resisting compliance on key issues that they perceive to affect their national interest. There have been continuing problems with fiscal policy, tax structure, and agricultural policy, and some countries still do not use the euro. Disagreements on foreign policy have also been evident, especially regarding the level of military involvement in the 1991 Persian Gulf War and the conflicts between Serbia and both Bosnia and the ethnic Albanians of Kosovo. In 1999, the EU countries agreed that they would create their own autonomous military force and a common policy on security and defense.

After the EU's indecisive response to the 1991 Persian Gulf War (the U.S.-led operation to drive Iraq's invading forces out of Kuwait), Belgium's Foreign Minister, Mark Eyskens, observed that Europe "is an economic giant, a political dwarf, and a military worm" (Kegley and Wittkopf 1995: 165). And the EU's role as an economic giant is somewhat tempered by the ongoing squabbles among member states unwilling to sacrifice sovereignty to it.

Despite its failure to achieve complete union and unanimity of action in all cases, it is clear that the EU is now a formidable player in international politics. Lester Thurow (2003) concluded that the balanced strengths of the EU will enable it to prevail in the global competition with the United States and Japan. Ironically, as more European countries become members, the power of the EU might be diluted rather than enhanced, because it will be more difficult to achieve consensus on major issues. The evolution of cooperative arrangements within the EU is one of the most fascinating and important developments for international relations in the early twenty-first-century world. If it does achieve political and military unanimity of action as well, the EU will be the undisputed superpower in the world. (This discussion is based on Europa 2008; Nugent 2008; and Kegley 2008.)

of a multistate, multipurpose confederation based on treaties for economic, political, cultural, and military cooperation among 27 European nations with a combined population of more than 497 million. Examples of security pacts are the North Atlantic Treaty Organization (NATO) and the Strategic Arms Reduction Treaties (START II, 1993, between the United States and Russia).

Some of the agreements are called **international regimes** to signify *a set of norms, rules, and procedures accepted by many countries that guide their behavior regarding a particular issue area*, such as arms control (e.g., the Nuclear Nonproliferation Treaty, 1968, now including 189 countries) or environmental protection (e.g., the 1997 Kyoto Protocol on greenhouse gas emissions, accepted by 178 countries). Many international regimes establish a permanent organization through which the member states can enact, modify, and implement the agreements and facilitate cross-national cooperation (Drezner 2007; Keohane 2005).

The direct, day-to-day interactions among most states are substantially governed by alliances, treaties, and regimes. Like other forms of international cooperation, such agreements are binding only as long as the participating states are willing to abide by the conditions of the agreement or are willing to submit disputes to some form of resolution. But such agreements can collapse for various reasons.

- Some participants might find that their national goals are not well served, so they ignore or violate the agreement. Thus, for example, countries sometimes conclude that their own national economic needs justify subsidies to their producers (e.g., farmers, steel producers) even if other countries object that such subsidies violate WTO agreements.

- Participants might have different interpretations of what actions are deemed acceptable under the agreement. After the 1991 Persian Gulf War, the United States (usually backed by the United Nations) repeatedly accused Iraq of violating elements of the peace treaty relating to the dismantling of its chemical and nuclear weapons capabilities, while Iraq insisted that it was complying with the agreements and that the United States was violating Iraq's sovereignty. This disagreement was the crucial justification that the United States presented for leading the invasion of Iraq in 2003.

- Fulfillment of the key objectives in an agreement might be impossible. For example, the Treaty of Locarno (1925) between Britain and Italy failed in its attempt to deter Germany from violating the borders of France and Belgium because Britain and Italy were not strong enough to counteract the reemergence and assertion of Germany's military power, and Italy's government eventually concluded that Italy's national interests were better served by becoming more pro-German.

International Law

The *broadest attempt to formalize and constrain the interactions among states* is **international law**. In 1625, Hugo Grotius, the "father" of international law, published *De jure belli et pacis* (*On the Laws of War and Peace*) (Grotius 1625/1957). This document emphasized **natural law**—*sensible forms of behavior that ought to guide the relations among states and restrain hostile or destructive interactions.*

Unfortunately, states often define "sensible" action according to their own political interests rather than shared abstract moral rules. Thus, by the nineteenth century, natural law had been supplanted by **positivist law**—*explicit written agreements that define both appropriate and unacceptable behaviors between states*, in the form of international treaties or conventions. Positivist laws have attempted to adjudicate geographic boundaries (e.g., the 12-mile limit on the territorial waters of states), to regulate states' use of environmental resources (e.g., laws limiting whale hunting in international waters), and to establish states' rights and limits over nonnational resources (e.g., the law of outer space).

The treaties and conventions of positivist law even attempt to distinguish acceptable from unacceptable behavior during conflicts between states. For example, the Helsinki Agreement binds combatants to use no glass-filled projectiles or other forms of violence that produce "unnecessary suffering." The Geneva Convention on "fair" war prohibits the use of poison gases and insists that captured soldiers be treated with dignity, although it does not preclude most of the terrible forms of suffering or death that a soldier can experience *before* he becomes a prisoner.

While positivist law has the great advantage of being formulated in explicit written agreements, the effectiveness of such agreements ultimately depends on the willingness of states to comply with them. Even if states sign a particular agreement, they sometimes openly violate the agreement and later deny accusations of such a violation. The International Court of Justice (the World Court) at The Hague was established in 1946 to adjudicate violations of positivist international law, serving as the highest judicial body in the world.

Part of the United Nations, the court has occasionally served as a valuable mechanism for conflict resolution between states. However, the court has jurisdiction and binding authority only if both parties to the dispute accept its ruling. Less than one-third of the member states of the United Nations have agreed to accept automatically the court's jurisdiction in matters affecting them. When the political or economic stakes are high or even when emotional elements of the disagreement are intense, states have often refused to accept the court's jurisdiction or to be bound by its judgments. The United States has taken cases to the court, but it is among the majority of states that rejects the court's automatic jurisdiction, as it did in a 1984 case brought by the Nicaraguan government, which objected to covert U.S. actions against it (such as mining Nicaraguan harbors).

Prior to the 1990s, the International Court of Justice was not particularly active. Between 1946 and 1991, it considered only 64 cases, gave advisory opinions in 19 cases, and handled very few cases that actually concerned violent conflicts between states. However, the court has averaged 14 cases per year since the mid-1990s, is dealing with more disputes involving political violence, and is now issuing numerous advisory opinions each year (Kegley and Wittkopf 2004: 585–586).

Another important recent development is the expanded use of international law to arrest and prosecute political leaders and other individuals who are accused of extensive human rights violations. Such trials can be handled by individual countries, as in the trial of Saddam Hussein in Iraq. Since 2002, a permanent International Criminal Court (ICC) at The Hague can take up cases of genocide, crimes against humanity, and war crimes if any of the 106 countries that support the court is not prepared to handle such a case in its national court system. In its first few years, the ICC has directly prosecuted only a few cases of human rights violations, such as those involving a Ugandan rebel leader and the late Slobodan Milosevic of Serbia.

The increased activities of these international courts reflect a growing interest in using international law more aggressively, not only to adjudicate disputes between states but also to hold individuals accountable for the ultra-violence perpetrated by their states. Do you think political leaders should be legally responsible before an international court system for the actions of their soldiers? More broadly, is it acceptable for a state to refuse the court's jurisdiction? What do you think would happen to international politics if all states automatically accepted the jurisdiction of the International Court of Justice and the ICC?

International Organizations

Transnationalism describes *a system of institutions in which key actors' loyalties and identities are not linked to any particular country.* **International organizations** is a broad term for many of the *transnational institutional mechanisms whose objectives* *are to influence the behavior and policies of states.* Some attempt to prevent or resolve conflict among states, although most focus on a specific issue area within the full range of economic, social, environmental, cultural, and political concerns that have global significance. There are two primary types of international organizations: intergovernmental organizations (IGOs) and international nongovernmental organizations (NGOs). A third type is multinational corporations (MNCs).

IGOs.   Members of **intergovernmental organizations** are states, not private groups or individuals. Although there are currently fewer than 300 permanent IGOs, they have vast potential to shape the politics across borders. States jointly establish IGOs for a variety of different purposes: to provide a forum for communication between states; to implement policies that respond to political, social, or economic problems transcending national boundaries; to enact international laws and treaties; and to intervene in disputes between states. Most IGOs are regional, such as NATO, the Association of Southeast Asian Nations (ASEAN), the Arab League, and the EU. Others have a global membership and focus, such as the World Health Organization (WHO), the International Monetary Fund (IMF), and the World Trade Organization (WTO), arguably the most controversial IGO in the current global system (see Box 11.2).

BOX 11.2

The WTO: Nasty Business?

No IGO is subject to more hostility and more intense political protest than the World Trade Organization (WTO). To its detractors, the WTO is "one of the most powerful, secretive and antidemocratic bodies on Earth," and the main results of its actions are to "preside over the greatest transfer in history, of real economic and political power away from nation-states to global corporations" and to "run roughshod over the rights of people and nations, causing all manner of environmental and social harms" (Mander 1999). Why are people saying such nasty things about the WTO?

In characterizing its own work, the WTO states that its main goal is "to ensure that trade flows as smoothly, predictably and freely as possible" among all countries, and that the primary result of its actions is "a more prosperous, peaceful and accountable economic world" (WTO 2008). Established in 1995, the WTO emerged from an international trading regime that had evolved over the prior 50 years under the General Agreement on Trade and Tariffs (GATT). It has 151 member countries, and most other countries are attempting to join. Located in Geneva, Switzerland, the WTO is run by a permanent staff of more than 600. It holds periodic meetings with representatives of all member countries (e.g., in Cancun, Mexico, in 2003; Hong Kong in 2005), and these meetings have provoked extensive, violent protests.

BOX 11.2 *(Continued)*

▶ **Filipinos participate in one of many worldwide protests of the WTO meeting in Cancun, Mexico.**

The WTO is committed to establishing policies that eliminate all barriers to global free trade (e.g., tariffs on imports, subsidies to producers, "dumping" strategies [selling goods abroad at below cost to cripple competitors]). WTO representatives and staff negotiate trade agreements that are then ratified by the governments of the member countries. The WTO enforces these agreements, sets penalties for countries that violate any agreement, and settles trade disputes between countries.

Critics assert that, as elite theory posits (recall Chapter 9), WTO rules and agreements primarily serve the interests of financial elites and multinational corporations that dominate the trade policy process and reap the greatest benefits from the decisions. The WTO can prevent a government from implementing any policy that constrains global free trade, even if the government judges that the policy is in its national interest or will benefit its citizens. In this view, the free trade agreements implemented by the WTO increase the profits of MNCs but reduce the power of workers, are indifferent to violations of human rights, fail to protect the environment, and even undermine the sovereignty of national governments. Opponents provide many graphic examples of these effects. For example, in its enforcement of free trade, the WTO has prevented governments from banning the sale of such imported products as: foods that have been genetically modified, fish caught in dolphin-killing nets, clothing made by child forced labor, and manufactured goods whose production releases toxic by-products into the environment. Moreover, although the WTO claims

BOX 11.2 *(Continued)*

its actions are associated with the increase in global prosperity, critics respond that inequalities across countries and within countries have both risen significantly since the WTO regime began (Global Exchange 2008; Wallach and Woodall 2004).

The many individuals negatively affected by the sweeping changes associated with globalization (discussed later in this chapter, especially in the Debate in 11) have increasingly focused on the WTO as the most visible source of their pain and as the prime target for their wrath. Yet many people in both the developed and developing countries enjoy the profusion of less expensive and higher quality imported products that WTO agreements make available for their consumption. Governments are locked in a love-hate embrace with the WTO: they appreciate the beneficial economic effects of global free trade when it opens new markets to their firms and when it improves the options of their citizen-consumers, but they resist WTO agreements and rulings that limit their freedom of action on either trade policy or economic policies that are advantageous to their firms and citizens. Only global corporations seem to find little about the WTO that they don't like.

The most powerful and wide-ranging IGOs in the twentieth century were two major international organizations: the League of Nations and the United Nations. The League of Nations was formed in 1921 (after World War I) as a mechanism for collective security against aggression. But Italian aggression in Ethiopia and Japanese aggression in Manchuria in the 1930s revealed that the League lacked the diplomatic, political, or military power to achieve its goal.

The United Nations (UN) was created in 1945 (after World War II) as an international organization dedicated to managing international security. In pursuit of this objective, the UN has five principal organs with specific functions. (1) The Security Council (SC) is considered the highest body within the UN to directly manage international conflicts, because it has the authority to pass binding resolutions that authorize the use of force, peacekeeping missions, and sanctions.. The SC membership includes five permanent members with veto power (China, France, Russia, United Kingdom, and United States) and ten rotating members. (2) The General Assembly (GA) has representatives from all 192 members of the UN and serves as a forum for discussion of global issues. Although the GA lacks the legal authority to pass binding resolutions, it oversees the entire UN budget as well as many specialized bodies. (3) The Economic and Social Council (ECOSOC) promotes economic and social cooperation and development. To achieve this goal, ECOSOC works with the General Assembly to coordinate and oversee most UN committees. (4) The Secretariat is the central bureaucracy, responsible for the UN's day-to-day operations and headed by its most visible representative, the secretary-general. (5) The International Court of Justice is the UN's primary judicial body, responsible for interpreting international law (described in the previous section). Figure 11.2 shows a number of the special units that function within the principal divisions of the UN.

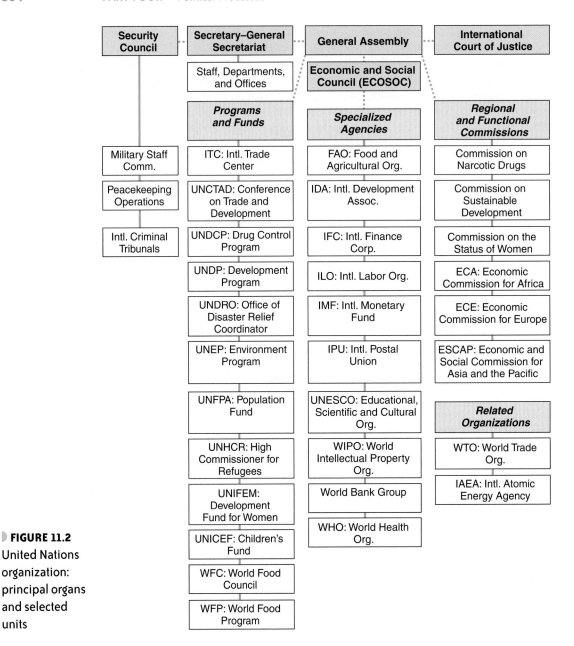

Security Council	Secretary–General Secretariat	General Assembly	International Court of Justice
	Staff, Departments, and Offices	Economic and Social Council (ECOSOC)	
	Programs and Funds	*Specialized Agencies*	*Regional and Functional Commissions*
Military Staff Comm.	ITC: Intl. Trade Center	FAO: Food and Agricultural Org.	Commission on Narcotic Drugs
Peacekeeping Operations	UNCTAD: Conference on Trade and Development	IDA: Intl. Development Assoc.	Commission on Sustainable Development
Intl. Criminal Tribunals	UNDCP: Drug Control Program	IFC: Intl. Finance Corp.	Commission on the Status of Women
	UNDP: Development Program	ILO: Intl. Labor Org.	ECA: Economic Commission for Africa
	UNDRO: Office of Disaster Relief Coordinator	IMF: Intl. Monetary Fund	ECE: Economic Commission for Europe
	UNEP: Environment Program	IPU: Intl. Postal Union	ESCAP: Economic and Social Commission for Asia and the Pacific
	UNFPA: Population Fund	UNESCO: Educational, Scientific and Cultural Org.	
	UNHCR: High Commissioner for Refugees	WIPO: World Intellectual Property Org.	*Related Organizations*
	UNIFEM: Development Fund for Women	World Bank Group	WTO: World Trade Org.
	UNICEF: Children's Fund	WHO: World Health Org.	IAEA: Intl. Atomic Energy Agency
	WFC: World Food Council		
	WFP: World Food Program		

▶ **FIGURE 11.2**
United Nations organization: principal organs and selected units

While the United Nations has a mixed record of success and failure in its central objective of maintaining global peace, it *has* improved the international political climate. At the least, the United Nations has been a highly effective setting within which rivals can engage in continuing diplomacy. Particularly within the Security Council and the General Assembly, UN officials and representatives from various countries can attempt to mediate conflicts and prevent escalation to war. The UN can also pass resolutions that might constrain certain countries from acting in opposition to the moral force of international public opinion (Ziring, Riggs, and Plano 2004).

Most directly, a UN *peacekeeping operation* can intervene between combatants. This is *an impartial, multinational military and civilian force authorized by the UN* Security Council with the consent of the disputing parties. The peacekeeping force literally stands between the combatants in the attempt to ease tensions, and it uses force only in defense. The United States and the Soviet Union used their veto power in the Security Council to block many potential peacekeeping initiatives during the cold war. In the post–cold war period (beginning in the late 1980s), the use of UN peacekeeping forces has expanded. Thus 45 UN peacekeeping operations have been deployed since 1990, compared with only 18 in the preceding 42 years (United Nations Peacekeeping Operations 2007). By its various actions, the United Nations has contributed to what former UN Secretary-General Dag Hammarskjold (1953–1961) called "preventive diplomacy"—limiting the extensive political and military involvement of major powers during conflicts between other countries. In 1988, the UN peacekeeping operations were awarded the Nobel Peace Prize.

Significantly, most of the post–cold war operations differ from earlier ones in that their central objective is to establish and promote *internal* peace among factions within a country. Of 16 peacekeeping missions active in 2007, for example, the primary objective in 12 (including the Democratic Republic of Congo [see Box 11.3], Haiti, Kosovo [see Box 15.2], Lebanon, and Sudan) was to prevent political violence among groups within the country. It has been difficult for UN forces to end the violence in these internal conflicts where both borders and the identity of combatants are ambiguous. However, a study of 124 UN peacekeeping operations in internal conflicts concludes that they have generally been successful in ending the violence and increasing the likelihood of greater democratization (Doyle and Sambanis 2000).

The United Nations also provides many nonmilitary services that enhance states' security, stability, and prosperity. Coordinated by the General Assembly and the Economic and Social Council, committees, agencies, and commissions, such as the World Health Organization (WHO); the United Nations Educational, Scientific, and Cultural

▶ **The United Nations contributes to world betterment in various ways, such as humanitarian aid programs (here, providing food in Haiti) and peacekeeping forces (here, in Lebanon).**

Organization (UNESCO); and the United Nations Conference on Trade and Development (UNCTAD), attempt to mitigate global problems and enhance the quality of human life in such areas as human rights, agricultural development, environmental protection, refugees, children's health, and disaster relief. These efforts are one important way to reduce human suffering and thus limit the conditions that might cause political violence.

The continuing level of political violence in the international system underscores the fact that the United Nations lacks the power to prevent all interstate conflict. Many states withdraw their support (financial and political) when UN actions are at variance with the states' perceptions of their national interest. However, through its agencies, its debates and resolutions, its continuous open forum for formal and informal communications between states, and its peacekeeping operations, the United Nations does contribute to greater cooperation and reduced conflict among states. For such contributions, Nobel Peace Prizes were awarded to the United Nations and former Secretary-General Kofi Annan in 2001 and to the UN International Atomic Energy Agency and its head, Mohammed Elbaradei, in 2005.

NGOs. The second type of international organizations is transnational **nongovernmental organizations**. NGOs are composed of *nonstate actors (private individuals and groups) who work actively in a particular issue area* to provide information, promote public policies, and even provide services that might otherwise be provided by government. NGOs work with each other, with governments, and with IGOs to address the full array of problems that cross state borders. Between 1960 and 2000, the number of NGOs active in at least three countries rose from 1,000 to more than 30,000. This includes about 5,000 major NGOs that are very active in a large number of countries (Weiss 1996). Transnational NGOs, which enjoy higher public trust than either governments or business, are using new strategies of engagement with business and have a growing economic base (more than $1 trillion). They are "increasingly important in shaping national and international politics, governance processes and markets" and are "amongst the most influential institutions of the twenty-first century" (Elkington and Beloe 2003).

NGOs are committed to furthering political and social issues with transnational dimensions. Although their issues tend to be regional or global, the actions and effectiveness of these NGOs can be analyzed in the same framework applied to the analysis of national interest groups (see Chapter 3). These groups encourage concerned individuals, groups, and even the governments of other states to write letters; organize demonstrations or boycotts; or engage in other political actions to pressure a government or transnational actor to change its practices (Keck and Sikkink 1998).

For example, you might be aware, from media, mailings, or other information sources, of the environmental protection actions of Greenpeace, the animal preservation goals of the World Wildlife Federation, or the lobbying to control destructive technologies by the Union of Concerned Scientists. Amnesty International, another well-known NGO, is concerned with protecting human rights and is engaged in campaigns to focus attention and pressure on governments that are violating the rights of their citizens. It is one of the leading NGOs among an expanding group of transborder organizations that promote the protection of human rights. Often local movements of human rights activists coalesce with others outside their state's boundaries to promote this issue.

The actions of some NGOs extend far beyond lobbying as they generate resources and actually deliver goods and services, such as the humanitarian medical services provided by Doctors without Borders. With the globalization of communications and greater mobility, many other groups, advocacy networks, and social movements are able to engage in a mix of persuasion and action, although most operate in only a limited set of countries. And while many transnational actors are admired for their pursuit of noble goals, some engage in illegal or violent activities that are relevant to states, such as the al-Qaeda terrorist network or international drug cartels.

MNCs.   It is also clear that the actions of many ***multinational corporations*** (MNCs, also referred to as TNCs—transnational corporations) have significant impacts on the politics within and between states. From a political economy perspective, MNCs are powerful firms, such as General Motors, Exxon, British Petroleum, Samsung, or Sumitomo, that produce and sell a diversity of goods in many countries in pursuit of private profit. The global impacts of major MNCs are based on their sheer economic weight as some of the richest institutions in the world. In terms of comparative economic power (measured as gross economic product in 2001), only 49 of the top 100 economic units in the world are countries, and 51 are multinational corporations (Kegley and Wittkopf 2004: Table 5.2).

The combination of three other crucial features of MNCs adds to their strategic importance in the global system. These features enhance the MNC's flexibility and bargaining power in dealing with the governmental institutions and the political economy in any state. First, a major MNC functions as a *globalized network*. Since its operations are spread across many countries, an MNC can rapidly move its activities in order to exploit opportunities and avoid problems in any host country and even in its home country. This enables the MNC to pressure governments into competing for a share of its operations by providing the MNC with large financial inducements (e.g., tax breaks, enhanced government services, bribes) and by minimizing the state's regulatory constraints on the MNC's undesirable activities (e.g., environmental impacts, labor practices, product safety).

A second feature of most MNCs is *product diversification*. The capacity to shift the balance of production among a variety of different goods (as well as to different locations) further reduces the MNC's dependence on any single country or any particular source of land, labor, or capital. And a third feature of an MNC is its *willingness to transform itself* in pursuit of economic advantage. To improve its profitability and stock price, an MNC might break off units into independent companies, engage in mergers, launch completely new areas of activity, or even shut down entire divisions.

All three of these strategic elements increase the MNC's autonomy, influence, and profitability at the expense of the host country and its government, which must continue to make costly concessions to compete for a share of the MNC's operations. The flexibility, ease, and speed with which an MNC can shift operations out of a country also increases the vulnerability of a state's political economy to unpredictable business decisions by MNCs over which a state has little control. Some critics identify an even broader set of negative impacts of MNCs on the global system. They claim that MNCs not only challenge the sovereignty and autonomy of the state as they avoid most of the laws and taxes of any state, but they also monopolize the production and distribution of important goods in the world marketplace and thus squeeze out small firms, and they also widen the economic gap between rich and poor countries (Keohane and Nye 2001; Russett, Starr, and Kinsella 2005; United Nations Commission on Transnational Corporations 1991). For all these reasons, "the MNC remains one of the most controversial actors in the international political economy" (Jenkins 1993: 606).

COMPETITION AMONG STATES

When the competing interests of states are stronger than their mutual interests, the states are unlikely to agree on a cooperative strategy. From the realist perspective in particular, states should expect this pattern to be a central feature of the international system. Recall that power is exercised when one actor uses its actions or resources to force another actor to do something that the other actor otherwise would not do (see Box 6.1). In the relations between states, there are frequent examples of "power politics." Short of using force, a state can either threaten or actually undertake an action that withholds something of value to another state in the attempt to induce compliance. States use such exchange power in many ways. If another state needs a good (a few of the thousands of examples are oil, military protection, a trade agreement, a useful technology, a loan, sensitive information), the power-exercising state might be in a position to provide this good, thus forcing the needy state to comply with its wishes. While such an exchange might be a friendly one between cooperating states, exchanges in international politics often occur somewhat more aggressively as the state controlling the resources forces compliance with its wishes. Virtually every day there are situations where one state alters its behavior under pressure from another state that effectively exercises exchange power.

When *a group of states combine to withhold a desired good in order to pressure a state*, the strategy can be called *sanctions*. To avoid using violence, sets of states or even the United Nations will apply such sanctions to a country whose behavior they want to alter. They might withhold food, medical supplies, replacement parts, or any other good. Recently there have been more attempts to apply "comprehensive" sanctions in which many important restrictions are placed on a state's acquisition or sale of good. During the 1990s, for example, there were 20 cases in which the United Nations successfully applied comprehensive sanctions to drive a country's leader from power or to force regime change (Cortright and Lopez 2002). Thus interstate relations are rich with situations where rivalries play out in highly competitive but nonviolent interactions.

Balance of Power

In situations where states have strong competing interests and where neither cooperative strategies nor exchange power approaches resolve the differences, direct conflict can still be avoided if a **balance of power** emerges. This occurs when there is *a rough equality in the power resources (political, economic, and especially military) that can be exercised by sets of competing states.* An actor is prevented from taking advantage of others because of the power that other actors have to retaliate.

The term *balance of power* is widely used and has many meanings. In the broadest sense, it implies that there is a rough equilibrium of power between competing states and this discourages any state from taking aggressive action against rivals because the state fears effective retaliation. Scholars of international relations particularly use this concept to refer to a regional or global balance of power that involves a number of states. Six key elements in this classic notion of balance of power, listed below, are especially associated with the political realist perspective (described earlier in this chapter; see also Kaplan 1957; Morgenthau 1993).

1. It is an attempt to maintain a general stability in the relations among states and to preserve the status quo.

2. It assumes that peace can be ensured only by a balancing of contending states because potential aggressors will be deterred only by overwhelming opposing power.

3. There are typically a few (usually four to six) major power states that are decisive in ensuring that the balance is sustained.

4. These states, and others, constantly create shifting alliances based only on self-interest and system equilibrium, never on friendship or ideology.

5. To prevent actions that seem to threaten the overall balance of the system, one or more power states must intervene in the affairs of a single state or the relations between states.

6. There will be periodic political violence and war because states must use force to preserve themselves and because the system is not always in such balance that all conflict between states is deterred.

Since the emergence of modern states in the seventeenth century, there have usually been only a few states that, at any point in time, had both the desire and the power to project their interests over many other states. Some scholars characterize the international relations dominated by European states during most of the period from the Peace of Westphalia in 1648 to the beginning of World War I in 1914 as a period of classic balance-of-power politics. Great Britain often played a major role as the "balancer." As Winston Churchill (1948) observed, "For 400 years the foreign policy of England has been to oppose the strongest, most aggressive, most dominating power on the continent, in joining the weaker states."

However, by the late nineteenth century, changes in the international system made balance-of-power politics less possible. The growing importance of both ideology and nationalism was especially significant because these factors limited the ease with which alliances between states were made and broken. This was most clear in the deep antipathy that developed between France and Germany, which would inevitably be on opposite sides of any conflict.

After World War II, the classic balance-of-power system was replaced by a *bipolar* balance-of-power system, in which the United States and its allies were generally balanced against the Soviet Union and its allies. The groups associated with each superpower were rigid in their ideological antipathy to the other bloc and were inflexible in their alliance formation. Thus the old pattern of flexible, nonideological balancing between a handful of independent states had broken down. In addition, the arena of between-state power struggles expanded from its narrow European base to a worldwide one. But the two blocs did prevent each other from achieving **hegemony**—*sustained domination of the international system.* And the military power on each side deterred them from fighting each other directly during a 40-year "cold" war (see page 387).

From the early 1970s until the breakup of the Soviet Union in 1991, the international system became increasingly *multipolar*. During these two decades, the coherence of the U.S. bloc and the Soviet bloc declined as powerful actors such as China, Japan, Western Europe, and groupings of "nonaligned" states began to act with greater independence. Although multipolar, this was not a classic balance-of power system, since alliance formation remained inflexible and guided by ideology. At the same time, the United States and the Soviet Union continued to be the preeminent global powers and to engage in a massive buildup of military capability and nuclear weapons.

In the post–cold war era, the state system continues to have multipolar elements, especially through the United Nations. However, the military and economic dominance of the United States suggests some characteristics of a *unipolar* period, in which the international system is generally controlled by a single "hegemon." The United States has often taken the lead in spearheading collective military action through the United Nations (e.g., the 1991 Persian Gulf War) or through NATO (e.g., the 1999 actions against the Serbs in Kosovo). In some cases, the United States has operated somewhat unilaterally (e.g., the military campaign against Afghanistan beginning in late 2001) or dominated a military "coalition of the willing" (the war against Iraq in 2003).

Balance of Terror

The enormous destructive capacity of modern military technologies was a key element that undermined traditional balance-of-power politics. War became far less controllable as an instrument of foreign policy between major states when each had the capacity to wreak massive devastation on the other and to risk equal destruction at home. The problem with this strategy of nuclear deterrence is that each state fears vulnerability: Does the rival have a numerical superiority in weapons or firepower? Does the rival have a technically superior system for attack or defense? Could a rival's first strike destroy one's own capacity for second-strike retaliation?

To overcome such uncertainties about mutual deterrence, a state expands its destructive capacity, numbers of weapons, and technical sophistication to a point where it has great confidence that under any conditions of conflict, it can inflict catastrophic and unacceptable damage on a rival. Thus the balance of power evolved into a balance of terror, a system of *mutually assured destruction (MAD)*. Even at this point, the fear of technological breakthroughs by rivals and the inherent desire for superiority induce each state to expand its military capability to an extraordinary, and excessive, magnitude. In the 1970s and 1980s, this continued expansion of military power and destructive capacity resulted in an arms race that produced nuclear arsenals capable of massive, even total, annihilation of humankind (see Figure 11.3). In short, balance-of-power politics became a dangerous and possibly irrational mechanism for regulating the relations among powerful states in the nuclear age.

Since 1990, the United States and Russia (the country that inherited most Soviet nuclear power) have negotiated significant reductions in nuclear weapons. Although the likelihood of a nuclear war between these two cold warriors has shrunk, U.S. President George W. Bush indicated that the United States would no longer be constrained by earlier nuclear weapons reductions agreements and intended to develop new

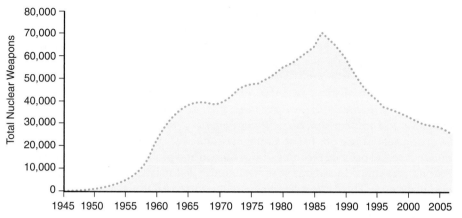

▌ **FIGURE 11.3**
Total number
of operational
nuclear
weapons,
1945–2006
Source: Federation of
American Scientists
(2007)

antimissile systems. Moreover, the stockpiles of operational nuclear weapons in key countries remain far in excess of MAD: Russia (5,670), the United States (5,160), China (145), France (350), the United Kingdom (160), Israel (200), and fewer than 100 each in India, Israel, Pakistan, and possibly North Korea (Bulletin of Atomic Scientists 2007). Indeed, of these eight countries, only France is not currently engaged in violent conflict. It is also clear that other states (e.g., Iran, North Korea) will soon (or already) have nuclear weapons capabilities.

And, in another dreaded scenario, it is possible that rogue actors such as guerrilla groups or terrorist cells could get access to a nuclear weapon or possibly even produce a primitive weapon, such as a dirty bomb. The Federation of American Scientists reports that the use of a dirty bomb by a terrorist group is a "credible threat." For example, the necessary materials could be "easily lost or stolen within the United States." A dirty bomb could contaminate tens of square miles, cause deaths from exposure to radioactivity, and require the demolition of buildings that would result in trillions of dollars of property damage. Terrorists' use of other chemical and biological weapons is also increasingly feasible and the level of death and destruction could be substantial (Federation of American Scientists 2007). For all these reasons, dangerous new forms of instability in the balance of terror are emerging (Cimbala 2000).

Domination and Dependence

While all states enjoy sovereign equality, it is obvious that some states are far more powerful than others. This section discusses the situation in which one state exercises substantial power over another. The capacity of one state to alter the actions of another state can be based on different forms of leverage, the primary three of which are listed here:

1. *Economic* leverage is based on the advantageous trade relations, financial interactions, or economic aid that the state can provide (or withhold from) another state.

2. *Military* leverage can be applied either negatively, via the use or threat of military action against a state, or positively, via military assistance in the form of protection, provision of military resources, or training.

3. *Political* leverage is derived from the ability of a state to affect the actions of another state through the use of its political resources, such as its negotiating skills, its effective political institutions, or its influence in interstate relations.

Colonialism/Imperialism.   During the twentieth century, particular attention focused on **colonialism** or *imperialism*, which is characterized by *one state having extensive dominance over another state, including manipulation or control of key economic and military structures for the benefit of the dominant state*. A state might have a variety of reasons for attaining mastery over another state. First, the subordinate state can provide resources, both human and physical, for the dominant state. Second, the subordinate state can be a controlled market for the products of the dominant state. Third, the subordinate state can serve important strategic functions, either as a buffer between the dominant state and its rivals or as a staging area for the dominant state's political or military objectives. Fourth, a state with a missionary zeal might dominate another state to ensure that its values (usually political or religious) guide the subordinate state. Fifth, a state might want to dominate another state to gain international prestige.

While all forms of colonial domination entail a mix of economic, military, and political control, dominant states have employed three different styles:

1. In the *segregationist* style of colonialism, the interaction is pure exploitation. The dominant state makes little or no attempt to improve the economic, political, or social systems in the subordinate state. This style generally characterized the relations of Belgium, Germany, and Portugal with their African and Asian colonial territories.

2. In the *assimilationist* style, the dominant state makes some attempt to transform the subordinate state into an external extension of itself. While the subordinate state is still being exploited, the institutions, knowledge, and culture of the dominant state are introduced to the elite of the subordinate state and become a basis for political, economic, and cultural development. This style is particularly associated with French colonialism in Africa and Asia and the extensive colonialism of the former Soviet Union.

3. In the style of *indirect rule*, the dominant state works with the traditional leaders and institutions of governance and culture in the subordinate state as intermediaries in its control, but it also introduces the modern forms of the dominant state that will eventually supplant traditional forms. The British approach to its vast empire is the classic example of indirect rule, and this mode of colonialism also characterizes the style of the United States in some Latin American and Pacific Rim states.

Neocolonialism.   In the 60 years since World War II, most states have willingly or reluctantly granted independence to their colonial holdings. But political independence does not necessarily end a state's subordination to a strong state. The label **neocolonialism** is given to *new, more indirect forms of domination and dependence that are nearly as powerful as those under colonialism*. Although the dominant state may officially withdraw its direct political and military presence, it can maintain domination, primarily by economic leverage. Through foreign aid, loans, technology transfer, military support, and economic intervention, the dominant state can continue to control many actions of a supposedly independent state. The dominant state's manipulations become relatively invisible, and its interests are served by a subtle alliance of a small elite within the subordinate country, MNCs, and other transnational actors, such as the IMF (Maxfield 1997; So 1990). These new forms of domination were described in the discussion of the dependency approach (in Chapter 10), which posits that the patterns established under colonialism have evolved into a *world system* of dominance and dependence that is global and systemic (Wallerstein 2004). The recent history of the Democratic Republic of Congo exemplifies how colonialism and neocolonialism can contribute to the plight of vulnerable Third World states (Box 11.3).

BOX 11.3

The Faces of Colonialism: Congo

The Democratic Republic of Congo is a large, resource-rich state (one-fourth the size of the United States) located in the center of the African continent. It encompasses more than 60 million people and 250 ethnic groups. King Leopold of Belgium sponsored expeditions down the Congo River and in 1879 claimed the area as his own private kingdom. In 1908, the area was placed under Belgian colonial administration as the "Belgian Congo." King Leopold's companies and Belgian-led military forces treated the local people with brutality, forcing the men into virtual slavery as workers in the mines and on the plantations as the natural resources were extracted with ruthless efficiency. The colonial regime provided only minimal education to the people and encouraged Catholic missionaries to teach the great virtue of obedience to (Belgian) authority.

The Belgians continued to exploit the resources of the Congo until internal resistance and the widespread liberation of African colonies made it clear that continued colonial rule was not possible. The Congo was granted its independence on June 30, 1960, and Belgium rapidly withdrew its military and administrative personnel and most of its financial and technical support.

Unprepared for self-rule, the Congolese elite broke into competing factions, and the country collapsed into political decay and civil war. The United Nations sent in a peacekeeping force, and the Soviet Union provided support to one faction. With assistance from Western countries (and the apparent assistance of the U.S. Central Intelligence Agency [CIA]), an army leader, Joseph Mobutu, led another faction to victory in the civil war and then assassinated the pro-Soviet prime minister.

In 1965 Mobutu, now army chief of staff, led a coup that overthrew the civilian government and installed himself as the leader of a one-party, authoritarian regime that ruled for more than three decades. Mobutu "Africanized" his society, changing

BOX 11.3 *(Continued)*

the country's name to Zaire and his own name to Mobutu Sese Seko ("all powerful one"). Despite Mobutu's repressive rule, several civil wars, the persistent failure of the economy, widespread corruption, and the massive diversion of funds to Mobutu and his cronies from state-owned mines, Mobuto's staunch anticommunism won him substantial economic and military support from the United States. His long tenure in office was completely dependent on neocolonialism—the foreign aid, loans, technology transfer, and military support he received from Western countries.

Zaire relied heavily on foreign corporations to build and maintain its mines, factories, and infrastructure facilities. The IMF (the consortium of Western banking institutions) loaned Zaire enormous amounts and repeatedly restructured Zaire's debt (the largest in Africa). In return, the IMF demanded "conditionality"—that Zaire implement crucial economic policies, including devaluation of the currency, lower real wages, and drastically reduced social welfare programs. There were extended periods when Zaire was obliged to allow its national banking system to be managed directly by a group of Europeans sent in by the IMF.

The combination of internal corruption, exploitation by foreign corporations, and IMF conditionality left few resources for the people of Zaire. The level of education continued to decline, the country could no longer feed itself, and the infrastructure system (e.g., roads, water supply, telecommunications) was in shambles. The real wages of urban workers fell to less than one-tenth of what they were at independence. Surrounded by the appalling poverty of most of the population, Mobutu was rumored to be the wealthiest person in sub-Saharan Africa, with holdings of more than $10 billion.

When the cold war ended, the United States found Mobutu to be an embarrassment and tried to pressure him to make democratic reforms. Mobutu finally allowed elections in 1993, but when his own candidate for prime minister was defeated, he ordered the armed forces to prevent the winning candidates from taking office. Instead, he installed a puppet government and sustained Zaire's "kleptocracy" (rule by thieves). Multinational corporations, however, still found much in Zaire to exploit, and they maintained their business dealings with Mobutu.

After years of worsening political decay, Mobutu's demise came suddenly. More than 1.2 million Hutus had crossed into Zaire to escape the ethnic chaos in two neighboring (Tutsi-controlled) countries, Burundi and Rwanda. A Zairean guerrilla group (composed mainly of Tutsis) that had been fighting against Mobutu was joined by many more Tutsis to expel the Hutu refugees. This expanded guerrilla army then returned to the civil war against Mobuto. Mobuto's corrupt regime was abandoned not only by his demoralized army and alienated citizenry, but also by the United States and the Western multinationals. As Mobutu fled the country in 1997, the guerrilla army's leader, Laurent Kabila, declared himself president and renamed the country the Democratic Republic of Congo. However, some Congolese groups refused to accept Kabila's rule and waged a destructive civil war to topple him. When Kabila was assassinated in 2001, his son, Joseph Kabila, took power.

From 1998 to 2003, military groups from eight countries engaged in vicious fighting in Congo in what became known as "Africa's World War." This complex mix of

BOX 11.3 *(Continued)*

civil war, ethnic conflicts, refugee issues, and exploitation of Congo's resources by neighboring countries was the bloodiest conflict since World War II, with at least 4 million deaths and millions of refugees. Although most regular military forces accepted a cease-fire and Joseph Kabila won a 2006 election, some groups have continued the violence.

Despite these changes of leaders and even the country's name, Congo's economic and political systems remain deeply dependent on Western capital. After 90 years under a brutal and exploitative colonial system, 50 years of "independence" have brought no blossoming of democratic politics, no sharing of the society's abundant resources among its people, no economic development. Rather, contemporary Congo is a tragic product of colonialism and neocolonialism as well as its own internal failings, a state characterized by poverty, corruption, oppression, economic chaos, political decay, and continuing dependence on foreign states and foreign economic actors.

Globalization?

According to one observer, "A new international system has now clearly replaced the Cold War: globalization. That's right, globalization—the integration of markets, finance and technologies in a way that is shrinking the world from a size medium to

GADO
DAILY NATION
Nairobi
KENYA

CARTOONISTS & WRITERS SYNDICATE http://CartoonWeb.com

Source: Gado, CartoonArts International/CWS.

a size small and enabling each of us to reach around the world farther, faster and cheaper than ever" (Friedman 1999a: 110). The new conventional wisdom is that the forces of globalization are reshaping everything, from international politics and economics to our individual values. In the past decade, discussions of globalization and its implications for the international system, economies, states, and individuals have proliferated.

What is globalization? As a working definition, **globalization** can be viewed as *the increasing integration of diverse economic, sociocultural, military, and environmental phenomena by means of dense networks of action and information that rapidly span vast distances around the world*. This definition is guided by the suggestion of Keohane and Nye (2000: 105) that we first define *globalism* as "a state of the world involving networks of interdependence at multicontinental distances." Two defining characteristics of such networks affect globalism: (1) they are increasingly dense, and (2) they involve extremely rapid transmission of phenomena across substantial, multicontinental distances. These networks allow the movement of people, goods, ideas, information, financial capital, and even biological substances. *Globalization* refers to an increase in the level of globalism (Keohane and Nye 2000).

What aspects of human existence are affected by globalization? It is particularly associated with economic factors: an international market political economy with private economic actors minimally constrained by states or borders, open capital markets, vigorous competition, and a reduction of state control over the economy. However, the linkages associated with globalization can affect many important aspects of our world. Thus Keohane and Nye (2000: 106–107) suggest four major domains of globalism: (1) *economic globalism*: the long-distance flows of goods, services, capital, and information that shape market exchanges (e.g., less costly imports, instantaneous transfers of financial capital); (2) *social and cultural globalism*: the movement of people, ideas, information, and images, which then influence the individuals, societies, and cultures into which they flow (e.g., MTV, international tourism); (3) *military globalism*: the long-distance networks of interdependence in which the threat or exercise of force is employed (e.g., mutually assured destruction, international terrorist networks); and (4) *environmental globalism*: the long-distance transport of materials and biological substances via natural movement (e.g., ozone depletion, bird flu) or via human agency (e.g., the intercontinental spread of SARS and HIV-AIDS).

There is heated debate about the overall impacts of globalization on individuals, countries, and the international system. The Debate in 11 summarizes a few of the central claims. As is often the case, there is considerable truth as well as substantial hyperbole associated with the assertions of both the advocates and the foes of globalization. It is clear that the extraordinary increases in the speed, distance, and density of networking have altered the global economic and sociocultural systems, facilitating capitalism and markets and richly connecting some peoples and groups. Yet most of the world's population continues to live, work, and experience life on the margins of those systems. There are powerful and contradictory forces at work. Some forces create enhanced interactions and shared identities across vast spatial and political boundaries, while other forces, reacting against globalization, intensify the importance of local activities and particularistic identities.

THE DEBATE IN 11

Is Globalization a Positive Development?

The evolution of the human race has brought us from small groups of self-sufficient hunter-gatherers to huge urban populations who rely on others for virtually every aspect of our existence. Many observers suggest that globalization—with its powerful forces that integrate economies, spread knowledge, and blend cultures—has shifted us to a new stage of human development. The global availability of more diverse goods and services, the vast worldwide communications network, and the widespread sharing of technological capabilities are presented as evidence that globalization is a positive force enhancing the quality of life for nearly all countries and peoples. However, others argue that the current forms of global integration have had extensive negative impacts on many countries and individuals. On balance, is globalization a positive development?

Globalization Benefits Most Societies and Individuals

■ A unified global market under globalization and free trade results in a more efficient system for the production and distribution of goods, due to lower prices and improved product quality. Moreover, financial capital flows quickly to the places where it will produce the highest, most effective return on investment.

■ Greater integration increases the transfer of technology and expertise across borders, resulting in the diffusion of best practices, more extensive innovation, and increased global productivity.

■ Higher productivity, higher-quality goods, and lower prices will generally "raise all boats." That is, these improvements will raise the level of material living standards and the prosperity enjoyed by larger numbers of people in many countries.

■ Globalization results in greater sharing and homogenization of culture and values across borders, creating a world with more shared understandings. This leads to a reduction in the kinds of nation-based differences that cause conflict (Fukuyama 1999).

■ Global communication enables individuals who share political interests but are dispersed geographically to engage in effective cooperation and mobilization, thus enhancing their political power.

■ As trade and economic interdependency increase in a global system, powerful economic and political actors view war and major armed conflict as disruptive and undesirable, and thus they will act to prevent them. Even more positively, powerful actors have strong incentives for cross-national cooperation.

Globalization Results in Many Negative Effects on Societies and Individuals

■ Globalization encourages production, capital, and jobs to move wherever costs are lowest and profits are highest, resulting in considerable economic instability from country to country and for many workers whose jobs are "outsourced."

■ Similarly, as production shifts to countries with the fewest regulations on labor and the least restrictive environmental standards, the results include a "race to the bottom" characterized by more hazardous working conditions, dangerous products, and environmental degradation.

The Debate in 11 *(Continued)*

- Globalization primarily benefits the most powerful economic actors in the world and thus is best understood as the newest form of neocolonialism.
- With globalization, the distribution of wealth grows even more unequal between core countries in the Global North and most countries in the Global South that are at the periphery of the international system (recall world systems theory in this chapter).
- As globalization produces more interdependency and mobility of goods, local problems spread quickly and can have global consequences, whether they are economic problems (e.g., the global economic crisis that spread from East Asia to many countries in the late 1990s) or dangerous pathogens (e.g., SARS).
- As local cultures, languages, and values are marginalized or eliminated, they are replaced by a mediocre, global homogeneity.
- In response to this destruction of their culture and their economic stability, many groups (e.g., nation based, religious) become mobilized, resulting in political disorder and violence as groups attempt to protect their identities and economic interests. Thus there is greater local and global instability.
- As national governments lose control of MNCs and economic activities, they will be weakened and less able to respond effectively to the growing negative impacts on their people and their economy. This will expose each country to more social turbulence and increase hostilities and conflicts between states.

More questions . . .

1. On balance, is globalization a positive development for you personally? For your country? For most people in the world?
2. Is it really the case that national governments can't use public policy to shape globalization more than they are shaped by it?
3. If globalization is the current general stage in human development, is it the "final stage"? If not, what might be the next stage after globalization?

Even as states are increasingly penetrated by outside forces, the states remain formidable actors in the international system. Thus it is possible that globalization could be substantially limited by the policy actions of the most powerful states. This might occur if those states conclude that their national interest (especially their prosperity and stability) is being undermined by globalization and if there is strong pressure to resist from powerful, well-organized internal groups harmed by globalization. Alternatively, states might cooperate with each other to coordinate their national policies in ways that limit the most negative effects of globalization. In this case, the calculus of the states would be, as in other forms of interstate cooperation, that collaborative approaches are the best means to serve their goals.

However, most analysts conclude that intentional state policies will not stop current globalizing trends. They emphasize that states have less and less capacity to control their participation in or insulation from the globalizing international system. Borders become more permeable to goods, people, capital, and ideas. There is also considerable skepticism that states can sustain sufficient cooperation in the brutally competitive system. Indeed, virtually all analysts assume that the forces of globalization are transforming the international system in ways that are probably not controllable and are certainly not understood (Barber 1995; Friedman 2007).

Competition in the Globalized World

The disintegration of the Soviet Union in 1991 is regarded as the crucial event ending the cold war era. The international system that is evolving in the new conditions of the post–cold war period is premised on the disappearance of the bipolar balance-of-power system dominated by a conflict between the U.S. bloc and the Soviet bloc and the shifts toward globalization described above. Four major trends are likely to be important in this evolution in the international system.

First, *military power* remains a significant factor in the relations among states. While the lessening of cold war tensions has resulted in some limits on worldwide military expenditure, more than $1 trillion per year is still being spent worldwide (SIPRI 2008). Despite the presence of multilateral military forces and multistate alliances, most military power remains under the control of individual states. If powerful and politically effective groups are increasingly threatened by globalization, it is possible that they will pressure their governments to be more active in protecting their citizens, their economies, and even their cultures. And leaders might become more assertive in response to the breakdown of borders and challenges to state sovereignty. This might produce protectionist and isolationist policies toward other states and the use of the state's military to protect and project the state's interests. It is quite likely that conflicts will be more frequent in a diffuse, multipolar world in which globalization and ethnonationalism are rampant. As was discussed earlier in the chapter, it is not obvious that the United Nations or any other actors have the will and capacity to prevent such conflicts.

Second, intense *economic competition* will split the developed countries that were allies during the cold war. In fact, competition among the major powers will pivot more on economic issues than on military or ideological issues. In the global economy, regional groupings have formed as states coordinate their policies with similar states ("harmonization") in order to protect the set of states from outside pressures. The EU might become this type of coordinating mechanism for its member states. The major economic competition might be among three groups: North America under leadership from the United States, the European Union, and an East Asian group under Japanese or Chinese leadership. Other regional economic groups have formed in South America and among the Muslim states of Central Asia.

Third, the state-centered system is evolving toward one in which *transnational entities* are extraordinarily important. The dynamics of globalization seem to be generally beyond state control, as does the extensive and growing power of the MNCs, described above. States might actually be willing accomplices of these transborder actors, since the most powerful elites controlling these states could reap substantial benefits from the globalized international order. IGOs such as the IMF and the WTO become the tools to facilitate further globalization.

Alternatively, states might continue to lose power to transborder, global actors and, as a consequence, lose their central role in structuring the international system. State borders have little significance for transnational actors. IGOs and NGOs pursue international agendas that are not shaped by the goals of individual states or negated by state sovereignty. A MNC can shift its resources and its operations from country to country in a single-minded pursuit of profit maximization within the global economy. Although located in a home country, MNCs have operations in other host countries as well. The MNC's loyalty to the prosperity and security goals of its home country can be limited or nonexistent. Such a system of weakened states might become more multipolar and anarchic, or the system might be dominated by a core set of nonstate, transnational actors who cooperate for mutual advantage.

Fourth, due to these trends and other factors, a *more complex international system* has emerged. As noted above, the United States has become such a dominant military power that the system has some unipolar (hegemonic) characteristics. Currently, 46 percent of the world's total military spending is by the Unites States alone (SIPRI 2008). However, the EU and other key countries, including China, Japan, Iran, and Russia, constitute potential poles in this new system, which is based on both military and economic power. As this diverse set of states and other actors jockey for position in a more fluid set of alliances and interstate relationships, a complicated multipolar system might be emerging. Scholars disagree about the extent to which this multipolar system will result and also whether it would be characterized by more international conflict than a bipolar system or hegemonic system. However, empirical research suggests that in the twentieth century, unlike the nineteenth century, aggressive competition and military conflict became more likely as the international system became highly diffuse and multipolar—rather like the system that seems to be emerging (Brecher and Wilkenfeld 1997; Kegley 2008: ch. 12, 14; Russett, Starr, and Kinsella 2008).

Some analysts conclude that the emerging international order will soon be dominated by "imperial corporations," whose globalized systems of production and distribution of goods, finance, technologies, and communications enable them to transcend sovereign states and shape the global system (Barnet and Cavanagh 1994; Falk 1993). For these reasons, some predict that a key conflict in the early twenty-first century will be between the MNCs or between MNCs and states (Heilbroner 1993; United Nations Commission on Transnational Corporations 1991). Do you think it would be desirable to have an international system dominated by transnational actors rather than by states? Would the relentless pursuit of profit produce a more peaceful or a more just world than the relentless pursuit of national interest and state power? Will there be a decrease or an increase in international political violence? This last question is among those that are addressed in Chapter 12.

KEY CONCEPTS

alliances
balance of power
colonialism
diplomacy
foreign policy
geopolitics
globalization
hegemony
intergovernmental organizations (IGOs)

international law
international organization
international regime
international relations
multinational corporations (MNCs)
mutually assured destruction (MAD)
natural law
neocolonialism

nongovernmental organizations (NGOs)
peacekeeping operation
political idealism
political realism
positivist law
sanctions
transnationalism
treaty
world system

FOR FURTHER CONSIDERATION

1. In the post-cold war period, the bipolar international system dominated by the equilibrium between the United States and the Soviet Union has ended. A new pattern must structure the relations among states. What is the most desirable pattern? What is the least desirable? What seems most likely for the international system in the early decades of the twenty-first century?

2. Can the United Nations, or *any* multinational body, be so effective in imposing an international order that major conflict between states becomes highly unlikely?

3. Who, if anyone, can judge whether there are appropriate conditions under which a country's sovereignty can be violated? What might such conditions be?

4. What is the most effective strategy to produce increased cooperation among key actors in the international system?

5. Is globalization likely to change the distribution of power among states and other transnational actors in significant ways? Who is likely to benefit most from globalization?

FOR FURTHER READING

Barnet, Richard J., and John Cavanagh. (1994). *Global Dreams: Imperial Corporations and the New World Order*. New York: Simon and Schuster. A rich, insightful, and often scathing analysis of the enormous power and impacts of the MNCs on the international system and the lives of citizens in many countries.

Dougherty, James E., and Robert L. Pfaltzgraff. (2001). *Contending Theories of International Relations*. 5th ed. New York: Longman. A readable and comprehensible explanation and assessment of the major theories of international relations.

Drezner, Daniel. (2007). *All Politics is Global*. Princeton, NJ: Princeton University Press. A persuasive argument is developed that strong states continue to remain the most powerful actors in the international system, despite globalization, through their leadership in international regulatory regimes.

Friedman, Thomas. (2007). *The World Is Flat: A Brief History of the Twenty-First Century*. 2nd revised ed. New York: Farrar, Straus and Giroux. The author offers his second readable exposition of globalization (following *The Lexus and the Olive Tree*, published in 1999). He argues that new technologies, especially information and communications technologies (e.g., the Internet, wireless mobile communication, integration software), are reducing both global productive inequalities and the obstacles to transborder activities in ways that are transforming the global political economy as well as political and social power.

Fukuyama, Francis. (2004). *State-Building: Governance and World Order in the 21st Century*. Ithaca, NY: Cornell University Press. The scholar famous for predicting "the end of history" due to the triumph of global capitalism revises his views to focus on how it is legitimate for the international community to intervene to attempt to establish viable political institutions in weak and failed states where the emergence of liberal democracy is not occurring naturally.

Gruber, Lloyd. (2000). *Ruling the World: Power Politics and the Rise of Supranational Institutions*. Princeton, NJ: Princeton University Press. The author argues that although countries decide voluntarily to transfer power to such supranational institutions as the

EU and NAFTA, many of the countries, and perhaps the international system itself, do not benefit from the increasing power of these supranationals.

Hasenclever, Andreas, Peter Mayer, and Volker Rittberger. (1997). *Theories of International Regimes*. Cambridge: Cambridge University Press. This comprehensive book presents the reader with different perspectives on international regimes, including realist, liberal, and cognitivist takes.

McCormick, John. (2006). *The European Superpower*. New York: Palgrave. A persuasive analysis of the emergence of the European Union as the major superpower in the new global system, where its multifaceted "soft power" will be more potent that the military approach that has empowered the United States.

Nugent, Neill. (2006). *The Government and Politics of the European Union*. 6th ed. Durham, NC: Duke University Press. A thorough description of the most significant regional alliance in the global system (and the subject of Box 11.1).

Parker, Geoffrey. (1998). *Geopolitics: Past, Present, and Future*. New York: Continuum. The emergence, development, and explanatory power of geopolitical thinking is explained, with particular emphasis on relevant themes of contemporary interstate relations, including ethnonationalism, globalization, inequality, and environmental degradation.

Pastor, Robert A., Ed. (1999). *A Century's Journey: How the Great Powers Shape the World*. New York: Basic Books. Noted scholars explore the foreign policy behavior and resulting international impacts during the twentieth century of each of seven major powers—China, France, Germany, Great Britain, Japan, Russia, and the United States. The authors illuminate the pervasive influence of these powers on the relations between states, the international political economy, and the international system.

Steans, Jill. (1998). *Gender and International Relations: An Introduction*. New Brunswick, NJ: Rutgers University Press. A comprehensible and thoughtful explanation of feminist perspectives on international relations theory, an approach that particularly challenges the key assumptions and interpretations of realist theory on such core topics as interstate relations, violence and militarism, and international political economy.

ON THE WEB

http://www.unsystem.org

The official Web site for the United Nations, including detailed information about many of its major agencies and programs.

http://www.unwire.org

An independent news service focusing on the United Nations and issues of global political concern.

http://europa.eu/index_en.htm

The official Web site of the European Union, with extensive information about the workings of the EU and its major institutional elements.

http://www.people.virginia.edu/~rjb3v/rjb.html

This wide-ranging Web site provides many links regarding matters of international relations, international law, and foreign policy.

http://www.aseansec.org/index.asp

On the official Web site of the Association of Southeast Asian Nations there are information and documents relevant to ASEAN and news about countries in the region as well as somewhat self-serving Web pages constructed by each member state.

http://www.nato.int/

This Web site focuses on military, strategic, and policy issues of importance to the North Atlantic Treaty Organization, a collective security association of 19 partner countries dominated by the United States and West European powers.

http://www.theglobalist.com

The Globalist, a "daily online magazine on the global economy, politics, and culture," offers a strong set of links to think pieces by many interesting commentators as well as relevant articles on issues in the global society.

http://www.g7.utoronto.ca/

The G8 Information Centre, developed by the University of Toronto, provides a wealth of information on the G8 (a cooperative institution with representatives from the major developed countries—the G7 plus Russia=G8), ranging from academic journal articles to recent summit information.

http://osce.org

The official Web site of the Organization for Security and Cooperation in Europe (OSCE), the largest regional security organization in the world, with 55 participating states from Europe, Central Asia, and North America, active in conflict prevention, crisis management, and postconflict rehabilitation.

http://www.apecsec.org.sg/

The electronic home of Asia-Pacific Economic Cooperation (APEC), an organization focusing on economic growth, cooperation, trade, and investment among 21 governments in the Asia-Pacific region, including Canada, China, Japan, Russia, and the United States.

http://www.oas.org/main/english/

The home page of the Organization of American States provides a comprehensive database of information regarding the group's activities and policies.

http://www.unhcr.org

The United Nations High Commissioner for Refugees is the agency that attempts to document the scale and details of the movement of populations across borders and to suggest appropriate policy responses to deal with the challenges of coping with the large numbers of dislocated people.

CHAPTER 12

POLITICAL VIOLENCE

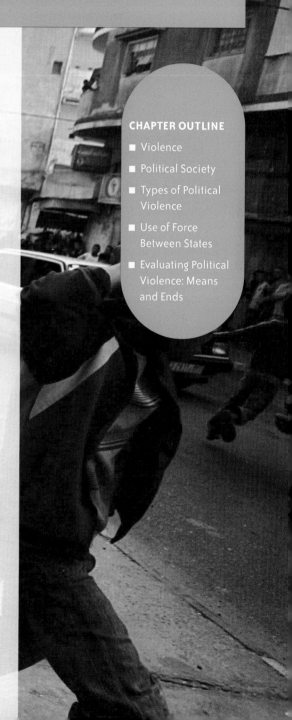

24 (real hours in the political world):

- Israeli tanks and soldiers crossed into the Gaza Strip and killed ten Palestinian militants they suspected of attacking an Israeli army post near the border fence.

- Gunfights between two rival factions of the National Liberation Front rebel group resulted in 21 deaths in a neighborhood on the outskirts of Bujumbura, Burundi.

- Maoist rebels killed three people and wounded five in a landmine explosion in India's Andhra Pradesh state, but they failed to kill their target, a member of parliament traveling in a bullet-proof car.

- Rebels from the Popular Revolutionary Army (EPR) launched six simultaneous attacks on gas and oil pipelines in Veracruz, Mexico, that caused explosions, fires and gas leaks, two deaths, and the forced evacuation of thousands of people.

- German secret police arrested three local men in their 20s, members of an Islamic jihad group who were planning massive car bomb attacks on military bases, pubs, the Frankfurt airport, and other sites frequented by U.S. citizens in Germany.

- Amid the ongoing anarchy in Somalia, mortars killed at least four in attacks on Villa Somalia, the presidential palace in Mogadishu.

- More than 200 Buddhist monks in Yangon, Myanmar, seized 20 government officials and burned vehicles in retaliation for their rough treatment by soldiers during a protest over rising prices.

- Fierce fighting and looting by Congolese rebel groups caused 10,000 people to flee their homes in the Goma area.

- Fifteen people waiting for a visit by the Algerian president were killed and 74 were wounded by a suicide bomber.

- Gunmen in Nigeria kidnapped 11 members of the governing People's Democratic Party (PDP). They demanded $4 million ransom and claimed their action was a protest because they were not paid after the PDP hired them to manipulate the results in a recent election.

- And in Iraq: 14 Shia militia members were killed by U.S. special forces in a firefight and airstrike in a residential neighborhood in West Baghdad; four U.S. Marines were killed in fighting with Sunnis in Anbar; four civilian Iraqis were killed in a roadside bomb in Baghdad; more than a dozen bodies were found in various part of Baghdad, the victims of torture and execution by Sunni and Shia death squads.

Such incidents of violence are often at the center of our awareness of the political world. On a given day, the media rarely report that the great majority of countries and billions of people experienced no bombings, kidnappings, riots, or revolutionary acts with a political motivation. Rather, the media are likely to report on the few settings that do experience armed conflict, riots, assassinations, terrorist incidents, and so on. In part, this selective reporting reflects our general fascination with the horror of violence. And in part, it indicates our underlying sense that such political violence is extraordinary, or even an aberration from politics-as-usual.

Violence is excluded from some definitions of politics, such as the group approach, since violence is viewed as a breakdown of politics, which is understood as consensus building and conflict resolution. Indeed, politics has been defined as "bloodless conflict" (Donovan et al. 1994). However, other definitions, including the class approach, treat conflict and violence as one possible, and perhaps even inevitable, form of politics. Indeed, in some approaches, political violence is portrayed as a positive force, producing necessary change and constructive outcomes. This chapter discusses the nature and dynamics of political violence.

VIOLENCE

Before the discussion can unfold, we need to consider briefly the concept of violence itself. The most common notion is that *violence* entails *the use of physical force, usually with the purpose of injuring or damaging the target of the violence*. In the political world, the tools of such violence can range from flying fists and bullets to nerve gas and nuclear missiles.

But notice that some analysts take a much broader view of violence. First, the *threat* of violence might be understood as a form of violence, even if the violent act is not committed. If someone points a gun in your face and you give her your money, you will probably view this interaction as a violent one, even if the person never fires the gun. Similarly, if a state points nuclear missiles at the state across its border but does not launch any, would you classify this as an act of violence? Is it a violent act if a group threatens to blow up a public building unless its demands are met? Is it a violent act if a group shouts down a speaker at a public rally? Do you think that such acts of intimidation and threat of force have a violent element, even if there is no actual physical injury or damage?

Second, an even broader view of violence includes various forms of subjugation and manipulation that do not involve even the threat of direct physical harm. For example, consider a group that is an "underclass" within a society. The group is subjected to discrimination in education, in health care, in jobs, in housing. This intentional pattern of systematic deprivation continues over time. The group is not targeted for any specific physical violence, but the economic and cultural systems provide the group with minimal opportunities to gain a significant share of the values in the society. Some would classify such oppression as a form of violence by the dominant group(s) against the fundamental rights of the deprived group to life, liberty, and the pursuit of happiness.

Thus **political violence** can be defined as *the use of actual physical violence or very serious threats of such violence to achieve political goals.* As you assess the role of violence in politics, however, consider the other ways in which the world of politics generates actions and impacts that "do violence" to many people. Although resorting to physical force is evident in politics, the more subtle forms of coercion and manipulation are more extensive, if less visible.

POLITICAL SOCIETY

Chapter 2 described the claim by Thomas Hobbes (1588–1679) that the formation of **political society** is an attempt to overcome the frequent reliance on force and violence in human interactions. As individuals use whatever means necessary to pursue their selfish interests, interpersonal violence is inevitable. To overcome such violence, Hobbes observes, individuals accept the *social contract* in an attempt to submit force to reason—to ensure that force becomes the *ultima ratio* (final resort), not the *prima ratio* (first resort). In essence, individuals cede to the state a monopoly over the legitimate use of violence, sacrificing their own right to use violence in exchange for a similar sacrifice from others.

Even if most people accept the social contract, some individuals and groups do not, arguing that the existing political society and its social contract have no authority over their actions. They believe that they have the right to engage in "justifiable" violence, which is based on such motives as the preservation of values, the restoration of order, self-defense, or retribution. They might further claim that they have never accepted the right of a particular government to command their obedience or that the political system is illegitimate (because it lacks a democratic mandate or because it has failed to deliver security, stability, and prosperity).

TYPES OF POLITICAL VIOLENCE

A simple taxonomy of political violence can be based on specifying the *source* of the violence and the *target* of that violence. Either party may be a state or an

Source	Target	
	Individual/Group	**State**
Individual/ Group	Crime Terrorism Nation-based conflict Class conflict	Riots/Rebellion Separatist violence Coup Revolution
State	Order maintenance Establishment violence State-sponsored terrorism	War

▶ **FIGURE 12.1**

Types of political violence

individual/group. Figure 12.1 distinguishes four categories of political violence. Although these categories help organize and clarify our discussion, this taxonomy is imperfect and the boundaries between categories are imprecise (hence the dashesd lines) because the states, groups, or individuals who engage in political violence are usually motivated by multiple objectives, can operate in fluid groupings, employ complex strategies, and focus on multiple targets.

State Violence Against Individuals or Groups

Given the state's monopoly of the legitimate use of violence, there are many instances in which the state's application of political violence seems justifiable. The state typically characterizes its own use of violence as an *order-maintenance* activity. The state's agents act as police officers, judges, and executors of punishment when individuals or groups seem to have violated the society's legal system. Thus the state might arrest, try, and punish an actor who breaks a criminal law, such as robbery, or a civil law, such as tax fraud. In such cases, most citizens are likely to support the state's efforts to create and maintain public order.

But some uses of violence by the state are more problematic. Recall Lenin's definition of the state as "a body of armed men, weapons, and prisons" (in Chapter 5). Because the state has the capacity to define the nature and severity of all "crimes," it is possible for the state to be highly repressive and discriminatory in its use of violence. *The state's excessive reliance on force and oppressive laws* can be called **establishment violence** and contrasted with the state's legitimate use of violence to maintain public order.

The boundary between a crime against society and a crime against the existing political order can blur. In some countries, political actions that oppose the current political leadership are treated as crimes. Thus political opponents become "enemies of the people" and are subject to constraints on freedom of action, deprivation of resources, imprisonment, and death. The state can also institute systematic policies of violence against certain groups that are not overt opponents of the regime but are blamed for problems faced by the state and thus are made scapegoats.

A key instrument of a state's power against its enemies is its security forces, which include official groups such as the regular military and the secret police as well as unofficial armed groups (e.g., Colombian paramilitary forces) and civilian vigilante groups (e.g., the Iranian Revolutionary Guards). Another form of state power is judicial systems and prison systems, which punish those whose behaviors displease the state. According to Amnesty International (2007), an NGO that monitors violations of individual civil rights by agents of the state, political prisoners are subjected to establishment violence in the majority (102) of contemporary states. In addition, the state can cause great suffering or even death to individuals through its power to withhold access to such rewards as good jobs, shelter, and welfare services.

In the contemporary world, extensive attention is paid to certain forms of political violence, especially violence between states (war) and individual/group violence (such as terrorism). This attention is understandable because such violence is dramatic and terrifying. But, according to an extensive analysis by political scientist R. J. Rummel (2008) of "death by government," the death toll from establishment violence far outweighs the deaths from war during the twentieth century. These data are summarized in Table 12.1.

According to Rummel, the deaths of more than 300 million people in the twentieth century are directly attributable to government violence and war. The most staggering aspect of these data is that fully 86 percent of these deaths are establishment violence. While about 41 million people were killed in wars, it is estimated that governments killed more than 260 million of their own citizens (including their colonial subjects)—the people they are supposed to serve. Rummel includes any murder committed by agents of the government, including genocides, politically motivated executions, massacres, and intentional famines. Most of these deaths through establishment violence have been the work of nondemocratic governments. Half of the deaths (50 percent) are attributable to communist regimes, about 9 percent are the responsibility of other totalitarian governments, and 26 percent are by authoritarian governments (Rummel 2008: table 1.2, table 1.6, figure 1.4, and later updates).

▶ **TABLE 12.1**
Death by Government in the Twentieth Century

	Total Deaths (millions)			
	Domestic	Foreign	All	Percentage of Total Deaths
Establishment violence	173	90	262	86%
By communist governments	145	8	153	50
By other totalitarian governments	1	26	28	9
By authoritarian governments	26	53	79	26
By democratic governments	0.2	2	2	1
War	10	31	41	14
TOTAL	182	120	303	100.0%

Note: The totals are rounded to the nearest million.
Source: Adapted from Rummel (2008), table 1.6; and updates communicated to the author from Professor Rummel by e-mail.

Rummel particularly emphasizes the massive death totals attributable to the twentieth century's "bloodiest dictators": Mao Zedong's regime in China killed 76.7 million between 1923 and 1976; Joseph Stalin's Soviet regime killed 42.6 million between 1929 and 1953; more than 20.9 million were eliminated by Hitler and the German Nazi regime (1933–1945); 10 million were killed by King Leopold in his colony of Congo (recall Box 11.3); and 2.4 million Cambodians died by execution and starvation under Pol Pot's regime (recall Box 10.4). If you need evidence of the fundamental importance of the state in determining the quality of citizens' lives, the 262 million deaths attributable to the citizens' own governments should be compelling.

Individual Violence Against an Individual

When an individual is the source of violence and another individual is the target, the violence is usually not explicitly political. Most such violence (e.g., murder, robbery, rape, assault, and certain crimes against property, such as burglary and arson) is best characterized as *ordinary crime*. Since only the state (and its agents) has a legitimate right to use violence (this is one definition of the state in Chapter 5 as well as in Hobbes's social contract notion), an individual who does violence without the approval of the state is normally in violation of the law. Even these ordinary crimes have an implicit political element, in the sense that the state is usually involved in determining what behaviors are criminal and then in apprehending violators, judging them, and punishing them on behalf of "the people." Notice also that in most societies, members of deprived or subordinate groups tend to engage in violent crimes far more frequently than members of the more advantaged classes. Do you think this pattern might suggest that the commission of some violent crimes and even the nature of the punishment have, in part, a subtle political origin?

There are instances where one individual engages in an act of political violence against another individual. For example, American presidents James A. Garfield in 1881 and William McKinley in 1901 were assassinated by individuals who seemed to be acting alone, primarily on political motives. Occasionally, a person's motivation for violence against a political actor is as much personal as political. In a famous example from 1804, U.S. Vice President Aaron Burr shot and killed distinguished Founding Father Alexander Hamilton in a duel. The two were bitter political enemies from rival political parties, but Burr was also offended by disparaging personal comments that he thought Hamilton had made about him. Burr challenged Hamilton to a duel, and after Hamilton shot in the air as gentlemen normally did, Burr mortally wounded Hamilton. In 2001, the king and queen of Nepal and six other members of the royal family were shot to death by the king's son, the crown prince, who had quarreled with his mother over his choice of a bride.

Group Violence Against an Individual

Most violence in which a person is targeted for political reasons, including assassinations, is committed on behalf of a group, even if the act is performed by a single individual. Box 5.2 described the assassinations of two Indian prime ministers, Indira Gandhi and her son Rajiv Gandhi seven years later. Although Indira Gandhi was killed by two guards and Rajiv Gandhi by one woman, in each case the assassins believed they were acting to further the political interests of their nationality group (the Sikhs and the Sri Lankan Tamils, respectively). U.S. President Abraham Lincoln was assassinated in 1865 as part of a broader group attack on the American political leadership, and some believe that President John F. Kennedy's assassination in 1963 can be attributed to more than one person. And the murders of former Lebanese Prime Minister Rafik Hariri (in 2005) and former Pakistani Prime Minister Benazir Bhutto (in 2008) each was the work of a suicide bomber, although organized groups or perhaps even governments were behind the attacks.

Terrorism.   An act is usually called **terrorism** when there is *premeditated, politically motivated violence by nonstate actors targeting a "noncombatant."* Bombs can be planted in public places such as markets or airplanes; civilians can be kidnapped or murdered; harmful chemicals can be placed in food, water, or air. Some analyses distinguish ***domestic terrorism***, when *both the terrorist and the victims are from the same country*, from ***international terrorism***—*incidents where the source and the target of the terrorism are citizens of different countries*. However, the patterns of cross-national population movement have become so complex that the key agency that tracks terrorism has discontinued this distinction (NCTC 2007).

The widespread perception that terrorism is increasing in frequency and in scale is generally supported by the data. In 2006, there were 14,000 attacks (an increase of 25 percent from 2005), 20,000 deaths (a 40 percent increase), and 38,000 nondeath injuries (a 60 percent increase). As Figure 12.2 indicates, most of those killed or wounded in terrorist attacks in 2006 were either in the Near East or South Asia. In fact, almost half of the terrorist incidents and nearly two-thirds of the deaths (13,340) in 2005 occurred in one country: Iraq. Only two other countries had more than 1,000 fatalities: India (1,256) and Afghanistan (1,042). While the taking of hostages (16,000 kidnappings) was down in 2006, the great majority occurred in only one country: Nepal (NCTC 2007). These regional patterns do change over time, with the war in

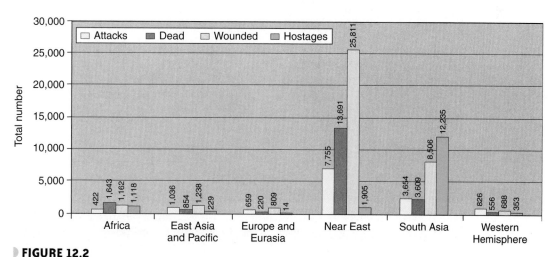

▶ **FIGURE 12.2**

Terrorist attacks and victims, by region, 2006
Source: NCTC 2007: 17

Iraq precipitating many of the casualties from terrorism circa 2005–2008. About a decade ago, for example, the Western Hemisphere had substantially higher numbers, especially due to kidnappings and killings in Latin America. Terrorism also occurs more frequently at present in countries with modest political freedom, in comparison to countries with substantial freedom or minimal freedom (Abadie 2004).

Some peoples, such as the Iraqis, Israelis, and Palestinians, despair of the recurrent terrorist attacks that make their lives feel so Hobbesian. In other countries, people are especially scarred by a particularly traumatic terrorist act. For Indonesians, it is the death of 202 people, mostly foreign tourists, in the 2002 bombings of two nightclubs in Bali by Indonesian militants. In Spain, it is the coordinated backpack bombings of Madrid commuter trains in 2004, killing 191 and wounding more than 2,000. And in the United States, of course, it is the events of September 11, 2001, the most massive terrorist attack in modern history. A well-organized group, composed mainly of Saudi Arabians, hijacked four transcontinental passenger airplanes departing from Boston, Newark, and Washington, D.C. Two of the planes were flown into the towers of the World Trade Center in New York, one crashed into the Pentagon near Washington, D.C., and the fourth crashed in a field in Pennsylvania after passengers struggled with the hijackers. The carnage was staggering, with almost 3,000 deaths, and the costs of the attack have been estimated at more than $300 billion. The events on September 11 have had continuing ramifications for many procedures and actions by the United States and a number of other countries.

For some, the central question regarding those who engage in terrorism is: Why use violence to harm noncombatants? The motives of political terrorists vary, but some combination of five rationales guide most such acts. First, the terrorists can attempt to punish an existing state (their own or another state) for perceived grievances,

▶ **People flee from the site where the two towers of the World Trade Center in New York are collapsing after a terrorist attack on September 11, 2001. The attack killed almost 3,000 people.**

even when noncombatants are the direct target of their actions. From the terrorists' perspective, no citizens of the targeted state are innocent of their state's misdeeds. (Recall the views of Osama bin Laden in Box 4.2.) Second, terrorists can attack a domestic group whom they wish to subordinate or retaliate against for previous offenses. This characterizes much of the recent violence in Iraq between Shia and Sunnis, or in Sudan's Darfur region by the Janjaweed. Third, the terrorist act can be a means to gain international publicity for the group's cause. Unlike those committing ordinary crimes, terrorists often claim credit for their violent actions and hope for extensive media coverage of such disturbing violence. Fourth, terrorists may seek to secure financial resources for the group's political activities or may demand the release of imprisoned members. Many acts of violence that involve hostages and ransom demands are this type. And fifth, an objective of terrorist violence may be to promote revolution—a strategy discussed later in this chapter.

Terrorism is undergoing ominous changes in the early twenty-first century. First and most important, terrorists have an increased capacity to inflict massive damage and disruption. The terrorists' ability to move people, information, weapons, and so on is enhanced by globalization, with its permeable national borders, extensive cross-border travel, and growing immigrant populations. Moreover, terrorists benefit from the rapid expansion of technologies that provide them with far greater destructive capabilities, ranging from computers (cyberterrorism) to chemical and biological weapons (bioterrorism) to weapons of mass destruction (WMD).

A second change is that many terrorists are now operating in very small cells (three to ten people) that are only loosely coupled with each other, making penetration and destruction of terrorist "networks" almost impossible. While there is some broad collaboration in training and provision of materials, most terrorist acts are carried out by small, isolated cells. Recall the discussion in Chapter 4 of the rise of the "bunch of guys" (BOGs) who mobilize and encourage each other to plan and undertake acts of violence that are otherwise out of character for the individuals in the small peer group (Sageman 2008).

A third change is that some groups, especially religiously motivated terrorists, now seem less constrained in the scale of death and destruction they are willing to inflict, even upon those who are noncombatants (Council on Foreign Relations 2005). Moreover, an increasing proportion of terrorist acts are committed by individuals who are not only willing to die for the cause, but actually intend to die in a suicide act.

There are ambiguities in the assessment of terrorism. One definitional problem is defining noncombatants. The media and politicians sometimes describe as terrorism an attack on military personnel, who are clearly combatants. But what about attacks on other armed personnel (such as police or security guards) or other agents of the state (such as judges or civilians working for the military)? One attempt to identify combatants states that they are "personnel in the military, paramilitary, militia, police under military command and control who are [on duty] in . . . areas . . . where war zones or war-like conditions exist" (NCTC 2007: 9). Others might argue that this definition of combatants is extremely narrow. Thus, while there is often agreement about the sheer terror associated with acts of political violence, it is not always clear to everyone whether such acts are best understood as terrorism or just brutal violence against "the enemy" in the service of some political goal.

In another distinction, some groups labeled "terrorists" are actually employees of a political system that uses them as "death squads" to eliminate opponents and to keep the citizens in line. For example, many accuse the Sudanese government of providing support to the Janjaweed who have brutally attacked certain ethnic groups in the Darfur region. And some terrorist groups are mercenaries subsidized by one state to perform violent acts against those from a rival state. In such cases, termed **state-sponsored terrorism**, *the actor who is actually the source of the political violence is best understood as another state*, not a group. The governments of these states are accused of either engaging in terrorist activities themselves or providing arms, training, safe haven, financial backing, and so on for international terrorists. The U.S. government designates five national governments as the primary state sponsors of terrorism: Cuba, Iran, North Korea, Sudan, and Syria.

With the proliferation of groups employing terrorist tactics, it is wryly observed that "one person's terrorist is another person's freedom fighter." The root problem with using terrorism as an analytic concept is that it has become a powerful and negative label in the manipulative language of politics. It is sometimes used regardless of the innocence of the victim, the identity of the actual sponsor of the violence, or the justifiability of the ends. The label communicates a disgust for extreme political violence against innocent individuals, but it can also be used to discredit any group that uses violent means to achieve its political ends or to condemn a group whose political ends, as much as its means, are unacceptable. Ultimately, the issue centers in moral and political values: Are there *any* circumstances in which group political violence against individuals is justifiable? If so, what kinds of violence are acceptable and under what circumstances? The Debate in 12 considers whether terrorism is ever justifiable.

THE DEBATE IN 12

Is Terrorism Ever a Justifiable Form of Political Violence?

Throughout history, some individuals and groups have engaged in political violence to achieve their goals. Few would argue that political violence is *never* justified. Indeed, most political theorists specify conditions under which people can legitimately engage in political violence against an unjust government. However, there must be many circumstances in which either the ends to which violence has been used or the means that are employed are unacceptable. In the contemporary world, some of the most serious concerns about political violence relate to the *victims*. In comparison to violent attacks against the military, police, or even political leaders, there are often considerably more objections to attacks that victimize people who have no direct link to the existing political regime. Indeed, a core element of the contemporary definition of *terrorism*, as a form of political violence, is the stipulation that the victims are "innocent" noncombatants. If the victims are noncombatants, is terrorism ever justified?

The Debate in 12 *(Continued)*

Some Terrorism Is Justified

- Individuals who engage in terrorist acts believe they are acting on behalf of many people, virtually all of whom are "innocents" and "noncombatants." These innocents are themselves a "violated" group who have been the victims of establishment violence or have experienced severe and prolonged oppression, which is also understood to be a form of violence.

- Terrorist tactics are employed as a last resort, but such actions are necessary because the oppressed group is prevented, by its exclusion from resources or by establishment violence, from using nonviolent political means to displace the oppressors. John Locke, in his *Second Treatise of Government* (1690), is among the many theorists who vigorously defend the right of an oppressed people to use violence against unjust governance.

- Innocent people might be harmed by terrorist acts in some instances, but they are the unlucky people who are in the wrong place at the wrong time. They are no different from the individuals that those with power call "collateral damage" when they are killed during state-sponsored violence.

- Many of the targets of terrorism are individuals who sustain and actively support the domination and violence of the oppressors, even if they do not necessarily wear the uniforms of combatants. They are certainly not "innocents."

- Ultimately, there are no true innocents: those who acquiesce to and enjoy benefits from the policies of the oppressors are also responsible for the harm caused to those who suffer. Those who gain life's advantages while accepting injustice and violence directed against the less advantaged cannot also claim immunity from responsibility and harm.

All Terrorism Is Indefensible

- The destruction of *innocent* lives for political gain is morally unacceptable, without exception.

- Only the state has the right to use violence under the conditions of the social contract. Thus any act of extreme political violence that is not committed by the representatives of the state is illegitimate, regardless of the targeted victim or motivation.

- Terrorism is tactically unwise because it pushes the existing regime to become even more aggressive and less willing to engage in dialogue and compromise (e.g., consider the response of Uruguay's government described below in Box 12.1).

- From a pragmatic perspective, terrorism is also tactically unwise because its ultraviolence alienates potential supporters, both within and outside the country. Eventually the terrorist group is isolated and without allies.

- There are considerably more cases where relatively powerless groups were able to replace an oppressive regime with persistent political mobilization than with terrorism.

- If the goal is to achieve social justice, there are effective nonviolent alternatives to terrorism, even for those who lack extensive political resources (e.g., nonviolent resistance to colonialism by India's Gandhi; the use of the electoral process, as in many postcommunist countries).

- History reveals that terrorism rarely succeeds in achieving the goals desired by the terrorists. Even those who do gain power by such brutal violence are usually driven from power by further violence before they attain the idealistic outcomes they sought. Indeed, they typically become as oppressive as those they have overthrown.

- The use of unrestrained violence for political ends becomes an ethical slippery slope into chaos. It establishes the right of every unhappy group to use "any means necessary" in the attempt to achieve its political ends

More questions . . .

1. Are those "noncombatants" who gain considerable benefits from an unfair political

The Debate in 12 *(Continued)*

regime truly innocents who should not suffer from the consequences of political violence directed against the regime?

2. Do the conditions, motivation, and political goals of the terrorists have any relevance in determining the acceptability of the action,

or is terrorism always wrong, regardless of conditions, motivation, and goals?

3. Is it possible to make a precise distinction between all terrorists and those who fight for freedom and justice?

Group Violence Against a Group

Nation-based violence.   Nationality groups are increasingly mobilized to demand political autonomy, a process grounded in a deep attachment to the group's identity, described in Chapter 5 as nationalism or ethnonationalism (Connor 1994; Conversi 2004; Gurr 2000). When the identities of two groups clash directly, *antagonism between these nation-based groups can result in political violence.* Indeed, such ***nation-based violence*** is the source of much of the political violence in the post-cold war period. Most of the major armed conflicts during this period have been between nation-based groups within countries, not between countries (SIPRI 2008: ch. 2).

In some cases, one or more groups attempt to establish their own sovereign state based on national identity, a situation discussed later in the chapter as separatist violence. However, in many instances, the nation-based groups are struggling against each other for political and cultural domination rather than for separation. The continuing violence between Hindus and Muslims in India (see Box 5.2) is a revealing example of how the antipathy between nationality groups can poison the relations between them as they attempt to share a country or even a remote village. In the southern African country of Angola, more than 1.5 million people died in the prolonged civil war (1975–2002) among three rival groups, each representing a different linguistic/ethnic region, who struggled for control of the entire country. The violence in Iraq reveals the deep antagonisms between groups within the Shia, Sunni, and Kurdish nations.

When *group political violence results in the murder of many members of one ethnic group by its rival,* it can be called ***genocide*** (Weitz 2005). The political system is often a partner in such situations, since its machinery of violence is employed by the dominant group. When the state organizes the campaign against an ethnic group, such genocide can also be classified as *establishment violence* (see Figure 12.1). Twentieth-century examples of genocide include the killing of Armenians by the Turks (in 1915), of 6 million Jews in Hitler's Germany (1933–1945), of the Tutsis by the Hutus in Rwanda (1963–1964), and of the Hutus by the Tutsis in neighboring Burundi (1988). Since 1990, the killing of nearly 1 million Tutsis in Rwanda, the Serbs' "ethnic cleansing" of civilian populations of Bosnians and of ethnic Albanians (in Kosovo), and the systematic violence against ethnic groups in Myanmar and Sudan have renewed international concern about preventing genocide and punishing those who are responsible for it.

Many of the recent conflicts are grounded in nation-based hostility but can also be a blur of class conflict, separatist violence, revolutionary struggle, and conflict between states, topics addressed below. What is clear is the massive toll that these conflicts levy on their populations. Table 12.2 provides data on just a few conflicts and some of the most visible indicators of human devastation. Most obviously, it lists the number of deaths attributable to political violence. In addition, the toll in disrupted lives is revealed by the number of people who have been forced by the violence to leave their homes and communities—there are currently 24.5 million internally displaced persons worldwide (IDMC 2007). Moreover, 13.9 million people have actually fled their country, crossing the border in an attempt to escape the violence. The great majority of these 40 million human beings, more than 70 percent of whom are women and children, live in squalor and unremitting hardship, homeless or surviving in miserable refugee camps.

Class conflict.   In some cases, intergroup violence might be attributable to an underlying *class conflict* (see Chapter 9), which is often linked to an ethnic or religious cleavage. In recent conflicts in Rwanda, Sudan, and Sri Lanka, for example, one of the groups in the conflict has dominant social, economic, and political power over the others. Thus class theorists argue that the "real" conflict in many settings is not actually due to religion or language or ethnicity, but to the inevitable class struggle that emerges from stratification and inequality. Of course, class conflict can occur between any strata, such as the peasant class against the landlord class or the capitalist class against the worker class, independent of any nation-based cleavage

▶ TABLE 12.2
Human Devastation from Recent Internal Violence and Ethnic Conflict

Country	Deaths[a]	Refugees[b]	Internally Displaced Persons[c]
Congo, D.R.	3,800,000	413,000	1,100,000
Sudan	2,100,000	648,000	5,535,000
Afghanistan	1,050,000	3,260,000	132,000
Rwanda	800,000	92,000	na
Burundi	550,000	394,000	100,000
Myanmar	500,000	693,000	500,000
Columbia	250,000	453,000	3,800,000
Iraq	250,000	1,687,000	1,700,000
Former Palestine	na	3,036,000	57,000
Uganda	na	na	1,700,000

[a]Deaths attributable to political violence.
[b]Refugees and asylum seekers who have left their country of origin (as of January 1, 2007).
[c]People driven from their home location due to persecution, armed conflict, or widespread violence (as of January 1, 2007).
Sources: IDMC (2007); World Refugee Survey (2007): table 7; Wright 1999.

that might reinforce the class distinctions. The group-based political violence in some Latin American countries, such as Colombia, Guatemala, and Mexico, seems best interpreted as a struggle between deeply unequal classes.

Individual or Group Violence Against the State

Individual or group political violence directed against the political system can have several causes. Be aware that the motivation underlying many acts of terrorism is actually to direct violence against a state, even if the immediate targets are noncombatants. In this section, we examine other forms of violence where the state is the target. At one extreme, such violence might be a person's or group's spontaneous outburst of frustration with life conditions. At the other extreme, the individual or group might have such deep-seated hostility against the existing political system that it undertakes a lengthy series of violent actions in order to overthrow the system.

Riots and rebellion.   When people find their political, social, or economic conditions intolerable, their frustration can escalate from demonstrations and civil disobedience to riots. *Riots* are usually *spontaneous and relatively disorganized group violence* against property, agents of the political system, perceived opponents in the society, or random targets. Riots are often triggered by a specific incident, such as the police shooting someone, or by an economic problem, such as a sudden large increase in the price of basic foodstuffs. Once riots start, they can spread as others are motivated to demonstrate their dissatisfaction with the political system or social conditions.

▶ **Citizens' frustrations with the policies of the state can trigger public demonstrations that lead to violent confrontations, as in this street battle between South Korean students and workers and the state's riot police.**

Riots are expressions of frustration in which there is an implicit or explicit demand for redress of grievances. The basic grievances might involve opposition to or support for certain public policies or political leaders. Black South Africans engaged in many riots in their ultimately successful opposition to apartheid during the 1980s. Mass protests and riots have forced many unpopular leaders from power in recent years (e.g., in Bolivia, Haiti, Indonesia, Lebanon).

Such political violence turns into **rebellion** when there is *more frequent, premeditated, and widespread violence, involving more people.* At this point, many of those engaged in violence have lost faith in the likelihood that the system will respond to their problems. This deterioration of citizen support and escalation of political action to more intense political violence are at the heart of Samuel Huntington's description of political decay (in Chapter 10).

The Palestinian Intifada ("uprising") is an example of a rebellion. Some leaders of the Palestinian movement decided that a rebellion would be an effective intermediate strategy, since neither negotiations nor terrorism had resulted in their gaining an independent state on lands held by Israel. When the Intifada began in 1987, people of all ages were encouraged to participate in limited political violence, mainly throwing rocks but not using firearms. The leaders hoped that world opinion would be sympathetic to the underdog rock throwers when the powerful Israeli military responded violently. Some claim that the Intifada is a key reason Israel agreed to negotiate a home rule settlement with the Palestinians (Khalidi 1993). When Palestinian groups concluded that the autonomy that Israel granted to the Palestine National Authority was inadequate and when Israel continued to expand its control over Palestinian territory, the Intifada was resurrected in 2000. This second Intifada became a more complex combination of a rock-throwing popular uprising and bloody terrorist actions, and the Israeli response has been more violent, resulting in high levels of death and destruction.

Separatist violence.   At the heart of most nation-based violence is the nationality group's struggle for autonomy—for the right to control its own political and cultural destiny. Groups engage in **separatist violence** *to achieve substantial (or total) political autonomy* from an unresponsive political system. If the separatist group is small and lacks political resources, it usually turns to acts of terrorism or attacks against specific individuals within the political system. This characterized the actions of the Irish Republican Army (IRA) throughout much of the twentieth century as it attempted to separate Northern Ireland from the United Kingdom and merge it with the Republic of Ireland. Targets of the IRA's bombs and murders were usually the British "occupying army" and members of the Protestant paramilitary groups in Northern Ireland. Separatist violence characterized recent activities by the Kurds against Turkey, by Chechens against Russia, and by Kashmiris against India.

Violent uprisings against colonial power have usually been one element in native people's political struggle for independence. In some cases, organization of the separatist violence has been weak or nonexistent. But in others, the separatist violence has been coordinated by an organized group, such as the Mau Mau versus the British in Kenya (1950s) and the Vietminh/Vietcong versus the French and then the Americans in Vietnam (1940s–1970s). The violent resistance (after 2003) to the U.S. military and its allies in postwar Iraq is also characterized by some as native opposition to foreign occupation.

A **civil war** results when *a significant proportion of the population in a region actively supports a separatist movement and political violence emerges on a large scale*. In the United States in the early 1860s, the political leaders of the slave-holding southern states decided that they no longer wished to be part of the American federation, and they announced that their states were seceding (withdrawing formal membership) from the federation. The central government rejected their request to secede, forcing 11 southern states to declare their independence, create a confederation, and initiate a military struggle against the central government. In the bloody American Civil War (1861–1865), the Union forces of the central government ultimately defeated the army of the Confederacy and forced the southern states to remain in the federation.

A similar civil war occurred in Nigeria in 1967–1970. The Ibo tribe, which differed from other major tribes in religion, language, and political traditions, attempted to secede from the Nigerian federation and create a separate state called Biafra. After four years of civil war and nearly a million deaths, the central government's army was victorious, and Biafra was stillborn as a state. In contrast, the Bengalis were successful in their separatist civil war against the central government of Pakistan (recall Box 5.2), and thus the new nation-state of Bangladesh was created (in 1971). Nation-based violence between Shia Muslims and Sunni Muslims in Iraq escalated by 2006 to a level some have characterized as civil war.

The devastating struggle among the Serbs, Bosnians, Croatians, Kosovars, and other nationality groups after the breakup of Yugoslavia in 1991 is a graphic example of separatist violence. These groups' differences in ethnicity, history, language, and religion all reinforced their separate national identities (see Box 15.2). Widespread separatist violence resulted from the groups' antipathy toward each other and their efforts to determine precisely what states would emerge and where the boundaries between the states would be.

Coup. A **coup** occurs when *the top leader or part of the leadership group is replaced by violent means or the explicit threat of violence*. Those carrying out the coup have no intention of overthrowing the entire political-economic order, although their opposition to the existing leadership can be based on differences in policy as well as on personal rivalry. Coups are a common form of leadership turnover in political systems that have no institutionalized procedures for leadership succession. Political violence against the top leadership group is typically organized by other members of the political leadership, by a rival political group, or by the military. An extreme example is Bolivia, where 190 coups occurred over a 156-year period ending in the 1980s. Bangladesh had 21 coups or attempted coups in its first 36 years of existence. Despite the enthusiasm with which many countries are democratizing their political systems in the last two decades, coups continue, ousting the leaders of Algeria, Afghanistan, Argentina, Bangladesh, Bolivia, Burundi, Comoros, Congo (Brazzaville), Democratic Republic of Congo, Ecuador, Ethiopia, Fiji, Gambia, Guinea-Bissau, Liberia, Mali, Mauritania, Niger, Pakistan, Sierra Leone, Somalia, Tajikistan, and Thailand, among others.

Revolution.   As Lennon (John, of the Beatles, that is) observed, "You say you want a revolution, well you know, we all want to change the world." A **revolution** is *a rapid and fundamental transformation of the state organization and the class structure* (Skocpol 1979). In contrast to the other forms of political violence against the state, the explicit objective of a revolution is to destroy the existing political system and establish a new one with a fundamentally different distribution of power and value allocations. After a revolution, new leadership takes power, claiming that it will reorganize the state, serve a new ideology, and allocate power and resources to different groups.

However, it can be difficult to specify the precise extent of system transformation that must occur to achieve "revolutionary" changes in the state organization, class structure, or distribution of values (recall the discussion in Chapter 10). When Colonel Muammar Qaddafi overthrew the hereditary king and installed a new revolutionary council committed to total egalitarianism (1969), it was clear that there had been a revolutionary change in the Libyan political system. Similarly, when Shah Reza Pahlavi and his "White Revolution" were overthrown and replaced by an Islamic theocracy (in 1979), there was a fundamental transformation in Iran's politics and society. But in many instances it is not clear whether the essential features of the political system have dramatically changed. This situation can occur either because the attempt to transform the political system is a charade or because it falls far short of its objectives. Although some of the most famous revolutions had occurred earlier (e.g., the American Revolution in 1776, the French Revolution in 1789, the Russian Revolution in 1917), there was a particularly large number of revolutionary movements and revolutions in the period leading up to and the decades just after the transition of many colonial territories to independent countries (especially from about 1950 to 1980).

Strategies for revolution.   Four broad strategies can be employed to achieve a revolution.

Strategy 1: Terrorism. As a revolutionary strategy, *terrorism* involves selective acts of violence, usually by small, organized cells of political activists that lack sufficient membership and resources to sustain a direct struggle against the existing state. Violence is used to disrupt public life and to provoke repressive responses from the state, and thus to foster political decay and undermine support for the state. The anticolonial resistance in Algeria is a clear example of the successful use of terrorism. A mixture of random public bombings, disruptions of infrastructure services, and violence against the agents of the colonial French led to a dramatic decline in the quality of life and provoked repressive responses from the French political and military authorities. As conditions deteriorated, France decided to abandon the ungovernable country, and the anticolonial/terrorist leadership, under Ben Bella, formed a new political system in 1962. (Gillo Pontecorvo's powerful film *The Battle of Algiers* documents this period.)

Obviously, terrorism, like other revolutionary strategies, does not always produce the expected results. Sometimes the terrorists are crushed without achieving any of their objectives, like terrorist groups in the United States in the 1960s. And sometimes the repression evoked by terrorism merely makes things worse, as in Uruguay (see Box 12.1). In Iran, leftist terrorists were successful in destabilizing Shah Reza

BOX 12.1

Terrorism Makes It Worse: Uruguay

Between 1903 and the early 1960s, Uruguay became widely respected as the exemplary Latin American democracy. It had a stable two-party system that was the basis of a liberal democratic government expanding social welfare and economic prosperity. But political decay emerged in the 1960s, grounded in economic decline, high inflation, and governmental incompetence and corruption. These failures spawned the Tupamaros, an urban guerrilla group that engaged in widespread violence and terrorism, especially kidnappings and assassinations, to overthrow the state and establish a more just political order. This terrorism completely undermined the citizens' confidence that the political system could maintain order. The civilian government was overthrown, not by the Tupamaros but by the conservative military in a 1973 coup.

The Uruguayan military dictatorship then launched a massive campaign to suppress not only the Tupamaros but all civilian opposition. During this period, Uruguay became known as "the torture chamber of Latin America," with widespread human and civil rights abuses. By 1979, more than one in a hundred of all Uruguayans were political prisoners, the highest proportion among all countries. And one-sixth of the population (a half-million people) lived in exile. The economic crisis worsened under the military regime, with inflation higher than 60 percent and unemployment higher than 30 percent. When the military promoted a referendum on a new constitution in 1980, 60 percent of the population rejected it.

Eventually the military allowed elections, returning governmental power to civilian rule in March 1985. Soon, political interest groups became active, press freedom was reestablished, and the independence of the judiciary was assured. Even the Tupamaros reemerged, not as a terrorist movement but as a political party (the Movement of Popular Participation) championing the interests of the poor.

There is considerable optimism that Uruguay has left behind its period of terrorism and repression and returned to its earlier democratic ways. It has been classified as a "free," liberal democracy by Freedom House (2008) since 1985 and now has the top score of 1.0. Its population of 3.5 million enjoys nearly universal literacy and good health care, and the economy has rebounded from the regional economic crisis of the late 1990s. Ironically, the Tupamaros' political party is now the largest party in the governing coalition, and its members from the guerrilla period now serve as presidents in both chambers of the legislature. The military is clearly uneasy with these developments, as well as the election of Uruguay's first leftist president (Tabare Vazquez) in 2005. Thus its security service continues extensive surveillance of key political and labor leaders as well as the media and remains in the background, watching quietly for signs of disorder (Goodwin 2005).

Pahlavi's regime, but it was the Islamic fundamentalists supporting the Ayatollah Khomeini who succeeded in grasping political power (1979) and forming a new political system even more unappealing to the leftists than the shah's. Nonetheless, terrorism continues to be the preferred strategy for certain revolutionary groups that lack widespread popular support, such as FARC in Colombia.

Strategy 2: Revolution from above. Historically, many revolutions resemble the revolution from above (Johnson 1983b). Violent resistance to the regime occurs primarily in the urban centers, especially the capital city. Usually, the rural areas have minimal involvement in the revolutionary struggle. At least some parts of the political elite and the military are sympathetic to or even supportive of the goals of the revolution. Typically, the final collapse of the old regime is rapid, as its leaders are killed or flee. The new political system then penetrates the countryside in an attempt to control the entire country. Twentieth-century examples of revolution from above include Gamal Abdel Nasser's replacement of King Farouk in Egypt (1952), Muammar Qaddafi's victory over King Idris in Libya (1969), the execution of communist Premier Nicholae Ceauçescu in Romania (1989), and the flight of socialist leaders Mengistu Mariam in Ethiopia and Said Barre in Somalia (1991).

Strategy 3: Guerrilla war. The essence of **guerrilla war** is *a long, protracted campaign of political violence against the state from rural bases*, although the fighting can be in both rural and urban areas. It is a direct struggle against the military, as the guerrilla forces persistently harass the regime's military and authorities by fighting in a hit-and-run style, suddenly attacking an exposed point and then disappearing into the population and the countryside. There is an effort to win the loyalty of the rural population by mixing intimidation and promises of reform. Eventually, the guerrillas gain control of the countryside and then march into the collapsing capital city. The Chinese revolution, culminating in victory in 1949, is the classic example. Mao Zedong observed that success in the revolution depended on the support of the rural peasants, for "without the poor peasants, there can be no revolution."

Many of the successful Third World revolutions after 1950 employed guerrilla warfare, including Cuba under Fidel Castro (1959), Vietnam under Ho Chi Minh (1975), and Zimbabwe (formerly Rhodesia) under Robert Mugabe (1980). This strategy is evident in recent struggles in Afghanistan, Algeria, Colombia, and Congo.

Strategy 4: Democratic revolution. **Democratic revolution** occurs when *legal, generally nonviolent political action is effectively mounted to achieve a fundamental transformation of the political system*. In one form, the population uses the democratic electoral process to select a leadership elite, which then dismantles the existing political system and creates a new one. Examples of this form are the rise of Hitler and establishment of the Third Reich in Germany (1933) and the election of the anti-Sandinista coalition in Nicaragua (1990).

In a second form, widespread but generally nonviolent resistance to a regime forces the elite to resign (Thompson 2003). The new leadership, though not initially elected, implements fundamental transformations in the political system. This occurred in such Soviet bloc states as Czechoslovakia, East Germany, and Poland in the late 1980s. More recently, there have been numerous instances of a third form that falls short of revolution but does involve extensive, generally peaceful demonstrations against a leader that result in resignation and the rapid installation of a significantly

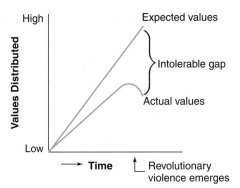

▶ FIGURE 12.3
"J-curve"
description of
revolution
Source: Derived from
Davies 1971.

different political regime. Among the many examples are the Philippines (2001), Georgia's "Rose Revolution" (2003), Ukraine's "Orange Revolution" (2004), and Kyrgyzstan's "Tulip Revolution" (2005).

Conditions for revolution.   The conditions under which political revolution occurs is an issue that has fascinated many people, especially those who want to analyze revolution and those who want to lead a successful revolution. The most widely cited studies of major historical revolutions include those by Hannah Arendt (1963), Crane Brinton (1957), Chalmers Johnson (1983b), Barrington Moore (1966), and Theda Skocpol (1979).

One long-standing explanation of revolution is substantial inequality, a factor emphasized in analyses from Aristotle to Karl Marx to contemporary theorists. A second general approach is the "theory of rising expectations," associated with Alexis de Tocqueville (1835/1945), James Davies (1971), and others. In this view, the key cause of revolution is a sudden increase in the disparity between the values that the population expects to enjoy from the government and the actual value distribution the population receives. It is also called the *J-curve theory* because, as indicated in Figure 12.3, the *disparity resembles an inverted J*, and revolutionary violence occurs when the disparity becomes substantial.

Empirical analyses have defined certain conditions that are associated with countries in which revolutions occur: (1) conflicting elites; (2) deep ethnic divisions; (3) rapid economic growth, especially when it is followed by a sharp decline in prosperity; (4) a relatively short history as an autonomous state; (5) divisive interventions by actors in the international system; (6) rapid population growth, especially a high proportion of younger people; and (7) social mobilization. None of these is a "necessary condition" for revolution, and unique events are critically important; but the probability of revolution increases as more of these conditions are present.

USE OF FORCE BETWEEN STATES

The final box in Figure 12.1 includes those cases in which both the source and target of violence are states. While this form is primarily referred to as a *war* (discussed in the next section), in some situations the use of violence between states is more limited (Gochman and Maoz 1984):

- In a *blockade*, the military (e.g., ships, troops, munitions) of one state is used to seal off territory (e.g., border crossings, harbors), preventing entry or exit by the rival state.

- In *state-sponsored terrorism*, the state provides financial or material support to groups committing occasional acts of political violence within the rival state.

- A state can engage in a brief, *single use of force*, such as a bombing raid, firing munitions into the enemy state, or rapid invasion for a specific purpose (e.g., the sabotage of a facility).

- In a *clash*, there is a brief engagement between the armed forces of two states, as in a border skirmish.

- In a **low-intensity conflict** *(LIC), a group uses conventional weapons in a rival's territory in a sporadic and prolonged manner that does not involve full-scale military conflict,* with the goal of inflicting maximum harm while suffering few or no casualties (Klare 1988). (The concept of LIC is also applied to situations in which a government or a powerful external state directs persistent uses of violent force against groups resisting the government, such as ethnonationalists or guerrillas.) Despite the label, the violence associated with low-intensity conflict *is* intense for those involved, especially the targets.

War

War *is interstate violence that is sustained and organized and (usually) involves hostilities between the regular military forces of the states.* Such violence is the ultimate mechanism for resolving conflict between states. For those who define politics as conflict resolution, war represents the utter failure of politics. But many probably agree with Karl von Clausewitz's famous dictum: "War is regarded as nothing but a continuation of political activity by other means" (Clausewitz 1833/1967: 87). Thus war is the use of violence by one state to achieve its political goals at the expense of another state.

Robert Ardrey (1966: 27), a well-known ethologist (a person who studies animal behavior to better understand human behavior), wryly observed that "human war has been the most successful of all our cultural traditions." Indeed, the study of world history is usually dominated by wars and recurrent episodes of organized violence among nations and states.

The elimination of war is not among the accomplishments of the modern world. The comprehensive analysis of major interstate wars between 1816 and 1980 found good news: wars are less frequent, are considerably shorter, and involve fewer states. But the bad news is that the number of wars "in progress" at any given time has increased substantially since 1900, and the total number of deaths from war has risen astronomically (Singer 1991; Sivard 1996). Moreover, the post-cold war context has not significantly reduced the number of major armed conflicts. Since 1990, more than half of the world's countries have suffered the enormous costs of a major armed conflict (SIPRI 2008: appendix 1A).

Few of the major recent conflicts are *conventional wars*—that is, wars that entail the direct, sustained confrontation of the military forces of two or more states within

▶ **With his machine gun and teddy-bear backpack, this Liberian preteen is among the world's rapidly growing number of child soldiers.**

a defined space, usually occurring on the soil of one of the combatants. Conflicts that do fit the definition of a conventional war include the Argentina–United Kingdom War (Falklands War, 1982), the Iran–Iraq War (1980–1988), the Iraq–Kuwait War (Persian Gulf War, 1990), the Ecuador–Peru War (1995), the Ethiopia–Eritrea War (1998–2000), and the Iraq–U.S.(-led coalition) War that began in 2003.

Many contemporary conflicts are more complicated mixes of internal, regional, and transborder combatants. While many are not classic wars, analysts combine them with war into a broader category: *major armed conflicts*. Major armed conflicts have three defining characteristics: (1) the use of armed force between two or more governments or one government and at least one organized armed group; (2) at least a thousand battle-related deaths in a year; and (3) conflict over control of the government or territory. In the last two decades, 20 to 30 major armed conflicts were being waged per year (SIPRI 2008).

Africa's "first world war" in Congo (see Box 11.3) seems a prototype of the contemporary unconventional war. At one level, it is an internal civil war between the military forces loyal to President Kabila and several large paramilitary groups that reject his authority to rule. Some of the cleavages underlying that conflict are regional, some are ethnonationalist, and some are based on merely personal animosity and ambition in a situation where no one has a legitimate mandate to rule. In addition, the conflict increasingly includes many non-Congolese combatants: ethnic-based paramilitaries from Rwanda and Burundi; regular military forces from Angola, Namibia, Rwanda, Uganda, and Zimbabwe; and UN peacekeeping forces. Another striking example of these complex "wars" is the bloody conflict in Israel and Palestine, where all forms of political violence collide (see Box 12.2).

The changing nature of many contemporary wars is most evident in the enormous increase in the proportion of civilian deaths. Whereas in World War I there was only one civilian death for every eight military deaths, in World War II there were

BOX 12.2

Ultraviolence Among the Children of Abraham: Israelis and Palestinians

Israelis and Palestinians share a common understanding of their beginnings, yet they split into two nations whose recent history is marked by ultraviolence. Perhaps more than anywhere in the world, virtually every type of political violence in Figure 12.1 occurs with depressing regularity. Helicopter gunships fire missiles at cars to assassinate leaders, suicide bombers kill and maim scores of innocents, bulldozers destroy neighborhoods of homes, bloody wars wreak havoc in several countries. How did things get so bad?

According to legend, the patriarch Abraham settled in and was eventually buried in the land of Canaan, near what is now Hebron, Israel, in about 2000 B.C.E. Abraham developed the foundational principles of a new religion, Judaism. The offspring of one of his two wives (son Isaac and grandson Israel) followed this new religion. The line descending from Abraham's other wife continued to live in the area and did not embrace Judaism. The teachings of Mohammed (born in Mecca in 570 C.E.) attracted most of this line to another new religion, Islam. Arab military conquests in the seventh to tenth centuries added to the near-total religious domination of Islam in the region.

"The children of Israel" (the Jews) lived in the Canaan area from about 1300 to 700 B.C.E. However, before that period and after it until the twentieth century, most of the Jews migrated to many countries. Almost everywhere, the Jews felt themselves to be a target of discrimination and described themselves as part of a wandering and dispersed ("diaspora") nation with no homeland. Thus, in 1897, European Jewish leaders founded the World Zionist Movement, whose central goal was to realize the ancient dream of a Jewish homeland and a sanctuary from anti-Semitism. After a debate in which various locations in Europe, Africa, Latin America, and the Near East were considered, the Zionists concluded that their target for a homeland was the "Promised Land" of Abraham's birth, known as Palestine. They began purchasing land and establishing colonies of Jewish settlers in Palestine. By the outbreak of World War I (1914), they owned 100,000 acres and 70,000 Jews had migrated to Palestine, living alongside more than 800,000 Arab Muslims (see Figure 12.4).

After the war, the United Kingdom was given a mandate to govern Palestine. Under pressure from European Jews, the British government agreed that it would assist the Jews in establishing a Jewish "home" in Palestine. As discrimination against the Jews in Europe reached horrendous levels with the rise of Nazism, the flow of Jewish immigrants to Palestine became a flood. By the outbreak of World War II, the number of Jews there had increased almost sixfold.

The Muslim Arabs in the Palestine area were increasingly distressed by this massive invasion of Jewish "foreigners." Their hostility provoked violence, terrorism, and guerrilla war between extreme groups of Arabs and Jews, as well as against the British occupying army. The recently founded United Nations proposed a plan to split

Box 12.2 *(Continued)*

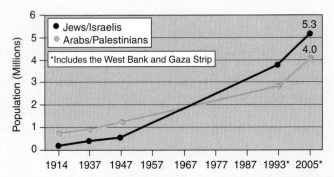

▶ **FIGURE 12.4**
Population in
Palestine/Israel
at key dates

Palestine into two states, maintaining Jerusalem as a shared city under UN trusteeship. The Jews accepted this plan in 1947, but the Arabs rejected it, angry that the invaders, who constituted only one-third of the population, would receive the majority (55 percent) of the land. Two hours before the British mandate in Palestine was to end in 1947, the Jewish leaders declared the founding of a new sovereign state, Israel. The next day, the armies of all the surrounding Arab states (Egypt, Lebanon, Syria, and Transjordan) declared war on Israel. The defeat of these armies by the Israeli Army resulted in 800,000 homeless Palestinians, many of whom fled to neighboring lands.

Full-scale war erupted three more times between Israel and its Arab neighbors (1956, 1967, and 1973). In each case, Israel defeated the Arab armies and conquered more land, the "Occupied Territories" (especially the West Bank and Gaza). By the late 1960s, these territories were inhabited by 1.2 million Palestinians, who were now an unwelcome nation subjugated within the Israeli state. More than 1 million additional Palestinians were exiles living in Jordan and other Arab states. Moreover, Jewish settlements continued to expand, establishing new outposts of Jewish control in the best land in the Occupied Territories.

Frustrated Palestinians formed active resistance groups, most notably the Palestine Liberation Organization (1964) and Hamas (1987). These groups were convinced that only political violence and the destruction of the state of Israel would enable them to regain control of their lands. The combination of civil disobedience, armed resistance, and terrorist acts by Palestinian groups, on the one hand, and the strong and often brutal responses by the Israeli military and Jewish militant groups, on the other hand, has resulted in an endless cycle of violence and retaliation. The more militant groups on each side assume that there are no innocents in the struggle, and they are willing to engage in "whatever means necessary" to protect their land.

The United States, the United Nations, and others have attempted to find an approach that will produce stability and peace in the region, but all agreements have collapsed. The United Nations is committed to a sovereign Palestinian state that will coexist with Israel, some Palestinian groups have renounced terrorism and accept the continued existence of Israel, and some Israelis, including the prime minister, agree that there should be Palestinian self-rule in a fixed territory. But the 2006 election of Hamas as the dominant party in Palestine's government renewed hostilities with Israel and led to a violent split among the Palestinians, with Hamas controlling Gaza and Fatah controlling the West Bank. Brutal violence continues, due to the fundamental distrust and antagonism between the various groups.

Beneath this basic story line there are extraordinarily complex subplots: factional struggles within each nation, disagreements about the level of acceptable compromise, and the complicated agendas of external actors (e.g., other Arab states, the United States, MNCs) regarding Islam, oil, terrorism, and so on. The land of Abraham has become the cauldron in which this volatile stew of violence boils furiously.

two civilian deaths for every military death. In the 1990s, nine out of every ten war deaths were *civilians*, and the major armed conflicts going on since 1990 have been killing more than half a million civilians each year (Sivard 1996: 7, 17). Even more distressing is the huge increase in the total number of deaths in war. Ruth Leger Sivard (1991: 20) notes that in the twentieth century, wars became "shockingly more destructive and deadly" and that there were four times more war deaths than in the preceding 400 years. The first decade of the twenty-first century has been even more deadly.

Worldwide, the more than $1.204 *trillion* per year that states spend directly on the military to support their security goals could, if reallocated to their prosperity goals, greatly enhance their citizens' quality of life. Total world military spending has increased by fully 37 percent between 1997 and 2006 (SIPRI 2008). The problem, of course, is that many policy makers believe that security goals have highest priority, and that without security, no other goals can be achieved. Yet in an era of high-tech warfare, virtually no one feels truly secure. This insecurity leads every state to push itself and its rivals into an accelerating, unending, and potentially devastating expansion of the capacity for massive political violence (recall the discussion of balance of power in Chapter 11).

What Causes War?

Are there fundamental causes of war? Studies have attempted to determine whether some states or their populations have particular attributes that result in a greater propensity to engage in war. These attributes include the state's size, economic system, political system, cultural features, geographic position, wealth, religion, and rate of modernization. Although studies have attempted to isolate the key characteristics of more "warlike" states, their findings are inconclusive, and there are always unique contingencies associated with particular wars. However, empirical research does suggest seven state characteristics that are generally correlated with the likelihood of war (Kegley and Wittkopf 2004: 411–418):

1. *Newer nations* are more likely to initiate war than are mature states.
2. War is more likely in states that have effectively *socialized their citizens to accept the government's actions* on national security.
3. The most warlike states have *rising prosperity* but are *relatively poor*, though not the very poorest states.

4. Countries with *desirable geopolitical features* (i.e., resources and location—recall Chapter 11) have a higher probability of warfare.

5. Countries *less well linked to the global economy* are more likely to engage in war.

6. States that are most *highly militarized*, and especially those that are rapidly expanding their military power, are more warlike.

7. Countries whose political culture reflects a high degree of *nationalism* are more warlike.

(8). The data also indicate that countries with market economies are as likely to participate in war as those with command economies and that democracies are as likely as nondemocracies to be involved in war.

The contemporary global system has created conditions that make many analysts (particularly those with the political idealist perspective described in Chapter 11) optimistic that war between the most powerful countries is highly unlikely. They emphasize two major forces that limit the likelihood of such wars: (1) democracy has spread to many major countries, and *established democracies rarely fight each other* (the **democratic peace**); and (2) globalization has increased countries' economic interdependence and the importance of transnational organizations, both of which cause countries to recognize their shared interests and create strong inducements for cooperation (Jervis 2002; Russett and Oneal 2001; but see Mansfield and Snyder 2002). However, realists point to the many significant interstate conflicts that continue, and they postulate that the dominance of a single great power (the United States) will ultimately decline, resulting in major conflict between it and rising powers (Mearshimer 2001).

Do you think some states have a more extensive history of interstate conflict than others? One comprehensive study analyzed the frequency with which more than 100 countries engaged in interstate conflict between 1816 and 1976. The analysis focused on 14 types of "militarized interstate disputes," including threats of force, displays of force, and uses of force described in this chapter. A state is considered to be in a dispute whether it is the initiator or the target of the conflict. Since some countries have considerably longer histories as states, the analysis measured disputes per year of the state's existence. The study concluded that less than one-third of the states, primarily major powers, initiated more than 70 percent of all disputes, were the primary targets of more than 60 percent of the disputes, and were also most likely to enter disputes among other countries. The five most dispute-prone states in the analysis, in order, are: Israel, the United Kingdom, India, the United States, and Pakistan, all of whom averaged more than one dispute per year. The next five are Germany, Russia/Soviet Union, France, China, and Italy (Gochman and Maoz 1984).

More recently, an empirical study has used 24 indicators such as conflicts, military expenditures, and relations with neighboring countries to measure the level of peacefulness of states, creating a "Global Peace Index." This index emphasizes a state's actions to sustain a situation of positive nonviolent conditions, not merely the presence of manifest violence. Among the 140 countries examined, the five *least* peaceful countries are Iraq, Somalia, Sudan, Afghanistan, and Israel. And the five most peaceful major countries are Denmark, Norway, New Zealand, Japan, and Ireland. Germany ranks 14th in peacefulness, and Italy and France are in the top 40, while the United States ranks 97th (Economist Intelligence Unit 2008).

At the "ultimate" level, there are three broad alternative explanations for the causes of war:

1. War can be attributed to *scarcity in nature*. Because the consumption goals of states are greater than the natural resources available, states undertake war to protect or capture resources from other states. Thus states struggle with each other for the control of such resources as people, food, minerals, and strategic locations (CNA 2007; Klare 2004).

2. War can be attributed to the *inadequacy of institutions*. In this view, neither the existing sociopolitical structure nor the rules governing the conduct among states are adequate to prevent states from using force to achieve their objectives. Thus states are guided by self-interest, and there are no conflict-resolution mechanisms that prevent the occasional eruption of large-scale interstate violence.

3. War can be explained by *human nature*. From this perspective, humans are innately aggressive as a biological species. Humans are virtually the only species that engages in widespread killing of its own kind. And humans, it is claimed, are acquisitive, competitive, and selfish by nature rather than by nurture. Thus war becomes a predictable group-level manifestation of these inherent qualities. A variation on this explanation emphasizes the critical importance of an aggressive leader who draws her country into war (Stoessinger 2007). This gender reference prompts the comment that there is a subfield of international relations theory that asserts female leaders are far less likely than males to resort to violence in interstate disputes (Tickner 2001).

The first and second explanations are clearly associated with the idealist perspective outlined in Chapter 11. And the third reflects the essence of political realism. Each of the three explanations of war also suggests possible "solutions" that might eliminate war:

1. If the problem is scarcity of natural resources, one might look to *technological solutions*, as states develop new techniques to use natural resources more efficiently and to develop abundant substitutes for scarce resources.

2. If the problem is inadequate institutions, the need is for *social engineering*—for the creation of organizational arrangements that more effectively structure the relations among individuals and states. In the political domain, this might ultimately entail the creation of a viable world government.

3. If the problem is human nature, the solution is found in *human engineering* by means of comprehensive political socialization or perhaps even genetic manipulation to create a population with the "proper" qualities.

There is some evidence to support each of these three general explanations of the causes of war. But there is also sufficient counterevidence so that none of the three positions is compelling as a complete explanation. Neither an abundance of natural resources nor advanced technology has stopped intergroup violence. And while there are societies whose members have not been driven by human nature into warlike behavior against their neighbors, no set of human institutions has been shown inevitably to generate war or perpetuate peace between states.

While the complete elimination of war might be impossible, it does seem that a combination of material abundance, effective institutions, and thorough socialization might reduce the incidence of war. This leads to more questions: Can this combination be identified and implemented by political actors? Might the solution not produce human conditions nearly as unpalatable as occasional wars?

EVALUATING POLITICAL VIOLENCE: MEANS AND ENDS

Political violence must be understood as a failure of institutionalized political action. A strong and persuasive normative perspective contends that political violence, especially within a country, is unacceptable, deviant behavior. Conservative ideology provides the most explicit condemnation of such violence, concluding that the only legacy of violence is to undermine order in the society. Moreover, the resort to violence is part of an erroneous belief that radical social change can lead to lasting improvements. As Englishman Edmund Burke (1729–1797) observed: "Time is required to produce that union of minds which alone can produce all the good we aim at. Our patience will achieve more than our force" (Burke 1790/1955: 197).

A contrary perspective argues that political violence is often the best or even the only mechanism for liberation from oppression and tyranny. This view contends that most societies are controlled by dominant elites who manipulate the state to serve their interests, not the collective good. If a government and its leaders refuse to be constrained by a limited mandate and are not responsive to the citizens, then the people have the right to overthrow them by any available means. Although this perspective is mainly associated with class theorists and Marxist ideology, the counterpoint to Burke is provided by another English political thinker, classical liberal John Locke (1632–1704), who argued that citizens create government to protect their rights to life, liberty, and property. If the existing government does not serve these purposes well, argued Locke, the people can and must revolt in order to replace tyranny and create a new and better government (Locke 1690/1963: 466).

Political violence can be a source of either progress or nearly universal suffering and chaos. Clearly, fundamental issues about means and ends are tied up with any assessment of political violence. On the one hand, if the maintenance of public order and political institutionalization are valued goals, you must consider whether resorting to political violence undermines longer-term prospects for peaceful, orderly governance. Many cynics would share Italian novelist Ignazio Silone's (1937) assessment: "Every revolution begins as a movement of liberation but ends as tyranny." On the other hand, if you value social and political justice, it is important to consider whether the processes of political violence can be a legitimate means of last resort to ensure such justice. Those who justify some forms of political violence might sympathize with African American Eldridge Cleaver's claim that "a slave who dies of natural causes will not balance two dead flies on the scale of eternity."

There are no tidy answers to the question of whether or when political violence is justifiable. Perhaps one way to organize your own assessment of political violence is to reflect on three basic questions:

1. Are the means of political violence unacceptable under *every* possible circumstance?

2. If you answered no, could an outcome emerge from the use of political violence that is so preferable to the existing situation that establishing the precedent of using political violence is justifiable?

3. If you answered yes to question 2, what specific circumstances would be necessary to justify the resort to political violence?

These issues about the conditions under which political violence might be legitimate are germane on an even larger scale regarding the justification of war. Despite the massive human and financial costs of war, few would support the proposition that there are absolutely no conditions under which war is justified. But what are the circumstances that justify war?

A classic justification is the doctrine of *self-defense*, a position associated with Augustine (354–430 C.E.). A victim of an unprovoked attack has the right to use violence as a means of protection. Apart from total pacifists, few would reject the principle of self-defense as a legitimate rationale for violence. But the application of this principle might be a subject of considerable disagreement, especially in relations among states. Here are some examples: Might state A engage in nonviolent actions that are so provocative that state B is justified in responding with violence? What if the initial violence against state B is by an actor from state A who does not have the sanction or the explicit support of state A? What if the violence by state A was unintentional? What if the initial violence is within the territory of state A but is perceived as directly harmful to citizens or interests of state B? What if state B uses violence to prevent state A from the (expected) use of far more substantial violence? What if the violent response of state B is of far greater magnitude than the violence by state A? Wars sometimes develop because of such patterns of misperception, accident, preemption, and incremental escalation (Schelling 1960).

Frequently, however, war is justified on a more ambiguous rationale associated with Ambrose (339–397 C.E.), as the *defense of universal principles*. In this view, "man has a moral duty to employ force to resist active wickedness, for to refrain from hindering evil when possible is tantamount to promoting it." In the contemporary world, however, it is difficult to identify truly universal principles in whose defense war is always justifiable. Even the interpretations of "active wickedness" and "evil" are not shared across all cultures. For example, many citizens in most countries believed that Iraq's Saddam Hussein was an evil ruler. However, most did not find this an adequate justification for U.S. President George W. Bush's insistence on a "preemptive" war, especially in the absence of compelling evidence that Iraq endangered other countries with weapons of mass destruction that could not be eliminated except by war.

In most cases of international political violence, a justification based on universal principles is invoked. State power is used against other states in the name of principles such as freedom, social justice, human rights, self-determination, territorial integrity, egalitarianism, religious freedom, religious orthodoxy, anticommunism, communism, and so on. But all states do not accept a single vision of natural law that provides universal principles to govern international relations. Moreover, the international system itself has not implemented powerful and effective institutional mechanisms that eliminate conflict. Thus occasional outbreaks of interstate conflict and war are inevitable.

The crucial point is that the context of international politics is essentially *amoral*. Recognizing this fact is the key to understanding most behavior in international relations, whether diplomatic activities, alliances, or war. In some instances, a state's actions in the international environment are constrained by the state's views of morality and universal principles. But in other instances, a state's decision makers might determine that virtually any action is acceptable if the action seems to further the state's security, stability, and prosperity goals. If either view is correct, what are the chances that contemporary states will ever meet the requirement of the UN Charter that states "settle their international disputes by peaceful means in such a manner that international peace and security, and justice, are not endangered"?

In the current technological era, the mechanisms for committing violence are more efficient, powerful, and horrifying than at any time in human history. The implications of this fact are especially evident in the relations between states. But even subnational political groups can now inflict massive and destructive political violence. Thus questions about the use of force and the balance between liberation and destruction are more pressing now than at any time in human history.

KEY CONCEPTS

civil war	guerrilla war	revolution
class conflict	international terrorism	riot
coup	J-curve theory	separatist violence
democratic peace	low-intensity conflict	state-sponsored
democratic revolution	nation-based violence	terrorism
domestic terrorism	political society	terrorism
establishment violence	political violence	violence
genocide	rebellion	war

FOR FURTHER CONSIDERATION

1. Is the state more to be feared than its enemies? Assess the implications of the prevalence during the twentieth century of "death by government," in which the state is the actor and the state's citizens are its target.

2. Summarize the key elements of a three-way debate between an absolute pacifist, a committed revolutionary, and yourself regarding the conditions under which political violence is justifiable.

3. It is suggested that much of contemporary political violence is nation based. Analyze the nation-based conflicts about which you are aware. Is most of the violence caused by fundamental antipathy between two nationality groups due to differences in ethnicity, religion, language, and so on? Or is the violence primarily motivated by other issues, such as inequality and class conflict, quest for power, geopolitics, or some other cause?

4. Must every revolution end in tyranny (as suggested by Ignazio Silone)? Can you identify a revolution that, by the criteria you establish, can be viewed as a success?

5. Which of the characteristics of warlike states on page 349–350 is most surprising to you? Why? What characteristic did you expect that is not among those listed?

FOR FURTHER READING

Brecher, Michael, and Jonathan Wilkenfeld. (1997). *A Study of Crisis*. Ann Arbor: University of Michigan Press. A comprehensive, usable database from the International Crisis Behavior project provides valuable information on 412 crises between 1929 and 1992, following the authors' thoughtful analyses of and generalizations about the patterns of interstate crises.

Cimbala, Stephen J. (2000). *Nuclear Strategy in the Twenty-First Century*. Westport, CT: Praeger. A provocative analysis of the implications of nuclear proliferation and high-tech warfare on the relations among states. Among other arguments, Cimbala explains why the danger of nuclear war is increasing, and why weaker states and marginal groups are gaining greater advantage from nuclear weapons than the major powers in the nuclear club.

Cinema of War. Film, in addition to literature, has often been a compelling visual and visceral medium for evoking the heroism and absurdity of war. Among the films that are especially effective are: Allan Dwan, *The Sands of Iwo Jima* (1949); Francis Ford Coppola, *Apocalypse Now* (1979, 2001); Samuel Fuller, *The Big Red One* (1980); David Lean, *In Which We Serve* (1942); Lewis Milestone, *All Quiet on the Western Front* (1930) and *Pork Chop Hill* (1959); Jean Renoir, *The Grand Illusion* (1937); and Oliver Stone, *Platoon* (1986).

Freedman, Lawrence, Ed. (1994). *War*. New York: Oxford University Press. A splendid collection of readings, ranging from the greatest classical treatments of the reasons for and the nature of war to significant contemporary analyses.

Goldstein, Joshua S. (2001). *War and Gender: How Gender Shapes the War System and Vice Versa*. Cambridge: Cambridge University Press. This widely discussed book explores why warfare is dominated by men, concluding generally that it is primarily due to culturally constructed male domination and "militarized masculine stereotypes" rather than genetic differences.

Goldstone, Jack A., Ed. (1994). *Revolutions: Theoretical, Comparative, and Historical Studies*. 2nd ed. San Diego, CA: Harcourt Brace. A readable set of articles that includes both detailed case studies of revolutions and more analytic work that attempts to develop generalizations about revolutionary violence.

Gourevitch, Philip. (1998). *We Wish to Inform You That Tomorrow We Will Be Killed with Our Families: Stories from Rwanda*. New York: Farrar, Straus and Giroux. A gripping exploration of the manner in which ethnonationalist rhetoric was used to mobilize the Hutu people to massacre almost one million Tutsis and Hutu moderates in Rwanda in the mid-1990s, while the international community was unwilling to intervene to prevent the genocide.

Gurr, Ted Robert. (2000). *Peoples Versus States: Minorities at Risk in the New Century*. Washington, DC: United States Institute of Peace Press. Based on the valuable Minorities at Risk Project database, the book is an exceptionally rich blend of data-based analyses and case studies of nation-based conflict.

Gutman, Roy, and David Rieff, Eds. (1999). *Crimes of War: What the Public Should Know*. New York: W. W. Norton. Authorities on the laws of war and experienced members of the media offer diverse and enlightening discussions on the legal and ethical issues regarding war crimes and international humanitarian law, with powerful commentaries on such cases as Cambodia, Chechnya, and Rwanda, and dramatic illustrations by photojournalists.

Hoffman, Bruce. (1998). *Inside Terrorism*. New York: Columbia University Press. A broad-ranging and troubling exploration of terrorism, with particular attention to the recent evolution of strategies and goals of terrorists.

Jenkins, Philip. (2003). *Images of War: What We Can and Can't Know About Terrorism*. New York: Aldine de Gruyter. A fascinating array of examples is provided to examine how stories about terrorism are transformed in public discussion, especially by the media.

Klare, Michael. (2001). *Resource Wars*. New York: Henry Holt. A persuasive argument about the "new geography of conflict" between states in the early twenty-first century. Grounded in specifics from such areas as the Persian Gulf and the Nile Basin, the argument is made that wars will increasingly be driven primarily by geopolitical struggles over scarce natural resources, such as water, oil, gas, minerals, and timbers.

O'Brien, Tim. (1990). *The Things They Carried*. New York: Doubleday Broadway Books. In 22 fictional short stories about an American military platoon in the Vietnam War, the author powerfully conveys universal themes regarding the horror of war from the perspective of the individual soldier.

Parker, Geoffrey, Ed. (2005). *The Cambridge History of Warfare*. 2nd ed. London: Cambridge University Press. An ambitious series of essays examining many aspects of war in the Western world, from ancient Greece through recent wars in the Middle East. A key theme is that Western technology and prosperity produced a dominant military that ensured Western global supremacy.

Sassoon, Siegfried. (1968). *Collected Poems: 1908–1956*. London: Faber and Faber. The deeply moving poems about war by a young British intellectual who suffered the horrific experiences of European trench warfare during World War I.

Singer, P. W. (2005). *Children at War*. New York: Pantheon. A scholar and former military advisor to the CIA explores the chilling and heartbreaking rise of children as soldiers in many conflict zones. He blends evidence and the actual commentaries of many child soldiers to describe how they are recruited and trained and become ruthless warriors.

SIPRI. (Stockholm International Peace Research Institute). http://www.sipri.se. A revealing yearly discussion and assessment providing comparative data on most states in the world, reflecting the current aspects of military expenditure, war, and arms control.

Stoessinger, John G. (2007). *Why Nations Go to War*. 10th ed. Boston: Bedford. A readable set of descriptive case studies of modern wars, particularly emphasizing individual behavior and motives, including World War I, Korea, Vietnam, India–Pakistan, Israel–Arabs, Iran–Iraq, and Yugoslavia.

Walter, Barbara F., and Jack Snyder, Eds. (1999). *Civil Wars, Insecurity, and Intervention*. New York: Columbia University Press. Centering on thoughtful case studies of the recent civil wars in Bosnia, Cambodia, Somalia, and Rwanda, important scholars analyze why the international community has not been particularly effective in either preventing the outbreak of or resolving civil wars.

Walzer, Michael. (1992). *Just and Unjust War*. 2nd ed. New York: Basic Books. A political philosopher presents a careful argument about the morality of war, grounded in the context of numerous actual wars.

Weiss, Peter. (1965). *Marat-Sade: The Persecution and Assassination of Jean-Paul Marat as Performed by the Inmates of the Asylum at Charenton Under the Direction of the Marquis de Sade*. New York: Atheneum. A brilliant play (and a dazzling film with the same title directed by Peter Brooks) offering a debate about revolution between Jean-Paul Marat, a leader of the French Revolution who attempts to retain his idealism about revolutionary change despite having become a victim of extremists, and the Marquis de Sade, the ultimate cynic.

Weitz, Eric D. (2005). *A Century of Genocide: Utopias of Race and Nation*. Princeton, NJ: Princeton University Press. A historian offers a compelling and readable comparison of the way in which four major genocides in the twentieth century (under Stalin, Hitler, and Pol Pot and in the former Yugoslavia) drew popular support through the strategic mixture of nationalism and racial identity.

ON THE WEB

http://www.amnesty.org

Amnesty International is the world's leading NGO monitoring establishment violence and human rights abuses and attempting to mobilize citizen support to pressure governments to end such actions.

http://wps.cfc.forces.gc.ca/en/index.php

The Information Resource Centre of the Canadian Forces College provides links to numerous sites detailing with current major international conflicts.

http://www.sipri.org

The site of the Stockholm International Peace Research Institute, which conducts research on questions of conflict and cooperation relevant to international peace and security, includes rich databases and significant articles on topics of peace and violence.

http://www.terrorism.com

The site of the Terrorism Research Center, Inc., which describes itself as an independent institute dedicated to research on terrorism, information warfare and security, critical infrastructure protection, homeland security, and other issues of low-intensity political violence.

http://mipt.org

The National Memorial Institute for the Prevention of Terrorism maintains one of the most comprehensive and current databases on more than 20,000 incidents of global terrorism.

http://www.usip.org

This site was established and is funded by the U.S. Congress with the goal of preventing conflict, ending current conflicts, and aiding in reconstruction after the hostilities.

http://www.nctc.gov

The National Counterterrorism Center has become the major source of information and data from the U.S. government regarding global terrorism.

http://www.un.org/terrorism/

On the official site of the United Nations, one can access both Security Council and General Assembly resolutions related to political violence.

http://www.ccc.nps.navy.mil/si/

The Center for Contemporary Conflict is hosted by the Naval Postgraduate School in California. The site provides information regarding current and emerging security concerns in all regions of the world, including many position papers and briefings.

http://www.hrw.org

The electronic home of Human Rights Watch provides access to an extensive database regarding human rights violations taking place throughout the international community.

http://www.sfcg.org

The site of Search for Common Ground, the world's largest NGO working on conflict resolution, is an excellent source for material on this topic.

http://www.historyguy.com

The electronic home of the "History Guy" provides a number of links to detailed information, articles and news reports related to political conflicts.

http://www.pcr.uu.se

The Conflict Data Project at Uppsala University (Sweden) maintains a rich and current database on armed conflicts in the world.

CHAPTER 13

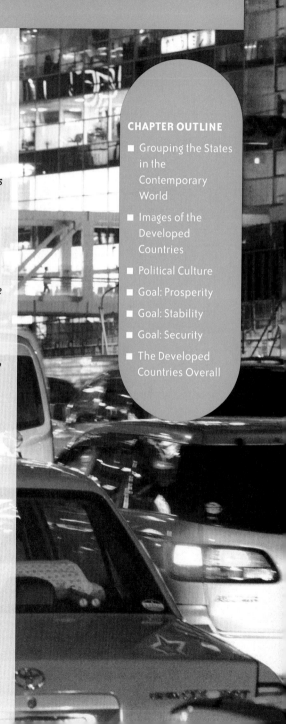

THE DEVELOPED COUNTRIES

N
o one that encounters prosperity does not also encounter danger.Heraclitus, 535–475 B.C.E.

The point in history at which we stand is full of promise and danger. The world will either move forward toward unity and widely shared prosperity – or it will move apart.

—*Franklin D. Roosevelt, 1882–1945, President, United States*

It will never be possible to stress enough the evil that the 35-hour week has done to our country. How can we retain this mad idea that by working less, we will produce more wealth and create jobs?

—*Nicolas Sarkozy. 1955–, President, France*

The question is not whether we are able to change but whether we are changing fast enough.

—*Angela Merkel, 1954–, Chancellor, Germany*

GROUPING THE STATES IN THE CONTEMPORARY WORLD

Chapters 13–15 aim at the near impossible: to characterize the key features of politics, both within and between the more than 190 countries in the contemporary political world. As you discovered in Part One, a central goal of political analysis is to develop general descriptions and explanations of political phenomena. To generalize about all these countries, it is desirable to use a taxonomic system that allows us to discuss and compare a few groups that include most states. It can also be illuminating to focus comparison on the countries that are in the same group.

Given the complexity and variations among states, no taxonomy is fully satisfactory. And different approaches to classification might make more sense, depending on the kinds of issues that are being explored. One of the most conventional ways to classify countries is by geographic region. It is not unreasonable to assume that countries that share geographic space also share other characteristics. Of course, this is not the case for all issues and all regional neighbors. Consider, for example, North Korea and South Korea, or Israel and Egypt. A regional classification of many of the countries in the world is the horizontal dimension in Table 13.1.

A second common approach to classification is based on level of economic development. The World Bank (2008), for example, uses GNI per capita to distinguish high-income economies, upper and lower middle-income economies, and low-income economies. It makes a yearly adjustment to the thresholds for each grouping and includes a variety of "economies" (ministates, territories) that are not member states of the United Nations. The World Bank approach is the vertical dimension in Table 13.1.

Either of these taxonomies is reasonable (as are others you might consider, such as democracies and nondemocracies; large, medium, and small countries; the different cultural "civilizations" proposed by Huntington (1996), etc.). However, this chapter develops an alternative taxonomy, primarily based on the concept of level of development, that provides the framework for grouping and analyzing countries in Chapters 13–15. This taxonomy is based on *two* dimensions of development. It begins with a measure of *economic development*. It then adds a *social development* dimension, guided by the broader conception of development discussed in Chapter 10.

Economic development. The most widely used measure of economic development is the total value of goods produced in a country divided by the population of the country. Box 8.1 described the two main indicators: GDP per capita and GNI per capita. The taxonomy created here utilizes GDP per capita but, unlike the World Bank, uses the form that includes the correction for purchasing power parity (PPP). As noted in Box 8.1, PPP seems a useful means to compare the relative levels of economic development in a manner that reflects the different value of money across countries.

Social development. To enrich the classificatory scheme, this book employs a second dimension, grounded in the types of organizational, technological, and attitudinal development discussed in Chapter 10. Every country is a mix of complex and

▶ **TABLE 13.1**
Distribution of Selected Countries by Development Level (GDP/capita) and Region

	Sub-Saharan Africa	East Asia and the Pacific	South and Central Asia	Latin America and Caribbean	North Africa and Middle East	Europe/Other
High Income Countries ($11,116 or more)		Brunei Japan New Zealand Singapore South Korea Taiwan		Barbados	Israel Kuwait Qatar Saudi Arabia United Arab Emirates	Austria Canada Czech Republic Denmark Estonia Finland France Germany Greece Iceland Ireland Italy Luxembourg Malta Netherlands Norway Portugal Slovenia Spain Sweden Switzerland United Kingdom United States
Upper Middle Income Countries ($3,596–$11,115)	Botswana *Equatorial Guinea* Gabon Mauritius Seychelles South Africa	Malaysia	Kazakhstan	Argentina Brazil Chile Costa Rica Dominica Mexico Panama Uruguay Venezuela	Lebanon Libya Oman Turkey	Bulgaria Croatia Hungary Latvia Lithuania Montenegro Poland Romania Russia Serbia Slovakia
Lower Middle Income Countries ($906–$3,595)	Angola Cameroon Rep. Congo Lesotho Namibia Swaziland	China Fiji Indonesia Philippines Thailand	Armenia Azerbaijan *Bhutan* Georgia Sri Lanka Turkmenistan	Bolivia Columbia Cuba Dominican Rep. Ecuador El Salvador Guatemala	Algeria *Djibouti* Egypt Iran Iraq Jordan Morocco	Albania Belarus Bosnia-Herzegovina Macedonia Moldova Ukraine

Legend: **Developed** Transitional **Developing** (*Least Developed*)

(Continued)

▶ **TABLE 13.1**

Distribution of Selected Countries by Development Level (GDP/capita) and Region (*Continued*)

	Sub-Saharan Africa	East Asia and the Pacific	South and Central Asia	Latin America and Caribbean	North Africa and Middle East	Europe/Other
Lower Middle Income Countries ($906–$3,595) (continued)				Guyana Honduras Jamaica Nicaragua Paraguay Peru	Palestine Syria Tunisia	
Low Income Countries ($905 or less)	Benin Burkina Faso Burundi Central African Rep. Chad Comoros Congo, Dem. Rep. Cote d'Ivoire Eritrea Ethiopia The Gambia Ghana Guinea Guinea-Bissau Kenya Liberia Madagascar Malawi Mali Mauritania Mozambique Niger Nigeria Rwanda Senegal Sierra Leone Somalia Sudan Tanzania Togo Uganda Zambia Zimbabwe	Cambodia Laos Mongolia Myanmar Nepal North Korea Vietnam	Afghanistan Bangladesh India Pakistan Kyrgyzstan Tajikstan Uzbekistan	Haiti	Yemen	

Developed Transitional **Developing** (*Least Developed*)

Note: The three major classifications are based on Figure 13.1; *Least Developed* is from World Bank (2008).

simple organizational structures, high and low technologies, different trajectories of health and welfare, modern and traditional attitudes. But in relative terms, there are substantial cross-national differences in countries' general levels on these social components of development. The four specific indicators in this index of social development measure the country's level of adult literacy, extent of urbanization, mortality rate to age five, and average number of televisions per household. Each country's values on these four indicators (weighted equally) are combined into scores ranging from 0 to 40. In combination, these measures reflect key underlying aspects of relative social development, as reflected in the pervasiveness of knowledge, urban lifestyles, health and longevity, and modern communications in the environment of the population. Figure 13.1 locates a selection of countries on the two dimensions and suggests labels for clusters of countries.

The Developed Countries of the Global North

The countries in the upper-right part of Figure 13.1 are primarily those usually referred to as the ***developed countries***; they are also called the ***Global North*** and the ***First World***. The developed countries group includes most of the countries with the highest levels of GDP per capita in the world, and these states also rank relatively high on the social dimensions of development. They are generally urbanized and secularized countries, with highly specialized and institutionalized organizational systems. The population enjoys relatively high levels of health and welfare. Their technological

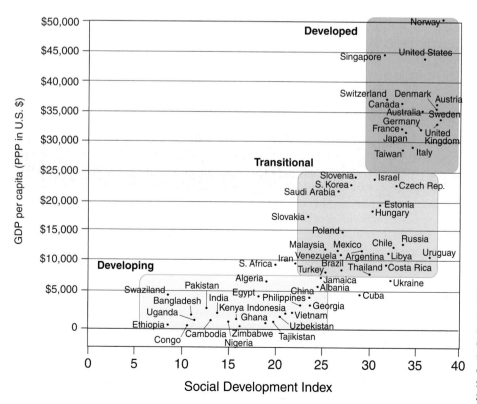

▶ **FIGURE 13.1**
Classification of selected countries based on economic and social development

Sources: World Bank 2008; UNDP, 2007

infrastructure is advanced, and most people are frequently and directly involved with advanced technologies of communications, transportation, and information. These developed countries are also sometimes referred to as (1) the *advanced industrial countries*, because of their large, sophisticated manufacturing sectors, or (2) the *postindustrial societies*, because of the growing dominance of the knowledge-based and service-based sectors of their economies.

The Developing Countries of the Global South

Social scientists, political actors, and the media frequently refer to a large group of countries as the *developing countries,* a term used in this book to designate a group of more than 140 countries. As you would expect, these countries have lower levels of economic development and are relatively less developed on the technological, organizational, and attitudinal dimensions than the developed countries. Thus, in Figure 13.1, the developing countries are primarily clustered in the lower-left quadrant.

Beginning in the late 1950s, many of these developing countries were also called the *Third World*. Initially, this term was applied in the context of the cold war (the late 1940s to the late 1980s) to those states that, by their own definition, were "nonaligned": the country's leaders claimed their country was not under the domination of either the United States and its allies (the *First World*) or the Soviet Union and its allies (the *Second World*). In the post-cold war world, some commentators still refer to virtually all developing countries as the Third World; however, other analysts contend that the term is no longer useful because these countries are so varied (Lewis 1999). Some analysts now refer to this group of countries as the *Global South* because nearly all of them are located geographically south of the developed countries (the *Global North*). The large cluster of countries explored in Chapter 14 as "the developing countries" is a diverse group. Chapter 14 will focus on this group and suggest other criteria by which it can be further categorized into subsets.

The Transitional Developed Countries

The developed countries and the developing countries are standard categories in analyses by governmental agencies and social scientists. But the countries in Figure 13.1 that are on the boundaries between these two broad groupings are particularly difficult to classify. At this time, the levels of economic or social development in these countries put them "in the middle." In this book, many of these countries in the middle of Figure 13.1 are called *transitional developed countries* to reflect their middle range, and sometimes their high rate of change, on one or both dimensions of development.

Although all the countries in the world are always in transition, Chapter 15 will distinguish and examine the two subsets of transitional countries identified in Figure 13.1. Each of these subsets is made up of countries with some important commonalities in their economic situation or political culture. These countries also face interesting challenges, and their approaches to achieving their goals are worth studying.

One subset is composed of some of the countries that emerged after the breakup of the Soviet Union as well as its former Eastern and Central European allies. This group of *postcommunist developed countries* (PCDCs) includes such states as Bulgaria, the Czech Republic, Estonia, Hungary, Poland, and Russia. These states are high on most dimensions of social development, especially in the attitudinal and organizational domains, and most have moderately high (by world standards) levels of economic development. Most are attempting to transform their economic systems from command oriented to market based and move their political systems toward democratization. The World Bank (2008) refers to them as the "transitional economies."

The second group of transitional countries examined in Chapter 15 is called the *newly industrializing countries* (NICs). The NICs (also called NIEs, newly industrializing economies) are characterized by rapidly growing, export-centered economies in which substantial value is added to goods during the production process (recall Chapter 10). Most NICs are included in one of two subgroups with distinctive regional and political-cultural differences: East Asia (e.g., Malaysia, South Korea, Thailand) and Latin America (e.g., Argentina, Chile, Mexico). On the economic dimension and increasingly on the social dimension, the leading NICs are reaching levels of development that approach those of some of the developed countries.

Thus Chapters 13–15 examine the developed countries, the developing countries, and the transitional developed countries. Each chapter describes critical issues for countries in these groups as they attempt to achieve the key goals of prosperity, stability, and security. We emphasize general patterns and similarities within each group, but you should keep these points in mind:

- There are substantial differences among states within each group, especially among the large number of states lumped together as the "developing countries."
- Each state has unique features that are lost in such generalized discussion.
- In some instances, a trait is more similar among certain states across groups rather than among all the states within one group.

As these qualifications suggest, this method of grouping countries for analysis and generalizations is not perfect. Like any taxonomy (see the Appendix), there is an attempt to create groups that can be distinguished analytically, are based on some specifiable criteria, and seem to make sense. However, not every country will fit neatly into a category. Examples of this in the framework in Figure 13.1 include some resource-rich (particularly oil) states in the Middle East and Africa and some PCDCs that have had particularly severe economic declines in the transition to market economies. The categories proposed here are acceptable if their use provides clarification and insight and, ideally, if they facilitate the development of generalizations and theory. As a political analyst, *you* should assess the utility of this taxonomy relative to alternative ways of grouping countries for analysis. The remainder of Chapter 13 focuses explicitly on the developed countries of the Global North.

IMAGES OF THE DEVELOPED COUNTRIES

When you think of countries in the developed world, what images come to mind?

Anyone reading this book has probably lived in at least one of the developed countries listed in Table 13.1. Among other things, you might envision large cities with tall buildings, extensive use of high technologies such as computers and cell phones, liberal democracies, an ethic of individualism, a generally high standard of living, and quality medical care.

What traits do *you* think best characterize life in the developed countries? As you come up with your own list, you might become aware of how difficult it is to capture complex reality with straightforward descriptors. The life of a poor farmer in rural Mississippi is different from that of a wealthy banker in Zurich, a housewife in a suburb of Yokohama, an unemployed factory worker in Milan, or a teenager in the Australian outback. This is a further reminder that the generalizations offered in these chapters will, at best, capture broad tendencies that oversimplify the diversity of political situations. We begin with a brief discussion of political culture in the developed countries.

POLITICAL CULTURE

Each of the developed countries contains a variety of political cultures. While the political cultures vary across countries and time, they can be characterized broadly in terms of the tension and balance between elements of the three ideologies outlined in Chapter 2: classical liberalism, conservatism, and democratic socialism.

Classical liberal ideology is the basis of the assertion by some individuals and groups in the developed countries that their governments have grown far too large and too interventionist. To promote greater individual and economic freedom, they believe their government should reduce its regulation of both the economy and behavior in private life and that it should facilitate globalization and free trade.

Conservatism shares with classical liberalism an antagonism toward the extensive use of government taxing and spending policies to redistribute wealth in the direction of greater equality. But those influenced by conservatism do advocate a strong role for government in preserving the global preeminence of the developed countries through military strength and an assertive foreign policy, in encouraging economic entrepreneurship, and in maintaining order within societies that seem increasingly disorderly. Conservatives also promote government policies that support the family, religious, and moral values that they believe are being undermined by modern culture and multiculturalism. For these reasons, conservatives are more uneasy with many of the social impacts of globalization.

In contrast, those influenced by democratic socialism advocate an activist state whose policies direct some of the developed country's substantial societal wealth to enhance the quality of life for all the citizens. Government policies should enable everyone to receive adequate education, health care, shelter, and security against economic hardship. And state policies should mitigate negative effects of the market-oriented political economy by regulating business practices and providing for infrastructure needs, such as transportation systems. Democratic socialists are also concerned about limiting the negative impacts of globalization, particularly the declining economic standing of many classes of workers and the degradation of the environment.

Since citizens enjoy relatively free political expression in the developed countries, there are strong and articulate advocates of each of these three ideologies, as well as proponents for an array of other ideologies such as environmentalism, fascism, feminism, and religious fundamentalism. This diversity of ideologies affects the belief systems of most individuals and the collective political culture of each country. As every developed country pursues the major political goals of prosperity, stability, and security, its policy decisions are influenced by the current ideological balance within its political leadership and its political culture, as well as by such factors as its history, culture, economic situation, and distribution of political power. In most of the developed countries, the period from 1945 to the mid-1970s was characterized by relatively greater support for policies associated with democratic socialism; since then, the balance has shifted back and forth, but generally toward more conservative and classical liberal values.

GOAL: PROSPERITY

The developed countries pursue the goal of prosperity (and its components of economic growth and development and welfare distribution) with great energy. The emphasis is on sustaining a high level of economic growth under the assumption that this will generate an expanding economic base that directly provides more material benefits to the population and also enables government to distribute greater welfare to the citizens.

Mixed Economy

To achieve prosperity, these countries have relied on a mixed political economy, which includes considerable private ownership and control of productive resources (land, labor, and capital) and substantial freedom in their use. Private actors are encouraged to use their resources aggressively to acquire desired goods, to produce goods, and to maximize their profit. Chapter 8 characterized the state's key roles in the mixed political economy: regulating the free market, providing guidance and incentives for production decisions, and redistributing some money and goods to less advantaged individuals in the society.

A central policy debate in most of the developed countries is the appropriate level of state activity in the political economy. Should the state reduce the taxes and state regulation imposed on private actors under the assumption that the market economy is most likely to stimulate greater production and higher economic growth, thus benefiting all? Or should the state capture more of the surplus and then redistribute it as welfare to the less prosperous? This debate is sometimes characterized as "growth versus welfare."

There is considerable variation in the extent to which the free market dominates in the political economy of specific developed countries. Each country's political economy shifts toward more or less emphasis on social democracy, conservatism, or classical liberalism as a result of current political and economic circumstances. One broad comparative measure of the public–private mix is the percentage of productive capacity (measured as GDP) that is in the public sector. The chart in Figure 13.2 indicates that this varies substantially, from more than 55 percent in Sweden and Denmark to only about 36 percent in Australia and the United States. The mixed political economy designation seems especially appropriate for countries in which public expenditure is about 45 percent or more of total GDP, which includes 10 of the 16 states in the chart.

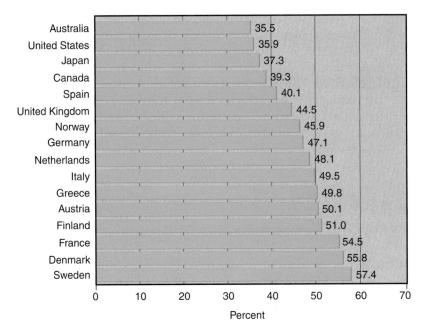

▶ **FIGURE 13.2**
General
government total
outlays as a
percentage of
nominal GDP in
selected
developed
countries (2005)
Source: OECD (2006):
table 25.

Mixed systems are usually evident in the Scandinavian states, the Benelux states (Belgium, the Netherlands, and Luxembourg), France, Austria, and Germany. Compared with the countries discussed below, taxation is more aggressive in the mixed systems, and more revenue is reallocated either as transfer payments or as subsidized goods and services (e.g., health care, housing, educational and cultural opportunities) to the citizens. The state is also more active in protecting individuals and groups from the actions of firms (e.g., price fixing, unsafe working conditions, job security, environmental degradation). In some of these social democracies, the public sector retains control or ownership of some major productive resources (e.g., energy, transportation) that have strategic importance for the country. In the international marketplace, domestic producers and workers are protected from aggressive or "unfair" foreign competition by means of tariffs and quotas on imports and subsidies for domestic production and consumption. These mixed economies are sometimes called **social market systems** because *the state encourages an extensive free-market economy but is also committed to social welfare distribution and income redistribution.* Box 13.1 describes the example of Sweden.

The *developed countries in which a larger proportion of economic activity is in the private sector,* designated as **market economies,** currently include Australia, Japan, Switzerland, the United Kingdom, and the United States. The state is oriented toward leaner, more limited government with lower taxes, less regulation of the economy, and reduced provision of goods by the state. Social welfare services are reduced toward a basic "safety net" with which the state protects individuals from only the harshest consequences of poverty. Government also reduces its constraints on economic activity (e.g., fewer antitrust actions, less protection of unions, deregulation). Private control of the productive system is extended, particularly by **privatization** (i.e., *the selling off of state-owned firms and the use of private firms to provide public goods and services*). Most states also reduce tariffs or quotas on imported goods and cut subsidies

BOX 13.1

The Social Market System: Sweden

Sweden is an example of the more progressive form of the social market system. A culturally homogeneous country of 8.9 million people, the state is committed to capitalism, with more than 90 percent of the economy in private hands. Economic policy facilitates increasing the distribution of Swedish goods in the world market. Sweden's prosperous economy ranks seventh in the world in GNI per capita (World Bank 2007).

At the same time, Sweden has one of the most expansive welfare states among the developed countries. About one-third of the national economic output is spent on social programs. Among the benefits available to all citizens at little or no direct cost are health care, higher education, child care, maternity/paternity leave, job training, and public transportation. Those suffering economic hardship receive substantial income supplements and support for amenities such as housing. As one example of Sweden's **social welfarism**, the state provides complete nursing home care to any elderly citizen for less than 5 percent of the actual costs. The regulatory policies of the state are also expansive in both economic and social life (e.g., environmental protection, working conditions). The state has even banned parental spanking to protect children against physical abuse. Some people describe systems like Sweden's as "cradle to grave" socialism.

Many celebrate Sweden as the model social democracy. A vigorous, multiparty parliamentary system operates under a constitutional monarchy, and there is active citizen involvement in the political process. Citizens are satisfied with the quality of life in their country. Sweden has one of the most equal distributions of wealth and income in the world. And it has the fifth highest quality-of-life score among the world's major countries on the Human Development Index.

One cost of social welfare has been high taxes. Total taxes paid by citizens and firms are about 57 percent of GDP, in comparison with about 38 percent in Germany and 30 percent in the United States. This tax burden reduces Swedes' disposable income and, along with regulatory policies, has made Swedish goods less competitive in the international market. The Social Democratic Party, which has promoted the social market approach, has dominated the national legislature for 65 of the last 75 years. Recently, the country has struggled with budget deficits, high unemployment and resistance to the level of taxation, and the Social Democrats were voted out in favor of a center-right coalition from 1991 to 1994, and again in 2006. But support for the policies of the left and green parties remains strong, and the Swedish population still seems willing to sustain one of the most social of the social market states.

on domestic production in order to encourage companies to be strong and competitive in the global market.

Certain domains, such as education, public safety, basic infrastructure (e.g., roads, sewers), and national defense, are primarily the responsibility of the public sector in all the developed countries. In the countries that are more committed to the social market, the state also tends to be very active in providing or subsidizing health care, housing, transportation, and income support. The market economies leave provision in these areas much more to the private sector.

Performance

The developed countries assess their prosperity primarily in terms of economic activity, usually measured as GDP per capita, and there is particular interest in the rate of change in GDP per capita over time. Former U.S. Secretary of State George Schultz reflected a widely shared view among leaders in the developed countries when he stated: "The immediate international imperative is...adequate growth. Without that, no one's objectives are achievable." But some accuse the developed countries of "growthmania." According to these critics, quality of life and citizen satisfaction are better measures of performance than an increasing GDP.

Figure 13.3 provides comparative data on GDP per capita (adjusted for purchasing power parity) for most developed countries. According to this indicator, these countries do enjoy considerable prosperity. In a ranking of GDP per capita (PPP) among 177 countries, the top five are Luxembourg, Norway, Singapore, the United States, and Ireland. All of the top 15 major states are developed countries in the classification scheme in Figure 13.1.

The *Human Development Index* (HDI) is the second measure of prosperity in Figure 13.3. This measure is computed by the UN Development Programme (2008) to reflect the quality of life enjoyed by citizens in a country. It is a composite index that gives equal weight to three indicators: "a long and healthy life, as measured by life

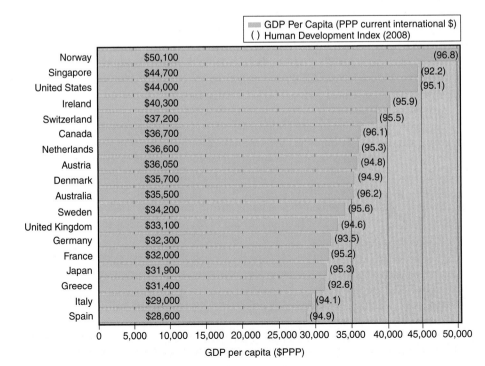

▶ **FIGURE 13.3**
Prosperity
measures for
selected
developed
countries
Source: World Bank
2008 ; UNDP 2008:
table 1.

expectancy at birth; knowledge, as measured by the adult literacy rate and . . . [school] enrollment levels; and a decent standard of living, as measured by GDP per capita (PPP US$)" (UNDP 2008: 394). The HDI scores range from 100 to 0.0; a score of 100 would indicate that all the country's citizens have attained the most desirable levels of health, education, and living standards. Broadly, a score of 80 or above currently represents a high level of human development (70 countries), scores in the 79–50 range represent "medium" levels of human development (84 countries), and a score below 50 indicates a relatively low level (21 countries) (UNDP 2008: table 1). A more comprehensive quality-of-life index might include many other indicators in addition to the three employed by the United Nations (see, e.g., Estes 1988). If you were attempting to create a comparative measure of the quality of life across many countries, what indicators would *you* include?

Every developed country in Figure 13.3 achieves a very high score of above 90.0 on the HDI. Norway and Iceland currently have the highest HDI score in the world (96.8), followed by Australia (96.2), Canada, Ireland (95.9). South Korea (92.1), Singapore (92.2), and Greece (92.6) currently have the lowest scores among the developed countries. Thus, on both a basic measure of economic production and a quality-of-life index that adds measures of literacy and health, the developed countries seem relatively successful in achieving their overall prosperity goals.

Challenges to Prosperity

Erratic economic growth.   Most developed states have periods of solid economic growth (about 4 percent or higher per year), and they averaged just above 1.8 percent annual growth in GDP per capita between 1990 and 2005 (World Bank 2007). However, there are also extended periods, such as in the early 1980s, the early 1990s, and again in the early 2000s, when many of the states have not sustained the high levels of economic growth that are the basis of their own definition of prosperity. Either there is low growth or, more seriously, there are periods of recession (a negative change in a key economic growth measure). Among the underlying problems that can result in periods of low growth are low productivity and high inflation.

First, *productivity* increases can decline, shrinking the level of profit and the rate of expanding production. This might be because of firms' failures to exploit new technologies, higher production costs, or government regulations and taxes that stifle the firms' productive efficiency. Second, a country can experience a period of significant *inflation*, which is a reduction in the exchange value of the currency that occurs when there is high demand for productive resources or goods relative to supply. Higher prices for the same products do not produce real growth. And they make domestically produced goods more costly and thus less competitive in the world market.

The competitive international economic system.   The economies of the developed countries can suffer from the economic effects of globalization. With the increasing power of multinational corporations and global markets, a government has less direct control over its political economy. As globalization increases the productive capacity of many countries, a developed country faces increasing competition from the developing countries, newly industrializing economies, and postcommunist countries, all of which tend to have lower production costs. As more jobs are outsourced and more goods are imported, a developed country's economic vitality can be drained.

The EU and the others.   The developed countries face not only the complexities of international competition and globalization, but also the multiple challenges of sorting out their economic relations with one another. Box 11.1 described the evolution of the European Union. While the EU offers economic advantages to its members, it also poses huge economic challenges for many of the developed countries. Internally, its members have persistent and serious difficulties reaching agreements on various aspects of economic policy. Member countries have resisted uniform policies (e.g., on agriculture, on the common currency, on contributions) and have continued to protect their national economic prerogatives. Some of the newer member states are considerably less developed and are a drain on resources. The Debate in 13 considers whether further integration within the EU is likely. Moreover, for the developed countries outside the EU, especially the United States and Japan, the combined economic power of the EU group constitutes a growing competitive threat (McCormick 2006; Thurow 2003).

Overall, low productivity, inflation, and international competition can each result in a reduction of income in the national economy, lower levels of production, higher levels of unemployment, trade deficits, and balance of payments problems. In recent years, virtually all of the developed countries, even such prosperous countries as Germany and Japan, have had problems sustaining economic growth in the competitive international economic marketplace.

Inequality of prosperity.   Another problem in some developed countries is the unequal distribution of their prosperity. Economic inequalities can be measured in various ways. One widely used measure, the "Gini index" of income inequality, computes a score in which a perfectly equal distribution of wealth in the population would equal 0.00 and a completely unequal distribution would score 1.00. As the Gini index increases, and especially as it is higher than about .40, the distribution is very unequal. A second measure of the inequality of prosperity is the ratio of the country's personal income that is held by the top 20 percent of the population relative to the lowest 20 percent.

Table 13.2 provides these measures of economic inequality for the populations in a selection of the world's countries. The table reflects the fact that many of the developed countries have relatively less wealth inequality than most of the developing countries and transitional countries to be considered in Chapters 14 and 15. Among developed countries, prosperity seems to be distributed most equally in the social market systems, including Denmark, Germany, Sweden, and Belgium, countries that have among the most equal distributions of income in the world. To a significant degree, this level of equality is attributable to the effects of sustained public policies that, as in Sweden's social market system, redistribute wealth to provide a diversity of state-supported services and subsidies. The political cultures in these states also tend to be more supportive of governmental actions that attempt to ensure a better quality of life for all citizens (Castles 2004).

However, some of the developed countries, such as Singapore, the United States and Japan do have higher levels of inequality. In general, there are higher proportions of the relatively poor in the developed countries where the values of classical liberalism and conservatism are dominant in the policy-making process. Public policies in such states focus less on reducing inequalities and distribute relatively less welfare through the provision of human services. In these countries

THE DEBATE IN 13

Is Continued Integration Within the European Union Likely?

As Box 11.1 described, the European Union (EU) was initially formed in 1952 and has now grown to 27 members. It has rapidly added member states in recent years (12 since 2004), and more states are requesting membership. In addition, although some states are not official members, they have unique arrangements with the EU. Some leading members, especially France and Germany, continue to promote a more integrated EU and a move toward a federation of closely coordinated states. At the same time, member states disagree on certain key issues, such as the use of the common currency (the euro) and the adoption of a new constitution, which would strengthen the level of EU integration. Thus a critical issue is whether the EU can sustain the path to greater integration in the face of so many new members and disagreements about policy (Nugent 2006).

There Are Strong Indicators that the European Union Will Continue to Become More Integrated

- The EU now has well-established legislative, executive, administrative, and judicial branches that function very effectively. These branches have representation from all member countries and exhibit strong political institutionalization.

- The combined talents of EU members and the aggregated GDP of its member states make the EU the most powerful economic actor in the world. Its combined economy, the world's largest, is characterized by diversity, growth, prosperity, and increasing integration that benefit all members.

- The collective security pact among EU members not only protects these states from war

with their European neighbors but also makes the EU so formidable militarily that no country in the world is likely to challenge one of its members. Thus the EU is enhancing the security of all its member countries.

- The relatively poorer countries in the EU recognize that they gain economic advantages by greater cooperation within the EU system of a common market, shared currency, and economic policies that generally assist the poorer member states.

- The relatively richer countries also have strong incentives for increased support of the EU, because they gain benefits from their access to educated, less costly labor and also to the markets in the poorer member states.

- As citizens with EU passports in a region without enforced borders increasingly travel, work, and communicate with those from other member states, their growing identity as Europeans will facilitate integration.

- Great strides have been made to harmonize policy in most important areas, increasing consensus on many EU policy issues (e.g., in education and agriculture).

There Are Strong Tendencies in the European Union that Undermine Integration

- It is extremely difficult to reach the required voting consensus on many of the major (and even minor) issues when there are 27 different countries, most still acting in their own national interests, and all 27 must agree on many of the important votes.

- There are continual conflicts among member countries over elements of the common economic policy. Not all the countries in the EU have accepted the euro as their national currency, which limits economic integration.

- The EU does not have a coherent military policy or a standing military. Countries have not always agreed on or cooperated in providing military forces to support EU security initiatives.

- The most powerful countries in the EU, such as Germany and France, expect to have substantial influence and control, given their population size and economic strength, but the smaller and less prosperous countries, such as Latvia and Poland, are sometimes unwilling to yield to them.

- The poorer countries expect large economic subsidies, but this is a serious burden on the prosperity of the wealthier countries in the EU, which also are attempting to cope with significant internal economic problems.

- The unrestricted immigration of people and labor among all the EU countries has resulted in increased cultural tension and animosity, especially in the more advanced and wealthy EU member states. Indeed, even the attempt of the EU to function in 23 different languages is an example of the challenges of coordinating 27 different cultures and the potential for misunderstanding and disagreements.

- The rejection of the EU Constitution by France and the Netherlands in 2005 reflects the continued importance of national sovereignty and the resistance to greater integration.

More questions . . .

1. Would further increases in the power and integration of the EU be a benefit or hindrance to the global society?

2. Might a more fully integrated EU surpass the United States as *the* major world power?

3. Is it unrealistic for the EU to require a consensus of all member states on key policies?

4. Should the EU deny membership to any more countries, so that it does not become even more complex, diverse, and unwieldy?

with greater income inequality, there tends to be a larger proportion of the population who do not enjoy a life of material well-being. About 130 million people in the developed countries live below the poverty line, and 100 million are homeless (UNDP 2001: 9). In the United States, the poorest 20 percent of households (which also tend to have more members) have less than one-eighth as much disposable income as the wealthiest 20 percent of households. About one in eight U.S. citizens is "in poverty," according to the government's own statistics, and one in five children is born poor. Such substantial and persistent inequality can produce a permanent "underclass" of citizens who are also disadvantaged in education, job skills, housing, health care, and most broadly, quality of life (Wilson 1987, 1996).

No developed country has permanently resolved the policy issues related to sustaining economic growth and distributing prosperity. These issues remain at the heart of the political debate in virtually all of these countries. Nevertheless, the developed countries have a better overall record than any other set of countries in the world in delivering higher absolute levels of prosperity to most citizens.

GOAL: STABILITY

The developed countries have been generally successful in achieving their stability goals of political institutionalization and order maintenance. Within a framework of representative democracy, the

> **TABLE 13.2**
Inequality in the Distribution of Income, Selected Countries

			Ratio of Income Top/Bottom 20%		
	Greater than 20:1	**16:1–20:1**	**11:1–20:1**	**6:1–10:1**	**5:1 or less**
.60+	**Sierra Leone**				
.50–.59	**Swaziland** Brazil **Colombia**	Chile South Africa	Malaysia Mexico		
.40–.49			Costa Rica **Cambodia**	**China** **Ghana** Iran **Kenya** **Nigeria** **Singapore** Thailand Turkey **United States**	
.30–.39				Canada Israel Poland Switzerland United Kingdom	Austria **Egypt** **India** **Indonesia** Russia South Korea Japan
.20–.29					Belgium Czech Rep. **Denmark** **Germany** Hungary **Norway** Sweden

(Gini Index — vertical axis label)

Legend: **Developed** Transitional Developed **Developing**

Source: World Development Indicators (2007).

politics of these states is characterized by the group approach (see Chapter 9), with multiple competing elites and groups. Although vigorous group politics creates some pressures, these states enjoy relatively high levels of social and political stability while allowing widespread participation in the political process and broad civil liberties.

Chapters 6 and 7 described the variation in the political structures of different developed countries. Most have parliamentary governments based on coalitions formed

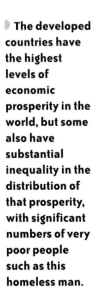

▶ **The developed countries have the highest levels of economic prosperity in the world, but some also have substantial inequality in the distribution of that prosperity, with significant numbers of very poor people such as this homeless man.**

within a multiparty system. And most are relatively stable, with alternating left then right governments (Great Britain) or coalitions (Denmark, Germany, and Sweden). A few experience instability due to the fragmented nature of the party system (Italy). Many countries have dual executives, often with a constitutional monarch (e.g., Great Britain, Japan, Sweden). There are a few hybrids with an elected president in addition to the cabinet and prime minister (e.g., Austria, France, recall Box 7.3). The United States is an exception as a presidential government with a two-party system, and Switzerland is an exception as a council system.

Political power is distributed rather than concentrated in a single governmental structure. Most are unitary states, although there are several federations (e.g., Canada, Germany, the United States). Even in the unitary states, policy implementation for many human and welfare services is the responsibility of local governments. The national legislatures are important actors in the policy process, with most being unicameral. These countries have large, efficient bureaucracies and relatively independent judiciaries. Chapter 3 indicated that the developed countries allow diverse modes of political participation by their citizens and that most countries have moderately high political involvement, at least with regard to elections and interest in politics.

Political Institutionalization

The developed countries have high levels of **political institutionalization**; that is, *substantial value and stability are attached to political structures and processes.* They are all constitutional democracies, and thus leaders and policies are constrained by the rule of law, and the rights of the ruled are guaranteed by law and tradition. Extensive political rights and civil liberties are enjoyed by the citizens, as reflected in the world's highest scores from Freedom House (2008), except for Singapore, which is only "partly free." Individuals and groups have substantial freedom to criticize and oppose the government and to engage in a wide variety of nonviolent political actions to change leaders and policies. Leaders operate with a limited mandate, leadership succession is regularized, and the selection of many public officials is based on citizen elections with genuine alternatives. While many countries have had well-supported parties of the extreme left and right, even these parties are generally committed to working within the democratic parliamentary system.

The governments in some of the developed countries have evolved over centuries by means of gradual and generally nonviolent mechanisms of political change. This pattern applies to such states as Belgium, Canada, Denmark, Great Britain, Sweden, Switzerland, and the United States. The distribution and uses of political power have changed as new groups gain admission to and influence in the political system, extending participation steadily until mass representative democracy is created. This "politics of inclusion" has drawn important groups into the political process and built their support for the political system, reducing their need to use extraconstitutional mechanisms such as violence to achieve their political goals.

In Great Britain, for example, more than 800 years of evolving political inclusion has ensured the stability of the regime. The basic story line is that the political system has very slowly drawn new groups into the political process, penetrating downward from the most powerful to the least powerful. During this period, starting in 1215, the substantial political powers of the hereditary monarch were defined, then constrained, and then limited greatly in the twentieth century. In parallel, the political powers and functional responsibilities of the national legislature, composed of the House of Lords and the House of Commons, were gradually extended. The elected Commons, which represented the less privileged classes, began as a weak second house, then slowly gained equality with the Lords, and finally, in the twentieth century, became the almost completely dominant house. And the Lords' membership eventually shifted from hereditary lineage among the top ranks of the upper class to life membership by appointment for those who had made distinguished contributions to the society.

Equally significant, the British electorate expanded steadily, as new classes of the population were granted political rights by lowering barriers based on wealth, gender, and age. So, for example, acts of Parliament reduced the restrictions on wealth as a qualification for the right to vote, increasing the electorate by almost 50 percent in 1832 and by more than 80 percent in 1867. In 1884, Parliament dropped property qualifications for voting and all working men were allowed to vote. All men over age 21 and married women over age 30 were given the right to vote in 1918; voting rights were extended to all adult women in 1928, and the voting age was reduced to 18 for men and women in 1969.

Political inclusion in Britain also affected the political party system, which adapted to the changes in the citizenry. For example, at the beginning of the twentieth century, a new Labour Party was formed to represent the British working class that had become a more important part of political society. Only in 1945 did the Labour Party gain enough seats in the Commons to form a government majority and enact significant new public policies that established "the welfare state" and greatly benefited the working class and the poor. Further adaptations in the party system have accommodated the growing national identity in Scotland, Northern Ireland, and Wales. While there are recurrent outbreaks of political instability in Britain, the politics of inclusion have been very effective in incorporating new political forces into the institutionalized political regime and sustaining a highly stable political system.

Some developed countries have substantially restructured their political system in the last 60 years. Many created new constitutional systems after World War II undermined the legitimacy of their previous political regimes, as in Austria, France, Italy, Japan, and Germany. Part of this process was to distribute power more broadly within the political system and to increase the participation and influence of the citizens. Democratic political processes are now firmly established in these younger democracies.

Order Maintenance

The developed countries have had varying levels of success in meeting the stability goal of order maintenance. This goal can be interpreted as the *absence of disorder* in the political, social, and personal domains. As discussed in Chapters 3 and 12, explicitly political violence includes illegal demonstrations, riots, rebellions, coups, and revolutions. Failure to maintain public order is also reflected in social disorders, such as murder, rape, robbery, white-collar crime, and organized crime, as well as in personal disorders, such as suicide and substance abuse (alcohol, drugs).

While a few of these countries have exceptionally high levels of order maintenance, such as Switzerland and Singapore (see Box 13.2), most are neither the most orderly nor the most disorderly in the political world. Overall, most citizens in most developed countries enjoy secure lives. The differences among the states can be substantial, however, and it is difficult to generalize. The Netherlands, Norway, and Japan, for example, have relatively low levels of social disorder such as violent crime. Yet Japan has one of the highest suicide rates in the world, alcohol abuse is high in Norway, and drug abuse is high in the Netherlands. France, Italy, and the United States, in contrast, are relatively high on most measures of social and personal disorder and are among the increasing number of developed countries with substantial problems related to substance abuse and drug-related crime and also underlying problems with alienated groups such as the lower classes and some immigrant populations. What explanations do you think best account for the fact that some of the developed countries seem to have such high levels of social and personal disorder?

Challenges to Stability

Value conflicts and disputes.   Since the developed countries allow open group politics, the active disagreements about specific policies and even about fundamental values can produce instability. As previously described, there is also intense

BOX 13.2

Welcome to the Brave New World: Singapore

Singapore has used government policy expansively to achieve order maintenance. A small island of 3 million people located off Malaysia, Singapore gained independence from Britain in 1963 and became a republic in 1965. Prime Minister Lee Kuan Yew exercised singular power for 31 years (until 1990) and guided the country to remarkable economic success. Its annual economic growth rate has averaged 8.3 percent since 1965. Its GDP per capita has risen dramatically, placing it near the top of all developed countries in terms of its overall prosperity.

Singapore is also notable for the remarkable social-control policies first instituted by Prime Minister Lee and the parliament he dominated for three decades. For example, to deal with traffic congestion, the government maintains a strict quota on the number of cars imported. An individual who purchases a new car must pay import duties and registration taxes that triple the car's market price. To reduce the massive yearly automobile registration fee, the driver can save $10,000 per year by purchasing a special red license that allows only nighttime and weekend driving. The high toll-road charges and other auto fees are used to subsidize an efficient system of mass transit.

©1994 LUCKOVICH—ATLANTA CONSTITUTION

Source: By permission of Mike Luckovich and Creators Syndicate, Inc

BOX 13.2 *(Continued)*

To promote financial responsibility and personal savings by its citizens, the government places 34 percent of each worker's wages in a special fund. The worker can use these forced savings only to buy government stocks, to purchase a house, or for retirement.

The state uses the media and the schools to support extensive campaigns to discourage certain behaviors, such as spitting in public, long hair on men, and littering. The stiff penalties imposed to enforce its social-control policies received worldwide attention in 1994 with the "flogging" of visiting American teenager Michael Faye for painting graffiti on automobiles. For many offenses, there are heavy on-the-spot fines: in U.S. dollar equivalents, $124 for driving without a seat belt, $250 for littering, $310 for eating on a subway, $310 for smoking in a restaurant. To prevent speeding, all taxicabs are equipped with a bell that begins to ring loudly as soon as the taxi exceeds the legal speed limit, and trucks have a yellow light on top that flashes when the driver goes too fast. Technological surveillance includes computerized camera systems that record the license plates of cars that violate traffic laws, and odor-activated video cameras in elevators that record anyone who urinates in the elevator (the person is also locked in). There is even a law against failing to flush after using a public urinal.

Singapore also instituted a set of not so subtle eugenics/population-control policies. Women with less than a high school education are given a government-subsidized home mortgage, but they lose the subsidy if they have a third child. To increase the low population "productivity" of college graduates, the government's Social Development Unit offers a computer-matching service for educated singles. One program, eventually discontinued, offered these smart singles a government-funded vacation at a romantic seaside holiday camp.

Because of such extensive policies of social control, Singapore has been subjected to jokes and serious criticism about its limitations on civil liberties. But no one denies that the country is exceptionally orderly, clean, and efficient. (This discussion is based on Sesser 1992.)

political debate regarding the degree to which the state should have an active role in the *political economy* and should distribute generous welfare benefits to various groups in the society.

Some enduring value conflicts center on disputes about the circumstances in which *state regulation of individual behavior* is legitimate. Such regulation might be justified to preserve social peace, promote the collective good, protect the rights and freedom of others, or protect the individual from himself and others.

In the United States, for example, state constraints on private behavior generate controversy, political disorder, and occasional violence regarding such areas of public policy as:

■ Abortion.

■ Development and use of private land.

- Discrimination/preferences (based on age, gender, ethnicity, sexuality).
- Educational curriculum (religious instruction, sex education, evolution versus intelligent design).
- Free speech (in the media, on the Internet).
- Homosexual rights.
- Ownership and use of firearms.
- Substance abuse (alcohol, drugs).

Multiculturalism and immigration.   Another source of instability in many developed countries is the response to multiculturalism and immigration. Some countries have a long tradition of *multiple nationalities*, such as Canada's English-speaking and French-speaking populations, the Walloons and Flemish in Belgium, and the English, Scots, Welsh, and Northern Irish in the United Kingdom. Demands for regional autonomy based on national identity have been a politically contentious and occasionally violent issue in some countries, such as Canada (Quebecois), Italy (Padania in the north), and Spain (Basques, Catalans). However, most developed countries are primarily struggling with the substantial increase in their cultural diversity in recent decades. Some of the instability is due to clashes between the majority ethnic group and "native-born" minorities, especially people of Afro-Caribbean or Arabic descent. For example, the concern about "home-grown terrorists" in England has soured relations between the Anglo majority and Britain's Muslims.

The instability in recent decades is particularly due to intensifying conflicts regarding *immigration*. Legal immigration within the EU, for example, has resulted in large enclaves of "foreigners" from Southern and Eastern Europe whose languages and customs grate on some in the ethnic majority in Western and Northern European countries. And *illegal* immigration is, in some countries, an even more disruptive issue, as in the United States, where the treatment of the 12 million individuals who have entered the country without permission is a major public policy puzzle. Every country has its policy debates about cultural diversity: the French ban the wearing of head scarves and other "religious symbols" in schools; American states pass laws that forbid bilingual education; the Danes reverse their open-door policy and place stringent restrictions on immigration. These kinds of responses have generated counterdemands for policies supporting multiculturalism and protecting minority rights (e.g., bilingualism in Canada, affirmative action in the United States). At this point, virtually every developed country is struggling with political and social instability caused by issues regarding immigration, multiculturalism, and tolerance of its nonnative populations.

Hyperpluralism and political polarization.   The political elites and governments are committed to working within the framework of representative democracy and group politics as they attempt to resolve value conflicts. They are generally successful in establishing compromises on issues that might become highly politicized.

However, Chapter 9 suggested that group politics are not well suited to situations in which value conflicts are intense and many groups are mobilized. The risk is

The Flag of the Unbridled Self-interests of America

13 ORIGINAL PACs

Source: © King
Features Syndicate

BY BORGMAN FOR THE CINCINNATI ENQUIRER

hyperpluralism, a situation in which *many effective groups are able to pressure the government to respond to their particular policy demands.* As the government attempts to satisfy all these different group demands, public policy can become contradictory or muddled. Even worse, the government might try to accommodate so many interests that it becomes somewhat paralyzed, unable to respond to all the competing demands (Edwards, Wattenberg, and Lineberry 2008: 326–329). If key groups become dissatisfied with government unresponsiveness and paralysis, they can make increasingly strident political demands, engage in aggressive political actions in support of their policy preferences, and produce high levels of political instability.

Some states, such as the Netherlands, Norway, and Switzerland, have reduced the incidence of serious disorder by nurturing a cultural style of social tolerance or by developing political institutions that accommodate competing groups (Eckstein 1966; Lijphart 1978, 1984). However, the governments of most developed countries tolerate hyperpluralism and political disorder. The risks of instability are especially great when there is substantial *political polarization* as *politics becomes a battleground between large, mobilized groups of the right and the left* and center parties and centrist policies are only weakly supported by the citizens. The political system has an extremely difficult time making policy and resolving conflicts, since it is often impossible to satisfy the opposing viewpoints. This type of polarization and instability occurs periodically in countries such as Britain, France, Italy, and Japan.

Domination and control.   Some analysts offer a far more critical description of how many developed countries maintain order. They describe societies in which the state controls its citizens by coercion rather than consensus, combining limited welfare distribution, extensive political socialization, and effective restraints on public life by the state's agents (e.g., the police, the bureaucracy, the judicial system). Some class and elite theorists also argue that most developed countries are controlled by a "hegemonic elite"—an extraordinarily powerful group that sustains its domination over a long period of time (Domhoff 2005; Esping-Andersen 1990; Poulantzas 1973). These theorists insist that politics in the developed countries is not a fair competition among groups, that the state is not a neutral referee, and that most public policies enable certain groups to maintain their advantaged position in society (see Chapter 9).

It is clear that the developed countries do have powerful and effective institutions that can shape the political process, control groups, and contain instability. Even the group politics explanation acknowledges that there are huge inequalities in the political resources available to different groups (Dahl 1961; Parenti 2007). There is no doubt that certain institutions and individuals (such as media baron Rupert Murdoch, described in Box 13.3) have extraordinary powers to shape political life in the developed countries. Yet most analysts and most citizens see no compelling evidence that these political systems are dominated by self-serving, nondemocratic elites. In response, radical (Marxist) theorists interpret such citizen views as evidence that the state *can* fool most of the people all of the time. One of the great (and perhaps impossible) challenges for political scientists is to develop an indisputable empirical analysis of how political power is exercised, how values are allocated, and how order is maintained in the developed countries.

GOAL: SECURITY

The first half of the twentieth century was a period with substantial insecurity, since it was marked by two massive multistate wars among the developed countries. While most of the states survived intact (there are notable exceptions, including Austria-Hungary after World War I and Germany after World War II), many states were devastated in human, material, and political terms by these wars. However, since the end of World War II in 1945, the developed countries have generally enjoyed success in the pursuit of their basic security goals, especially survival and freedom. Arguably, the greatest security victory of the developed countries during the recent period is the collapse in 1990 of the communist state in the Soviet Union, their major adversary. In the early twenty-first century, these countries are still establishing new arrangements for security in the altered, post-cold war global system.

The Era of Colonialism

Some developed countries have been extremely successful at extending their influence or control over other states in order to enhance their own security goals. Belgium, France, Germany, Japan, Portugal, Spain, and the United States dominated vast colonial territories until the mid-twentieth century. In 1945, Great Britain was the leading colonial power, controlling more than one-fourth of the world's population in its worldwide empire.

BOX 13.3

Media Mogul Murdoch

Information is one of the critical resources that can shape politics in any society. If the control and dissemination of information are concentrated in the hands of a few major actors, the possibility of elite domination increases. Rupert Murdoch, an Australian who is now an American citizen, stands tall among a small group of media moguls who are shifting global media power toward private actors (Hachten and Scotton 2003). Among the other influential members of this group are Emilio Azcarraga Jean of Mexico (Grupo Televisa) and Prime Minister Silvio Berlusconi of Italy (Mediaset TV).

Murdoch started with the ownership of two Australian newspapers. He then began a 50-year process of leveraging his holdings to acquire more and more media resources in other parts of the world. Some of his vast holdings are multichannel satellite networks (including BSkyB in Britain, Star TV in Asia, and Sky Latin America), Fox broadcasting (Fox television and Twentieth-Century Fox films), DirecTV, the *Wall Street Journal*, the London *Times*, *TV Guide*, MySpace.com, the global HarperCollins publishing house, and the Barnes and Noble bookstore chain. The reach of his media is truly global, including intensive saturation in the United States, United Kingdom, Australia, and 53 countries in Asia and the Middle East.

What is critical is not merely the fact that Murdoch controls the world's most extensive media empire, but how he uses it to wield political influence. Murdoch himself has commented: "For better or for worse, our company (News Corp) is a reflection of my thinking, my character, my values." A staunch political conservative, his newspapers and television networks openly support conservative candidates and policies, such as the Iraq War, and are antagonistic to most of those on the left, such as trade unions and liberal Democrats. Murdoch's media are known for their strong political bias, low-brow content, and sensationalism.

The closest advisor of former British Prime Minister Tony Blair comments: "[Murdoch's] presence was always felt. No big decision could ever be made . . . without taking into account the likely reaction of three men, Gordon Brown [a top cabinet member, and Blair's successor as prime minister], John Prescott [Blair's deputy prime minister], and Rupert Murdoch. On all the really big decisions, anybody else could be safely ignored" (Campbell 2007). There is clear evidence, for example, that Murdoch forced Blair to promise in 2004 that Britain would hold a referendum on the proposed EU Constitution (which Murdoch would oppose vigorously in all his media). After helping Murdoch gain a waiver allowing him to own the *New York Post* newspaper as well as a New York television station, the governor of New York, Mario Cuomo, observed that while other newspapers might provide a politician with one editorial, "With Murdoch, he gives you the whole paper, page 1 to page 96, every day for six months—for you or against you." And when Murdoch acquired the esteemed *Wall Street Journal* in 2007, one of its reporters wrote: "Rupert is my boss. . . . So I am now an underling in the world's most evil corporate empire" (Foley 2007).

Although most of the content of Murdoch's media is not explicitly political, there can be little doubt that his information and "infotainment" empire helps shape the ideas and views of millions of people on every continent.

Colonialism was a means by which many of these countries furthered virtually all of their security goals. Although their colonial holdings are now independent states, some developed countries continue to exert their power through neocolonialism, as Chapter 11 described. From the perspective of many developing countries, the developed countries have very much "had it their own way" in promoting their security interests and projecting their will in the international political arena.

The Cold War Period

From World War II until the late 1980s, the security-oriented actions of virtually all the developed countries were powerfully influenced by *the international struggle between the United States and the Soviet Union*, generally called *the cold war*.

During the cold war period, U.S. policy was based on the assumption that the main threat to the security of the developed countries was the Soviet Union, its allies, and the worldwide expansion of communism. In this view, the freedom, influence, and even survival of the developed countries depended on strong military power to counterbalance the Soviet bloc. As the leading advocate of this bipolar balance-of-power perspective, the United States had a foreign policy based on at least two core elements.

First, the United States used military power in an attempt to deter Soviet military activity outside of the Soviet Union and its European satellites. The United States was the key actor in NATO, a mutual security pact among the developed countries, and it was prepared to undertake military actions anywhere in the world that Soviet activities threatened its conception of international stability. As part of their massive capacity for war, the extensive nuclear arsenals of the United States and the Soviet Union created a balance of terror—mutually assured destruction (MAD)—in which neither side was willing to initiate direct military hostilities against the other (see Chapter 11).

Second, the United States applied its considerable military, economic, and political power to influence the actions of many developing countries. It provided support to pro-American, anticommunist regimes—for example, in Congo (Zaire), El Salvador, and South Korea—and to many nonaligned Third World states, and it attempted to destabilize leftist or pro-Soviet regimes (e.g., in Afghanistan, Cuba, Grenada, North Korea). This policy was generally successful, but the United States suffered its most costly setback in its direct military involvement and ultimate defeat in Vietnam (1964–1975).

Not all political elites in the developed countries shared the United States' perception of a clear bipolar struggle between the forces of good and evil. Some states (e.g., Austria, Finland, Switzerland) maintained a position of neutrality during the cold war. Others (e.g., Denmark, France, Greece, Italy, New Zealand, Sweden) emphasized a more conciliatory policy of détente ("relaxation" of tensions) with the Soviet bloc, based on the view that both blocs had common interests in maintaining their superior position internationally and preventing a global nuclear war. This latter view became more widespread by the late 1980s, due to Soviet leader Mikhail Gorbachev's effective peace initiatives.

Challenges to Security in the Post-Cold War Period

By 1990, with a speed that stunned the world, the Soviet bloc countries and even the Soviet Union were transformed (see Chapter 15). These countries moved away from communism and toward democratic politics and market political economies. They sought economic cooperation rather than military conflict with the United States and Western Europe. The cold war seemed to end with the unification of East and West Germany (1990) and particularly with the breakup of the Soviet Union (1991) into 15 countries.

In the *post-cold war period*, the global military power of the United States is unmatched, and the United States alone accounts for 46 percent of the military expenditure of the entire world (SIPRI 2008). Although the United States projects its military power extensively in some cases, as against Iraq in 2003, most developed countries emphasize collective security arrangements, through the United Nations and regional security pacts. As the developed countries reformulate their approaches to security, they are influenced by at least four major security challenges, described next.

Disorder in the developing countries.   Most major political violence occurs in developing countries, as it did during the cold war period. From Afghanistan to Colombia to Iraq to the Sudan to Zimbabwe, complex patterns of disorder have persisted, despite various strategies of intervention by the developed countries and international organizations. In each situation, governments of the developed countries must weigh the security benefits from stabilizing a distant part of the international system against the substantial costs of intervening and the difficulty (impossibility?) of maintaining stability in many of those countries (Falk 1999).

Proliferation of weapons.   The heavy armaments of Russia and the United States have been significantly reduced by agreements during the post-cold war period (e.g., START II). However, this period is also characterized by the expansion of military power in many states, the ease with which chemical and biological weapons can be acquired, and the sale of weapons of mass destruction to all who can pay for them. Equally serious is the widespread distribution of "light weapons" (e.g., guns, shoulder-fired missiles, land mines) to irregular forces in countries everywhere, because such weapons cause most of the casualties from political violence (Klare 1997). The developed countries, which lead the world in the production and sales of military hardware, have failed to implement effective strategies to prevent the further proliferation of all these kinds of weapons. Indeed, the United States and Germany (along with Russia) are the largest suppliers in the global market for weapons.

Globalization of terrorism.   While the great majority of terrorist acts are committed in developing countries, some developed countries are among the top terrorist targets. The 2002 bombings at Bali nightclubs that killed mostly tourists and the political violence in Iraq against Western corporate employees, journalists, and even aid workers are examples. Moreover, globalization has facilitated the extensive movement of people and information that has placed cells of terrorists in all countries in the Global North. Such groups committed the deadly attacks on the U.S. World Trade Center in September 2001 and on the mass-transit systems in Madrid (2004) and London (2005). The developed countries have never been more vulnerable to terrorist attacks by individuals from the Global South.

International economic relations.   In the absence of a common military enemy, economic competition for markets and resources has become a source of more conflict. As noted earlier, the most powerful actors at the center of this global economic competition are the developed countries themselves as well as multinational corporations (see Chapter 11). But the newly industrializing economies (see Chapter 15) and many developing countries are intensifying this competition. The developed countries can no longer dictate to their advantage where the desirable jobs are, how scarce resources (e.g., energy, food) are allocated, and most important, who garners the maximum benefits and profits in the global marketplace. Fierce economic competition between states, regions, and multinational corporations could be the greatest source of insecurity for the developed countries in the era of globalization (Thurow 2003).

THE DEVELOPED COUNTRIES OVERALL

In terms of pursuing the broad goals of prosperity, stability, and security, the developed countries of the Global North generally have the highest levels of "success" in the world. These states have the most developed systems of economic production, having evolved political economies that effectively mix capitalism and democratic socialism. The majority of productive resources remain under private control, but in most developed countries, the state has established a substantial program of welfare distribution to the citizenry. Most of their citizens enjoy a higher standard of living than is available to the majority of people in any other part of the world.

By exercising their considerable economic, military, and political power in the global system, the developed countries have also met their security goals. They have a strong record of survival, influence, and even control over other political systems. In the pursuit of security goals, the developed countries achieved "victory" in the cold war against the Soviet Union and its global promotion of communism. The leading developed countries still exercise their power energetically to maintain their advantages in the international system.

The success of the developed countries in achieving prosperity and security is not unqualified. While most citizens enjoy a high material standard of living, others live in relative poverty and despair, and such inequalities might be the Achilles' heel of their prosperity. Also, critics, especially in developing countries, argue that the developed countries have maintained their prosperity by exploitation—historically, of the poor within their own societies, and more recently and more systematically, of the populations and resources of other states, by means of neocolonialism and military intervention (see Chapter 14). They have not reached the top by being passive or generous. And security issues have become more complex as the Soviet threat, which encouraged cooperation among the developed countries, has been replaced by more diverse threats. These include increasingly violent regional instabilities in the Global South, the insecurities associated with the current forms of terrorism, and the complex destabilizing impacts of globalization on relations with allies, competitors, and adversaries.

The developed countries, perhaps because of their prosperity and security, have maintained relatively open, fair, and stable group politics. Democracy and political equality do not prevent enormous inequalities in political influence and political power. And there are tensions between the commitment to individual freedom and limited government, on the one hand, and state intervention to increase equality of outcomes, on the other. While pluralism has occasionally been severely strained, a wide range of political beliefs and actions are tolerated. Many individuals and groups are able to mobilize their political resources to influence the processes of government and decision making, and citizens do have the right to select among leadership elites at regular intervals. In comparison with other countries during the past 50 years, the developed countries receive high marks for maintaining constitutional, participatory politics.

KEY CONCEPTS

cold war
developed countries
developing countries
First World
Global North
Global South
Human Development
    Index (HDI)

hyperpluralism
market economy
newly industrializing
    countries (NICs)
political institutionaliza-
    tion
political polarization
post–cold war period

postcommunist
    developed countries
privatization
social market system
social welfarism
Third World
transitional developed
    countries

FOR FURTHER CONSIDERATION

1. How would you further classify the developed countries into two or more subsets? What criteria would you use?

2. In the current period, what is the greatest threat to the stability of the Global North? What is the most appropriate strategy to reduce that threat?

3. Consider the issue of hyperpluralism. Do you think a country can be *too* democratic? What are several of the strongest arguments on each side of this question?

4. Write a script or role-play (with others) a situation in which a classical liberal, a conservative, and a democratic socialist discuss the virtues and failings of a particular developed country.

5. If you were to create a "quality of life" index, what measures would you include? Rank the importance you would attach to the various measures, and explain why you have given those rankings.

6. How should the desirable level of distribution of prosperity among citizens in a society be determined? Should the state do anything to ensure that prosperity is distributed more equally among its citizens? What actions by the state are appropriate and might be effective?

FOR FURTHER READING

Almond, Gabriel, G. Bingham Powell, Kaare Strom, and Russell J. Dalton, Eds. (2008). *Comparative Politics Today: A World View*. 9th ed. New York: Longman. Solid case-by-case studies of selected developed countries (England, France, Germany, Japan, and the United States) as well as Brazil, China, Egypt, India, Mexico, Nigeria, and Russia, employing Almond's structural-functional concepts (recall Chapter 5).

Bastow, Steve, and James Martin. (2003). *Third Way Discourse: The Crisis of European Ideologies in the Twentieth Century*. Edinburgh: Edinburgh University Press. An exploration of the roots, the current forms and challenges facing alternative "Third Way" ideologies (blending socialism and neoliberalism), including Italian socialism, British New Labour, ecologism, and neo-fascism.

Burgess, Anthony. (1970). *A Clockwork Orange*. Harmondsworth, UK: Penguin. A dystopian novel describing a near-future Britain in which youth gangs rule the mean streets of a divided and amoral society. Stanley Kubrick's chilling film was based on this book.

Castles, Francis G. (2004). The Future of the Welfare State: Crisis Myths and Crisis Realities. New York: Oxford University Press. A thoughtful, empirically-grounded analysis of how current conditions, especially globalization and the changing population demography, are shaping the evolution of the welfare state policies in 21 Global North countries.

Freeman, Richard. (2000). *The Politics of Health in Europe*. Manchester, UK: Manchester University Press. The contemporary health care systems, as well as the policy debates regarding those systems, are effectively described for major European countries (France, Germany, Italy, Sweden, and the United Kingdom), which range from social market to more neoliberal orientations regarding the state role in health care.

Huber, Evelyne, and John D. Stephens. (2001). *Development and Crisis of the Welfare State: Parties and Policies in Global Markets*. Chicago: University of Chicago Press. A revealing explanation of the expansion of the welfare state and state policies of welfare redistribution in the developed countries from 1950 to 1980, and then the substantial reduction of those welfare programs since that time.

Kennedy, Paul. (1987). *The Rise and Fall of the Great Powers*. New York: Random House. A sweeping analysis of how countries such as the United Kingdom and the United States become the strongest in the world and then decline.

Pharr, Susan J., and Robert D. Putnam, Eds. (2000). *Disaffected Democracies: What's Troubling the Trilateral Countries?* Princeton, NJ: Princeton University Press. A strong and diverse set of essays exploring the extent to which citizens in the advanced democracies have lost confidence and trust in their political leaders and political institutions, and even in democratic processes.

Pinder, John and Simon Usherwood (2007). *The European Union: A Very Short Introduction*. 2nd ed. New York: Oxford University Press. A solid (and brief) exploration of the institutions, processes, and challenges of the European Union as it attempts to extend its roles, power, and effectiveness.

Thurow, Lester C. (2003). *Head to Head: Coming Economic Battles among Japan, Europe, and America*. New York: William Morrow. A rich study of the post-cold war shift in which the key conflicts will be economic ones among the developed countries. Thurow concludes that the united Europe of the EU seems to have the resources to prevail in the emerging economic competition among the EU, Japan, and the United States.

Wilensky, Harold. (2002). *Rich Democracies*. Berkeley: University of California Press. Using case studies, interviews, and quantitative data, a distinguished political scientist offers a comprehensive and compelling perspective on how the 19 "rich democracies" have evolved over the last half-century, with particular attention to social policy and a focus on the interplay among the form of political economy, political institutions, and key political actors.

ON THE WEB

http://europa.eu/index_en.htm

The official Web site of the European Union provides detailed information about each EU member state.

http://www.oecd.org

The Organization for Economic Cooperation and Development is a cooperative association of 30 member countries, primarily the developed countries plus a few of the most economically advanced countries in East Europe and Asia. The OECD site provides information about its activities as well as data on member states.

http://www.coldwar.org/resources.html

The home page of the Cold War Museum contains a number of fascinating online exhibits and an online discussion forum regarding this important period.

http://www.weu.int/

The electronic home of the Western European Union provides extensive information regarding the organization's activities and policies.

http://www,usa.gov

The official Web portal for the U.S. government, the site offers many links to the agencies and information associated with the various governmental institutions in the United States.

http://www.canada.gc.ca/

The official Web site of the Canadian government, with links to the agencies of the central and provincial governments.

http://www.cnn.com/SPECIALS/cold.war/

An educational and entertaining introduction to the cold war is provided by CNN, with historical documents, details of the arms race, clips of key actors, and more.

http://ukonline.direct.gov.uk

The Web site for the government of the United Kingdom, with multiple links to government agencies, services, and information.

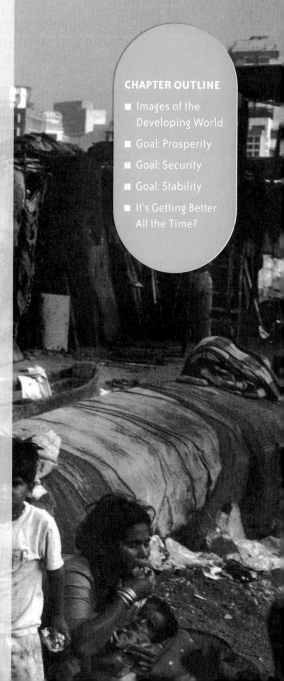

CHAPTER 14

THE DEVELOPING COUNTRIES

Many people are poor because they live in countries that are poor. Because they are poor, these countries do not have the resources—finance, technology, and skills—they need to extricate themselves from their predicament. This vicious circle has become more pronounced with globalization. Because they lack the human, financial, physical and institutional resources required to take advantage of globalization, these countries are unable to reap its benefits and are becoming marginalized in the world economy. Like certain individuals or regions within a country, the countries themselves are, in a sense, caught in a "poverty trap". They therefore require special help to change the conditions in which they find themselves.

—*UN Development Agenda: Development for All (2007)*

IMAGES OF THE DEVELOPING WORLD

What is your image of *developing countries?* It might be dusty villages where poor and uneducated people scrape out a subsistence diet from their small farms. It might be large cities where some people live and work in modern, technologically advanced settings but are surrounded by a huge, dense population living in poverty and squalor. It might be a huge state attempting to govern a billion people or a small island state with a population of fewer than 50,000. It might be a country successfully adopting European political forms of representative democracy, popular participation, and freedom of opposition, or a despotism where the small governing clique ruthlessly eliminates all opposition and change in leadership occurs only through political violence.

Developmental Classification

Somewhere in the 150+ developing countries, with their combined population of more than 5.2 billion people, all of these disparate images are accurate. There are even a variety of ways in which particular countries can be defined as "developing." The classification approach used by the World Bank designates all countries with a GNI per capita below $11,115 as a developing country (middle income or low income). As discussed in Chapter 13, this book uses a more multifaceted classificatory scheme (Figure 13.1). One dimension is GDP per capita, adjusted for purchasing power parity; the second dimension is an index of the country's overall level of social development, based on four key indicators of literacy, urbanization, health, and communications.

Chapter 13 also noted that several other labels are applied to the developing countries. They are sometimes referred to as the *Global South*, in contrast to the *Global North*, the geographical location of the great majority of the developed countries analyzed in Chapter 13. The label *Third World* is still widely used, although its derivation is from the cold war period and some analysts now suggest that the term is too vague, analytically and politically (Lewis 1999). The United Nations, among others, also identifies the 50 "least developed countries" in the Global South (UNDP 2007). These states, which include more than half a billion people and are predominantly in Africa, are identified by their very low levels of wealth, health, and literacy and by their economic vulnerability. This group of countries (also sometimes called the "Fourth World") shows the fewest signs of progress toward overcoming the development gap with other countries.

All of these labels for the developing countries are a useful shorthand for common traits attributed to states that, relative to the developed countries and even most of the transitional countries discussed in Chapter 15, are less economically developed, are less modern, and have a lower overall standard of living. Most also have high birthrates (sometimes higher than their economic growth rates) and youthful populations (in more than 40 developing countries, at least 45 percent of the population is below the age of 15).

This chapter attempts to specify dominant patterns and general trends among the developing countries, although generalizations oversimplify political reality and are subject to qualifications. The countries of the Global South encompass many different histories, traditions, religions, and political ideologies, and they do not share a single political culture. They also have different strategies of development and approaches to politics.

As you read this chapter, and especially as you formulate your own understanding about the developing countries, be sensitive to the variation *across* these states and, in many cases, *within* each state. Just as the most developed countries have some people living in abject poverty and primitive conditions, even the poorest developing countries have advanced technology, and some citizens enjoy enormous wealth and an exceptionally high standard of living.

Regional Classification

Although this chapter generalizes across all developing countries, it sometimes uses region as a second element of classification. Table 13.1 did suggest some region-based clustering based on economic development levels. Excluding the world's ministates, most developing countries in sub-Saharan Africa are low-income countries, and most countries in Latin America, the Islamic Middle East, and North Africa are middle-income countries. Before this chapter engages in generalizations regarding the pursuit of prosperity, security, and stability in the developing countries, it is illuminating to note some broad regional differences.

East Asia and the Pacific. One regional group includes East Asian developing countries, as well as the few Pacific island states (with population of at least 300,000). Most of these countries have been traditional, village-based agrarian societies until recently, and most cope with the challenges of multiple ethnicities. China dominates this group in human and historical-cultural terms, given its huge size (1.3 billion people), the dispersion of ethnic Chinese to many of the other countries, the diffusion of Confucian culture, and China's attempts to dominate many of its neighbors. Most of these countries had a late experience with colonialism, which never penetrated too deeply into the societies. China and some of the other East Asian countries (e.g., Cambodia, North Korea, Vietnam) have a recent history of communist political regimes that have been brutal and repressive. This region is also the site of some of the developing world's most successful emerging economies in recent decades, including several "Asian Tigers" that have advanced to developed-country status (e.g., Singapore, Taiwan) and such NICs as the "Little Dragons" (e.g., Malaysia and Thailand).

South Asia and Central Asia. The Central Asian group is primarily composed of the "Stans"—countries with nomadic, kin- and clan-based social organization, localized power bases and weak central authority, and cultures that have been dominated by Islam for hundreds of years. The primary colonial experience for most of the "Stans" (but not Pakistan) occurred late, when they were annexed by the Soviet Union in the early twentieth century and were socialized in its totalitarian social order, if not its command economy model. The South Asian group, composed mainly of the multistate, multiethnic Indian subcontinent (recall Box 5.2), did have considerable colonial penetration from the late seventeenth century as part of the British Empire. India, Bhutan, and Sri Lanka differ from most other developing countries in the region in their Hindu culture. While similar to the Islamic societies in reinforcing a rigid, traditional, male-dominated social order, these Hindu cultures are also highly stratified on the basis of caste. Huge India (1.1 billion) is arguably the only institutionalized democracy in the region. While India's villages remain traditional, some of its urban areas have evolved into the site of substantial economic growth and development, driven by its large sector of well-educated, technology-savvy, English-speaking men and women.

North Africa and the Middle East.   This region includes the dozen states and ministates of southwest Asia (e.g., Iraq, Iran, Saudi Arabia) as well as the five North African states that are on the Mediterranean Sea and are dominated by the Sahara Desert (Algeria, Egypt, Libya, Morocco, and Tunisia). Most of the peoples of North Africa and the Middle East are Islamic in religion and culture and mainly Arabic in ethnicity and language (Persian Iran is an exception). The area has major geopolitical importance because of its petroleum resources as well as its strategic location, including its waterways. Much of the region was controlled by the Ottoman Empire between 1453 and 1918. In the nineteenth and twentieth centuries, Europe exercised colonial power mainly through indirect economic and military involvement, but European values and structures did not penetrate most of these states. Many remain socially conservative and somewhat tribal-feudal. Economically, most of these countries are in the middle-income group, although several of the small oil-rich states are quite wealthy (e.g., Kuwait, United Arab Emirates).

Sub-Saharan Africa.   Despite its substantial natural resources, sub-Saharan Africa (the African continent excluding the states of North Africa listed above) is the poorest and least economically developed region in the world. About two-thirds of the world's poorest countries (as measured by GDP per capita) are in this region. After the abolition of the slave trade, the experiences with colonialism in most of these states were late, occurring between the 1880s and the 1950s, and were extremely intensive and exploitative. Currently, these countries are generally in a neocolonial situation, with limited control over their own resources and a dependency on foreign financial and technological assistance. A strong sense of national unity is rare because colonial powers created states that arbitrarily merged many nationality groups that had no historical commonality. More than two-thirds of the population in these countries is rural, although increasing numbers of people are migrating to cities. In many countries, the authority of the central, modern state is weak, and national political, social, and economic structures lack institutionalization.

Latin America.   There are two subsets of countries in Latin America. One subset is countries that tend to be relatively advanced in both economic and social development, with a substantial technological sector. Most of these states have achieved sufficient development to be classified among the NICs (to be discussed in Chapter 15): Argentina, Brazil, Chile, Costa Rica, Mexico, and Uruguay. Direct colonial control of these states was early, and most were granted independence before the mid-nineteenth century. In most, there is a strong national identity that corresponds to the country's geographic boundaries, and the state has considerable political institutionalization. Other well-institutionalized structures in these societies include the armed forces, the church, and an upper-class elite. Most of these states are highly urbanized (more than 80 percent of the population throughout Latin America now lives in cities).

A second subset of Latin American countries is composed primarily of the small states of Central America and the Caribbean. These small states (e.g., Honduras, Nicaragua) and hundreds of Caribbean islands (e.g., Jamaica, Haiti) are extremely diverse in culture and geography. Compared with the rest of the region, these states tend to have longer colonial legacies and to be less developed and less urban. The Caribbean states have an ethnic-cultural heritage that is African and Asian (and, secondarily, English and French) more than Indian and Hispanic (the heritages that predominate in the rest of Latin America).

GOAL: PROSPERITY

All developing countries strive for the benefits of prosperity associated with economic growth and development and welfare distribution. While the developing countries employ the same economic strategies as the more developed countries, many of them have had only limited success in achieving prosperity. Figure 14.1 presents two prosperity measures for selected developing countries.

GDP per capita is the common measure of prosperity, although it can be difficult to determine in the many developing countries that have less extensive cash-based economies. A striking aspect of Figure 14.1 is the low GDP per capita in many countries, especially in comparison with the developed countries (recall Figure 13.3). The 61 low-income developing countries have an average GDP per capita (PPP, or purchasing power parity) of only $2,531 (and as low as $610 per year measured in unconverted form). The GDP per capita (PPP) in the least developed countries is only $1,499 (UNDP 2008: table 14).

A very low GDP per capita suggests limited production of goods within the society, but it does not reveal the additional fact that these goods are often very unequally distributed and that even the most basic goods are minimally available to many people. For example, 1 billion people in the Global South live on less than $1 per day, and 2.5 billion live on less than $2 per day, conditions of severe poverty. More than 850 million experience chronic hunger, eating less than the daily subsistence level of calories, and one-third of children are malnourished and underweight. More than 800 million adults are illiterate, and more than 1 billion have no access to clean water (UNDP 2006: ch. 1). These stark statistics might be hard to fully grasp, but they are graphic illustrations of the difficult life conditions that are also evident in the low Human Development Index scores of many developing countries (Figure 14.1), with the very lowest scores predominantly in Africa and Asia.

There is a broad correlation between GDP per capita (in PPP) and quality-of-life scores , but the relationship is far from perfect. For example, Oman and Panama have virtually identical HDI scores, although Panama's GDP per capita is less than half of Oman's. In a particularly dramatic example, while Vietnam has a higher HDI score (73.3) than South Africa (67.4), Vietnam's GDP per capita is only about one-fourth that in South Africa. Assessing such variations, the United Nations concludes: "So, with the right policies, countries can advance faster in human development than in economic growth. And if they ensure that growth favors the poor, they can do much more with that growth to promote human development" (UNDP 2001: 13). It is clear that political

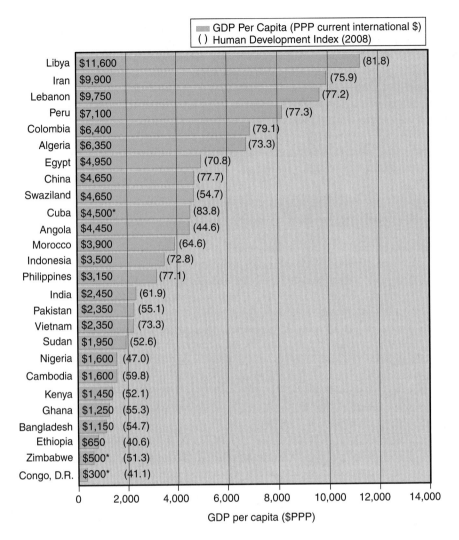

FIGURE 14.1
Prosperity
measures for
selected
developing
countries
*Estimate from
CIA 2008
Sources: World Bank
2008; UNDP 2008:
table 1.

The chart is titled with a legend: GDP Per Capita (PPP current international $) and ( ) Human Development Index (2008).

Country	GDP per capita ($PPP)	HDI (2008)
Libya	$11,600	(81.8)
Iran	$9,900	(75.9)
Lebanon	$9,750	(77.2)
Peru	$7,100	(77.3)
Colombia	$6,400	(79.1)
Algeria	$6,350	(73.3)
Egypt	$4,950	(70.8)
China	$4,650	(77.7)
Swaziland	$4,650	(54.7)
Cuba	$4,500*	(83.8)
Angola	$4,450	(44.6)
Morocco	$3,900	(64.6)
Indonesia	$3,500	(72.8)
Philippines	$3,150	(77.1)
India	$2,450	(61.9)
Pakistan	$2,350	(55.1)
Vietnam	$2,350	(73.3)
Sudan	$1,950	(52.6)
Nigeria	$1,600	(47.0)
Cambodia	$1,600	(59.8)
Kenya	$1,450	(52.1)
Ghana	$1,250	(55.3)
Bangladesh	$1,150	(54.7)
Ethiopia	$650	(40.6)
Zimbabwe	$500*	(51.3)
Congo, D.R.	$300*	(41.1)

GDP per capita ($PPP)

choices (such as decisions regarding the distribution of prosperity, the education of women, and the response to ethnic differences) *can* have a powerful impact on the quality of citizens' lives. As states attempt to make the right choices to achieve human development and economic growth, they must cope with a competitive global economy in which they face substantial disadvantages. Before assessing their strategies for development, we must consider certain key obstacles to prosperity.

Obstacles to Prosperity

High birthrates.   On average, each woman in the developing world has more than three children. The United Nations recently estimated that the population of the developing countries is likely to grow from 5 billion to about 8 billion by the mid-twenty-first century. Such population growth is a key obstacle to achieving prosperity (recall that the standard measure of prosperity is GDP *per capita*) in developing countries. More people result in greater demands on existing resources such as land, fuel, and water, and the poorest countries do not fare well in global competition for these finite resources. The projected population increase creates the need in the developing countries for more than 1.2 billion new jobs, hundreds of millions of new schools and houses, and a significant expansion in health care just to maintain the existing, low standard of living. Yet more than 40 percent of the women in the developing countries do not have easy access to family planning. Until governments in developing countries take decisive action to limit population (see Box 14.1), they will have few or no surplus resources for economic expansion and an increased level of welfare distribution (Kegley and Wittkopf 2004: 356–360; Mitchell 1998; UNDP 2008).

BOX 14.1

Can the Population Bomb Be Disarmed?

Before we hit the year 2000, the world population had reached 6 billion, and nearly 80 million babies are born each year. The population of the developing countries grew from fewer than 2 billion in 1950 to 5.1 billion in 2004. Although birthrates in almost all countries have declined in recent years, the developing world is still projected to be home to 5.9 billion in 2015 and 8 billion by 2054. Between 2000 and 2050 world-wide, 19 out of 20 births and virtually all the population growth will occur in the developing countries. Already, China and India *each* has a larger population than the combined populations of all the developed countries (World Bank 2006).

Some analysts regard the large and growing population in most developing coun-tries as the major cause of problems—economic stagnation, famine, nationality con-flicts, global warming, and desertification. An underlying concern is that the sheer number of people is becoming so large that the regenerating capacity of the earth will be overwhelmed by the depletion of resources and degradation of the environment (e.g., cutting down the rain forests, polluting the water and air, depleting fossil fuels). Thus some observers call this situation a *population bomb* that can wreak havoc on humanity as extensive as nuclear bombs could (Ehrlich and Ehrlich 1990).

Governments in developing countries offer extraordinarily different policy responses to overpopulation. Some countries have essentially taken a *Darwinian approach* to population control. Lacking either the will or the capacity to attack the problem, they allow the natural forces of famine and disease to cull their populations. They provide neither effective birth-control programs nor adequate prenatal and post-natal care; health care is minimal, and there are few successful policies to boost agri-cultural productivity. Recurrent images of shocking famine, disease, and death appear

BOX 14.1 *(Continued)*

Cartoonists & Writers Syndicate

Source: Kal, CartoonArts International/CWS

from Congo, North Korea, Somalia, and other countries. Overall, more than 200 million people have died in the past 20 years from hunger-related diseases.

The most common policy response to overpopulation is to offer *mild incentives* for birth control. The Mexican government, for example, implemented an extensive public relations campaign on television, radio, billboards, and print media, attempting to persuade its largely Catholic population that "small families live better." India is among the developing countries that distribute free birth-control devices; however, since more than two-thirds of the village women in India are illiterate, many do not use the oral contraceptives properly.

A few countries implement *aggressive public policies* to limit population. China is best known for its combination of rewards and sanctions. The government authorizes each couple to have only one child. If a couple has a second child, that child is not qualified to receive most of the free welfare benefits, such as health care. If the couple has a third child, the couple also loses welfare benefits for the first child. Since many Chinese have a strong culturally based bias toward male children, special cash

BOX 14.1 *(Continued)*

awards are given to families that have a single female child. The government offers a free abortion to any woman who requests one. It also authorizes certain women to monitor the menstruation of all women in their workplace, farm, or village to ensure that there are no pregnancies among women who do not have approval to have a baby. A woman with an unapproved pregnancy is subjected to substantial peer pressure to get an abortion, since the baby will be the financial responsibility of the entire work group and the parents will receive no additional compensation from the state.

In the last decade, the birthrates in many developing countries have dropped significantly. And some analysts argue either that technological innovations have outpaced and will continue to outpace the problems of an expanding population or that it is morally wrong to limit people's right to bear children (see, e.g., Simon 1998). Nonetheless, most analysts agree that the population increases in the developing countries continue to pose serious global threats to the environment and that the failure of governments to deal with the population problem is undermining their pursuit of prosperity, stability, and security.

Inefficiency and corruption. The search for prosperity is also thwarted by high levels of inefficiency, corruption, or both (see, e.g., Isbister 2006). One source of organizational inefficiency is the limited availability and ineffective use of modern technologies. Many developing countries have been unable to maintain efficient economic infrastructure systems, such as those for transportation and information. Another major source of productive inefficiency is the absence of Weberian bureaucracies (as defined in Chapter 6) in most of these states. The functioning of the political economy is hampered because citizens cannot assume that those who work in public and private organizations will behave predictably or follow rules.

An even more serious obstacle to prosperity is corruption. Chapter 6 noted that the terms *baksheesh* ("something given"), *chai* ("tea"), and *mordida* ("the bite") describe the private payoffs that organizational personnel (from high-ranking leaders to low-level functionaries) expect to receive before they will assist citizens. Widespread corruption demoralizes the population and drains productive energy from the political economy. Corruption exists in every society, yet it seems especially pervasive in public and private organizations in the Global South. According to Transparency International (2007), an NGO that measures levels of corruption in more than 160 countries, 59 of the of the 60 most corrupt countries are in the Global South (including ten that emerged from the former Soviet Union, and Russia is the other country in the bottom 60). Among the world's 30 *least* corrupt countries, all are high-income countries of the Global North (except middle-income Chile).

Neocolonialism. The discussions of the dependency approach in Chapter 10 and of colonialism and neocolonialism in Chapter 11 (including the example of Congo in Box 11.3) reveal that a developing country's political independence does not necessarily end its subordination to the developed countries and global institutions. **Neocolonialism** describes *a more informal and indirect, but still extensive, control of the resources, the economic systems, and even the political systems of developing countries by powerful external actors* (Wallerstein 2004; Weatherby 2008). These patterns have become even stronger with increased globalization. The developed countries, international financial institutions, and multinational corporations are the major sources of the financial capital, advanced technologies, and product distribution systems that many actors in developing countries need to compete in the international marketplace.

Dependence on primary commodities for export.   Until the last several decades, most developing countries relied on the export of a few primary commodities (raw materials, such as oil or minerals, and agricultural products, such as coffee or bananas) to generate foreign exchange capital. In turn, they imported most manufactured goods and advanced services from the more developed countries. This reliance systematically disadvantaged many developing countries, since the prices of primary goods fluctuate greatly and have decreased relative to the prices of manufactured goods over time. Most countries in the Global South have now substantially diversified their mix of exports; the percentage of manufactured products increased from 24 percent in 1970 to 71 percent by 2005. But the reliance on primary commodities for export remains a significant problem for some countries, especially the least developed countries (where 66 percent of exports are primary commodities). Sub-Saharan Africa (70 percent) and the Arab states (75 percent) are most heavily dependent (UNDP 2006: table 16; Kegley and Wittkopf 1995: table 8.1).

The Quest for Prosperity: Strategic Choices

Developing countries must deal with the challenges and obstacles noted above, which leave them less in control of their own prosperity, and with political economies that are especially vulnerable to the behaviors of the leading developed countries as well as the global corporations and institutions that are associated with the developed countries. A developing country must make choices in at least five key strategic areas in its broad approach to economic development in the global system: (1) the balance between state control and the market; (2) the balance between import substitution and export promotion; (3) the mix of manufacturing products, services, and commodities; (4) the role of agriculture; and (5) the extent of collaboration with foreign capital. While developed countries face similar choices, they are especially crucial in the developing countries.

Statism versus neoliberalism.   A basic policy decision for a developing country is whether to foster economic growth by means of greater state control of the political economy or a more market-oriented approach (see Chapter 8). After independence, many developing countries opted for **statism**—*more extensive state control of the political economy*—because they assumed that economic dependency and underdevelopment could best be overcome by a strong centralized effort to plan and control the production and distribution of goods in the society. In this approach, the state's role is expansive—it owns major industries and natural resources (nationalization), controls production decisions, regulates prices and wages, protects domestic producers from foreign competition, and encourages import substitution.

By the late 1980s, most developing countries had rejected this approach because of its disappointing results and shifted to a strategy of **neoliberalism** (the *market-oriented development approach* described in Chapter 10). This strategy of neoliberalism has four key features:

1. Government regulation of both industry and agriculture is dramatically reduced, and many government-owned industries are privatized (sold to private entrepreneurs).

2. There is an emphasis on globalized free trade, the reduction of trade controls (e.g., tariffs, quotas), and export promotion.

3. The economy is open to foreign direct investment and active participation by multinational corporations.

4. A combination of tax cuts and substantial reductions in public spending, especially on welfare services, further limits the government's role.

Producing for domestic consumption or export.   As described in Chapter 9, every political economy produces some goods and services for its own population and some for export to other countries. And some products are imported from other countries because of cost and quality considerations. Ideally, a developing country will export goods with greater value than the goods it imports to avoid a "balance of payments" deficit and an increase in borrowing.

A developing country can use public policy to influence its mix of imports and exports. One policy option is ***import substitution**—a country decreases the share of goods that are imported by producing more of those goods internally*. The government can exhort the citizens to buy internally produced products (e.g., "Buy Nigerian!") or it can provide subsidies to its firms or consumers in order to lower the prices of internally produced goods and services. A more common tactic is trade protectionism—the use of tariffs and other procedures to discourage imports or make imports more expensive than domestically produced goods. In the current globalized economic system, powerful economic actors (e.g., the WTO, the IMF) apply considerable pressure on developing countries to eliminate such protectionism and allow free trade.

A second policy option is ***export promotion**—firms are encouraged to produce goods and services that can be exported and sold at a profit in the global economy*. The government might implement policies that provide its domestic firms with an advantage over global competitors. The effect of such policies could be a well-trained labor force, less restrictive environmental policies, subsidized materials, less costly regulations on business practices, lower taxes on firms, and so on. In recent decades, virtually all developing countries have attempted to introduce policies that facilitate export promotion. This strategy has been used very effectively by the Asian NICs and, more recently, by countries such as China and India.

The mix of manufactured goods, services, and commodities.   Every political economy also seeks to diversify by producing a wide variety of goods and services. Under colonialism and neocolonialism, developing countries have been excellent sources of cheap raw materials (primary *commodities*) and intermediate (minimally transformed) goods. Developing countries still sometimes reap substantial profits from the export of such commodities as oil, coffee, and diamonds, but the prices of most exportable commodities are subject to sharp drops, and they usually rise more slowly than the prices of manufactured goods. Thus, as noted above, many developing countries are shifting to the production of manufactured goods and services.

Industrialization is a classic strategy for increasing economic development and hence prosperity via manufacturing. The aim is to use labor and capital to transform commodities into intermediate goods (e.g., cotton to cloth, trees to lumber, ore to steel, water to electricity) and then into more refined and valuable goods (e.g., clothing, furniture, televisions, trucks). For example, Bangladesh and Indonesia produce an increasing share of the shoes and clothing that are exported. More electronic equipment, furniture, cars, and other relatively sophisticated goods in the global marketplace are now being manufactured in countries such as China, Brazil, and the Philippines.

In the postindustrial period, there is increasing emphasis on producing *services* (e.g., data entry, tourism) and knowledge-based goods (e.g., banking, computer software) instead of traditional "hard" manufactured goods. For example, India's large population of well-educated, English-speaking technical workers has made it an international center for such activities as writing computer software and staffing call centers.

Most developing countries attempt to achieve growth by stimulating manufacturing and the provision of services for both export and internal consumption. They can create some competitive advantages over the developed countries in these areas, particularly due to their lower overall costs of production (e.g., lower wages, fewer regulations regarding worker safety and environmental protection, lower taxes, cheaper access to commodities). This encourages both national and multinational companies to operate in those countries.

The role of agriculture.   Food is a crucial commodity in all economies. Globally, 37 percent of all workers are still engaged in agriculture, and the percentage is considerably higher in most developing countries (Trumbull 2007). With the goal of producing a sufficient amount of food to meet societal needs, the political regimes of some developing countries established statist control over agriculture. The state organized farmland into large farms and developed a plan for production based on shared labor and technology. This approach was most fully implemented in command economies, such as Cambodia, China, Cuba, and Tanzania. State-controlled agriculture was not successful, because most rural people resisted social restructuring and were not motivated to work as hard for the general welfare as for their own profit.

Consequently, nearly all developing countries now encourage market-based production of cash crops by private farmers or local collectives (Isbister 2006). Small farms still produce half of the food grown in developing countries. But in most developing countries with a large rural population and low market prices (e.g., Bangladesh, Ghana, Indonesia, Kenya), most farms produce little more than is necessary for family subsistence. The goal is to transition to *commercial agriculture*, a system where people produce a surplus of food that can be sold in a market. This generates cash for rural people and also provides food to support a growing urban population. And if workers produce food for export, the financial capital that is generated can be reinvested in either rural or urban economic development. The successful transition to commercial agriculture requires public policies that facilitate (1) stable and attractive prices within a reliable market, (2) an efficient system of distribution, and (3) increased crop yields, especially with mechanization, better irrigation systems, and the green revolution.

In many countries, innovative technologies were introduced in recent decades that were intended to substantially increase agricultural productivity. This ***green revolution*** is based on *new farming technologies—hybrid grains, chemical fertilizers, and pesticides*. These technologies doubled average yields for rice, corn, and wheat in the Global South between 1960 and 1996. However, the costs of the components of the green revolution, especially fertilizers and pesticides, have risen dramatically. Moreover, unanticipated negative consequences from high-tech farming emerged.

In Indonesia, for example, the green revolution dramatically increased rice yields in the 1970s. By the early 1980s, however, these new farming technologies caused huge areas to be devastated by insect infestation. First, eliminating traditional methods of crop rotation had allowed the insect population, especially brown hoppers, to explode. Second, the new hybrid rice breeds were far less resistant to infestation. And third, the increasing use of pesticides actually increased the ratio of pests to "good" insects. Thus Indonesia implemented aggressive policies in 1986 that reversed these high-tech strategies. Strict laws prohibited the use of most pesticides and required farmers to use biological sprays that protect the good insects. The government instructed farmers to return to traditional crop-rotation strategies and to use natural fertilizers such as dung and clover rather than the chemical fertilizers. The results of Indonesia's partial retreat from the green revolution were very positive. By the mid-1990s, pesticide use was down nearly 80 percent and Indonesia's crop yields had rebounded.

Many developing countries have turned to agricultural self-help programs based on the use of natural farming techniques, "appropriate technologies," and environmental sensitivity. For example, a tree-planting program in Niger (initially sponsored by CARE, the Cooperative for American Relief to Everywhere) has produced more than 7.4 million tree-covered acres whose soil is protected from wind and erosion (Polgreen 2007). As the trees mature, crop yields have increased more than 20 percent. Small farmers in neighboring Burkina Faso have been taught to use a simple level (provided by Oxfam, the Oxford Committee for Famine Relief) to survey their flat croplands. Groups of farmers then build low rock walls and dams that direct rainwater into areas where it moistens land for planting and then replenishes groundwater and wells, both of which irrigate crops and provide well water for year-round vegetable gardens. Increasingly, farmers are attempting to balance the use of modern technology with more traditional methods to stabilize agricultural productivity.

While self-help programs and the use of appropriate technologies have been beneficial, the pressures to provide food and fuel remain intense in many of the least developed countries, especially due to the growing population, social disorder, and impacts of climate change. Thus many rural people engage in extensive deforestation, overgrazing, and aggressive farming techniques that exhaust the soil, destroy forests, and harm ecologically sensitive areas. The environmental consequences are severe. It is estimated that during the 1990s, mainly in the Global South, 6.25 million square

miles of timberland disappeared, 250 billion tons of arable topsoil vanished from croplands, and deserts claimed 5.3 million square miles (an area about one and a half times
the size of the United States) (Population Institute 1992; Worldwatch 2003). Ironically, some of the most successful small farmers are those producing lucrative but illegal cash crops such as coca and opium rather than legal crops, whose international
prices tend to fluctuate greatly.

In agriculture, an additional challenge is that the developing countries generally
suffer from substantial competitive disadvantages relative to the developed countries.
The governments of the Global North pay their own farmers agricultural subsidies
(on crops such as sugar, rice, and cotton) that enable their farmers to make a profit
even when selling (below cost) at prices lower than the prices of crops imported from
the Global South. This results in a loss of $24 billion per year by the countries in the
Global South. In addition, the developed countries employ protectionist trade policies that prevent developing countries from selling agriculture exports in the Global
North that would generate an additional $40 billion per year (International Food
Policy Research Institute 2003).

Collaboration with foreign capital.   Economic growth in any country requires a
stable political and economic environment that provides a trained and disciplined
workforce, effective use of technologies, an efficient infrastructure for distributing
goods, and the infusion of financial capital. Most developing countries are challenged on all these dimensions and especially suffer from the absence of sufficient
capital. Such financial capital is needed to invest in the production system, to purchase imports, and to distribute welfare benefits to a needy population. Since their
internal financial resources are often too limited to serve all these needs, many developing countries look to the Global North and its major national and multinational
corporations and financial institutions for three types of financial capital: foreign
aid, direct foreign investment, or loans.

Foreign aid. Most aid from the developed countries has been in the forms of
shared technology, grants and loans (with no expectation of repayment), and debt
forgiveness on existing loans. Many developing countries argue that the Global North
"owes" them such aid as compensation for decades or even centuries of colonial and
neocolonial exploitation that greatly benefited the developed countries and left the
developing countries with depleted resources and severe underdevelopment. While
the provision of aid is sometimes altruistic, the developed countries increasingly offer
such aid with strings attached that serve their own self-interest: economic (to obtain
resources, to open markets for their own goods and services); political (to establish
alliances or a political sphere of influence, to exclude ideological rivals); or military
(to deploy strategic military power in Global South territory).

Foreign direct investment. Consistent with the ideology of neoliberalism described
above, most developed countries, MNCs, and financial institutions offer **foreign direct
investment (FDI)**, not aid. That is, they *invest in the developing country's firms or set
up their own firms within the country*. Most developing countries accept such foreign
involvement in their economy on the assumption that capital, jobs, and other economic benefits will "trickle down" to their population (Maxfield 1997).

Loans. The simplest approach to acquiring financial resources is to borrow funds
from the international financial community, composed primarily of major banks and

Source: Gable,
CartoonArts
International/
CWS

coordinated by the International Monetary Fund and the World Bank. Loans offer an enticing short-term solution for securing funds to finance economic growth and distribute welfare benefits to the population. Eventually, however, resources must be found to repay both the loans and the interest on those loans.

Microcredit. Recently, an innovative approach to investment has emerged in many developing countries. This strategy recognizes that effective entrepreneurial activities often begin with small, local firms. However, billions of people in developing countries have virtually no capital with which to start their own small enterprises. Therefore energetic but poor individuals are provided with ***microcredit***—*tiny loans* to enable them to launch such ventures (Box 14.2). Women, who perform a substantial majority of all work in the developing countries, have been the recipients of 84 percent of this financial assistance. Microcredit approaches are now utilized in more than half of all developing countries, and loans have been extended to more than 113 million poor people. Fully 82 million of these are the world's very poorest, earning less than $1 per day (Microcredit Summit Conference 2006). Many governments and NGOs are actively expanding their efforts to provide such small-scale, local financial support due to the success of this strategy. Of course, this modest level of internal capital does not substitute for the continuing need for a large-scale infusion of capital from the international community.

Current Outcomes

Each developing country has established its own mix of strategies for gaining prosperity based on its economic history, resources, political leadership, and many other factors. Given the realities and pressures of globalization, most developing countries currently pursue some version of market-oriented (neoliberal) and export-oriented

BOX 14.2

Poor Women and Development: Microcredit in Bangladesh

Virtually every economic development project requires financial capital. Such funds are typically provided by national or global banking institutions to companies and other major economic actors who have a record of business success. However, a very different approach was crafted by some innovative thinkers in the Third World. Professor Muhammad Yunus and his colleagues in Bangladesh began with a bold and visionary assumption: that "millions of small people with their millions of small pursuits can add up to create the biggest development wonder." Yunus built on the novel concept of "microcredit." That is, he assumed that if motivated individuals in humble circumstances were given access to a small amount of financial capital, they would use their creativity and energy to establish successful small firms.

In 1976, Yunus and his associates established the Grameen Bank in order to test their faith in the untapped entrepreneurial abilities of ordinary women and men. The bank makes small loans to those Bangladeshis who present promising ideas and show willingness to work hard to implement them. These small loans, averaging $160, are extended to people without land or assets—people too poor to qualify for traditional bank loans. Before microcredit, most of these people had no option for borrowing except from intermediaries who charged extremely high interest rates, thus worsening their economic situation. In contrast, the Grameen Bank offers these small loans at a reasonable interest rate and allows an extended time for repayment.

A notable feature of the Grameen Bank's microcredit program is that 97 percent of the 7.2 million borrowers are women. Prior to receiving a loan from the bank, the typical female borrower had never controlled much money. Most of the women have used the funds effectively, establishing a diversity of small businesses in their communities: such enterprises as paddy husking and lime making; such services as storage, marketing, and transport; and such manufacturing activities as pottery making, weaving, and garment sewing.

Overall, the women have been reliable borrowers and prudent entrepreneurs. Kept on track by peer pressure and peer support, the women repay their loans in tiny weekly payments and use their businesses to move themselves and their families out of poverty. Surprising virtually everyone in the global financial community, more than 98 percent of the borrowers fully repay their loans from the Grameen Bank. Eventually, many of the women reapply for larger loans as they expand their business enterprises. These loans have provided a rich base of small businesses and economic growth for the country. And, according to the bank, microcredit has "enabled women to raise their status, lessen their dependency on their husbands, and improve their homes and the nutritional standards of their children."

Microcredit has now spread to 94 percent of the villages in Bangladesh. More than $6.4 billion has been lent, and more than 10 percent of the Bangladeshi population has benefited directly from microcredit. About 70 other developing countries have replicated the methods of the Grameen Bank, and these loans have assisted more than 133 million clients and more than 465 million family members worldwide. The Grameen Bank remains a remarkable and inspiring model of the capacity of poor women and microcredit to be a powerful source of economic development. In recognition, Yunus and the Bank were awarded the Nobel Peace Prize in 2006. (This discussion is based on information from Grameen Bank, http://www. grameen-info. org.)

development. Government and economic leaders have generally opened their countries' economies to international competition and to global capital. Virtually all countries have attempted to diversify their production mix between commodities, manufacturing, and services.

Both individual cases and aggregate statistics provide useful information about the recent performance of developing countries in the overall pursuit of prosperity. Table 14.1 reveals the varied success of developing countries during the recent period. Although each country has its own unique configuration of growth, inflation, and borrowing, certain broad patterns are evident:

- A few states have enjoyed strong economic growth with only moderate inflation and little reliance on borrowing (e.g., China, India, and Vietnam).
- A second pattern is a solid level of economic growth tempered by modest inflation and loan obligations (e.g., Bangladesh, Egypt, and Swaziland).
- A third group has solid growth but is burdened by substantial inflation or debt dependency (e.g., Armenia, Ghana, and Iran).
- A fourth group has minimal growth but no serious inflation or debt dependency (e.g., Morocco, Pakistan, and the Philippines).
- Another group has low economic growth yet substantial inflation, high debt burden, or both (e.g., Nicaragua, Nigeria, and Turkey).
- Some developing countries have actually suffered an overall decline in GDP per capita since 1990 (Kenya, Kyrgyzstan) and several have also suffered hyperinflation (Angola, Congo).

Aggregate regional data provide a broader perspective. The annual GDP per capita growth rate between 2000 and 2006 is highest in East Asia (8.4 percent), led by China. The annual growth in South Asia is 6.5 percent, followed by Eurasia (5.4 percent), sub-Saharan Africa (4.3 percent), the Middle East and North Africa (4.1 percent), and only 2.3 percent in Latin America (World Bank 2007).

These differences between countries and regions are one aspect of "uneven development." The distribution of prosperity at the *individual* level is also uneven. Look back at Table 13.2 on the distribution of wealth. Most of the countries with huge inequalities in the distribution of prosperity are in the Global South. This conclusion

> **TABLE 14.1**

Economic Indicators for Selected Developing Countries

State	GDP per Capita: Average Annual Growth Rate, 1990–2005	Inflation: Average Annual Change in Consumer Price Index, 1990–2005	Total Debt Service as Percentage of Exports, 2004
China	8.8%	5%	3.10%
Vietnam	5.9	3	N/A
India	4.2	7	18.9
Bangladesh	2.9	5	5.3
Egypt	2.4	7	6.8
Iran	2.3	21	N/A
Peru	2.2	15	26
Indonesia	2.1	14	22
Ghana	2.0	26	7.1
Nicaragua	1.8	19	6.9
Turkey	1.7	64	39.1
Philippines	1.6	7	16.7
Morocco	1.5	3	11.3
Angola	1.5	393	N/A
Pakistan	1.3	8	10.2
Algeria	1.1	11	19.5
Nigeria	0.8	24	15.8
Rwanda	0.1	11	8.1
Saudi Arabia	0.1	0	N/A
Kenya	−0.1	12	4.4
Kyrgyzstan	−1.3	13	20
Zimbabwe	−2.1	36	3.4
Congo	−5.2	424	N/A

Source: World Bank 2008 (most recent data available reported for each country).

is even more clear in Figure 14.2, which lists the 21 countries with the world's most unequal distributions of income. Eighteen of the 21 are in the Global South. The other three are newly industrializing countries (discussed more fully in Chapter 15). These countries have extremely high Gini index scores, ranging from 74.3 in Namibia to 50.1 in Zimbabwe. Notice also that virtually all of these countries are in either sub-Saharan Africa (10) or Latin America and the Caribbean (11). It should be noted that a small proportion of the quartile of the world's countries with the most *equal*

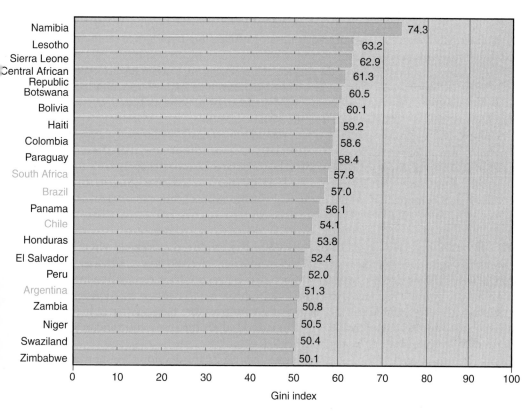

▶ **FIGURE 14.2**
Countries with
the world's most
unequal income
distributions
Source: World Bank
(2007): table 2.7.

distributions of wealth are in the Global South. This group includes Armenia, Pakistan, Uzbekistan, Kyrgyzstan, Ukraine, Bangladesh, Yemen, and Egypt.

In many developing countries, both the decisions of the political system and the actions of the international financial community have resulted in an array of policies that have generally increased the economic advantages of the wealthier groups and reduced welfare benefits to the less advantaged sectors of the population. The result is that more than a billion people in the Global South have experienced a substantial *decline* in their standard of living since the late 1980s. In Latin America, for example, the average income per person in 2002 was lower than in 1980, and 36 percent of the population was in poverty (measured as less that $2 per day). More than 75 percent of the population lives in poverty in sub-Saharan Africa, and population growth has resulted in a 34 percent increase in the total number of poor (World Bank 2001). At a minimum, developing countries need to feed their own populations. Yet one in seven people suffers from lack of sufficient calories, and the number of deaths from the effects of hunger is tragic: 10 million per year, including 16,000 children per day (UNWFP 2007).

In many developing countries, becoming more integrated into the global economy has resulted in a decrease in real wages, rising unemployment, and greater income inequality. Given such problematical results, some leaders, particularly in Latin America (e.g., Hugo Chavez in Venezuela, Evo Morales in Bolivia), are attempting to formulate a new policy approach. This approach allows participation in the global economy but shelters the country's economy from global free trade. Moreover, it emphasizes public policies that aim to improve the quality of life of all groups in the society, especially by providing substantially more welfare distribution, social services, and jobs for the poor and others most disadvantaged by neoliberalism. Bolivia's President Evo Morales is clear in his condemnation of the neoliberal model: "The worst enemy of humanity is U.S. capitalism. That is what provokes uprisings like our own, a rebellion against a system, against a neoliberal model, which is the representation of a savage capitalism. If the entire world doesn't acknowledge this reality, that the national states are not providing even minimally for health, education and nourishment, then each day the most fundamental human rights are being violated" (http://en. wikipedia. org/wiki/Evo_Morales).

The balance sheet.   The pursuit of prosperity has produced extremely uneven results across the developing countries. There are some clear positives. First, economic diversification and growth have occurred in many countries, especially those that successfully implemented market-oriented approaches to industrialization and agricultural development in recent years. Some countries that have sustained high levels of economic development, such as China and India, offer inspiration and possible models for other developing countries.

Second, the overall economic growth rates per capita for developing countries averaged more than 3.0 percent per year in 1990–2005, compared with only 1.8 percent

▶ **School days in Cairo. Education is a top priority in many countries that are attempting to achieve both social and economic development.**

in the developed countries. Indeed, the developing countries had higher average annual growth in GDP per capita (2.5 percent) than high-income countries (2.1 percent) for the period 1975–2005 (UNDP 2008: table 14). And third, the "average person in the developing world" is living longer (on average, 16 years longer than in 1960), is healthier and better educated, and has a higher real income (it has doubled in the past 30 years) and more material possessions than at any prior time (UNDP 2005: 25).

However, there are also three negatives in the pursuit of prosperity. First, the financial, industrial, and commercial-agricultural sectors in most developing countries continue to be characterized by dependency on the developed countries and multinational corporations. While more than two-thirds of developing countries' total exports are now manufactured goods (excluding oil-exporting countries), most countries still must borrow money to pay for imports, to support limited welfare distribution, and to repay their foreign loans. The positive spin is that the countries in the Global South have improved their debt burdens in the last decade, and their debt as a percentage of export earnings now averages 7.0 percent. Regionally, the highest debt burdens in the developing world are currently in South Asia (15.4 percent average) and Latin America (22.9 percent) (UNDP 2008: table 18). The less positive spin is that the countries of the Global South do still remain net importers of capital, technology, manufactured goods, oil, and even food.

Second, the gap in the level of general prosperity between the Global South and the Global North continues to widen. The material and physical conditions of life are much harsher for the average person in the developing countries—per capita GNI is less than one-twentieth as large, life expectancy is about 19 years shorter, and economic well-being is far more elusive. Slightly higher economic growth rates in developing countries do not close these huge absolute differences. For example, even if the developed countries were to stop growing today, Latin America would not catch up until 2177, given its current growth rate (UNDP 2005: ch. 1).

Third, economic prosperity is very uneven across developing countries. Growth is particularly concentrated in East Asia and somewhat in South Asia, while other areas of the developing world have languished. Moreover, focusing on growth rates alone can deflect attention from a broader notion that the essence of prosperity is economic and social betterment for most of the population. Growth statistics can reflect increased total output that does not necessarily produce a better life for most citizens. Inequality in the distribution of prosperity is increasing in most developing countries, and especially in those that have had the greatest recent success, such as India, China, and other countries in South Asia. There are serious shortcomings in the pursuit of prosperity during a period when, despite apparent global economic growth, 1 billion people in the developing world experience a *deterioration* in their standard of living.

Prognosis

Many developing countries are rich in human and natural resources. Yet most have not been able to sustain a solid level of economic development or to distribute a modest level of welfare to most of the population, let alone do both. This seems unlikely to change in a period characterized by turbulence in the global economy, an increase in direct foreign economic involvement, and pressure to reduce government spending on citizens' welfare. The perplexing question for most leaders is how to convert their resources into prosperity, given underdevelopment, a disadvantaged position in a harshly competitive international environment, and the substantial challenges to their security and stability described in the next sections.

GOAL: SECURITY

The developing countries search for security in the face of pervasive insecurity. Their problems are grounded in low levels of political and economic development, which reduce their capacity to control their own population and resources and make the state vulnerable to intervention by other states. Paradoxically, this relative weakness can also lead a state to be more aggressive in its interstate relations, both as a defensive reaction against perceived threats and as a means to divert its citizens' attention from internal problems.

Interstate Violence

At any given time, most developing countries are *not* involved in violent interstate disputes. However, most wars since 1950 and most instances of major armed conflict have occurred in the Global South, often between neighboring states (Cruikshanks 2000; SIPRI 2008). The following list offers five explanations for the frequent interstate violence between *adjacent* developing countries:

- The *geographic boundaries* between some states do not correspond to the boundaries of historically established nations, so conflict develops in an attempt to realign states with nations.
- Differences in the *cultures* of two states, especially differences grounded in nationality, political ideology, or religious belief, can produce animosities so strong that violence erupts.
- States often look covetously at valuable *resources* in neighboring states and sometimes attempt to gain control of those resources by force.
- States with severe *internal problems* can use neighboring states as scapegoats, redirecting internal frustration into violence against those states.
- Conflict between states can be encouraged by the *actions of other states* that are attempting to serve their own national interests.

Most interstate conflicts between adjacent developing countries involve a combination of these reasons. The Iran-Iraq War, described in Box 14.3, is an example of a conflict resulting from the interrelated impacts of nationality, resources, ideology, internal problems, and external influences. As noted in Chapter 12, these conflicts only occasionally expand into a war (e.g., Cambodia-Vietnam, China-India, Eritrea-Ethiopia, India-Pakistan). It is more common for the conflict to take the form of a more limited "militarized dispute" short of war (e.g., Cambodia-Thailand, Colombia-Ecuador, D.R., Congo and its neighbors, India-Pakistan).

Occasionally, there are interstate conflicts between a developing country and a developed country *on its border*. Most notable have been the five wars and many militarized disputes since 1948 between Israel and the neighboring Arab states, especially

BOX 14.3

The Third World War: Iran and Iraq

The brutal war between Iran and Iraq, which raged from 1980 to the 1988 cease-fire, illustrates the complex causes of interstate violence between neighboring countries in the developing world even among states that share a religious culture—in this case, Islam. Iraq's effort to regain total control of the Shatt al Arab was the manifest reason for the war, which began officially when Iraq invaded Iran in September 1980. The Shatt al Arab, a narrow strait between the two countries, has strategic value as a trade outlet to the Persian Gulf. In addition, these five factors are partial causes of the long-standing hostilities that resulted in war:

1. There is historical, nation-based hostility between the Iranians, whose ethnicity is Persian, and the Iraqis, who are predominantly Arab.

2. There have been periodic disputes along the Iran-Iraq border, which was established after World War I, because of attempts by the Kurdish nationality (whose region, Kurdistan, is along the border) to establish autonomy from the Iraqis, and also because of Iranian support for separatist political violence by the Kurds.

3. The Kurdistan area has valuable oil resources that both Iraq and Iran want to control.

4. The Iranian revolution (January 1979) brought to power a fundamentalist Shia Muslim regime under the Ayatollah Khomeini. The Shia Muslims are deeply antagonistic to the religion of the Sunni Muslim minority, who dominated a Shia majority in Iraq under President Saddam Hussein. There was also a history of personal animosity between Khomeini and Hussein.

5. Internal political difficulties in each country, and especially major economic problems in Iran after the revolution, provoked each state to redirect the frustrations of its population against the enemy across the border.

Moreover, the actions and intentions of many other states were significant factors. For example, Egypt and other Arab states supported Iraq's war effort because of their desire to prevent Shia Islamic fundamentalism from spreading to their states. Syria, an Arab country that had long been in conflict with Iraq, was a primary supporter of non-Arab Iran. When Shah Reza Pahlavi's pro-American Iranian government was replaced by a strongly anti-American Iran under Khomeini, who was deeply resentful of U.S. support for the shah, the United States began to aid Iraq. The U.S. shift toward Iraq caused cold war rival the Soviet Union to limit its long-standing support for Iraq. And some arms-producing states, such as Brazil and France, sold large quantities of weapons to both countries.

The war was devastating to the human and economic resources of both Iran and Iraq, causing more than 1 million casualties. After the cease-fire in August 1988 stopped the fighting, Iran withdrew from international military struggle and focused on

BOX 14.3 *(Continued)*

pursuing its own prosperity and stability goals. It slowly normalized its relations with other states and achieved slight economic growth. However, the cease-fire provided no solution to the complex regional conflicts. Disputes regarding borders, resources, and religion were again among the reasons that Iraq invaded Kuwait in 1990. This time, the United States organized a major multinational military response against Iraq, which suffered another massive toll, with high casualties (estimates range greatly, between 10,000 and 500,000) and extensive destruction of its infrastructure.

War often produces unexpected fallout. After the war, Iraq, under its defiant and dictatorial leader, Saddam Hussein, continued to provoke military reaction. In a 2003 war waged against Iraq by a multistate coalition led by the United States and Britain, the Hussein regime was quickly driven from power. However, postwar Iraq was unable to establish a stable government and the country was devastated by a violent internal war among nation-based factions (especially Shia, Sunni, and Kurdish groups) and against the "occupation army." Iraq became the site of more than half of the world's incidents and deaths from terrorism and a country broken by ongoing political violence. Meanwhile, in Iran, a fundamentalist, theocratic government consolidated its power, risked dangerous conflict with Western countries due to its nuclear program, and promoted cooperation with its new best friend, the Shia majority in Iraq.

Syria, Egypt, and Jordan. A developing country can also be the target of military intervention by a neighboring developed country. For example, the Soviet Union was concerned about the political decay in neighboring Afghanistan. It dispatched more than 115,000 troops to set up and defend Afghanistan's Marxist government, but it became entrenched in a long guerrilla war in which 1 million Afghans died and the Soviets retreated in defeat (1979–1987).

When a developing country has been involved in interstate conflict with a *nonadjoining* state during the postcolonial period, the other combatant is usually a developed country that uses force to serve its strategic, economic, or ideological interests in an internal war (e.g., the United States in Haiti in 1994; France in the Central African Republic in 1996). Occasionally, the conflict escalates into a conventional war (e.g., between the United States and North Vietnam in the 1960s, between the United Kingdom and Argentina in 1982, and between the U.S.-led coalition and Iraq in 2003).

Some argue that the entire period of colonialism and neocolonialism should be understood as the sustained use of military, economic, and psychological violence by the developed countries against the developing countries. Thus some actors in the Global South feel justified in directing political violence against a developed country that they perceive to be a source of oppression, claiming that they are doing so in self-defense—as exemplified by the sponsorship of terrorist activities against Europeans and Americans by some countries (e.g., Syria) and groups (e.g., al-Qaeda).

A striking feature of the post-cold war period has been the increasing use of international peacekeeping forces to provide security (see Chapter 11). In 2006, for example, 15 of the 16 active UN peacekeeping operations were in developing countries

(United Nations Peacekeeping 2007). Unlike earlier UN operations, most of these recent ones (including 11 of the 15 current ones) are primarily attempts to maintain *internal* stability within a developing country rather than to intervene in an interstate dispute. A related, emerging form of intervention is the use of external force on humanitarian grounds—usually to protect an ethnic minority that is the target of widespread violence by the state (Falk 1999). However, such "humanitarian intervention" is often controversial because it violates a state's sovereignty (recall the Debate in 5).

The search for security can be extremely costly. Many developing countries devote a substantial amount of their limited resources to military expenditure. In 2004, they spent more than $155 billion on their militaries, including more than $100 million per day on arms, ammunition, and other military hardware. In the last decade, military spending has been increasing rapidly in *every* region of the Global South: the Middle East (a 78 percent increase), South Asia (74 percent), North Africa (54 percent), sub-Saharan Africa (55 percent), and East Asia (40 percent) (SIPRI 2007). Obviously, these huge military expenditures can enhance security and stability. But empirical analyses suggest that greater military might is actually associated with a *higher* probability that a state will be involved in interstate conflict (Bremer 1980). Moreover, expenditures on the military represent resources that are not available for economic development and social welfare.

Economic Security

The fact that many developing countries have such fragile economic systems is also a crucial element in their quest for security, because a *state's goal of autonomy*—of controlling its own destiny—depends in part on its *capacity to resist external manipulation of its political economy*. When the developed countries and multinational corporations provide economic and technological assistance, they expect to have substantial influence and to receive generous benefits, such as favorable regulations and advantageous trade relations. And since developing countries owe more than $2 trillion to the financial institutions of the developed world, those institutions expect some control over the country's internal affairs.

This economic intervention has come most explicitly from the ***International Monetary Fund***, a consortium of financial institutions that sets economic policy and monitors the behavior of global lenders and debtors. To grant additional loans or to reschedule payments on existing loans, the IMF requires "conditionalities"—the debtor state must fulfill specific conditions that the IMF sets. The IMF's conditions often include requirements that the state implement a *structural adjustment program* (SAP), which increases the debtor state's openness to the global economy by facilitating free trade and direct foreign investment. Also, SAPs usually require the state to reduce public spending, with particularly severe reductions in the distribution of welfare services to its population, as well as currency devaluation, cuts in wages, and privatization of state-owned firms.

Leaders in some of the major developing countries have recently become more vocal in their opposition to key elements of economic globalization, especially to the economic and trade policies associated with conditionality. The "Group of 21," including the largest developing countries, has organized a more coordinated resistance, demanding global economic and trade policies (implemented through the WTO) that do not put them at such severe disadvantage in relation to the Global North. In addition, some developing countries are now attempting to organize their own regional free-trade zones to increase their autonomy from the developed countries. Such trade zones have emerged among states representing more than half of Latin America's population (Mercosur), including Argentina, Brazil, Paraguay, Uruguay, and six associate members, and among a set of Islamic states with 300 million people, including Iran, Kazakhstan, Pakistan, and Turkey.

However, the political and financial elites in nearly all developing countries seem to believe that their interests are best served by cooperation with the developed countries and the international financial community, and that loss of some control over their political economy and even over their policy processes is an acceptable cost. This continuing need for support is captured in a paradoxical comment by Kenya's former President Daniel Arap Moi: "No country can maintain its independence without assistance from outside." In the contemporary political world, no state can survive as an independent entity. But the developing countries are particularly dependent on outside assistance in many forms, especially economic and technological. Because they are susceptible to influence, manipulation, or even control by other states, few of them can escape this economic component of their insecurity.

GOAL: STABILITY

Many countries in the Global South find that achieving stability is as elusive as achieving prosperity and security. They have not been able to establish structures that maintain social order and ensure stable functioning of the political system through time.

Challenges to Political System Effectiveness

Recall (from Chapter 10) Kwame Nkrumah's credo: "Seek ye first the political kingdom and all else shall be added unto you." This perspective places primary importance on the political system as the crucial instrument for achieving the developing country's goals. It is assumed that the leaders will effectively use the state's policies and structures to create the conditions needed to increase the country's prosperity, security, and stability.

However, in many developing countries, the political system is a flawed instrument for achieving these goals because the state's effectiveness and stability are limited by a variety of factors. Some are the same factors that threaten prosperity and security:

- The citizens in many developing countries have *little shared culture* or purpose. Rather, historical nationality cleavages grounded in ethnicity, religion, and language become the basis for intense political competition and conflict over value allocations (Barber 1995; Huntington 1996).

- *Other actors in the international environment*, particularly states and major economic institutions (such as multinational corporations), often use the developing country to achieve their own goals. Typically, their actions reduce the state's political capabilities (see Chapter 10) by disrupting its control over its population and economy (Isbister 2006).

▶ **Election day. Long lines reflect the value that citizens in many developing countries attach to democracy. The military presence reflects the continuing need to maintain order.**

■ Most developing countries lack the economic capacity to produce sufficient goods, so they provide an *inadequate level of material well-being* for the majority of their populations. Moreover, many also have among the world's most unequal distributions of wealth (recall Table 13.2 and Figure 14.2). The economic elite and often the political elite enjoy a very high standard of living, an island of luxury in a sea of desperately poor people. Insufficient prosperity is always a potential source of political frustration, conflict, and instability, and severe inequality in the distribution of the existing resources makes the situation even more volatile (Wiarda 2003).

Two additional obstacles to stability are more direct consequences of the political situation within the country:

■ Many of these states *lack a tradition of limited mandate*—an institutionalized, nonviolent procedure for the periodic transfer of power from one government leader to another. Despite recent trends toward democratization (described below), there are still developing countries where the top leader has been replaced more often by political violence, such as a coup or an assassination, than by a genuine election. For example, during the 1980s, only 3 of 170 leaders in sub-Saharan Africa left power voluntarily.

■ These countries *lack political institutionalization*; that is, their political structures and roles are not infused with value and lack extensive capabilities (see Chapter 10). The political institutions in most developing countries (South American states are the general exception) have existed for fewer than 60 years. When subjected to the (inevitable) internal and external pressures, these political institutions function ineffectively or break down in political decay (Aguero and Stark 1998; Bratton and van de Walle 1997; Sorensen 2007; Linz and Stepan 1996).

The Decline of Political Order

Political decay.   Samuel Huntington's (1968) model of political decay, described in detail in Chapter 10, is based on the problems of instability in developing countries. The postcolonial history of Ghana (see Box 14.4), like the case studies of Cambodia, Congo, India, and Uruguay in other boxes in this book, includes

BOX 14.4

A Model of Hope, Decay, and Renewed Hope: Ghana

Historically, the Gold Coast of West Africa was dominated by the Kingdom of the Asante tribes and had trade linkages with many European powers. The British conquered the area only in 1901, gaining colonial control of the region. As the new state of Ghana, it was the first colonial territory in sub-Saharan Africa to gain its independence, in 1957. Its early leader, Kwame Nkrumah, became an articulate spokesman for African freedom and independence in the postcolonial era.

There was widespread optimism that Ghana would be the model of political and economic development. In the decade before independence, an active multiparty system was created and free elections were held. Nkrumah and his Convention Peoples Party (CPP) won the first postindependence election. But significant problems arose immediately, including economic shortfalls associated with a decline in world cocoa prices and widespread corruption and inefficiency within the CPP and the government bureaucracy.

Unfortunately, everyone lacked experience with the parliamentary style of government-versus-opposition. Other parties and groups vehemently criticized the failures of the CPP ("a party of incompetents") and the extensive powers exercised by Nkrumah ("a dictator"). These criticisms embarrassed, threatened, and angered Nkrumah and the CPP, and so they passed laws restricting opposition activities. Opponents protested verbally and then violently. The government responded with even more repressive measures, arguing that any opposition was unpatriotic.

The government became more and more autocratic. An election in 1960 was obviously rigged, and a referendum of support for the government in 1964 was a farce. By the 1965 election, legal opposition was virtually eliminated, and all CPP candidates were declared elected. Both the economy and the social order were in collapse, and Nkrumah was behaving like a dictator. In 1966, the army intervened, overthrowing Nkrumah and installing a "temporary" military junta.

From 1966 to 2000, Ghana alternated between civilian governments and military regimes. By coups in 1972, 1978, 1979, and 1981, military officers took control of the government in the face of civilian incompetence and corruption. A young air force officer, Flight Lieutenant Jerry Rawlings, led the last two coups. By 1981, Rawlings

BOX 14.4 *(Continued)*

was convinced that his leadership and solutions were superior to those of civilian governments. Despite several assassination and coup attempts, he ruled continuously from 1981 until 2000.

Whereas Nkrumah attempted to install a command economy, Rawlings used political power with equal purposefulness to shift to a market economy. He collaborated with the International Monetary Fund to secure loans, implement a structural adjustment program, denationalize most public corporations, and radically cut public services. Ghana's economic performance has improved since 1990, in the sense that GDP per capita has been growing slightly, at an average of 1.9 percent per year, and inflation is being "held down" to an average of 26 percent (see Table 14.1).

Under international pressure, Rawlings allowed a free presidential and parliamentary election in 2000. Opposition leader John Kufuor, an Oxford-educated lawyer, became president in the first peaceful, democratic transition of power in Ghana's history, and he was reelected in a fair election in 2004. Freedom House now classifies Ghana as a "free" electoral democracy. The state that was going to be a model for postindependence Africa provided a depressing example of Third World authoritarianism, dependency, economic stagnation, and recurrent political decay for nearly 50 years. Can Ghana now, at last, sustain democratic stability and successful development and be a hopeful model for other developing countries struggling with political decay and turbulent histories?

episodes of serious political decay. In many developing countries, the combined effects of national independence, some modernization, some economic development, increasing social mobilization, and their political leaders' rhetoric cause the population to have high expectations that they will enjoy increased prosperity and a higher standard of living.

Since the political economy is usually unable to deliver sufficient goods (e.g., jobs, housing, health care, food) to meet these expectations, citizen support for the political leadership and institutions declines. As Chapter 10 indicated, leaders attempt various strategies, such as promises of better times or repression. But if citizens' patience and tolerance continue to drop, the result is usually an increase in political decay—noncompliance with the political system, strikes, riots, terrorism, nation-based violence. In some cases, new charismatic or authoritarian leadership reestablishes order; in some cases, order requires external intervention (e.g., by the United Nations or another country); and in some cases, there is a lengthy period of chaos in a failed state where no one is able to maintain order. In nearly all these cases, two major casualties are democratic processes and political institutionalization (Bratton and van de Walle 1997; Onwumechili 1999; Sorensen 2008; Linz and Stepan 1996).

Military regimes.   Until recently, the new political leadership that restored order in many developing countries often came from the military. There are three reasons the military emerges under conditions of political decay. First, a key norm within the military is a *commitment to order*, a norm that induces the military to act when the existing leadership has failed to maintain social order. Second, the military has the *capabilities to exercise power effectively*, since it is the most highly institutionalized and disciplined organizational structure in most developing countries. Third, the military has the *capacity to subdue disorder*, since it usually controls the greatest concentration of force and violence in the society.

As in the example of Ghana (in Box 14.4, and recall Box 10.4 on Cambodia and Box 11.3 on Congo), the emergence of strong military leadership has been a recurrent pattern in the countries in the Global South. In the early 1980s, for example, military regimes were in power in 15 of the 22 major Latin American states and in 20 of the 26 major sub-Saharan African states. By the mid-1990s, the military in most developing countries had accepted the professional norm that it should support the civilian regime and prevent political decay, but that it should not seize power. Thus a substantial number of developing countries are now "protected democracies" in which a strong military does not take direct political control but instead protects the political leadership and democratic processes in exchange for public policies that the military supports, such as maintaining social stability and the military's privileged status in society (Colburn 2002; Loveman 1994). In some cases, members of the military are still inclined to take political power in countries experiencing political decay, especially in sub-Saharan Africa and South Asia (e.g., in the Central African Republic in 2003, Thailand and Fiji in 2006, Bangladesh in 2007). In such instances, the military actors claim that they are restoring order, honesty, and democracy, but they usually establish an authoritarian regime and corruption recurs.

Internal war.   When political decay becomes so extensive that no groups, not even the military, can maintain order, a country is likely to become embroiled in internal war—either civil or revolutionary. In some countries (e.g., Cambodia, Nepal, Peru, the Philippines), variations of Marxism continue to appeal to frustrated groups that are persuaded their situation fits Marx's revolutionary call that the people have nothing to lose but their chains.

While the appeal of Marxist ideology has diminished in most developing countries, fundamental power struggles and deep inequalities among groups remain. Conflict is fueled by some combination of ethnonationalist, class, and regional cleavages. In the past decade, rival groups competing for power and control of resources reduced Afghanistan, Burundi, Colombia, Congo, Haiti, Iraq, Ivory Coast, Liberia, Sudan, Sierra Leone, Sri Lanka, and Somalia to near anarchy.

Major internal violence in developing countries is almost always supported by other states, which pursue their own national interests while providing financial or military assistance to combatants. Syria and Israel invade Lebanon; Uganda, Rwanda, and Burundi intervene in Congo; Libya, France, and the United States assist factions in the civil war in Chad; the United Nations intervenes in Congo, East Timor, Ivory Coast, Kosovo, Lebanon, and Sierra Leone. Indeed, a key element in the pervasive insecurity *and* instability of developing countries is the ease with which other states can pursue their own policy goals within the context of internal violence in these states.

Democratization

The trend toward **democratization** analyzed in Chapter 10 is evident in the Global South. Most developing countries are under considerable pressure to shift away from authoritarian and military regimes toward regimes with an elected leadership, a multiparty system, and open, pluralist politics. Two key sources of this pressure are citizen groups demanding political rights and the governments and financial institutions of the Global North.

Figure 14.3 summarizes the levels of freedom in Global South countries, according to Freedom House (2008). A "free" country grants its citizens extensive political rights (e.g., to form political parties that represent a significant range of voter choice and to engage in vigorous, open political opposition) and civil liberties (e.g., protection of religious, ethnic, economic, linguistic, and other rights). A country that is "not free" substantially limits these rights and liberties. "Partly free" means that there are significant political restrictions and violations of civil liberties, even though the country might be an electoral democracy (recall pages 166-168).

The spread of democratization is most extensive in *Latin America*. In 2008, every country in the Western Hemisphere had an electoral democracy, except Cuba, the only "not free" country in the region. Recently some countries, such as Bolivia and Ecuador, weathered serious episodes of political decay that earlier would almost certainly have resulted in a military coup. Some, including Argentina, Haiti, and

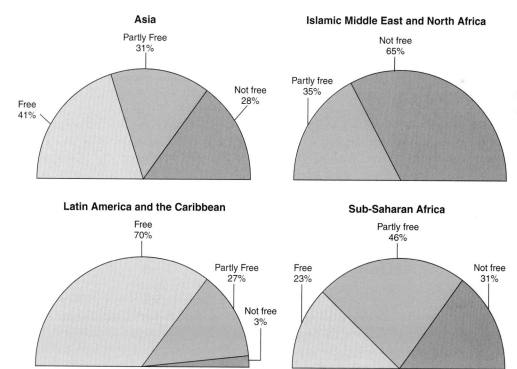

▶ **FIGURE 14.3** Levels of freedom in the developing countries, by region, circa 2007

Source: Freedom House (2008).

Venezuela, defeated coup attempts. Freedom House (2008) classifies more than two-thirds of the Latin American countries as fully "free" democracies (including Brazil, Chile, Costa Rica, Mexico, and Uruguay) (see Figure 14.3). Among the nine "partly free" countries are Colombia, Guatemala, Nicaragua, and Venezuela.

In *Asia*, the spread of democratization is mixed. China emphatically crushed the prodemocracy movement in Tiananmen Square in 1989. Cambodia, Myanmar, North Korea, Pakistan, Thailand, and Vietnam are also among 11 Asian developing countries that are classified as "not free." Twelve more (including Bangladesh, Malaysia, and the Philippines) are only "partly free." The 16 "free" countries include Indonesia, South Korea, and India, still the world's largest democracy, although it has been battered occasionally by political decay, including parliamentary deadlock, assassination, and extensive violence among Hindus, Muslims, and Sikhs. Electoral democracies are functioning in 59 percent of the Asian countries, although some are fragile and under persistent pressure from dissatisfied groups.

Although less than two-fifths of the countries in *sub-Saharan Africa* are electoral democracies, this is the region's highest level on this measure since independence. Freedom House (2008) classifies 11 of the 48 countries as "free," led by South Africa and Botswana, while 22 are "partly free" (e.g., Kenya, Nigeria) and 15 are "not free" (e.g., Angola, Congo, Zimbabwe). One analyst concludes that the prospects for further democratization are good in nearly half of the countries in the region (Barkan 2002).

Even many of the developing countries of the *Islamic Middle East* and *North Africa* have introduced elements of democratic politics. Most countries now have multiple political parties and elect their political leadership (e.g., Egypt, Iran, Morocco), while others at least have a democratically elected legislature (e.g., Jordan). However, many are best understood as illiberal democracies, since the existing leadership dominates the political system and opposition groups are severely restrained. Turkey is the region's only electoral democracy (Freedom House 2008). Not one Islamic country in the region is "free," and only 6 of 17 (Bahrain, Jordan, Kuwait, Morocco, Turkey, and Yemen) are "partly free."

Overall, democratization has expanded substantially in the Global South during the last two decades. Most regimes have granted some political rights to individuals and groups and have raised the level of elite accountability through elections. While the old elites have retained power in some elections, there are also many countries, especially in Latin America and Asia, where power has passed democratically to former opposition groups.

However, the current wave of democracy (discussed in Chapter 10) might already be ebbing in every region of the Global South (Schedler 2006; Wiarda 2003, 2004). Freedom House describes a global "pushback" against democracy and groups advocating political freedom and human rights (Puddington 2008). There are still some traditional coups, as in 2001, when the Ecuadorian military overthrew its president. Many recent elections lack legitimacy. For example, when Venezuela conducted an election for the legislature in 2005, all five main opposition parties boycotted what they felt were unfair manipulations of the media and the electoral process by President Hugo Chavez. Candidates of his party won all 167 seats, and the turnout was only 25 percent. In Iran, the religious leadership banned more than 90 percent of reformist candidates from the 2008 legislative elections, ensuring victory for the conservatives.

In the aftermath of questionable elections, many leaders have been driven from power by popular uprisings. In recent years, such "soft coups" have removed leaders from power in Bolivia, Georgia, Haiti, Kyrgyzstan, Paraguay, Peru, and Ukraine. While this "people power" has some virtues, it offers a mixed message about accepting the outcome of an election and the legitimate tactics for replacing leaders.

In general, the positive developments that have facilitated democratization in the Global South are balanced against three negative factors. First, these societies face the major destabilizing forces discussed in this chapter. Second, many elites do not have a genuine commitment to democratic practices. And third, these democratic regimes often have limited political institutionalization. "Hero" by well-known Egyptian cartoonist Toughan reflects the demoralizing obstacles to political and economic development facing citizens in many developing countries (see below).

Political Approaches

For those who do first "seek the political kingdom" as the primary instrument for achieving societal goals, the fundamental question is: What political approach will

HERO.!

Source: Toughan, CartoonArts International/CWS

increase the likelihood of prosperity, security, and stability? Developing countries pursue these goals within various political frameworks. One method for categorizing these frameworks is to consider the political approach taken regarding two basic issues: resource equality and democratic participation.

Resource equality concerns the extent to which the political system attempts to produce an equal distribution of key economic and social values (e.g., wealth, income, status, housing, health care, education, jobs). The state's authoritative allocation of these values can result in either greater equality or greater inequality. *Democratic participation* concerns the extent to which the people are mobilized into active and meaningful involvement in the political process. As discussed in Chapter 7, at the nondemocratic theoretical extreme, one person has all the political power in a country and all others are prevented from any political action. At the democratic extreme, every citizen has an equal role in political decisions and actions.

Obviously, there is no actual political system on either end of the continuum for either resource equality or democratic participation. Figure 14.4 indicates four ideal-type political approaches that have different orientations toward the desired mix of equality and democracy: (1) conservative authoritarianism, (2) modernizing authoritarianism, (3) revolutionary socialism, and (4) constitutional democracy. The next sections describe features of each.

Conservative authoritarianism.   *Conservative authoritarian* regimes *attempt to preserve the traditional socioeconomic order and culture* and have little or no commitment to resource equality or democratic participation. Certain groups, defined by lineage, ethnicity, class, religion, military power, or some other trait, enjoy great advantages in the distribution of economic and social power. This socioeconomic elite, with support from the government apparatus, exercises substantial control over the political economy. Most people are allowed little or no role in the political process. Political repression of the mass can be based on traditional practices, especially those associated with religion, or on state actions, especially those implemented by such agents of the state as the police and the military.

Greater political stability tends to occur in conservative authoritarian states that have minimal commitment to egalitarianism and where those groups engaged in order

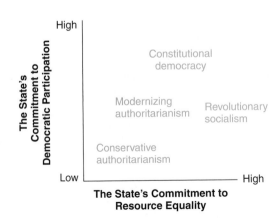

▶ **FIGURE 14.4**
Ideal-type
political
approaches

maintenance are well organized and loyal to the elite. Contemporary examples of such political systems are Haiti, Nepal, Saudi Arabia, Somalia, and Tajikistan.

Modernizing authoritarianism.   A *modernizing authoritarian* regime is dominated by an elite group that *desires to preserve culture and tradition*, but the elite *accepts that some development is inevitable and perhaps even desirable*. These states can have well-institutionalized organizational structures in the public sector, and technocratic elites within the bureaucracy can be a key group within the ruling coalition. Typically, most of the political economy is under private control, and the state works cooperatively with economic actors.

Substantial economic and social inequalities remain, and the elites make no major attempt to reduce them. Rather, there is an assumption that economic development will have an indirect, trickle-down effect and will eventually raise the absolute level of economic and social power of the less advantaged. Many of these states claim to be evolving slowly toward democracy, but popular political participation is limited and opposition is restrained. State leaders put a strong emphasis on stability and allocate considerable state resources to order maintenance. Military leaders are often a prominent part of the political elite. Modernizing authoritarianism characterizes such regimes as China, Egypt, Indonesia, Kenya, Morocco, Nigeria, and Syria.

Revolutionary socialism.   *Revolutionary socialist* regimes have *a strong commitment to economic and social equality and use political power to achieve this goal*. The leadership contends that a small, unconstrained political elite is essential to reduce the massive inequalities in the society. This leadership acts on behalf of the population, asserting totalitarian control over the political economy and the society. The citizens are mobilized, but only to support the policies of the elite, and there is no effort at genuine democratization. Extensive state-controlled political socialization, through the educational system, social groups, culture, and the media, indoctrinates citizens to serve collective interests. These states also employ repression and sanctions to induce desirable behavior.

China under Mao Zedong is a clear example of revolutionary socialism. Few current regimes follow this approach, although Cuba, Libya, North Korea, and the military regime in Myanmar display aspects of revolutionary socialism. Laos and Cambodia under the Pol Pot regime (described in Box 10.4) emphasized sanctions and repression of the masses.

Constitutional democracy.   *Constitutional democracies* promote *open politics in which citizens are allowed considerable political rights and civil liberties*. The leaders are directly accountable to the citizens and accept a limited mandate by means of an electoral system with genuine alternatives. The state engages in some welfare distribution, particularly to those in greatest need, but there is no attempt to use public policy to achieve substantial economic equality.

Botswana, India, and Jamaica are among the states that have generally maintained constitutional democracies in the last 30 years. As noted, many countries in the Global South have evolved toward constitutional democracy since the mid-1990s. These countries still face substantial pressure to limit democratic processes when they undergo the inevitable problems and disorder in the pursuit of prosperity, security, and stability.

Which route?   Every state attempts to attain prosperity, security, and stability. But in terms of the dimensions depicted in Figure 14.4, leaders must make fundamental choices about the approach they use to pursue these goals. The rhetoric of political leaders in most developing countries (but not in conservative authoritarian regimes) includes a vision in which their society ultimately achieves both a high level of political democracy and considerable social and economic equality—the upper right corner in Figure 14.4. The key question is: What is the most effective route to reach that "ideal location"?

The route the state takes will be influenced by many factors that its leaders cannot control in the short run: a country's political culture, its geopolitical situation, its nationality composition, its history of political institutions and leaders, its relations with other states, and so on. Within these constraints, political choices *can* be made. One set of major policy choices concerns the structure of the political economy, especially the level and nature of state involvement in the economic system. And Figure 14.4 reflects two other key choices regarding the emphasis on attaining political democracy and on achieving social and economic equality.

IT'S GETTING BETTER ALL THE TIME?

In both political forms and goals, there are no fundamental differences between those of the developing countries and the developed countries. Any developing country's selection of a particular political approach or political economy is dependent on many factors, especially its leaders, history, geopolitics and current circumstances. *Economic* underdevelopment is obviously the main factor distinguishing the countries of the Global South from those of the Global North, but *political* underdevelopment is the pivotal problem if the political system is to be used as the crucial instrument for social and economic change.

Regardless of their political approach, virtually all developing countries face difficult challenges as they attempt to use the political system to achieve prosperity and security. Most have valuable natural resources and a population that is willing to apply its energies to achieve these goals. However, their underdevelopment places them at an enormous disadvantage in the contemporary world, with its patterns of political, military, and economic inequality.

The Debate in 14 asks whether there will always be a Third World. For many of these states, especially the low-income developing countries, it is possible that *no* political approach and *no* form of political economy can simultaneously achieve all their major goals. The leaders of any developing country must make very difficult decisions about how to gain partial success on some of their goals. Some objectives will have to be sacrificed in the quest for others, and there is no assurance that *any* objective can be accomplished.

In the globalized world, the obstacles are formidable, and determining the best strategy is baffling. At every turn, the underlying political choices are fundamental: freedom versus security, economic development versus welfare, political equality versus economic equality, democracy versus efficiency, aid versus independence, neoliberalism versus statism, guns versus butter. Yet there are grounds for some optimism. Since 1990, the low-income countries have achieved some

THE DEBATE IN 14

Will There Always Be a Third World?

Virtually every country strives for a higher level of development. Most developing countries have been labeled part of the Third World at some point. While other terms are more favored today, "Third World" is still widely used to characterize a large number of countries that have a relatively low level of economic development, measured as GDP per capita. The label might encompass as many as 150 countries that are not yet "developed" to the level of countries in the Global North; but a more limited classification might include the 53 "low-income economies" and some or most of those (55) defined as "lower-middle-income" economies (World Bank 2008). Some analysts predict that these less developed countries will close the gap with the more developed countries, given the homogenizing dynamics of globalization (see Chapter 11). Others claim that substantial inequality between countries is an essential feature of the global system, and that continuing economic inequality is inevitable in a world of limited resources, free trade, disparities in technology, and hegemonic power relations. The poor countries, it might be said, will always be with us. Will there always be a Third World?

The Third World Is on a Path to Development

- Numerous economic and social indicators reveal significant improvement in the conditions and also the trajectory of development for the set of countries known as the Third World.

- In the developing countries, life expectancy has increased from 55.6 years to 66.1 years (1970–2005); the literacy rate has increased from 68.8 percent to 76.7 percent (1990–2005); the mortality rate for children under 5 (per 1,000) has decreased from 167 to 83 (1970–2005) (UNDP 2008).

- Overall, the Third World experiences higher economic growth rates than the high-income countries. Since 2000, low-income countries have grown at an annual rate of 6.5 percent, compared with 2.3 percent in the high-income countries (World Bank 2008).

- The mobility of capital, the transfer of technology across borders, and the extensive outsourcing of economic activity associated with globalization are producing substantial and increasing economic and social benefits for the Third World.

- The huge growth in international trade nearly tripled the volume of trade generated by low-income countries between 1970 and 1990, to $203 billion (World Bank 2005).

- The overall debt service (as a percentage of exports) that burdened most developing countries was cut in half in less than a decade, from 16 percent in 1990 to only 7 percent in 2004.

- The number of people living in severe poverty in the Third World decreased from 1.4 billion in 1981 to 1 billion in 2001, despite the increase in total population (World Bank 2005).

- If "Third World" is merely a label for those countries that are *relatively* poor, even while the absolute standard of living rises to a reasonable level for most of the population in most developing countries, then there will always be a Third World, but only because some countries will continue to be less rich than others.

The Third World Will Never Disappear

- The developed countries continue to enjoy enormous competitive advantages over the Third World, in terms of their control of capital flows, their greater technological capacity

The Debate in 14 *(Continued)*

and innovativeness, and their military and political power. These advantages helped generate the current vast inequalities between rich and poor countries, and there is no reason to assume that the rich countries will allow these advantages to wither.

- Powerful global institutions such as the WTO and multinational corporations generally operate in ways that favor the developed countries over the Third World. Globalization has resulted in increasing inequality between the world's rich and poor countries (Third World Network 2006).

- Despite higher growth rates and claims of convergence, the absolute differences between the Third World and the developed countries remain huge. For example, even if the developed countries were to stop growing from this moment forward, it would take Latin America until 2177 and sub-Saharan Africa until 2236 to catch up (World Bank 2005: 37).

- In real terms, the external debts of Third World countries have actually increased by more than 25 percent between 1990 and 2003 (World Bank 2005).

- There are more people in the Third World living on less than $2 per day in 2004 than there were in 1981 (World Bank 2005).

- A select set of developing countries will successfully reach a high level of development (such as some of the NICs). However, overall, there are few data to suggest that there will be any dramatic reduction in the dependency and poverty of many Third World countries, relative to developed countries.

More questions . . .

1. Might globalization and free trade generate some hardships and greater inequalities for some Third World populations in the short run but ultimately have very positive impacts on productivity, trade, and prosperity in their countries?

2. Is it a satisfactory situation if most people in Third World countries are increasingly better off in terms of life expectancy, literacy, caloric intake, and so forth, yet the relative disparities in quality of life between the Global North and the Third World increase?

improvements: life expectancy has increased by 1.8 years (to 58.7), adult illiteracy has declined from 45 percent to 37.7 percent, debt service has been reduced from 23 percent to 9.7 percent of exports, and the number of "free" countries has increased. Perhaps it is getting better, even if not in every developing country and not all the time.

KEY CONCEPTS

conservative
  authoritarianism
constitutional democracy
democratization
export promotion
foreign direct investment
Global South

green revolution
import substitution
International Monetary
  Fund
microcredit
modernizing
  authoritarianism

neocolonialism
neoliberalism
revolutionary
  socialism
statism
Third World

FOR FURTHER CONSIDERATION

1. Assess the claim that the label "Third World" has no meaning, either analytical or political, in the globalized, post-cold war world.

2. Are the problems in achieving economic development in the developing countries attributable primarily to the actions of the developed countries, or are they best explained by domestic circumstances in these countries?

3. Choose a real (or imaginary) developing country, and specify its conditions. Given your country's conditions, what political and economic arrangements make the most sense for progressing toward the key development goals you emphasize?

4. Is political violence in the developing countries likely to be greater or less during the next ten years compared with the past ten years? Why?

5. In addition to greater economic prosperity, what conditions seem most likely to sustain the shift to democratization in many developing countries? In particular, what forms or arrangements of political structures are most important?

FOR FURTHER READING

Andersen, Roy, Robert Seibert and Jon Wagner. (2008). *Politics and Change in the Middle East.* 9th ed. New York: Prentice Hall. A multidisciplinary, comparative introduction to the political systems and challenges in this important region.

Calderisi, Robert. (2007). *The Trouble with Africa: Why Foreign Aid Isn't Working.* New York: Palgrave. A very controversial argument by a former World Bank official that the low level of economic growth in sub-Saharan Africa is primarily attributable to short-comings in the institutions and especially the cultures of many African countries, including the problematic "African character" evident in elite behavior.

Diamond, Larry, Marc F. Plattner, and Daniel Brumberg. (2003). *Islam and Democracy in the Middle East.* Baltimore, MD: Johns Hopkins University Press. A broad-ranging series of short pieces from diverse viewpoints explore the question of why the recent "wave of democracy" has not swept across the Islamic Middle East, examining many specific countries as well as broad issues of democracy and Islam.

Ehrlich, Paul R., and Anne H. Ehrlich. (1990). *The Population Explosion.* New York: Simon and Schuster. Updating the earlier arguments in *The Population Bomb*, the Ehrlichs mount a powerful case that overpopulation in the developing world will lead to actions that result in catastrophic deterioration of the planet's resources.

Isbister, John. (2006). *Promises Not Kept: Poverty and the Betrayal of Third World Development.* 7th ed. Bloomfield, CT: Kumarian. A sensible and balanced analysis of the difficulties that have prevented most developing countries from achieving sustained development, exploring both the external and the internal obstacles to prosperity.

Li, Cheng. (1997). *Rediscovering China: Dynamics and Dilemmas of Reform.* Lanham, MD: Rowman and Littlefield. An insightful description of the powerful changes sweeping over China at both the individual and the institutional level, based on Li's personal observations and interviews.

Mehta, Ved. (1993). *A Portrait of India.* New Haven, CT: Yale University Press. A sensitive characterization of one of the most complex and intriguing developing countries.

Nugent, Paul. (2004). *Africa Since Independence: A Comparative History*. New York: Palgrave Macmillan. A richly comparative discussion of the evolution of many important African countries covering the entire postcolonial period.

O'Donnell, Guillermo, Philippe Schmitter, and Laurence Whitehead, Eds. (1986). *Transitions from Authoritarian Rule*. Baltimore, MD: Johns Hopkins University Press. Important case studies regarding the development and decline of rule by the military and technocrats, especially in Latin American countries.

Onwumechili, Chuka. (1999). *African Democratization and Military Coups*. Westport, CT: Praeger. A sobering and occasionally encouraging characterization of 40 years of struggle to establish democracy in African countries and to limit the tendency toward violent takeovers and authoritarian rule by the military.

Schedler, Andreas, Ed. (2006). *Electoral Authoritarianism: The Dynamics of Unfree Competition*. Boulder, CO: Lynne Rienner. These articles examine authoritarian regimes that hold elections, which the book contends are the most common form of political regimes in the developing world. They focus on the impacts of such elements as elections, the military, constitutions, and external actors.

Simon, Julian. (1998). *The Ultimate Resource 2*. Princeton, NJ: Princeton University Press. A powerful critique of those, like the Ehrlichs, who predict disaster due to overpopulation and environmental degradation. It argues that the ultimate resource (people producing knowledge and then applying it as technology) will outstrip problems.

Skidmore, Thomas, and Peter Smith. (2005). *Modern Latin America*. 6th ed. New York: Oxford University Press. A helpful comparative introduction to society and politics in Latin America.

Weatherby, Joseph N., et al., Eds. (2008). *The Other World: Issues and Politics of the Developing World*. 8th ed. New York: Longman. Thoughtful general chapters on colonialism, women and development, and political economy precede informative chapters focusing on each region of developing countries.

Wiarda, Howard J., Ed. (2004). *Authoritarianism and Corporatism in Latin America—Revisited*. Gainesville: University Press of Florida. The book argues that the apparent shift toward democratization in many Latin American countries is illusory. Rather, these countries still have strongly entrenched authoritarian and corporatist power structures.

World Bank. (Yearly). *World Development Report*. New York: Oxford University Press. Systematic yearly statistics on the economic, financial, and demographic aspects of development for more than 180 states. Each annual issue also emphasizes a key theme (e.g., 2001 on poverty, 2003 on sustainable development, 2006 on equity and development, 2007 on climate change), with a strong emphasis on the developing countries.

Yunus, Muhammad. (2008). *Creating a World Without Poverty: Social Business and the Future of Capitalism*. New York: Public Affairs Publishing. A remarkable vision from the inspiring Nobel Prize winner who established the Grameen Bank (Box 14.3) in which he sketches a business model that would enable every family to live with dignity and security.

ON THE WEB

http://allafrica.com

This site links to hundreds of current, Africa-focused newspaper articles as well as more than 900,000 articles in a searchable archive.

http://www.arab.net

Rich information on such aspects as the government, culture, business, and geography of every country in the Middle East and North Africa is provided as well as coverage of current news and issues.

http://menic.utexas.edu

The Middle East Network Information Center, hosted by the University of Texas, Austin, provides a vast number of sites with information regarding such areas as the politics, culture, and economic development of countries in the Middle East.

http://lanic.utexas.edu/index.html

The Latin American Network Information Center, hosted at the University of Texas, Austin, provides a vast number of Internet-based information sources about all countries in Latin America.

http://www.undp.org

The Web site for the United Nations Development Programme, a key unit of the United Nations that specializes in issues of economic and political development.

http://www.aseansec.org/

On the official Web site of the Association of Southeast Asian Nations are information and documents relevant to ASEAN, news about countries in the region, and somewhat self-serving Web pages constructed by each member state.

http://www.unctad.org

This part of the home page of the United Nations Conference on Trade and Development focuses on issues regarding the world's least developed countries.

http://un.org/womenwatch/

This French-based bilingual site provides links to various research, documents, organizations, and activities that concern the role of women in the development process.

http://www.twnside.org.sg/

Based in Malaysia, the Third World Network provides a strong perpective through a diversity of analyses, policy papers, and information on the full range of issues facing developing countries, including trade and development, environment, human rights, and globalization.

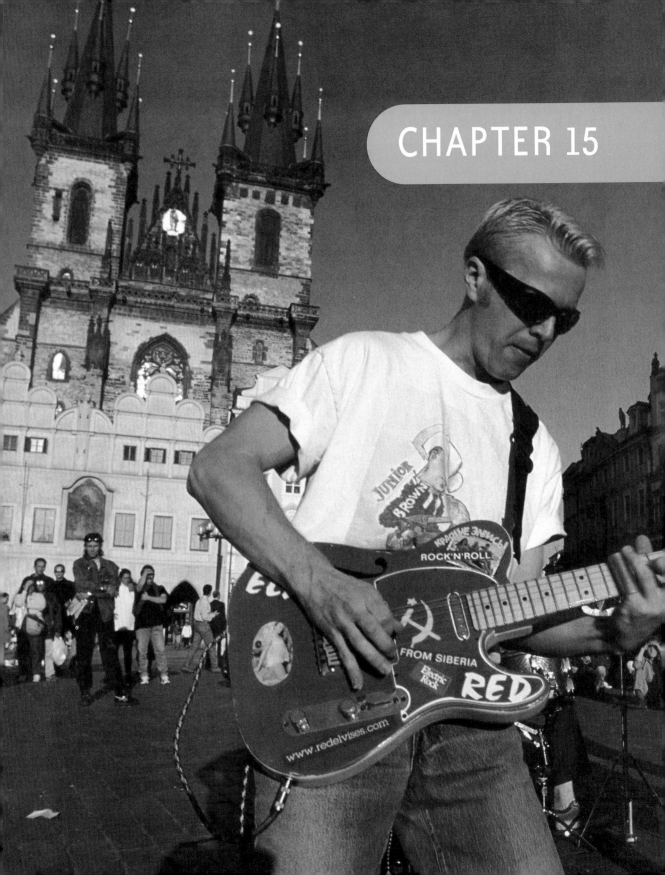

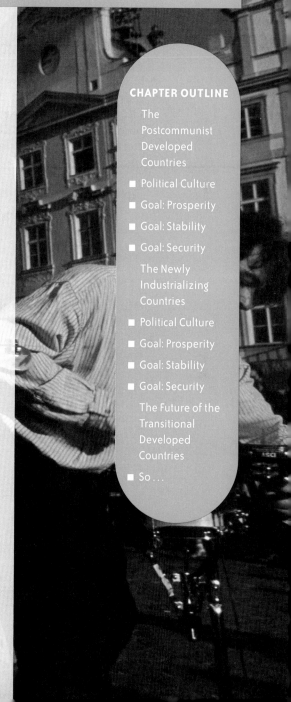

CHAPTER 15

THE TRANSITIONAL DEVELOPED COUNTRIES

Anyone who doesn't regret the passing of the Soviet Union has no heart. Anyone who wants it restored has no brains ... Our aims are absolutely clear: They are a high living standard in the country and a secure, free and comfortable life.

—*Vladimir Putin, 1952- , Prime Minister, Russia*

My commitment will be to travel with you on yet another stretch of this great promenade of freedom we have been opening ... The priority for my government is that there will be development for everyone, equally.

—*Michelle Bachelet, 1951-, President, Chile*

We have to construct a hopeful, happy, and rich nation. To this end, I propose "Korea 747 Vision," which delineates our economic commitment that the Korean economy will grow at least 7 percent every year, and in ten years per capita income will reach 40 thousand US dollars and the Korean economy will become the 7th largest globally.

—*Lee Myung-Bak, 1941-, President, South Korea*

Even in a dynamic world, the forces of change seem especially powerful in certain countries, including the two groups of *transitional developed countries* whose characteristics were defined in Chapter 13: (1) the postcommunist developed countries of the former Soviet bloc and (2) the newly industrializing countries. The countries in each group were identified in Table 13.1. They can be distinguished from most developing countries in the Global South (see Chapter 14) because they rank higher on the economic or social dimensions of development, but they have not reached the levels of the developed countries (see Chapter 13) on one or both dimensions.

As noted in Chapter 13, the criteria for including or excluding a country from one of these development groups are imprecise and subject to interpretation. The two groups of countries are singled out for examination in this chapter because they are in particularly notable periods of transition. It is possible that the changes these countries are undergoing will ultimately result in levels of economic and social development comparable to those in the most developed countries. But they face significant obstacles that might prevent them from achieving such high levels in the near future, and some of these countries might evolve in ways that result in their eventual reclassification within the group of developing countries. Currently, they are revealing case studies of "countries in the middle" within our framework of analysis. This chapter explores the broad patterns of changes and the obstacles facing each group.

THE POSTCOMMUNIST DEVELOPED COUNTRIES

After the Soviet bloc broke up in the late 1980s and early 1990s, 28 new national political systems emerged, including 15 states from the former Soviet Union. Many NGOs treat this set of 28 countries as a group. Freedom House (2008) clusters these countries as "Nations in Transit," and the World Bank (2008) refers to the entire group as "Europe and Central Asia" (it includes Western Europe as part of another group of "high-income economies"). However, based on the classification scheme in Figure 13.1, our analysis excludes from the transitional group those 12 postcommunist countries that still seem to have the characteristics of other developing countries (e.g., Albania, Armenia, Azerbaijan, Georgia, Moldova, Tajikistan).

Thus this chapter focuses on only the 16 countries from this group that are at moderate levels on economic and social development and are called the *postcommunist developed countries (PCDCs)*. These PCDCs include some of the states that emerged from the Soviet Union (e.g., Armenia, Belarus, Estonia, Kazakhstan, Latvia, Lithuania, Russia) and most of the states that evolved from the Soviet Union's previous allies in Central and Eastern Europe (e.g., Bulgaria, Croatia, the Czech Republic, Hungary, Macedonia, Poland, Romania, Serbia, Slovakia, Slovenia). These countries have a combined population of about 240 million.

The PCDCs are currently engaged in a process of substantial economic and political transformation. Until the late 1980s, these countries were communist states and were trying to achieve prosperity, stability, and security under the structure of a command political economy and totalitarianism (for 60 years in the Soviet Union and 40 years in Central and Eastern Europe). Since about 1990, these states have abandoned their communist ideologies and attempted to transform themselves into more market-oriented political economies and to implement democratic politics. These sweeping changes were the watershed events in the shift in the international system to the post-cold war period (described in Chapter 13).

Figure 13.1 in Chapter 13 reflects that these countries are relatively advanced on the social development dimension. Their populations are well educated and mainly urban, and they are incorporating high-tech systems into their economies and their private lives. The states have adopted democratic political processes and are institutionalizing them in varied degrees. The political economies in most states were significantly depressed during the economic transitions in the 1990s, but their GDP per capita measures are now increasing and three have now reached the level of high-income countries. Some citizens in these countries support the shift to a market economy, although others are dissatisfied with the effects of this change on themselves and on their society. Thus their current quest for prosperity, stability, and security entails adjustment from "traditional" communist approaches to these newer forms of politics and economics. The next sections briefly describe key elements of the communist approaches that shaped these political systems for two to four generations and then characterize the current systems.

POLITICAL CULTURE

The peoples of the PCDCs have a rich and complicated history shaped by many political cultures. Most of the former Soviet Union was ruled autocratically by the Russian czars for three centuries before the Russian Revolution of 1917. The rest of the region was controlled during much of the same period by great empires, including the Ottoman Turkish Empire in Eastern Europe (e.g., Bulgaria, Macedonia, Romania) and the Austrian (Hapsburg) Empire in Central Europe (e.g., the Czech Republic, Hungary, Poland). Only in the late nineteenth century did independent states emerge in Central and Eastern Europe. The political cultures of these states are strongly influenced by their history of oppressive rule and by the multiple nationalities that live within the boundaries of most of these states.

Under Communism

The dominant influence on the political culture in these states from 1945 to 1985 (and from 1917 in the Soviet Union) was *Marxist-Leninist socialism* (see Chapter 2). This political philosophy began with Karl Marx (1818–1883) and evolved after the Russian Revolution through the decisions of such Soviet leaders as V. I. Lenin (in power 1917–1924), Joseph Stalin (1927–1953), and Mikhail Gorbachev (1985–1991). There was an attempt to establish a political culture guided by four central concepts. First, consistent with the class approach (described in Chapter 9), individual societies and the international system are characterized by *stratification* and *class struggle*. Over time, the lower classes overthrow the oppressive class above them, and the new group in power reshapes the political economy to benefit its members.

Second, the political economy must serve a basic goal: producing *equality* in the distribution of societal resources, regardless of a person's status, role, age, gender, ethnicity, or any other such factor. Third, until such equality is achieved, politics must be *guided by an ideological elite*, the Communist Party, which controls the state and the economy, makes all policy decisions, and monitors the behavior of everyone. And fourth, when the transformation to communism is complete, the coercive state is no longer necessary and a true *people's democracy* is established. The state will, in the language of Friedrich Engels, "wither away," to be replaced by "the administration of things" and by widespread democratic participation in politics at the local level.

Postcommunism

The postcommunist political culture favors democracy and group politics and rejects the monopoly of power by the Communist Party. It also insists that the political economy must abandon extensive state control and state ownership, shifting toward a market political economy, private ownership, and greater freedom of action for firms and individuals. Most people, especially younger people and those who are relatively prosperous, accept this new political culture based in democracy and free market economics. However, the economic and social problems associated with the transition to the postcommunist system have been so severe in some PCDCs that key elements of Marxist-Leninist political culture continue to have a strong hold, particularly on older generations and those disadvantaged by the new system. In Russia, for

"It's going to be tough switching over to individual private enterprise."

example, a plurality of adults in 2003 still identified the Communist Party as the party that best represents the interests of "all Russian people" (Murphy 2003; Torcal and Montero 2006).

While these two conflicting political cultures continue to complicate the politics in many of the PCDCs, greater prosperity in most of these countries is reducing the support for the Marxist-Leninist vision. The next three sections characterize these countries' strategies for achieving the basic goals of prosperity, stability, and security.

GOAL: PROSPERITY

Under Communism

To achieve the goal of the equal distribution of abundant goods and material welfare to the entire population, the principal strategy was the *command economy*, as described in Chapter 8. The state and the Communist Party, guided by a comprehensive plan, attempted to control society's valued resources so that the economy benefited all the people, not just the rich and privileged.

Performance.   Under communism, these countries had relatively high scores on most quality-of-life measures (such as the Human Development Index). At the individual level, virtually every citizen had access to inexpensive or free health care, education, food, and shelter, and most had economic security against such problems as illness and old age. However, these countries' economic performance (on such measures as GDP per capita) was disappointing relative to the developed countries (with which they compared themselves). Most did rank in the upper one-third of the world's states, between fifteenth (the former East Germany) and forty-ninth (the former Yugoslavia).

Problems.   Although basic goods were distributed to most people, there were persistent shortages of many goods and services, and overall quality was poor. Three inherent problems with command political economies were particularly important (recall Chapter 8). First, there were *inadequate incentives* to hard work and innovation. Contrary to the Marxist ideal, workers with no wage incentives had minimal motivation to work efficiently for the good of all. And managers were cautious because the penalties for not following the economic plan were greater than the rewards for successful innovation. Second, *overcentralization* and rigid planning created an economy that was not responsive either to short-term opportunities and problems or to local circumstances. And third, the economy's overemphasis on heavy industry and the military resulted in *insufficient capital investment* in machinery and modern technologies (e.g., computers) to stimulate productivity gains in agriculture, light industry, and consumer goods (Blasi, Kroumova, and Kruse 1997).

Postcommunism

Many countries (e.g., Hungary, Poland, Yugoslavia) had already begun introducing elements of a market and encouraging some profit seeking by firms in the 1980s. Soviet leader Mikhail Gorbachev accelerated these changes with his support for economic *perestroika* ("restructuring") (Medvedev 2000). Since the early 1990s, the PCDCs have attempted to achieve a rapid transition to a market political economy. Private firms produce goods for profit, and the prices of most goods are determined by supply and demand. Central planning has been abandoned, and most state-owned enterprises have been sold to private actors ("privatized") or shut down. Some countries (e.g., the Czech Republic, Poland, Romania) opted for rapid and extensive market reforms (sometimes called *shock therapy*). Other countries (e.g., Hungary, Russia, Slovenia) chose a more gradual (*reformist*) approach based on slower changes in the political economy (Rutland 1999).

Performance.   Regardless of the approach, most PCDCs initially experienced a substantial decline in GDP, high unemployment, hyperinflation (inflation averaged higher than 100 percent per year in all but two of the PCDCs), and widespread personal economic hardship (World Bank 1996: table A3). At the individual level, the real income of most people dropped substantially, cuts in welfare services were deep, and unemployment soared. The number of people in absolute poverty increased enormously in less than a decade—from about 14 million people just prior to the "fall of communism" in 1988 (4 percent of the population) to 147 million in 1996 (40 percent of the population).

By the late 1990s, the economies and also the living standards of many people in most of the PCDCs were improving. By 2006, most of the PCDCs were averaging a

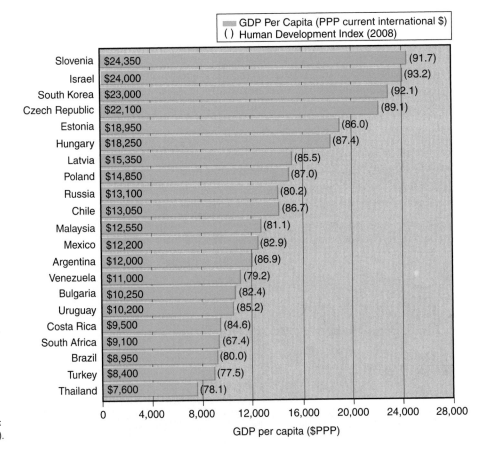

FIGURE 15.1
Prosperity measures for selected transitional developed countries
Source: World Bank (2008); UNDP (2008).

healthy 4–6 percent annual growth (World Bank 2006: table 1). Virtually all of the postcommunist countries in Central Europe and the Baltics are now upper-middle-income countries. Figure 15.1 indicates that GDP per capita is higher in most PCDCs than in most of the NICs to be analyzed later in this chapter. And several countries (e.g., Slovenia, the Czech Republic, Estonia, and Hungary) are now approaching the economic levels of some developed countries. This economic prosperity and their legacy of social development from the communist era (e.g., high literacy, low infant mortality) result in relatively high scores on the Human Development Index. But the economic transition in Russia, described in Box 15.1, lagged behind that of many other PCDCs. And Russia still has significant pockets of abject poverty, as do some of the other less-prosperous PCDCs.

BOX 15.1

Russian Roller Coaster

Russia's transition to a market economy has received continuing international attention, not because its transition is typical of that in most other PCDCs, but because Russia is the most prominent country in the region, given its size and international significance. Although the leaders did not opt for shock therapy, the Russian economy underwent a steady process of privatization in the 1990s. By 1996, 72 percent of large and midsized enterprises and nearly 90 percent of small shops and retail stores were under private ownership.

However, the political leadership was reluctant to implement fundamental economic reform. About two-thirds of the enterprises that were privatized moved into the hands of insiders from the old communist regime (dominated by powerful entrepreneurs called "oligarchs"), whose agenda was to acquire the society's economic assets at bargain prices and then exploit those assets ruthlessly in get-rich-quick schemes. Economic development was stifled by this *crony capitalism—the tendency for members of the old Communist Party elite to use their connections to reemerge as the new economic elite.* Meanwhile, the state retained ownership of some of the most inefficient enterprises, which operated at significant losses. Domestic production shrank steadily. Corruption pervaded every aspect of economic life. Overall, the state was ineffective in guiding the economy, controlling public spending, or extracting taxes.

In the decade after 1989, the Russian economy plummeted. There was hyperinflation (e.g., prices increased twenty-six-fold in 1992 alone), direct foreign investment dried up, and foreign debt was greater than 90 percent of GDP. Many people worked for months without being paid. Indeed, the economy had disintegrated to such an extent by the late 1990s that, by one estimate, about 80 percent of the country's business transactions were being conducted in barter trade (Goldman 1998).

Life conditions severely declined for many Russians. The state could no longer afford to provide social services to a population increasingly ravaged by unemployment and inflation. Real GDP per capita plunged 50 percent, the Human Development Index actually dropped from 91 to 77, and the percentage of people who lived below

BOX 15.1 *(Continued)*

the poverty line increased from 2 in 1989 to 50 in 2000. A significant increase in the inequality of wealth is reflected in the huge rise in the Gini index (from .215 to .487) between 1988 and 1999. By 1999, the richest one-tenth of the Russian population was earning more than 23 times the wages of the poorest tenth.

The political and social systems were also transformed dramatically. The new constitution opened the system to multiparty democracy and personal freedoms. The orderly, if dull and oppressive, society under communism disappeared. By late in the decade, Freedom House classified Russia as an electoral democracy with a free press and expanding political rights and civil liberties. However, these political transitions were not deeply institutionalized, and economic and social disruptions distorted and undermined political liberalization. The result was unstable governments, ineffective policies, and citizen disillusionment. Soon Russia was characterized by severe political decay, endemic corruption, and distressing environmental degradation. Serious crime increased tenfold between 1989 and 1999.

Moreover, there was another major economic crisis in 1998. In one year, the ruble lost 70 percent of its value, hyperinflation returned, and the number of people living below the subsistence level nearly doubled. Thus, among all these negative effects of the transition from communism, the three top problems identified by the citizens were directly related to economic performance: price increases, rising unemployment, and the "crisis in the economy" (VCIOM 1999). People's daily lives and the political economy had been so negatively affected that four-fifths of those surveyed in 2001 said they wished the old Soviet Union still existed, and in another survey only one in four Russians (27 percent) disagreed with the conclusion that it would be better (for Russia) had "everything in this country remained as it was prior to 1985" (that is, when the country was still communist and authoritarian) (Peterson 2001; VCIOM 1999).

Then, supported by high international oil prices (a strong export), assistance from the global financial community, and expanding consumer demand, the Russian economy began to surge upward. Since 2000, the economy has grown each year, averaging 6.8 percent annually, the highest among major countries. Capital investment has been high, inflation is under 10 percent, and foreign debt has declined significantly. Many Russians have benefited from this economic recovery, as real personal income has also increased by an average of 12 percent per year during this period. The budget is balanced, wages are being paid, inequality has been substantially reduced, and a 13 percent flat tax is generating considerably more revenue for government operations.

There are now two tiers of Russians. Prosperity and optimism are more evident among the population living in major cities, especially Moscow, and among the young; poverty and disillusionment are more common in nonurban areas, especially in the villages, and among the older generations of Russians who have lost nearly all the social services and welfare they received during the communist era.

While the economic conditions are improving, the political system has reversed its democratic course. Former President (now Prime Minister) Vladimir Putin has reasserted strong authoritarian control, jailing rivals, stifling political opposition, and muffling the media. Political rights and civil liberties have dropped to nearly the levels under communism, and the Freedom House (2008) classification of Russia has dropped to "not free."

BOX 15.1 *(Continued)*

Thus both economic and political transitions in postcommunist Russia have been roller-coaster rides, with promising highs and gut-wrenching drops. Most Russians have no idea where this ride will take them now. (This discussion is based on CIA 2008; Goldman 2003; McFaul and Stoner-Weiss 2004; Millar 1999; Roberts and Sherlock 1999; and Schleifer and Triesman 2000).

Challenges.   Since their political economies now function like all other market systems in the global economy, the postcommunist developed countries face all the formidable challenges to sustaining prosperity that confront the developed countries, as detailed in Chapter 13. The more advanced PCDCs (e.g., Slovenia, Czech Republic, Hungary, and Estonia) are on a positive path of economic growth as free market economies and, barring some unforeseen calamity, will complete the transition to developed countries (as measured in Figure 13.1) within the next decade.

However, for Russia and some of the other PCDCs (e.g., Bulgaria, Romania, the Balkan states), the path is more difficult and success less certain. These states must meet three major challenges for a more successful transition. First, the state and key economic actors must fully *institutionalize free market mechanisms* (e.g., capital markets, business contracts, business law), which did not exist under the command economy. Some countries have been reluctant to shrink the state sector too rapidly because the closure of state enterprises eliminates many jobs and the subsidized goods (e.g., food, electricity) that they produce. They have also been slow to eliminate the extensive regulatory obstacles to the formation of private firms.

Second, these states must *establish an appropriate level of welfare distribution* for the many people whose material living conditions have declined significantly. These people have faced the dual hardship caused by economic turbulence and the fact that the state has drastically reduced its large subsidies for food, shelter, health care, education, transportation, and other benefits, and has eliminated its extensive transfer payments to the financially disadvantaged.

Third, these PCDCs must *ensure that the vigorous new group politics does not undermine economic policy making*. Many citizens have used their new democratic rights to vote out of power each set of incumbent leaders and parties, whom they blame for the negative impacts from economic transitions. This results in substantial political instability and makes it difficult for any political leadership to implement tough economic policies and also retain popular support (Hanson 2001; McFaul and Stoner-Weiss 2004).

GOAL: STABILITY

Under Communism

For communist political regimes, a basic assumption was: prosperity + equality = stability. That is, social and political stability would result because the people were satisfied with the relatively equal distribution of abundant goods and services. This equation achieved only partial success. Before they abandoned communism, most of these countries had among the world's most equal distributions of wealth, including 8 of the 14 most equal countries (World Bank 1999: table 5). Also, the state provided free or subsidized education, food, and welfare goods, such as housing and health care, and people believed the system would take care of them in times of need. There was some inequality. Novelist George Orwell's ironic observation in *Animal Farm* (1945/1964) that "everyone is equal, but some are more equal than others" aptly applied, because certain groups, such as professionals, urban citizens, and especially Communist Party members, were favored in the distribution of material goods and status.

In terms of the stability equation, however, the key problem under communism was the insufficient *level* of prosperity, not the degree of inequality. The failure of the economy to generate greater material abundance was a major source of citizen dissatisfaction. These states promised far more material well-being than they could deliver, causing alienation in some of the population and undermining support for the political system.

Instruments of social control. To ensure stability in the absence of prosperity, these states utilized four key instruments of social control over many aspects of people's lives:

1. *Rewards and sanctions.* Those who were obedient were rewarded with such benefits as higher priority for desired goods, job advancement, and status awards such as public recognition. In contrast, those who failed to obey the rules of the communist system lost basic welfare benefits and those who committed serious offenses were imprisoned.

2. *The agents of political socialization.* The educational system, mass social organizations (e.g., youth clubs), and all the state-owned media constantly reinforced the values of loyalty, obedience, and service to the society.

3. *The Communist Party.* Party members, an honor extended to only about 10 percent of the population, were expected to encourage everyone to support party policies and to report anyone's inappropriate behavior to the authorities.

4. *The governmental apparatus.* The huge bureaucracy, the police, and the military firmly controlled most aspects of social and organizational life.

Performance. These mechanisms of social control resulted in a high level of stability. The occasional outbreaks of collective violence (e.g., uprisings in Hungary in 1956, Czechoslovakia in 1968, and Poland in 1956, 1968, and the 1980s) were firmly suppressed. The normal pattern of collective life was stable, with the party and the state in firm control. People generally behaved in accordance with the rules of the regime because the mechanisms of control were effective and also because the people accepted a life that, though dull, was safe and secure. The rates of crimes against people (e.g., murder, rape, assault) and crimes against property (e.g., burglary, theft) were much lower than those in such developed countries as the United States. Although crime was low, individual frustration in such oppressively stable systems manifested itself at the personal level in relatively high rates of substance abuse (e.g., alcoholism) and family problems (e.g., divorce, child abuse) (Goldman 1998).

Opposition to the Communist Party became more open and personal freedoms expanded significantly during the 1980s, with an enormous boost from Soviet Premier Mikhail Gorbachev's policy of *glasnost*—a tolerance of public discussion and criticism of the political, economic, and social systems. Then, in 1989, the citizens in every East European country filled the streets, demanding political and human rights. After decades of repression, the Communist Party leaderships capitulated in country after country, lacking either the will or the capacity to retain power. A signal moment was November 9, 1989, when the Berlin Wall, the most notorious symbol of the Iron Curtain, was opened, allowing a joyous reunion of 1 million East and West Berliners. Except in Romania (where events corresponded to a revolution from above), the dramatic changes occurred in these countries with so little violence that they are best described as "democratic revolutions" (see Chapter 12). By December 1991, even the Soviet Union "died" and was replaced by 15 independent countries.

Postcommunism

In most countries, the new leaders who emerged after 1989 were committed to sweeping transformations of the political system as well as the political economy. These countries adopted new constitutions that established hybrids which distribute power between a president and a legislature-plus-prime minister selected through proportional representation (mixed-member) electoral systems (Chapter 7). Elections are fair, open, and competitive, often with a large number of political parties. These multiparty systems include liberal parties that support rapid transition to a market economy, nationalist parties that focus especially on issues of ethnic identity, and "reformist" parties that advocate a market system with a "social face," retaining some communist-era state distribution of welfare and state control of key sectors of the economy (Grzymala-Busse 2002). Political discourse is wide ranging and unconstrained, and virtually all groups and political parties (even the reform communists) accept the outcome of actively contested elections among genuine alternatives. Thus 12 of the 16 PCDCs have made a successful transition to liberal democracy and are classified as "free" by Freedom House (2008).

One PCDC (Macedonia) is "partly free," and three (Belarus, Kazakhstan, and Russia) are "not free," according to Freedom House (2008). These countries have reasserted authoritarianism though with more political rights and civil liberties than during the communist period (Schnetzer 2003). Box 15.1 noted that since Vladimir Putin's regime began in 2000, Russia has steadily reduced democratic practices, political rights, and civil liberties. Neighboring Belarus has imposed Soviet-era restrictions on democratic practices such as free speech, press freedom, and political opposition and has retained a command political economy. All of the PCDCs, whether democratic or authoritarian, have attempted to maintain stability during their transition periods, and all face challenges related to social disorder, nationality issues, and globalization.

Social disorder.   Inequality has increased during the postcommunist period in most PCDCs. In the absence of communism's strong commitment to minimize differences based on class, gender, and age, there is notably more *social* inequality in virtually all these transitional countries The increases in both poverty and wealth have also led to more *economic* inequality; yet many of these countries, including Belarus, Hungary, the Czech Republic, and Bulgaria, still have among the highest levels of income equality in the world (measured by the Gini index of inequality; recall Table 13.2).

The combination of free-wheeling capitalism, the decline in communist-era social controls, and increases in poverty and inequality have resulted in a rise in *social disorder*. This is reflected in a decline in obedience to laws and rules and is particularly evident in the high incidence of crime. In many regions, the police are either ineffective or corrupt, and citizens live in fear of organized crime, random criminal violence, and even the police (McFaul 1998). In Russia, more than 4,000 mafia crime groups are engaged in widespread extortion, auto theft, drug peddling, burglary, and other criminal activities. In the first five years of postcommunism, for example, reported serious crimes increased 270 percent in Romania, 222 percent in Bulgaria, and 105 percent in Poland (Murphy 1995). While the rates of increase are now modest, countries that were accustomed to almost no violent crime under communism are now attempting to cope with distressing levels of crimes against both people and property.

Nationality conflicts.   A few nationality groups, such as the Poles and the East Germans (who were reunited with their West German brothers and sisters in 1990), now live in ethnically homogeneous states. In 1993, Czechoslovakia broke peacefully into two states based on its two main ethnic groups (Czechs and Slovaks). However, *ethnonationalism* (recall Chapter 5) threatens the stability of most PCDCs because virtually all have significant minority populations. In most of the countries, marginalized nationality groups are increasingly active in demanding greater autonomy. The

▶ **Chechen rebels threaten Russian prisoners of war captured during a bloody battle in the Chechens' ethnonationalist struggle for regional autonomy.**

majority group has often responded by aggressively asserting its domination (Bunce 2003). Thus internal nation-based conflict has produced disorder in many PCDCs, with particular hostility directed against Russians and the Roma (gypsies). Some conflicts have exploded into separatist violence, most extensively in highly multinational Russia (e.g., Chechnya and Ingushetia). And Yugoslavia, a complex multiethnic state under communism, became a brutal battleground as different nation-based groups fought to define the boundaries of a set of new states (see Box 15.2).

BOX 15.2

Out of Many, One; and then Many Again: Yugoslavia

Like many countries, Yugoslavia was forged from many nationalities by the heat of history, military might, and strong leadership. Historically, the Balkan area included several ministates that had been dominated by the Austrian Hapsburg Empire and the Ottoman Turkish Empire. The first Yugoslav state, formed after World War I had diminished the former imperial powers, was a royal dictatorship called the "Kingdom of the Serbs, Croats, and Slovenes" and renamed Yugoslavia ("Land of the South Slavs") in 1929. The lack of shared national identity among the various ethnic groups became most obvious during World War II. In a brutal civil war, the Slavs killed more of one another in interethnic fighting than were killed in Yugoslavia by the invading Nazis. The area was divided among the Germans, Italians, Albanians, Hungarians, and Bulgarians. Croatia declared independence and became an ally of the Germans.

After the war, Josip Broz Tito, a shrewd and charismatic leader of the resistance to the Nazis, took political power. Tito united the various groups (six republics and two autonomous regions) into a federation that was fragile at first but eventually gained stability and relative prosperity. He installed a collective executive that shared power among the various ethnic groups. Although Tito was a communist, he established an economy that allowed substantially more enterprise and initiative than the command economies in other East European states. Tito also established an independent foreign policy, making political and economic alliances with West European states as well as with members of the Soviet bloc.

The country remained stable after Tito's death in 1980, but then the turbulence in Eastern Europe in the late 1980s reawakened the nationalist animosities within Yugoslavia. The key protagonists were 9 million Serbs (generally Greek Orthodox, pro-communist), 4.5 million Croats (Catholic, noncommunist), 2 million Slovenes (Catholic, noncommunist, and the most prosperous group in the country), 4.5 million Bosnians (Muslim), 2 million Macedonians (Greek Orthodox, with strong links

BOX 15.2 *(Continued)*

to northern Greece), and 600,000 Montenegrans (Greek Orthodox, pro-Serbian, and with a history under their own king).

In 1991, the Macedonians, Croats, and Slovenes rejected the authority of the central government located in Belgrade in the Serbian region. Each group declared independence. Macedonia and Slovenia managed to secede with minimal violence. Despite international recognition of Croatia and a United Nations-arranged cease-fire, a bloody, if sporadic, struggle occurred between Croatia and the Serb-dominated Yugoslav armed forces until 1995.

Bosnia also declared independence, in March 1992, but did not gain immediate recognition. Serbs, about one-third of the population within Bosnia, launched a bloody civil war as Bosnians and Serbs each attempted to secure as much of the region of Bosnia-Herzegovina as possible for their emerging states. In devastating town-to-town fighting, Serbian and Bosnian paramilitary groups murdered and brutalized each other as well as civilians. Eventually, a settlement was imposed by the United Nations and the EU, based on a federation of two semiautonomous regions and a complex three-person presidency representing all key ethnic groups.

Serbia was the site of the next explosion of violence, in Kosovo, an impoverished southern province. About 90 percent of the Kosovo population are ethnic Albanians, whose desire for autonomy resulted in a revolutionary guerrilla war in the late 1990s. While the United Nations attempted to intervene, Serbian President Slobodan Milosevic encouraged the local Serbs to engage in ethnic cleansing. Within months, the great majority of ethnic Albanians were either dead or in exile. Massive airstrikes by NATO reestablished the rights of the ethnic Albanians to inhabit Kosovo, and they returned, turning their hostility against local Serbs. In 2006, Montenegro voted for independence from Serbia, and Kosovo claimed its independence in 2008.

It is possible that this exceedingly complex and brutal turf war over the boundaries of new states-in-formation is reaching a resolution. The region has engaged in a substantial ethnic reordering in which borders now coincide roughly with nationality identity. This might end most of the violent conflicts that produced hundreds of thousands of refugees, serious episodes of ethnic cleansing, and more than 250,000 deaths in the 1990s. There are continuing tensions in the region and, more ominously, bitter divisions in some locations where two ethnicities must try to coexist. Kosovo's sovereignty is contested. Bosnia-Herzegovina attempts a delicate balance among three antagonistic ethnic groups. Several ethnic groups resent the war crimes trials of their national heroes (e.g., Serb Mladic, Croatian Norac) for war crimes. There is hope that the Balkans will be brought into the European community with no further balkanization (Brown 1999; CIA 2008; Rupnik 1999).

Entry into Europe and the global system. After decades of relative isolation, most PCDCs have fully entered the global economy and have established new relationships with Western Europe. Ten Central and East European PCDCs have joined the European Union since 2004 (recall Box 11.1). As conditions for membership, these states demonstrated, to the satisfaction of all existing EU member states, that their political institutions are stable and democratic and that they have effectively functioning market political economies. In contrast, Russia and several other PCDCs have not made these transitions and remain outside the EU, resulting in considerable tension between the two groups. All of these transitional economies are attempting to establish their niche in the complex global economy. Many can offer a well-educated, disciplined, and low-wage labor force, which gives their manufacturing and service sectors some competitive advantages in relation to the more developed countries in the EU. Thus foreign direct investment has been flowing in. However, this advantage is under threat from the much lower wage labor available in the developing countries.

Overall. Most of the postcommunist developed countries have established effective democratic political practices and institutions. The speed and apparent depth of these changes are remarkable, given their previous experiences under communism. However, a few PCDCs, most notably huge, influential Russia, have been much less receptive to democratization and have retained the authoritarianism of the past, with its limits on political rights and civil liberties. For this latter group of countries, the transition to a stable and effective postcommunist political system is more uncertain and more vulnerable to the kinds of political disorder and violence described in such analyses as Huntington's conception of political decay (see Chapter 10).

GOAL: SECURITY

Between its foundation in 1917 and its demise in 1991, the Soviet Union placed exceptionally high importance on security goals. By that standard, the 1990s was a disaster for the Soviet Union and its allies in Central and Eastern Europe. In December 1991, the Soviet Union disappeared, replaced by 15 states that are based on historical ethnic and regional boundaries. East Germany, the strongest state economically, also disappeared, having merged with West Germany in 1990. Yugoslavia fractured into multiple states, and Czechoslovakia split in two. All this seems remarkable for a "Soviet Empire" that was judged an adversary equal to the powerful United States during the four-decade cold war. A brief consideration of the security situation in the Soviet Union and Eastern Europe during the cold war aids our understanding of the different security issues that these states now face.

Under Communism

History and geopolitics.   In Halford John Mackinder's (1996) famous nineteenth-century geopolitical analysis, Eastern Europe and Russia were the essential "heartland": control of that region would ensure world dominance. These areas have been battlefields for the last 200 years, including devastating invasions by the French under Napoleon and by the Germans under Hitler.

After World War II, the Soviet Union perceived itself to be surrounded by increasingly hostile, anticommunist threats to its survival. To the east, Japan, a historical military adversary, evolved into a major capitalist world power. To the southeast, China, with its huge population and alternative vision of communism, displayed growing combativeness. To the southwest, the militancy of Islamic fundamentalism presented a clear danger, given its antipathy to communism and the large population of Muslims in the Soviet Union's southwestern regions. To the west were the major capitalist powers, with their deep animosity to the communist systems and with NATO's devastating military (including nuclear) capabilities stretched along almost half of the Soviet bloc's border.

Military power.   To protect itself against all these real or perceived threats to its survival, the Soviet Union aimed for unchallengeable military power. In order to create a buffer zone between itself and its rivals, it gained control over territory on all sides, annexing some areas into the Soviet Union and creating a bloc of subservient states in Central and Eastern Europe. This bloc built what was arguably the world's most powerful military for conventional warfare, and the Soviet Union was not far behind the NATO allies in air power and nuclear capabilities.

The cold war rivalry between the Soviet Union and the United States dominated the bipolar international system, spawning a huge military buildup, an arms race, and the mutually assured destruction (MAD) discussed in Chapter 11. Soviet leaders from Stalin to Gorbachev opted for guns over butter, spending 9–15 percent of GNI on defense in the late 1980s. Such high military expenditure substantially reduced the resources available for economic growth and the distribution of welfare and is arguably the main reason for the demise of the Soviet system (Medvedev 2000).

Postcommunism

The postcommunist period has fundamentally altered the security situation for the PCDCs. Ten former members of the Soviet security bloc joined the old enemy, NATO, despite strong opposition from Russia. Russia's military spending dropped almost 85 percent during the 1990s, but it is still ranked fourth in the world in total military expenditures (SIPRI 2008). Russia maintains its military machine, including a large standing army and the second largest nuclear arsenal in the world, with 5,670 operational nuclear warheads (*Bulletin of Atomic Scientists* 2007). Most of Russia's neighbors, including many PCDCs, are uneasy about its assertive foreign policy since 2000, as Russia has rearmed and seeks to rebalance the power of Russia and its allies against the United States (McFaul 2007). In retrospect, the international system had become relatively secure under the strong bipolar security regime dominated by the United States and the Soviet Union. According to balance-of-power analyses, the current evolution toward a more diffuse, multipolar international system will increase insecurity in the relations among states (see Chapter 11). One of the major challenges for all countries, including the postcommunist developed countries, is how to adapt to the end of the bipolar system in an era of globilization.

THE NEWLY INDUSTRIALIZING COUNTRIES

During the past several decades, one group of countries has been particularly successful in attempting the transformation from developing to developed countries. These countries have been labeled the *newly industrializing countries (NICs)*. Many international organizations (e.g., the World Bank) now refer to them as the newly industrializing economies (NIEs). A NIC is distinguished by its economic transition to become a major exporter of manufactured goods and services and by its sustained high economic growth rate.

The NICs are rising faster than most other developing countries in the analytic framework presented in Figure 13.1. To this point, only a few NICs in Asia (e.g., South Korea) have been fully successful in advancing on both the economic and social dimensions. (Indeed, two NICs—Singapore and Taiwan—have recently been "promoted" to the developed countries group, based on their performance levels on the critera in Figure 13.1.) Certain Latin American countries, especially Argentina, Chile, and Mexico have also advanced considerably toward achieving the level of development and sustained growth characteristic of the leading NICs.

There are other countries, mainly in Asia (e.g., Malaysia) and Latin America (e.g., Brazil, Uruguay, and Venezuela), that have reached the levels of development that place them in the NIC group. And a few countries outside of these two regions (e.g., Israel, Turkey, South Africa) are currently difficult to classify but are arguably NICs based on their location in Figure 13.1, as is China (recall Box 10.3). This section discusses the key political and economic transitions that are occurring in the NICs of Asia and Latin America. Although some commonalities are identified, these two groups are discussed separately.

POLITICAL CULTURE

Generally, the Asian NICs share a social and political culture that is influenced by such ethical-religious philosophies as Buddhism, Taoism, and most notably, Confucianism. Indeed, many analysts conclude that Asian cultural norms, and Confucianism in particular, are the critical factor that accounts for the notable success of the NIC approach in Asian countries compared with Latin America or other regions (Compton 2000; Fallows 1995; Huntington 1991; but also see the *Economist* 1998). These norms emphasize hard work, acceptance of authority, and subordination of personal needs to collective goals. Box 15.3 explores the critical linkages between Asian political culture and economic development.

The political cultures in Latin American NICs have some similarities to those of the Asian NICs. The Catholic Church is an important institution that traditionally encouraged obedience to a hierarchical authority system and the subordination of current rewards to eventual benefits. Similarly, Latin American social structure has generally been based on hierarchical class strata and a dominant ruling class whose members are in charge of the economic and political systems. However, Latin American cultural norms generally place less importance than Asian ones on mass education, hard work, and the pursuit of collective goals relative to personal advancement.

BOX 15.3

Confucius Says . . . : Culture and Development

Important scholars such as Max Weber (1958a) and R. H. Tawney (1938) have linked crucial elements of a society's cultural norms with its success in implementing capitalist economics. Recently analysts have asked: How can we explain the particular success of the leading Asian NICs in achieving economic development, given a global system that seems to favor the more developed countries (recall the dependency approach discussion in Chapter 10)? Many answers have emphasized the powerful positive influences of Confucian cultural norms (Compton 2000). Based on the teachings of a fifth-century B.C.E. Chinese intellectual, *Confucian culture* stresses that *individual action must be based on what is best for the group and for society as a whole.* Harmony and cooperation are always to be sought, and disunity and conflict must be avoided. Society is shaped by a series of superior-subordinate relationships in which obedience must be offered: by subject to ruler, by child to parent, by younger to elder, and by female to male.

In political terms, Confucianism places the highest value on *order, stability, and discipline* within a framework of hierarchical authority. The ruler, the parent, and the boss must be obeyed unquestioningly. The individual's responsibilities and public duty have priority over his individual rights and interests. Such principles powerfully support

BOX 15.3 *(Continued)*

a political system in which authoritarianism is natural and acceptable. The political elite is justified in taking any action that maintains harmony and order or that serves the broader interests of the society, regardless of the costs to individuals or interest groups (e.g., political parties, unions, students). Other key cultural norms include the beliefs that making and saving money are virtuous and that individuals (traditionally, males) should achieve the highest possible level of education and learning.

Analysts suggest that this combination of norms has encouraged behaviors that facilitated capitalist development in the late twentieth century. These behaviors include the discipline and loyalty of employees to the firm, the subordination of personal needs and prosperity to the goals of the nation, the high propensity to save (and invest), and the acceptance of close linkages between the state and the economic elite (Fallows 1995). Obviously, many other factors are also critical for economic development, including the availability of necessary resources, the activities of economic competitors, the quality of economic and political leadership, the security of the country, and so on (*Economist* 1998). But most agree that Confucian cultural norms have been a very positive force in the economic transition of the Asian NICs.

Broadly, political authoritarianism has been linked with the political cultures of both regions. The Latin American region is particularly associated with a popular acceptance of leaders, often with a military background ("caudillos"), who exert extremely strict control over the political system. Latin American political cultures have typically assumed that there would be political competition but that it would be hegemonic, involving the alternation between elites rather than open competition among truly opposing groups (Aguero and Stark 1998; Lozada 2003). Many Asian political cultures have also accepted, and perhaps even preferred, strong, authoritarian leaders. However, they have placed considerably less premium on political competition and group struggle, given the value attached to consensus and hierarchy by Asian political cultures.

GOAL: PROSPERITY

The most successful NICs, particularly those in Asia, have pursued prosperity by employing variations on the ***developmental-state approach*** described in Chapter 10: (1) an export-oriented market political economy, but with an activist state whose policies enable firms to be more profitable; (2) close cooperation between firms and government to target niches in which export goods can be sold; and (3) government support of the agrarian sector, including the redistribution of land and encouragement of commercial agriculture.

This approach emphasizes the primacy of economic development relative to political or social development (Fallows 1995; Johnson 1996; Simone 2001). State expenditures are directed toward improving the economic infrastructure (e.g., transportation systems, communications networks) and educating the labor force.

Government policy encourages savings and investment rather than consumerism, and it limits wage rates for workers. Only as economic development reaches high levels is there a shift toward policies that enable citizens to acquire more consumer goods and that increase the state's welfare distribution to less advantaged citizens.

While the broad strategy of the Asian NICs is similar, there are significant differences among these states. For example, the South Korean government supported and protected a few very large national firms called *chaebols* (e.g., Hyundai, Goldstar, Samsung), which produce a broad diversity of manufactured goods. In contrast, Malaysia has allowed more extensive involvement of foreign multinational corporations, especially from the United States and Japan, as it focused on manufacturing, particularly electronics components.

Government economic policies in most Latin American NICs have been less interventionist than those in Asia. For example, the governments have generally been less involved in firms' production decisions, less active in agrarian reform and rural land redistribution, and less controlling regarding the role of multinational corporations in their economies. Many Latin American countries abandoned statist strategies only in the last several decades, adopting developmental-state or neoliberal approaches (Triesman 2004).

Because most Latin American NICs have a substantial endowment of natural resources and farm lands, their governments have generally attempted to balance their development policies to support not only manufacturing and service industries but also the extraction and processing of commodities (e.g., foods, oil, minerals). Additionally, the longer history of active electoral politics in the Latin American NICs has had numerous consequences for economic policy, including more extensive distribution of social welfare goods by the state to secure votes and fewer restrictions on trade union activities. The NICs in each region are influenced by a global power: the Japanese economy has affected development in the Asian NICs, and the vast economic system of the United States has had even greater impacts on economic development in Latin America, and for a much longer period.

Performance. In general, all the NICs have relatively high levels on both GDP per capita and the Human Development Index (Figure 15.1). This is based on solid economic growth rates (see Figure 15.2 and Table 15.1). Although the Latin American NICs began at higher levels of prosperity than the Asian NICs in 1960, the Asian NICs have generally had more consistent increases since that time. The leading Asian NICs sustained economic growth rates averaging about 7 percent annually during the period from 1980 to 1995, placing them among the fastest-growing economies in the world. They had positive trade surpluses and high levels of capital accumulation, and their firms became competitive in the international marketplace across a wide range of goods.

By the mid-1990s, the original Asian "tigers" (e.g., Singapore, South Korea, Taiwan) had been joined by a group of "little dragons" (e.g., Malaysia, Thailand) that also seemed to be on a fast track of rapid and sustained economic development. Then in 1997, the economies of most Asian NICs experienced a severe and unexpected decline. Their currencies lost value, stock markets collapsed, banks and other major firms went into bankruptcy, and direct foreign investment dried up. These economic

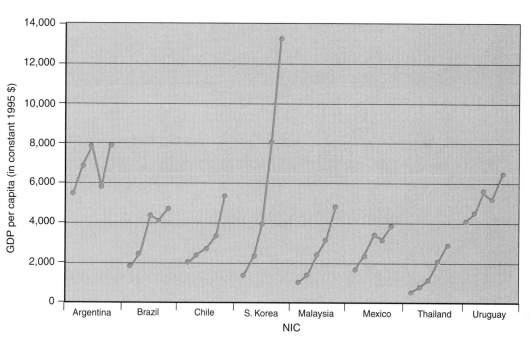

▌ **FIGURE 15.2**
Changes in
prosperity
measures for
selected
transitional
developed
countries,
1960–2005

disruptions negatively affected almost every economy in East Asia and then spilled over into the economies in other "emerging markets," particularly in such transitional countries as Brazil and Russia. After aggressive intervention by the International Monetary Fund, most Asian NICs recovered their economic momentum within a few years and thus have sustained solid growth since 1990 (Table 15.1). However, the "magic" of the Asian NICs as invulnerable engines of economic growth and increasing prosperity had been debunked (Mahon 1999; Winters 1998).

   Only a few Latin American NICs, such as Chile, approached this admirable rate of persistent growth since 1990. Most Latin American NICs tamed hyperinflation but had only sporadic periods of economic growth, averaging less than 3 percent annually (Hakim 1999). Recently, growth in GDP per capita has been erratic, with Chile and Costa Rica generally highest but most others averaging less than 2.0 percent per year (Table 15.1). Many Latin American NICs experienced recurring periods of economic decline and inflation, rather like their less-developed regional neighbors (recall Chapter 14). Mexico suffered a "peso crisis" in 1994, Brazil's economy has been highly volatile (see Box 15.4), and the economies of Argentina and Uruguay dropped precipitously in 2002. The core causes of these economic problems in the Latin American NICs are disputed, but many analysts attribute them to the same sorts of weaknesses listed above for such PCDCs as Russia. Privatization, corruption, international competition, and exploitation by multinationals and "crony capitalists" have taken a severe toll in Latin America (Hakim 1999; Heredia 1997; Mahon 1999).

   As the Latin America NIC economies have been buffeted by the forces of severe economic volatility and globalization, their governments have implemented structural

> **TABLE 15.1**
Economic Growth and Decline in Selected Transitional Developed Countries, 1990–2004

	Average Annual Growth/Decline in GDP per Capita, 1990–2005	Average Annual Inflation Rate, 1990–2005
Postcommunist Developed Countries		
Poland	4.3%	16.0%
Estonia	4.2	12.0
Hungary	3.1	15.0
Slovakia	2.8	7.8
Croatia	2.6	40.6
Croatia	2.6	4.6
Belarus	2.2	144.6
Kazakhstan	2.0	29.7
Czech Republic	1.9	5.2
Romania	1.6	66.5
Bulgaria	1.5	67.6
Russia	−0.1	53.5
Newly Industrializing Countries		
South Korea	4.5	4.3
Chile	3.8	6.3
Malaysia	3.3	2.9
Thailand	2.7	3.7
Costa Rica	2.3	13.5
Turkey	1.7	64.2
Israel	1.5	6.6
Mexico	1.5	14.8
Argentina	1.1	7.1
Brazil	1.1	86.0
Uruguay	0.8	22.3
South Africa	0.6	7.4
Venezuela	−1.0	37.6

Note: Inflation is measured as annual change in the consumer price index.
Source: UNDP (2008): table 14.

adjustment programs required by the International Monetary Fund. Cuts in government spending and restrictions on the money supply have resulted in increased unemployment and reductions in government services. Some of the population enjoys an extremely high standard of living, material possessions, and quality services (e.g., health care, education), and Argentina, Chile, Costa Rica Mexico, and Uruguay have HDI scores in the mid-80s (see Figure 15.1). However, many people in some Latin American NICs have suffered a serious reduction in their standards of living over the last three decades. Those who are very poor experience a life as harsh as that in many of the developing countries. In addition, the inequalities of income and wealth in

BOX 15.4

Order and Progress in Brazil: Sometimes

The motto on the Brazilian flag is "Order and Progress." The vision of order and progress has guided much of Brazilian policy since the founding of the republic in 1889, but recent circumstances have cast doubt on its ability to realize this vision. Brazil is the fifth largest country (in area) in the world, with a population of 188 million and vast natural resources. In many ways Brazil reflects the promise of development in the twenty-first century—but it also epitomizes the troubles associated with that quest.

Progress

From the mid-1960s to the mid-1970s, the Brazilian state took the lead in guiding industrialization, both emphasizing import substitution and promoting exports. The involvement of international capital and foreign corporations was encouraged. The results were impressive. Brazil's economic development was praised worldwide as a "miracle," with yearly growth averaging 10 percent. Brazil's economy is larger than that of all the rest of South America and is now the tenth largest in the world. It is a leader among the developing countries in the production of many goods, including such agricultural exports as coffee, sugar, and cocoa; such minerals as tin, gold, iron ore, and bauxite; and such industrial goods as textiles, cement, automobiles, weapons, and machinery. Since 1970, life expectancy has increased 12 years (to age 72), infant mortality has dropped to one-third its former level, and adult literacy has risen to 89 percent.

Order

Politically, Brazil is a constitutional democracy. The government is a federal republic, with an elected president who has dominant power over the bicameral National Congress. It has a multiparty system, universal and compulsory voting, an independent judiciary, and a partly free press. Its Freedom House rating is "free," and its citizens enjoy relatively high levels of political rights and civil liberties. The large state bureaucracy has maintained social and political order, with minimal class-based conflict, and Brazil is often cited as one of the world's most successful multiracial societies. A strong military ensures Brazil's security and sovereignty.

Progress?

The economic miracle was built on a weak statist base, fueled by debt-led growth, and deeply dependent on external support for finance capital, technology, and markets. Much of the growth was in the 600 state-owned companies, many of which were extremely inefficient and eventually went bankrupt. The emphasis on industrial development has had many negative consequences: The agricultural sector has atrophied,

BOX 15.4 *(Continued)*

resulting in 2 million landless peasants and the need to import basic foods. In urban areas, the upper and middle classes have received most of the benefits of uneven development, and there are large numbers of working poor and unemployed.

Brazil has the world's fourth widest gap between rich and poor. After years of miracle growth, the economy came close to collapse in the early 1980s and again in the mid-1990s. The average annual growth rate for the entire period from 1975 to 2005 was only 0.7 percent, coupled with hyperinflation averaging about 85 percent per year since 1990 (reaching a staggering high of 2,864 percent in 1990). Despite new economic policies, the privatization of many state-owned enterprises, and recent control of inflation, annual growth since 1990 still averages only 1.1 percent. Brazil's foreign debt is the largest within the transitional countries or Global South—more than $220 billion and more than half of annual GDP. Consequently, under structural adjustment pressures from the international banking community, reductions in social spending leave almost half of Brazil's huge population with a very low standard of living.

Order?

Since 1930, the military has deposed six top political leaders. The military, supported by the middle class, seized power most recently in a 1964 coup against an elected government that was judged too sympathetic to the needs of the many rural and urban poor. The military government was repressive and ruthless, crushing leftist opposition, censoring the press, and compiling one of South America's worst records of

▶ **Brazilian President da Silva promises land reform for 400,000 rural families in an emotional speech at a campsite of landless workers.**

human rights abuses. An elected president took office in 1985 after 21 years of authoritarian military rule, and a new constitution was implemented in 1988. Since that time, the recurrent economic problems have provoked a huge rise in social disorder. Crime rates are extremely high; urban riots are frequent, especially in the huge shantytowns surrounding the cosmopolitan cities; and there is violence between peasants and landholders, who are disputing the government's announced but unfilled promises of land reform.

One recent president (Collor de Mello) was forced to resign due to a massive corruption scandal. When the next president (Fernando Henrique Cardoso) was elected in 1995, the citizens reflected their disgust with government: one in three Brazilians abstained in the presidential election, and blank (protest) votes outnumbered votes cast for any senate candidate in 22 of the 26 states. Luiz Inacio Lula da Silva, a former metalworker and union organizer, was swept into power in October 2002 and reelected in 2006. But the first leftist president in four decades has struggled with his supporters' unmet expectations, corruption scandals, and a fractious legislature composed of more than a dozen major political parties, many of whose members actually change parties between elections and are primarily loyal to their regional political bosses. The Brazilian flag's proud announcement of "Order and Progress" flaps ironically over the building where these politicians attempt to govern. (This discussion is based on CIA 2007; Goodwin 2005; and World Bank 2007.)

several of the NICs are among the most severe in the world and are getting worse. Brazil, Chile, and Argentina are all among the 20 countries with the world's highest levels of wealth inequality (recall Figure 14.2).

These are some of the reasons for the active opposition to neoliberalism and globalization and the concern for social welfare that are increasingly evident in the Latin American NICs and voiced by current leaders in Brazil, Bolivia, Chile, Ecuador, Mexico, Uruguay, and the region's most prominent leader, Venezuela's Hugo Chavez. It is also notable that the region's four most visible political "champions" of neoliberalism in the late 1990s—Argentina's Carlos Menem, Chile's Augusto Pinochet, Mexico's Carlos Salinas de Gortari, and Peru's Alberto Fujimori—were eventually subject to criminal charges, under house arrest, or exiled from their countries. Thus the issues associated with economic liberalization policies pervade not only the strategies of industrialization but also the dynamics of political stability and democratization in the NICs.

GOAL: STABILITY

The governments of the Asian NICs have been particularly concerned about maintaining a highly stable and orderly social system. As Box 15.3 indicated, political conflicts, social disorder, and labor agitation are viewed as serious impediments to economic development as well as contrary to Confucian cultural norms about appropriate social relations. Another reason the Asian NICs value stability is the assumption that the economic system thrives in an environment of order and predictability. Thus, until recently, governments in the Asian NICs have been centralized, authoritarian, and repressive (Simone 2001). For example, South Korea was dominated by three autocratic presidents between 1948 and 1987. Malaysia's Mahathir Mohammed retired in 2003 after 22 years in power. Some Asian NICs have been less successful in maintaining order. Thailand has suffered nearly 20 successful or attempted coups since 1932. The most recent military coup occured in 2006, after an election boycotted by all major opposition parties.

Apart from consistently democratic Costa Rica, strong political leaders and a hegemonic class elite were also characteristic of most Latin American NICs in the second half of the twentieth century. Chile, Uruguay (recall Box 12.1), and Argentina alternated between periods of rule by a civilian government and by authoritarian military regimes that, in most cases, came to power by violence and ruled repressively. Mexico was dominated nationally by a single, socially conservative political party, PRI, from 1929 until 2001.

By the late 1980s and early 1990s, most NICs had begun a process of democratization that is proceeding at varying rates in different countries. In 1992, South Korea held its first fair and actively contested presidential election with a genuine multiparty system. Thailand returned to its recent pattern of democratic elections in 2007. Vigorous and competitive democratic politics reemerged in the 1990s in place of repressive regimes in Argentina, Chile, Malaysia, and Uruguay. With the 2000 election of Vicente Fox, even PRI in Mexico lost its one-party dominance of the national political system (recall Chapter 7).

Along with positive effects, the combination of democratization, greater prosperity, and economic volatility has generated forces of instability in many NICs. In general, the NICs that have achieved the highest levels of economic development now also seem the NICs most able to cope with these disruptive forces. They have adapted best to the expansion of political democratization and to the instability associated with competitive group politics, social change, and vigorous public debates over such issues as the allocation of resources and the shape of the political economy. This is particularly the case in the more prosperous Asian NICs.

However, key groups, especially the middle classes in Latin America, have displayed little support for their political systems (Colburn 2002; Torcal and Montero 2006). Serious instability was evident in rioting in Argentina (2002) resulting in the succession of five "presidents" in less than three weeks, an attempted coup in Venezuela (2002), and the turbulent recent political history of Brazil described in Box 15.4 (Lozada 2003). Two recent Costa Rican presidents have been jailed for corruption. In 2007, only 30–36 percent of those surveyed in Argentina, Brazil, Chile, and Mexico indicated they were "satisfied" with the way democracy was working in their country (Latinobarometro 2008: Table 21).

A particular source of instability is those groups that have been most negatively affected by cutbacks in government welfare and by the recurring periods of economic crisis. Frustration and political violence are evident from the large numbers of poor and politically marginalized groups, such as the peasants in the Chiapas region of Mexico, students and labor union members in South Korea, and the Indian populations in Brazil. Moreover, instability that occurs outside the borders of a NIC can spill over into disruption and violence in that NIC, as in Chile (from Peru), Malaysia (from Indonesia), and South Korea (from North Korea). The mix of economic volatility, inequality, and widespread political disillusionment continues to generate serious challenges to the stability of many of the NICs.

GOAL: SECURITY

The borders of Latin American states were established in the nineteenth century and have been relatively stable for more than 150 years. While there have been occasional political disagreements between the Latin American NICs and their neighbors in recent decades, these rarely reach the level of militarized disputes. Interstate war involving these states was rare in the twentieth century. While the NICs' considerable military strength could be deployed for protection against neighboring states, it has been more actively engaged in maintaining internal order, either by supporting the political leadership or by overthrowing it and seizing political power.

Some of the most significant threats to security have been from the former colonial powers that limited the Latin American NICs' autonomy and freedom of action, particularly the United States, Spain, and Great Britain. Indeed, the most notable conventional war since 1950 that involved a NIC is the Falklands War between Argentina and Great Britain in 1982. This conflict resulted from the Argentine military government's attempt to seize islands off its coast that remained under the colonial dominion of Britain. Argentina's defeat in a short war, like the deep penetration into Latin American economies by the developed countries and their financial institutions, was a reminder that dependency and subordination persist in the postcolonial period.

Despite their effective policies to promote internal stability, the Asian NICs operate in a region where there are significant external threats to security. Japan brutally occupied most of these countries during World War II (and, in the case of Korea, from 1905). South Korea has the particular challenge of dealing with the huge differences in political economy and ideology in relation to its militaristic brothers and sisters in North Korea, a conflict that began with the Korean War (1950–1953). Despite recent discussion of reunification, tensions remain high, especially with the possible development of North Korea's nuclear weapons capabilities.

From a broader perspective, the Asian NICs perceive China, Japan, and Russia as major military and economic powers in the region that might have geopolitical designs on them. These three countries rank fourth, fifth, and seventh in the world in total military expenditures. With the exception of South Korea, none of the Asian NICs has sufficient military power to resist the advances of a strong country. Thus most have relied on the protection of an interested "big brother" (e.g., Great Britain, the United States) or the international security regime (e.g., the United Nations) to provide sufficient military power to protect their borders. Moreover, the Asian economic crisis was a clear indicator that these transitional countries are all extensively connected to the global economy, resulting in considerable economic dependence on key actors such as the European Union, Japan, the United States, and the International Monetary Fund.

THE FUTURE OF THE
TRANSITIONAL DEVELOPED COUNTRIES

While the two sets of countries discussed in this chapter are quite different from each other, most of these countries-in-transition share both optimism and uncertainty about their futures. These countries have experienced considerable political, social, and economic development in recent decades; yet these development dynamics could disrupt the relative stability and prosperity they have enjoyed.

The Postcommunist Developed Countries

The PCDCs are attempting to make dramatic transformations, having abandoned political institutions, a political culture, and a political economy that provided generations of citizens with stability and security, though with disappointing levels of prosperity. Unlike the Asian NICs, where economic development preceded political democratization, the PCDCs are engaged in a simultaneous transition to both democratic politics and a market economy. Coping with both forms of change at once can be especially disruptive. The citizens in the postcommunist developed countries have high expectations about the standard of living their governments should provide. Thus there is a particular risk of an intolerable gap emerging between expectations and reality in the achievement of prosperity, stability, and security (recall the J-curve theory in Chapter 12).

Shifts to a market political economy and a democratic political system require extensive institutional adaptation and citizen tolerance. The PCDCs that began the process with the highest levels of economic development and the greatest population homogeneity seem to have been particularly successful in "harmonizing" their systems with other countries in the European Union (Schnetzer 2003). In most of this group that is now part of the EU, the practices of liberal democracy seem to be functioning relatively well, the private sector has grown, and the probability of improvements in prosperity and quality of life seems high. Some are on a trajectory to rise into the most developed country group in Figure 13.1 within a decade.

Political leadership and the political system are generally under more pressure in Russia and other PCDCs outside of the EU, where the levels of prosperity and stability have been disappointing in the postcommunist period. The economic decline has been so severe that some European postcommunist countries (e.g., the Ukraine and Georgia) that still remain relatively high on social development have dropped into the developing world category in Figure 13.1, at least temporarily. The disillusionment of citizens in Russia and these countries has been widespread, and the drift toward authoritarianism might swamp the efforts at democratization. Inequality and economic hardships, combined with weakened economic safety nets, have further heightened the challenges facing these countries, where the upward transition has stalled.

The NICs

Some of the NICs (e.g., South Korea, Chile, Mexico, Argentina, Costa Rica), rather like the leading PCDCs, seem to be on a promising trajectory to close the gap with some of the more developed countries in achieving prosperity, stability, and security. However, for most of the emerging NICs, current efforts at transition to a fully developed economic system and to political democracy will result in a mix of positive and negative effects. Economic growth and development offer the promise of rising standards of living for a larger proportion of the population as the market generates more products.

To the extent that their political economies become more diversified and resilient, the emerging NICs should also have increased control over their own destiny in the global economy. Yet the uncertainties and speed of change in the global economy are extremely high, and thus the transitions in the NICs might be favorable or unfavorable. The sudden and precipitous decline in the economic fortunes of many Asian NICs in the late 1990s is compelling evidence that economic growth is reversible and that its foundations can be substantially less solid than they appear. Few of these transitional countries have escaped crony capitalism, dependency, and overspeculation in currencies, property, and stocks.

There are now deepening democratization and stronger civil societies in many NICs. These factors provide increased resistance to a return to the authoritarian politics that still remain a possibility in some of the NICs in both Latin America and Asia. Among the greatest challenges facing the NICs are sustaining solid economic growth and responding to the aspirations of the population, especially where poverty is widespread and inequality remains high.

Next?

There are promising signs that democratic practices are becoming more deeply institutionalized and that economic growth can be achieved. However, the transitions to full democratization and economic development entail considerable disruption and dislocation. The dynamics in the transitional developed countries are complex, and positive political, economic, and social outcomes are not inevitable. It is evident that no one fully understands how to sustain solid economic growth in the current international environment, and thus prosperity in the transitional countries is vulnerable to many forces that their leaders cannot control. Most of the countries examined in this chapter are likely to confront periods when false steps, political decay, disruptions from the external environment, or bad luck could severely challenge their pursuit of prosperity, security, and stability. Some will achieve the high levels of economic and social development of the most developed countries. Each of these transitional countries strives to be in that group, sooner rather than later, later rather than never.

SO . . .

THE FINAL DEBATE

What Time Is It?

Novelist Charles Dickens opens *A Tale of Two Cities* with his famous observation: "It was the best of times, it was the worst of times. It was the age of wisdom, it was the age of foolishness. . . . It was the spring of hope, it was the winter of despair." Many people might consider this an apt description of the political world as we complete the first decade of the twenty-first century. As you reach the end of this book, it is reasonable for you to consider what *you* now think about the political world. How would you characterize the political world today?

It Is the Worst of Times

- There is now far greater possibility of the use of weapons of mass destruction than at any point in human history. Our weapons arsenals have far more power and efficiency than ever before, and only a few of the 25,000 existing nukes could literally end most life on Earth. Not only is there a proliferation of governments that can deploy dangerous weapons, but now other, more reckless actors, including rogue states and terrorist groups, are also able to either steal or manufacture nuclear, chemical, or biological weapons that can do massive harm.
- Our applications of technology are out of control. The development and uses of many technologies are often driven by self-serving motives, short-term thinking, and indifference to their negative impacts. It is no coincidence that the huge expansion of technological capacity has occurred during a period in which humans have killed far more of their race than at any other time in history, environmental degradation has reached frightening levels, the loss of community and social trust is severe, and global inequalities are at their starkest levels.

- Many governments seem incapable of effective governance—that is, they seem unable to make and implement wise policy decisions that respond to the complex demands presented by diverse groups with conflicting agendas and different ideologies. Governments are increasingly constrained by insufficient global resources to satisfy all needs. While more countries are democracies, this has not led to beneficial increases in political knowledge, participation, or commitment to democratic principles. And contemporary political institutions have not changed the underlying reality that power corrupts.
- Globalization has undermined the capacity of governments to protect their economies from manipulation by global capital and multinational corporations, to protect their workers from the loss of jobs, or even to protect their national cultural norms and values from being undermined by outside influences that are alien and undesirable. Both the clash of civilizations between hostile worldviews and the intolerance between nation-based groups seem to be generating more, and more dangerous, conflicts.
- *The bottom line: we live in a world of uncertainty and insecurity where the general welfare of humankind is not nurtured or protected.*

It Is the Best of Times

- The danger of a catastrophic nuclear war between the United States and the Soviet Union, whether intentional or accidental, is no longer a grave risk. All the major nuclear powers have actually reduced their stockpiles. Since the end of the cold war, the United Nations has been much more active in collective peacekeeping operations, and there are now comparatively few interstate wars. The

The Final Debate *(Continued)*

fact that democracies do not fight with each other is another positive factor as an increasing majority of countries embrace democracy.

- Technology (i.e., applied knowledge) in its many forms has vastly expanded human powers of control and production. With wise policies from our governments to guide the development and application of technologies, we have the capacity to provide sufficient resources to ensure that every human being has the food, health, knowledge, and material goods for a long and satisfying life.
- Democracy and political institutionalization have spread to more political systems than ever. As citizens experience the value of open political discussion and of selecting their leaders in fair and competitive elections, they become more engaged and take more

responsibility for dealing with the political issues in their country and the world. They define the political rights and civil liberties of all citizens, they demand more effective governance from political actors, and they support leaders who further the goals of prosperity, stability, and security.

- Globalization has increased the quality, affordability, and accessibility of almost every good and service that people need. We share information and ideas, trade goods and services, and recognize that what happens everywhere has consequences for our own welfare. The incentives and interdependency encouraging us all to get along have never been greater.
- *The bottom line: more people live longer and with a higher quality of life than at any point in history.*

There are complex questions in the political world, and sometimes, despite our desire for clarity and closure, there is no simple answer. It is quite possible that this is both the best and worst of times, and that there are grounds for both hope and despair.

Many people look to their political system to provide solutions in a complex world. But many also seem to think that political systems are a major source of obstacles preventing their achievement of goals. This book's central objective has been to increase your understanding of the political world through the discussions and many examples that have hopefully helped you (in Popper's expression from Chapter 1) "to see more clearly than before."

Voltaire observed, "If we believe absurdities, we shall commit atrocities." The political world is full of disagreement, hyperbole, and ruthless competition. Political science cannot necessarily make the world a better place; its primary role is to increase our understanding about how politics works. Such understanding can be the basis of insights: about different conceptions of how politics should be organized, about the basis of any real political disagreements that require response, about mechanisms for conflict resolution, and about how to organize ourselves in the pursuit of specific (private, group, national, or global) interests within a framework of the common good.

As individuals, we often feel powerless in the face of the massive power mobilized in the political world. But every individual—even you!—can affect what happens. The democratic ideals that are widely celebrated in the political world are based on the assumption that people, individually and collectively, can make a difference. First, if you approach political questions with knowledge, insight, and sensitivity, you can better understand how to think and act in the political world. Second, you can communicate your own political demands and supports in order to influence the policies that are made by actors in the political system. Third, you can become a political activist as a shaper of public opinion, a leader of a political group, or a public official. The American novelist F. Scott Fitzgerald observed: "One should be able to see that things are hopeless and yet be determined to make them otherwise." In the political world, things are not hopeless unless people like you fail to think, to understand, and to act.

KEY CONCEPTS

Confucian culture
crony capitalism
developmental-state
    approach

Marxist-Leninist socialism
newly industrializing
    countries (NICs)
people's democracy

postcommunist developed
    countries (PCDCs)
transitional developed
    countries

FOR FURTHER CONSIDERATION

1. Why has Russia not followed the path toward democracy that seems so successful in most of the other postcommunist developed countries?
2. Under what, if any, conditions might the cold war be revived?
3. Develop an argument for including any of the NICs in Figure 13.1 in the group of more developed countries considered in Chapter 13.
4. Is there any element in the NIC development strategy that seems particularly difficult to implement in countries outside of Asia?
5. Explore similarities and differences between Confucian culture and Latin American Catholic culture as mechanisms supporting social order.

FOR FURTHER READING

Alexander, James. (2000). *Political Culture in Post-Communist Russia: Formlessness and Recreation in a Traumatic Transition*. New York: St. Martin's. From detailed studies of two Russian towns, the author offers an illuminating explanation of the difficulties associated with the "traumatic transition" from authoritarianism to a more liberal democratic political culture and the continuing impacts of broader Russian cultural traditions.

Fallows, James. (1995). *Looking at the Sun: The Rise of the New East Asian Economic and Political System*. New York: Pantheon. A readable and insightful analysis of the interplay among political culture, politics, and political economy in the Asian NICs.

Flynn, Norman. (2000). *Miracle to Meltdown in Asia*. New York: Oxford University Press. The rise and sudden crisis in the Asian NICs are thoughtfully analyzed, with particular attention to the balance of power among the market, cronyism, and authoritarianism in governing the state and guiding the political economy.

Goldman, Marshall. (2003). *The Piratization of Russia: Russian Reform Goes Awry*. New York: Routledge. A revealing critique of the poor choices and political deals that have plagued the privatization of Russian assets.

McFaul, Michael. (2001). *Russia's Unfinished Revolution: Political Change from Gorbachev to Putin.* Ithaca, NY: Cornell University Press. The challenges facing Russian political leaders during the 1990s are thoughtfully explained within the context of the author's view that the period is best understood as one of revolutionary transformation without the use of revolutionary language or symbolism.

McFaul, Michael, and Kathryn Stoner-Weiss, Eds. (2004). *After the Collapse of Communism: Comparative Lessons of Transition.* London: Cambridge University Press. Leading scholars explore critical issues in the strengths and failings of the various strategies for political, economic, and social transition in the PCDCs.

Medvedev, Roy. (2000). *Where Is Russia Going?* Trans. George Shriver. New York: Columbia University Press. A lengthy but insightful exploration of the difficulties during the Yeltsin era of what Medvedev, a key advisor to both Mikhail Gorbachev and Boris Yeltsin, believes has been a too-radical transition to a market economy.

Simone, Vera. (2001). *The Asian Pacific: Political and Economic Development in a Global Context.* 2nd ed. New York: Longman. A thorough comparative study of the political and economic development of the 15 countries of East and Southeast Asia, with particularly strong treatment of China, Japan, and the Asian NICs.

True, Jacqui. (2003). *Gender, Globalization, and Postsocialism: The Czech Republic After Communism.* New York: Columbia University Press. A rich combination of the study of the dynamics of change in a postcommunist society with the way in which gender roles are affecting those changes and being changed by them, all within the context of globalization.

Thomas, Robert. (1999). *The Politics of Serbia in the 1990s.* New York: Columbia University Press. An interesting approach to understanding the political dynamics and power struggles in Serbia, the key protagonist in the chaotic Balkans, emphasizing an analysis of what was being said (as well as done) by the key actors, especially the late Slobodan Milosevic.

ON THE WEB

http://www.aseansec.org/index.asp

On the official Web site of the Association of Southeast Asian Nations, there are information and documents relevant to ASEAN, news about countries in the region, and somewhat self-serving Web pages constructed by each member state.

http://lanic.utexas.edu/index.html

The Latin American Network Information Center, hosted at the University of Texas, Austin, provides a vast number of Internet-based information sources about the politics, economics, culture, and other areas of the Latin American NICs.

http://www.ce-review.org/

Transitions Online provides detailed information regarding political and cultural issues relevant to these postcommunist developed states.

http://www.russiajournal.com/

An online daily English-language newspaper published in Moscow that provides a perspective on the politics and society of Russia.

http://www.europeanforum.net

The European Forum for Democracy and Solidarity offers country-by-country information on politics and economics for the postcommunist developed countries from the perspective of the European Social Democrats.

APPENDIX

POLITICAL ANALYSIS

The mind rests in explanation.

—Aristotle

This book began with the claim that, in a democracy, men are more likely to vote than women. You were encouraged in Chapter 1 to read this Appendix on political analysis as you considered this question about the relationship between gender and voting and as you assessed the data in Table 1.1. Chapter 1 defined **political analysis** as the attempt to describe and explain political phenomena. This Appendix will introduce you to some of the basic tools political theorists use for political analysis—that is, for conceptualizing, collecting, and analyzing data about actual political phenomena. After a brief discussion of such data, we shall consider how to read data like those in Table 1.1 and how to draw a tentative inference based on those data. Most of the Appendix describes four broad approaches used for political analysis: taxonomic analysis, formal analysis, functional analysis, and relational analysis.

Source: FRANK & EARNEST reprinted by permission of Newspaper Enterprise Association, Inc.

DATA IN POLITICAL ANALYSIS

Many political analyses rely on data assessment. *Data* can be defined as any observations, facts, statistics, or other forms of information that attempt to measure or represent some aspect of reality. The data used in political analysis can be characterized on different dimensions, including the style of measurement, the level of analysis, the composition, and the time dimension.

1. *Style of measurement.*
   a. ***Nominal data** measure by applying names to phenomena that have some common characteristic.* Examples: male voters or female voters; Conservative, Labour, or Liberal parties in Britain; democratic, authoritarian, or totalitarian governments.
   b. ***Ordinal data** rank phenomena in an order,* such as from higher to lower, bigger to smaller, greater to lesser. Examples: more-developed countries or less-developed countries; voters who are older than 65, voters between 35 and 65, or voters younger than 35; political party systems that have one major party, two major parties, or many parties.
   c. ***Interval data** are like ordinal data, but they also have a numerically equal distance between any two adjacent measures*—the distance from 5 to 6 is the same as the distance from 81 to 82. Example: the George H. W. Bush presidency of 1989–1993 (four years) was exactly half as long as the Ronald Reagan presidency of 1981–1989 (eight years).
   d. ***Ratio data** are like interval data, but they also have a real zero point.* Examples: a country's total expenditure on defense in a specific year; the number of citizens participating in antigovernment rallies; the percentage of seats in the legislature held by a particular political party.

2. *Level of analysis.* Political data can be measured at different levels of combination regarding the class of phenomena. Examples: at the individual level, the strength of a particular individual's loyalty to a political party; at the group level, the strength of party loyalty among all. Asian Americans; for a geographic area, the total number of seats in the EU Parliament or the number from each member country.

3. *Composition.* Data can measure a single phenomenon, such as a political leader's age or a country's rate of inflation in a particular year; or they can be measures that aggregate phenomena, such as the percentage of total votes cast for all conservative political parties in an election or a country's average annual rate of inflation over ten years.

4. *Time dimension.*
   a. ***Cross-sectional data** measure a single point in time.* Example: a country's GDP per capita in 2000.
   b. ***Longitudinal data** measure several points through time.* Example: a country's GDP per capita in 1970, 1980, 1990, and 2000.

The example in Chapter 1 of voting in the 1976 and 2004 presidential elections uses data that are nominal (men versus women), ratio (percentages), and aggregated (for many people) in a cross-sectional analysis (only one election). You might think of data as dry statistics, but the data in political analysis are rooted in real-world events. If properly analyzed, relevant data can increase our political knowledge on an endless list of questions. Examples: Are countries that spend the greatest amount on military preparedness more likely to avoid war? Is religion or social class a better predictor of whether a Scot will vote for the Labour Party? How much longer is average life expectancy in rich countries than in poor countries?

ON READING TABLES

Table A.1 (which shows the same data as Table 1.1 in Chapter 1) provides data from two presidential elections in the United States. Does this table help you to clarify the relationship between gender and voting level in democracies? Since political analysis often includes data presented in tables, it is useful to know the basic steps for reading them. When you examine a table such as Table A.1, you should first establish precisely what the data are about. The title of the table and the names given to the variables (the key concepts measured in the table) indicate what the analyst who created the table thinks it reveals. But the analyst can be misleading or mistaken, so it is worthwhile to assess whether the phenomena measured by the data correspond to the labels given to the variables, whether the data seem relevant to the analytic question, and whether the data seem accurate.

Next you should examine the data in the table. What do the data measure? Table A.1 provides data on the percentage of men and women who did or did not vote in the election of the U.S. president in 1976 and 2004. How are such tabular data read? Is either of these two statements supported by the 2004 data in the table?

1. Forty-four percent of those who did not vote were men.
2. Forty percent of the women did not vote.

> **TABLE A.1**
> Analysis of Table 1.1: Participation of Eligible Voters in the 1976 and 2004 U.S. Presidential Elections by Gender

	1976	
	Men	*Women*
Voted	a. 77%	b. 67%
Did not vote	c. 23%	d. 33%
Yule's $Q = +.24$		

	2004	
	Men	*Women*
Voted	a. 56%	b. 60%
Did not vote	c. 44%	d. 40%
Yule's $Q = -.08$		

It is useful, especially when there are percentages in a table, to examine how the columns (up and down) and the rows (across) are formed. In the case of percentages, find any direction(s) in which the data add to 100 percent. In this table, the columns add to 100 percent. Thus statement 2 is supported by the table and statement 1 is not. Can you see why this is so?

In many cases, the analyst uses more sophisticated techniques than tables in order to assess the relationships between variables. Box A.1 discusses the relational modes of analysis and considers the use of statistical techniques to examine these relationships. It also explains the meaning of the Yule's Q statistics in Table A.1.

BOX A.1

Assessing Relationships
Between Phenomena

To interpret most quantitative analyses in political science (and most other social sciences), you need to understand a bit about the meaning of the most commonly used statistics (e.g., Pearson's r, regression analysis, factor analysis). Ideally, you will take some statistics coursework so that you understand the logic and assumptions of the statistics being employed.

The simplest relational statistics (e.g., Pearson's r, *tau beta*, Spearman's *rho*) usually range in value between +1.00, which indicates a perfect positive relationship between the variables, and −1.00, which indicates a perfect negative relationship between the variables. Many of these simple statistics will also have a *significance* level—an indication of how likely it is that the observed relationship between the variables might have occurred by chance. This is normally measured in terms of this chance probability: .05, .01, .001. The smaller the probability of a chance relationship, the greater the analyst's confidence that the variables are actually associated.

In the case of two variables, a +1.00 correlation would look like graph A in Figure A.1: as one variable increases one unit in value, the other variable increases at a corresponding rate. For example, you would find a +1.00 correlation if each $100,000 spent on congressional political campaigns increased voter turnout by 1 percent. A −1.00 correlation would look like graph B. Rarely do real-world phenomena in political science come even close to a perfect positive or negative correlation.

A correlation statistic close to .00 means that there is virtually no linear relationship between the two variables, as in graph C. For example, you are likely to find that campaign expenditure levels have no consistent relationships with voter turnout rates. Political phenomena are often extremely complex and subject to many influences, so they typically have little or no systematic relationship with other factors that you might consider. Thus, in many political analyses, the statistical associations are low or statistically insignificant. The strongest statistical relationships for interesting political data are usually at moderate levels of correlation, in the range of ±.10 to ±.35, as in graph D.

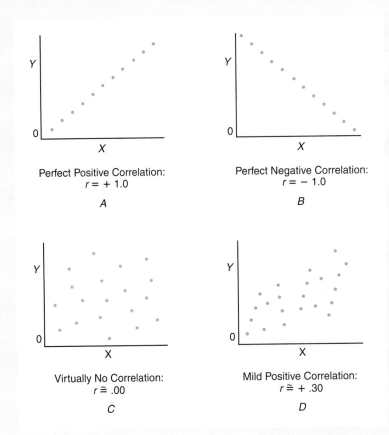

FIGURE A.1
Correlation relationships between two hypothetical variables, X and Y

You can look at simple arrays of data, like those in Table A.1, and draw your own conclusions. Graphical representations (like the four scattergrams in Figure A.1) are another straightforward way to assess data. Each point in the figures represents one case, located at its appropriate value on each of the two variables in the analysis. This visual mapping of cases can provide useful insights about the nature of the relationship between two variables.

As the data become more complex, statistics can help inform your judgment. Table A.1 indicates that the correlation between gender and voting in the 1976 election data is ±.24, using a very simple correlation statistic for 2×2 tables called "Yule's Q." The correlation of ±.24 suggests that in these data there is a moderate, systematic relationship between male gender and higher probability of voting. In the 2004 data, the relationship between gender and voting appears less pronounced, and this judgment is supported by the Yule's Q of −.08, which indicates that there is virtually no systematic relationship.

While most statistics of association require a calculator or a computer, you can calculate Yule's Q yourself for any 2×2 table: (1) multiply the values of the two cells on each diagonal: $a \times d$ and $b \times c$; (2) subtract the two products: $ad-bc$; (3) add the two products: $a+bc$; (4) divide $ad-bc$ by $ad+bc$; (5) the result of this division should be a correlation score, ranging between +1.00 and −1.00. The formula for Yule's Q is thus: $(ad-bc)/(ad+bc)$. (Unlike the case for most correlation statistics, a positive Yule's Q means that the ad diagonal is stronger than the bc diagonal.)

Beyond simple statistics and graphs, political scientists have an array of sophisticated data-analysis techniques to examine questions using quantitative data. Most of the techniques are elaborations on the basic idea of examining whether the values on phenomena seem to be systematically related to each other.

The use of statistics and other quantitative techniques can be helpful in political analysis. The more demanding task for the analyst is to use careful judgment to decide whether the relationship identified by such techniques has *substantive* significance. The key question is: Do the tables, statistics, and other data provide useful insights about political processes or about how political phenomena are associated?

MODES OF POLITICAL ANALYSIS

Chapter 1 indicated that political science has little theory in the strictest sense of the term; that is, it does not have a set of precise, systematically related generalizations. However, most contemporary political analysis does strive to make our understanding of politics more general, precise, and systematic by ordering empirical data with one of these four modes of political analysis: taxonomic, formal, functional, or relational.

Taxonomic Analysis

Aristotle (384–322 B.C.E.), the father of political analysis, was interested in distinguishing different types of Greek city-states. He classified them by using a concept derived from earlier work by Herodotus (c. 484–425 B.C.E.): the size of the ruling group. Aristotle defined three categories: the city-state might be ruled by one person, by a few people, or by many people.

This is an example of **taxonomic analysis**: *the orderly arrangement of some political phenomena by developing a set of distinct categories.* Most political analysis begins with a taxonomy—a set of categories that classify data into different types. The categories within a taxonomy establish the crucial concepts that define the analysis. The criteria for naming the types and for classifying phenomena into each type are arbitrary in the sense that they are established by the analyst on the basis of substantive concerns. But the categories ought to be exhaustive (all cases are classified), mutually exclusive (no case fits into more than one category), and comparable (all categories are distinguished by the same criteria). Relevant data might be of any type, although they are usually nominal or ordinal.

▶ **Aristotle**

Aristotle's three categories of city-states are sufficient to create a taxonomy. But to enrich his analysis, Aristotle also employed a second concept: the group(s) whose interests the ruler serves. His two categories were: (1) the ruler(s) could rule in the general interest, or (2) the ruler(s) could rule in self-interest. Thus Aristotle's taxonomy of governments had two central concepts, each based on nominal data, resulting in the six categories displayed in Table A.2. Aristotle then provided names for each category in the taxonomy. He labeled as a **monarchy** any city-state in which one person ruled in the general interest; if a few ruled in their own interests, the system was called an **oligarchy**. Notice that Aristotle labeled the most perverse case, where many attempt to rule in their self-interests, a *democracy!*

▶ **TABLE A.2**
Aristotle's Taxonomy of Political Systems

How Many Rule?	In Whose Interest?	
	General	*Self*
One	Monarchy	Tyranny
A few	Aristocracy	Oligarchy
Many	Polity	Democracy

Aristotle used his taxonomy for political analysis by placing each Greek city-state in one of the six categories. Athens, for example, was classified as an aristocracy. Notice that a taxonomy organizes data, but it does not answer the *how* and *why* questions. To explore such questions (e.g., Is a prosperous middle class more likely in an oligarchy? Under what conditions does a polity transform into a democracy?), the analyst must move beyond taxonomic analysis.

Formal Analysis

Suppose you want to travel around New York City on the subway. If you are unfamiliar with New York, you will probably use a subway map, which indicates the spatial relationships among different subway stations and identifies the stations where one subway line connects with another.

A subway map is an example of the product of formal analysis. A **formal analysis** *specifies abstract forms that correspond to the reality in which the analyst is interested.* The analyst attempts to "model" reality by defining and interrelating concepts so that the linkages among the concepts in the formal analysis reflect the dynamics and interactions among the actual phenomena. Some formal analyses have the same physical form as the actual phenomena being modeled, such as a miniaturized version of an automobile engine. But most formal analyses use symbol systems as abstract representations of the phenomena, such as a subway map, a schematic drawing of the circuitry in a radio, or a mathematical formula for the trajectory of an object moving through space.

Most formal analyses of political phenomena are recent. Some political scientists have attempted to devise schematic diagrams that represent how some aspect of politics works. In one well-known example, David Easton (1965) developed an abstract diagram, composed of boxes and arrows, that attempts to characterize the flow of activities by which decision makers in the political system establish public policies. Their decisions are influenced by the resources available in the environment and the pressures they experience from various groups. This "political system model" is explained in detail in Chapter 5.

An array of formal analyses called **rational choice theory** (or *public choice theory*) has become an important approach in political science. Applications of rational choice theory can be quite complex, but they share two basic features. First, they attempt to represent political processes primarily by means of mathematical formulations or systems of symbolic notation. From the perspective of advancing a science of politics, such formal theories are given special prominence because they aim to be general, systematic, abstract, and testable in actual settings.

Second, it is assumed that political actors (e.g., voters, legislators, political parties) behave purposefully. The approach does not assume that all political actors behave with complete rationality all the time, but it does assume that their behavior is goal oriented and calculating. Both their preferences for various outcomes and their calculation of the costs, benefits, and likely success of different strategies to achieve those outcomes can be formulated as quantified indicators or as systems of symbols (Mueller 2004).

To introduce the rational choice approach in a nontechnical manner, we offer several simple examples grounded in the logic of the approach. The Debate in 4 (see Chapter 4) employs the approach to assess whether it is rational for an individual to vote in a U.S. presidential election. The following paragraph describes another brief example (without the mathematics) of how the approach is applied.

Political scientist William Riker (1962) has posited the theory of the "minimum winning coalition." This is a mathematical representation linked to the well-known saying "To the victors go the spoils." That is, the benefits of any policy decision in a legislature will tend to be distributed among those who have voted in favor of the decision. However, Riker argues, as the coalition voting for the policy becomes larger, the benefits must be distributed among more people (or the groups each person represents), and thus a smaller share of benefits is available to each coalition member. In order to assure each coalition member of the largest possible share of benefits, there is a tendency to create a coalition that has just enough participants to ensure victory—hence the idea of a minimum winning coalition. This concept is developed as a formal theory through specification of mathematical equations that relate the size of the decision-making group, the size of the coalition, and the amount of resources available for distribution. (For an empirical analysis of national legislatures that challenges Riker's theory, see Strom 1989.)

Functional Analysis

Suppose someone asks you how a car works. You are likely to discuss the key structural components of a car's engine and power train, such as its carburetor, pistons, and driveshaft. You might then detail the processes of the internal combustion engine, noting how an ignited fuel expands in an enclosed area, pushing a series of mechanisms into directed motion. This style of description and explanation is the basis of functional analysis. **Functional analysis** *describes the contributions of a certain element (process or structure) to the activities of the phenomenon under study*.

In political science, one widely used form of functional analysis identifies certain functions (i.e., processes) that occur within a political system, and it describes how and by what structures the functions are performed. Some scholars, such as Gabriel Almond and his colleagues (2008), have defined certain functions, including political communication, rule adjudication, and interest articulation, that must be performed in every political system.

Applications of functional analysis are described in Chapters 5, 10, and 11. As a brief example here, we can consider the interest articulation function. Individuals might want their government to spend more on preschool care or to protect their right to own handguns. The processes by which individuals communicate these specific interests to others in the political world are called *interest articulation*. According to functional analysis, this communication of political needs and wants is a necessary function in every effective political system. Most functional analysts also describe and explain how structures perform these types of functions. Thus interest groups emerge to amplify the shared interests of many individuals. For example, the National Rifle Association uses various strategies to promote many individuals' concerns about gun ownership to those who make and implement government policies on firearms.

Related to functional analysis is constitutive analysis. ***Constitutive analysis*** *assumes that political functions can be explained primarily in terms of one fundamental concept.* (Indeed, every scientific discipline strives to discover, ultimately, the fundamental structure or process that accounts for more complex phenomena.) Among the concepts that have been proposed as the central one to explain politics are the interactions between groups, classes, or roles.

Constitutive theories are discussed in various chapters, especially in Chapter 9, which presents the elite, class, and group approaches to explaining politics. As an example, Karl Marx's (1867) theory of politics pivots on one key concept: class. In every historical period, society is divided into a set of classes based on the distribution of economic power. The structure of classes determines political and social relations as well as economic relations. In political terms, the class structure determines who wields political power, for what purposes, and for whose benefit. The role of the state and the dynamics of political change are also explained in terms of class relations.

Relational Analysis

Box 1.3 (in Chapter 1) and Table A.1 consider the question of voting differences between men and women: Is there some relationship between an individual's gender and the likelihood that she or he votes? This is typical of the kinds of questions addressed by relational analysis.

The central goal of **relational analysis** is to *discover and explicate the systematic connections between phenomena.* The basic question is always: Are political phenomena linked? For example: Are democratic countries more stable than nondemocratic countries? Are older people more politically conservative than younger people? Are states dominated by Islam more warlike than states dominated by Hinduism? What conditions are associated with greater equality in the distribution of wealth?

Both formal analysis and functional analysis also assume connections, but relational analysis tries merely to identify the connections between phenomena. It does not attempt to model or schematize the connections as does formal analysis. And it does not focus on crucial functions, as does functional analysis. There are two levels of relational analysis: (1) correlational analysis and (2) causal analysis. To determine whether there is a systematic association between variables, most correlational and causal analyses use various statistical techniques. These statistics provide a mathematical appraisal of the extent to which change in one phenomenon is systematically related to changes in one or more other phenomena. Box A.1 provides further information about such statistics.

Correlational analysis.   **Correlational analysis** *determines whether there is a statistically probable relationship between two variables.* It does not presume, as does causal analysis (discussed in the next section), that one variable actually is the agent that causes change to occur in another variable. It merely assesses the strength and direction of an association between variables. Many empirical attempts to understand politics begin with the establishment of a correlation between political phenomena.

For example, evaluating the linkage between gender and voting in Table A.1 is an example of correlational analysis. The table and the Yule's Q statistic both seem to support the tentative conclusion that, for 1976 at least, there is a modest *correlation* (i.e., *a systematic, statistically probable association*) between gender and voting. While this seems correct, there are obvious problems with using this election as the basis for a broader generalization about gender and voting. First, it examines only a single election. The relationship is not evident in the 2004 electoral data. In fact, women outvoted men in every U.S. presidential election after 1980. You might pursue this research on U.S. elections by asking: Is this a new trend or a temporary deviation from a 50-year pattern?

Second, a generalization about democracies might also consider elections other than the presidency and certainly should analyze other democracies. For example, any generalization might take into account an analysis of British and German national elections since 1970, in which there is no correlation between gender and voting rates (Walker 1988: table 1). A third problem with the evident pattern between gender and voting in the 1976 data will be explored later in this section.

Causal analysis.   **Causal analysis** goes beyond correlational analysis because it *explicitly identifies one phenomenon as the effective agent that brings about changes in another phenomenon.* Much of the language in political analysis is loosely causal, implying that there is a cause-and-effect relationship between two variables. However, causal analysis is the only approach that attempts an explicit empirical test of cause and effect. Causal analysis presents the "If X, then Y" mode of explanation described in Chapter 1. Here X is the *independent variable* that, given a certain value, actually causes Y, the *dependent variable*, to change in a particular way.

An example of causal analysis links the electoral system and the number of political parties. In his book *Political Parties*, French political scientist Maurice Duverger (1954) contends that the type of electoral system *causes* the number of effective parties to increase or decrease. In particular, he offers two hypotheses:

1. Plurality electoral systems (in which the candidate who receives the most votes wins) reduce the number of major political parties toward two.

2. Electoral systems with proportional representation (in which candidates are elected to the legislature in proportion to their party's share of the total vote) and with multimember districts (more than one legislator per district) allow more than two major parties (see Box 7.1).

Political analysts have tested Duverger's hypotheses using data from various electoral systems (e.g., Riker 1982; Taagepera and Shugart 1989: ch. 13). Table A.3 presents data from 20 democratic countries for the period from 1945 to 1965. Do you think the data in Table A.3 support Duverger's hypothesis? Why?

DRAWING CONCLUSIONS FROM EMPIRICAL ANALYSES

The purpose of empirical analysis is to increase our knowledge about politics. It is especially important that the analyst draw appropriate conclusions. In political analysis, as in politics, things are often not what they seem. Let us consider some

▶ **TABLE A.3**

Relationship Between Number of Political Parties and Type of Electoral System

Number of Parties[†]	Electoral System[*]	
	Plurality	Other
Two	23	4
More than two	7	73
Yule's $Q = +.97$		

Note: Based on data from 20 Western democracies in elections of legislative representatives between 1945 and 1965.
[*]In plurality or "first-past-the-post" systems, the party/candidate with the largest number of votes wins a seat in the legislature, and all other parties/candidates gain no seats. In "other" systems, there is some form of proportional representation or vote transfer (see Box 7.1).
[†]Number of political parties with at least 5 percent of the seats in the legislature.
Source: Rae 1971.

of the potential problems, using the causal analysis of electoral systems and party systems as an example. You probably concluded that the data in Table A.3 support Duverger's hypothesis. Do we now know that the electoral system causes different types of party systems? Yes, maybe.

Yes: There is certainly some persuasive empirical evidence for such a conclusion. And, on logical grounds, it does seem reasonable that the electoral system might cause variations in the number of parties that survive over time.

Maybe: The political analyst must always be cautious in drawing conclusions and making generalizations. Several questions should be considered:

1. Are the data and methods appropriate? Did the analysis use accurate, relevant data and the correct analytic techniques? Is the sample of nations or the time period examined typical? Does this generalization also hold for non-European nations? Were systems divided between "plurality" and "other" in a manner consistent with Duverger's hypothesis?

2. Are the analyst's inferences about cause and effect persuasive? Might the dependent variable (in this case the number of political parties) actually have a significant effect on the presumed independent variable (the electoral system)? That is, since the parties in most legislatures have the power to establish the electoral system, certain parties might try to implement an electoral system that perpetuates their power via the existing party system.

3. Are there plausible rival hypotheses? Is there another independent variable, not considered in this analysis, that might better account for the pattern of values on the dependent variable? It is possible that both the number of parties and the electoral system are related primarily because each is correlated with the third variable? For example, the number of fundamental issues that divide the electorate might have the greatest effect on the number of major parties if

one party emerges for each pattern of positions on the fundamental issues (Taagepera and Shugart 1989).

When political scientists use the scientific method, other analysts might raise any of these kinds of "problems" with a conclusion. The data, the methods, or the inferences might not stand up to such scrutiny. In our examination of Duverger's claims about the causal relationship between electoral systems and number of parties, none of the three problems just listed seems to undermine the analysis. Until one of these types of criticisms is supported persuasively, we can have some confidence that the generalization about the causal relationship is correct—that electoral systems do seem to cause certain types of party systems to evolve over time.

But the gender and voting analysis based on the 1976 election data in Table A.1 is an example of how an initial causal inference can be challenged. The three potential problems must be considered in an assessment of whether the data reveal that gender differences do cause different probability of voting:

1. The data and methods do seem appropriate. However, a generalization (even limited to the United States) certainly requires more than a single case.

2. The posited cause-and-effect relationship seems reasonable. This is the only possible direction of causality, since voting certainly cannot "cause" gender. Also there are reasonable explanations for why men might vote at higher rates than women. Can you think of at least one?

3. However, to make a compelling argument that the data reveal causality, it would be necessary to ensure that there is no other causal agent (i.e., no plausible rival hypothesis) that better explains voting levels or that creates the apparent relationship between gender and voting. While the analyst can never disprove every competing hypothesis, it is important to examine and reject the most plausible ones.

Let us reexamine the 1976 voter turnout data in Table A.1. Can you propose another explanation for the incidence of voting in the United States that is as plausible as gender? Among those you might suggest are age, social class, occupation, interest in politics, identification with a political party, and education level. Table A.4 provides the relevant data on one of these—education level—for our analysis of voting in 1976. Do these data alter your judgment about the importance of gender?

One reasonable interpretation of Table A.4 is that the 1976 election revealed a considerable difference between men and women in the incidence of voting among those with minimal education but virtually no difference in the levels of voting between men and women who have a college education. In the absence of further analysis (and many further analyses could be attempted), these data about education seem to reduce the power of gender as an adequate causal explanation of voting. One might infer, at least on the basis of Table A.4, that both education and gender were important in 1976 but that the impact of gender was powerfully altered by education level. This closer look should suggest to you that if you were developing a causal theory of voter turnout, you would need to consider many variables and diverse data.

This example reveals a common challenge for most of the interesting questions addressed by causal analyses of politics: There are almost always clusters of plausible

> **TABLE A.4**
> Participation of Eligible Voters in the 1976 U.S. Presidential
> Election, by Gender and Education Level

	Percentage Who Voted	
Education Level	Men	Women
Grade school	72	50
High school	69	64
College	86	84

explanatory factors that seem interrelated. For example: What accounts for a person's decision to vote for the conservative People's Party in Austria—class, education, family experiences, occupation, wealth, beliefs about society, attitudes toward governmental leaders, or something else? What factors lead a group to undertake revolutionary violence—political oppression, poverty, corrupt government officials, charismatic leadership, unequal distribution of wealth, foreign domination, or something else?

KNOWLEDGE AND POLITICS REVISITED

Chapter 1 suggested a number of ways it is possible to know things about the political world. Your understanding of politics does not need to be grounded in the scientific method and in empirical analysis. Insight and understanding about politics might be based on the method of authority or the method of personal thought, or they might be derived from other sources such as literature, films, or art.

In the attempt to develop precise and valid generalizations about politics, however, most contemporary political scientists use some form of the scientific method and some of the modes of political analysis described in preceding sections. Whatever types of data and modes of analysis they use, political scientists generally accept the notion that all aspects of their research should be subject to scrutiny and challenge by other analysts. Most also agree that their hypotheses, inferences, generalizations, and theories must be subject to some empirical test of validity. Although various sources of knowledge can provide you with insights about politics, this book emphasizes the modes of political analysis described in this Appendix as the best means for broad understanding of the political world.

KEY CONCEPTS

causal analysis	functional analysis	ordinal data
constitutive analysis	interval data	political analysis
correlation	longitudinal data	ratio data
correlational analysis	monarchy	rational choice theory
cross-sectional data	nominal data	relational analysis
formal analysis	oligarchy	taxonomic analysis

GLOSSARY

Adjudication: Every society creates and enforces rules and laws regarding the proper forms of behavior for individuals and groups. The adjudication function attempts to interpret and apply the relevant rules or laws to a given situation. Most political systems have established judicial structures (e.g., criminal courts) whose primary role is adjudication.

Administration: The general term used to describe the machinery and processes through which rules and policies of an organization are applied and implemented. It is a core function of political systems and is usually one of the four basic institutional structures (along with executives, legislatures, and judiciaries). (See also *Bureaucracy*.)

Assembly system: A form of collective leadership in which a large group, usually constituted as a legislature, is clearly dominant over the executive. Examples: the United Nations; the European Parliament.

Associational interest group: A type of political interest group organized specifically to further the political objectives of its members. Examples: the British Medical Association; Common Cause. (See also *Interest group*.)

Authoritarianism: (1) A political system generally characterized by little or no commitment to equality or democratic participation and by a strong emphasis on order and stability. The political behavior of the population is severely constrained. In many countries, authoritarian regimes are dominated by a military elite. (2) A personality syndrome, associated particularly with political and social attitudes and behavior, in which the individual tends to: revere strong leadership; draw sharp boundaries between the identity group and all others; be intolerant of unconventional behaviors; and exhibit considerable hostility toward minority groups.

Authority: (1) A source of knowledge about the political world. The method of authority involves the appeal to any document, tradition, or person that is believed to possess the controlling explanation regarding a particular issue. (2) The legitimacy attached to the decisions of the political system, in the sense that people willingly accept those decisions as binding, independent of their own self-interest.

Balance of power: A configuration of power among a set of states in which there is a broad equality in the power resources (political, economic, and especially military) that can be exercised by competing states. Through a system of shifting alliances, no state or group of states is able to achieve a preponderance of power. Thus stability and the status quo are usually sustained, since states will intervene to prevent a serious imbalance that might lead to domination.

Bureaucracy: Though often used as a synonym for administration, bureaucracy has been defined, especially by Max Weber (1958a), as a particular structure and style through which administration can operate. Structurally, bureaucracy is characterized by hierarchical organization and a highly specialized division of labor. Members of the bureaucracy behave according to specific rules of action so that treatment of each case is relatively predictable and nondiscriminatory. (See also *Administration*.)

Capitalism: One of the great "isms," explicitly linking politics to political economy, capitalism is a system that corresponds loosely to a market economy. In this system, private economic actors are generally free from state constraints and the state engages in only limited efforts to shift resources among private actors. Capitalism is founded on the philosophy of laissez-faire economics. There is no assumption that capitalism requires a particular form of political processes to function efficiently.

Causal analysis: A type of relational analysis, causal analysis goes beyond correlational analysis because it explicitly identifies one phenomenon as the effective agent that brings about changes in another phenomenon. Causal analysis presents the "If X, then Y" mode of explanation, where X is the independent variable that, given a certain value, actually causes Y, the dependent variable, to change in a particular way.

Civil war: A form of political violence that occurs when a significant proportion of the population within a region actively supports a separatist movement and political violence emerges on a large scale. Examples: Sudan (since 1983); U.S. Civil War (1861–1865).

Class approach: An analytic explanation of the value allocation process (politics) based on a core notion of stratification—structured inequality in the distribution of key values in society. The class approach centers on an examination of the tactics of class domination and the dynamics of class struggle. Class theory is particularly associated with the writings of Karl Marx (1867/1981) and later forms of Marxist theories.

Classical liberalism: One of the major Western political ideologies. In classical liberalism, the highest value is placed on each individual's natural rights to life, liberty, and property and the freedom of the individual to pursue these rights as an independent actor. Government plays a very limited role under classical liberalism, which celebrates a laissez-faire economy and discourages government attempts to create material equality (although equality of opportunity is important). Political thinkers associated with classical liberal thought include John Locke (1632–1704), Adam Smith (1723–1790), and John Stuart Mill (1806–1873).

Colonialism: A situation of dominance and subordination in the relations between two states. One state asserts substantial power and control over the other, based on military, economic, and/or political power. The goals of the dominant state might include: to extract resources, to control a market for its products, to use the strategic location, to instill its own values into members of the subordinate state, or to obtain international prestige. Most areas that were colonial holdings became independent in the decades after 1945.

Command economy: A type of political economy in which the state assumes total control of virtually all significant factors of production. The state replaces or eliminates the role of private owners of land, labor, and capital; makes all production decisions; and determines the value of all goods. The state owns, plans, controls, and regulates all major economic activity. (Compare with *Market economy*.)

Communism: One of the major "isms" linking politics and political economy, communism is a system that is closely associated with the command political economy. Based on the theories of Karl Marx (1867/1981) and others, the key to communism is the socialization of resources—the notion that the state must maintain control of society's land, labor, and capital. Although it is primarily an economic system, communism also emphasizes an ideological commitment to economic and social equality among all of its citizens. It also posits that until such equality is achieved, government and politics must be guided powerfully by a unified leadership. Examples: Cuba; the former Soviet Union.

Confederation: A loose association of states. In a confederation, each state delegates some power to a supranational central government but still retains primary power, and its compliance is always conditional. Confederations are usually created when states decide that the performance of certain functions is enhanced by structured cooperation with other states. Example: the United Nations.

Conservatism: One of the major Western political ideologies, at the core of conservatism is the commitment to sustain traditional values and forms of behavior and to maintain social order. Tradition and religion, rather than reason, are viewed as the most reliable sources for guiding society. There is loyalty to the nation and antipathy to egalitarianism. The writings of Edmund Burke (1790/1955) provide a good example of conservative thought.

Constitution: A set of statements that describes the fundamental rules of a political system, including a characterization of the core activities of major political structures. Most constitutions are a single, written document, such as the U.S. Constitution, but some are embedded primarily in major statutes, precedents, and legal decisions.

Constitutional regime: A political system that operates in terms of the rule of law, as defined in the constitution, and that ensures effective restraints on the power holders. The defining feature of a constitutional regime is that the state does attempt to fulfill the provisions of its constitution.

Core: Refers to the set of states, firms (especially multinational firms), and financial institutions that have enormous power and influence in the global system and the international political economy. The core, primarily located in the developed countries, dominates the world's "periphery," composed of institutions and peoples that have minimal power and are primarily located in the developing countries. Core is a crucial concept of the dependency approach, which is an explanation of both the relations between states and the development process.

Corporatism: A corporatist state is characterized by extensive economic cooperation between an activist state and a set of large organizations that represent actors who control major productive resources. In the hope that there will be cooperation and consultation (rather than conflict) among the state, big capital, big owners, and big labor, the leaders of these groups are given great influence in working with the state to make and implement policy on key political economy issues.

Correlational analysis: A form of relational analysis that determines whether there is a statistically probable relationship between two variables. The analysis does not conclude that one variable is actually the agent that causes change to occur in another variable (as in causal analysis) but merely assesses the strength and direction of the association between variables. Correlational analysis is often a key step in any empirical attempt to understand politics.

Council system: A political system in which a small group shares collective leadership and is responsible for both executive and legislative functions. All members of the council have relatively equal power, so decisions and actions are based on the will of the council majority or council consensus. Examples: mayor-council systems and boards of supervisors in many American local governments.

Coup: Occurs when the top political leader or leadership group is replaced by violence or the explicit threat of violence. A coup is a common form of leadership turnover in political systems that have no accepted and enforceable procedures for leadership succession. Examples: replacement of Wahid in Pakistan (1999); ouster of Aristide in Haiti (2004).

Democracy: A political system in which governance is accomplished by leaders whose authority is based on a limited mandate and who are elected by a universal electorate. Such an "electoral" democracy becomes a "liberal" democracy when the population selects among genuine alternatives and also has significant rights to political participation, expression, and opposition.

Democratic socialism: A variation of socialist ideology that treats greater egalitarianism as its primary goal but also assumes that its goals can and should be implemented by a government that comes to power and rules by democratic means, not by violence and repression. Under democratic socialism, the government might own some of the major economic resources and regulate much of the economy, but it does not attempt to plan and control all aspects of the economic system. (See also *Socialism.*)

Democratization: The effort to institutionalize democratic political regimes more fully and deeply, especially in countries with limited democratic processes. Analyses often try to measure the extent of democratic consolidation and to specify the political, economic, and social conditions conducive to further democratization.

Dependency approach: This claims that an economic and political hierarchy exists in which many actors take advantage of those with less power and resources. At the top are the most-developed countries, and the poor people and the villages of the developing countries are at the bottom. Some analysts claim that many of the difficulties facing the less-developed countries stem from their vulnerability to, and dependence on, the more highly developed countries and the transnational institutions they control.

Dependent variable: The *Y* variable whose value changes as a result of changes in some other specified (independent) variables. Causal analysis presents the "If *X*, then *Y*" mode of explanation, where *X* is the independent variable that, given a certain value, actually causes *Y*, the dependent variable, to alter in value in a particular way.

Dictatorship: A political system in which political leaders are not subject to a limited mandate but have absolute power and authority. The citizens have no regular and realistic opportunity to replace such political leadership in a nonviolent manner.

Dual executive: A political system in which one actor, the head of state, performs the more ceremonial aspects of top leadership and embodies the nation, while another actor, the head of government, is responsible for the more political aspects of the executive role. (See also *Executive.*) Example: The United Kingdom has Queen Elizabeth (head of state) and Prime Minister Gordon Brown (head of government).

Economic development: This occurs as more and more households and firms within a country are engaged in ever-higher levels of production and consumption. Based on greater control of the environment and resources, more (and more complex) goods are produced and exchanged, and the GDP gets larger relative to the number of people sharing in the market.

Electoral system: The framework by which the votes of citizens are converted to specific selections of candidates who have a mandate to hold office. There are many variations, some based on selection proportional to votes cast and others based on the selection of the candidate with most (plurality) or at least half (majority) of the votes.

Elite approach: An analytic explanation of the value allocation process (politics) in which the political world is characterized by political stratification, the segmentation of the population into separate groups with greater or less power. There are only two major strata—those that do more of what there is to do (in the policy process) and that get more of the resources that are available, and those that do less and get less. These two groups are called the political elite and the mass, respectively. Key elite theorists include Gaetano Mosca (1896/1939) and C. Wright Mills (1956).

Ethnonationalism: A powerful attitude of identity with and support for others perceived to share a key nation-based trait (e.g., ethnicity, religion, common geography). There is often animosity between groups with different nationality identities. This animosity has become a particular problem that produces conflict and violence, both within and between states, because the nationality identities of many people are not coterminous with the borders of their state.

Executive: The branch of the political system composed of a leader or group of leaders who are responsible for defining and managing the implementation of public policy. A broad definition of the executive includes not only the chief executive (e.g., mayor, governor, prime minister, president, queen) but also the entire administrative system.

Fascism: A political ideology that places fundamental importance on the unity and harmony of government and society and is defined particularly by its opposition to forces that might weaken that collective unity. It further assumes that the top leader is the embodiment of the natural will and that all individuals and groups must obey the will of the leader. It is both antisocialist and antidemocratic. Fascism had major impact on twentieth-century history and is particularly associated with such regimes as those of Adolf Hitler ("Nazism") in Germany (1932–1945) and Benito Mussolini in Italy (1922–1943).

Federation: A political system in which there is a constitutional division of power and functions between a central government and a set of regional governments, usually known as states, provinces, or cantons. Power is shared among the levels of government, and no level has legal power to dominate any other level in all policy domains. Examples: Brazil; Canada; Mexico; the United States.

Formal analysis: Specifies abstract forms that correspond to the reality in which the analyst is interested. The formal analyst attempts to "model" reality. Most formal analyses use symbol systems as abstract representations of the phenomenon under study, such as a subway map or David Easton's (1965) political system model.

Functional analysis: Describes the contributions of a certain element (process or structure) to the activities of the phenomenon under study. For example, one form of functional analysis identifies certain functions or processes (e.g., political communication, rule adjudication) that occur within a political system and describes how and by what structures the functions are performed.

Geopolitics: An analytical method that assumes that the geography of a state—its particular geographical location and also its physical characteristics, natural resources, and human resources—can significantly affect the domestic and foreign policy actions of the state.

Globalization: The increasing integration of diverse economic, sociocultural, military, and environmental phenomena by means of dense networks of action and information that span vast distances around the world. These networks dramatically increase interdependence among actors within the international system and within such environments as the economic system and the environmental system.

Group approach: An analytic explanation of the value allocation process (politics) that is grounded in the concept of the group—any aggregate of individuals who interact to pursue a common interest. Within this approach, politics can be understood as the interaction among groups that are pursuing their political interests, and policy decisions are the outcome of that group process. It is assumed that any particular individual can belong to many different groups and has some political resources that can be used in an attempt to influence policy decisions.

Guerrilla war: Violent opposition to an existing regime by means of a long, protracted campaign primarily from rural bases. Fighting is typical in a hit-and-run style, with extensive efforts to win the support of the peasants and the creation of new political institutions prior to collapse of the old regime.

Hegemony: The existence of an extraordinarily powerful group (a "hegemonic elite") or country ("hegemon") that sustains its domination over other actors for a long period of time.

Hybrid system: A political system that attempts to blend the desirable aspects of both the presidential and cabinet systems of government. Hybrid systems have a prime minister and an elected legislature that can both enact and implement policies, but they also have a president who may have relatively equal power with the cabinet or may have key specific, but limited, powers. Examples: France; Russia.

Hyperpluralism: A situation in which many effective groups are able to pressure the government to respond to their policy demands. As the government tries to satisfy them all, public policy can become contradictory or muddled. At worst, government may become paralyzed, unable to respond in the face of strong competing demands.

Independent variable: The variable in a cause-and-effect hypothesis or explanation that produces change in another variable. In the "If X, then Y" mode of explanation, X is the independent variable that, given a certain value, actually causes Y, the dependent variable, to change in a particular way.

Interest group: A group that directly attempts to influence the allocation of public values or other actions of those in the political system. It may undertake political action, provide goods or services to political actors, or provide data and information to those within the political system in its attempts to achieve its political objectives. It may also exert influence through compliance or noncompliance with the government policy process.

Intergovernmental organizations (IGOs): A political actor whose members are states, not private groups or individuals. IGOs can shape the cooperative relations among states, some or all of whom are their members. States form IGOs to provide a forum of communication among states, to enact international laws and treaties, and to intervene in disputes between states. Examples: European Union; NAFTA; NATO.

International law: A broad attempt to establish principles and rules that formalize and constrain the interactions among states. Positivist law, or written agreements between states in the form of international treaties or conventions, is the basis for international law.

International organization: A broad term that refers to many of the cross-national institutions whose objectives are to influence the behavior and policies of states. The two primary forms are NGOs (nongovernmental organizations) and IGOs (intergovernmental organizations). Examples: Amnesty International; the United Nations.

International regime: A set of norms, rules, and procedures that are accepted by many countries and guide their behavior with each other in a particular issue domain. Examples: the World Trade Organization on trade relations; the Nuclear Nonproliferation Treaty.

International relations: One of the four major subfields within political science that examines the political relations between countries and the dynamics within the worldwide system of states. Subjects of analysis include foreign policy, interstate conflict and conflict resolution, and international law.

Judicial review: In political systems where the judiciary is relatively independent, the judiciary can interpret or even revoke the policy decisions and actions taken by the other political structures, thus exercising the power of judicial review. In the United States, for example, the Supreme Court exercises the power of judicial review when it declares that a law passed by Congress is unconstitutional.

Judiciary: An important branch of most political systems, the system of courts and personnel that determine whether the laws of the society have been transgressed, and, if so, whether and what type of sanctions ought to be imposed on the transgressor.

Legislature: The political structure in which, typically, policy issues are discussed and assessed and public policies are enacted by a set of elected or appointed legislators. Although a particular legislature may not exercise these powers, most have three broad roles: (1) enacting legislation, (2) representing the citizenry, and (3) overseeing the executive.

Liberal democracy: A political system that not only is an electoral democracy (periodic elections, limited mandate) but also ensures extensive political rights (e.g., parties promoting genuine alternatives, opposition) and civil liberties (e.g., freedom of expression, religion, and the media).

Market economy: A type of political economy in which there is near-total private control of land, labor, and capital. Every actor has direct control over his or her own factors of production, and production decisions are essentially the sum of all private actors' decisions. The exchange value of goods is decided by the market. The state is generally quite passive in a market economy, enforcing rules and providing minimal protection to economic actors. (Compare with *Command economy*.)

Marxist-Leninist socialism: A variant of socialist ideology heavily influenced by the writings of Karl Marx and the interpretations by V. I. Lenin. It begins with three assumptions regarding the changes necessary to produce the key goals of equality and social justice: (1) it might be necessary to use violence to overthrow the old economic order, (2) a powerful government is necessary to restructure the economic system, and (3) a small dictatorial leadership group must manage the government and effect the economic and social changes. This group will be unnecessary when equality is achieved and can be replaced by decentralized citizen-run politics. (See also *Socialism*.)

Micropolitics: An analytic focus on individual and small group political processes, with a particular emphasis on how the individual understands the political world and how the individual acts politically.

Mixed economy: A political economy that attempts to combine the strengths of both market and command economies while also minimizing their shortcomings. Control of the means of production is shared between the state and private actors. The state's rules, actions, and direct involvement in the economic system guide some production, distribution, and pricing decisions and also moderate and limit the market behavior of private households and firms.

Monarchy: (1) A political system with a hereditary sovereign, often called a king or queen. (2) Analytically, a political system in which one person exercises a very large proportion of political control.

Nation: A sociopolitical unit defined by a deeply shared fundamental identification among a set of people based on shared ethnicity, language, descent, culture, religion, or geographic space. The nation is a major group, beyond the family, with whom the individual identifies very powerfully.

Nationalism: A strong affection and commitment to the well-being of the nation with which one identifies, in comparison with minimal concern for those outside the nation. Nationalism can become the underlying principle shaping people's loyalty and willingness to make sacrifices for the protection and enhancement of the nation and its collective interests.

Natural law: Refers to sensible, widely accepted norms of behavior that ought to guide the relations among states and individuals and that should restrain hostile or destructive interactions.

Neocolonialism: New forms of domination and dependence between states that have emerged in the decades (after World War II) since the end of colonialism. Although direct occupation by colonial powers was ended at independence, domination has been extended in some cases by the manipulation of such power resources as economic aid, technology transfer, military support, and economic intervention.

Neoliberalism: An approach to economic development that emphasizes a reliance on a local and global free market that is guided by entrepreneurs who shape decisions about the production and distribution of goods. The state plays a minimal role in the political economy, and public spending is focused on infrastructure support (e.g., transportation, education) rather than welfare distribution.

Nonconstitutional regime: A political system in which there is persistent nonenforcement of crucial limits on the rulers and/or protection of the rights of the ruled, especially those limits and rights specified in a constitution and other key legal documents. Most authoritarian or totalitarian regimes are nonconstitutional.

Nongovernmental organizations (NGOs): National or transnational associations that are not part of the governmental/state apparatus but are committed to the promotion of an issue with national or international policy dimensions. (In the latter case, the association is called an international nongovernmental organization.) Members are groups and individuals who combine their knowledge and financial and political resources to pursue a shared objective. Examples: Amnesty International's monitoring of human rights; Medecins sans Frontiers (Doctors Without Borders) provisions of medical assistance.

Normative political knowledge: Answers questions about what ought to be rather than simply providing descriptions and explanations of what is. Examples of normative questions: Should there be limits on free speech?; How much and what types of health care should the state provide?

Oligarchy: Literally, rule by the few. Hence, a political system in which a small number of actors dominate the resource allocation process, usually serving their own interests.

Parliamentary (cabinet) government: A political system in which the executive and legislative functions and structures are fused. The people elect the legislature (parliament), whose majority empowers a cabinet, which then empowers one of its members to be the chief executive, usually called a prime minister or premier. The cabinet devises, drafts, and implements most policies, although they must be enacted by the legislative majority. Examples: Italy; the United Kingdom.

Participatory democracy: Democracy in its classic sense as government of and by all the people. There is active, direct participation by all citizens in the authoritative allocation of values.

Party system: The configuration of political parties in a political system. Party systems are generally classified according to the number of political parties and the nature of the interactions among the parties in the governing process.

Political analysis: The attempt to describe and explain political phenomena that strives to make understanding of politics more general, precise, and systematic, and ultimately to generate and test theories.

Political belief system: The configuration of an individual's political orientations across an array of political issues. Many political beliefs are evaluative orientations, which synthesize facts (cognitive orientations) and feelings (affective orientations) into a judgment (evaluative orientation) about some political phenomena.

Political culture: The general configuration of a particular people's (e.g., a nation's or a country's) political beliefs. It characterizes those cognitive, affective, and evaluative orientations that are dominant among those people. Many explanations of political behavior and political processes are grounded in interpretations of political culture.

Political decay: The phenomena that occur when there is a decline in the capacity of the political system and especially its effectiveness in maintaining order. It can be manifest in such collective behavior as demonstrations, protests, rebellion, and other forms of political violence. It is often associated with extensive demands that the political system cannot meet and with the loss of citizen support for the political system. According to Samuel Huntington (1968), the probability of political decay increases as a state has a lower level of political institutionalization.

Political development: The specifically political aspects of development and modernization. It can refer either to a set of characteristics of the political system or to the process through which those characteristics are increased. The key characteristics of more-developed political systems can include: (1) the concentration of power in the central state; (2) "modern" forms of political organization, such as institutionalized party systems and effective bureaucracies; (3) complex and extensive forms of individual and group political behavior; and (4) expanded capabilities of the political system to maintain order, manage the environment, meet the demands of the citizens, and so on.

Political economy: The combination, in theory or in practice, of politics and economics. The political system and the economic system are inextricably intertwined because many of the decisions made by the political system have significant impacts on the economy and activities within the economic system have major impacts on the state. Two ideal-type political economies are the market economy and the command economy.

Political elite: A general term for those individuals who have relatively high levels of power, influence, interest, knowledge, and involvement in political life. It is the stratum of the population that does more of what there is to do (in the policy process) and gets more of what there is to get (in the allocation of values).

Political idealism: A perspective, especially in international relations theory, that posits that human nature is basically good and thus states have a natural tendency to be cooperative and even altruistic. Political institutions can then be shaped to facilitate the emergence of these cooperative, nonviolent tendencies in the relations among states.

Political ideology: A comprehensive set of beliefs about the political world, including a specification of desirable political goals and the best way to achieve those goals, based on particular assumptions about human nature, the relation of the individual to society, and the desirability of equality.

Political institutionalization: The extent that political organizations and procedures have acquired value in the eyes of the population and the stability to withstand significant pressure. It is measured by the political system's capacity to regulate its citizens, respond flexibly to citizen demands, extract and distribute resources efficiently, and adapt to changing circumstances.

Political participation: The term applied to all modes of the political actions by individuals and groups. The broad goal is to influence the actions or selection of political rulers. Modes of political participation for an individual range from listening to political discourse to voting to taking part in a demonstration to holding political office.

Political party: An organized group that attempts to capture political power directly by placing its members in government office. The political party is the broadest institution in most political systems that links individuals and groups to the state, and it can organize the activities of those participating in government. It also aggregates political interests into a comprehensible set of policy goals.

Political realism: A perspective, especially in international relations theory, that assumes that people are naturally disposed to behave selfishly and that this self-interested orientation extends to the behavior of states. The fundamental goal of each state is to ensure its own security and survival by maximizing its power. Interstate conflict is likely to be a recurring event, and states sometimes use balance-of-power strategies to limit the frequency of major conflicts.

Political resources: Something that can influence the actions and decisions of political actors, such as social status, money, legality, special knowledge or skills, ability to mobilize large numbers of people, visibility in the media, and control of productive capabilities. According to the group approach, political resources are of many forms and widely distributed. According to the class and elite approaches, one or a few types of political resources are critical, and control of those resources tends to be concentrated in a limited group.

Political science: A set of techniques, concepts, and approaches whose objective is to increase the clarity and accuracy of understandings about political phenomena. This academic discipline is labeled a "science" in the United States because most political scientists use the scientific method to establish shared knowledge about the political world.

Political socialization: The process through which individuals acquire their cognitive, affective, and evaluative orientations toward the political world. Some of the most important agents (sources) are the family, the schools, peer groups, the media, and culture.

Political society: Formed when individuals cede to the state a monopoly over the legitimate use of violence, sacrificing their own right to do violence to others in exchange for a similar sacrifice from others. Thomas Hobbes (1651) called this agreement among individuals the *social contract*.

Political system: A (formal) theoretical concept that attempts to model the fundamental structures, processes, and institutions of politics. According to David Easton (1965), the defining feature is its authoritative allocation of values for the collectivity.

Political violence: The use of physical violence, or very serious threats of such violence, to achieve political goals. The modes range from nuclear war to assassination to riots. Some analysts define as political violence other activities that do not entail physical violence, such as racial epithets or ethnic discrimination.

Politics: The process through which power and influence are used to promote certain values and interests and to determine who gets what, when, and how in a given society.

Positivist law: Explicit written agreements, often enacted by legislatures and interpreted by judiciaries, that specify appropriate and unlawful behaviors as well as the sanctions for the latter. In the form of treaties or conventions between states, positivist law is the basis of international law.

Power: Exercised when A (one actor) induces B (another actor) to behave in a manner in which B would not otherwise behave. One taxonomy classifying the forms of power includes force (coercive power), exchange (economic power), and mutuality (integrative power).

Presidential government: A political system in which there is a separation of executive and legislative power and structures. This is meant to ensure a system of checks and balances in the policy process, with the legislature taking primary responsibility for policy making and the president (the executive) taking primary responsibility for policy implementation (although in practice these distinctions may be blurred). The president and the members of the legislature are elected independently, for fixed terms. Examples: Mexico; the United States.

Privatization: The selling off of state-owned firms to private actors and/or the use of private firms to provide public goods and services.

Public policy: Any decision or action by a governmental authority that results in the allocation of a value. A taxonomy of public policies could be based on the functional area of the policy (e.g., environmental, trade), the overall effects of the policy (e.g., redistributive, symbolic), or the stages of the policy process (e.g., problem definition, evaluation).

Rational choice theory: An array of formal analyses that share two basic features: (1) they are attempts to represent political processes primarily by means of mathematical formulations or systems of symbolic notation, and (2) it is assumed that the behavior of political actors is goal oriented, based on self-interest, and calculating. Examples: game theory; minimum winning coalition theory.

Relational analysis: Approaches to political analysis that specify the systematic connections between sets of phenomena, revealing either patterns of association (correlation) or causality.

Representative democracy: A form of electoral democracy in which citizens elect people to represent them in the governing process and to allocate values on their behalf for the collectivity. Also known as a republic.

Revolution: A rapid and fundamental transformation of the state organization and of the allocation of values in a society. A revolution often involves the use of force and violence to destroy the existing political system.

Social market system: A political-economic system in which the state encourages the operation of an extensive free-market economy but is also committed to social welfare distribution and some income redistribution, within the context of a democratic political process. Contemporary examples: Germany; Sweden.

Social welfarism: A set of ideological orientations and public policies that aim to ensure that all citizens receive an adequate quality of life in such domains as education, health care, housing, and employment opportunities. Usually characterized by relatively high taxes, more extensive resource allocations (e.g., transfer payments or subsidized goods and services), and more active state intervention to protect citizens against the behaviors of those firms or others whose actions reduce the quality of life. Example: Sweden.

Socialism: One of the major Western political ideologies in which the most important goal is to provide a high-quality, relatively equal standard of living for all. Each individual is encouraged to increase the collective good of all in an environment that encourages cooperation and sharing. Government plays a crucial role as it attempts to use its allocation of values and control of resources to increase the material, social, and political equality of all citizens. Two major variations are Marxist-Leninist socialism and democratic socialism.

Sovereignty: The premise that each state has complete authority and is the ultimate source of law within its own boundaries. It assumes that all states are equal before the law and that each state has the right to protect its territory against any aggression or intervention.

State: (1) The legal notion of the state is that it is a "territorially bound sovereign entity." (2) In the general language of political science, "state" usually refers to the organizational units, institutions, and individuals that perform the political functions for a national territorial entity, such as France or Nigeria. (3) The state can also be defined as the entity with a monopoly on the legitimate use of violence to enforce the laws and decisions of the society.

Statism: A state-centered strategy for facilitating economic development. The statist approach emphasizes the importance of strong state action to support and guide the production and distribution of goods by the political economy. The state typically plans and regulates major aspects of the political economy and might own and operate key economic sectors.

Taxonomic analysis: Approaches to political analysis that establish the orderly arrangement of phenomena into a set of categories that classify those phenomena/data into different types. Categories should be exhaustive, mutually exclusive, and differentiated by consistent criteria. The categories of a taxonomy establish the crucial concepts that structure the analysis.

Territorial integrity: A concept closely associated with sovereignty, it is a premise of international law that holds that a state has the right to resist and reject any aggression, invasion, or intervention within its territorial boundaries.

Terrorism: Premeditated violence serving an underlying political objective, in which the target of violence is a "noncombatant." As a revolutionary strategy, terrorism involves selective acts of violence, usually by small, organized cells of political activists.

Totalitarianism: A political regime that demands complete obedience to its extensive rules regarding not only politics but virtually all aspects of life, including culture, economics, religion, and morality. It might prescribe and proscribe the behavior and thoughts of its population in every domain of existence. Examples: contemporary North Korea; the Soviet Union under Joseph Stalin.

Transnationalism: A system of institutions and relationships in which key actors' loyalties and identities are not linked to any particular country. Many of these powerful actors are multinational corporations (MNCs) such as General Motors, Exxon, and Sony, and other important transnational actors include the International Monetary Fund, OPEC, NATO, and other IGOs and NGOs. Increasingly, MNCs and other transnational actors hold international economic power, shape global culture and communications, and operate outside the legal control of states.

Treaty: A formal agreement between states that they will cooperate or assist each other militarily, economically, or politically. A treaty carries a stronger expectation of compliance than an alliance. Examples: NATO; Nuclear Nonproliferation Treaty.

Unitary state: A political system in which the central government holds all legitimate power. The central government may delegate power or functional responsibilities to territorial units (often called departments, regions, or prefectures), but those delegated powers and functions can be revoked at any time. Examples: China; France; Japan; the United Kingdom.

War: Interstate violence that is sustained, organized, and usually involves hostilities between the regular military forces of the states. War is the ultimate mechanism for attempting to resolve power struggles and conflict between states. Examples: Iran-Iraq War; Korean War.

REFERENCES

Abadie, Alberto. (2004). "Poverty, Political Freedom, and the Roots of Terrorism." Cambridge, MA: KSG Working Paper 04-043 (October).

Abrahamian, Ervand. (1993). *Khomeinism: Essays on the Islamic Republic*. Berkeley: University of California Press.

Achebe, Chinua. (1959). *Things Fall Apart*. New York: Fawcett.

Agnew, John. (2003). *Geopolitics: Re-Visioning World Politics*. London: Routledge.

Aguero, Felipe, and Jeffrey Stark, Eds. (1998). *Fault Lines of Democracy in Post-Transition Latin America*. Miami, FL: North-South Center Press.

Almond, Gabriel, and Sidney Verba. (1963). *The Civic Culture*. Princeton, NJ: Princeton University Press.

Almond, Gabriel, G. Bingham Powell, Kaare Strom, and Russell Dalton, Eds. (2008). *Comparative Politics Today: A World View*. 9th ed. New York: Longman.

Amnesty International. (2007). *Amnesty International Report 2007*, http://web.amnesty.org/report2007.

Ardrey, Robert. (1966). *The Territorial Imperative*. New York: Atheneum.

Arendt, Hannah. (1963). *On Revolution*. New York: Viking Press.

Bachrach, Peter, and Morton Baratz. (1962). "The Two Faces of Power." *American Political Science Review* 56 (December): 947–952.

Barber, Benjamin R. (1995). *Jihad Versus McWorld*. New York: Random House.

———. (2004). *Strong Democracy: Participatory Politics for a New Age*. 20th anniv. ed. Berkeley: University of California Press.

Barkan, Joel. (2002). "The Many Faces of Africa." *Harvard International Review* (Summer): 14–18.

Barnet, Richard J., and John Cavanagh. (1994). *Global Dreams: Imperial Corporations and the New World Order*. New York: Simon and Schuster.

Baumgartner, Frank, and Beth Leech. (1998). *Basic Interests: The Importance of Groups in Politics and Political Science*. Princeton, NJ: Princeton University Press.

Beah, Ishmael. (2007). *A Long Way Gone*. New York: Farrar, Straus and Giroux.

Becker, Ted, and Christa Slaton. (2000). *The Future of Teledemocracy*. Westport, CT: Praeger.

Bennett, W. Lance. (2008). *News: The Politics of Illusion*. 8th ed. New York: Longman.

Bentley, Arthur. (1908/1967). *The Process of Government*. Cambridge, MA: Harvard University Press.

Berrebi, Claude. (2007). "Evidence About the Link Between Education, Poverty, and Terrorism Among Palestinians." *Peace Economics, Peace Science, and Public Policy* 13 (1): article 2.

Bill, James, and Robert Hardgrave. (1981). *Comparative Politics: Quest for Theory*. Lanham, MD: University Press of America.

Bimber, Bruce. (2003). *Information and American Democracy: Technology and the Evolution of Political Power*. New York: Cambridge University Press.

Birnbaum, Jeffrey H. (1993). *The Lobbyists: How Influence Peddlers Get Their Way in Washington*. New York: Times Books.

Black, Cyril. (1966). *The Dynamics of Modernization*. New York: Harper and Row.

Blasi, Joseph R., Maya Kroumova, and Douglas Kruse. (1997). *Kremlin Capitalism: Privatizing the Russian Economy*. Ithaca, NY: Cornell University Press.

Blinder, Alan, and William Baumol. (2008). *Economics*. 11th ed. Belmont, CA: Thompson.

Boulding, Kenneth E. (1989). *Three Faces of Power*. Newbury Park, CA: Sage.

———. (1993). "Power." In *The Oxford Companion to Politics of the World*, ed. Joel Krieger, pp. 739–740. New York: Oxford University Press.

Brams, Steven J., and Peter Fishburn. (1983). *Approval Voting*. Cambridge, MA: Birkhauser Boston.

Bratton, Michael, and Nicolas van de Walle. (1997). *Democratic Experiments in Africa: Regime Transitions in Comparative Perspective*. New York: Cambridge University Press.

Brecher, Michael, and Jonathan Wilkenfeld. (1997). *A Study of Crisis*. Ann Arbor: University of Michigan Press.

Bremer, Stuart. (1980). "National Capabilities and War Proneness." In *Correlates of War, II*, ed. J. David Singer, pp. 57–82. New York: Free Press.

Brinton, Crane. (1957). *The Anatomy of Revolution*. Rev. ed. New York: Vintage.

Brown, Justin. (1999). "Lowdown on a High Strung Corner of Europe." *Christian Science Monitor*, March 16, 12–13.

Bueno de Mesquita, Bruce. (2006). "Game Theory, Political Economy, and the Evolving Study of War and Peace." *American Political Science Review* 100 (November): 637–642.

——, and George Downs. (2005). "Development and Democracy." *Foreign Affairs 84* (September/October).

Bulletin of Atomic Scientists. (2006). "Nuclear Pursuits." http://www.thebulletin.org/article_nn.php?art_ofn= so03norris.

——. (2007). http://www.thebulletin.org/content/media-center/announcements/2007/01/17/doomsday-clock-moves-two-minutes-closer-to-midnight.

Bunce, Valerie. (2003). "Rethinking Democratization: Lessons from the Postcommunist Experience." *World Politics* 55 (January): 170–189.

Burke, Edmund. (1790/1955). *The Works of Edmund Burke*. New York: Harper and Row.

Calderisi, Robert. (2007). *The Trouble with Africa: Why Foreign Aid Isn't Working*. New York: Palgrave.

Campbell, Alastair. (2007). *The Blair Years: The Alastair Campbell Diaries*. New York: Knopf.

Cantril, Hadley. (1965). *The Pattern of Human Concerns*. New Brunswick, NJ: Rutgers University Press.

Carbone, Giovanni M. (2007). "Political Parties and Party Systems in Africa: Themes and Research Perspectives." *World Political Science Review*. http://www.bepress.com/wpsr/vol3/iss3/art1.

Carroll, Susan, and Richard Fox, Eds. (2006). *Gender and Elections: Shaping the Future of American Politics*. New York: Cambridge University Press.

Castells, Manuel. (2000). "Materials for an Exploratory Theory of the Network Society." *British Journal of Sociology* 5 (January/March): 5–24.

Castles, Francis G. (2004). *The Future of the Welfare State: Crisis Myths and Crisis Realities*. New York: Oxford University Press.

Center for Responsive Politics. (2006). http://www.opensecrets.org.

Central Intelligence Agency. (2008). *World Factbook 2008*. http://www.odci.gov/cia/ciahome.html.

Chadwick, Andrew. (2006). *Internet Politics: States, Citizens, and New Communications Technologies*. New York: Oxford University Press.

Chinese Consulate (2007). Consulate General of the People's Republic of China in New York. http://www.nyconsulate.prchina.org.

Cimbala, Stephen. (2000). *Nuclear Strategy in the Twenty-First Century*. Westport, CT: Praeger.

Clausewitz, Karl von. (1833/1967). *On War*. Ed. and trans. Michael Howard and Peter Paret. Princeton, NJ: Princeton University Press.

CNA Corporation. (2007). *National Security and the Threat of Climate Change*. Alexandria, VA.

Colburn, Forrest. (2002). *Latin America at the End of Politics*. Princeton, NJ: Princeton University Press.

Coles, Robert. (2003). *Bruce Springsteen's America: The People Listening, a Poet Singing*. New York: Random House.

Compton, Robert W. (2000). *East Asian Democratization: Impact of Globalization, Culture, and Economy*. Westport, CT: Greenwood.

Connor, Walker. (1994). *Ethnonationalism: The Quest for Understanding*. Princeton, NJ: Princeton University Press.

Chinese Consulate-General. (2007). http://www.china-embassy.org/eng/gyzj/t398678.htm.

Converse, Philip. (1964). "The Nature of Belief Systems in Mass Publics." In *Ideology and Discontent*, ed. David Apter, pp. 224–240. Glencoe, IL: Free Press.

Conversi, Danielle, Ed. (2004). *Ethnonationalism in the Contemporary World: Walker Connor and the Study of Nationalism*. London: Routledge.

Corothers, Thomas. (2002). "The End of the Transition Paradigm." *Journal of Democracy* 13 (January): 5–18.

Cortright, David, and George Lopez, Eds. (2002). *Smart Sanctions: Toward Effective and Humane Sanctions Reform*. Lanham, MD: Rowan and Littlefield.

Council on Foreign Relations. (2005). *What Is Terrorism?* http://cfrterrorism.org/terrorism/introduction.html.

Cruikshanks, Randall. (2000). "Conflict Resolution in the Other World." In *The Other World: Issues and Politics of the Developing World*, 4th ed., ed. Joseph Weatherby et al., pp. 78–109. White Plains, NY: Longman.

Cutright, Phillips. (1963). "National Political Development: Measurement and Analysis." *American Sociological Review* 20: 253–264.

Dahl, Robert. (1961). *Who Governs? Democracy in an American City*. New Haven, CT: Yale University Press.

——. (1971). *Polyarchy: Participation and Opposition*. New Haven, CT: Yale University Press.

——. (1991). *Democracy and Its Critics*. New Haven, CT: Yale University Press.

——. (2006). *A Preface to Democratic Theory*. Expanded ed. Chicago: University of Chicago Press.

Dahl, Robert, and Bruce Stinebrickner. (2003). *Modern Political Analysis*. 6th ed. New York: Pearson.

Dahrendorf, Ralf. (1959). *Class and Class Conflict in Industrial Society*. Stanford, CA: Stanford University Press.

Dalton, Russell. (2008). *Citizen Politics: Public Opinion and Political Parties in Advanced Industrial Democracies*. 5th ed. Washington, DC: CQ Press.

Davies, James C. (1971). "Toward a Theory of Revolution." In *When Men Revolt and Why,* ed. James C. Davies, pp. 134–147. New York: Free Press.

Davis, Richard. (1998). *New Media and American Politics.* New York: Oxford University Press.

Davis, Winston. (1987). "Religion and Development: Weber and the East Asian Experience." In *Understanding Political Development,* ed. Myron Weiner and Samuel Huntington, pp. 221–280. Boston: Little, Brown.

Demick, Barbara. (2003). "U.S. Gets a Bad Name in South Korea." *Los Angeles Times,* July 12, A3.

Derbyshire, Denis, and Ian Derbyshire. (2000). *Encyclopedia of World Political Systems.* New York: M. E. Sharpe.

Diamond, Larry. (1992). "Economic Development and Democracy Reconsidered." In *Reexamining Democracy: Essays in Honor of Seymour Martin Lipset,* ed. Gary Marks and Larry Diamond, pp. 93–139. Newbury Park, CA: Sage.

———. (1999). *Developing Democracy: Toward Consolidation.* Baltimore, MD: Johns Hopkins University Press.

———. (2000). "The Global State of Democracy." *Current History* 99 (December): 412–418.

———. (2003). "Universal Democracy?" *Policy Review Online.* http://www.policyreview.org/jun03/diamond.html.

Dolan, Julie Ann, Melissa Deckman, and Michele Swers (2007). *Women and Politics: Paths to Power and Influence.* New York: Prentice Hall.

Domhoff, G. William. (2005). *Who Rules America? Power and Politics.* 5th ed. Boston: McGraw-Hill.

Donovan, John, Richard Morgan, Christian Potholm, and Marcia Weigle. (1994). *People, Power and Politics.* 3rd ed. New York: Random House.

Doyle, Michael W., and Nicholas Sambanis. (2000). "International Peacebuilding: A Theoretical and Quantitative Analysis." *American Political Science Review* 94 (December): 779–801.

Drezner, Daniel. (2007). *All Politics Are Global.* Princeton, NJ: Princeton University Press.

Duverger, Maurice. (1954). *Political Parties.* New York: Wiley.

Easton, David. (1953). *The Political System.* New York: Knopf.

———. (1965). *A Framework for Political Analysis.* Englewood Cliffs, NJ: Prentice Hall.

Eckstein, Harry. (1966). *Division and Cohesion in Democracy: A Study of Norway.* Princeton, NJ: Princeton University Press.

Economist. (1998). "What Would Confucius Say Now?" *Economist,* July 25, 23–24, 28.

Economist Intelligence Unit. (2008). Global Peace Index. http://www.visionofhumanity.com/introduction/index.php.

Edwards, George, Martin Wattenberg, and Robert Lineberry. (2008). *Government in America.* 13th ed. New York: Longman.

Ehrlich, Paul R., and Anne H. Ehrlich. (1990). *The Population Explosion.* New York: Simon and Schuster.

Eifert, Martin, and Jan Ole Puschel, Eds. (2004). *National Electronic Government: Comparing Governance Structures in Multi-Layer Administrations.* London: Routledge.

Elgie, Robert, Ed. (1999). *Semi-Presidentialism in Europe.* New York: Oxford University Press.

Elkington, John, and Seb Beloe. (2003). *The 21st Century NGO: In the Market for Change.* London: SustainAbility.

Erikson, Erik. (1958). *Young Man Luther.* New York: W. W. Norton.

———. (1969). *Gandhi's Truth.* New York: W. W. Norton.

Esping-Andersen, Gosta. (1990). *The Three Worlds of Welfare Capitalism.* Princeton, NJ: Princeton University Press.

Estes, Richard. (1988). *Trends in World Social Development.* New York: Praeger.

Europa: Gateway to the European Union. (2008). http://europa.eu.int/index_en.htm.

Evans, Emmit B., Jr., and Dianne Long. (2000). "Development." In *The Other World: Issues and Politics of the Developing World,* 4th ed., ed. Joseph Weatherby et al., pp. 53–77. White Plains, NY: Longman.

Evans, Peter, Ed. (1997). *State-Society Synergy: Government and Social Capital in Development.* Berkeley: University of California Press.

Evans, Peter, Dietrich Rueschmeyer, and Theda Skocpol, Eds. (1985). *Bringing the State Back In.* New York: Cambridge University Press.

Fagen, Richard. (1964). *Cuba: The Political Content of Adult Education.* Stanford, CA: Hoover Institute.

Falk, Richard A. (1993). "Sovereignty." In *The Oxford Companion to Politics of the World,* ed. Joel Krieger, pp. 851–854. New York: Oxford University Press.

———. (1999). "The New Interventionism and the Third World." *Current History* 98 (November): 370–375.

Fallows, James. (1995). *Looking at the Sun: The Rise of the New East Asian Economic and Political System.* New York: Random House.

Federation of American Scientists. (2007). Biological and Chemical Weapons Control. http://www.fas.org/main/content.jsp?formAction=325&projectId=4.

Fendrich, James. (1993). *Ideal Citizen: The Legacy of the Civil Rights Movement.* Albany, NY: SUNY Press.

Foley, Stephen. (2007). "Planet Murdoch." *Independent* (London). August 2, 2–5.

Franda, Marcus. (2002). *Launching into Cyberspace: Internet Developments and Politics in Five World Regions.* Boulder, CO: Lynne Reinner.

Frederick, Howard H. (1993). *Global Communication and International Relations.* Belmont, CA: Wadsworth.

Freedom House. (2007). *Freedom of the World.* http://www.freedomhouse.org.

———. (2008). *Freedom of the World.* http://www.freedomhouse.org.

Friedman, Thomas L. (1999a). "DOScapital." *Foreign Policy* 113 (Fall): 110–127.

———. (1999b). *The Lexus and the Olive Tree: Understanding Globalization.* New York: Farrar, Straus and Giroux.

———. (2007). *The World Is Flat: A Brief History of the Twenty-first Century.* 2nd revised ed. New York: Farrar, Straus and Giroux.

Global Exchange. (2008). "Top Reasons to Oppose the World Trade Organization." http://www.globalexchange.org.

Gochman, Charles S., and Zeev Maoz. (1984). "Militarized Interstate Disputes, 1816–1976." *Journal of Conflict Resolution* 18 (December): 588–615.

Goldman, Marshall I. (1998). "The Cashless Society." *Current History* 97 (October): 319–324.

———. (2003). *The Piratization of Russia.* New York: Routledge.

Goodwin, Paul. (2005). *Latin America.* 11th ed. New York: McGraw-Hill.

Graber, Doris A. (2001). *Processing Politics: Learning from Television in the Internet Age.* Chicago: University of Chicago Press.

———. (2005). *Mass Media and American Politics.* 7th ed. Washington, DC: CQ Press.

Grotius, Hugo. (1625/1957). *De Jure Belli et Pacis [On the Laws of War and Peace].* New York: Macmillan.

Grzymala-Busse, Anna M. (2002). *Redeeming the Communist Past: The Regeneration of Communist Parties in East Central Europe.* Cambridge: Cambridge University Press.

Gurr, Ted Robert. (2000). *Peoples Versus States: Minorities at Risk in the New Century.* Washington, DC: U.S. Institute of Peace Press.

Gwartney, James, and Robert Lawson. (2007). *Economic Freedom of the World: 2006 Annual Report.* http://www.freetheworld.com.

Hachten, William A., and James Scotton. (2006). *The World News Prism: Global Information in a Satellite Age.* 7th ed. New York: Wiley.

Hakim, Peter. (1999). "Is Latin America Doomed to Failure?" *Foreign Policy* 113 (Winter): 104–119.

Hanson, Stephen E. (2001). "The Dilemmas of Russia's Anti-Revolutionary Revolution." *Current History* 100 (October): 330–335.

Hearnshaw, F. J. C. (1933). *Conservatism in England.* London: Macmillan.

Hechter, Michael. (2000). *Containing Nationalism.* New York: Oxford University Press.

Heilbroner, Robert. (1993). "The Multinational Corporation and the Nation-State." In *At Issue: Politics in the World Arena,* ed. Steven L. Speigel, pp. 338–352. New York: St. Martin's Press.

———. (1994). *Twenty-First Century Capitalism.* New York: W. W. Norton.

Heredia, Blanca. (1997). "Prosper or Perish?: Development in the Age of Global Capital." *Current History* 96 (November): 383–388.

Heritage Foundation. (2005). *Index of Economic Freedom 2005.* http://www.heritage.org/research/features/index/countries.cfm.

Heyne, Paul, Peter Boettke, and David Prychitko. (2006). *The Economic Way of Thinking.* 11th ed. New York: Prentice Hall.

Hobbes, Thomas. (1651/1958). *Leviathan.* Oxford, England: Clarendon.

Holley, David. (2001). "Kofi Annan Accepts Nobel Peace Prize." *Los Angeles Times,* December 11, A15.

Hunter, Floyd. (1953). *Community Power Structure.* Chapel Hill: University of North Carolina Press.

Huntington, Samuel P. (1968). *Political Order in Changing Societies.* New Haven, CT: Yale University Press.

———. (1987). "The Goals of Development." In *Understanding Political Development,* ed. Myron Weiner and Samuel Huntington, pp. 3–32. Boston: Little, Brown.

———. (1991). *The Third Wave: Democratization in the Late Twentieth Century.* Norman: University of Oklahoma Press.

———. (1996). *Clash of Civilizations and the Remaking of the World Order.* New York: Simon and Schuster.

Huxley, Aldous. (1932). *Brave New World.* London: Chatto and Windus.

IDMC (Internal Displacement Monitoring Center). (2007). http://www.internal-displacement.org.

Inglehart, Ronald, and Christian Welzel. (2005). *Modernization, Cultural Change, and Democracy: The Human Development Sequence.* New York: Cambridge University Press.

Inkeles, Alex. (1997). *National Character: A Psycho-Social Perspective.* New Brunswick, NJ: Transaction.

Inkeles, Alex, and David Smith. (1999). *Becoming Modern: Individual Change in Six Developing Countries.* Cambridge, MA: Harvard University Press.

Inkeles, Alex, et al. (1985). *Exploring Individual Modernity.* New York: Columbia University Press.

International Food Policy Research Institute. (2003). http://www.ifpri.org.

Isbister, John. (2006). *Promises Not Kept: Poverty and the Betrayal of Third World Development.* 7th ed. Bloomfield, CT: Kumarian Press.

Iyengar, Shanto. (1994). *Is Anyone Responsible? How Television Frames Political Issues.* Chicago: University of Chicago Press.

Jenkins, Barbara. (1993). "Multinational Corporations." In *The Oxford Companion to Politics of the World,* ed. Joel Krieger, pp. 606–608. New York: Oxford University Press.

Jennings, M. Kent, Gregory Markus, and Richard Niemi. (1991). *Youth-Parent Socialization Panel Study, 1965–1982*. Ann Arbor, MI: Interuniversity Consortium for Political Research.

Jensen, Michael, James N. Danziger, and Alladi Venkatesh. (2007). "Civil Society and Cyber Society: The Role of the Internet in Community Associations and Democratic Politics." *Information Society* 23: 39–50.

Jervis, Robert. (2002). "Theories of War in an Era of Leading-Power Peace." *American Political Science Review* 96 (1): 1–14.

Johnson, Chalmers. (1983a). *MITI and the Japanese Miracle*. Stanford, CA: Stanford University Press.

——. (1983b). *Revolutionary Change*. 2nd ed. London: Longman.

——. (1996). *Japan: Who Governs? The Rise of the Developmental State*. New York: W. W. Norton.

Juergensmeyer, Mark. (2003). *Terror in the Mind of God: The Global Rise of Religious Violence*. Rev. ed. Berkeley: University of California Press.

Kahler, Miles. (2002). "The State of the State in World Politics." In *Political Science: State of the Discipline*, ed. Ira Katznelson and Helen Milner. New York: W. W. Norton.

Kaplan, Morton. (1957). *System and Process in International Politics*. New York: Wiley.

Karatnycky, Adrian, and Peter Ackerman. (2006). "How Freedom Is Won: From Civic Struggle to Durable Democracy." http://www.freedomhouse.org/template.cfm?page=137.

Keck, Margaret, and Kathryn Sikkink. (1998). *Activists Without Borders: Advocacy Networks in International Politics*. Ithaca, NY: Cornell University Press.

Kegley, Charles W., Jr. (2008). *World Politics: Trend and Transformation*. 12th ed. New York: Thompson Wadsworth.

Kegley, Charles W., Jr., and Eugene Wittkopf. (1993). *World Politics: Trend and Transformation*. 4th ed. New York: St. Martin's.

——. (1995). *World Politics: Trend and Transformation*. 5th ed. New York: St. Martin's.

——. (2004). *World Politics: Trend and Transformation*. 9th ed. New York: Thomson Wadsworth.

——. (2006). *World Politics: Trend and Transformation*. 11th ed. New York: Thomson Wadsworth.

Kellner, Douglas. (1990). *Television and the Crisis of Democracy*. Boulder, CO: Westview.

Kennedy, Paul. (2006). *The Parliament of Man: The Past, Present, and Future of the United Nations*. New York: Random House.

Keohane, Robert O. (2005). *After Hegemony: Cooperation and Discord in the World Political Economy*. Princeton, NJ: Princeton University Press.

——, and Joseph Nye. (2001). *Power and Interdependence: World Politics in Transition*, 3rd ed. New York: Longman.

Kerpelman, Larry. (1972). *Activists and Nonactivists: A Psychological Study of American College Students*. New York: Behavioral.

Khalidi, Rashid I. (1993). "Intifada." In *The Oxford Companion to Politics of the World*, ed. Joel Krieger, pp. 463–464. New York: Oxford University Press.

Klare, Michael T. (1988). "Low-Intensity Conflict." *Christianity and Crisis* (February): 11–14.

——. (1997). "The New Arms Race: Light Weapons and International Security." *Current History* 96 (April): 173–178.

Klein, Hans. (2001) "The Feasibility of Global Democracy." *Journal of Policy, Regulation, and Strategy for Telecommunications* 3 (August 2001): 333–345.

Knight, Kathleen. (2006). "Transformations of the Concept of Ideology in the Twentieth Century." *American Political Science Review* 100 (November): 619–626.

Koopmans, Tim. (2003). *Courts and Political Institutions: A Comparative View*. Cambridge: Cambridge University Press.

Kuhn, Thomas. (1996). *The Structure of Scientific Revolutions*. 3rd ed. Chicago: University of Chicago Press.

Laitin, David D. (2002). "Comparative Politics: The State of the Subdiscipline." In *Political Science: State of the Discipline*, ed. Ira Katznelson and Helen Milner. New York: W. W. Norton.

Larkey, Edward. (1990). "Rock Music and Cultural Theory in the German Democratic Republic." In *Politics in Familiar Contexts*, ed. Robert L. Savage and Dan Nimmo, pp. 215–224. Norwood, NJ: Ablex.

Lasswell, Harold. (1960). *Psychopathology and Politics*. New York: Viking.

Latinobarometro. (2008). http://www.latinobarometro.org.

LeDuc, Lawrence, Richard Niemi, and Pippa Norris, Eds. (2002). *Comparing Democracies 2: New Challenges in the Study of Elections and Voting*. Newbury Park, CA: Sage.

Lenski, Gerhard. (1966). *Power and Privilege: A Theory of Social Stratification*. New York: McGraw-Hill.

Levi, Margaret. (2002). "The State of the Study of the State." In *Political Science: State of the Discipline*, ed. Ira Katznelson and Helen Milner. New York: W. W. Norton.

Levitt, Steven D., and Stephen J. Dubner. (2008) *Freakonomics: A Rogue Economist Explores the Hidden Side of Everything*. New York: Harper Collins.

Lewis, Martin. (1999). "Is There a Third World?" *Current History* 98 (November): 355–358.

Lijphart, Arend. (1978). *Democracy in Plural Societies*. New Haven, CT: Yale University Press.

——. (1984). *Democracies: Patterns of Majoritarian and Consensual Government in Twenty-One Countries*. New Haven, CT: Yale University Press.

Lindblom, Charles E. (1977). *Politics and Markets: The World's Political-Economic Systems*. New York: Basic Books.

———. (2003). *The Market System: What It Is, How It Works, and What to Make of It*. New Haven, CT: Yale University Press.

Linz, Juan J. (1993). "Authoritarianism." In *The Oxford Companion to Politics of the World*, ed. Joel Krieger, pp. 60–64. New York: Oxford University Press.

Linz, Juan J., and Alfred Stepan. (1996). *Problems of Democratic Transition and Consolidation: Southern Europe, South America, and Post-Communist Europe*. Baltimore, MD: Johns Hopkins University Press.

Lipset, Seymour Martin. (1988). *Revolution and Counterrevolution: Change and Persistence in Social Structures*. Rev. ed. New Brunswick, NJ: Transaction.

Locke, John. (1690/1963). *Two Treatises on Government*. New York: New American Library.

Loveman, Brian. (1994). " 'Protected Democracies' and Military Guardianship: Political Transitions in Latin America, 1978–1993." *Journal of InterAmerican Studies and World Affairs* 36 (Summer): 114–130.

Lovenduski, Joni. (2005). *Feminizing Politics*. London: Polity.

Lozada, Carlos. (2003). "Think Again: Latin America." *Foreign Policy* 135 (March/April): 18–26.

Lukes, Steven. (2005). *Power: A Radical Review*. 2nd ed. London: Palgrave-Macmillan.

Lupia, Arthur, and Mathew McCubbins. (1998). *The Democratic Dilemma: Can Citizens Learn What They Need to Know?* Cambridge: Cambridge University Press.

Machiavelli, Niccolò. (1517/1977). *The Prince*. Trans. and ed. Robert M. Adams. New York: W. W. Norton.

Mackinder, Halford John. (1996). *Democratic Ideals and Reality*. Washington, DC: U.S. Government Printing Office.

Macridis, Roy, and Steven Burg. (1997). *Introduction to Comparative Politics: Political Regimes and Political Change*. 2nd ed. New York: Addison-Wesley.

Mahon, James E. (1999). "Economic Crisis in Latin America: Global Contagion, Local Pain." *Current History* 98 (March): 105–110.

Mander, Jerry. (1999). "Regarding the WTO." *International Forum on Globalization*. http://www.ifg.org/media.html.

Mansfield, Edward D., and Jack Snyder. (2002). "Democratic Transitions, Institutional Strength, and War." *International Organization* 56 (Spring): 297–304.

March, James G., and Johan P. Olsen. (1989). *Rediscovering Institutions: The Organizational Basis of Politics*. New York: Free Press.

———. (2006). "Elaborating the 'New Institutionalism.' " In *The Oxford Handbook of Political Institutions*, ed. R.A.W. Rhodes, Sarah Binder, and Bert Rockman. Oxford: Oxford University Press.

Marx, Karl. (1867/1981). *Capital*. Trans. David Fernbach. New York: Vintage.

Marx, Karl, and Friedrich Engels. (1848/1978). "The Communist Manifesto." In *The Marx-Engels Reader*, 2nd ed., ed. Robert Tucker, pp. 482–500. New York: W. W. Norton.

Maslow, Abraham. (1954). *Motivation and Personality*. New York: Harper and Row.

Masters, Roger D. (1992). "How Television Has Transformed American Politics." *Public Affairs Report* (November): 7–9. Berkeley, CA: Institute for Governmental Studies.

———. (2001). "Biology and Politics: Linking Nature and Nurture." *Annual Review of Political Science* 4 (June).

Maxfield, Sylvia. (1997). *Gatekeepers of Growth: The International Political Economy of Central Banking in Developing Countries*. Princeton, NJ: Princeton University Press.

McClelland, David. (1961). *The Achieving Society*. Princeton, NJ: Van Nostrand.

McCormick, John. (2006). *The European Superpower*. New York: Palgrave.

McFaul, Michael. (1998). "Russia's Summer of Discontent." *Current History* 97 (October): 307–312.

———. (2007). "New Russia, New Threat." *Los Angeles Times*, September 2, M8.

McFaul, Michael, Nikolai Petrov, and Andrei Ryabov. (2004). *Between Dictatorship and Democracy: Russian Post-communist Political Reform*. Washington, DC: Carnegie Endowment for International Peace.

McFaul, Michael, and Kathryn Stoner-Weiss, Eds. (2004). *After the Collapse of Communism: Comparative Lessons of Transition*. New York: Cambridge University Press.

McLellan, David, Ed. (2007). *Marxism After Marx*. 4th ed. New York: Palgrave.

Mearsheimer, John J. (2001). *The Tragedy of Great Power Politics*. New York: W. W. Norton.

Medvedev, Roy. (2000). *Where Is Russia Going?* Trans. George Shriver. New York: Columbia University Press.

Meisner, Maurice. (1999). *Mao's China and After*. 3rd ed. New York: Free Press.

Meisner, Maurice, and Gareth Schott. (2006). *Mao Zedong: A Political and Intellectual Portrait*. London: Polity Press.

Meyer, David S., and Sidney Tarrow, Eds. (1997). *The Social Movement Society: Contentious Politics for a New Century*. Lanham, MD: Rowman and Littlefield.

Meyer, David S., Nancy Whittier, and Belinda Robnett. (2003). *Social Movements, Identity, Culture, and the State*. New York: Oxford University Press.

Meyer, Josh. (2007). "Small Groups Now a Large Threat," *Los Angeles Times*, August 16, A1, A10.

Microcredit Summit Conference. (2006). http://www.microcredit-summit.org.

Milbrath, Lester, and M. L. Goel. (1982). *Political Participation*. Lanham, MD: University Press of America.

Milgram, Stanley. (1974). *Obedience to Authority*. New York: Harper and Row.

Millar, James R. (1999). "The De-development of Russia." *Current History* 98 (October): 322–327.

Miller, Roger LeRoy. (2007). *Economics Today*. 14th ed. New York: Addison-Wesley-Longman.

Mills, C. Wright. (1956). *The Power Elite*. New York: Oxford University Press.

Mitchell, Jennifer D. (1998). "Before the Next Doubling." *World Watch* (January/February): 20–27.

Moore, Barrington. (1966). *The Social Origins of Dictatorship and Democracy*. Cambridge, MA: Harvard University Press.

Morgenthau, Hans J. (1993). *Politics Among Nations*. Brief ed. Revised by Kenneth W. Thompson. New York: Knopf.

Mosca, Gaetano. (1896/1939). *The Ruling Class*. Trans. Hannah Kahn. New York: McGraw-Hill.

Mueller, Dennis. (2004). *Public Choice III*. New York: Cambridge University Press.

Murphy, Dean. (1995). "East Europe P.D. Blues." *Los Angeles Times,* February 28, H1, H4.

Murphy, Kim. (2003). "Takeover of Polling Firm Causes a Stir." *Los Angeles Times,* August 23, A3.

NCTC (National Counterterrorism Center). (2007). *A Chronology of Significant International Terrorism for 2006.* http://www.NCTC.gov.

Nelson, Joan. (1993). "Political Participation." In *The Oxford Companion to Politics of the World,* ed. Joel Krieger, pp. 720–722. New York: Oxford University Press.

Neuman, W. Russell. (1999). *The Gordian Knot: Political Gridlock on the Information Highway*. Cambridge, MA: MIT Press.

Niemi, Richard G., and Herbert Weissberg. (2001). *Controversies in Voting Behavior*. 4th ed. Washington, DC: CQ Press.

Nimmo, Dan, and James E. Combs. (1990). *Mediated Political Realities*. 2nd ed. White Plains, NY: Longman.

Norris, Pippa. (2004). *Electoral Engineering: Voting Rules and Political Behavior*. Cambridge: Cambridge University Press.

Norris, Pippa, and Ronald Inglehart. (2004). *Sacred and Secular: Religion and Politics Worldwide*. New York: Cambridge University Press.

Nugent, Neill. (2006). *The Government and Politics of the European Union*. 6th ed. Durham, NC: Duke University Press.

———. (2004). *European Union Enlargement*. New York: Palgrave Macmillan.

O'Connor, Karen, and Larry Sabato. (2007). *The Essentials of American Government*. 8th ed. New York: Longman.

Onwumechili, Chuka. (1999). *African Democratization and Military Coups*. Westport, CT: Praeger.

Orwell, George. (1945/1964). *Animal Farm*. Middlesex, England: Penguin.

———. (1949/1967). *1984*. Middlesex, England: Penguin.

Oxfam (2007). *Africa's Missing Billions: International Arms Flow and the Cost of Conflict*. http://www.oxfam.org.uk.

Packenham, Robert. (1998). *The Dependency Movement: Scholarship and Politics in Development Studies*. Cambridge, MA: Harvard University Press.

Parenti, Michael. (2007). *Democracy for the Few*. 8th ed. New York: Wadsworth.

Parker, Geoffrey. (2000). *Geopolitics: Past, Present, and Future*. London: Pinter.

Pei. Minxin. (1999). "Economic Institutions, Democracy, and Development." Paper presented at World Bank Conference on Democracy, Market Economy, and Development, Washington, DC, February 26.

Peterson, Scott. (2001). "Jaded Hope: Russia 10 Years Later." *Christian Science Monitor,* August 17, 1, 7–8.

Physicians for a National Health Program. (2007). http://www.pnhp.org.

Popper, Karl. (1963). *The Open Society and Its Enemies*. Vol. 2. New York: Harper and Row.

Population Institute. (1992, September). Untitled pamphlet. Washington, DC: Population Institute.

Poulantzas, Nicos. (1973). *Political Power and Social Classes*. London: Sheed and Ward.

Przeworski, Adam. (1985). *Capitalism and Social Democracy*. Cambridge: Cambridge University Press.

———. (1993). "Socialism and Social Democracy." In *The Oxford Companion to Politics of the World,* ed. Joel Krieger, pp. 832–838. New York: Oxford University Press.

———. (2004). "Democracy and Economic Development." In *The Evolution of Political Knowledge*, ed. Edward D. Mansfield and Richard Sisson. Columbus, OH: Ohio State University Press.

Przeworski, Adam, Michael Alvarez, Jose Antonio Cheibub, and Fernando Limongi. (2000). *Democracy and Development: Political Institutions and Well-Being in the World, 1950–1990*. New York: Cambridge University Press.

Putnam, Robert. (1993). *Making Democracy Work: Civic Traditions in Modern Italy*. Princeton, NJ: Princeton University Press.

Pye, Lucian W. (1962). *Politics, Personality, and Nation-Building*. New Haven, CT: Yale University Press.

———. (1985). *Asian Power and Politics: The Cultural Dimensions of Authority*. Cambridge, MA: Belknap Press.

Rae, Douglas. (1971). *The Political Consequences of Electoral Laws*. New Haven, CT: Yale University Press.

Ranney, Austin. (2001). *Governing: An Introduction to Political Science*. 8th ed. Englewood Cliffs, NJ: Prentice Hall.

Reppy, Susan. (1984). "The Automobile Air Bag." In *Controversy*, 2nd ed., ed. Dorothy Nelkin, pp. 161–174. Beverly Hills, CA: Sage.

Riker, William. (1962). *The Theory of Political Coalitions*. New Haven, CT: Yale University Press.

———. (1982). "The Two Party System and Duverger's Law." *American Political Science Review* 76 (4): 753–766.

Riker, William, and Peter Ordeshook. (1973). *An Introduction to Positive Political Theory*. Englewood Cliffs, NJ: Prentice Hall.

Roberts, Cynthia, and Thomas Sherlock. (1999). "Bringing the Russian State Back." In "Explanations of the Derailed Transition to Market Democracy," pp. 477–492. *Comparative Politics* 39 (July).

Robinson, Simon. (2003). "Iraqi Textbooks: X-ing Out Saddam." *Time,* July 21, 18.

Rocha, Geisa Maria. (2002). "Neo-Dependency in Brazil." *New Left Review* 16 (July/August): http://www.newleftreview .net/NLR25001.shtml.

Rodrik, Dani. (1999). *The New Global Economy and Developing Countries*. Washington, DC: Overseas Council.

———, Ed. (2003). *In Search of Prosperity: Analytic Narratives on Economic Growth*. Princeton, NJ: Princeton University Press.

Rosenau, James, and Ole Holsti. (1986). "Consensus Lost, Consensus Regained?" *International Studies Quarterly*: 375–409.

Rosenberg, Shawn. (1988). *Reason, Ideology, and Politics*. Cambridge: Polity.

———. (2002). *The Not So Common Sense: Differences in How People Judge Social and Political Life*. New Haven, CT: Yale University Press.

Rousseau, David. (2005). *Democracy and War*. Stanford, CA: Stanford University Press.

Royo, Sebastian. (2002). "A New Century of Corporatism?" In *Corporatism in Southern Europe—Spain and Portugal in a Comparative Perspective*. Westport, CT: Praeger.

Rueschemeyer, Dietrich, Marilyn Rueschemeyer, and Bjorn Wittrock. (1998). *Participation and Democracy East and West: Comparisons and Interpretations*. Armonk, NY: M. E. Sharpe.

Rueschemeyer, Dietrich, Evelyne Huber Stephens, and John Stephens. (1992). *Capitalist Development and Democracy*. Chicago: University of Chicago Press.

Rummel, R. J. (2008). *Death by Government*. http://www .hawaii.edu/powerkills/.

Rupnik, Jacques (1999). "The Post-Communist Divide." *Journal of Democracy* 10 (January): 57–62.

Russett, Bruce, and John R. Oneal. (2001). *Triangulating Peace: Democracy, Interdependence, and International Organizations*. New York: W. W. Norton.

Russett, Bruce, Harvey Starr, and David Kinsella. (2008). *World Politics: The Menu for Choice*. 9th ed. New York: Thomson Wadsworth.

Rustow, Dankwart. (1967). *A World of Nations: Problems of Political Modernization*. Washington, DC: Brookings Institution.

Rutland, Peter. (1999). "The Revolutions of 1989 Revisited." *Current History* 98 (April): 147–152.

Sadowski, Yahya. (1998). "Ethnic Conflict." *Foreign Policy* 31 (Summer): 12–23.

Safran, William. (2008). *The French Polity*. 7th ed. London: Longman.

Sageman. Marc. (2008). *Leaderless Jihad: Terror Networks in the Twenty-First Century*. Philadelphia: University of Pennsylvania Press.

Salisbury, Robert H. (1990). "The Paradox of Interest Groups in Washington, D.C.: More Groups and Less Clout." In *The New American Political System*, rev. ed., ed. Anthony King. Washington, DC: American Enterprise Institute.

Salisbury, Robert H., John P. Heinz, Robert L. Nelson, and Edward O. Laumann. (1991). "Triangles, Networks, and Hollow Cores: The Complex Geometry of Washington Interest Representation." In *The Politics of Interests,* ed. Mark P. Petracca, pp. 130–149. Boulder, CO: Westview.

Sassen, Saskia. (1996). *Losing Control?: Sovereignty in the Age of Globalization*. New York: Columbia University Press.

Savage, Robert L., and Dan Nimmo, Eds. (1990). *Politics in Familiar Contexts: Projecting Politics Through Popular Media*. Norwood, NJ: Ablex.

Schedler, Andreas, Ed. (2006). *Electoral Authoritarianism: The Dynamics of Unfree Competition*. Boulder, CO: Lynne Rienner.

Schelling, Thomas. (1960). *The Strategy of Conflict*. Cambridge, MA: Harvard University Press.

Schleifer, Andrei, and Daniel Triesman. (2000). *Without a Map: Political Tactics and Economic Reform in Russia*. Cambridge, MA: MIT Press.

Schmitter, Philippe C. (1993). "Corporatism." In *The Oxford Companion to Politics of the World*, ed. Joel Krieger, pp. 195–198. New York: Oxford University Press.

Schnetzer, Amanda. (2003). *Nations in Transit 2003: Milestones*. http://www.freedomhouse.com.

Schumpeter, Joseph. (1950). *Capitalism, Socialism, and Democracy*. 3rd ed. New York: Harper and Row.

Sesser, Stan. (1992). "A Nation of Contradictions." *New Yorker,* January 13, 37–68.

Shugart, Matthew Soberg, and John M. Carey. (1992). *Presidents and Assemblies: Constitutional Design and Electoral Dynamics*. New York: Cambridge University Press.

Shugart, Matthew Soberg, and Martin P. Wattenberg, Eds. (2001). *Mixed-Member Electoral Systems: The Best of Both Worlds?* Oxford: Oxford University Press.

Silone, Ignazio. (1937). *Bread and Wine*. Trans. Gwenda David. New York: Harper and Row.

Simon, Julian L. (1998). *The Ultimate Human Resource 2*. Princeton, NJ: Princeton University Press.

Simone, Vera. (2001). *The Asian Pacific: Political and Economic Development in a Global Context*. 2nd ed. New York: Longman.

Singer, J. David. (1991). "Peace in the Global System: Displacement, Interregnum, or Transformation?" In *The*

Long Postwar Peace, ed. Charles W. Kegley, pp. 56–84. New York: HarperCollins.

SIPRI (Stockholm International Peace Research Institute). (2008). *The SIPRI Yearbook*. http://www.sipri.org.

Sivard, Ruth Leger. (1991). *World Military and Social Expenditures 1991*. Washington, DC: World Priorities.

———. (1996). *World Military and Social Expenditures 1996*. Washington, DC: World Priorities.

Skinner, B. F. (1948). *Walden Two*. New York: Macmillan.

Skocpol, Theda. (1979). *States and Social Revolutions: A Comparative Analysis of France, Russia, and China*. New York: Cambridge University Press.

Sniderman, Paul M. (1975). *Personality and Democratic Politics*. Berkeley: University of California Press.

Sniderman, Paul M., et al. (1991). "The Fallacy of Democratic Elitism: Elite Competition and Commitment to Civil Liberties." *British Journal of Political Science* 21 (August): 349–370.

Snyder, Jack. (2000). *From Voting to Violence: Democratization and Nationalist Conflict*. New York: W. W. Norton.

So, Alvin Y. (1990). *Social Change and Development: Modernization, Dependency, and World-System Theories*. Newbury Park, CA: Sage.

Sophocles. (1967). *Antigone*. Trans. E. F. Watling. Middlesex, England: Penguin.

Sorensen, Georg. (2007). *Democracy and Democratization: Processes and Prospects in a Changing World*. 3rd ed. Boulder, CO: Westview.

Spagnoli, Filip. (2003). *Homo-Democraticus: On the Universal Desirability and the Not So Universal Possibility of Democracy and Human Rights*. Cambridge: Cambridge Scholars.

Spencer, William. (2008). *Middle East*. 10th ed. New York: McGraw-Hill.

Stein, Howard. (2006). "The World Bank and the Application of Asian Industrial Policy to Africa: Theoretical Considerations." *Journal of International Development* 6 (3): 287–305.

Stoessinger, John G. (2007). *Why Nations Go to War*. 10th ed. Boston: Wadsworth.

Stone Sweet, Alec. (2000). *Governing with Judges: Constitutional Politics in Europe*. Oxford: Oxford University Press.

———. (2004). *The Judicial Construction of Europe*. Oxford: Oxford University Press.

Strauss, Leo. (1959). *What Is Political Philosophy?* New York: Free Press.

Strom, Kaare. (1989). *Minority Government and Majority Rule*. New York: Cambridge University Press.

Sunstein, Cass. (2001). *Designing Democracy: What Constitutions Do*. New York: Oxford University Press.

———. (2002). *Republic.com*. Princeton, NJ: Princeton University Press.

Taagepera, Rein, and Matthew S. Shugart. (1989). *Seats and Votes*. New Haven, CT: Yale University Press.

Tawney, R. H. (1938). *Religion and the Rise of Capitalism: A Historical Study*. Middlesex, England: Penguin.

Third World Network. (2006). http://www.twnside.org.

Thompson, Leonard. (1966). *Politics in the Republic of South Africa*. Boston: Little, Brown.

Thompson, Mark R. (2003). *Democratic Revolutions: Asian and Eastern Europe*. London: Routledge.

Thoreau, Henry David. (1849/1981). *Walden and Other Writings*. Ed. J. W. Krutch. New York: Bantam.

Thurow, Lester C. (1997). *The Future of Capitalism*. New York: Penguin.

———. (2003). *Head to Head: Coming Economic Battles Among Japan, Europe, and America*. New York: HarperBusiness.

Tickner, J. Ann. (2001). *Gendering World Politics*. New York: Columbia University Press.

Tocqueville, Alexis de. (1835/1945). *Democracy in America*. New York: Knopf.

Torcal, Mariano, and Jose Ramon Montero. (2006). *Political Disaffection in Contemporary Democracies: Social Capital, Institutions, and Politics*. London: Routledge.

Transparency International. (2007). http://www.transparency.org.

———. (2008). http://www.transparency.org.

Triesman, Daniel. (2004). "Stabilization Tactics in Latin America: Menem, Cardosa, and the Politics of Low Inflation." *Comparative Politics* 36 (July): 399–419.

Truman, David. (1951). *The Governmental Process*. New York: Knopf.

Trumbull, Mark. (2007). "Great Global Shift to Service Jobs." *Christian Science Monitor*, September 4, 1, 10.

United Nations Commission on Transnational Corporations. (1991). *Recent Developments Related to Transnational Corporations and International Economic Relations*. New York: United Nations.

UNDP (United Nations Development Programme). (2001). *Human Development Report 2001*. http://www.hdr.undp.org/reports.

———. (2006). *Human Development Report 2006*. http://www.hdr.undp.org/reports.

———. (2007). *Human Development Report 2007*. http://www.hdr.undp.org/reports.

———. (2008). *Human Development Report 2007/2008*. http://www.hdr.undp.org/reports.

United Nations Peacekeeping Operations. (2007). http://www.un.org/Depts/dpko/dpko/home.shtml.

UNWFP (2007). United Nations Food Programme. http://www.wfp.org.

VCIOM. (1999). Russian Center for Public Opinion and Market Research. "Russian Citizen Survey" (March). http://www.russiavotes.org.

Verba, Sidney, and Norman Nie. (1972). *Participation in America*. New York: Harper and Row.

———. (1975). "Political Participation." In *Handbook of Political Science, vol. 4*, ed. Fred Greenstein and Nelson Polsby. Reading, MA: Addison-Wesley.

Verba, Sidney, Norman Nie, and Jae-on Kim. (1978). *Participation and Political Equality: A Seven-Nation Comparison*. Cambridge: Cambridge University Press.

Verba, Sidney, Kay Schlozman, and Henry Brady. (1995). *Voice and Equality: Civic Voluntarism in American Politics*. Cambridge, MA: Harvard University Press.

Victoroff, Jeff. (2005). "The Mind of the Terrorist: A Review and Critique of Psychological Approaches." *Journal of Conflict Resolution* 49 (February): 3–42.

Waldron, Jeremy. (2006). "The Core of the Case Against Judicial Review." *Yale Law Journal* 115 (2006): 1346–1406.

Walker, Nancy. (1988). "What We Know About Women Voters in Britain, France, and West Germany." *Public Opinion* (May–June): 49–55.

Wallach, Lori, and Patrick Woodall. (2004). *Whose Trade Organization?: The Comprehensive Guide to the WTO*. 2nd ed. New York: New Press.

Wallerstein, Immanuel. (1974). *The Modern World System*. New York: Academic Press.

———. (1980). *The World System II*. New York: Academic Press.

———. (1991). *Geopolitics and Geoculture: Essays on the Changing World System*. New York: Cambridge University Press.

———. (2004). *World-Systems Analysis: An Introduction*. Raleigh, NC: Duke University Press.

Walter, Barbara. (2007). "You Can't Win with Civil Wars." *Los Angeles Times* (October 2, 2007): A17.

Wattenberg, Martin. (2008). *Is Voting for Young People?* New York: Pearson Longman.

Weatherby, Joseph. (2008). "The Old and the New: Colonialism, Neocolonialism, and Nationalism." In *The Other World: Issues and Politics of the Developing World*, 6th ed., ed. Joseph Weatherby et al., ch. 2. New York: Longman.

Weatherby, Joseph, et al. (2008). *The Other World: Issues and Politics of the Developing World*. 8th ed. New York: Longman.

Weber, Max. (1951). *The Religion of China: Confucianism and Taoism*. Ed. Hans H. Gerth. New York: Free Press.

———. (1958a). *From Max Weber: Essays in Sociology*. Ed. Hans H. Gerth and C. Wright Mills. New York: Oxford University Press.

———. (1958b). *The Religion of India: The Sociology of Hinduism and Buddhism*. Trans. Hans Gerth and Don Martindale. New York: Free Press.

Weiss, Thomas, Ed. (1996). *NGOs, the UN, and Global Governance*. Boulder, CO: Lynne Rienner.

Weitz, Eric D. (2005). *A Century of Genocide: Utopias of Race and Nation*. Princeton, NJ: Princeton University Press.

Welzel, Christian. (2007). "A Human Development View on Value Change." http://margaux.grandvinum.se/SebTest/wvs/articles/folder_published/article_base_83.

Weyland, Kurt. (1999). "Neoliberal Populism in Latin American and Eastern Europe." *Comparative Politics* 31 (July): 379–400.

White, Gordon (1998). "Constructing a Democratic Developmental State." In *The Democratic Developmental State: Political and Institutional Design*, ed. M. Robinson and Gordon White. New York: Oxford University Press.

Wiarda, Howard J. (1997). *Corporatism and Comparative Politics: The Other Great "Ism."* Armonk, NY: M. E. Sharpe.

———. (2003). *Political Development in Emerging Countries*. Belmont, CA: Wadsworth.

———, Ed. (2004). *Authoritarianism and Corporatism in Latin America—Revisited*. Gainesville: University Press of Florida.

Wilensky, Harold. (2002). *Rich Democracies*. Berkeley: University of California Press.

Wilson, Edward O. (1978). *On Human Nature*. Cambridge, MA: Harvard University Press.

Wilson, Graham K. (1991). "American Interest Groups in Comparative Perspective." In *The Politics of Interests*, ed. Mark P. Petracca, pp. 80–95. Boulder, CO: Westview.

Wilson, William Julius. (1987). *The Truly Disadvantaged*. Chicago: University of Chicago Press.

———. (1996). *When Work Disappears*. New York: Knopf.

Winters, Jeffrey A. (1998). "Asia and the 'Magic' of the Marketplace." *Current History* 97 (December): 418–425.

Wolin, Sheldon. (1960). *Politics and Vision*. Boston: Little, Brown.

Woo-Cumings, Meredith, Ed. (1999). *The Developmental State*. New York: Cornell University Press.

World Bank. (1996). *World Development Report 1996*. New York: Oxford University Press.

———. (1999). *World Development Report 1998–1999*. New York: Oxford University Press.

———. (2001). *World Development Report 2000–2001*. New York: Oxford University Press.

———. (2005). *World Development Report 2004–2005*. New York: Oxford University Press.

———. (2006). http://www.worldbank.org (subscription service). Also available in World Bank (2006). *World Development Indicators*. New York: Oxford University Press.

———. (2007). *World Development Report 2006–2007*. New York: Oxford University Press.

———. (2008). World Development Report 2007. New York: Oxford University Press.

World Refugee Survey. (2007). U.S. Committee for Refugees and Immigrants. http://www.refugees.org.

World Trade Organization. (2008). *What Is the World Trade Organization?* http://www.wto.org.

World Values Survey. (2006). http://www.worldvaluessurvey.org.

Worldwatch. (2003). *State of the World 2003*. Washington, DC: Worldwatch Institute.

Woshinsky, Oliver. (1995). *Culture and Politics*. Englewood Cliffs, NJ: Prentice Hall.

Wright, Erik Olin. (1998). *The Debate on Classes*. London: Verso.

Wright, Robin. (1999). "Wars of Identity." *Los Angeles Times*, April 3, A15.

Wrong, Dennis. (1995). *Power: Its Forms, Bases, and Uses*. Brunswick, NJ: Transaction.

Zakaria, Fareed. (2003). *The Future of Freedom: Illiberal Democracy at Home and Abroad*. New York: W. W. Norton.

Zaller, John R. (1992). *The Nature and Origins of Mass Opinion*. New York: Cambridge University Press.

Ziring, Lawrence, Robert E. Riggs, and Jack C. Plano. (2004). *The United Nations: International Organization and World Politics*. 4th ed. Belmont, CA: Wadsworth.

Zukin, Cliff, et al. (2006). *A New Engagement?: Political Participation, Civic Life, and the Changing American Citizen*. New York: Oxford University Press.

CREDITS

INDEX